Beyond Yugoslavia

Eastern Europe After Communism
Sabrina Petra Ramet, *Series Editor*

Since the collapse of communism throughout Eastern Europe, 1989–1990, the societies of the region have begun searching for new social and political formulae, setting new tasks, and facing new challenges. New social forces have arisen, such as nationalism and chauvinism, and preexisting social institutions and groupings, such as the churches and feminist groups, have intensified their activity. Above all, Eastern Europe is dominated, in the years following the collapse, by the twin tasks of democratization and privatization, tasks that are complex and multifaceted, with consequences that reach far beyond the formal goals associated with these processes.

This new series is designed to provide a set of windows on the changing realities of Eastern Europe and to chart these societies' courses as they attempt to deal with the legacy of communism and the problems of transition. This volume looks at the processes leading up to the breakup of Yugoslavia and the consequences thereof. Future volumes will examine the security context and offer perspectives on other countries in the region.

Books in This Series

The New Eastern Europe and the World Economy, edited by Jozef M. van Brabant

FORTHCOMING

Albania, edited by Elez Biberaj
Romania, edited by Trond Gilberg
Security, edited by Robin Remington
Eastern Germany, edited by Patricia Smith
Hungary, edited by Ivan Volgyes
Czech Republic, edited by Sharon Wolchik
Slovakia, edited by Sharon Wolchik

Beyond Yugoslavia

Politics, Economics, and Culture
in a Shattered Community

EDITED BY

Sabrina Petra Ramet
and Ljubiša S. Adamovich

LONDON AND NEW YORK

First published 1995 by Westview Press

Published 2018 by Routledge
52 Vanderbilt Avenue, New York, NY 10017
2 Park Square, Milton Park, Abingdon, Oxon OX14 4RN

Routledge is an imprint of the Taylor & Francis Group, an informa business

Copyright © 1995 by Taylor & Francis

All rights reserved. No part of this book may be reprinted or reproduced or utilised in any form or by any electronic, mechanical, or other means, now known or hereafter invented, including photocopying and recording, or in any information storage or retrieval system, without permission in writing from the publishers.

Notice:
Product or corporate names may be trademarks or registered trademarks, and are used only for identification and explanation without intent to infringe.

Library of Congress Cataloging-in-Publication Data
Beyond Yugoslavia : politics, economics, and culture in a shattered community / Sabrina Petra Ramet and Ljubiša S. Adamovich, ed.
   p. cm.
  Includes bibliographical references and index.
  ISBN 0-8133-1953-9
  1. Yugoslavia–Economic conditions–1945-1992. 2. Yugoslavia–Politics and govemment–1980-1992. 3. Yugoslavia–Social conditions. I. Ramet, Sabrina P., 1949- II. Adamović, Ljubiša S.
HC407.B39 1995
338.9497–dc20   94-35987
                                                  CIP

ISBN 13: 978-0-367-01481-0 (hbk)
ISBN 13: 978-0-367-16468-3 (pbk)

For our spouses,
Christine and Ann

Contents

Preface	ix
Introduction: The Roots of Discord and the Language of War, *Sabrina Petra Ramet*	1

PART ONE
Adumbrations of the Breakup

1	The Avoidable Catastrophe, *Dennison Rusinow*	13
2	The Dissolution of Yugoslav Historiography, *Ivo Banac*	39
3	The Armed Forces of Yugoslavia: Sliding into War, *Marko Milivojević*	67
4	Media: The Extension of Politics by Other Means, *Jasmina Kuzmanović*	83

PART TWO
The Republics

5	The Serbian Church and the Serbian Nation, *Sabrina Petra Ramet*	101
6	Democracy and Nationalism in Croatia: The First Three Years, *Dijana Pleština*	123
7	The Bosnian Crisis in 1992, *Paul Shoup*	155
8	Slovenia's Road to Democracy, *Sabrina Petra Ramet*	189
9	The Macedonian Enigma, *Sabrina Petra Ramet*	211
10	Politics in Montenegro, *Milan Andrejevich*	237

viii

PART THREE
Economics

11 Economic Transformation in Former Yugoslavia, with
Special Regard to Privatization, *Ljubiša S. Adamovich*   253

12 Foreign Economic Relations, *Oskar Kovač*   281

13 Environmental Issues and Policies, with Special
Attention to Montenegro, *Svetlana Adamović and
Vukašin Pavlović*   301

PART FOUR
Foreign Relations

14 Relations with the Superpowers, *Branko Pribičević*   331

15 Yugoslavia's Relations with European States,
Zachary T. Irwin   349

PART FIVE
Culture and Society

16 The New Democracy—With Women or Without Them?
Rada Iveković   395

17 "Only Crooks Can Get Ahead": Post-Yugoslav Cinema/
TV/Video in the 1990s, *Andrew Horton*   413

18 The Catholic Church in a Time of Crisis, *Jure Kristo*   431

PART SIX
Conclusion

The Yugoslav Crisis and the West, *Sabrina Petra Ramet*   453

About the Editors   477
About the Contributors   479
About the Book   484
Index   485

Preface

Planning for this book was begun in early 1988. The initial invitations were issued in August–September 1989, and organizational work related to an eventual conference was begun in 1990. By early 1991, it was apparent that the long-feared breakup of Yugoslavia had become irreversible and was now imminent, and at that point, we reassessed the project and redesigned it, adding the section entitled "The Republics" in order to give individual attention to each of the six constituent republics of what once was socialist Yugoslavia.

This book was designed as a joint Yugoslav-American cooperative enterprise, and care was taken to invite some of the most accomplished scholars and experts working in the field. Chapters were contracted from scholars working in the US, Britain, Germany, Serbia, Croatia, Slovenia, and Macedonia. Regrettably, neither of the two scholars from Slovenia and neither of the two scholars from Macedonia came through, and only one of the two scholars from Germany finally offered a chapter for the book. In addition, although great effort was expended in attempting to obtain a chapter on the Serbian political scene from a distinguished Serbian scholar, eventually our efforts in that connection proved unavailing, as first one and then another Serbian scholar left us empty-handed. The result was that we were constrained, for the sake of structural balance, to move the Serbian Orthodox Church chapter from the social issues section of the book to the "Republics" section, even though it only partially covers the terrain covered by other chapters in this section. Nor was it our original intention that the Slovenia and Macedonia chapters be contributed by one of us; this solution was forced on us by the withdrawal of the scholars contracted for these chapters. Yet, for all the travails that this book has gone through—travails that are by no means unique, but are, on the contrary, thoroughly familiar to any who have participated in collaborative projects—we believe that this book makes a unique contribution to the existing literature, both in terms of the breadth of its coverage and in terms of the range of opinion offered herein.

Our original intention was to hold the conference in Dubrovnik, with November 1991 as the prospective date. But by July 1991, it seemed increasingly likely that Dubrovnik would shortly come under siege and we decided to convene our meeting somewhere outside the country. Later that year, when Dubrovnik was in fact besieged by Serbian forces, the international center in which we would have met was completely destroyed by bombardment. Meanwhile, our conference was rescheduled for 9–11 June 1992, in Budapest, Hungary. The final versions of all chapters except the conclusion were completed in early 1993 and reflect the situation at that time.

We are deeply indebted to IREX for generously funding our conference and related expenses as well as for providing a publication subsidy to Westview Press, to Obrad Kesić of IREX, who provided valuable assistance at every stage in the process, to the East European Institute in Budapest for providing fine facilities for our conference, and to Susan McEachern of Westview Press for her consistently efficient work and wise counsel in connection with this project. We also wish to thank Karen Walton, who coded the computer discs used to generate this book.

Ivo Banac's chapter, although presented at the conference in Budapest, was first published in *American Historical Review* (October 1992), and we are grateful to the editors of that journal for permission to reprint the article here. Sabrina Ramet's chapter on Slovenia was first published in *Europe-Asia Studies* (1993), and we are likewise grateful to the editors of that journal for permission to reprint the article in question.

Finally, we should like to note what a pleasure it has been working with each other on this book. Collaboration on a book can often strain a relationship, but in this case, the entire collaboration proceeded so very smoothly and with such pleasure on both sides that it seems only appropriate to celebrate our successful collaboration publicly here.

Sabrina Petra Ramet
Ljubiša S. Adamovich

Introduction

The Roots of Discord and the Language of War

Sabrina Petra Ramet

No more serve your brutal war-lords, join our dance!
No more slavery, join our dance!
Oh dance to our sun! Oh dance to our sun!
Cruel war priest of proud walled city
Feared this dancing madness,
Led his brutal army out to battle,
Slew all dancers, burned alive the Mad Dancing Girl,
She danced in flames until she was ashes.
> —Alan Hovhaness, American composer,
> in the text to his "Lady of Light"
> (1968)

Such nonsense—wanting to put Serbs, Croats, and Albanians into one state each. The Balkans are the most mixed region in Europe, all people should learn to live together instead of making this absurd attempt to create ethnically cleansed states.
> —Kiro Gligorov, President of Macedonia[1]

I

I used to believe that nationalism had both beneficial and harmful incarnations. After more than three years of inter-ethnic savagery in former Yugoslavia, I am no longer certain of the supposed beneficial incarnations, and am more inclined to believe that it is better to suppress nationalism altogether rather than to water a plant that may bear such poisonous fruit. For a "good nationalist" it is nothing to kill a member of the "enemy nation"; on the contrary, it is a point of duty, the fulfillment of which is expected to be *rewarded* both in this life and in a supposed hereafter in which the Supreme Deity himself is seen as favoring one's own nation.

The founding of the Yugoslav state at the end of 1918 was accompanied by much fanfare, both among South Slavs and in the West, about the triumph of the principle of national self-determination. This fanfare notwithstanding, the Yugoslav state quickly revealed internal fragility as a result of fundamental differences over its structure and appropriate orientation toward national differences. The interwar kingdom lasted exactly 23 years before it slid, under the impact of the Nazi-fascist occupation, into an internal civil war between Croatian *Ustaše*, Serbian Chetniks, and communist Partisans. Tito rebuilt a new Yugoslavia on the ashes of the old, and the second Yugoslavia lasted 46 years—exactly twice as long as the first Yugoslavia—before once again sliding into interethnic war. Both the interwar kingdom and the Tito regime began by attempting to impose a centralized regime, and gradually came to realize that, in the context of multinational Yugoslavia, only a decentralized model had any hope of success. But decentralization also had its foes, who argued alternatively that the approach was inefficient, unnecessary, and even "unmodern."[2]

The consequent perennial tensions between advocates of centralism and advocates of decentralism (or even confederation), whether in the interwar era, the Tito era, or the post-Tito period, produced an atmosphere of perpetual crisis, in which monumental energies were rivetted on every issue and in which economic, developmental, structural, personnel, and policy questions were inevitably translated into ethnic/national questions. The instability of both the interwar and postwar political formulas lent Yugoslav politics a perennial sense of urgency, but simultaneously prevented the regimes from setting priorities on the basis of anything other than ethnic and national grounds. In the early 1980s, for example, Sergej Krajgher of Slovenia headed a commission which prepared a report which made various recommendations for economic stabilization. Among other things, his recommendations would have entailed some compromise with the practice of near-confederal decentralization, itself a concession to the "national question." As a result, the Krajgher report was stillborn.

Alongside this perpetual crisis, there have been recurrent pressures from Yugoslavia's discontents. Thus, as Ljubo Boban has noted, ". . . the Ustaša [wartime Croatian fascist] movement itself was a direct product of the Yugoslav state and its Great Serbian hegemonist policies."[3] The communists wanted to avoid the mistakes of the interwar kingdom, but ironically, made the same mistake of provoking nationalist resentment. After 1971, important sectors of the Croatian public were alienated, and after the Albanian riots in Kosovo in 1981, the Serbian public became both more disenchanted with the federalized state and more vulnerable to manipulation.

Introduction: The Roots of Discord and the Language of War 3

One of the debates which the Serbs' expansionist war against Croatia and Bosnia has reinforced, but which actually began at least eight years prior to the outbreak of the war, has to do with the question as to whether the war was inevitable or not. The mere fact that various scholars, including myself,[4] warned in the months between October 1990 and February 1991, that the outbreak of ethnic war was imminent makes it clear that the country's drift toward strife was increasingly evident, and not some sort of unpredictable thunderbolt. There were, of course, optimists and these scholars took a very different approach, and stressed, on the contrary, the possibility for containment of the crisis and for negotiated settlements.[5]

And yet, there was some point at which war became inevitable. For the most bright-eyed optimists, that day was 26 June 1991, the day that JNA tanks actually rolled into Slovenia. A more pessimistic interpretation might argue that civil war became inevitable when Slobodan Milošević, a committed Serbian nationalist, took the helm of power in Serbia toward the end of 1987. Milošević's ascent to power was, of course, a turning point, but despite the escalation of tensions which accompanied his rise, it was probably not until the arming of the Serbian civilian population in the summer of 1990 that internal ethnic war became, strictly speaking, "inevitable." The danger of civil war had, however, been growing for years, and ordinary citizens had openly talked of their fears of civil war for at least three years prior to that summer.

The perpetual Yugoslav crisis was often seen largely in national terms and indeed, the national question affected every sphere of social life.[6] But the crisis was also reflected quite autonomously in these sundry spheres, so that, for example, as the Yugoslav economy soured over the course of the 1980s, policy-makers and economic managers instinctively shifted the brunt of the suffering onto women. As of the end of 1990, thus, some 70 percent of unemployed persons in Yugoslavia were women.[7] Similarly, the increase in nationalist chauvinism in the country between 1989 and 1992 also contributed directly to a new male chauvinism and to increased difficulties for women. Or, to take another example, the gathering political and social crisis confronted the leading Churches (chiefly the Catholic Church and the Serbian Orthodox Church) with new challenges, new opportunities, and new "rules of the game." The result is that both the Catholic and the Orthodox Church have adopted a more strident tone in public discourse and public debate since the withering away of communism.

II

Accompanying the war against the "enemy" is a war against "enemy ideas," and consequently an effort to alter not merely boundaries but language as well. Bullets can terminate resistance on the battlefield, but resistance—even if, as in history's most one-sided clashes, only a spiritual resistance—continues all the same, as long as any of the vanquished nation are alive and remember. Only a successful imposition of one's own preferred "national script" holds out the promise of a still more complete victory, in which even the survivors know only the history written by the victors. The war about language is at the same time a war for the minds of one's own nation, a war to consolidate ranks around the "national idea," as defined and rendered in the national script being propounded. Nation as victim or as hero, as justified by God or fate or history, as old or new, as united or divided by unjust forces—nation is the value at the heart of many such struggles over language.

Newsreports inevitably focus their attention in the first place on the purely military level on which wars are waged, and to a somewhat lesser extent, on the diplomatic-political and economic levels (which include such matters as embargoes, illicit trade, price manipulations, and so forth). But there are other levels of warfare which are also concomitants of the process. While one might enumerate a number of additional levels, including cultural, sexual (re. this, see Rada Iveković's chapter), and religious, I shall focus here only on the linguistic level.

In this process of the dissolution of Socialist Yugoslavia, the linguistic struggle has been waged at various levels. First, there is the renaming of towns and villages. Titograd, thus, has reverted to its historical name, Podgorica, and sundry Hungarian villages in Vojvodina have been given Serbian names, even though no Serbs have lived there. The Edvard Kardelj University of Ljubljana is no longer called such. And the Serbs and Croats alike have concocted their own names for lands they have seized: e.g., the Serbian designation of part of Croatia as the "Krajina," and the Croatian designation of Croat-occupied Herzegovina as "Herzeg-Bosna." This argument about the names of places has extended to the province of Kosovo, which Serbs lately call Kosmet, as they did from 1945 to 1968 (reviving, thus, a name repugnant to the Albanians), and to Macedonia (which the Greeks are willing to concede, at most, is "former Macedonia"), and even to the name "Yugoslavia," with Croatian resentment that the Serbs and Montenegrins have chosen to call their truncated state by this name.

Second, there is a conscious effort to find "appropriate" names for the enemy. The Serbs, for example, started calling the Croats "Ustaša" already in 1989, two years before the outbreak of war, suggesting that Tudjman's program is pure fascism. The Croats, offended by this usage, have themselves replied by calling the Serbs "Chetniks," but in this case, the name carries no sting, because many of the Serbs are in fact proudly calling themselves Chetniks. On other fronts, the Serbs have taken to calling the Albanians "Shiptars" (even though in Serbo-Croatian, Albanians

Introduction: The Roots of Discord and the Language of War   5

have wanted to be called "Albanci"), and the Muslims "Islamic fundamentalists." Tito is a special case here, in that Milošević has insisted on calling him "Broz" (Tito's actual family name), at the same time forcing the Serbian media to follow his lead.

Third, at least some citizens have considered it necessary, in times of war, to change their names, in order to assert their patriotism or just to preserve their lives and property. *Nedeljna Dalmacija,* a Split-based weekly, presented evidence in January 1993 of a wave of Croatian citizens, mostly Serbs, who had changed their names since 1991. As the newspaper explained, these people "for reasons well known to themselves want to nullify the awkward national sound of their own names through this action."[8]

And fourth, there has been a drive to purify the language itself, manifested, in Croatia, chiefly in a pseudo-Croatization of Croatian, involving the coining of new words with indigenous derivation and the revival of archaic Croatian-only words, and, in Serbia, in the suppression of the Latin alphabet (which had been widely promoted in Tito's day) in favor of an exclusive use of the Cyrillic alphabet, which both Serbs and Croats have associated with Serbian culture.

In addition to these four broad areas, there are also a number of specific areas of controversy, such as those surrounding the words "minority" and (as already mentioned briefly) "Yugoslavia," and the nature of the war itself.

Let us take our first case, the word "minority." *Webster's New World Dictionary of the American Language* defines "minority" as "less than half of a total; a group, party, or faction with a smaller number of votes or adherents than the majority."[9] The word has, thus, a purely mathematical reference, and accordingly, 49 percent of a population constitutes a minority, while 51 percent of a population constitutes a majority. For reasons having to do with the nature of Titoism's claims vis-a-vis the nationalities question,[10] the Yugoslavs never allowed, in the years following World War Two, that there were *any* "minorities" in the country, although under a strict definition of the word, there were *only* minorities, since even the largest group (the Serbs) constituted less than 40 percent of the total. As long as the state was at peace, however, this question as to whether the Macedonians, let us say, were a "minority" within Yugoslavia, or a "nation" within Yugoslavia (why not both?) seemed a quibble, and most observers seemed content to let the Yugoslavs reject mathematical concepts and choose more subjective ideological concepts. With the dissolution of the state, however, has come the strange spectacle of Serbs within Croatia insisting that, with 11.6 percent of the population of that republic, they were "not a minority," while their co-ethnics in Bosnia insisted that with 32 percent of the population of Bosnia-Herzegovina, they were also "not a minority" of the population of Bosnia. The consequence drawn from this language, as Paul Shoup explains in his chapter, was a rejection of the concept of majority rule, or of any concept of self-determination by a majority vote. This, in turn, opened up the prospect of an infinite spiral: when areas of Serbian concentration in Croatia declared their secession from Croatia, areas of Croatian concentration within those Serbian areas declared their secession from the Serbian secessionist area. Had war not intervened to resolve the issue, Serbian families living in the areas of Croatian density within the largely Serbian regions of Croatia could have declared their secession from the Croatian secessions from the Serbian secessions from the Croatian republic, which was seceding from Yugoslavia. What we have is something along the lines of a "this is the house that Jack built" formula, and is, in fact, the logical consequence of the rejection of the principle of majority rule which lay at the heart of the Titoist enterprise and which has been taken over by the ruling nationalists in both Serbia and Croatia.[11]

Another word which has been disputed in this war is the word "Yugoslavia." Until June 1991 everyone knew what "Yugoslavia" meant. But when Slovenia and Croatia declared their independence, the question immediately opened as to whether Yugoslavia was splitting up, or whether, rather, Slovenia and Croatia were seceding from a Yugoslavia which still existed. The controversy continued even after the declarations of independence by Bosnia-Herzegovina and Macedonia. At the heart of the issue was Belgrade's claim that Serbia and Montenegro constituted "Yugoslavia," and should enjoy the privileges of being the successor state to Yugoslavia (for example, retaining membership in international bodies). Belgrade later reinforced this claim by declaring the formation of the "Federal Republic of Yugoslavia"—not a "new" state, the world was told, but a reorgnization of the old "Socialist Federated Republic of Yugoslavia."

And finally, there is the matter of the war itself. Were Serbia and Croatia to agree on the terminology to describe the war, there would be considerable cause for surprise. But, on the contrary, they have construed the war rather differently.[12] In Serbia's eyes, there is a profound difference between the war with Croatia and the war with Bosnia. The former has been consistently portrayed in the Serbian media as a war to liberate unjustly persecuted Serbs from the claws of a fascist regime. That war is thus seen as political in nature. FRY President Dobrica Ćosić told Greek state television in January 1993 that the Croats were waging a "genocidal war" against the Serbs, adding that "entire villages have been burnt down."[13] By contrast, the Serbian press has repeatedly argued that the war against Bosnia is a "religious war," occasioned by the need to defend Serbian Christians against Islamic "fundamentalism." Thus, Tanjug, the official Serbian press agency, cited Dobrica Ćosić to the effect that ". . . a religious war is taking place in the Balkans and . . . is acquiring international dimensions, especially because of the presence of the Mujaheddin warriors in Bosnia-

Herzegovina."[14] In a typical effort to drive this point home, the politically rabid Belgrade daily *Politika ekspres* reported (falsely) in March 1992 that Ismet Kusumagić, described as a minister in the Bosnian government of Alija Izetbegović, was demanding that Islamic Shariat law be made the basis of civil law in Bosnia-Herzegovina.[15] By contrast, in Croatian eyes and media portrayals, there is ultimately no difference between Serbia's war against Croatia itself and Serbia's war against Bosnia. Both are seen as wars of territorial expansion, stoked by inflaming nationalist chauvinism and inter-ethnic hatreds. Ironically, it was Slobodan Milošević himself who warned, in January 1990, about the danger of "national and religious hatreds" which could "spring from out of the darkness concealing them into the light of day, the hatreds that led us into a fratricidal war in the past, a war which we well know was such that its consequences will burden the consciousness even of the generations that are yet to be born."[16]

III

It will be years before the full consequences of the war are known. Most Western news reports are based either on battlefield observation or on visits to the respective capital city. Ignored are the various towns and villages which are not under siege, but which, typically, bear the brunt of the burden of war: the capital city is, as a rule, the last to feel shortages. This is why Western journalists' and other travelers' reports that shops in Belgrade and Zagreb are full of goods (qualified, at high prices) miss the point, which is that the war is indeed destroying the economies of these republics, gutting entire communities and driving huge numbers of people below the poverty line. Kragujevac, once a thriving industrial town, has been economically ravaged by the war, and many local Serbs are without work and roam the streets idly: random crime in Kragujevac has soared since early 1992, as a result.[17] Again, the Serbian economy has slid steadily downwards, enduring an inflation rate of 19,810 percent in 1992.[18] According to renowned Yugoslav economist Oskar Kovač, up to 90 percent of enterprises in the Federal Republic of Yugoslavia (Serbia and Montenegro) may go bankrupt before the end of 1993, with many markets permanently lost to Serbian firms.[19] Health services and medical protection have likewise deteriorated in the FRY since the outbreak of the war, and Belgrade authorities feared widespread food shortages by the end of 1993, in the event that the international embargo was not lifted (or more effectively circumvented).[20] There are, of course, always those who profit during times of hardship and scarcity, and consistent with this pattern some Belgrade firms have chalked up sizeable profits recently.[21] But by November 1992, there were already nearly 3 million unemployed in Serbia and the number was rising.[22]

The situation is, of course, worse in Croatia, whose labor force of 1.2 million persons must sustain the burden of financing the 270,000 unemployed (as of December 1992), 550,000 refugees, and 667,000 pensioners. Recently, the Croatian economy has been marking up an annual budget deficit of $2.5 billion, and Croatian authorities announced steep tax increases to take effect in January 1993.[23] Industrial production has fallen in Croatia— by 28.5 percent in 1991 alone and by another 28.1 percent in the first six months of 1992[24]—while inflation, which roared at 609.9 percent in 1990, slowed to 122.6 percent in 1991, and has crept upwards again to 384.3 percent in the first six months of 1992. Exports declined 24.7 percent in 1991, and another 19.3 percent in the first seven months of 1992.[25] In the Serbian Krajina, which was always the poorest region in Croatia, there have been reports of the exhaustion of food supplies, and the emigration of locals to Slovenia and inner Serbia.

Bosnia's economy is completed gutted, with entire industrial sectors physically destroyed or damaged beyond simple repair. Moreover, much of the transport infrastructure linking Bosnia with Croatia and linking parts of Bosnia has been destroyed, chiefly by Serbian militias, according to news reports. And even those republics not involved in the fighting, viz., Slovenia and Macedonia, have been affected by the war: the disruption of trade connections, the restrictions of the UN imposed trade embargo on Serbia and Montenegro, and, in Macedonia's case, the derivative Greek blockade have all hit these economies hard.

The result is a region seriously impacted by the war—whether in terms of lives lost, or in terms of the destruction of the economic infrastructure necessary for those who survive to make their way. The old Yugoslavia, which died a stormy death as rising nationalism tore it limb from limb, has not only been politically dismantled, thus. It has also been psychologically scarred and economically retrogressed, while all the while, the new muses of war have elaborated national scripts to celebrate this new purgatory (with its moments of sheer hell) as if it were heaven.

Notes

1. In interview with *Profil* (Vienna), 30 November 1992, p. 57, trans. in FBIS, *Daily Report* (Eastern Europe), 1 December 1992, p. 60.

2. Radoslav Stojanović, *Jugoslavija, nacije i politika* (Belgrade: Nova knjiga, 1988).

3. Ljubo Boban, "Still More Balance on Jasenovac and the Manipulation of History," in *East European Politics and Societies*, Vol. 6, No. 2 (Spring 1992), p. 215.

4. See my article, "The Breakup of Yugoslavia" , in *Global Affairs*, Vol. 6, No. 2 (Spring 1991), p. 97.

5. Bogdan Denitch, *Limits and Possibilities: The Crisis of Yugoslav Socialism and State Socialist Systems* (Minneapolis: University of Minnesota Press, 1990); and V.

Introduction: The Roots of Discord and the Language of War 9

P. Gagnon, Jr., "Yugoslavia—Prospects for Stability" in *Foreign Affairs* Vol. 70, No. 3 (Summer 1991). Also Dennison Rusinow, "To Be or Not to Be? Yugoslavia as Hamlet," in *UFSI Field Staff Reports*, 1990–91 series, No. 18 (June 1991).

6. Including even the rock scene: for discussion of this lesser known dimension, see Sabrina Petra Ramet, *Balkan Babel: Politics, Culture, and Religion in Yugoslavia* (Boulder, Colo.: Westview Press, 1992), chapter 5 ("Rock Music").

7. Cynthia Cockburn, "A Women's Political Party for Yugoslavia: Introduction to the Serbian Feminist Manifesto," in *Feminist Review*, No. 39 (Winter 1991), p. 156.

8. *Nedeljna Dalmacija*, as quoted in *Borba* (Belgrade), 20 January 1993, p. 12, trans. in FBIS, *Daily Report* (Eastern Europe), 2 February 1993, p. 48.

9. *Webster's New World Dictionary of the American Language*, 2nd College Ed. (Cleveland, Ohio: William Collins and World Publishing Co., 1976), p. 906.

10. For discussion, see Sabrina Petra Ramet, *Nationalism and Federalism in Yugoslavia, 1962-1991*, 2nd ed. (Bloomington, Ind.: Indiana University Press, 1992).

11. Zoran Djindjić offers a somewhat different approach, arguing that insofar as old Yugoslavia has ceased to exist, so too have old Croatia, Serbia, Bosnia-Herzegovina, and Macedonia, leaving only peoples with legitimate rights, but not preexisting legitimate states, as is usually supposed. This argument would, of course, appeal to the Greeks. See Djindjić's "Jugoslawien—ein unerwünschter Staat," in *Die Neue Gesellschaft, Frankfurter Hefte*, Vol. 38, No. 9 (September 1991), p. 775.

12. The remainder of this paragraph draws freely from my essay, "Delegitimation and Relegitimation in Yugoslavia and After," in George Andreopoulos (ed.), *International Security in Eastern Europe*, forthcoming from Greenwood Press.

13. Tanjug (26 January 1993), in FBIS, *Daily Report* (Eastern Europe), 27 January 1993, p. 44.

14. Tanjug (17 October 1992), in FBIS, *Daily Report* (Eastern Europe), 20 October 1992, p. 37.

15. *Politika ekspres* (Belgrade), 31 March 1992, summarized in Tanjug (31 March 1992), in FBIS, *Daily Report* (Eastern Europe), 1 April 1992, p. 42.

16. *Politika* (Belgrade), 22 January 1990, p. 2.

17. *Borba* (6 November 1992), p. 11.

18. Tanjug (1 February 1993), in FBIS, *Daily Report* (Eastern Europe), 2 February 1993, p. 53.

19. *Ibid.*

20. Re. medical services, see Tanjug (3 February 1993), in FBIS, *Daily Report* (Eastern Europe), 4 February 1993, p. 52; re. food shortage, see Tanjug (25 January 1993), in FBIS, *Daily Report* (Eastern Europe), 26 January 1993, p. 62.

21. *Politika* (5 November 1992), p. 11.

22. Tanjug (13 November 1992), in FBIS, *Daily Report* (Eastern Europe), 16 November 1992, p. 40.

23. *Financial Times* (12 December 1991), p. 8.

24. *Vjesnik* (28 March 1992), p. 2, trans. in FBIS, *Daily Report* (Eastern Europe), 20 April 1992, p. 32; and *Neue Zürcher Zeitung* (30 September 1992), p. 16.

25. *Neue Zürcher Zeitung* (30 September 1992), p. 16.

PART ONE

Adumbrations of the Breakup

1

The Avoidable Catastrophe

Dennison Rusinow[1]

Historians and social scientists are adept at retrospectively discovering why whatever happens was always inevitable, as if the various efforts to produce some alternative result had never had any prospect of success whatsoever. So it is with the violent disintegration of Yugoslavia in 1991. Scholars are already busy following the media in describing Yugoslavia as an "artificial" state (whatever that means) and an ill-fated experiment that was doomed to shatter once Tito's dictatorship was no longer there to hold it together. The deep cultural, religious, historical, and socio-economic differences among its peoples and their allegedly ancient or even primordial hatreds of one another are why its creation was unnatural and its disintegration inevitable.

This is a doubly flawed argument. The hidden premise of the purportedly particular and fatal "artificiality" of the Yugoslav state is that only homogeneous single-nation nation-states are "natural" and therefore sustainable or even legitimate. Leaving aside as a quibble the counter-argument that *all* states are human (and contingent) artifacts and thus "artificial," this historically and theoretically debatable and much debated premise is far from self-evident and at best a potentially misleading over-simplification of a complex set of modern cultural and political phenomena.[2] Secondly, the contention that some or all of the South Slav peoples have always hated one another so much that only Royal and then Communist dictatorships could temporarily suppress their urge to largescale reciprocal violence is contradicted by the historical record. Except for devastating casualties in inter-communal civil war within a wider triune war[3] during World War II, which occurred in exceptional circumstances and with external (Axis) provocation, most of them have lived in relative peace—although not necessarily in harmony—for most of the centuries that two or more of them have cohabited in many countrysides and towns. With cooperation as common as conflict, inter-communal violence has been as sporadic and usually low-level as in other multi-cultural states and regions that are normally regarded as also conflict-prone but fundamentally stable communities. Although easily subject to sentimental, romantic exaggeration, the "anecdotal evidence" of inter-faith and inter-ethnic marriages, families and friendships and of shared feast-days and house-raising is too impressive in quantity and in spatial and temporal distribution to be dismissed as marginal or irrelevant.

As will be argued below, Yugoslavia's second disintegration actually became "inevitable" only shortly before it occurred, and primarily because the calculations and/or ineptitude of post-Tito politicians from several regions and nations, superimposed on a decade of mounting economic, political, and social crisis that had "de-legitimized" the regime and system but not yet the state, transformed endemic tensions and conflicts among its diverse nationalities into collective existential fears for their communal survival that progressively infected them all. What *was* inevitable (and therefore widely considered a powerful inhibition) was that Yugoslavia's deconstruction, if consummated in haste and by unilateral actions, would be violent rather than peaceful. Even then, however, the magnitude of hatreds released and the inhuman brutality of the violence are comprehensible only as the results of deliberate incitement and exploitation, by the same politicians, of historical or personal memories of ancient and recent wrongs and stereotypes that a Bosnian Serb, speaking for her own nation, calls "things [that] slumbered in the hearts of many Serbs, but it took an industry of hate to revive them."[4]

"The Improbable Survivor," Stevan Pavlowitch's title of a book about "Yugoslavia and its problems" published in 1988, is an apt description of the country that his title and text implicitly assumed would somehow and improbably continue to survive in some form.[5] Yugoslavia was always a doubtful and problematic creation: a multi-national anomaly in the age of nationalism and nation-states, and a union of diverse peoples, endowed by separate histories with distinct cultures and more or less distinct languages, acute differences in economic development and interests, and in several cases already fully developed, widely diffused, and essentially competitive national consciousness and "national ideologies." They soon discovered that they had little in common except "the Yugoslav idea" and the similarities of language, myths of origin, and aspirations to be free of foreign domination on which it was based.[6] But survive it did, "improbably" and despite the interval of its destruction by the Axis in 1941 and the civil war and attempted mutual genocide that followed, from 1918 until 1991.

Yugoslavia was not the creation of Woodrow Wilson's Fourteen Points and the peace process of 1919–20, although these facilitated and consummated its creation, or solely the re-creation of Tito and his Communist-led

The Avoidable Catastrophe 15

National Liberation Struggle, although these were essential to its restoration. It was created in 1918 and re-created in 1943–45 by patriotic South Slavs who believed that some form of union—although they might disagree about the form—was preferable to separate nation-states that would be small, weak, vulnerable to renewed foreign domination, still multi-national (except Slovenia) and condemned by the ethnic map and competing nationalist ideologies to a plethora of minorities and a plague of reciprocal irredentisms.

This is the essence of "the Yugoslav idea," twice born and triumphant over competing national ideas and nationalist programs and now, along with the Yugoslav state, twice dead and buried.[7] Its strength is its recognition of the impossibility of drawing the borders of true (nationally homogeneous) nation-states where nations are so scattered and inter-mingled, and the inevitability of irredentist conflicts and minority problems within and among supposedly national states imposed on such an ethnic patchwork. It particularly recognized the importance of these problems for the Serbs, Croats, and Serbo-Croatian- or Croato-Serbian-speaking Slavic Muslims (since 1968 officially a separate nation), whose diasporas outside their historical matrix-states (for present purposes considered to be the late federation's republics of Serbia, Croatia, and Bosnia-Herzegovina) constituted 25.6 percent, 20 percent, and 19 percent of their respective total numbers in the census of 1991, taken just before "ethnic cleansing" began to change their distribution.[8] It is no coincidence that the principal advocates of the Yugoslav idea were Croats, Serbs, and Muslims from those parts of Croatia and Bosnia-Herzegovina cohabited by two or all three of these peoples. Its primary weakness was its advocates' failure to recognize the existence, or else fully to comprehend the implications, of competition from the earlier or later development of full-fledged national consciousness and national ideologies among Croats, Serbs, Slovenes, some Montenegrins, and eventually also Macedonians and Muslims.

In its later evolution—when "Illyrianism" had become "Yugoslavism" after the demise of the idea of Illyrians as the common ancestors of all South Slavs—advocates of the Yugoslav idea sought to cope with this problem in one of two ways. The first, which has been called "integral Yugoslavism" or "Yugoslavist unitarism,"[9] was by denying the separate nationhood of Serbs, Croats, and Slovenes alike, or seeking to supersede it, by either positing the existence of a single "Yugoslav nation" (subdivided into ethnolinguistic and perhaps other historically-formed "tribes" or merely "names") or by creating one (later called "nation-building"). The second, found in all phases of the "Titoist answer" to the national question except its drift toward integral Yugoslavism, circa 1953–62,[10] was by recognizing separate nationhoods and seeking constitutional and other formulae for a multinational state of related peoples with shared interests and aspirations.

There are significant differences between the first and second deaths of the Yugoslav idea and the Yugoslav state. The Yugoslav idea was "de-legitimized" for non-Serbs (especially Croats) in the first Yugoslavia primarily by perceptions of Serb hegemony, and of King Aleksandar's "Yugoslav nation" as Serbianization, that were largely valid. However, the first Yugoslavia was destroyed by Axis invasion and policy; whether it might otherwise have survived, perhaps even finding ways of regaining or finally winning the loyalty of more or most of its non-Serb citizens, remains a hypothetical "might-have-been." The second Yugoslavia, on the other hand, disintegrated entirely from within and against the overt wishes of all interested foreign powers, although it can be and has been argued that the timing of foreign recognition (or non-recognition) of seceding republics affected the later stages and violence of the process. Moreover, de-legitimation of the Yugoslav idea in the second Yugoslavia had more complex and differentiated causes and came later in its history: significant in magnitude and effect only in the 1980s, first intensely felt (or openly expressed) by traditionally pro- Yugoslav Slovenes, and eventually also affecting many Serbs, who came to regard "Tito's Yugoslavia" as an anti-Serb conspiracy.

By the end of the 1980s (the precise year is arguable) it was clear that Yugoslavia in its current form could not survive. Although for different reasons and with conflicting ideas about what form of "third Yugoslavia" or no Yugoslavia should replace it, the kind of union that most were now critically rather than admiringly calling "Tito's Yugoslavia" was no longer wanted by almost any of them. Most of the exceptions, apart from mostly older officers in "his" army whose loyalty to his legacy for a time resembled the post-Ataturk attitude of Ataturk's army, were Bosnians and Macedonians with particular reasons to fear all of the alternatives more than they might also dislike the hybrid of federalism and confederalism created by Tito's last (1974) Constitution and its interpretation in practice.

This was not true when Josip Broz Tito died ten years earlier, in May 1980. As foreign witnesses reported at the time,[11] the grief and consternation registered by almost all Yugoslavs when it finally happened were genuine and suffused with apprehensive hope for the future of the united Yugoslav state he symbolized as its principal builder and maintainer. The smoothness of the transition and the attitude of increasingly free and critical mass and specialized media during the following two years of deepening economic woes suggested that his successors were receiving a benefit-of-the-doubt honeymoon of transposed legitimacy that they proved incapable of exploiting.

This is not to say that most were content under single-party and authoritarian (but no longer "totalitarian" or centralized) Communist rule, "self-management market socialism" that was only marginally a market

The Avoidable Catastrophe 17

or self-managed, and constitutional and political arrangements under which most people regarded "their" nation as exploited or disadvantaged. But most apparently still agreed with the dictum attributed to Father Antun Korošec, the Slovenes' principal political leader in the pre-war, Serb-dominated Yugoslav Kingdom, that even a bad Yugoslavia is preferable to no Yugoslavia.

By the summer of 1989, none of Korosec's heirs in Slovenia as (at that time) current and reform-Communist or future and anti-communist political leaders seemed able to recall his dictum. Instead, members of both groups were using the same words, in a kind of litany, to call Yugoslavia "a 70-year-old mistake that should finally be rectified." By the following spring I was hearing much the same thing in Croatia and even in Serbia.[12]

How the atmosphere illustrated in these anecdotes changed so decisively in a single decade is a tale of the progressive "de-legitimation" of Tito's successors, the regime and system, and finally the state itself. It also explains how and why the Yugoslavs spoiled the comparative advantages, derived from earlier experiments and experience with markets, market mechanisms, and political quasi-pluralism, that should have enabled them to move toward a genuine market economy and stable multi-party political systems faster and with greater success and less pain than Europe's other post-Communist societies.

In part defused and in part suppressed but never solved by "the Titoist solution"—consisting of a state for each South Slav nation[13] in an increasingly genuine federation, economic decentralization, and cultural autonomy under a centralized but multinational and supposedly "internationalist" Communist dictatorship—the national question was still the country's most ominous unfinished business when Tito's death removed the system's ultimate arbiter and linchpin. With the Communist Party (officially the League of Communists of Yugoslavia) as well as the Yugoslav state otherwise already thoroughly "federalized" or even quasi-"confederalized" into eight competing regional-national party-states,[14] the potential for its rearmament, figuratively and literally, was manifest.

The decade following Tito's death was marked by permanent economic crisis and declining living standards. The downward spiral was harder on morale and confidence in the regime and one another because it came after three decades in which rising expectations reflected and anticipated the continuation of dramatic growth in public and private income and expenditures and quality of life for most people in most places—although from very low starting levels and in the 1970s largely funded by various forms of borrowing against the future that came due, disastrously, in the 1980s.

In 1982 and thereafter, congresses and other forums of the League of Communists and the Federal Assembly repeatedly and formally agreed, with increasing directness and intensity, that the primary culprit was the latest, unworkable version of self-management socialism and quasi-markets, which should be speedily reformed and largely dismantled in favor of a full-fledged market economy ("real" markets for capital and labor as well as goods and services). Corresponding action was perpetually vitiated by non-adoption or non-implementation of all such reforms, and in most years even effective macro-economic policies.[15] "Official" definitions of the crisis, from party and government forums, expanded from merely "economic" to "economic and political" to "social" and "systemic." Although other inhibitions also played a role, this dismal record was in large part because the 1974 Constitution required the consensus of all eight republics and provinces, with differing economic and political interests and "national" leaderships to interpret and promote them, for decision-making in severely limited areas of federal competence. Furthermore, implementation and enforcement of the results, if any, were largely by republican rather than federal organs. Centralized and centralizing solutions were unacceptable to powerful republican and provincial "Party Barons," which was enough to block them in any case, and to almost all of their constituents and clients except Serbs; decentralized ones were ineffective, often inappropriate, complicating, and above all tended to magnify differences. Meanwhile, each successive year of unremitting economic crisis, manifestly dysfunctional political institutions and behavior, and growing social and inter-communal tensions further eroded the dwindling acceptability (legitimacy) of the regime and system. The only surprise lay in the perverse patience of most Yugoslavs, and therefore the slowness of this process.

The centrality of the national question, with the federal units and their leaders regarded as national states and leaderships and nationalism(s) functioning in a vicious circle as both consequence and cause of failure to cope with economic crisis and the regime's dissolving legitimacy, was built into this equation. The details and dynamics of political paralysis, revision and "de-mystification" of Partisan and postwar "Titoist" history as an additive to the system's de-legitimation, the emergence of what has been described as "apocalypse culture" (a *Zeitgeist* as well as specific, usually critical works anticipating and prescribing for dramatic change), and the cause-and-effect role of competing nationalisms in all of these have been described and analyzed elsewhere.[16] However, the gradual evolution of stalemate and crisis from what former U.S. Ambassador David Anderson calls "nationalist/historical/religious/cultural strains"[17] of an endemic but usually containable kind into a life-threatening challenge to the existence of a single Yugoslav state arguably would not have happened without the addition of a new factor: collective existential fear, refracted from group to group until almost all were affected.

Perhaps the primary reason why those strains between Yugoslavia's diverse peoples never before seriously threatened the survival of the sec-

The Avoidable Catastrophe

ond Yugoslav state is that none of the major national communities, however much each considered itself disadvantaged or exploited, felt that the existence of its members *as a national community* was actually endangered, either in its "own" Republic (for the six South Slavic "state nations") or Autonomous Province (for the non-Slavic Albanians of Kosovo) or as a numerically significant minority in another Republic (e.g., the Serbs of Croatia).

This had not been the case in Serb-dominated inter-war Yugoslavia, where most non-Serbs came to feel threatened as national communities by Serbianization in the guise of proclamations and policies designed to meld them into a single "Yugoslav nation." (The chief exception was the Slovenes, who were protected by distance, compactness, their own language, and the deals their leaders struck with Belgrade, and who still perceived *Deutschtum* and *italianità* as the primary threats to their territory and cultural community both within and outside Yugoslavia.) No such existential fear was credible in Tito's federal Yugoslavia.[18] Here each South Slav nation, and after 1968 even the formerly oppressed Albanian "nationality" in Kosovo, enjoyed (or in the Muslim case shared) the protection and promotion of its cultural and national identity provided by a *de jure* or *de facto* republic and a national-Communist political elite of its own. Their diasporas, officially part of their respective state-nations and not minorities ("nationalities"), possessed a measure of corresponding protection under the Yugoslav umbrella, which at least united all Serbs (as the largest and most sensitive diaspora nation) in a single if federal state. To this extent, Tito's strategy of containing divisive nationalisms through a combination of territorial-national autonomy and a balance of power and grievances among the contenders (especially between Serbs and non-Serbs) may have provided a more viable solution to the national question than is generally recognized today, when its instability and ultimately "transient" nature is retrospectively manifest.[19] Indeed, it may have done more to preserve both peace and unity than his ability to blow the whistle when he thought it was not working, as he did to topple "nationalist" and "liberal" leaderships in Croatia and elsewhere in 1971–72. The problem after 1980 was not only the lack of such a whistle-blower. Quasi-confederal federalism, the legacy of Tito's strategy in its final phase, was no longer working in practice. It was also increasingly challenged in principle by the most numerous nation, the Serbs, who were coming to regard it as a plot, based on the principle that "a weak Serbia is a strong Yugoslavia," to keep them divided and powerless in a state they believed they had done the most to create and defend.

Kosovo provided the time-fuse, and Slobodan Milošević provided the detonators, for a chain-reaction of explosions in which first Serbs and then Albanians, Slovenes, Croats, and others came to believe, often to the point of obsession, that part or all of their nation was already or could be faced with extinction as a national community living where history (either ancient or more recent) and the modern doctrine of national self-determination give it an inalienable right to live and to govern itself.

The Kosovo problem is in origin and recent history a classic case of conflict between one people's historic and another's ethnic claim to the same territory. Kosovo is sacred to Serbs, for whom it is the cradle of their culture, church, and statehood and the place where their epic defeat in 1389 led to their infamous "five hundred years under the Turkish yoke." They like to call it "our Jerusalem," suggesting a strong emotional attachment and right to a place that was once theirs and then lost. As a result of later (including recent) migrations and staggeringly high Albanian birthrates in this century, about 90 percent of Kosovo's population now consists of Albanians, mostly Muslim. The Kosovo problem is therefore also a double minority and after 1968 a double irredentist problem: for Albanians as a minority in Yugoslavia, and for Serbs and Montenegrins as a minority in Kosovo. It is further complicated by the poverty, both relative and absolute, that affects and embitters most members of both communities.

In the spring of 1981, eleven months after Tito's death, it entered its current and acute phase when mass demonstrations by Albanians, demanding the Province's transformation from a *de facto* into a *de jure* Republic, were violently suppressed. Throughout the 1980's further repression, the dispatch of police reinforcements and army units to the Province, and widespread violations of civil rights periodically calmed but never quelled a simmering Albanian rebellion, which was abetted by purged but still resistant Albanian political and intellectual elites and Provincial Party and government leaders. The exodus of the Province's dwindling Slav minority continued unabated.[20]

Until 1987 the Kosovo problem, although intractable, seemed likely to continue to be a Yugoslav Northern Ireland: festering on and doomed to periodic violence, but basically containable within the Province.[21] Then the bitterness and aggravation of nationalist passion engendered in Serbs everywhere by the Albanian challenge to Serbian suzerainty and the relic of a Serb community in Kosovo found a focus and mobilizing force in the person of Slobodan Milošević, President of the Presidency of the League of Communists of Serbia since the preceding year. Seizing on the plight of Serbs and Serbdom in Kosovo, Milošević rode the tiger of aroused Serb nationalism to unchallengeable personal power in Serbia (and through proxies in Montenegro), to the destruction of Kosovo's (and Vojvodina's) autonomy in all but name, and to the defense of Serbs and Serbdom wherever else these might be threatened in fact or in his and his supporters' fancy. For a scripture he had a "Memorandum" drafted by the Serbian Academy of Science and Arts in 1986, detailing the injustice and discrimi-

The Avoidable Catastrophe

nation suffered by Serbia under Tito's rule and calling for remedy through a unified and strong Serb community and state.[22]

By March 1989, when he became President of Serbia's state presidency under a new constitution also marking the effective end of the autonomy of the two provinces, Milošević could boast that Serbia—if not yet all the Serbs—had finally been reunited. In consonance with historic Serb preference, as the largest nation with the largest diaspora, for a centralized ("unitarist") Yugoslavia in which they assume they will play the leading role and can better protect that diaspora, he had also launched a further campaign for a strengthened federal center, both governmental and in the League of Communists.[23]

In the process, and in the reactions of non-Serbs to a strategy they perceived as an attempt to reimpose both Serb and Communist hegemony throughout Yugoslavia, the Kosovo poison spread to the rest of the country.[24]

Slovenes were the first to express widespread concern that Milošević's strategy, and the nationalist passions that were being fanned and exploited in its service, could presage threats not only to their autonomy but to their longer-term survival as a small nation in a Serb- and Milošević-dominated Yugoslavia. Slovene calls for a loose confederation of "sovereign" states or outright secession multiplied inside as well as outside the Republic's Communist establishment. By 1989 conflict between Slovenia and Serbia, escalating from mutual accusations and threats to boycotts, temporarily took over from Serb-Croat issues as the centerpiece of the national question.

As Milošević extended his claim to be the knight-errant of Serbdom to the diaspora Serbs of Croatia and Bosnia-Herzegovina, and as Croatia's Serbs responded (in rural regions where they were a majority) with demonstrations decrying "cultural genocide" by the Croatian regime and calling for autonomy, the Croats of Croatia and the Slavic-Muslim plurality and Croat minority in Bosnia-Herzegovina were increasingly prone to similar fears. So were nationally conscious Macedonians, recalling their definition as "South Serbs" and Serbianization policies in the first Yugoslavia, and those Montenegrins who believed that they are a Montenegrin nation rather than merely the best and fiercest Serbs.

A vicious circle of reciprocal fears, fueled by deliberate incitement of memories that had slumbered in the hearts, was on its way to becoming a vicious spiral of mutually self-fulfilling prophecies. Its first acute and eventually violent vortex, as described below, was in parts of Croatia with local Serb majorities or large minorities. Here actions and reactions based on fears for Serb national and Croatian territorial integrity or survival would feed on one another—with the first aggravated by especially awful local experience of the Ustaše (Croatian fascist) regime's attempt to exterminate Croatia's Serbs during the Second World War and the second by the region's

22   *Dennison Rusinow*

strategic location astride crucial communications between continental and Dalmatian Croatia—until both were increasingly valid.

Defied by first one and then most of the republics, the writ of federal authorities, highly limited in content throughout the 1980s, had meanwhile ceased to run in almost all matters. The way Serbia's new constitution was adopted in March 1989, parts of the Slovenian one proclaimed that September, and legislation to implement both of these violated the federal constitution with impunity.[25] Emotional expressions of hypertrophied national sentiments mounted almost everywhere. In these circumstances apparently irreconcilable confrontation between a joint Slovene-Croatian proposal for a loose confederation that Serbia's rulers found totally unacceptable and a Serbian-inspired proposal for a "modern federation" (more centralized than Yugoslavia's since the 1950s), which Slovenes and Croats rejected out of hand, seemed to presage a break-up and violence to prevent or consummate it.

1990 began with the evaporation of the League of Communists of Yugoslavia, and with it Slobodan Milošević's putative strategy to restore a more centralized federation.[26]

The party's demise came before dawn on 24 January 1990, with a dramatic adjournment *sine diem* of its 14th and last Congress. It had been convened six months ahead of schedule at the request (a contingency authorized by the party statute) of the Vojvodina League of Communists, now a satellite of Milošević's Serbian Party. This suggests that Milošević believed that the time was right for his bid for a revitalized and re-centralized communist party, which he could control, and through which other, recalcitrant Republican leaderships could be tamed as Tito had tamed them.

If so, he had miscalculated—and not only because of increasing resistance to his apparently hegemonic intentions in most of the country. In the weeks between the summons to Congress and its convening a revolutionary wave swept across the rest of eastern Europe, toppling Communist regimes and promising democratic elections and market economies everywhere except in Albania. In Yugoslavia, until recently but no longer the proud bellwether of "liberalization" and "marketization" under Communist rule, these events reinforced a trend toward acceptance of multi-party elections and their own conversion into Socialist or Social-democratic parties that was already well underway among Slovenian and Croatian Communists and gathering steam in Macedonia and Bosnia-Herzegovina. In December "reform-Communists" in these republics, which Milošević had already described as forming "an unprincipled anti-Serb coalition," won majorities that exceeded some of their own expectations[27] in the regional party congresses that had preceded and increasingly influenced federal congresses since 1969.

The Avoidable Catastrophe 23

The Slovene delegation arrived committed to walk out if the Congress failed to accept a still looser (confederal) "League of Leagues," endorsement of multiparty elections, and a strong stand in favor of "human rights" throughout the country (read: Kosovo), all of which Milošević's cohort of delegations from Serbia, the formally separate parties in Vojvodina and Kosovo, and Montenegro were bound to oppose. At the end of four days of acrimonious debates, the Slovenes finally did walk out. After a dramatic confrontation at the podium between Milošević and Croatian party President Ivica Račan—Serb against Croat again, without the Slovenes as buffer and foil—a rump session eventually agreed with Račan's insistence that the Congress could not continue without one of the League of Communists' constituent regional parties.

The Communist Party or League of Communists of Yugoslavia, creator and sustainer of the second Yugoslav state, had self-disintegrated. Little else was left to support the continuance of that state except the residue of "the Yugoslav idea" and its rationale, a motley of federal organs with diminishing authority, and the Army with its 70 percent Serb and Montenegrin officer corps. And the confrontation between Milošević and Račan marked the return to center-stage in the Yugoslav drama of rivalry and conflict between Yugoslavia's two largest nations, with large diasporas in one another's homelands and intermingled in Bosnia-Herzegovina to magnify the risks.

The sole and momentary exception to the rule of diminishing federal authority was the President of the Federal Executive Council (federal government), Ante Marković, whose demonstration of leadership in launching the most comprehensive and hopeful economic reforms of the post-Tito era was elevating his visibility and popularity at the moment of the Yugoslav Party's Congress and demise. Perhaps also in a momentary reflexive search for a substitute pan-Yugoslav symbol, public opinion polls that spring identified him as the country's most popular politician, even in Serbia. In June I listened to people in Belgrade and Zagreb discussing, more in hope than in fear or with any evidence that it might happen, the possibility of an Army-supported, time-limited "Roman dictatorship" (their term, although more recent Turkish precedents also come to mind) to permit Marković to draft and impose a new constitution, and to create democratic country-wide parties, over the heads of Republican-national Party leaderships. But Marković dithered, and the window of opportunity for some kind of "Marković solution" disappeared, if it ever existed, before he finally announced the formation of his own pan-Yugoslav "Party of Reform Forces" in late summer, and too late.

What was left of the Yugoslav idea was meanwhile suffering the consequences of its co-optation by the Communist Party, under the now increasingly dubious slogan of South Slav "brotherhood and unity," into the

24   *Dennison Rusinow*

discredited when not passionately despised corpus of Titoist-Communist ideology and propaganda. If Communists had promoted it, according to the logic of the new times, it must have been a bad and probably nefarious idea.

By the end of 1990 all six republics had held genuinely if imperfectly competitive multi-party elections: in Slovenia and Croatia in April-May, in Macedonia and Bosnia-Herzegovina in November, and in Serbia and Montenegro in December.[28] As a reflection of voter preferences, the results and mandates they bestowed were sometimes more ambiguous (even discounting the net effects of some fraud and more pressure as unmeasurable) than the parliamentary majorities and governments they produced. In Croatia and Serbia the electoral arithmetic of single-member constituencies transformed mere electoral pluralities into decisive one-party parliamentary majorities, in Serbia further inflated by an Albanian boycott of the elections. In Slovenia the parliamentary majority and government represented a coalition of seven anti-communist but otherwise heterogeneous parties, called Demos, none of which received as many votes as the "reform-Communist" party or its former youth organization. And in Macedonia the formation of a non-party "government of experts" followed three months of fruitless attempts to assemble a working majority in parliament. Moreover, the public stances of the winning parties or coalitions tended to ambiguity on the vital question of the future shape of Yugoslavia and its alternatives.

Four of the six elections produced non-Communist majorities and governments, although these included co-opted or former Communists, including three heads of state: Presidents Milan Kučan of Slovenia (President of the Slovene party from 1986 to 1989), Franjo Tudjman of Croatia (although out of the party and anti-communist for 20 years), and Kiro Gligorov of Macedonia. The exception was Alija Izetbegović, who became President of Bosnia-Herzegovina's seven-member collective State Presidency; in prison a decade earlier for activities and an "Islamic Declaration" that the regime then and his opponents in the 1990s considered "Islamic fundamentalist," he was now head of his Republic's more militant Muslim party. All of the new governments, including the Communist ones in Serbia (where the ruling party had renamed itself the Socialist Party of Serbia in July 1990) and Montenegro, can fairly be described as nationalist in orientation and policy—except in trinational Bosnia-Herzegovina, where precentages of the electorate voting for Muslim, Serb, and Croat parties were almost exactly proportionate to the national composition of the population. There the new collective state presidency and government were for the moment precariously multinational and pledged to defend the civic peace and territorial integrity of their Yugoslavia-in-miniature—an impossible prospect if the greater Yugoslavia were to disintegrate.

The Avoidable Catastrophe

Wherever these new governments or individual leaders enjoyed a strong parliamentary majority and a weak or divided opposition, they tended to display authoritarian instincts. One example was their attempts (largely successful) to substitute their own for Communist control over mass media, especially television.[29] A malicious observer might describe their behavior as an attempt to substitute "the dictatorship of the proletariat," which was that of its Communist "vanguard," with "the dictatorship of the nation," meaning themselves as its tutors. Where the former was intolerant of other classes, the latter tends to be intolerant or at least insensitive toward other nations and national minorities within its jurisdiction: Serbs in Croatia, Muslims and Croats as well as Albanians in Serbia, "Southerners" (*Juznjaci*) of all kinds in Slovenia, and others.

In the months after their elections, the governments of Slovenia, Croatia, and Serbia watched their popularity slipping in public opinion polls, primarily (they and press commentaries assumed) because they were seen to be doing little about the still deteriorating economy but possibly also in reaction to their political behavior: authoritarian in Serbia and Croatia and high-handed and blundering in Slovenia. Tri-national government in Bosnia-Herzegovina passed through stalemate to effective disintegration and domination by its Muslim part.[30] In March 1991 Milošević's hold on Serbia was seriously challenged when the army was called in to disperse a peaceful demonstration by the combined opposition in Belgrade, resulting in two deaths and sparking a five-day occupation of the city center by protesting students and others. Milošević made concessions and seemed to be in serious political trouble.

In each case the government concerned found some way to refocus popular attention on its nation's respective national traumas and national enemies, to reiterate that "Only Unity Saves the Serbs" (or Croats or Slovenes, although it is a Serb slogan of great antiquity), and thus to recoup popularity and silence dissenting voices. In doing so they ignored (and in the process also gradually eliminated) the possibility that declining popularity might also reflect alarm over policies on the national front and in inter-republican relations that seemed to be leading toward a breakup, for which none of them as yet had a clear mandate or evidence of majority support (even in Slovenia,[31]) and a strong probability of ensuing violence, which almost no one yet wanted.

In a double confrontation, with one another and with their own fearful and volatile constituencies (and opposition parties, some more radically nationalist than they), the nationalist politicians in charge of Serbia, Croatia, Slovenia, and the Muslim, Serb and Croat parties in Bosnia-Herzegovina were painting themselves, some purposefully and some by mismanagement, into corners furnished with policies and promises that they could not realize without risking a civil war or abandon without their own political demise. These were national salvation for Slovenes and Croats through secession, and for Serbs through unity in a single (either Yugoslav or Greater Serbian) state. But there were also several occasions when these politicians might have escaped cornering, if some had possessed the will and others the skill, in ways that would either preserve some form of loose association or provide a mechanism for a gradual, peaceful, and consensual divorce. The right combination of will and skill was always lacking.

With parliaments and governments that could claim to enjoy the mandate and legitimacy bestowed by democratic election in place by the end of 1990 (except in Macedonia, where the new government was finally installed only in March 1991), formal negotiations about the future of their common state, postponed until all could claim this mandate, began again. Their centerpiece was a series of meetings of top republican and federal leaders, the first on 26–27 December 1990, and the last on 6 June 1991, which became known as "YU-summits" ("YU" for Yugoslavia).[32] The Slovenes and/or the Croats boycotted or walked out of some of them. The rest and a parallel series of bi-lateral meetings between republican leaders produced just enough apparent progress to warrant optimistic evaluations by participants and most of the media, which were quickly betrayed by contradictory interpretations back in republican capitals.

The initial basis for these negotiations was provided by "A Confederate Model Among the South Slav States" first tabled by the state presidencies of Croatia and Slovenia on 4 October 1990, along with a draft "Treaty of the Yugoslav Confederation" by the Croatian Presidency, and "A Concept for the Constitutional System of Yugoslavia on a Federal Basis," which reflected Serbian preference for a federation with enhanced central powers.[33] The differences seemed unbridgeable, but some (especially Bosnian and Macedonian) participants stubbornly continued to try, and the rest at least pretended to. The final attempt to build a bridge—a compromise proposal that tilted toward the Croato-Slovenian "Confederate Model" but retained some central monetary, fiscal, and other macro-economic controls— was presented by Presidents Izetbegovic of Bosnia-Herzegovina and Gligorov of Macedonia at a YU-summit of the six republican presidents on 6 June 1991, where it was unanimously accepted as a basis for further discussion at their next meeting.[34] Like its predecessors, this last agreement or pretence of agreement was quickly overtaken by events, this time in the form of door-slamming secessions and civil war. The meeting of 6 June was to be the last YU-summit.

Whether and for whom these negotiations and other efforts to defuse an increasingly explosive situation were sincere or gestures deemed necessary for a variety of reasons—to win time to arm; to shift or share the blame for unpopular or undesirable outcomes; to persuade, enlarge, and mobilize one's own constituency or to reduce and demobilize the other side's;

The Avoidable Catastrophe 27

or for all of these and other reasons—are debatable questions. They are also important as part of a bigger question, also hotly debated on the basis of selective and currently inadequate evidence: were some already so set on the path to unilateral secession or to maintaining the present or a more centralized union by force that the die was already cast? In any case, other developments were meanwhile making a break-up more rather than less likely. These included:[35]

On 23 December 1990, 89 percent of the 94 percent of the Slovene electorate who went to the polls voted, in a referendum organized by the Demos government, for "an independent and sovereign Slovenia" that the government promised to deliver at the end of six months, as a fully independent state, if the other five republics had not by then agreed to a loose confederation in a "League of Sovereign States." Legal and other preparations for separation, already underway, were accelerated and suggested that the deadline was serious.

On 15 March 1991, the Serbian regime precipitated a six-day constitutional crisis in the eight-member collective Presidency of Yugoslavia that merits additional attention because it set the stage for its effective destruction two months later. It began when Borislav Jović, Serbia's member of the Presidency and its President-for-a-year (to 15 May), resigned after his proposal that the Presidency unleash the army against internal unrest was voted down, 5-3, with Kosovo's member, Riza Sapundxija, unexpectedly voting with the majority. The members from Vojvodina and Montenegro also resigned, and Milošević declared that "Serbia will not recognize a single decision by the Federal Presidency." The Serbian parliament "relieved" Sapundxija as Kosovo's member and elected Sejdo Bajramović in his place, thereby exercising powers vested by the Federal Constitution in the parliament of Kosovo that the Serbian parliament had (also unconstitutionally) dissolved the previous summer. Amid growing furor in Yugoslavia and abroad, and no or a negative reaction by the army, Jović's resignation was formally rejected by the Serbian Assembly on 20 March. Back to square one, except that Montenegro, Vojvodina, and Kosovo would be represented by their presidents until their new members of the Federal Presidency were both elected and confirmed by the Federal Assembly, which was delayed by the Bajramović irregularity until 16 May.

On 16 March, the second day of the Presidency crisis, a new version of reiterated declarations of autonomy by a Serbian National Council, purporting to speak for the Serb majority in a region in Croatia they called "Krajina" (see below), became a declaration of separation from Croatia. It was followed two weeks later by a declaration of union with Serbia.

On 25 March Presidents Milošević and Tudjman met at Karadjordjevo, a hunting lodge in Vojvodina once favored by Tito, for private talks that reportedly included discussion, on the basis of a map or maps, of a partition of Bosnia-Herzegovina between Serbia and Croatia. There had already been other indications that Milošević, apparently recognizing the bankruptcy of his putative earlier strategy for a more centralized Yugoslavia and unwilling to accept a looser one, had shifted to Greater Serbia as a less desirable but more feasible vehicle for Serb unity and his own ambitions. Reversing an earlier position, he was now prepared to accept the right to "national self-determination" (including secession) for Slovenes and Croats as national communities, but not for republics as territorial entities and only if Serbs in Croatia and Bosnia were accorded the same right. He and other Serbian leaders were also issuing repeated warnings that Serbia would demand changes in inter-republican boundaries, which they termed administrative, arbitrary, and "Titoist," if Yugoslavia either disintegrated or became a confederation.

This two-steps-forward-one-step-back approach to the precipice on the political front was replicated, and becoming violent, in the countryside. Most serious confrontations and ensuing violence in this period occurred in the former Habsburg Military Frontier (*Vojna Krajina*) in Croatia (beginning in August 1990) and then in central and finally eastern Slavonia (in March and May 1991 respectively). These regions, in which Croats and Serbs have cohabited for centuries,[36] would also be the first battle-zones in the War of Croatian Secession later in 1991, and the first proof—with Bosnia chronologically the second and Kosovo logically the third—that Yugoslavia could not and would not disintegrate in peace.

Croatian Krajina is a largely mountainous, poor, and sparsely inhabited territory curling around the border with Bosnia. Serbs (or "Vlahs") settled here, with Habsburg encouragement, as free warrior-peasants pledged to drop their ploughs and seize their guns to confront Turkish incursions (the enemy changes, but the tradition persists), and are a majority or a large minority in most localities. They are a majority of the sparse population in six *općine* (counties) in the karstic and inhospitable Knin region, where 89,551 Serbs were 77 percent of 117,000 inhabitants in the 1991 census, and in six *općine* in nearby Banija and Kordun, where 73,481 Serbs accounted for 65 percent of the 1991 population. Memories of genocide by the fascist Ustaše during World War Two and never-again determination are particularly strong in Banija and Kordun, where some of the worst wartime atrocities occurred; Serb-Croat competition for the Knin region's scarce arable land and jobs made it a breeding ground for intense nationalist sentiments since at least the early 20th century. In Slavonia, which is far more fertile and densely populated, 83,558 Serbs constituted sizeable minorities (more than 25 percent) in six *općine* (four in central Slavonia and two on the Serbian border in eastern Slavonia), but outnumbered Croats only in central Slavonian Pakrac; an additional 116,902 Serbs were less than 25 percent of the population in other Slavonian *općine*. Furthermore, all of

The Avoidable Catastrophe

the Serbs of the 18 Croatian *općine* where they were a majority or large minority accounted for only 42 percent (or with the rest of Slavonia 62 percent) of Croatia's 581,000 Serbs.[37] The rest, including large numbers in Zagreb and other urban centers, were in effect ignored—"consigned by Serbia to assimilation" was the ironic comment of one of them in a July 1992 conversation—in the political and then battlefield campaign for the union of all Serbs in one Greater Serbian or rump Yugoslav state. In this sense Krajina was a contrived test.

From the Knin district in and after August 1990, when Croatia's new paramilitary "special" police and armed Serbs first confronted one another in the context of a locally organized "plebiscite" on autonomy for the region that Croatian authorities vainly attempted to prevent, to Pakrac and Plitvice (Lika) in early and late March respectively, and to Borovo Selo (eastern Slavonia) on 2 May 1991, the fuse lit by Milošević in Kosovo sparked a series of increasingly violent detonations. The first serious number of casualties and fatalities were incurred at Borovo Selo and in lesser incidents on the same and following days in Dalmatia and Krajina. Some date the beginning of civil war, and thereby the end of the endgame over the evitability and fashion of the disintegration of Yugoslavia, to Borovo Selo; for others the point of no return was Plitvice.[38]

In the political arena the endgame began on 15 May the day Stipe Mesić of Croatia was in line to become President of Yugoslavia's Presidency but did not. In what should have been a purely formal election by his peers (under a schedule for rotation among the eight federal units laid down when the Presidency was created), Mesić received only four votes, one short of the required majority. Jović and the presidents of Vojvodina and Kosovo (standing in, like President Momir Bulatović of Montenegro, for new members not yet confirmed to replace those who resigned or were "relieved" in March) voted "no." Bulatović abstained because, he explained, the Federal Assembly had insulted Montenegro's equality by not yet approving its new member of the Presidency. In a new vote on the following day, after the Federal Assembly hastily confirmed the three new members in what was assumed to be a *quid pro quo* arrangement for Mesić's election, all three joined Jović in voting against him. These maneuvers precipitated another constitutional crisis, from which the federal Presidency, parliament, and government in effect never emerged alive.[39]

On the following Sunday and under the influence of these events, Croatia's voters went to the polls in a referendum with two questions and a foregone conclusion. With a turnout of 84 percent, which suggested that most Croatian Serbs stayed away, more than 90 percent voted "no" to the first question: "Are you in favor that the Republic of Croatia remains in Yugoslavia as a united federal state . . . ?" Approximately the same majority, 94 percent, voted "yes" to the second: "Are you in favor that the Republic of Croatia, as a sovereign and independent state which guarantees cultural autonomy and all civic rights to Serbs and other nationalities in Croatia, may join in a league of sovereign states with other republics . . . ?"

The wording of the second question, as several voters eagerly pointed out to a foreign observer,[40] did not explicitly endorse or commit the government to secession, which still appeared to be a reserve option—without a deadline of the kind the Slovene government had committed itself to in December. On 11 May, to be sure, President Tudjman had reiterated on television that Croatia would secede "the day after Slovenia"; but he had gone on to explain that Croatia could not secede "the day before" because of three problems (which would presumably still be there on the day after): its large Serb minority, a world not yet ready to recognize an independent Croatia, and lack of assurances ("unlike Slovenia") that the Yugoslav army would not intervene.

On 20 June both Croatian President Tudjman and Slovenian President Kučan reportedly assured American Secretary of State James Baker, who was visiting Yugoslavia, that their governments would not take precipitate action.[41] Five days later both republics seceded, Croatia ahead of Slovenia but by hours rather than a day. Despite imposition by the European Community of a three-month moratorium on "implementation" of secession (from early July to early October 1991) and other external efforts to save the unsaveable, further disintegration in the form of further secessions and civil war was now truly inevitable. Only the Slovenes made their escape almost unscathed.

Responsibility for the break-up of Yugoslavia and the catastrophe of (inevitably?) ensuing civil war is shared, but far from evenly. By far the largest portion belongs to Milošević, who wanted Yugoslavia and did his utmost until late in the game to keep it together, but with a unitarist and Serbian nationalist vision and methods that massively promoted disintegration and violence. His successful bulldozing of opponents and critical media in Serbia, of the autonomy of Vojvodina and Kosovo, of the independence of Montenegro, and of the basic rights and liberties of Albanians, along with convincing indications that these were only the first items on an agenda for Serbian and personal hegemony throughout Yugoslavia, sent Slovenes, then Croats, and ultimately Muslims and Macedonians scurrying to the exits. Then his alternative or revised strategy for a rump Yugoslavia or Greater Serbia that would still permit all Serbs to live in one united state, under Milošević, ensured that at least Croatia and Bosnia-Herzegovina would not escape without the violent rendering of their lands and people that began in Slavonia in July 1991.

Slovenes who were dedicated to independence at any cost to themselves, but also to their neighbors, have a different kind and magnitude of

The Avoidable Catastrophe   31

responsibility for the break-up and ensuing violence, which was brief and limited for them but not for others.

Total independence for Slovenia was the procedurally negotiable but fixed goal of many Slovene intellectuals and both Communist and "alternative" (non-Communist) politicians by the summer of 1989, as noted previously, and some of these had been contemplating it even pre-Milošević.[42] The steps to achieve this goal and their timing, as these unfolded in the months before 25 June 1991, closely resembled the more cautious of two detailed strategies that were being debated by some of these same people, in or close to the new Demos government, in the summer of 1990.[43] They are therefore responsible, with help from Milošević, for having achieved what they wanted. But Slovenia's geographic location and homogeneous population (90 percent Slovene and almost no Slovenes in other republics) made it a special case. Everyone, by 1990 apparently including Milošević (whose subsequent behavior suggested that he was trying to drive the Slovenes out, not keep them in), acknowledged that Yugoslavia could in principle survive Slovenia's departure alone. The co-responsibility for the violent break-up of the *rest* of Yugoslavia of these people, and of the Demos coalition and public opinion they manoeuvered and led to secession in June 1991, derives largely from their ethnocentric self-preoccupation and growing indifference to the fate of their fellow South Slavs, including their Croat partners in "confederal model" proposals, whom they abandoned in their calculated rush for the exit. Their timing worked for them, but it pushed the Croats further and faster than was wise: Tudjman's declaration that Croatia would secede "the day after Slovenia," when the good reasons he gave for not doing so the day before would not have gone away, implicitly recognized the possibly fateful damage that the defection of Croatia's chief ally would inflict on Croatia's negotiating strength if Croatia lingered; but it may also have been targeted across the western border, in a final effort to deter the Slovenes from forcing the Croats to abandon hope for a solution less risky than secession at this time and in these circumstances.[44]

As for the Croats, their most fateful errors and greatest contribution to ensuring that civil war would follow their declaration of independence grew out of the insensitivity (at least) of Tudjman and his government and party toward Croatia's Serbs and their historically justified fears of becoming second-class citizens, or worse, in a Croatian nation-state dominated by Croatian politicians unwilling or considering it politically inexpedient to dissociate themselves from the fascist satellite "Independent State of Croatia" and its genocidal policies toward Serbs and other non-Croats in that state. Mojmir Krizan, who is otherwise sympathetic to Croatian positions and dilemmas, describes this "series of errors concerning the Serbs in Croatia" as follows:

The political culture of the Serbs of Krajina was wrongly evaluated, or completely left out of consideration. This culture has been shaped by the centuries-long autonomy and warlike tradition of warrior-peasants, the living memory of genocide in the "Independent State of Croatia," identification with Yugoslavia as the state in which all Serbs are united, and complete ignorance of liberal-democratic values. It is therefore understandable that the Serbs of Krajina would oppose with force the Croatian leadership's effort to create an independent, centralistic and perhaps (with parts of Bosnia and Herzegovina) territorially expanded state of "the Croatian people." It was a further burden that this leadership never clearly disassociated itself from the Ustasha-state and failed to integrate the Serbs symbolically and institutionally in the new Croatian state.[45]

Would the story have been very different if the new Croatian government had promptly granted autonomy to Krajina, in blatant and suggestive contrast to Milošević's dismantlement of the existing autonomy of Kosovo and Vojvodina? The answer is probably yes. Even if it is true that by 1990 nothing would deter efforts by Milošević and Krajina Serbs to create Greater Serbia, or the Yugoslav Army from trying to hold Yugoslavia together by force, pre-emptive recognition and accommodation of Serb fears and grievances would have complicated and might have frustrated these intentions and/or their implementation.[46]

If, as argued here, Yugoslavia's break-up was not inevitable from the day of its creation or even when Tito died, when did it become inevitable? A variety of dates and events can be nominated. These range from Milošević's dramatic espousal of the Serb cause in Kosovo on the night of 24–25 April 1987, or his capture of the Serbian Party at its Central Committee's Eighth Session that autumn to Borovo Selo and Mesić's non-election in May 1991, or even to the accomplished facts of unilateral Croatian and Slovenian secessions on 25 June. I tend to opt for no earlier than the summer of 1990, when new Slovene and Croatian governments were playing with scenarios for getting out, but were far from committed[47] and still looking for alternatives or at least a gradual, negotiated, consensual, and in the process possibly and partly reversible divorce. They were also aware (and could be encouraged by the fact) that their reform-communist predecessors, together with Bosnian and Macedonian Communists in what Milošević had called "an unprincipled anti-Serb coalition," had thwarted Milošević's earlier pan-Yugoslav hegemonic pretensions and at least temporarily confined him to his base in "reunited" Serbia and Montenegro. At the other end of this time-spectrum, Borovo Selo and Mesić's non-election can with greater certainty be seen as the final nail in the coffin of Yugoslavia, which was left without a legitimate head of state or illusions about the nature and potency of Milošević's revised ambitions, and ready for burial. Yugoslavia was dead before its corpse

The Avoidable Catastrophe

was dismembered by the secession of Croatia and Slovenia—although delay in issuing an internationally valid death certificate and the timing and way in which its heirs were and were not recognized would tragically prolong and aggravate its increasingly violent and brutal postmortem agony.

When civil war became the inevitable denouement of break-up is easier to answer. It was when more than homogeneous and expendable Slovenia followed the path to secession—namely multi-national Croatia, with a large and armed Serb minority unwilling to accept living in a unitarist and intolerant Croatia and enjoying the support of Serb irregulars, the Serbian regime, and the Serb-dominated Yugoslav army. Torn apart by Serbian and Croatian irredentisms (alternately competitive and cooperative) and Muslim pretensions (whether defensive-reactive or premeditated), Bosnia-Herzegovina could not long remain immune. Therewith we return to the conflict and dilemma between the basic rationale of "the Yugoslav idea" and its nationalist competitors: Serbs, Croats, Slavic Muslims, and others condemned by their dispersal and extensive areas of co-habitation to live together, and condemned by competing national cultures, consciousness, and ideologies to find it extraordinarily difficult.

Notes

1. Portions of this chapter have been adapted from Dennison Rusinow, "To Be Or Not To Be? Yugoslavia As Hamlet," in *Field Staff Reports*, 1990–91/No.18 (June 1991).

2. Important contributors to the debate include Elie Kedourie ed. and intro., *Nationalism in Asia and Africa* (New York: Meridian, 1970), Ernest Gellner, *Nations and Nationalism* (Ithaca: Cornell Univ. Press, 1983), Benedict Anderson, *Imagined Communities* (London: Verso, 1983), and Eric Hobsbawm, *Nations and Nationalism since 1780* (Cambridge: University Press, 2nd ed., 1992).

3. Simultaneously a complex multi-party guerrilla war against foreign occupiers and two kinds of civil war: inter-communal and over the country's future political and social order.

4. Gordana Knezevic, associate editor of the Sarajevo daily *Oslobodjenje*, as quoted by John F. Burns, "Hate Was Just an Ember, But Oh, So Easy to Fan," in *New York Times* (17 January 1993), p. E-4.

5. Stevan K. Pavlowitch, *The Improbable Survivor—Yugoslavia and its problems: 1918–1988* (Columbus: Ohio State University Press, 1988).

6. See especially Ivo Banac, *The National Question in Yugoslavia* (Ithaca and London: Cornell University Press, 1984), the seminal study of the conflict between "the Yugoslav idea" and competing Serb and Croat national consciousness and "national ideologies" up to 1921, and Aleksa Djilas, *The Contested Country* (Cambridge, Mass.: Harvard University Press, 1991), which has a longer time-frame and is more sympathetic to the Yugoslav idea.

7. The Serbo-Montenegrin "Federal Republic of Yugoslavia" declared in April 1992 has not been recognized internationally as legal heir or "rump" continuation of either previous Yugoslavia.

8. Data based on the 1991 census, here and below, are from Ruža Petrović, "The National Composition of Yugoslavia's Population," in *Yugoslav Survey*, Vol. 33 (1992), No. 1, pp. 3–24.

9. The second by Banac, in *The National Question* and "Post-Communism as Post-Yugoslavism: The Yugoslav Non-Revolutions of 1989–1990," in Ivo Banac (ed.), *Eastern Europe in Revolution* (Ithaca: Cornell University Press, 1992), pp 168–187.

10. Paul Shoup, *Communism and the Yugoslav National Question* (New York: Columbia University Press, 1968), for the wartime to 1967 period, and Dennison I. Rusinow, "Unfinished Business: The Yugoslav 'National Question'," in *American Universities Field Staff Reports*, 1981/No. 35 (August 1981).

11. E.g., Dennison I. Rusinow, "After Tito . . . ," in *American Universities Field Staff Reports*, 1980/No. 34 (July 1980).

12. I recorded this Slovene litany and its Croatian and Serbian analogues during 1989–90 visits to the three republics.

13. Except the Muslim nation, which "shared" explicitly tri-national Bosnia-Herzegovina with that Republic's Serbs and Croats and was not fully recognized as a separate nation until 1968.

14. Studies in English of the process and consequences include Steven L. Burg, *Conflict and Cohesion in Socialist Yugoslavia* (Princeton, N.J.: Princeton University Press, 1983); Sabrina P. Ramet, *Nationalism and Federalism in Yugoslavia, 1962–1991*, 2nd ed. (Bloomington, Indiana: Indiana University Press, 1992); April Carter, *Democratic Reform in Yugoslavia—The Changing Role of the Party* (London: Frances Pinter, 1982); and contributions by Wolfgang Höpken, Dennison Rusinow, and others in Pedro Ramet (ed.), *Yugoslavia in the 1980s* (Boulder: Westview Press, 1985).

15. The only notable exception, late and during the endgame of Yugoslavia's dissolution, was the Marković government's initially successful "shock therapy" reforms of 1990, which several republican governments subsequently sabotaged. For a useful summary of these measures and accomplishments, see Robin Remington, "The Federal Dilemma in Yugoslavia," in *Current History* (December 1990), pp. 407f.

16. Including the sources cited in Note 14. For "apocalypse culture" see Pedro Ramet, "Apocalypse Culture and Social Change in Yugoslavia," in Ramet (ed.), *Yugoslavia in the 1980s* [note 14], pp. 3–21. For one view of a key issue in historical revisionism, Robert Hayden, "Recounting the Dead: The Rediscovery and Redefinition of Wartime Massacres in Late and Post-Communist Yugoslavia," in Rubie Watson (ed.), *Memory and Opposition Under State Socialism* (Santa Fe: School of American Research, 1993). My own periodic "snapshots" of the process are in *UFSI Reports*, 1982/Nos. 39 & 40 (December 1982), 1983/No. 3 (April 1983), and 1986/No. 21 (November 1986).

17. In "Yugoslavia in the 1990s: A Very Uncertain Future," unpublished essay dated 22 May 1991.

18. Apart from a flurry of renewed anxiety (and effective opposition by non-Serbs) when a shortlived campaign for "Yugoslavism" in the late 1950s and early

The Avoidable Catastrophe 35

1960s seemed to resemble "the Yugoslav nation" as a camouflage for Serbianization after 1929 (see sources cited in Note 10). This did not, however, stop some non-Serbs, including political and cultural elites, from believing in and producing sophisticated arguments to document new forms of Serb political, cultural, and economic hegemonism.

19. Aleksa Djilas, *The Contested Country* [note 6], p. 187.

20. Numerous studies and commentaries in non-Yugoslav languages on the background and dynamics of the Kosovo problem in the early 1980s include Jens Reuter, *Die Albaner in Jugoslawien* (Munich: R. Oldenbourg Verlag, 1982); Ramet, *Nationalism and Federalism* [note 14], pp. 187–201; Sami Repishti, "The Evolution of Kosova's Autonomy Within the Yugoslav Constitutional Framework," Paul Shoup, "The Government and Constitutional Status of Kosova," and other contributors to Arshi Pipa and Sami Repishti (eds.), *Studies on Kosova* (Boulder, Colo.: East European Monographs, 1984). Dennison I. Rusinow, "The Other Albania: Kosovo 1979," in *American Universities Field Staff Reports*, 1980/Nos. 5–6 (January 1980) is a first-hand report on the situation 18 months before the 1981 explosion.

21. Serb unhappiness with Albanian "nationalism and irredentism" in Kosovo, the exodus of the province's remaining Slavs, and Serbia's division and reduction to "inner Serbia" through de facto republican status for Kosovo and Vojvodina was voiced in the Central Committee of the Serbian party as early as 1968 (by historian Jovan Marjanović and writer Dobrica Ćosić, who were criticized and dropped from the committee). However, popular reactions even to developments after 1981 were notably muted and often despairing ("Kosovo is lost!") until galvanized by Milošević in 1987.

22. "Memorandum SANU," published in *Naše teme* (Zagreb), Vol. 33, no. 1-2 (1989), pp. 128–163. The second part, entitled "The Situation of Serbia and the Serb Nation" (pp. 147–53), contains the catalog of grievances and remedies that became the "Bible" of Serbian nationalism in the following years.

23. Descriptions and critical evaluations of Milošević's methods and role include Sabrina P. Ramet, "Serbia's Slobodan Milošević: A Profile," in *Orbis*, Vol. 35, No. 1 (Winter 1991), pp. 93–105; Sabrina P. Ramet, *Social Currents in Eastern Europe: the Sources and Meaning of the Great Transformation* (Durham, N.C.: Duke University Press, 1991), ch. 7; Banac, "Post-Communism as Post-Yugoslavism" (see Note 8); and Mojmir Krizan, "Nationalismen in Jugoslawien," in *Osteuropa*, Vol. 42, No. 2 (February 1992), pp. 121–140. Critical Serb analyses include Dragiša Pavlović, *Olako obećana brzina* (Zagreb: Globus, 1988); and Slavoljub Djukić, *Kako se dogodio vodja* (Belgrade: Filip Visnjic, 1992).

24. Krizan, "Nationalismus in Jugoslawien," pp. 123–127, presents a useful (but incomplete and somewhat prejudiced) chronology of these developments from 1986 to October 1991. Rusinow, "To Be Or Not To Be?," pp. 5–11, summarizes and interprets the same to early June 1991.

25. Robert Hayden, "A 'Confederal Model for Yugoslavia'?," paper presented at the annual meeting of the American Association for the Advancement of Slavic Studies in Washington, D.C., 22 October 1990; Robert Hayden, "Constitutional Nationalism," in *Slavic Review*, Vol. 51, No. 4 (Winter 1992); and Robert Hayden, "The Beginning of the End of Federal Yugoslavia: The Slovenian Amendment Crisis of

1989" (Pittsburgh, Pa.: Carl Beck Papers, No. 1001, December 1992), which argues that amendments to the Slovene constitution adopted in 1989 "made the civil war of 1991 virtually inevitable."

26. The following is based on Rusinow, "To Be Or Not To Be," pp. 5ff, a more detailed eye-witness account.

27. Interview with Branko Caratan (then a leader of the "reform" wing of the Croatian party), Zagreb, 17 May 1991.

28. For more detailed summaries and analyses, see Steven L. Burg, "Nationalism and Democratization in Yugoslavia," in *The Washington Quarterly*, vol. 14, no. 4 (Autumn 1991), pp. 5–19; Rusinow, "To Be Or Not To Be," pp. 6–9; and reports by Milan Andrejevich in Radio Free Europe, *Report on Eastern Europe*, especially vol. 1, nos. 8 (23 February 1990), pp. 31–33; 18 (4 May 1990), pp. 33–39; 20 (17 May 1990), pp. 22–26; 48 (30 November 1990), pp. 25–32; 49 (7 December 1990), pp. 20–27; and vol. 2, no. 3 (18 January 1992), pp. 26–32.

29. As described by Jasmina Kuzmanović in this volume.

30. As described by Paul Shoup in this volume.

31. An unpublished public opinion poll taken by Ljubljana University's Research Institute of the Faculty of Sociology, Political Science, and Journalism in early 1990, which may have given the leadership pause for thought, showed a majority of Slovenes still in favor of belonging to a looser and preferably "confederal" Yugoslavia, if this could be achieved.

32. The first round included the collective 8-member Presidency of Yugoslavia, the presidents of the republics, and others. The second, beginning in March, was for presidents of the republics but not the Presidency, whose legitimacy was being challenged by parallel developments. Communiques and press releases from the first round and parallel bilateral meetings of republican leaders are assembled in "Documents on the Future Regulation of Relations in Yugoslavia," in *Yugoslav Survey*, Vol. 32 (1991), No. 1, pp. 3–26.

33. All published in English translation in *Review of International Affairs*, Nos. 973 (20 October 1990) and 974 (5 November 1990). Subsequent issues of this quasi-official Belgrade periodical have usefully published other (including UN, CSCE, and EC) "Documents on Yugoslavia" as inserts.

34. Texts and commentaries in major Yugoslav newspapers in the week before and days after the meeting.

35. Based on Yugoslav press accounts at the time and on interviews in Belgrade and Zagreb in May 1991.

36. For historical overviews, from the contemporary perspective of a politically moderate Croatian Serb, see Drago Roksandić, *Srpska i hrvatska povijest i "nova historija"* (Zagreb: Stvarnost, 1991), and *Srbi u Hrvatskoj* (Zagreb: Vjesnik "posebno izdanje," 1991); also *Bosna i Hercegovina–ogledalo razuma*, a collection of articles, extracts, and maps published as booklet by IGC Borba, March 1992.

37. Adolf Karger, "Die serbischen Siedlungsräume in Kroatien," in *Osteuropa*, vol. 42, no. 2 (February 1992), pp. 141–146, with tables and map based on results of the 1991 Yugoslav census.

38. For the former dating, see Strobe Talbott, "The Serbian Death Wish," in *Time* (1 June 1992), p.74; Plitvice is the candidate of friends of this writer in Zagreb. Other ominous developments in this period included a tense stand-off between

The Avoidable Catastrophe

Croatian and Yugoslav army units in January 1991, which was defused when Tudjman, the Federal Presidency, and the army agreed to a compromise solution to the issue that had provoked it; but others followed.

39. They all lingered on, powerlessly, until the rump Presidency (the three Serbian and Montenegrin members) deposed the government and Federal Assembly in October 1991 and itself became irrelevant.

40. The present writer, who was in Belgrade on May 15 and in Zagreb on May 19.

41. David Binder, "Baker Weighing a Break With Belgrade," in the *New York Times* (21 April 1992), p. A3.

42. Both Carole Rogel, "Slovenia's Independence: A Reversal of History," in *Problems of Communism*, Vol. 40, No. 4 (July–August 1991), pp. 31–40, and Krizan, "Nationalismus," pp. 134–137, emphasize the seminal importance of what Rogel calls the "landmark issue," subtitled "Contributions to a Slovene National Program," of the Ljubljana intellectual journal *Nova Revija*, No. 57 (March 1987), and the role of Slovene fascination with the concept of "civil society" in the formation of Slovene separatism. See also Tomaz Mastnak and Lynne Jones, "Behind the ethnic rivalry," in the *Times Literary Supplement*, 19 July 1991, p. 6.

43. As described to the author by one of the strategists, on a not-for-attribution basis, in Ljubljana in August 1991.

44. An interpretation suggested by fellow-watchers of the broadcast (11 May 1991) of this otherwise curious statement.

45. Krizan, "Nationalismus," p. 138.

46. Izetbegović's and other Bosnian Muslims' share of responsibility for the catastrophe, described by Paul Shoup in this volume, became apparent and relevant to the larger picture only in 1992.

47. The Slovenes who were (see above) influential but with one or two exceptions not members of the government.

2

The Dissolution of Yugoslav Historiography

Ivo Banac

I

In May 1979, one year before Tito's death, the specialists on the history of Yugoslav unification gathered at one of those ritualistic congresses that Communist neo-traditionalism churned up with typical mastodonic grace. They gathered at Ilok, a sleepy Croatian town on the Danube, downstream from Vukovar, within sight of the Franciscan church in which St. John of Capistrano was laid to rest in 1456. But, unlike the swallows that mark the return of spring to the California mission named after the same warrior-saint, the historians at Ilok marked the points of appui for the lines of historiographic combat. To be sure, the four days at Ilok gave ample space to the usual drones of *faktografska istoriografija*, the tiresome and unimaginative unfoldings on the agreeable minutiae of Yugoslav unity. Still, this congress was unlike all previous gatherings of its kind. For behind the facade of stock phrases about "bourgeois historiography," "liberal integralist ideology," and "strategic imperialist aims and interests of big financial capital," one could hear entirely new tones and interpretations that went contrary to the celebratory intentions of the meeting. Instead of the solemn rite on the sixtieth anniversary of Yugoslavia, the proceedings were marred by several speakers, notably Momčilo Zečević, a Belgrade historian and specialist in Slovenian history, who took on several sacred cows.

In a report that one participant characterized as "shock therapy," Zečević asserted: first that there existed a one-sided ideology and policy of treating the Yugoslav unification and the ideas that charted its course as if the "Yugoslav idea [were] an ancient and unilinear aspiration, created before the formation of nations, as a process that was coordinated in its motives and interests, and constantly on the rise"; second, that the official historiography overstated the importance of the supposed unitary trends, such as the nineteenth-century Illyrian movement in Croatia; third, that there have been few systematic analyses of the "Serb national question, as a historical, state-juridical, and national interest of the Serb people"; fourth, that there existed (and presumably still exist) real national interests of each specific national community in Yugoslavia (now former Yugoslavia) that may not always be reconcilable, precluding at the same time the possibility of reducing Serbian interests to mere "national interests of the Serbian bourgeoisie"; fifth, that historiography ignored the religious question—"a factor of [the] first order in our area, including in the struggle for the establishment of Yugoslavia," which was inflamed by the three "leading churches [sic], Catholic, Orthodox, and Islamic," notably by the anti-Yugoslav Vatican; sixth, that, due to "political and pedagogical motives," historiography "remained obstinately silent about the fratricidal attacks among the Yugoslav peoples in the course of the First World War"; and last, in general, that the "reasons for mutual distrust and conflict among the participants in the unification of Yugoslavia . . . were complex and deep and could not be solved in an offhand manner, with various declarations, resolutions, and similar political and juridical acts."[1]

In 1979, Yugoslav historiography, or, more exactly, its dominant institutional part, was still bound by the ideology of the Titoist party-state. Hence, seen retrospectively, Žečević's paper marked the beginning of erosion of the Titoist interpretation of South Slav history. It is a curiosity of the Yugoslav Communist regime that it failed to codify its thinking on a series of historical questions that had been controversial since the beginning of the Yugoslav state (1918). Nevertheless, the pragmatic consensus of Communist historical interpretation was summed up in Tito's report to the Fifth Congress of the Communist Party of Yugoslavia (CPY) in 1948. Tito assumed that the unification was innately good: "The unification of the South Slavs was needed and had to be accomplished. This was the idea of the most progressive people in the lands that were called South Slavic." But he also recognized that the new state was burdened with inevitable conflicts from the very beginning, because of Great Serbian hegemony under the monarchy of the Karadjordjevices and "bourgeois power." He singled out Montenegro and Croatia as the two South Slav lands in which the unification was resisted by the populace and thereafter imposed by the Serbian and Entente (mainly French) troops. He also implicated the non-Serbian bourgeoisie in the success of the Great Serbian project, because it feared the "revolutionary movement of the masses" more than Serbian hegemony.[2]

As for the nature of the interwar regime, Tito described it as the "dictatorship of the ruling Yugoslav bourgeoisie, headed by the king," which

The Dissolution of Yugoslav Historiography

put on a democratic mask until 1929, when "King Aleksandar was obliged to throw off that mask, trample the constitution and . . . openly proclaim a monarcho-fascist dictatorship."[3] After the assassination of Aleksandar in 1934, the successive regimes, notably those of Prime Ministers Milan Stojadinović and Dragiša Cvetković (1935–41), did not mitigate the severity of the dictatorship ("this was not the democratization of the country, but its fascisization under the influence of Italian and German fascism"). The Cvetković-Maček agreement of 1939, which sought to "solve" the Croatian question, was "in one sense, a division of power between the Serbian and Croatian bourgeoisie."[4] Tito was particularly harsh with Vladko Maček, the leader of the Croat Peasant Party (HSS), for his anti-communism and leniency with the Croat pro-fascist Ustašas. As for the April war of 1941, when Yugoslavia was attacked and quickly occupied by the Axis powers, Tito held that "as is well known, the Yugoslav army capitulated, owing to the treachery and cowardice of the generals, after twelve days of weak resistance."[5] It goes without saying that his version of wartime history was devoid of any sympathy for Draža Mihailović, the leader of the predominantly Serbian Chetniks, who, according to Tito, represented "the last remnant of armed power of the old, rotten, bourgeois order, [which] in no case wanted to struggle against the occupiers but, at all costs, wanted to safeguard the old bourgeois social order under the occupation."[6] As for the Communists, "without the leading role of the CPY [Communist Party of Yugoslavia], we would today have no new Yugoslavia . . . Nor would one be able to imagine the realization of brotherhood and unity of our peoples."[7]

II

Since 1948, this version of Yugoslavia's twentieth-century history was maintained in institutional historiography without regard to Communist party membership. The Yugoslav historical establishment, represented by a generation of historians born before 1918, such as Vaso Čubrilović, Dragoslav Janković, and Jorjo Tadić in Serbia; Vaso Bogdanov, Ferdo Ćulinović, and Jaroslav Sidak in Croatia; Bogo Grafenauer and Fran Zwitter in Slovenia; and Anto Babić and Branislav Djurdjev in Bosnia-Hercegovina, was preoccupied, with exceptions, with the pre-1918 period. Although they occasionally disagreed, their disagreements were not subversive of the Titoist historical interpretation, which was further serviced by a somewhat younger establishment of historians specializing in the history of the CPY (Pero Damjanović, Jovan Marjanović, Pero Morača, and Vlado Štrugar). Both establishments, after accounting for disparities in age and interest, generally cohered in a series of joint projects, beginning with bibliographic guides on historical publications (published for the world congresses of historians in 1955, 1965, and 1975), two volumes of the History of the Peoples of Yugoslavia (1953, 1959), and in various encyclopedia projects, notably the two editions of the Encyclopedia of Yugoslavia (1955–71, 1980–91).

From the end of the 1960s, however, it became increasingly clear that the unity of Yugoslav historiography was dependent upon the unity of the regime. The demise of Yugoslavia in the 1990s cannot be traced to a single factor, nor was it only an aspect of regime fragmentation. Nevertheless, the internal troubles inside the Titoist establishment—the emergence, in the 1960s, of a reformist bloc with a strong base in the northwestern republics and the associated correlation between systemic reform and administrative decentralization (genuine federalism)—had immediate repercussions in historiography. The publication of the third volume of the *History of the Peoples of Yugoslavia*, which was to deal with the critical period of nineteenth and twentieth century national integration and statebuilding, kept being postponed and never came to pass. There were growing polemics over controversial aspects of twentieth-century history. In 1963, General Velimir Terzić brought out his monograph, *Jugoslavija u aprilskom ratu 1941* (Yugoslavia in the April War of 1941), in which he attributed Yugoslavia's swift fall to the treason of Croatian leaders, notably Maček, who supposedly "after 1930 . . . sought the help of the Axis powers and worked on—and planned beforehand—the destruction of Yugoslavia. In fact, [he and his associates] for the most part chose treason, which was clearly manifested in the April war."[8] At the Eighth Congress of the League of Communists of Yugoslavia (LCY), held in Belgrade in December 1964, Tito himself gave vent to an oblique criticism of "nationalist manifestations in historiography," by denouncing "instances of indirect claims that aver some kind of primacy of one national history over the others."[9]

Tito's authority concealed the cleavages in what was still the single center of power. Ever the master of political balance, Tito expected historians to bestow, without favor, the proper measure of praise and censure on each national community. But he himself started providing increasingly different measures in historical scorekeeping. In 1966, Tito forced the leading Serbian Communist, Aleksandar Ranković, out of the LCY leadership, signalling, among other things, greater leeway for the critics of Serbia's role in Yugoslav history—but only up to a point. In short, Tito wanted to take centralism, with its political locus in Serbia, a few notches lower in general regard without stirring up a great deal of fuss.[10] By January 1970, the Croatian Communists took the struggle against centralism one step further. In repudiating Yugoslav unitarism, a tendency favoring the amalgamation of the Serbs, Croats, Slovenes, and other South Slavs into a supranational Yugoslav nation, Croatian communist leader Savka Dabčević-

*The Dissolution of Yugoslav Historiography*43

Kučar stated that no form of nationalism was attractive or without danger for Yugoslavia and its individual peoples, warning that "unitarism is in fact only a form of nationalism of the stronger nation in the variant of great state chauvinism."[11] The pace of confrontation with centralism and unitarism, especially in its Serbian version, was at issue. Hence, the nervous and inconclusive nature of historical polemics in the early 1970s.

Opposition to centralism and unitarism came largely as an unexpected gift to Croatian historiography, which did not really take full advantage of the opportunity.[12] Indeed, establishment historians in Croatia were exposed to harsh censure by nonacademic practitioners such as Zvonimir Kulundžić, who berated their timidity and lack of patriotism.[13] But where the historians were still reluctant, other intellectuals ventured forth. The reading public was elated by the poet Vlado Gotovac's stinging attacks on Belgrade scholars Miroslav Pantić and Jorjo Tadić, who invested considerable energy in denying or ignoring the Croatian character of Dubrovnik's prestigious literary and historical heritage. Playing on Tadić's textual scholarship, Gotovac charged that a "merchant's invoice is more important to [Tadić] in determining the national character of [Dubrovnik] than the city's whole spiritual tradition."[14] Tadić's posthumously published defense of the unitarist character of Dubrovnik went beyond the scope of his theme to affirm the traditional unitarist view that religion was the facile—and erroneous—dividing line between the Orthodox Serbs and Catholic Croats. In an allusion to the newly proclaimed policy of viewing Bosnian Muslims as a nation, he offered his opinion that "we are endeavoring to proclaim one of our religious communities as a nation, which is a unique case in present-day Europe."[15]

The tense early 1970s can only be understood as a conflict over the future of Yugoslavia. The centralist and unitarist bloc held that the distinctions between the nationalities were being blurred and that Yugoslavia could be homogenized on the traditions—real or invented—of forceful Yugoslavism. In practice, this meant the extirpation of non-Serb nationalisms, always interpreted as separatist and potentially fascistic, and the quiet absolution of Serbian history and political practice from the sin of supremacy. The remission of the supremacist offense was permitted precisely because "Great Serbian hegemony," willingly or unwillingly, regardless of its historical record, became an auxiliary to Yugoslav national amalgamation. Hence, when Tadić questioned his critics' unfavorable view of "insatiable centralist circles of Great Serbian monarchy," he credited the latter with the adoption of Yugoslavism and linked his critics with the anti-Yugoslav and fascistic Ustašas.[16]

The decentralist bloc proceeded from the demonstrable fact that amalgamation did not take place and concluded that this was not a setback but a benefit of Yugoslav unity. The decentralists stood by the historically evolving and separate national identities of each of the South Slavic nations, starting with the clearly distinct Serbs, Croats, and Slovenes, but including the Macedonians and Montenegrins, whom the Yugoslav Communists had recognized as distinct Yugoslav nations already in the 1930s and thereafter treated accordingly. This roster of "nations" was completed in 1968 with the addition of the Bosnian Muslims. In addition, a number of non-Slavic "nationalities," notably the Albanians of Kosovo and the Hungarians of Vojvodina, were recognized as unassimilable components of the multinational Yugoslav state and therefore entitled to every protection of identity, language, and culture, including contacts with their co-nationals in neighboring states (Albania, Hungary). The decentralist logic was that Yugoslavia would better cohere, or would at least be a less repressive place, if the threat of assimilation to any constituent nation, or for that matter to the supposedly supranational Yugoslav community, could be permanently removed. Hence, when Gotovac attacked various unitarists, he did not fail to point out that "those who see only an insignificant remnant of history in every sign of national identity, no matter what sort of revolutionary ideas they have in their heads, are really aiding dogmatists and conservatives, are really giving a chance to their programs, to their terrorist voluntarism."[17] Obviously, the ideology of Yugoslav socialism itself became an instrument in the contention between the centralist/unitarist and decentralist/distinctivist camps.

The contention was soon tested in historiography but at an unseasonable hour. In December 1971, at the Twenty-First Session of the LCY Central Committee, Tito disturbed the political equilibrium by striking at the League of Communists of Croatia. He accused its leaders, Savka Dabčević-Kučar and Miko Tripalo, previously his closest collaborators in the struggle against centralism, of being soft on Croatian nationalism and of stressing the sovereignty of Croatia at the expense of Yugoslavia's collective sovereignty and state unity, moreover, to the detriment of socialist statehood, defined as a "community of working people," not as a national state.[18] This seemingly abrupt change in course inaugurated a nasty campaign against Croatian nationalism, attended by arrests, mass firings, and expulsions from the party, denunciations, and censorship. The brief synthesis of *Povijest hrvatskog naroda* (History of the Croatian People), by Trpimir Mačan, whose outside reviewer was Franjo Tudjman, was withdrawn from the market and destroyed.[19] In a separate development, Tudjman was arrested and sentenced to two years in prison on charges of belonging to a "counterrevolutionary nationalist group."[20] It was in this context that Vladimir Dedijer (1914–90), Tito's biographer, sometime dissident, and gadfly, announced the publication of *Istorija Jugoslavije* (A History of Yugoslavia), stating that "there were some objections to the fact that [the book] will not be called the 'History of the Peoples of Yugoslavia.' It is good that the

The Dissolution of Yugoslav Historiography   45

Twenty-First Session of the LCY [Central Committee] took place. Had it been otherwise, the 'History of Yugoslavia' would have appeared, perhaps, only in an English edition."[21]

Dedijer clearly meant to challenge the decentralist/distinctivist camp in its hour of trial. Excepting the authors of the book's premodern sections, notable and highly respected Belgrade historians Ivan Božić and Šima Cirković, the volume had a decidedly centralist bent. Writing on the twentieth century, Dedijer himself contributed one of his typically journalistic and quaint pieces that had much colorful detail but little analysis.[22] It was Milorad Ekmečić (b. 1928), a Serbian historian at the University of Sarajevo, who stepped forward with a series of interpretations on nineteenth-century developments that challenged the decentralists' basic premises. In particular, he advanced the thesis that nationhood based on language was the only concept of nation-building that can be traced to progressive rationalist and romanticist premises. This permitted his defense of the Serbian language reformer and national ideologist Vuk Karadžić (1787–1864), who rejected the traditional identification between Serbdom and Orthodoxy in favor of an assimilationist notion that Serbs were defined by their language, meaning the štokavian dialect common to almost all Serbs, most Croats, and all Bosnian Muslims. Since Karadžić and his followers failed to assimilate Croats and Muslims through the construction of Serbian "linguistic" nationhood, Ekmečić concluded that religion was to blame: "The basic democratic conception of a nation depended on the premise that [nations] should not be tied directly to religion but to a secular factor. Having attempted to realize this idea, the South Slav awakeners succeeded only partially in their literary and cultural tasks, whereas the backward agrarian reality of the Balkans of the time prevented the success of their political tasks."[23]

Ekmečić went on to claim that the "failure of this agrarian society to build a secular idea like language [sic] (the only possible democratic conception of society) into the foundation of nationhood meant that the subsequent South Slav history would be marked by this failure, thereby determining its whole purport."[24] As a result, Ekmečić could not fail to see traces of religious—specifically, Catholic—obstructionism in all anti-unitarist movements, even when they were perfectly secular, as in the case of Ante Starčević's Party of (Croatian State) Right. By implication, the anti-unitarist policy of the LCY was also seen as somehow connected with the Catholic Church; this leap of faith that was made by Ekmečić would characterize a significant portion of Serbian opinion some twenty years later.

As it happened, the work of Dedijer and Ekmečić appeared in print in the fall of 1972, at approximately the same time as Tito's attempt to reimpose discipline on the reluctant leadership of the Serbian Communists, thereby reestablishing balance in Yugoslavia's political system. Serbian

Communist "liberals," led by Marko Nikezic and Latinka Perović, were not the proponents of centralism. In fact, they were the first Serbian leaders in the history of Yugoslavia to have retreated from centralist ambitions. Nevertheless, they also understood the struggle against centralism as the emancipation of Serbia from the tutelage of the federal center. This position won them some reprieve from Serbian nationalists but only heightened Tito's suspicions. In the words of Latinka Perović, "whereas the other republics could always, with more or less reason, point to Serbia by attacking centralism in Tito's presence, criticism of centralism from Serbia itself was understood as a direct challenge to Tito."[25] After Tito removed the Croat leadership, the Serbs' reluctance to jump on the bandwagon of the antinationalist campaign was seen as covert nationalism.[26] Nikezić and Perović resigned on 21 October 1972. Attacks on Serbian nationalism could then focus on Dedijer and Ekmečić.

III

The "turn" of 1971–72 represented a retreat from democratization but not from Titoist federalism, which was defended and promoted by the increasingly repressive LCY. The polemics against Dedijer and Ekmečić were therefore marked by repressive federalism, which was predicated on "sweeping up before one's own threshold," that is, on repudiating the "nationalism of one's own nation." For example, Serbian historian Branislav Gligorijević questioned Dedijer's economic analysis, which he saw as devoid of "an accurate picture about the foundations of the Serbian bourgeoisie's hegemony." Djuro Stanisavljević, a Serbian social historian from Croatia, questioned Dedijer's figures on Serbian war losses in Yugoslavia and Ustaša Croatia. ("Should the figures refer to the total number of Serbs killed during the war, then the figure of 200,000 is only insignificantly exaggerated. Should we believe the number of 600,000 Serbs killed in Croatia alone, and then take a look at the censuses of the last forty years, we would have to question the motives of those who make such claims.") And Momčilo Žećević criticized Dedijer for "leaving the impression that animalistic Serbophobic attitudes existed in Slovenian bourgeois political circles."[27] But there was also a type of Marxist anti-hegemonism among the critics of the *History of Yugoslavia*, for example, when the Bosnian Muslim historian Avdo Sučeška complained about the "insufficiently accented issues of class" in the book and then proceeded to note that this tendency was particularly damaging to the history of Bosnian Muslims, "who are barely noticeable in this book."[28]

Although swipes at Serbian biases were permitted if couched in Marxist rhetoric, this accommodation was less likely in "post-nationalist" Croatia.

The Dissolution of Yugoslav Historiography

To be sure, the establishment Croatian historians strongly criticized Ekmečić and Dedijer. Mirjana Gross, in particular, made short work of Ekmečić's double standard. ("[Ekmečić] believes that the ideology of the Party of Right had many elements similar to the great nationalist movements of the [twentieth] century; first of all because of [its belief in] the 'geopolitical basis of nations.' I wonder why this bias should be ascribed only to the ideology that sought to gather the South Slav population, which it considered Croatian, into a Croatian state, and not to the ideology that sought to gather the South Slav population, which it considered Serbian, into a Serbian state?"[29]) For all that, the freedom of debate was increasingly restricted as Croatia slipped into the period of "Croatian silence," which lasted until 1989. This was the age of unbridled sectarianism without genuine belief, administered by an alliance of dogmatists and opportunists. Stipe Šuvar, Croatia's doctrinal watchdog, initiated periodic attacks on the humanistic intelligentsia. A typical example of these one-sided ideological combats was the assault in 1978 on Zvonimir Kulundžić's uneven biography of the peasant author, Slavko Kolar. Mounted by Goran Babić, a talented poet in Šuvar's service, it included an ominous warning that exposes of unitarism in scholarship were subversive of the Yugoslav socialist system: "This is all about a struggle for or against socialism; and everything else is nothing but a smoke screen and noise whose aim is to conceal the basic course of this counterrevolutionary activity garbed in a literary, scholarly, and artistic robe, like a monk's habit. In order to disguise this, accusations of unitarism are being showered down upon us."[30]

In fact, the debate about the *History of Yugoslavia* was the last major historical debate in the oppressive atmosphere of late Titoism. The pursuit of politics through historiography wound down by the middle of the 1970s, at the time of Tito's last legislative effort. The constitution of 1974 was meant to establish repressive federalism as a political *perpetuum mobile*. Its basic feature was a system of unceasing rotation of and representation by the republican leaders, redefined to include, to the chagrin of Serbia's opinion makers, the leaders of Serbia's two autonomous provinces, Vojvodina and Kosovo. Analogous subsystems operated in every area of public interest, including historiography; the congresses of historians kept rotating from republic to republic.[31] However, while the architects of revolving machines always attempt to free the motion of their constructions from the influence of every physical force, Tito's *perpetuum mobile* was meant to highlight the visible hand of the party. That was the system's structural weakness, as became evident with Tito's death in 1980.

The Serbian leadership, however reliably Titoist after 1972, grumbled against the constitution as early as July 1977. It seized on the passing of Tito as a signal to begin the unraveling of the federalist era. The opportunity for launching the debate on the constitutional order, primarily over the liabilities of Serbia's "parcelization" into three federal units, presented itself in the spring of 1981 with the commencement of demonstrations by Albanian students in Kosovo. Henceforth, the Serbian intelligentsia and political elite were on a campaign against Tito's constitution. Their calls for the diminution of Kosovo's autonomy could only be accomplished by exaggerating the Albanian menace and by reopening every historical underpinning of Tito's federalism. The sparring at the historians' congress in Ilok was the parent of this effort.

History's utility to Yugoslav politics was not a debatable premise in 1981. It is more difficult, however, to account for the speed with which the new political vacuum prompted an outpouring of revisionist works, almost exclusively in Serbia. Most of these works, at least initially, dissected the history of the system and its demiurge. Ironically, it was Dedijer, the "Partisan Michelet," as he was called in a poignant obituary, who first lifted the hand that had written Tito's official biography against his erstwhile master.[32] Dedijer's *Novi prilozi za biografiju Josipa Broza Tita* (New Contributions to the Biography of Josip Broz Tito), published in 1981, demythologized the late dictator and portrayed him as a lecher and schemer, dissembler and master of craftiness, bon vivant and tyrant, charismatic leader and pacesetter in "excessive retortion" (Dedijer's euphemism for the execution of "enemies").[33] Though maintaining the appearance of amity for his subject, Dedijer clearly delighted in breaking every taboo, from Tito's participation in the Austro-Hungarian units on the Serbian front in 1914 to the negotiations between his Partisan forces and the Germans in 1943, from the Comintern's policy toward Yugoslavia to the responsibility for the reckless endangerment of imprisoned Communist leaders in Croatia (the abortive Kerestinec escape of 1941). This ungraceful book, a cabbage head on a makeshift body, full of unrelated provocations, including Dedijer's obsession with "revolutionary suicides" and vituperative epithets directed against Alojzije Cardinal Stepinac, Archbishop of Zagreb and Metropolitan of Croatia, provoked a storm of protest. It was also widely read and set the course for an entire line of iconoclastic volumes by Serbian authors.[34]

An admirer of Dedijer has claimed that *Novi prilozi* "definitely mark[ed] the end of illusions that our history can be written according to traditional foreign models, in which everything is subordinated to dry documents and conclusions of political forums . . . Our true history . . . for better or worse, is still exclusively oral."[35] Small wonder that Dedijer's overstated revisionism legitimated sensationalist debunking and diminished genuine scholarship.[36] Nevertheless, the book that Gojko Nikoliš, veteran Communist and dissident, had touted as the "most sensational of all that have appeared in our epoch and on our soil" opened the door for the pretensions of more serious Serbian scholars, who were frequently also more politically sophisticated than Dedijer.[37] Whether they were party loyalists,

The Dissolution of Yugoslav Historiography

like Branko Petranović or Momčilo Žećević, or dissidents bent on challenging the political monopoly of the LCY, like Vojislav Koštunica and Kosta Čavoški, their parallel activities weakened the established interpretations of wartime and postwar developments and contributed to the growing sense of resentment among the Serbian public, frustrated with the party's inability to "pacify" Kosovo, undo the constitution of 1974, and reconstruct a strong centralized administration favorable to Serbian national interests.

Branko Petranović's *Revolucija i kontrarevolucija u Jugoslaviji, 1941-1945* (Revolution and Counterrevolution in Yugoslavia, 1941–1945), published in 1983, was an early and relatively moderate contribution to the reinterpretation of the Yugoslav war along the lines of Serbian national communism. Petranović clearly had his blind spots (the Catholic Church, Croatian and other non-Serbian nationalisms, liberal institutions), but he usually succeeded in keeping his feelings under control and certainly committed no major offenses against professional standards. His principal innovation was the ideological redefinition of the Chetnik movement. Even though Petranović made no effort to obscure the growing collaborationism of the Chetniks, he broke with the canons of Communist historiography in stating that the "most significant antifascist manifestation among the Serbian bourgeoisie was connected with the Chetnik organization of Dragoljub-Draža Mihailović."[38] As antifascists, that is, a complex set of collaborators, the Chetniks thereby were associated with an anticommunist "counterrevolution" of the Western type.

This position, which was infinitely more favorable than that of mere "fascist hirelings," could be further elaborated. Andrej Mitrović, a Serbian historian of more pronounced liberal orientation, seized on Petranović's dualistic distinction between "revolution" (communism) and "counterrevolution" (everything else) to introduce a somewhat more nuanced triad of "liberalism, communism, and fascism." In his words,

> I want to stress this triad precisely because we have really only two phenomena—revolution and counterrevolution—in the title that Petranović offered us, whereas, at the time [of the war], the history of Europe developed under the aegis of three possibilities. Moreover, it must be understood that a war front did not exist between the world of socialism and capitalism but between the coalition of a socialist state [the USSR] and liberal states, on one side, and the fascist states, on the other. This confrontation, as a general European model, is interesting in relation to [Petranović's] thesis that the revolutionary front collided with the counterrevolutionary front on our soil. On international soil, we had three fronts, of which two had made a coalition against the third, that is, after all changes were accounted for, since the socialist state was in coalition with a fascist state at the beginning of the war.[39]

Where was the "third front" of liberalism? To Mitrović, this was the continuity of the interwar Yugoslav state, ever in conflict with "Central European imperialism," in which Serbia represented the most dependable ally of liberal Western Europe, meaning Britain and France. Petranović did not take this reinterpretation to its logical conclusion, although he insisted throughout the book that the "international-legal life of a temporarily defeated [Yugoslav] state was not extinguished" during the war.[40] Even though he penned extremely straightforward passages that left no doubt about the CPY's dependence on the Comintern's "alien state policy garbed . . . in proletarian internationalism,"[41] he was not prepared to see the exiled royal government as a credible liberal force or to endow its Chetnik agency with the mantle of pluralism. To be sure, the collection of sources which he edited together with Momčilo Žećević[42] was criticized for allegedly downplaying Chetnik massacres,[43] but the expanded edition of his *Istorija Jugoslavije 1918-1988* (History of Yugoslavia, 1918–1988), whose printing was in part financed by the research and publications fund of the LCY Central Committee, contained a new and impassioned denunciation of Great Britain and America's "deception of the democratic world" by supporting the Chetniks until the summer and fall of 1942.[44] Petranović's preference was for a Serbian-led federal (and Communist) Yugoslavia, not for Serbian dominance at any price.

If the number of books sold is any indicator, Petranović's audience was vast, but his social impact, sanitized as it was by official prizes and LCY graces, was nonetheless limited. It was otherwise with the innocently titled monograph, *Stranački pluralizam ili monizam: Društveni pokreti i politički sistem u Jugoslaviji 1944–1949* (Party Pluralism or Monism: Social Movements and the Political System in Yugoslavia, 1944–1949), which bore the cachet of the Belgrade Praxis group.[45] The book's authors, social scientists Vojislav Koštunica and Kosta Čavoški, turned the cheaply printed edition of a thousand copies into a political fire bomb. Their theme was the source of "tactical craftiness" applied by the CPY to create an impression during the war that it was in favor of a multiparty political system, only to establish Communist political hegemony after the seizure of power. Individual chapters discussed the various methods that the Communists used to marginalize, silence, and eliminate alternative political organizations, as well as the issues at stake in the conflict between the Communists and the adherents of political pluralism. Not surprisingly, Koštunica and Čavoški found the sources of Yugoslav Communist practice in Bolshevik monism and insistence on the monopoly of power. The party polemicists quickly denounced the book as a "plaidoyer for a multiparty system" and an "extremely controversial and tendentious book without precedent in our postwar history."[46] Although the authors made no special reference to the nationality question, their fa-

The Dissolution of Yugoslav Historiography 51

vorable view of the predominantly Serbian Democratic Party of Milan Grol suggested a noncommunist Serbian model of pluralism.

IV

The oppositional themes in Serbian scholarship roused the LCY watchdogs in the other republics. But it was the Croatian conservatives, still on guard against heterodox thinking in their own backyard, who were particularly alarmed by the new trends in Serbian publishing. Stipe Šuvar, Croatia's chief LCY ideologist, summoned 165 historians and party activists to Zagreb in October 1983 for a two-day conference awkwardly titled, "Historiography, Memoir-Publicistic, and Feuilleton Production in the Light of Ideational Controversies." Serbian historians clearly did not wish to confer legitimacy on a meeting that was expected to lash out at Belgrade's ideological latitudinarianism. Of the 70 invitees who did *not* attend, 34 were from Belgrade and Novi Sad, including such notable historians as Šima Cirković, Dragoslav Janković, Andrej Mitrović, Pero Morača, Čedo Popov, Branko Petranović, and Momčilo Žećević.[47] Šuvar set the tone for the conference by stating that the time had come for "us" to stop being defensive: "The League of Communists today, more than ever before, must show its ability and strength as the collective intellectual leadership of the working class, must organize the struggle of ideas over real issues and in the right way."[48] Following Šuvar's lead, alarms were sounded by most participants. Retrospectively, the warnings of Vojan Rus, who predicted "three or four Lebanons" in Yugoslavia should the proponents of a multiparty system have their way, seem exaggerated only in their chain of causality.[49] The preventive measures were accordingly misplaced.

Šuvar cautioned against the "harmful consequences of all suspicious intrigues in historiography . . . in the sphere of multinational relations." He noted the thesis that the "CPY was a tool of the Comintern in weakening and wrecking [interwar] Yugoslavia, and that it even carried out an assigned mission of cutting up . . . the new Yugoslavia, especially by setting back and breaking up some of our nations."[50] He clearly aimed at national protectionism in Serbian historiography. As an object lesson in how to deal with nonconformist historians, his assistants soon whipped up two controlled witch hunts in Zagreb. In January 1984, Zagreb's Yugoslav Lexicographical Institution published the first volume of *Hrvatski biografski leksikon* (The Croatian Biographical Lexicon). The biographies of 1,751 notables written by 270 authors aided by 40 editorial assistants, covering the surnames from A to Bi, contained, according to Ines Šaškor, examples of "insufficient Marxist critical evaluatin of the contributions of individual personalities to national history."[51] In April 1984, Goran Babić wrote a convulsive article in which he cited several hundred clerics in the lexicon's published and projected list of subjects, charging that this "reactionary publication" revived an "enormous number of totally marginal people whose sole historical 'merit' was a monk's habit or some black garb, not to mention that there are criminals among them."[52] And, in June 1984, the ideological commission of Zagreb's League of Communists of Croatia (LCC) City Committee organized a discussion of the suspect publication.[53] Then, in December 1984, Croatian hardliners mounted a campaign against a newly published survey of the Croatian film industry, *Izmedju publike i države: Povijest hrvatske kinematografije 1896-1980* (Between Public and State: A History of Croatian Cinematography, 1896-1980).[54] The book was denounced as an anticommunist "pamphlet" in which "no sentence is accidental and almost all are tendentious."[55]

The lessons in repression were not assimilated in Serbia. Unlike the Croatian intellectuals, whose spirits were cowed, Serbian intellectuals, historians especially, whether Communists or noncommunists, became increasingly more daring in their publications. They were not intimidated by the drones of the historical establishment and their ideological warnings at the Eighth Congress of Historians of Yugoslavia (Arandjelovac, October 1983)[56] or by the antics of Šuvar and Babić. Unfortunately, they were also increasingly more nationalistic. In 1983, Velimir Terzić brought out a new and expanded version of his book on the collapse of Yugoslavia in the April war of 1941 in which he repeated his old theses about Croatian betrayal and thereby provoked bitter recriminations from Zagreb.[57] Desanka Pešić's book on the Communist nationality policy from 1919 to 1935 was essentially a rehabilitation of Šima Marković (1888–1938), secretary of the CPY's Central Party Council in 1919, a leading Serbian Communist, and leader of the Right faction in the party disputes of the 1920s, whose position on the nationality question—notable for its opposition to alliances with the mass movements of non-Serbian nationalities—was favorably reevaluated as a classic Leninist position. Pešić's principal theme was the danger of using "national struggle as a tool of class struggle," thereby permitting "the dominance of national ideology" in Communist politics. This view implied that Serbian disinterest in Croatian or Albanian national movements was good communism. Pešić made this even more explicit by denouncing the Communist "treatment of the Serbian people [in the interwar period] as strictly *exploitative*" and by arguing that the Communists generally overlooked the relevance of the "Serbian question," that is, the integration of the Serbs within a single state.[58]

Rehabilitation of dethroned Serbian leaders of the interwar period was a further step in the revival of Serbian national claims. Some journalists started promoting King Aleksandar, assassinated in Marseilles in October 1934 by Italian-backed Croatian and Macedonian terrorists, as the "first

The Dissolution of Yugoslav Historiography 53

victim of fascism in Europe."[59] But it was historian Djordje Dj. Stanković's biography of Nikola Pašić (1845–1926) that initiated the trend in scholarship. Pašić was the leader of the Serbian Radical Party, prime minister of Serbia and Yugoslavia, and chief architect of Serbian predominance in the unified Yugoslav state.[60] In his work, Stanković avoided the uncritical attitudes of pre-war Serbian historians who viewed Pašić's efforts in the unification of Yugoslavia as selfless determination to liberate all the Serbs, Croats, and Slovenes from foreign rule. And he took aim at postwar Marxist historians who blamed Pašić not only for opposing the democratic aspirations of the masses but (after having opted for Serbian hegemony instead of Yugoslav cooperation) also for wrecking all offers of agreement with the South Slav bourgeoisie of the former Austro-Hungarian territories. Instead, he insisted that Pašić was solving the "Serb national question," that is, the unification of all Serbs within a single state, which, according to Stanković, necessarily promoted the interests of the other South Slavs. This sort of "Yugoslavism," defined essentially as a Serbian interest, lay at the heart of the nationality disputes of the 1980s and was hence an accompanying factor in the political disputes.

The wave of Serbian historical revisionism, attended as it was by the appearance of revealing memoirs by various Communist leaders[61] and publications on Masons and other creators of "secret histories,"[62] could not by itself be a decisive threat to the stability of nationality relations as long as it was not an immediate instrument of political contention. All of that changed with the rise of Slobodan Milošević (b. 1941) to party leadership in Serbia, when the conclusions of political historiography became fully operational in Serbia's confrontation with the autonomous provinces of Kosovo and Vojvodina and indeed with the "constitution defenders" in the other republics and in the federal center. Among the curiosities of these intricate struggles was the fact that Milošević rose to power as an orthodox Titoist ready to use "administrative measures" against dissidents. This did not prevent the Serbian Academy of Sciences and Arts (SASA), increasingly a nationalist and anticommunist bastion, from lending its authority to Slobodan Milošević.

In May 1985, at the annual meeting of SASA, members decided to organize a commission that would be charged with coordinating a draft memorandum on the current situation in Yugoslavia. The commission included two historians—Radovan Samardžić and Vasilije Krestić. A draft of the document came into the possession of a Belgrade daily in September 1986. According to one version, orthodox Titoists in the federal center, perhaps connected with the conservative federalists outside Serbia, wanted an affair that would embarrass the Serbian leadership and demonstrate its laxity toward nationalism. "The Memorandum of SASA" was the perfect foil for the diminishing luster of Titoist communism. Its authors argued

54

Ivo Banac

that the confederalist tendencies in the constitution of 1974—not any other systemic weaknesses—were the source of Yugoslavia's growing difficulties. The root of the problem was the primacy of national over class interest that the CPY inherited from Stalin's Comintern:

> The strategy of the Comintern [in the interwar period] derived from an estimate that after the absence of proletarian revolution in Western Europe, the Communist parties of Eastern, Central, and Southern Europe must rely on national movements, even if they were explicitly antisocialist and founded on the idea of national as opposed to class unity. Stalin was active in demolishing all resistance to this strategy (for example, in the case of Šima Marković, one of the CPY's founders). In this spirit, Sperans (Edvard Kardelj) formulated and developed his theory on the national question in his book *Development of the Slovene National Question* [1939], which mainly served as an ideational formula for the development of Yugoslavia toward a confederation of sovereign republics and provinces, a formula finally realized in the constitution of 1974. The two most developed republics [Slovenia and Croatia], which realized their national programs with the promulgation of this constitution, today stand as stubborn defenders of the existing system.[63]

The memorandum contained a series of charges about the economic and political discrimination that Serbia allegedly suffered under the Tito regime. Once again, the cause was found in the supposed "revanchist" policy that the Communists imposed on the Serbs, whom they treated as a nation of oppressors, centralists, and gendarmes. Moreover, the "economic subjugation of Serbia" was carried out by an alliance of Croatian and Slovenian Communists. Croatia and Slovenia shared a similar historical fate, the same religion, and an aspiration toward the greatest possible independence. As the most developed republics, they also shared common economic interests, which were sufficient reasons for a lasting coalition in attempts to realize political domination. This coalition was deepened by the longstanding collaboration between Tito and Kardelj, the two most important political figures of postwar Yugoslavia, who enjoyed unquestioned authority in the centers of power.

The "anti-Serb coalition" promoted the virtual separation of Kosovo and Vojvodina from Serbia proper, "genocide" against the Serbs of Kosovo, the disintegration of Serbian culture along republic lines, and "Serbophobia". The Serbs of Croatia were deprived of their institutions and exposed to assimilation: "Excepting the [wartime] period, never have the Serbs of Croatia been so imperiled as today. A solution to their national status is becoming a political question of the first order." The memorandum concluded with a call for the revision of the constitution by making Kosovo and Vojvodina "real constituent parts of the Republic of Serbia,"

The Dissolution of Yugoslav Historiography

by abolishing the confederalist elements of the constitution, and, failing that, by defining Serbia's economic and national interests, presumably outside Yugoslavia.[64]

The novelty of the memorandum was its questioning of Yugoslavia as the optimal solution for the Serbs. Usually, the non-Serb national movements hurled accusations at Yugoslavia on account of various Serbian advantages in the common state. Now, the leading Serbian intellectual institution cast its own aspersions on Yugoslavia. The memorandum shocked and compromised the Communist leadership of Serbia. Although Slobodan Milošević left an impression that he "purposely did not wish to be clear" on the question of the memorandum, he gained considerably from its publication. According to one view, he was privately already in favor of the memorandum's theses. He openly adopted them "two years later as his programmatic orientation. As a result, this document later gained far greater significance than when it originally appeared."[65] The historiography that rose in its shadow represented more than a move toward historical revisionism. It became an agency of aggressive national aggrandizement, clearly in service of Milošević's political program—the establishment of a strong and unified Serbia that would, once again, be capable of dominating Yugoslavia and, failing that, go its own way together with all the territories in which the Serbs lived, including portions of Croatia and most of Bosnia-Hercegovina.

Several Serbian historians—members of or associated with the Serbian Academy of Sciences and Arts—played a major role in this transformation. Academician Dr. Vasilije Krestić had a history of controversial publications before the memorandum. His collection *Srpsko-hrvatski odnosi i jugoslovenska ideja* (Serbo-Croat Relations and the Yugoslav Idea), published in 1983, portrayed the ideology of South Slav reciprocity (Yugoslavism) among the Croats as essentially a case of self-interest that promoted Croatian supremacy over the Serbs and Slovenes. The Croatian Yugoslavists, according to Krestić, "accepted cooperation with Serbia and together with it and under its leadership sought to solve the South Slavic and Eastern Question only when they found themselves in a hopeless position and when all of their plans for primacy among the South Slavs, which [the Croats] would have had in a federally organized [Habsburg] Monarchy, ended in failure."[66] Far more damaging was Krestić's 1986 article "On the Origin of the Genocide of Serbs in the Independent State of Croatia," in which he used ten quotes (spanning the period from 1700 to 1902), accounts of four incidents, and unpublished observations by a Croatian politician to claim that the "genocide against the Serbs in [Ustaša] Croatia is a specific phenomenon in our [Serbian] centuries-old common life with the Croats. The protracted development of the genocidal idea in certain centers of Croatian society . . . [which] did not necessarily have some narrow—but rather a broad—base, took deep roots in the consciousness of many generations."[67] Krestić's article became the sole academic inspiration for the increasingly less specific assertions about the "genocidal nature" of the Croats, a theory that justified the Serb insurgency in Croatia in 1990–91.

The Serbian Academy's most serious misstep before the Memorandum was the publication of Veselin Djuretić's *Saveznici i jugoslovenska ratna drama* (The Allies and the Yugoslav War Drama), published in 1985, which was condemned as a "defense of the Chetnik movement."[68] This poorly researched and written work aroused undeserved attention on account of its intentionally provocative message, which found sponsorship in SASA's Balkanological Institute. Djuretić set out to prove that the "myth of Serbian hegemony" contributed to the Allies' misreading of interwar Yugoslav developments, prevented proper appreciation of the dimensions of genocide inflicted on the Serbs by Croatian Ustašas, and created a need to impose symmetrical culpability for wartime carnage on both Croats and Serbs, thereby prejudging the choice of local clients in favor of antinationalist Communists instead of equally antifascist but nationalist Chetniks. In Djuretić's conclusion, unlike the other nationalities that were on one or another embattled side, the Serbs were uniquely divided between the Communists and the Chetniks. Serbian nationalists (Chetniks) were unable to counter the myths of Serbian hegemony and pro-Partisan sentiment among the Croats. Indeed, the "Croatian and Muslim extremism (Ustašism)" succeeded in transforming itself into Communist "official policy," thereby hoodwinking the undisciplined and nationally "unconstituted" Serbs. The result was that the Serbs could choose only between the acceptance of the Partisans and death.[69] Although Djuretić's book was temporarily banned, Serbian polemicists defended his views against the criticisms of the "Zagreb circle,"[70] as did, more moderately, professional historians like Petranović.[71]

The final product of the SASA line was the monograph by academician Milorad Ekmečić, *Stvaranje Jugoslavije 1790–1918* (The Creation of Yugoslavia, 1790–1918), which appeared in 1989, the year of Milošević's reintegration of Kosovo and Vojvodina, of his militant speech at Gazi Mestan at the 600th anniversary of the Serbian defeat on the Field of Kosovo, when he said that the Serbs are "once again in battles and before battles. They are not armed battles, though that is not to be excluded."[72] In his sophisticated narrative, which stands head and shoulders above the primitive efforts of Djuretić, Ekmečić returned to his old themes about the Catholic hand in the failure of Yugoslav integration. He was far more explicit in his speech at the public forum of Budva, Montenegro, on 25 October 1990, when he charged that "it is not the tragedy of Yugoslav communism that it historically failed to lift culture out of the vault of inferiority before religion, thereby preventing [culture] from becoming the foundation of a new association. The tragedy is that communism acquired this role."[73]

The Dissolution of Yugoslav Historiography

Insisting on the culpability of the Catholic Church, Ekmečić claimed that the "whole past of Yugoslav unification depended on the ability of Churches to rationalize the division of a single linguistic cake. That is, during the [nineteenth and twentieth] centuries, the Yugoslavs were united only to the extent that the Catholic Church failed in maintaining Croatian and Slovenian separatism." The South Slavs did not rise to full unitarism because "the Churches divided us." Hence the future of Yugoslavia could go either against the influence of religion (especially Catholicism) and into "clericalism" and dissolution.[74] By 1991, in the wake of the collapse of communism throughout Eastern Europe, the dissolution was at hand. Following the legalization of opposition parties 1989–90, and the victory of the opposition in the 1990 elections in Slovenia, Croatia, Macedonia, and Bosnia-Hercegovina, Serbia and the Yugoslav People's Army became increasingly isolated and determined to accept no further confederalization, much less independence, of the constituent republics. The declarations of independence by Slovenia and Croatia in June 1991 and the war that followed prompted an obituary for Yugoslavia in a leading Serbian cultural weekly: "Croatia and Slovenia are exiting from Yugoslavia with the Communist dowry, leaving behind them, in a garbage can, all the symbols, rituals, and party cards with which they acquired the dowry. Moreover, they are exiting from that notorious party and ideological state with spoils that they never would have won on the field of battle."[75]

The non-Serb reaction to the rise of nationalist historiography in Serbia was inadequate and late. Moreover, as we have already seen in Croatia, much of this effort was mounted by orthodox Titoist polemicists, not genuine historians. Only in the late 1980s did real scholars like Ljubo Boban,[76] Bogdan Krizman, and Dušan Biber start responding to the avalanche of double standards and distortions. They were joined by demographers who took up the exaggerated claims about the war losses of 1941–45, the stock subject of nationalist historiography.[77] Most non-Serbian historians were silent or equivocating. Given the tight control of party censorship in Croatia, Bosnia-Hercegovina, Kosovo, and almost everywhere outside Serbia proper except in Slovenia, popular historical works were rare and usually written by amateurs. Professional historians went about their business, avoiding political history in favor of noncontroversial social studies. The few Serbian historians who raised their voices against the deluge were isolated in intellectual ghettos.[78]

"Today it is impossible to say," Milošević argued at Gazi Mestan, "what is historical truth and what is legend in the battle of Kosovo. This is no longer even important."[79] Yugoslav historiography could not survive the notion that the distinction between historical truth and popular legends was not a matter of importance. It could not survive the notion that there were different truths, negotiated by professional historians. The one-sided

58   *Ivo Banac*

war of historians is notable because legends and ideological distortions were often promulgated by the best historians, not by amateurs. Yugoslav historiography was never harmoniously arranged. Now, it no longer exists. This means that the historiographies of the successor states will be unequal in harmony, quality, and orientation, according to the level of ideologization in each. The historical guild will have a difficult task in removing not only the heritage of the Communist *dirigisme* but also the consequences of the postcommunism chasm. This chapter has suggested that the dissolution of Yugoslav historiography occurred because of the continuity of partisan loyalties to changing ideological banners. It cannot answer why so many changed their Marxist allegiances (if such they were) so quickly (if they did so) to introduce (or reflect) the new political requirements. The consequences for historiography, but also for ordinary human lives, are vast.

V

In 1984, amid various historical polemics, Mexican writer Roberto Salinas Price tickled the fancy of the Yugoslav public with his novel theory about the location of Homeric sites. Troy, he claimed, was really at Gabela, a Hercegovinan village on the right bank of the Neretva River, downstram from Capljina. Frustrated classicists, whose inability to anticipate Salinas' theories became a source of considerable disparagement in the press, responded with a sardonic quiz, whereby the most gullible respondents were proclaimed Trojans: "You have a stomach of steel, a real Trojan stomach, despite the Bronze Age. You can devour everything, nothing can make you ill, nothing can surprise you. You are blessed because you have believed but cannot see. Yours is the Kingdom of Troy."[80]

At the time of this writing, the Neretva valley is a great cauldron of war, Capljina and Gabela are among the many towns and villages that the Yugoslav People's Army has bombed in April and May 1992 in its war against Bosnia-Hercegovina. The Trojan fancy has turned into Hecuba's veiling. But it is Ilok, more so than the bombed slopes of the Hercegovinan Ida, that has produced the most graphic images of the Yugoslav war. In October 1991, slightly more than twelve years after the memorable congress that initiated the war of historians, the army obliged 10,000 Croats to leave Ilok. Instead of performing a solemn rite on the seventy-third anniversary of Yugoslavia, the people of Ilok packed their cars and carts with everything they could carry and took off toward the west. A photograph of a kerchiefed grandmother being searched by two stern army women is particularly memorable.[81] "No terms can be made with Fate. I have just now seen Cassandra dragged away by force."[8]

The Dissolution of Yugoslav Historiography 59

Notes

This chapter was originally published in *The American Historical Review*, Vol. 97, No. 4 (October 1992). Copyright by The American Historical Association. Reprinted by permission of the author and of the journal.

1. Momčilo Žećević, "Nekoloko pitanja istoriografiji o jugoslovenskom ujedinjenju," in Nikola B. Popović (ed.), *Stvaranje jugoslovenske države* (Belgrade: Institut za savremenu istoriju, 1983), pp. 439–441, 446–448.

2. Josip Broz Tito, "Politički izvještaj," in *Peti kongres Komunističke partije Jugoslavije: Izvještaji i referati* (Belgrade: Kultura, 1948), pp. 24–26.

3. *Ibid.*, p. 29.

4. *Ibid.*, pp. 50, 53.

5. *Ibid.*, pp. 63–65.

6. *Ibid.*, p. 94.

7. *Ibid.*, pp. 128–129.

8. Velimir Terzić, *Jugoslavija u aprilskom ratu 1941* (Titograd: Grafički zavod, 1963, p. 664, note 1. This book provoked a storm of criticism in Croatia, prompting political condemnations in the party press. According to one critic, "One gets the impression that [Terzic] proceeded from an a priori assumption that the collapse of royal Yugoslavia and its army was not caused, first of all, by its regime, untenable relations among its nationalities, corruption and lack of preparedness on the part of state and military leadership, and the aggression of fascist powers within a specific international situation, but that the causes of collapse must be sought among the consequences of this order of things, mainly in one consequence—the behavior of individual peoples in the April war, above all in the Croatian developments and in the behavior of the Croatian people as a whole."—Stjepan Šćetarić, "O političkim i vojnim uzrocima sloma Jugoslavije," in *Putovi revolucije*, Vol. 2 (1964), Nos. 3–4, pp. 498–499.

9. Josip Broz Tito, "Uloga Saveza komunista u daljnjoj izgradnji socialističkih društvenih odnosa i aktualni problemi u medjunarodnum radničkom pokretu i borbi za mir i socijalizam u svijetu," in *Osmi kongres SKJ* (Belgrade: Kultura, 1964), p. 35.

10. In his concluding remarks at the plenum that censured Ranković (July 1966), Tito clearly had Serbia in mind as the "center of nationalist deviations that have manifested themselves even in the ranks of Communists," but then he quickly added, "Let's not now have only Belgrade in mind. Belgrade is the city of all South Slavs. There are a great number of Croats, Slovenes, Macedonians, Bosnians, and Montenegrins in Belgrade. That is a Yugoslav city, and all of us are responsible for what happens in it."—Cited in *Četvrti plenum Centralnog komiteta Saveza komunista Jugoslavije* (Belgrade: Komunist, 1966), p. 97.

11. Savka Dabčević-Kučar, "Bratstvo i jedinstvo na elementima onogo što nas spaja u samoupravnom socijalizmu," in *X sjednica Centralnog komiteta Saveza komunista Hrvatske* (Zagreb: Vjesnik, 1970), pp. 6–7.

12. Notable exceptions were the works of Franjo Tudjman, currently the president of Croatia, and Trpimir Mačan, a historian of broad synthetic interests and a uniquely poignant reviewer of historical literature, but neither belonged to the academic establishment. For an insight into the concerns and criticisms of leading

60 *Ivo Banac*

Croatian historians in the early 1970s, see Mirjana Gross, "Hrvatska historiografija na prekretnici?," in *Kritika*, no. 14 (September–October 1970), pp. 642–654. The article is mainly concerned with the lack of institutional support for and adequate funding of Croatian historians.

13. Kulundžić went for the jugular in stating that the misfortune of Croatian historiography lay in its domination "by men who served the previous regimes quite subserviently and who, for their own personal reasons, out of their guilt complex, transported their own sins onto the whole nation, thereby developing what we usually refer to as the *guilt complex* of this whole people."—Zvonimir Kulundžić, *Tragedija hrvatske historiografije: O falsifikatorima, birokratima, negatorima, itd . . . itd . . . hrvatske povijesti*, 2nd ed. (Zagreb: Published at the author's expense, 1970), pp. 7–8. Arguing that the Ustaša complex—a sense of guilt for the anti-Serbian crimes of the Ustašas—was self-imposed, Kulundžić stated that the source of the problem rested with "us intellectuals who did not, sufficiently persistently and systematically, always and at every opportunity, place the Ustaša symbol of *U with a bomb* alongside the Chetnik symbol of *skull and bones*, Ustaša daggers and clubs alongside Chetnik curved knives and saws, [Ante] Pavelić alongside [Milan] Nedić and [Kosta] Pečanac . . . Just as only a small, insignificantly small portion of Serbs can be called by the extremely odious name of *Chetnik*, so, too, among the Croats, there was only a handful of bloodthirsty madmen in whom the beast was awakened and whom we can christen with the terrible name *Ustaša*."—Kulundžić, *Tragedija hrvatske historiografije, p. 6.*

14. Vlado Gotovac, "Autsajderski fragmenti: Svitak treći," in *Kritika*, no. 8 (September–October 1969), p. 557.

15. Jordo Tadić, "Šablasti kruže Jugoslavijom," in *Istorijski časopis*, Vol. 18 (1971), p. 49.

16. *Ibid.*, p. 50.

17. Gotovac, "Autsajderski fragmenti" [note 14], p. 559.

18. Josip Broz Tito, *Govori druga Tita* (Zagreb: Vjesnik, 1971), p. 8.

19. The contents of this handy book were hardly controversial. In fact, the author's balanced position was evident in all sensitive questions that mattered to the authorities. The book's offense had more to do with the known political liabilities of author and reviewer than with its biases. To be sure, there was also the sin of omission. The whole postwar section consists of the following three sentences: "In a state community with the other nations and nationalities of the Socialist Federal Republic of Yugoslavia, the Croatian people live and prosper in the Socialist Republic of Croatia. [This republic] is a result of the joint struggle of Croats and Serbs, and of all South Slav nations, in the National Liberation War [i.e., World War Two]. It is the realization of the Croatian people's right to liberty, statehood, and independence."—Trpimir Mačan, *Povijest hrvatskog naroda* (Zagreb: Školska Knjiga, 1971), p. 228.

20. Tudjman was charged, among other things, with calling for a reexamination of the historical circumstances that contributed to the never-ending Croatian struggle for survival. On Tudjman's role in historical controversies, see Željko Kruselj, "Franjo Tudjman—biografija," in Tomislav Pušek (ed.), *Franjo Tudjman* (Zagreb: Globus, 1991), pp. 41–116.

21. "Istorija," in *Politika* (Belgrade), 30 March 1972, p. 13.

The Dissolution of Yugoslav Historiography

61

22. Dedijer did not fail to promote many questionable views, notably on the supposedly vast anti-Serbianism of the Slovenian Catholic press in 1914, "genocide" against the Serbs of "Bosnia-Hercegovina and parts of Croatia" in World War One, exploitation of economically backward regions of interwar Yugoslavia by Slovenian and Croatian finance capital, "peasant spontaneity" in the activities of the Croatian Peasant Party, and his own favorite themes of "spheres of influence" and "uniqueness of the Yugoslav revolution."—Ivan Božić, Šima Cirković, Milorad Ekmečić, and Vladimir Dedijer, *Istorija Jugoslavije* (Belgrade: Prosveta, 1972), pp. 383–384, 394–396, 424–426, 432–433, 529.

23. *Ibid.*, p. 236.

24. *Ibid.*, p. 244.

25. Latinka Perović, *Zatvaranje kruga: Ishod političkog rascepa u SKJ 1971/1972* (Sarajevo: Svjetlost, 1991), p. 195.

26. The issue of Dubrovnik, more precisely its depiction as a city of "stokavian-speaking Catholics" but not Croats, in the book *Srpski narod i njegov jezik* (Belgrade: Srpska književna zadruga, 1971), by the Serbian philologist Pavle Ivić, was used by the new leadership of Croatia to attack Serbian nationalism and, by implication, the Serbian leadership that took no repressive actions against it. See Perović, *Zatvaranje kruga* [note 25], p. 398.

27. Momčilo Žećević, "Istorija Jugoslavije," in *Gledišta*, Vol. 14, No. 3 (March 1973), pp. 275, 290, 297.

28. *Ibid.*, p. 264.

29. Mirjana Gross, "Ideja jugoslavenstva u XIX stoljeću u 'Istoriji Jugoslavije'," in *Časopis za suvremenu povijest*, Vol. 5 (1973), no. 2, p. 15.

30. Goran Babić, *Možda uzaludno: Polemike* (Zagreb: Globus, 1983), p. 167.

31. The penultimate meeting was at the spa of Arandjelovac, in Serbia, in 1983. The last ever, ominously, at Kosovo's capital, Pristina, in 1987.

32. Branislav Milošević, "Partizanski Misle," in *Vreme* (Belgrade), 10 December 1991, p. 27.

33. Vladimir Dedijer, *Novi prilozi za biografiju Josipa Broza Tita*, vol. 2 (Rijeka: Liburnija, 1981), *passim*.

34. The "federal" daily, *Borba*, the durable bastion of orthodox Titoists, organized a round table on Dedijer's book on 6 January 1982. Participants characterized the volume as "contributions to Dedijer's squaring of accounts with the revolution that he has deserted" (Julijana Vrcinac), "a common but profoundly calculated political pamphlet, imbued with profound anti-socialism, anti-communism, and anti-Marxism, devised to glorify [Milovan] Djilas and his blackest liberal orientation" (Djuradj Stanisavljević), and "contributions against Josip Broz Tito, his deeds, and our revolution" (Joco Marjanović). In his discussion, Jovan Pavičević clearly recognized the complicated array of xenophobic and paranoid attitudes that were typical of "old cadres": I often asked myself after [reading] this book, perhaps even earlier, is the Western public, American and Western public generally, really interested in our National Liberation Struggle, since already in 1953 Dedijer started writing books for the West? What is this now? Does America really want to know how to make revolution, does it want an example? Or is something else at work here—the destabilization of socialist Yugoslavia? Is this not Dulles's policy: do not attack communism from the outside, but from the inside?" Milovan

62

Dželebdžić ended his discussion on an ominous note: "All of this should be borne in mind, lest we experience some new trauma, some new civil war, some new massacre."—Branko Jovanović (ed.), *Razgovor o knjizi Vladimira Dedijera "Novi prilozi za biografiju Josipa Broza Tita"* (Belgrade: Borba, 1982), pp. 14, 39, 43, 78, 84.

35. Milimir Marić, "Komesar za ishranu radoznalih," in *Duga* (Belgrade), 10 July 1984, p. 43.

36. Among the sensationalist works published in the wake of Dedijer's *Novi prilozi*, the following were notable: Vjenčeslav Ćencić, *Enigma Kopinić*, 2 vols. (Belgrade: Rad, 1983); and Dragan Kljakić, *Dosije Hebrang* (Belgrade: Partizanska Knjiga, 1983). Both stressed the dependence of Yugoslav Communists on the Comintern and raised suspicions about the continuity of nationalist "deviations" in the Communist Party of Croatia. Both also touched on the persecution of those Yugoslav Communists, the so-called Cominformists, who sided with Stalin and the Cominform resolution in the Soviet-Yugoslav split of 1948. Simultaneously, there appeared a series of novels and plays on the Goli Otok concentration camp, which the Yugoslav security police prepared for the incarceration of the Cominformists. The most important of these works were: Antonije Isaković, *Tren 2: Kazivanja Ceperku* (Belgrade: Prosveta, 1982); Slobodan Selenić, *Pismo/glava* (Belgrade: Prosveta, 1982); and Dušan Jovanović, *Karamazovi* (Belgrade: Nezavisna izdanja, 1984). The publication of these highly charged fictional works put pressure on historians to "solve" the questions that the litterateurs posed.

37. "Novi prilozi . . . od prigovora do osporavanja," in *Vjesnik* (Zagreb), 10 March 1982, p. 5.

38. Branko Petranović, *Revolucija i kontrarevolucija u Jugoslaviji (1941-1945)*, 2 vols. (Belgrade: Rad, 1983), Vol. 1, p. 129.

39. Andrej Mitrović, "Nedovršena slika," in *Politika* (15 October 1983), p. 10.

40. Petranović, *Revolucija i kontrarevolucija* [note 38], Vol. 1, p. 99.

41. *Ibid.*, Vol. 2, p. 82.

42. Branko Petranović and Momčilo Žećević (eds.), *Jugoslavija 1918/1984: Zbirka dokumenata* (Belgrade: IRO Rad, 1985).

43. Anto Milušić, "U povodu najnovije zbirke dokumenata o Jugoslaviji . . . ," in *Časopis za suvremenu povijest*, Vol. 18 (1986), no. 1, p. 111. For the authors' responses, see Branko Petranović and Momčilo Žećević, "Odgovor na napis Anta Milušića 'U povodu najnovije zbirke dokumenata o Jugoslaviji'," in *Časopis za suvremenu povijest*, Vol. 18 (1986), no. 3, pp. 116–121.

44. Branko Petranović, *Istorija Jugoslavije 1918–1988*, 3 vols. (Belgrade: Nolit, 1988), Vol. 2, p. 186.

45. Vojislav Koštunica and Kosta Čavoški, *Stranački pluralizam ili monizam: Društveni pokreti i politički sistem u Jugoslaviji 1944–1949* (Belgrade: Center for Philosophy and Social Theory, 1983).

46. Pero Pletikosa, "Pledoaje za višestranački sistem," in *Vjesnik* (20 September 1983), p. 3; and Mirko Arsić, "Tendenciozna 'rekonstrukcija'," in *Politika* (6 August 1983), p. 12. In his attack on Koštunica and Čavoški, Arsić was especially insistent on the special role of the CPY as a party "in the great historical sense." Since the authors were incapable of such obeisance, they were "incapable of comprehending the logos of Yugoslav socialist revolution." Under a barrage of partisan attacks, the authors were themselves obliged to plead that "it is malicious to claim that we

are in favor of a multiparty system."—Nastaša Marković, "Kiselo grozdje," in *Danas* (27 September 1983), p. 19.

47. Also missing were Mirjana Gross, Dragovan Sepić, and Jaroslav Sidak, three of the most prominent Croatian historians, all of them likewise invited to the conference.

48. Stipe Šuvar, "Historija revolucije tiče se nas svih," in Ivan Perić (ed.), *Historija i suvremenost: Idejne kontroverze* (Zagreb: Centar CK SKH za idejno-teorijski rad "Vladimir Bakarić," 1984), p. 9.

49. Vojan Rus, "Izmedju liberalističkih i dogmatskih revizija," in Perić (ed.), *Historija i suvremenost* [note 48], p. 131.

50. Šuvar, "Historija revolucije tiče se nas svih" [note 48], p. 14.

51. Ines Šaškor, "I zločinci—'znameniti Hrvati'," in *Nedjeljna Dalmacija* (Split), 25 August 1985, p. 22.

52. Goran Babić, "Voćna salata ili pomirenje svih Hrvata," in *Oko* (Zagreb), 26 April 1984, pp. 5, 8–9.

53. Sanja Vrhovec (ed.), *Aporije Hrvatskog biografskog leksikona* (Zagreb: Centar za idejno-teorijski rad GK SKH Zagreb, 1984). Although most participants did not share Babić's view that the edition was an "expression of spiritual counterrevolution," critical and even denunciatory tones prevailed in the discussion.

54. Ivo Škrabalo, *Izmedju publike i države: Povijest hrvatske kinematografije 1896–1980* (Zagreb: Znanje, 1984).

55. Mira Boglić, "Povijest ili pamfleti," in *Vjesnik: Sedam dana* (12 December 1984), pp. 12–13; and R. Arsenić, "To nije istorija," in *Politika* (8 March 1985), p. 10.

56. Ratko Peković, "Kako oživeti vreme," in *Duga* (5 November 1983), pp. 30–32.

57. Velimir Terzić, *Slom Kraljevine Jugoslavije 1941*, 2 vols. (Belgrade: Narodna Knjiga, 1982–83). For a response from a leading Croatian historian, see Ljubo Boban, "Izvod iz strogo povjerljive kombinatorike Velimira Terzića. A ponešto i o drugim kombinatorikama," in Perić, *Historija i suvremenost* [note 48], pp. 263–275.

58. Desanka Peić, *Jugoslovenski komunisti i nacionalno pitanje (1919–1935)* (Belgrade: Rad, 1983), pp. 143–144, 283.

59. Milomir Marić, "Lovna jednog kralja," in *Duga* (4 November 1984), pp. 30-32.

60. Djordje Dj. Stanković, *Nikola Pašić i jugoslovensko pitanje*, 2 vols. (Belgrade: BIGZ, 1985).

61. On 18 September 1987, at a session of the League of Communists of Serbia (LCS) Central Committee, General Nikola Ljubicic, Tito's longtime minister of defense, denounced the flood of Serbian memoirs: "Here, you see, we have memoirs of Koca Popović, Milovan Djilas, Vojan Lukić, Mirko Marković, Mirko Perović, Milija Kovačević, Gustav Vlahov, Patriarch Dozić, Radivoje Jovanović, Ljubodrag Djurić, and I don't know who else. What will it mean for Serbia when all of these memoirs are published, and what will the world think of us?" Cited in Slavoljub Djukić, *Kako se dogodio vodja: Borbe za vlast u Srbiji posle Josipa Broza* (Belgrade: Filip Višnjić, 1992), p. 160.

62. See especially Zoran D. Nenezić, *Masoni u Jugoslaviji (1764–1980): Pregled istorije slobodnog zidarstva u Jugoslaviji—Prilozi i gradja* (Belgrade: Narodna Knjiga, 1984). Nenezić insinuated that Tito and Kardelj were Masons and that they belonged to the pro-federalist Masonic lodge with Juraj Krnjević and Juraj Šutej, lead-

64

Ivo Banac

ers of the Croatian Peasant Party. See Nenezić, *Masoni*, pp. 417, 634, 646, 649, 665. For a polemic on this issue, see Letters to the Editor, in *NIN* (7 October 1984), pp. 4–6, 8. Fascination with the Masons was not exclusive to Serbia. For a Croatian equivalent, see Ivan Mužić, *Masonstvo u Hrvata: Masoni i Jugoslavija* (Split: Crkva u svijetu, 1983).

63. "Memorandum SANU," in *Duga* (June 1989), p.26.

64. *Ibid.*, pp. 36, 38–40, 42–43, 44, 46, 47.

65. Djukić, *Kako se dogodio vodja* [note 61], pp. 111, 121.

66. Vasilije Dj. Krestić, *Srpsko-hrvatski odnosi i jugoslovenska ideja* (Belgrade: Narodna Knijiga, 1983), p. 150.

67. Vasilije Krestić, "O genezi genocida nad Srbima u NDH," in *Književne novine* (15 September 1986), p. 5.

68. "Dr Djuretić iskljucen iz Saveza komunista," in *Politika* (6 November 1985), p. 6. The author and the book's two reviewers (Zoran Lakić and Savo Skoko) were expelled from the LCY.

69. Veselin Djuretić, *Saveznici i jugoslovenska ratna drama*, 2 vols. (Belgrade: Narodna Knjiga, 1985), Vol. 2, pp. 251, 253.

70. The phrase belongs to Milorad Vucelić, who charged that criticisms against various Serbian publications stem from "aggressive and orthodox monopolists in the public, journalistic, cultural, and ideational-political life of Croatia's capital." See Milorad Vucelić, "Protiv nove militantnosti," in *Književne novine* (1 October 1985), p. 2. Slovenian historian Dušan Biber was actually the most devastating critic of Djuretić's book. See Dušan Biber, "Naučna kuliserija jednog političkog pamfleta: U povodu knjige V. Djuretića, Saveznici i jugoslovenska ratna drama," in *Časopis za suvremenu povijest*, Vol. 17 (1985), no. 3, pp. 95–119.

71. Vidojko Veličković (ed.), *Stručna rasprava o knjizi dr Veselina Djuretića "Saveznici i jugoslovenska ratna drama"* (Belgrade: SANU, 1985), pp. 12–33. Djuretić had the last word on the controversy at the height of Milošević's power in 1991: "We [Serbs] gave up our second chance for the formation of our state after the end of World War Two. In the course of that war, we fought under different banners, but we experienced the most ironical position, that is, that the international dimension of our struggle became the means for the total destruction of Serbian lands; that our blood, shed in the name of nebulous socialist or Communist ideas, in the name of the ideology of Mother Russia, that is, in league with Russia, which was in the hands of Satan, was used for the destruction of Yugoslavia and Serbian lands." Since Communist federalism succeeded in destroying the Serbian lands, relief will come from the decommunized homeland of communism that Djuretić just visited: "into the center of Russia—New Russia which is in its slow but inevitable birth pangs, we have thrown a people that had disappeared, disappeared from Russia's vision, only to emerge as a cosmic people. I am referring to the Serbs."—Veselin Djuretić, "Nova Rusija i Srbija," in *Pogledi* (6 September 1991), pp. 40–41.

72. Slobodan Milošević, "Ravnopravni i složni odnosi uslov za opstanak Jugoslavije," in *Politika* (29 June 1989), p. 4.

73. Milorad Ekmečić, "Budućnost Jugoslavije," in *NIN* (16 November 1990), p. 55.

74. *Ibid.*, p. 56. Ekmečić did not indulge in the crude anti-Catholic propaganda that arose in Serbia in the late 1980s. He simply legitimated the anti-Catholic literature of Dragoljub R. Živojinović, Vladimir Dedijer, and Milan Bulajić. On this

The Dissolution of Yugoslav Historiography 65

subject, see Ivo Banac, "The Fearful Asymmetry of War: The Causes and Consequences of Yugoslavia's Demise," in *Daedalus*, No. 121 (1992), pp. 161–163, 173.

75. Miodrag Perišić, "Kraj Jugoslavije," in *Književne novine* (1 July 1991), p. 1.

76. For Boban's diligent efforts, see his *Kontroverze iz povijesti*, 3 vols. (Zagreb: Školska knjiga, 1987, 1989, 1990).

77. The skillful and moderate work by an emigre Serbian statistician, Bogoljub Kočović, was supplemented by a Croatian demographer, Vladimir Žerjavić. See Bogoljub Kočović, *Žrtve Drugog svetskog rata u Jugoslaviji* (London: Naša reč, 1985); Vladimir Žerjavić, *Gubici stanovništva Jugoslavije u drugom svjetskom ratu* (Zagreb: Jugoslavenstvo Viktimološko Društvo, 1989); and Vladimir Žerjavić, *Opsesije i megalomanije oko Jasenovca i Bleiburga* (Zagreb: Globus, 1992).

78. The following works of three quite different scholars are notable: Ivan Djurić, *Istorija—pribezište ili putokaz* (Sarajevo: Svjetlost, 1990); Andrej Mitrovic, *Raspravljanja sa Klio* (Sarajevo: Svjetlost, 1991); Drago Roksandić, *Srbi u Hrvatskoj* (Zagreb: Vjesnik, 1991); and Drago Roksandic, *Srpska i hrvatska povijest i 'nova historija'* (Zagreb: Stvarnost, 1991).

79. Milošević, "Ravnopravni i slozni odnosi" [note 72], p. 3.

80. Roberto Salinas Price, *Homer's Blind Audience: An Essay on the Iliad's Geographical Prerequisites for the Site of Ilios* (San Antonio, Tex.: Scylax Press, 1983); Bruna Kuntić-Makvić, "Veliki prigodni kviz: Jeste li Trojanac?" in Zlatko Šešelj (ed.), *Troja i kako je steći* (Zagreb: Latina et Graeca, 1985), p. 82.

81. Dejan Orsić, "Ilok: Egzodus Hrvata," in *Arena* (Zagreb), 26 October 1991, pp. 2–5.

82. Euripedes, *Trojan Women*, verses 616–617.

3

The Armed Forces of Yugoslavia: Sliding into War

Marko Milivojević

On 26 February 1991, a Yugoslav People's Army (YPA) military prosecutor in Zagreb formally indicted Col.-Gen. (retired) Martin Špegelj, Defense Minister of Croatia, for allegedly organizing and coordinating "the criminal act of armed rebellion."[1] Now reportedly performing his duties while under heavy guard in Zagreb, Špegelj faced at least five years' imprisonment if convicted. The YPA high command, headed by the Federal Defense Secretary, Col.-Gen. Veljko Kadijević, seemed determined to see Špegelj arrested and tried, even at the risk of a shooting war with the paramilitary armed forces (militia or police) of President Franjo Tudjman's Croatian Democratic Union (CDU) government.

Exactly one month earlier, an eleventh hour Serbian-Croatian summit accord defused an escalating confrontation that Tudjman described as being "on the verge of civil war,"[2] following his talks in Belgrade with Federal President Borisav Jović and President Slobodan Milošević of Serbia. This deal, reportedly made under intense American and British government pressure, agreed that Croatia would demobilize its militia reserves in return for a reduction in the combat readiness of YPA forces in Croatia. An enhanced combat readiness that involved the operational deployment of 5th Military District (HQ: Zagreb) troops, armor and combat aircraft in a way that was more akin to a wartime mobilization than the regular military movements of peace time.

Typically, this patched-up exercise resolved nothing of any importance. Though the Tudjman government did demobilize its militia reserves, it did not disband them, as provocatively demanded by the "final" ultimatum of the Federal Defense Secretariat on 23 January, when the YPA threatened to "enhance the combat readiness of its units . . . if all mobilized armed

68   *Marko Milivojević*

groups on the territory of the Republic of Croatia fail to be disbanded immediately."[3] The YPA, though it did reduce the combat readiness of its forces in Croatia, then immediately undermined the spirit of the Serbian-Croatian accord of the 25th by stepping up its anti-Špegelj campaign in February.

Reportedly covertly supported by Milošević's Serbian Socialist Party (SSP) government in Belgrade, this anti-Špegelj, and thus anti-CDU, struggle by Kadijević's YPA was given a veneer of legality on 9 January, when Jović, a close ally of Milošević, pushed through a Federal State Presidency order authorizing the federal army to disarm all illegal armed groups in the country (i.e., Tudjman's militia, although this was not explicitly stated until the 23 January ultimatum). Significantly, Kadijević was present at the session when this provocative order was passed, despite the vigorous protests of the Slovenian and Croatian members of the Federal State Presidency.[4]

The 9 January session of the State Presidency also considered two highly pertinent letters from the Slovenian and Croatian governments, which demanded the immediate depoliticization of the YPA. Though more or less rejected by Jović after much acrimony at that time (according to Croatian sources),[5] this political demand was to become absolutely central thereafter, as the YPA's political role became more overtly threatening to the CDU government in Zagreb and, more indirectly, to the DEMOS (Democratic Opposition of Slovenia) government in Ljubljana. Following the crisis of 23–25 January and its immediate aftermath in relation to Špegelj, the total depoliticization of the YPA is now a vital precondition for a negotiated peaceful solution to the country's ongoing political crisis.

The crisis now reached the point where the breakup of Yugoslavia became not only possible but increasingly probable in the not too distant future. Slovenia, following an overwhelmingly pro-independence plebiscite in December 1990, formally committed itself to a negotiated separation from the Yugoslav federation by June 1991 at a joint session of the three chambers of the Slovene Assembly on 20 February 1991. Addressing the joint session, President Milan Kučan stressed that if a negotiated separation was not possible, then Slovenia would go its own way without an agreement.[6] The Milošević-Kadijević-YPA axis in Belgrade, now increasingly committed to a reconstituted Greater Serbia in the Balkans, seemed possibly prepared to let Slovenia go, but to do everything in its power—up to and including a full-scale war—to prevent Croatia, within its present borders, from going the same way.

The large Serbian minority population in Croatia (11.6 percent of its total population) is at the root of this conflict. In August 1990, three months after the CDU was elected to power in Zagreb, Serbs in the Knin area of northern Dalmatia staged an armed uprising with the covert aid of both Milošević and the YPA,[7] whose local military forces enabled the self-styled

The Armed Forces of Yugoslavia: Sliding into War

Serbian Autonomous Region of Krajina (SARK) to survive indefinitely, thereby showing that Tudjman's militia was effectively powerless in a third of Croatia's territory.

This affair, along with related disturbances in various Serbian areas in Croatian Slavonia, became more serious later. Tudjman's government, having promulgated a new unitary and implicitly secessionist Croatian constitution in December 1990, then went on to follow Slovenia's *de facto* exit from the Yugoslav federation in February 1991. Thus, if Slovenia formally separated itself from the federation, so would Croatia. This explicit linkage then prompted the breakaway government of the SARK to formally secede from Croatia in March 1991, thereby sowing the seeds of yet more Serb-Croat conflict in the republic in the future.[8]

This development, needless to say, was warmly welcomed by the Milošević government in Belgrade. Having promulgated a new unitary Serbian constitution in September 1990, and having gained a seemingly decisive electoral mandate for his brand of national communism in the Serbian election of December of the same year, Milošević now hardly bothered to conceal his ambition to reconstitute the Greater Serbia of December 1918.[9] The first phase of this policy, the abolition of the former autonomous provinces of Vojvodina and Kosovo, was completed in 1990. The next phase, a radical redrawing of Serbia's present borders at the expense of Croatia, Bosnia-Herzegovina, and Macedonia, would ultimately lead to war in June–July 1991.

This slide into war was already crystal clear in Croatia. In Bosnia-Herzegovina, ruled by an anti-communist coalition government dominated by the Slavic Muslim Party of Democratic Action (PDA) since the elections of November 1990, an extremely complicated and politically sensitive ethnic mix existed: 40 percent Slavic Muslim, 32 percent Serb, and 18 percent Croat. Any attempt to force this republic—the geopolitical linchpin of Yugoslavia—into a Greater Serbia, or a Greater Croatia, could only lead to war. The PDA government of President Alija Izetbegović also made it clear that if Slovenia and Croatia left the Yugoslav federation, then Bosnia-Herzegovina would do the same.[10] Similar sentiments also now prevailed in Macedonia, whose reformed communist-nationalist (IMRO-DPMNU, Internal Macedonian Revolutionary Organization-Democratic Party for Macedonian National Unity) coalition government (formed in January 1991) had the Macedonian Assembly unanimously adopt a declaration on a sovereign and independent Republic of Macedonia, which included the right to secede from the Yugoslav federation.[11]

Even Milošević's allies in Montenegro, whose League of Communists of Montenegro (LCM) won a landslide electoral victory in December 1990, were generally hostile to the idea of becoming a part of a Greater Serbia, although they would have little choice in the matter when the federation collapsed altogether in the course of 1991. Such serious obstacles to a reconstituted Greater Serbia, however, did not bother Milošević at that time. This is because he was now reasonably confident of getting anything he wanted from Croatia or any other republic that got in his way on account of his strong alliance with the communist-controlled YPA (70 percent of whose high command and officer corps was Serb).

Despite its supranational Yugoslav pretensions, Kadijević's YPA was becoming, arguably, little more than an instrument for the forcible advancement of Milošević's pan-Serbian ambitions.[12] As such, it was a serious threat to Milošević's numerous enemies, although the political revolutions of 1990 in Yugoslavia reduced its politicized role from that of being the party-army of a communist Yugoslavia to becoming the *de facto* party-army of Milošević's Serbian government.

The Politics of the YPA in the Post-LCY Era

With the dramatic collapse of the League of Communists of Yugoslavia (LCY) at its 14th and, as it turned out, final Extraordinary Congress in January 1990, the YPA was deprived of its former political role virtually overnight. The former ruling LCY had historically committed itself to maintaining a politicized party-army as a means of both preserving its own monopoly of political power and tightly controlling its military establishment, and thus all the military forces under its command. The YPA was an army that thus would "not accept any role as a depoliticized force confined to its barracks," according to the former President of the YPA's party organization, the late Admiral Petar Šimić.[13]

This insistence on maintaining a political role that had no legitimate means of expression after January 1990, coupled with the marked hostility of the YPA high command to the idea of genuine political pluralism, was to be the cause of serious political conflict between the army and those it regarded as its "enemies" throughout 1990. In the case of Slovenia, the most politically innovative of Yugoslavia's six republics, this conflict actually began in earnest in September 1989, when various military leaders, and Šimić in particular, strongly and publicly objected to the republic's new constitutional amendments—particularly the one restricting the Federal State Presidency's jurisdiction in declaring a state of emergency in Slovenia without the prior consent of its National Assembly.[14]

This blatant political interference was followed by crude intimidation in April 1990, when the YPA attempted to file criminal charges (thrown out by the Maribor public prosecutor) against Jože Pučnik, the DEMOS presidential candidate in Yugoslavia's first free and fair elections in over fifty years. At the same time, another provocation took place when Kadijević

The Armed Forces of Yugoslavia: Sliding into War 71

took it upon himself to mount an unwanted "inspection tour" in the republic, which is part of the 5th Military District.[15]

In May 1990, when Tudjman's CDU was elected to power in Croatia, the YPA used Federal President Jović's alarmist inaugural speech as an excuse to illegally and secretly order the disarming of Territorial Defense Force (TDF) units in Slovenia, Croatia, and other parts of the country.[16] Though this order was in part blocked and reversed by the new anti-communist governments in Slovenia and Croatia—with the help of Ante Markovic's Federal Executive Council (FEC)—it was highly indicative of how Kadijević and the YPA high command (nominal supporters of the Yugoslav Prime Minister, but more and more covert allies of Milošević) actually regarded the new political order in Yugoslavia's two northern republics.

A particular hostility was reserved for Tudjman's CDU government in Zagreb, whose power was shown to be purely nominal in the face of YPA military power during, and for a long time after, the Serb uprising in the Knin area in the summer of 1990. Though Slovenia had no Serb minority population for the YPA high command and Milošević to play with, its DEMOS government was effectively powerless to prevent YPA provocations in the republic, such as the forcible seizure of the Slovene TDF headquarters in Ljubljana by military police in October 1990.[17]

At the end of the previous month, in a move that was to lead directly to the very verge of war in January 1991, Kadijević's Defense Secretariat issued a then little-noticed statement that declared that the YPA would not permit Yugoslavia's republics to maintain military forces that were outside the federal military structure or its direct operational control. So-called "urgent steps" were then promised to stop such military forces emerging,[18] although little was actually done to prevent the development and arming of local armed forces by both the Slovenian and Croatian governments (the only exception being the raid on the Ljubljana TDF building in October).

In November 1990, just as the local reformed communists went down to an absolutely humiliating defeat at the hands of the PDA and its future coalition partners in Bosnia-Herzegovina's elections, Kadijević and other top YPA leaders, active and retired, founded their own orthodox communist movement: the League of Communists, Movement for Yugoslavia (LC-MY).[19] This effectively scuttled Marković's League of Reform Forces (LRF) created the previous July, given the presence of Kadijević and other FEC members in the leadership of the LC-MY. The message of the latter was simple: the YPA would not tolerate an electoral victory in Serbia by Vuk Drašković and his strongly anti-communist nationalist Movement for Serbian Renewal (MSR), and that people should vote for Milošević and his Socialist Party.[20]

How much this clear YPA threat helped Milošević gain a stunning electoral victory over Drašković in December is hard to determine exactly, but it may well have been as significant a factor in the elections as the SSP's iron grip on the Serbian media. Given that Serbia, and particularly Belgrade's 1st Military District, is the politico-military nerve center of the YPA and its associated military industries, it is hard to see how a MSR government could have come to power peacefully in Belgrade had it won the elections. It thus may well be that only Milošević's victory averted a complete military takeover of Serbia to, at the very least, save national communism in that republic and, by extension, the whole of Yugoslavia.

The YPA, Milošević, and Greater Serbia

Though nominally supportive of the policies of Federal Prime Minister Marković since March 1989, the YPA high command had in fact become increasingly partial towards Milošević's policies and plans since then, and especially during 1990 when a full Milošević-Kadijević-YPA axis developed in favor of a reconstituted Greater Serbia in the Balkans. During 1988 and for most of 1989, this elective affinity with Milošević was largely indirectly expressed in the form of not saying anything remotely critical of what was happening in Serbia in relation to Kosovo. Thus, otherwise highly vocal YPA leaders had nothing to say about Serbia's constitutional amendments of March 1989, which effectively stripped the republic's two autonomous provinces of all their powers (Vojvodina and Kosovo were abolished altogether in the new Serbian constitution of September 1990).[21] This silence was in sharp contrast to Šimić's harsh criticisms of the Slovene constitutional amendments of September 1989.

Just before the promulgation of these controversial Serbian constitutional amendments, the Federal State Presidency ordered the mobilization of YPA units into Kosovo in February 1989, when the province was in violent turmoil in protest against Milošević's politically provocative and highly repressive policies in the area. This was the fourth such deployment since 1945 (the others being 1968 and 1981). One year later, in February 1990, yet another YPA deployment took place in Kosovo; this time involving around 15,000 troops, most of whom were from Serbia (Nis), Macedonia (Skopje) and Montenegro (Titograd). They were backed up by 2,000 extra paramilitary militia troops from Serbia's Internal Affairs Ministry.[22] As in 1981 and 1989, this more or less permanent show of brute military force not only failed to halt Serb ethnic Albanian conflict in Kosovo, but actually exacerbated it in many highly dangerous ways. As of March 1991, for example, a general revolt was considered imminent in Kosovo, following intolerable repression and deprivation locally and revolutionary turmoil in nearby Albania.[23]

The main local political force, the Kosovo Democratic Alliance (KDA), is now convinced that a peaceful settlement with the Serbs, and Milošević in particular, is impossible. This can only mean revolt, a full-scale civil war and, if circumstances permit it, secession in favor of a reunified Greater Albanian state in the area. Milošević, who has staked everything on winning the ongoing civil war in Kosovo, can only nominally exercise control of the area by force, which means a permanent YPA presence. His militia and secret police cannot hold Kosovo on their own, and especially if it erupts into a general revolt supported by imported weapons and other assistance from nearby Albania and other parts of Yugoslavia.

This is the ultimate Serb nightmare. Another is the *de facto* alliance currently being forged between the KDA (also well-connected to old and new political forces in Albania), the PDA in Bosnia-Herzegovina and the largely Slavic Muslim area of Sandžak in Serbia, and the other main ethnic Albanian political force in the area, the Party of Democratic Prosperity (PDP) in nearby western Macedonia.[24] Such an alliance would represent over five million Muslims, who together constitute a major obstacle to Milošević's plan for a Greater Serbia, which also faces the enmity of the Slovenes, Croats and Hungarians (or Vojvodina).[25]

In retrospect, the stepping up of repression in Kosovo from the spring of 1990 onwards was itself the preface to Milošević's political metamorphosis in favor of a Greater Serbia later the same year. A change that was obviously speeded up by the DEMOS and CDU electoral victories in the spring of 1990. In June 1990, in an important speech to the Serbian Assembly, Milošević first outlined his vision of an independent Serbian state, which would, he suggested, emerge if Yugoslavia became a loose confederation in the future, as was then being demanded by both Slovenia and Croatia. Secondly, and far more dangerously, he raised the question of the fate of the Serbian diaspora outside Serbia in Croatia and Bosnia-Herzegovina, noting in passing that his proposed independent Serbian state would protect these Serbs against unspecified enemies, and therefore implicitly suggesting that he was contemplating a radical change of Serbia's 1945–91 borders in favor of a reconstituted Greater Serbia.[26]

In July 1990, Kosovo again came to the fore when the Serbian Assembly literally closed down the provincial assembly and government in Priština, following a pavement session of the former (caused by being locked out of the assembly building), where ethnic Albanian delegates adopted a declaration of sovereignty and formally repudiated the validity of the Serbian constitutional amendments of the previous March.[27] The following month, the Knin uprising took place, leading to the subsequent formation of the SARK, thereby leading to a cycle—still in progress—of provocative and implicitly expansionist pan-Serbianism outside Serbia proper, and further moves towards a unitary and, in the case of Kosovo, highly repres-

74   *Marko Milivojević*

sive Greater Serbian state structure inside Serbia itself. These processes
that were supported by the Greater Serbian opposition spearheaded by
the Movement for Serbian Renewal, whose objection to Milošević was only
on account of his by then purely nominal communist credentials.[28] His
strong and aggressive Greater Serbian nationalism was largely politically
untouchable, even by his barely tolerated MSR opponents.

On 28 September 1990, Serbia's new constitution was promulgated.
Highly unitary and giving immense powers to the republic's President,
the constitution is a good guide to Milošević's thinking on the possible
future development of a whole variety of issues, including his relations
with the country's federal armed forces. In this regard, the constitution
explicitly gives President Milošević, *inter alia*, the power to be the commander-in-chief of the Serbian armed forces in the event of Yugoslavia's
breakup and, by implication, the end of the YPA as presently organized.[29]
On the very same day as the new constitution became operative, Kadijević's
Defense Secretariat issued its now notorious statement on non-federal military forces.

This may or may not have been a coincidence, but it was certainly sym-
bolic of the growing political bond between Milošević and the YPA, whose
LC-MY of November was on the same ideological wavelength as the SSP.
For Milošević, this bond had a crucial personal touch: his influential wife,
Mirjana Marković, was an important political figure in both the SSP and
the LC-MY. Following the historic events of December 1990 in Slovenia
(plebiscite), Croatia (constitution) and Serbia (election), the Milošević-
Kadijević-YPA axis was fully formed and poised to make its first moves in
pursuit of a Greater Serbia in the first month of the New Year, aided and
abetted by Jović in the State Presidency.[30]

The Politics of War in Yugoslavia

Politically, a war of one sort or another had become essentially inevitable in Yugoslavia by the end of 1990 and was certain to break out in 1991
or 1992 at the latest. The latest phase of the country's seemingly perennial
crisis, whether it be in Croatia, Kosovo, or Serbia proper, contained a considerable potential for widespread political violence, which was also deeply
rooted in the country's turbulent recent history. The Serb-Croat conflict in
Croatia over the SARK, Pakrac, and Špegelj was clearly the most dangerous in terms of bringing about a war. However, Kosovo, in a state of semi-
civil war for most of the past decade, was just as dangerous, while the
violent opposition-organized anti-communist demonstrations in Belgrade
in March 1991 add a new and highly disturbing aspect to Serbia's volatile
politics, which could also profoundly affect politics in the country's other

republics. During these disturbances, when two people were killed and hundreds injured by the Serbian police, 1st Mililtary District YPA troops and armor were deployed on the streets of Belgrade for the first time since 1945. However, a YPA plan to impose a general state of emergency throughout the country was rejected by a majority of the State Presidency, which prompted the resignation of Jović, whose master, Milošević, then went on to say that his government no longer recognized the authority of the State Presidency.[31]

These ominous developments have both increased the probability of a war and Kosovo-type levels of repression in Serbia itself, where the Milošević-Kadijević-YPA alliance may well have to use ever more extreme methods to stay in power as the local economy collapsed, political life became ever more polarized and, as ever, Kosovo threatened to explode into a general anti-Serb revolt.

Following the events of March 1991, when the YPA high command failed to obtain a legalized military takeover, the option of a classic coup seemed to be on the agenda. Any number of pretexts, genuine or possibly manufactured for the purpose, could have made themselves available to those attempting to justify some sort of military takeover. Further violent turmoil in Belgrade, for example, could serve as just such a pretext. Or events in Kosovo; or in relation to Croatia—the possibilities are numerous. A number of historical precedents were now also being openly discussed in, among other places, the YPA weekly newspaper, *Narodna Armija*, where General Kenan Evren's military coup in Turkey in 1980 is a firm favorite among those so inclined in the YPA high command.[32] The only other relevant precedent, General Jaruzelski in Poland in 1981, was not so popular for obvious reasons, although it was arguably more relevant to Yugoslavia than was the one carried out in Turkey a year before.[33]

On the crucial issue of the timing of such a military takeover, this may well be determined by the perceived emergence of a serious political or military threat to the YPA's very existence as an institution, where fighting for survival would be the name of the game. In this regard, some in the YPA high command were now convinced that such a threat—albeit more political than military—now existed, and that a coup should consequently be launched immediately. The leading advocate of such views was reported to be Col.-Gen. Blagoje Adžić, the YPA Chief-of-Staff, and hence the figure responsible for putting together the logistics of a military takeover. The key figure, Kadijević, was thought to be more cautious on tactical grounds, arguing that the threat that did exist, though certainly serious, was not enough to go beyond what was attempted in March 1991, if only for the moment. Otherwise, far more real was the economic threat posed to the YPA's traditionally bloated budget by the ongoing fiscal and monetary collapse of the federal government, whose central bank was reportedly making emergency loans from its falling official reserves to meet day-to-day YPA and federal government expenses beginning in early February 1991.[34]

At the same time, a now infamous briefing, produced by the YPA's political (SK-PJ) directorate, was circulated to the troops of the 5th Military District. Based on Kadijević's recent statements, this document contained much that is frankly incredible (such as seeing the collapse of communism as a Western plot), but some of the material was in the real world. Thus, one of the major practical priorities of the YPA was to find stable and secure sources of finance for itself.[35] This is easier said than done. In 1989, defense expenditures were just under the equivalent of US $3 billion (around 5 percent of Gross Material Product), which were mostly derived from the federal government (50 percent of whose budget went on defense).[36] During 1990, as virtually all of Yugoslavia's republics (including Serbia) stopped paying any taxation revenues into the federal exchequer, the high defense budget had to be drastically cut in real terms, as it could not be sustained. In 1991, only National Bank of Yugoslavia (NDY) reserves were keeping the YPA alive financially.

Obviously, such emergency measures could only be short-term. As the YPA high command faced the real possibility of having no income at all from federal sources sometime in 1991, so the probability increased of its going for the military takeover option discussed earlier in order to survive as an institution. Though such a coup would plunge Yugoslavia's already collapsing economy into even worse chaos, it would also give the YPA endless opportunities for plunder pure and simple to sustain itself economically in at least the short-term. Beyond that, however, the military, under the control of hardline nationalist communists like Adžić and Kadijević, would not have a clue about dealing with Yugoslavia's worsening economic problems.[37] Kadijević's so-called "thoughts" on the subject, as outlined in the 5th Military District briefing, were predictably meaningless: gradual economic reform of the sort that has failed in Yugoslavia over the last quarter of a century.

There are, however, still a number of political and other constraints acting upon the YPA high command as regards any possible military takeover in the future. Firstly, though now less importantly than was once the case, the fear that an attempt at a coup would fatally undermine the internal cohesion of an army that is around 50 percent conscript, and in which around one in four conscripts is an ethnic Albanian.[38] Such a collapse would almost certainly take place upon an attempt at a coup, leaving a purely Serbian Army to fight a civil war in pursuit of, firstly, its own survival and, secondly, a Greater Serbia—a development that has now become reality. The fear of such a scenario coming about almost certainly explains the tactical caution of Kadijević during the crisis of March 1991.

The Armed Forces of Yugoslavia: Sliding into War 77

Secondly, we may consider negative foreign responses to either a direct war or a military takeover (an act of war by any other name as well), in a part or the whole of Yugoslavia. A number of interested foreign governments have already warned the YPA about the external political and other consequences it would face in the event of a coup, while the key variable in eventually putting together the Serbian-Croatian accord of 25 January 1991 was extensive political and economic pressure from the U.S. Ambassador, Warren Zimmerman, and the British Foreign Office. Similar pressure was almost certainly brought to bear during the crisis of March 1991. A letter that asked for unspecified American support against the YPA was also sent.[39] The sort that Tudjman had in mind—military assistance—was not an offer, but effective diplomatic pressure was available to be used to save the peoples of Yugoslavia from themselves.

The Military Capabilities of the Armed Forces of SFR Yugoslavia

Looking at the various armed forces operative (in 1991) in Yugoslavia, it is clear that there is a basic and quite fundamental assymetrical division between them as regards their respective military capabilities. On the one hand, there is the YPA, a combined service cadre (professional)—conscript army of around 200,000 troops (around 50 percent professional; 50 percent conscript), who are deployed in six Military Districts and one Maritime Military Region, and organized into 3 corps HQs, 12 infantry divisions (10 active, 2 reserve), 9 infantry brigades (3 mechanized, 3 motorized, 3 light), 8 independent tank brigades, 3 mountain brigades, 10 artillery regiments, 6 anti-tank regiments, 11 anti-aircraft artillery regiments, 4 SAM (SA-6) regiments (Army Ground Forces—144,000 troops, 94,500 conscripts); 6 naval bases, with 5 submarines, 3 frigates, 71 patrol and coastal combatants, 35 amphibious craft, 7 support vessels, 2 marine brigades, 25 coastal defense artillery batteries (Navy—11,000 troops, 4,500 conscripts); 2 air corps, with 431 combat aircraft and 150 armed helicopters, plus one airborne brigade, 14 SAM (8 SA-2, 6 SA-3) air defense battalions, 15 anti-aircraft artillery regiments (Air Force—33,000 troops, 4,500 conscripts); plus 15,000 paramilitary Frontier Guards under the control of the Army Ground Forces.

A respectable armed force even by First World standards, the order of battle of the YPA's core, its army ground forces, includes 1,570 main battle tanks, around 1,000 armoured vehicles of various types, 1,751 towed artillery pieces of various types (plus a smaller number of self-propelled artillery systems and multiple rocket launchers), 3,000 120-mm mortars, 1,700 anti-tank guns of various types, and around 4,000 air defense guns of various types.[40] Logistical back up for this armed force is provided by relatively sophisticated military industries, which are capable of producing—

by a mixture of indigenous and licensed production—all types of infantry weapons and ammunition; soft-skinned military vehicles; armoured vehicles, including main battle tanks; light and heavy artillery; light submarines; larger naval platforms; helicopters; and advanced fighter ground attack aircraft.[41] Few completed weapons systems are now imported outright by the YPA.

The eventual opponents of the YPA, on the other hand, were the republican Slovenian and Croatian remnants of the former YPA reserve, the Territorial Defense Forces, and the para-military militias (police) of these two republics. The former, a para-military militia of just over 800,000 troops in full wartime mobilization, was (in 1991) a lightly armed force with very little armor and no aircraft. The equipment that it did have was mainly obsolescent and thus no match for the front line units of the YPA.[42] It had, however, relatively well stocked infantry weapon/ammunition armories all over the country, which the YPA tried to seize—particularly in Slovenia and Croatia—in the spring of 1990. The Slovenian and Croatian police, though now reinforced with some new special and well-armed units, were mostly poorly armed with old infantry weapons and with even fewer heavier armaments/armored vehicles than local TDF forces, now known as Home Guards. Logistically, these forces were at a disadvantage in relation to the YPA, as most of the country's military industries were in Serbia. The Kragujevac-based Zavodi Crvena Zastava (ZCZ), for example, was Yugoslavia's largest general vehicle producer, but one of its key divisions, the Sporting Gun and Defense Weapon Plant, produced all the country's infantry weapons and ammunition.[43] Since May 1990, no ZCZ weapons or ammunition have been sold to Slovenia and Croatia on the direct orders of the YPA.[44] All of these data are relevant to understanding the situation before the secessions of Croatia and Slovenia and the subsequent collapse of the YPA.

This forced both the Slovenian and Croatian forces to seek to fill their weapons requirements abroad, and particularly in nearby Hungary and Austria, where certain agencies and individuals were prepared to supply relatively small quantities of various items, including anti-armor and anti-aircraft missiles, at a high price.[45] In addition, large numbers of private citizens—particularly in Croatia—were buying all types of weapons (principally automatic rifles) abroad and smuggling them into the republic, which was soon awash with them. The Serb minority in Croatia, especially in the SARK around Knin, was also heavily armed. For months, only a tense stand-off between Tudjman's militia and local YPA forces prevented a murderous free-for-all in the area. Similar situations, where armed civilians operate in informal militias or criminal gangs, developed in Bosnia-Herzegovina, Montenegro, Macedonia, and, of course, Kosovo. They were more often than not tacitly and even covertly supported by the various local and external political authorities to which they owed at least nominal allegiance.

At the governmental level, the DEMOS and CDU governments both established coordinating organs to better control and expand their respective armed forces, and to make the best use of all the relevant local resources available for the defense of their respective republics. In January 1991, for example, the Council for National Defense and Protection of the Constitutional Order was set up by Tudjman.[46] In the same month, a Slovene-Croatian Agreement on Joint Defense and Security Cooperation was signed by the defense and interior ministers of the two republics, which agreed, *inter alia*, to use all legal means—including the armed forces—at their disposal, to protect and defend themselves "in the event of armed intervention against the legal bodies and citizens of the two republics."[47] Following the creation of this rudimentary common defense policy, large scale military exercises took place in both republics during the following month. Internal security precautions are also very strict in both republics, and especially in Croatia, where every key facility and political personality is now under very heavy guard.

In the war, therefore, the YPA has certainly had the military edge over its opponents, even though it has reverted to being a purely Serbian Army, which also includes Serbian TDF forces and the para-military militia troops of the Serbian Internal Affairs Ministry, plus assorted civilian militias and gangs inside and outside Serbia. The Serb-dominated YPA high command and officer corps certainly did everything in its power to have unreliable non-Serb officers removed after the initial military fiasco in Slovenia. The new Serbian Army also benefits greatly by the extensive military industries based in Serbia.

Slovenia and Croatia alone are now thought to have around 200,000-250,000 para-military (TDF/Home Guards and militia/ police) troops, active and reserve, under arms and ready to fight.[48] This far exceeds the number of Serb YPA troops in the 5th Military District, whose various barracks and bases are, with the exception of Knin, completely surrounded and under heavy local police surveillance. Though far better armed than the local opposition, these forces and their facilities are relatively fixed targets, and as such are vulnerable to local countermeasures. As the war has expanded and as Serbia and Croatia have tenaciously contested areas of dispute, casualties and property damage have mounted rapidly. All are losers in what is very quickly turning into the nightmare of a Balkan Lebanon.

Notes

1. Prosecutor's office statement carried by *Tanjug* (Belgrade) on 26 February 1991, quoted in "Military Indicts Croatian Defense Minister and Seven Others," *Reuters*, Belgrade, 26 February 1991.

2. Quoted in *Independent on Sunday* (London), 27 January 1991.

3. Federal Defense Secretariat statement carried by *Tanjug* (Belgrade) in Serbo-Croat on 23 January 1991, translated and reproduced in BBC Monitoring Service, *Summary of World Broadcasts* (hereinafter *SWB*), Part 2, Eastern Europe, 25 January 1991, EE/0979, p. B/13.

4. Respectively, Janez Drnovšek and Stipe Mesić, who walked out of the session attended by Kadijević, as reported by Radio Ljubljana in Slovene (9 January 1991), translated and reproduced in *SWB*, 11 January 1991, EE/0967, p. B/13.

5. HINA (Croatian News Agency) reported by Radio Zagreb (9 January 1991), translated and reproduced in *SWB*, 11 January 1991, EE/0967, p. B/13.

6. Text of report of speech by Milan Kučan carried by *Tanjug* (Belgrade) in Serbo-Croat on 20 February 1991, translated and reproduced in *SWB*, 22 February 1991, EE/1003, p. B/8.

7. Particularly Kadijević, a Knin Serb, and the YPA Chief-of-Staff, Col.-Gen. Blagoje Adžić, another Serb. The then Federal Interior Secretary, Col.-Gen. (retired) Petar Gračanin (Serb) was also reportedly involved in this affair. For this, see "Yugoslavia: The Brink," in *Eastern Europe Newsletter* (London, hereinafter *EEN*), Vol. 4, No. 17 (27 August 1990), p. 2.

8. *The Independent* (London), 2 March 1991.

9. Milošević adopted this position in 1990, having previously failed to become a second Tito in a unitary communist Yugoslavia, which he, more than any other politician, unwittingly destroyed. For this, see Sabrina P. Ramet, "Serbia's Slobodan Milošević: A Profile," in *Orbis* (Philadelphia), Vol. 35, No. 1 (Winter 1991), pp. 104-105.

10. This formulation arises out of the PDA's 1990 electoral manifesto commitment to an independent Bosnia-Herzegovina within, it was then hoped, a confederal Yugoslavia. For this, see: "Yugoslavia: War Sirens," in *EEN*, Vol. 4, No. 18 (10 September 1990), pp. 7–8.

11. This was done on 25 January 1991, and reported by *Tanjug* (Belgrade) in English on the same day, reproduced in SWB, 29 January 1991, EE/0982, p B/11

12. Which is not to say that it does not have its own political and economic reasons for behaving as it does now. For this, see "Yugoslavia: The Waiting Game," in *EEN*, Vol. 5, No. 4 (February 1991).

13. Remark made in a speech in Split on 29 September 1989, and reported in *Politika* (Belgrade), 30 September 1989, quoted in Milan Andrejevich, "The Military's Role in the Current Constitutional Crisis," in *Report on Eastern Europe* (Radio Free Europe/Radio Liberty, Munich, hereinafter *REE*), 9 November 1990, p. 26.

14. Milan Andrejevich, "The Military's Views on Recent Domestic Developments," in *Radio Free Europe Research*, REE (October 1989), p. 15.

15. Milan Andrejevich, "Military Attempts to File Charges Against Slovenian Presidential Candidate," in *REE* (27 April 1990), p. 40.

16. "Yugoslavia: Milošević's Metamorphosis," in *EEN*, Vol. 4, No. 12 (11 June 1990), p. 6.

The Armed Forces of Yugoslavia: Sliding into War 81

17. *The Independent* (6 October 1990).

18. Andrejevich, "The Military's Role" in [note 13], p. 24.

19. "Yugoslavia: The Generals' Intentions," in *EEN*, Vol. 4, No. 24 (3 December 1990), p. 6.

20. This SK-PJ/SSP link had a strong personal aspect for Milošević, whose wife, Mirjana Marković, was both a prime member of the SK-PJ and a guest of honor at its first conference in December 1990, as reported by *Tanjug* (Belgrade) in Serbo-Croat on 24 December 1990, translated and reproduced in *SWB* (1 January 1991), EE/0959, p. B/14.

21. First drafted in July 1988 by the Serbian Assembly, the forcible imposition of these constitutional amendments in Kosovo was to be the cause of violent disturbances in the area, culminating in the death of over a hundred people during clashes between ethnic Albanians and Serbian security forces. For this, see Marko Milivojević, *Descent Into Chaos: Yugoslavia's Worsening Crisis, European Security Study No. 7* (London: Institute for European Defense & Strategic Studies, 1989), p. 10.

22. Milan Andrejevich, "The Yugoslav Army in Kosovo: Unrest Spreads to Macedonia," in *REE* (23 February 1990), p. 38 & note 3 (p. 40).

23. "Yugoslavia: The Waiting Game," in *EEN*, Vol. 5, No. 4(18 February 1991), p. 5.

24. For the Serbian media, which is dominated by conspiracy theorists of one sort or another, this Slavic Muslim-Albanian alliance is itself part of what one Milorad Jorganovic sees as a 'conspiratorial Ljubljana-Zagreb-Priština axis' against the Serbs (commentary in Albanian by Radio Priština on 18 February 1991), translated and reproduced in *SWB* (20 February 1991), EE/1001, pp. B/13–B/14.

25. Though relatively quiet when compared to the ethnic Albanians of Kosovo, the Hungarians of Vojvodina—represented by the Democratic Union of Magyars of Vojvodina (DUMV)—are now becoming increasingly restive in response to Milošević's policies in the area. Two recent incidents are typical. In February 1991, the Serbian Assembly rejected a DUMV call for a nationality ministry in the republic (reported by Budapest home service on 5 February 1991, translated and reproduced in *SWB* (8 February 1991), EE/0991, p. B/13), and the DUMV rejected a SSP (Vojvodina) claim that it was a secessionist and separatist organization hostile to Yugoslavia (reported by *Tanjug* (Belgrade) in Serbo-Croat on 18 February 1991, translated and reproduced in *SWB* (20 February 1991), EE/1001, p. B/14).

26. Speech published in *Politika* (Belgrade), 26 June 1990, translated and reproduced in Foeign Broadcast Information Service (FBIS), *Daily Report* (Eastern Europe), 26 June 1990, pp. 51–55.

27. "Yugoslavia: Sliding into War," in *EEN*, Vol. 4, No. 14 (11 July 1990), p. 3.

28. Drašković, the MSR leader, is even more extreme than Milošević on some issues, such as his call for the forcible repatriation of all Yugoslavia's ethnic Albanians into nearby Albania. For this, see *Independent on Sunday* (London), 25 February 1990.

29. *The Guardian* (28 September 1990).

30. *The Guardian* (29 January 1991).

31. *Independent on Sunday* (10 march 1991); and *The Guardian* (16 March 1991).

32. EEN (3 December 1990), p. 6. For the Evren coup itself, see Mehmat Ali Briand, *The Generals' Coup in Turkey: An Inside Story of 12 September 1980* (London: Brassey's Defense Publishers, 1987).

82 *Marko Milivojević*

33. For the Jaruzelski precedent, see Marko Milivojević, "The Yugoslav People's Army: Another Jaruzelski on the Way?," in *The South Slav Journal* (London), Vol. 11, Nos. 2–3 (Summer/Autumn 1988), pp. 1–18.

34. *EEN* (18 February 1991), p. 4.

35. "Generals' Last Stand," in *EEN*, Vol. 5, No. 3 (4 February 1991), p. 2.

36. For overall defense expenditures, see *The Military Balance, 1989–1990* (London: International Institute for Strategic Studies, 1989), p. 92; for their share of the federal budget, see *Yugoslavia: Country Profile, 1990–91* (London: Economist Intelligence Unit, 1990), p. 26.

37. F. Stephen Larrabee, "Long Memories and Short Fuses: Change and Instability in the Balkans," in *International Security* (Cambridge, Mass.), Vol. 15, No. 3 (Winter 1990/91), p. 71.

38. For this and other constraints acting upon the YPA, see Marko Milivojević, "The Political Role of the Yugoslav People's Army in Contemporary Yugoslavia," in Marko Milivojević, et al. (eds.), *Yugoslavia's Security Dilemmas: Armed Forces, National Defence and Foreign Policy* (Oxford: Berg, 1988), pp. 56–59.

39. "Balkan Bust-up," in *EEN*, Vol. 5, No. 5 (4 March 1991), p. 2.

40. *The Military Balance*, [note 36], pp. 92–93

41. Marko Milivojević, *Yugoslavia's Military Industries*, Bradford Studies on Yugoslavia No. 16 (Bradford: Research Unit in Yugoslav Studies, 1990), p. 8 (Fig. 1).

42. *The Military Balance*, [note 36], p. 92.

43. James P. Nichol, "Yugoslavia," in James E. Katz (ed.), *Arms Production in Developing Countries* (Lexington, Mass: Lexington Books, 1984), p. 349.

44. "Yugoslavia," *EEN*, Vol. 5, No. 2 (21 January 1991).

45. Often with the assistance of shady middlemen, though this was publicly denied by the Slovene Defense Minister, Janez Janša. For this, see "Slovene Defence Minister on sources of weapons for republican army" (Belgrade home service in Serbo-Croat on 19 January 1991), translated and reproduced in *SWB* (23 January 1991), EE/0977, p. B/5.

46. "Croatian Council for National Defence Set Up" (reported in *Tanjug* (Belgrade) in Serbo-Croat on 4 January 1991), translated and reproduced in *SWB*, 9 January 1991, EE/0965, p. B/14.

47. "Croatian-Slovene Agreement on Defence and Security Cooperation Published" (reported in *Tanjug* (Belgrade) in Serbo-Croat on 13 February 1991), translated and reproduced in *SWB* (15 February 1991), EE/0997, p. B/17. The agreement was signed on 20 January 1991.

48. For the will to fight, see *The Guardian* (21 January 1991).

4

Media: The Extension of Politics by Other Means

Jasmina Kuzmanović

When questions are asked about reasons for the Yugoslav breakup and about the savage war inflicted on two former Yugoslav republics, the media are among the first to be blamed. This is why it is necessary to highlight, in the introduction to this chapter, one of the most widespread and deeply rooted myths in contemporary consciousness: the myth of "objective reporting." In spite of decades of state-controlled media, the public of former Yugoslavia has obviously been indulging in that myth, just as many Western media consumers have—which is probably the result of years of "Americanization," as our communist soul-keepers would have put it. The myth of "objective reporting" was especially alive in television reporting; the picture was there, after all, and cameras just cannot lie. Or can they? After Vukovar, Dubrovnik, Sarajevo, and many other places had been seen by "the camera's objective eye," not to mention described by objective pencils and pads, or on objective recorders, it became clear that technology does not necessarily breed objectivity. In real life, "objective reporting" is restricted by two major facts. First, reporters function as extended arms of networks or newspapers which are, at best, market-oriented corporations or, at worst, the government's mouthpieces. In both cases, they are susceptible to pressure. Second, the reporter's unique way of receiving, processing, and editing information necessarily reflects his or her value system, including prejudices, education, and emotions. "Objectivity," the phenomenon we so like to treasure, exists only in the eye of the beholder. But the public are not media experts; and even if they might not take for granted everything they read, the majority still take for granted everything they see.

In the early 1970s, British mass media expert Peter Golding wrote that "the main theme concerning mass media is the reconciliation that needs to

84   *Jasmina Kuzmanović*

be made between the information and value people derive from direct personal experiences and those they receive from the media."[1] Golding concluded that "it is fair to say that [the] media play their most significant role in imparting values in areas of comparative abstractedness, distance, unfamiliarity and inaccessibility, while behavior and attitudes about personally experienced circumstances are more directly the result of the situation surrounding these circumstances."[2]

And what can be better described as "distant, unfamiliar, and abstract" than the destruction and deaths in distant cities, the suffering of unfamiliar people, and the alleged sense of "threat" in countrymen living 500 kilometers away? War is the perfect situation where the media not only reflect reality (as is supposedly their main function) but also *create* reality, especially so if the conflict takes place in an already existing atmosphere of war-mongering and if the public has to rely on only one information system. Since 1987 (the year Slobodan Milošević came to power in Serbia), one of the most crucial issues in former Yugoslavia has been who controls the information space.

The Breakup Begins

The information space of socialist Yugoslavia was for decades sectioned along republic borders. Each of the republics and two autonomous provinces had a local broadcasting system (Radio-Television Skopje, RTV Ljubljana, RTV Novi Sad, etc.) and one or more major newspaper corporations (*Vjesnik* in Zagreb, *Politika* in Belgrade, *Oslobodjenje* in Sarajevo, etc.) The electronic media and usually one daily newspaper (*Vjesnik* in Croatia's case, *Politika* in Serbia's case, *Delo* in Slovenia) served as the semi-official mouthpiece of the republic government. Editorial policies and staff, especially those of the electronic media, were closely monitored by the Communist Party's Central Committee of the republic in question. A head of one such RTV system was traditionally the member of the republican Central Committee himself. In the second half of the 1980s, gradual liberalization of the social climate in general encouraged a number of newspaper and magazines to adopt a more liberal and democratic outlook: above all, the weekly *Danas* in Zagreb, the weekly *NIN* in Belgrade, the bimonthly *Start* in Zagreb, and the alternative/youth weekly *Mladina* in Ljubljana. The typical strategy of the "liberated medium," such as *Start*, was to establish its name with articles on culture, entertainment, art, or life-style, areas not so closely watched by party watchdogs, in which Western values and attitudes have been promoted. Eventually the space of real politics was conquered, to the point that in 1989, the year before the first free elections in Croatia, the editorial board of *Danas* had more or less been determining

Media: The Extension of Politics by Other Means　　　　　85

the next move of Croatia's party Central Committee.[3] The market for printed media went beyond republican borders, making it an era of huge circulations for many magazines. In the late 1980s, *Danas* racked up a circulation of 180,000—an all-time high—with one fifth of sales being outside Croatia. The situation was similar with Belgrade's *NIN*, which reached a circulation well above 200,000, while Ljubljana's provocative weekly *Mladina* even managed to break the language barrier and sell more than 100,000 in Slovenia and other republics.

The late 1980s set major media standards for democracy in all, or almost all, republics. Those few months in Croatia, after the communists were pressed by a series of East European "velvet revolutions" into permitting the multi-party system in November 1989, and before the first free elections in April 1990, are still regarded as the high point for freedom of the press in recent Croatian history. This phenomenon was a kind of trademark of the Yugoslav media in transition from communism to national democracies. In spring 1990, the war-mongering on behalf of the major part of the Serbian media had been going on undisturbed for more than two years, ever since Slobodan Milošević came to power. Communist governments in other republics seemed unable to respond to state-promoted national hysteria from Belgrade, breeding a sense of helplessness and confusion among their citizens. In Croatia, the reluctance of the then leaders to react in any way to rising Serbian nationalism had been taunted by the Zagreb media as "Croatian silence."[4] The elections in Slovenia and Croatia were held in these conditions, which inevitably blew wind into the sails of the more nationalist parties. The oppositional coalition DEMOS won in Slovenia, and the center-right Croatian Democratic Community won in Croatia. Later in 1990, nationalist parties won the elections in Macedonia and Bosnia-Herzegovina. Only Serbia and Montenegro had reelected the communist-turned-socialist parties by the end of 1990. Political changes throughout the country also hit the media. Yugoslavia was now evidently breaking along national lines, and most of the media had to follow suit. One obvious expection was a supranational or transnational television channel, YUTEL (Yugoslav Television), founded in 1990 in Sarajevo, then a model city of a melting pot Yugoslav style. YUTEL was headed by a Croat from Belgrade, Goran Milić, and had a nationally mixed crew. YUTEL reported about Serbian aggression against Croatia with a certain distance, avoiding any judgment, and searched for an "independent approach." In so doing, YUTEL pleased neither side and was condemned by both Serbian and Croatian officials as a subtle version of "enemy propaganda." But as Serbian aggression continued and spread to Bosnia-Herzegovina, YUTEL's line of equidistance from both the aggressor and the victim came under stress. Torn by internal disagreements and the sheer impossibility of maintaining "neutrality" in the middle of a besieged city, YUTEL closed down in May 1992.

The Slovenian media have had the most successful transition to democracy of the six republics. The national newspaper corporation *Delo* publishes several periodicals and the daily *Delo*, a paper whose reputation for integrity has not changed since the elections. The oppositional daily *Slovenec* was launched in June 1991, joining other opposition periodicals. The youth or alternative weekly *Mladina* had been the most liberal and provocative periodical from 1985 to the end of the communist era. During this period, *Mladina* pursued issues of free speech with intensity, probed Tito's posthumous personality cult, and became the first periodical in Yugoslavia to publish interviews with dissidents. *Mladina* was also the first to criticize the spending and totalitarian ways of the Yugoslav People's Army (YPA), as well as its complicity in Palestinian terrorism. The periodical *Tribuna* and the satirical *Pavliha* had traditionally been accentuating the Slovenian social and political scene. Radio-Television Ljubljana changed its name to RTV Slovenia. During the "war of nine days" in June 1991, when the Yugoslav People's Army attempted unsuccessfully to break Slovenia, the media played a good part in the tiny republic's defense. Slovenia was the first Yugoslav republic to proclaim independence in June 1991, attracting hundreds of foreign journalists to Ljubljana. The new government immediately took control of Slovenia's borders with the West, prompting the Yugoslav People's Army to strike back with tanks and MiG jets. Since all air and almost all road exits were instantly closed, six hundred foreign journalists temporarily imprisoned in Ljubljana's center, "Cankarjev dom," had nothing else to do but to feed the world with news on Slovenia. National radio and television adopted, overnight, a 24-hour special war schedule. Slovenian Minister for Information Jelko Kačin began appearing next to the Defense Miniter (Janez Janša) in daily news conferences in Cankarjev dom. In contrast to the Slovenes' modern and articulate strategy for the media, the Yugoslav People's Army responded with old-time propaganda, having uniformed generals hold threatening TV monologues. It was a media *Blitzkrieg* and Slovenia won hands down, speeding up the Army's defeat and its withdrawal from the republic.

In February 1992, the Slovenian Ministry for Information proposed a new Information Bill. The Bill can be described as descriptive rather than restrictive, and it admits "information censorship only in cases of immediate military danger." *Delo's* commentator Dragica Konade wrote, "It is one Information Act too many . . . And who actually needs a Ministry for Information?"[5] At the end of April 1992, the Slovenian Parliament decided to postpone the adoption of the Information Act. If the ideal soil for free expression is a society whose government does not attempt to legislate information, Slovenia seems to be on its way to newsroom paradise.

The major print media of Macedonia—the daily *Nova Makedonija* and the weekly *Večer*—survived the free elections in 1990 with little turmoil.

Media: The Extension of Politics by Other Means

Radio-Television Skopje changed its name to Radio-Television Macedonia, after some protest from the People's Democratic Party, the principal party of the Albanian minority, Macedonia's largest ethnic minority. In September 1991, the national agency TAM (Telegraph Agency Macedonia) was founded. This meant that after Slovenia and Croatia, Macedonia had also turned its back on the official federal news agency Tanjug, which in recent years had been increasingly identified with Serbian interests. Prior to the establishment of TAM, the Macedonian public had been informed about the Serb-Croat war mainly through Tanjug. In April 1992, after the publisher of *Nova Makedonija* purchased printing works abroad, Minister for Information Martin Trenevski called for a police investigation of the purchase, citing corruption. After the investigation, the daily was cleared of charges. Since it turned out that the minister had acted alone, without notifying the prime minister, the editorial board of *Nova Makedonija* turned to the government for an explanation.

A protest meeting for freedom of speech was held in March 1992 in Skopje. About 2,000 people attended, asking for the demonopolization of information space in Macedonia. The meeting was organized by the Forum for Media Freedom and Democracy, the establishment of which, some months earlier, had been prompted by official intimidation of *Republika*, Macedonia's first independent daily.

Montenegro held its free elections comparatively late, in October 1990. The election campaign had rocked the self-indulgent state media and opened space for politically provocative issues for the first time in half a century. Six journalists in the republic's main daily, *Pobjeda*, felt it was time to ask for a share of freedom. They claimed, in an open letter to the editorial board, that the paper openly favored only the governing Socialist Party, and the People's Party. "We felt that it is high time to establish the criteria for media coverage of the election campaign, so that we could create a non-partisan daily, the future of which would not depend on an election victory," said the letter. *Pobjeda's* editor-in-chief, Šćepan Vuković, had accepted the game of democracy and had offered his resignation, but it was refused by the paper's editorial board. After the communists were reinstated in power as socialists, journalism fell back to state-controlled normality. The monotonous media scene changed in October 1990, as the first independent Montenegrin weekly, *Monitor*, was founded as a shareholding company of 150 shareholders. From the beginning, *Monitor* was printed in Latin lettering, in *Oslobodjenje's* printing house in Sarajevo. This recourse had been taken in order to circumvent the monopolistic Montenegrin publisher, *Pobjeda*. The circulation varies around 25,000. *Monitor* has gathered a number of Montenegrin journalists who had been employed elsewhere, but unable to speak their mind in newsrooms of *Pobjeda* or the national broadcasting station, Radio-Television Montenegro.

For the first two years of its existence, *Monitor* has been highly critical of the current socialist government of Montenegro. It has offered a different perspective and has often run stories from other Yugoslav publications, diminishing the impact of the government-imposed information blockade. The weekly has been subjected to government pressure and less formal ways of intimidation, including physical threats to reporters and editors. But it has managed to survive.

"The old spirit of losers must be replaced by the spirit of winners"— with these words, current Montenegrin Prime Minister Milo Djukanović announced the personnel changes in the national broadcasting system in spring 1991, immediately after he assumed his position.[6] Three top people of RTV Montenegro were swept off by Djukanovic's orders: Milutin Radulović, acting general manager of Montenegro Television; Čedomir Lješević, manager of Radio Montenegro; and Danilo Burzan, editor-in-chief of Radio Montenegro. In so doing, Prime Minister Djukanović acted in accordance with his authority. For under the republic's Act on Public Enterprises, which under Montenegrin law regulates the national radio and television, the government is entitled to appoint editors and managers in the state media. Several weeks prior to this media purge, the united opposition had proposed to the Montenegrin Parliament that the authority over the top appointments in the state media should be given to the parliament. The proposal was rejected by a two-thirds majority of the 120-member parliament. In September 1991, six television journalists who had occasionally contributed to *Monitor* were fired from RTV Titograd. The Montenegrin Professional Journalists' Association issued a sharp protest, pointing out the "totalitarian, repressive manner" of the action.[7]

Bosnia-Herzegovina and its media have long abstained from the Serb-Croat "paper war." When the Croatian Democratic Community won the 1990 elections, one of its first moves was to replace the general manager of the national television station. But in Bosnia, when a loose coalition of three national parties came to power in November 1990, they left the media alone for the first several months. The major daily *Oslobodjenje* and the periodicals *Večernje novine* and *Svijet*, and the alternative weeklies *Valter* and *Voks*, all carried on according to new standards won during the election campaign. The republic's first Information Minister, Velibor Ostojić, worked prior to the elections as a language editor for the national radio, but by the end of 1990, Ostojić was to announce a "major cleaning" in the media scene.[8] (Ostojić has since joined Serbian irregular forces in Bosnia-Herzegovina.)

It was to be expected that the tripartite coalition would soon change the national structure of people employed in the state media, and bring it into line with the demographic pattern in Bosnia-Herzegovina. The republic's media, and especially the national television, had been tradi-

Media: The Extension of Politics by Other Means   89

tionally dominated by Serbs (34 percent of the population), while Croats and Muslims, on the other hand, were underrepresented. In this fledgling democracy, government and media found themselves, at first, frequently at odds. The Muslim Party for Democratic Action even considered asking its supporters to boycott the chief daily *Oslobodjenje*, and Sarajevo's TV anchor introduced Bosnian President Alija Izetbegović, who had been imprisoned by the communists for political "crimes," as "a former convict and the president of Bosnia-Herzegovina."[9] But the government soon struck back and took control.

Where Montenegro's journalists could indulge in wishful thinking, Bosnia's journalists were confronted with undisguised repression. In March 1991, the Bosnian government proposed to the parliament to amend the existing Information Act. The most controversial part of the proposal was that managers and editors of the state media should be appointed by the parliament, and not, as before, elected by media employees. Reporters and other media employees responded with a protest meeting in Sarajevo. On the surface, it looked like a classic case of supporters of freedom of speech on one side and repressive government on the other. But the deeper controversy between the conflicted parties was pointed out by the Sarajevo writer Miljenko Jergović: "Top people in the state media suffer from a severe lapse of memory; they have completely forgotten how and by whom they were appointed to these positions in the first place. That is, most of them had first been visiting the party's Central Committee, and then comrade so-and-so would recommend them to some editor-in-chief. They had to be ideologically pure to get the job."[10] In spite of the protests, the parliament adopted the amended Information Act in April 1991.

But the issue of national representation lingered on. In summer 1991, the Croatian Democratic Community of Bosnia-Herzegovina claimed that Croats and the Croatian language were still insufficiently represented in the media. Serbian Democratic Party leader Radovan Karadžić was at that time supporting the idea of three national televisions, i.e., three distinct Sarajevo television channels. (Karadžić's idea was eventually realized in mid-April, when the Serbian news agency SRNA was founded in Sarajevo's suburb of Pale. It was two days after the war in Bosnia-Herzegovina had started.)

When Serbian aggression on Croatia became aggravated in fall and winter 1991, Bosnian media generally assumed an equidistant attitude. This attitude survived even the national referendum on independence, and it lingered almost to the day when some Bosnian Serbs, helped by the Yugoslav People's Army, rebelled and ignited ethnic warfare against their fellow Bosnians.

Bosnia-Herzegovina has for so long been a model of coexistence in the Balkans. This factor, in combination with a deeply rooted communist idea

90   *Jasmina Kuzmanović*

that the media should be "educational," resulted in a curious phenomenon. For the first several weeks of the war, Sarajevo TV was pleading and preaching, rather than reporting on what was going on. For the most part, it was well intended pleading, summoning its viewers to "reason," but at the same time, it was pathetically out of touch with reality and usually also with elementary professional standards. When the shootings started in mid-April and the first Serbian barricades in Sarajevo were erected, television speakers would invariably call to all three ethnic leaders to "stop the chaos" and "save the city," as if all three were equally responsible for creating that chaos.

During those few weeks when the war in Bosnia started but political communication was still possible (or so it seemed), the two Sarajevo networks—the official Television Bosnia-Herzegovina, and YUTEL—turned a new page in the history of the contemporary media, both professionally and ethically. They played a most explicit political role, in the most direct game of life and death, more than any media have ever played. Romanian television and its role in overthrowing Ceauşescu pales in comparison. While Sarajevo was under fire, YUTEL's editor-in-chief Goran Milić established a live telephone contact in the studio with both Alija Izetbegović, the president, and Radovan Karadžić, the Serbian leader. Milić made them talk to each other and had himself tried to talk them into temporary reconciliation, while citizens of Sarajevo watched this most intense talk-show ever. (It was as if CNN's Bernard Shaw had had Saddam Hussein and George Bush on studio lines and had tried to talk them into peace.) When the Federal People's Army kidnapped President Izetbegović in April 1991 and held him for one day, Television Bosnia-Herzegovina's anchor initiated a live telephone contact between imprisoned Izetbegović, his keeper the army general, and members of the Bosnian presidency.

Were the Sarajevo journalists right in taking politics into their own hands? Was it a major violation of professional standards, or just a desperate attempt to save the city and themselves? The answers are hard to find, since professional standards and ethics have never anticipated such situations. In both cases, the meddling of Sarajevo television journalists eventually did not work out. They did not help change history, though they had certainly jumped right in the middle of the process. Quite apart from all rules, the television was these days making history in Sarajevo, not only recording it.

As attacks on Sarajevo intensified throughout May, Television Bosnia-Herzegovina was faced with political changes and growing professional challenges. Only those staff—Muslims, Croats, and Serbs—who were loyal to the Bosnian government remained in the television building. Because of targeted mortar and shell attacks, they worked in shifts of several days, bravely covering the city and airing very impressive footage. By the end

Media: The Extension of Politics by Other Means 91

of May, Sarajevo reporters issued an appeal addressed "to the world." It was sadly reminiscent of the famous appeal issued by the director of Budapest Television in 1956, who addressed Europe, while Soviet tanks were rolling in, with news that he and his staff were dying for "European culture and civilization." The Sarajevo appeal said: "The television building was hit by shells more than a hundred times, was rocketed six times, the Army has occupied seven of our transmission towers and killed six of our employees. We implore you, journalists of the world, to inform your governments and international organizations about this crime in the center of Europe. We still air the program."[11]

Not long after this appeal, the power supply to the city was cut and Sarajevo Television stopped broadcasting. But the daily *Oslobodjenje* has persisted to this day, publishing a shorter version of the paper every day under almost impossible conditions.[12] In November 1991, the paper's editor-in-chief, Kemal Kurspahić, and deputy editor, Gordana Knezević, were awarded for courage in journalism by the International Women in Media Foundation.

The Paper War

"Surrender—all resistance will be forcefully broken." Such leaflets were dispersed by YPA jets in Slovenia in June 1991, marking the end of the Serbian paper war and the beginning of the real one. The Serbian media war started almost a decade ago, and at first was aimed only against the Albanians in Kosovo. The major Belgrade newspaper enterprise *Politika* and its namesake dailies *Politika* and *Politika ekspres* led the media charge, followed by the electronic media, the weekly *Duga*, and the daily *Večernje novosti*. The idea was to demonize the Albanians, by calling them thieves, rapists, illiterate, murderous,[13] and by creating a general atmosphere where the Albanians would be viewed, and increasingly treated, as second class citizens. In this period, the notion of "genocide" against the Serbian people appeared in the printed media for the first time since World War Two. The turning point in history of both Serbian politics and media was the Eighth Conference of the League of Communists of Serbia in 1987, when Slobodan Milošević seized power in Serbia and instantly began to purge the Belgrade printed and electronic media. This year marked the beginning of a new era in Serbia, in which almost all media, with the exception of the federal daily, *Borba*, alternative radio station B-92, and later, the independent weekly, *Vreme*—have functioned as government mouthpieces. And unlike some ordinary repressive system that uses the media to keep its subject under control, this government was getting ready for war, and needed the media to prepare the battlefield.

Kosovo has been under YPA occupation and emergency measures since 1988, and almost all Albanian journalists have lost their jobs at Television Priština and the Albanian language daily, *Rilindja*. Having dealt with the Kosovo media, Milošević hushed the disobedient voices in the northern Serbian province of Vojvodina. When his loyalists unconstitutionally usurped power in Vojvodina's government and parliament in fall 1988, they first deposed the top people in Radio-Television Novi Sad and the major daily, *Dnevnik*. The dailies of Vojvodina's national minorities—Hungarian, Ruthenian, and Slovak—at first showed resistance. But when the Serbian aggression on Croatia began, it was ever harder for them to maintain an independent position. In October 1991, during the army siege of Vukovar, Vojvodina's parliament concluded that the national daily, *Dnevnik*, had "extensively and objectively reported on conflicts from Slavonia, Baranja, and Western Srem. Doing so, *Dnevnik* managed to break the information blockade and neutralize the impact of propaganda from the Croatian media."[14] But the minority press did not earn any praise. "[These dailies] have not respected agreements, and the conclusion on editorial policies," said Vojvodina's Prime Minister, Radoman Bozović. "They have openly supported separatism in the northwestern republics of Slovenia and Croatia; they have fabricated lies and attempted to count up which nationalities lost how many in the reserve forces."[15] In the same breath, Bozović threatened the Hungarian daily, *Magyar Szö*, with "serious personnel changes."[16] In April 1992, a new purge took place in the province's media: the editor-in-chief of Hungarian weekly *Het nap*, the editor of the periodical *Poljoprivrednik*, the editor-in-chief of *Magyar Szö*, the whole editorial board of the student periodical *Index*, and even the editor-in-chief of the obedient daily, *Dnevnik*, were all replaced. Employees of *Magyar Szö*— 132 of them—had organized a referendum for their prospective editor-in-chief, Miklos Marotti, casting 129 negative votes and 3 invalid. Marotti was nevertheless appointed to the job. In 1991, a number of criticial journalists organized the Independent Journalist Association of Vojvodina. Since June 1991, they have organized a number of activities against the state-imposed information blockade, like "informal news" or news reading in the streets of Novi Sad (similar daily news readings had been organized previously along Belgrade's main boulevard, the Terazije). In early 1992, the Association sent a letter to Helsinki Watch, stating that Serbian official reports on human rights and freedom of speech in the republic were untrue and incorrect. But the oppression has continued, urging an increasing number of journalists, especially non-Serbs, to flee or give up journalism.

If war is just the extension of politics by other means, as von Clausewitz said, then the Serb-Croat war proved that the media may also figure as an

Media: The Extension of Politics by Other Means   93

extension of politics, in this case of war, "by other means." In fact, the media played an active role in bringing on the war. From late 1987 to spring 1990, Serbian state-controlled media published and aired a number of materials that evoked events from World War Two, always in a partial light and dwelling, in particular, on the crimes committed against Serbs by special units of the Croatian *Ustasha*. The Belgrade magazine *Duga* published five serials on *Ustasha* crimes in World War Two, during those months.

Duga's columnist Brana Crnćević, writing in his weekly column "Serbian affairs," has pursued the theme of an alleged "inherently genocidal nature" of Croats. Other typical stories in *Duga* or the daily *Politika ekspres* in that period dealt with accusations of Croatian and Slovenian exploitation of the Serbian economy for that last half century or even longer, or how Serbian factories were removed immediately after World War Two to Slovenia for alleged strategic reasons.[17] Anti-Croatian and anti-Slovenian feelings were stoked and blown up by state media, with generous help from prominent writers and academics. Serbian poet Matija Bećković coined a phrase about today's Serbs as "remnants of a slaughtered nation."

In spring 1990, before the elections in Croatia and Slovenia, the media demonization of non-Serbs, especially Croats, was at its peak. *Politika* and *Duga* referred to most of Croatia's newly founded parties, including the Croatian Democratic Community, as "ultra-nationalist" or "*Ustasha*-like."[18] On the other hand, Serbs in Croatia have invariably been described as deprived of their political and national rights, threatened, and "barehanded"—this last attribute lingered on even after it became evident that a good part of this "barehanded people" managed quite nicely with rifles, mortars, and rocket launchers.

During and after the elections, several privately funded periodicals were started in Croatia. Two of them, *Slobodni tjednik* and *Globus*, have survived the first months and built circulations of 100,000 and more. After three years of national hysteria in most of the Serbian media, national passions were now running high in Croatia. *Danas* magazine, which tried to hold to an objective and calm perspective, experienced a decline in circulation from 180,000 at the time of the 1990 elections to 60,000 just before the war. Radio-Television Zagreb changed its name to Croatian Television; instead of transforming itself into the state television, it soon became the mouthpiece of the party in power. *Slobodni tjednik* was on the rise, selling the tabloid version of national politics, running unverified and often completely concocted stories, and depicting all Serbs in Croatia as self-evident suspects for treason. In *Slobodni tjednik*, and to some extent the weekly *Globus*, the Serbian war press has finally found a sparring partner. Several months later, the real war began. By this time, the Serbian and Croatian media market had closed within their respective republic boundaries.

94   *Jasmina Kuzmanović*

Reporters in Helmets[19]

The war between Serbia and Croatia has from the start also been a war for interpretation: the interpretation of what is going on, who is defending and who is attacking, and what is the "truth." (In recent years, "truth" has been a much misused word: in 1987, in Kosovo, Serbs even established a "Committee for Truth.")

The struggle for the "correct" interpretation has made reporters and journalists who were covering the war obvious targets, since many of them were endangering the other side's idea of "truth" or, in some cases, the official interpretation of their own side. In the eyes of conflicted parties, a domestic reporter is automatically partial; he or she is just another warrior in the information war. And the death toll of unfortunate information warriors soon grew more rapidly than in any other modern war.

The first victims were two Austrian reporters killed during the June 1991 war in Slovenia. The Yugoslav People's Army launched a mortar attack on their jeep at the Brnik Airport. According to the International Journalist Assocation, 20 journalists were killed in Croatia between June 1991 and February 1992; two Russian journalists have been reported missing since September 1991. Of the killed, seven journalists were Croatian, four of them working for Croatian Television. Croatian and foreign journalists were killed by sniper fire, grenade or mortar fire, by Serbian irregular and Yugoslav People's Army forces. A British reporter working for ITN was also shot by sniper fire while reporting from the Croatian frontline near Osijek; two Swiss reporters stepped into a mine field surrounding YPA barracks in Petrinja. One Serbian journalist, reporting for the Belgrade daily *Večernje novosti*, reportedly died in cross fire. Four members of a Television Belgrade crew were found on the road between Petrinja and Glina, which is Croatian territory under Serbian control. The war in Bosnia-Herzegovina claimed more lives. A Slovenian journalist died in a shell explosion in Sarajevo, a CNN producer was shot by sniper fire on the way from Sarajevo airport, and several other journalists were also wounded.

Some journalists have clearly violated the code of ethics for war reporters. *Duga's* Nebojša Jevrić has repeatedly written how he took part in fighting and looting on the Serbian side near Knin in Croatia, while researching his story. *Duga's* editorial board praised Jevrić and another reporter for having taken part in that action. Reporters like Jevrić prompted ex-YUTEL journalists like Jela Jevremović and Ljerka Draženović to write an incriminating essay on "Reporters—War Criminals" for the Slovenian periodical, *Republika*, in fall 1991.

As a part of the war of interpretation, one of the most crucial media issues was, of course, naming the enemy. The Serbian and Montenegrin

Media: The Extension of Politics by Other Means

electronic media have not set up precise terminology, varying from "*Ustasha* forces" to "Tudjman's black legions." Some Belgrade Television reporters have used Croatian old-new words (words that were banned in communism, like "bojovnik" or "časnik") and have given them derogatory meanings. As for the Serbian irregulars, the terms "reserve forces" and "defenders" have been the terms of choice in all the state-controlled media in Serbia and Montenegro. In particular situations where the YPA and Serbian irregulars were besieging a city or area with a clear Croatian majority, paradoxes took place. "The defenders of Mirkovci [a Serbian village] have encircled Osijek," Belgrade Television reported in October 1991. Later, when Serbian irregulars attacked the Croatian city of Zadar and fought a battle near Maslenica Bridge, Montenegro Television reported that "the defenders of the bridge are progressing toward the city."

Croatian media first dropped the word "Yugoslav" in talking about the Yugoslav People's Army. Croatian Television eventually decided on the expression "Serbian-Chetnik Army," sometimes adding the modifier, "occupational." Other media used "Chetniks," "terrorists," "rebels," "fighters for Greater Serbia," "Serbian Army," and sometimes just "Serbs."

The war over interpretation has also been a war for radio frequencies. It had started in spring 1991, when the first illegal Serbian radio station began broadcasting in Petrova Gora (Radio Petrova Gora). Illegal Serbian radio stations also appeared in Mirkovci, Celarac, and Sveta Nedjelja. The Croatian Television transmission tower on Sljeme above Zagreb was twice hit by army rockets in fall 1991.

The Press in Croatia

At the moment when Western sanctions were imposed on Serbia at the end of May 1992, the free press in Serbia was represented only by the independent weekly *Vreme*, founded in November 1991. Alternative radio B-92 and the independent TV channel Studio B have been the only electronic media to deviate from official policies. By the end of 1992, further purges ensued in state-run Belgrade Television, throwing a large number of journalists out of work.

Croatian national radio and television have officially remained state or official media. In reality, they have been under the full control of the party in power—the Croatian Democratic Community. In fall 1991, a special Act on Information in War was passed, that introduced censorship for revealing information that could harm the country. Penalties included police seizure of the entire circulation of the issue in question, and a prison term of up to five years for a journalist or editor. In May 1991, the Law on Information returned to the status before the war. Except for two private weeklies, *Globus* and *Slobodni tjednik*, the rest of the printed media are in various degrees of government control.

The Croatian press in general has suffered due to the war and rapidly falling standards. Respected periodicals like *Start* or the entertainment weekly *Studio* went bankrupt, and others experienced significant losses in circulation. One of these was the official daily, *Vjesnik*, which in spring of 1992 fell to an all-time low of 20,000. The paper, briefly renamed *Novi Vjesnik*, partly recovered when the Croatian authorities gave it financial support in April 1992.

The Croatian government has repeatedly proclaimed that the privatization of socially owned property is one of its main aims. The governmental Agency for Restructuring and Development was authorized, in 1991, to supervise the process throughout Croatia. In April and May 1992, the agency repeatedly refused to allow the transformation of the independent weekly *Danas* into a private corporation, although the prospective buyer and the weekly had fulfilled all legal prerequisites. *Danas* was experiencing financial difficulties, and the buyer was willing to assume its debts and other obligations, as well as to continue to publish it. In early June 1992, the governmental agency, whose job it was to protect social property in the transition period, declared *Danas* bankrupt. Its journalists and editors gathered around private publisher Emil Tedeschi and founded *Novi Danas* that same month. The first two issues were sold out. But state-controlled publisher, *Vjesnik*, which maintains a virtual monopoly over the distribution and sales of Croatian press, subsequently proscribed *Novi Danas* and refused to place it on the news stands. Banned from the market and troubled with financial difficulties, *Novi Danas* folded in September 1992. At that moment, its predecessor, the bankrupt, socially-owned *Danas*, was still waiting to be "privatized." Then, in January 1993, *Danas* was resurrected, but in a pro-government incarnation; this new version of *Danas* is run by journalists close to the Croatian Democratic Community. The major episode in the national farce of media privatization thus ended.

Croatia entered 1993 with a damaged reputation regarding freedom of the press and with only one independent daily, the Split-based *Slobodna Dalmacija*. The financially successful newspaper corporation that publishes the namesake daily as well as the weekly *Nedjeljna Dalmacija*, began the transformation into a shareholding company in 1990, under the existing federal (i.e., Yugoslav) laws. But in October 1992, the ubiquitous Agency for Privatization imposed a managing board on the publisher. In spite of protests from journalists' associations from all over the world, *Slobodna Dalmacija's* independence seemed, as of early 1993, doomed.

Freedom of speech has lately been receiving other blows. In late May 1992, Croatian public prosecutor Vladimir Šeks started the investigation against six prominent Croatian journalists. One of them, Denis Kuljis, the editor-in-chief of *Globus*, was indicted under paragraph 197 of the Criminal Code, for having spread false and alarming news. Four journalists have been indicted for libel against Croatia's president, Franjo Tudjman.

In the second half of 1992, the Croatian pro-government press, including the privately-owned *Globus*, developed a passion for discovering "Yugo-nostalgists" or "spiritual fifth-columnists."[20] The catchphrase was applied to anybody who publicly voiced any criticism of the government or the ruling party, or expressed dissatisfaction with some aspect of everyday life.

The idea that in time of war, the whole people should abandon even constructive criticism prevails in most of the Croatian media. It has also opened space for power games that have long ago ceased to be just the idiosyncracies of the transient period. And though it is true that young democracies need time to put their houses in order, it still does not stop the outside world from counting.

Conclusion

"The Voice of Freedom," blazed the headline of the front page editorial of *Slobodna Dalmacija* on 13 March 1993. Ironically, the editorial was written by the new editor-in-chief of the Split daily, installed there by the pro-government managing board. Thus, the last independent Croatian daily was finally "privatized" into a shareholding society, with three government-owned banks and the Croatian Fund for Privatization holding an equity of more than 60 percent of the stocks. *Slobodna Dalmacija* was the last in the long chain of unfortunate dailies and weeklies which lived to be transformed from socially owned companies into private enterprises. Some—like the political weekly *Danas* or biweekly *Start*—died in the process. But for the chief national dailies, Zagreb's *Vjesnik* and *Večernji list*, and Split's *Slobodna Dalmacija*, the privatization process ended in the government's hands, with governmental institutions as major shareholders. Instead of being privatized, Croatian print media were *nationalized*.

13 March 1993 marked the end of an era in Croatia. What looked promising in 1989, ended in a crackdown in 1993. Croatian media have returned to the pre-democratic dark ages, with bleak prospects for reawakening in the near future.

Serbia, where the media situation was relatively better off as of spring 1993, is often regarded as Croatia's nemesis. But once the war had started, to compare the media situation in Serbia to the one in Croatia has seemed exceedingly unfair. While one third of Croatian territory was seized by Serbia, every square inch of Serbia and Montenegro has remained intact. And though the Croatian government has misused the aggression on the

98   *Jasmina Kuzmanović*

country as an excuse to silence the media, the extreme vulnerability of truncated Croatia remains a fact. On the other hand, one often wonders if Croatian or Muslim or some other troops were only 25 kilometers from Belgrade, would there, in that case, also be *Vreme* and independent TV-channel *Studio B* and independent radio *B-92*?

This question, though impossible to answer, offers a different perspective and even has a certain prognostic quality. Obviously, the future of the media in each country of former Yugoslavia depends on the outcome of the present crisis. If Croatian territories are not reintegrated in the near future, it will result in internal dissatisfaction and disillusionment. Political extremism would prevail and true democracy would be even further away. If, on the other hand, Serbia (where 30 percent of the vote at the 1992 elections was won by the neo-fascist Radical Party and its leader Vojislav Šešelj) is not denazified in the near future, the deepening political crisis will further affect the media.

Notes

1. Peter Golding, *The Mass Media* (London: Longman, 1974), p. 102.

2. *Ibid.*

3. Jelena Lovrić, "Hrvatski ključ za Jugoslaviju," in *Danas* (13 February 1990), p. 7.

4. Jelena Lovric, "Novo izdanje idejnog plenuma," in *Danas* (26 April 1988), p. 13.

5. Dragica Kunade, "Država, mediji in pravica javnosti," in *Delo* (18 February 1992).

6. Luka Brailo, "Strogo kontrolirana javnost," in *Nedjeljna Dalmacija* (10 March 1991), p. 12.

7. Croatian News Agency (HINA), "Otkaz novinarima koji su suradjivali s Monitorom," in *Vjesnik* (11 September 1991).

8. Mladen Mirosavljević, "Opet poslušnici," in *Vjesnik* (21 February 1991).

9. Senad Avdić, "Istina u tri dijela," in *Danas* (2 April 1991, p. 28).

10. Miljenko Jergović, "Poltronski žurnalizam," in *Nedjeljna Dalmacija* (14 April 1991).

11. Jasmina Kuzmanović, "Kletve s balkona," in *Nedjeljna Dalmacija* (27 May 1992).

12. In March 1993, *Oslobodjenje* was still being published.

13. Fahrudin Radončić, "Teku dani kosmara," in *Danas* (13 March 1990), p. 21.

14. Yugoslav News Agency (TANJUG), in *Vjesnik* (28 October 1991).

15. *Ibid.*

16. *Ibid.*

17. Marinko Čulić, "Čega sa boje Srbi," in *Danas* (29 May 1990), p. 13.

18. *Ibid.*

19. Darko Hudelist, serial "Reporteri pod sljemom," in *Slobodna Dalmacija* (April–May 1992).

20. Dubravko Horvatić, "Duhovni petokolonasi," in *Tomislav* (January 1993); and "Hrvatske feministkinje siluju Hrvatsku," in *Globus* (11 December 1992), by Globus' Investigative Team.

PART TWO

The Republics

5

The Serbian Church and the Serbian Nation

Sabrina Petra Ramet

That religion and nationalism are interrelated, figuring at times as alternative dimensions of a complex identity, is well known. Likewise, it is well known that religious fervor may reinforce nationalist fervor and vice versa. What is less often noted is the full panoply of reasons why this relationship is not constant among cases. Clearly, the theology and nature of the Church structure must have some role here, as likewise the ethnic makeup of the population of the state, and of the Church itself. But other factors impinge as well, including the history of the nation and of the Church—which may indeed be a crucial determinant as to whether the Church can, let us say, refer to itself as "the nation's Church." And, as we shall see below, elite manipulation of public consciousness may transform both nationalism and its relation to religion.

It is readily understood that any particular "religion" is not "religion in general," but a specific embodiment modulated through a particular historic prism and with features and contents specific to itself. But while the diverse contents of religion have been studied in extenso, there has been far less attention to the fact that the content of nationalism may also vary. While the fact that the content of nationalism varies from case to case, stated in this bald way, will scarcely surprise anyone, there have been few if any systematic efforts to identify different forms of nationalism. I myself began to develop my own typology in essays published in 1989[1] and 1991.[2] This current essay represents, thus, the third stage in my effort to develop a theoretically-based typology of nationalism.

Any typology is inevitably founded on specific criteria for categorization. The criteria I have selected are: first, a portrayal of the world to the nation (as threatening, as indifferent or mixed, or as beckoning); and second, a nation's recollection of its past (as triumphant, as uncertain, or as cataclysmic). These dual measures yield the following matrix:

102   *Sabrina Petra Ramet*

TABLE 5.1   TYPOLOGY OF NATIONALISM

Recollection of the Past

<table>
<tr><td rowspan="4">Perception
of the
World</td><td></td><td>Triumphant</td><td>Uncertain</td><td>Cataclysmic</td></tr>
<tr><td>Threatening</td><td>Defiant</td><td>Defensive</td><td>Traumatic</td></tr>
<tr><td>Indifferent
or Mixed</td><td>Muted</td><td>Muted</td><td>Problematic</td></tr>
<tr><td>Beckoning</td><td>Heroic</td><td>Entrepre-
neurial</td><td>Messianic</td></tr>
</table>

These measures are not selected arbitrarily; on the contrary, they relate to the two issues which are the most sensitive, and ipso facto the most powerful, for both individuals and collectivities.

Nations are animated by one or another form of nationalism, which may come into sharper focus at certain points of time, typically during crisis and always during war. For some nations, such as the English and the French, past history has often been remembered above all as an endless series of triumphs and accomplishments, and the world is seen as a non-threatening, even beckoning arena for rewarding activity on the part of the nation. Their nationalism is of the *heroic* type.[3] Nations with a more uncertain image of the past may nonetheless see the international environment as a beckoning arena, and I characterize their nationalism as *entrepreneurial*. Here I would include the Japanese and the Italians. Entrepreneurial nationalism invests the national culture with positive value, but lacks the bravado of heroic nationalism.

Nations which have experienced their history as cataclysmic may nonetheless aspire to play a large role in the world arena; their past experience of cataclysm (or crucifixion) drives them to overcome that past by an act of redemption. Hence, this combination of ingredients produces a *messianic* reaction such as characterized Polish nationalism in the nineteenth century.

When the international environment is perceived as indifferent or mixed, nationalism is toned down. Here, a perceived triumphant or uncertain past will produce a *muted* nationalism (as, for example, among the Austrians, the Slovenes, and the Canadians), while a more cataclysmic experience of history is compatible with an indifferent or mixed perception of the world only when the national identity itself is *problematic*. Examples of groups with problematic nationalism have included, at certain points of time, the Macedonians, the Bosnian Muslims, arguably the Montenegrins.

Finally, when the international environment is viewed as threatening, an entirely different configuration of psychological reactions results, producing a higher quotient of aggressive behavior. When the environment is experienced as threatening, the nationalist posture is *defiant*; twentieth-century Arab nationalism, which has repeatedly exploded into violence, is probably a good example of this type. The heroic, entrepreneurial, or messianic options are simply not open to the Arabs, thus, both because their view of the world focuses on threat and—distinguishing it from the entrepreneurial and messianic types only—because they nonetheless remain convinced of their ability to achieve triumph, however that may be defined at one juncture or another.

When the past is remembered as highly uncertain, nations which see a threatening world around them are apt to adopt a *defensive* posture. Defensive nationalism does not aspire to save the world (as in messianic nationalism), or to parade its glories (heroic), or to expand its influence (entrepreneurial), or to fight and defeat a threatening world (defiant). It seeks rather to defend the core interests of the nation itself; the very name highlights the purely inward concerns of this type. I believe that Croatian nationalism over the past two centuries is a good example of defensive nationalism.

And finally, when a nation both recalls its past as rife with suffering, catastrophe, and cataclysm, and views the world as threatening, the result is *traumatic* nationalism. I shall argue that in the years since 1986, Serbian nationalism has assumed a specifically *traumatic* cast, drawing its energy, by habit and by nature, from a reinterpretation of Serbia's history in terms of suffering, exploitation, pain, and injustice. Serbian nationalism has not always been traumatic in character; it has become so only as a result of successful elite manipulation.

Indeed, no nation is locked into a given type of nationalism for all time; perceptions may change, new experiences may modify the equation, and changes of boundaries and, through migration, of the population may all affect the nation's sense of self. But equally, these types of nationalism possess inertial force and tend to be self-sustaining and self-reinforcing in the absence of major shock from the outside. Obviously, to the extent that one or another type of nationalism may be dominant in a given nation (for a given period of time), the content of nationalism will have a major impact on the nationalist posture of any religious organization.

Psychologists Daniel Yankelovich and William Barrett point out, in the context of an analysis of *individual* trauma, that "traumas are most likely to take place in the early years of development before the child has learned to handle large amounts of instinctual cathexes."[4] Traumatization creates a point of vulnerability, which, by mechanisms of psychological transference, may be extended even to experiences not actually related to the original trauma but analogized by the subject because of some perceived similarity. Transference is, by nature, irrational.[5] In the case of *collective* trauma, by extension, the traumatizing event may be taken to occur at some early point in the perceived history of the given nation. Transference figures as a source of neurotic behavior, insofar as it elicits reactions, whether individual or collective, which not only are not rational, but are systematically and identifiably associated with the original trauma. As I noted in 1989, "an individual who has experienced trauma approaches phenomena associated with the trauma experience with trepidation, and responds to new phenomena in terms of the earlier trauma, even if the present circumstances are different."[6] Trauma, thus, has the effect of partially incapacitating the victim of trauma, who often fixates on some specific event to which the individual attributes great significance. Indeed, "trauma cannot nurture itself without some symbolic focus,"[7] which, where nations are concerned, is often a military defeat, hence interpreted as national catastrophe. Beginning in 1986, with the circulation of a famous memorandum in the Serbian Academy of Sciences, the Battle of Kosovo of 1389 has come to be viewed as the Serbs' "great cataclysm." In the battle, an invading army of the Ottoman Sultan had defeated a mixed army of Serbs and Albanians in the service of Tsar Lazar of Serbia, although the fact of the Serb-Albanian coalition has been played down. The Serbs certainly had attributed great historical and national importance to the battle before 1986. But it was only after 1986 that the battle became associated, in the minds of many Serbs, not merely with the birth of the nation, but with specifically traumatic energy.

One of the characteristics of traumatized persons is a strong drive to reenact the original trauma. Psychoanalysts believe that this compulsive behavior reflects the repressed desire " . . . either to undo the trauma—by getting back to the time before it happened—or to master it by repeating it."[8] In fact, psychoanalysts posit "a general automatic repetitiousness of human behavior, especially of neurotic human behavior."[9] Not all repetition is intentional or chosen, of course, and there is always the risk that repetition, whether intentional or not, may reinforce and deepen the original trauma. In the case of the contemporary Serbian Orthodox Church, the memories of World War Two (as it is now recalled) manifestly reinforce the trauma focused on the image of Kosovo in the fourteenth century; indeed, Patriarch German, long-time patriarch of the Serbian Orthodox Church, declared in 1990 that the Serbian Church had been "traumatized" by the war.[10]

Repression (of one's inner drives) is a possible response to traumatization,[11] and in Tito's time, the Serbian Orthodox Church, in fact, had no alternative but to repress its nationalist instincts and drives. Another possible response is to internalize the violence done to self, in the process kindling hatred and resentment, and turn the violence outward. In a 1990 essay entitled "Hatred as Pleasure," psychologist Otto Keinberg noted that " . . . hatred, a derivative of rage, may give rise to highly pleasurable aggressive behaviors: sadistic enjoyment in causing pain, humiliation, and suffering; and the glee derived from devaluating others. Each of these

The Serbian Church and the Serbian Nation

behaviors might be rationalized as an expression of righteous indignation or even expressed in unmitigated, explosive violence that obscures its very origin."[12]

Hatred rooted in trauma is characterized by the generality, rather than specificity, of the feeling of rage. That is, it is not just that the Turks won the Battle of Kosovo in 1389, or even just a question of grief over the deaths of some 200 innocent Orthodox priests in World War Two (according to one Serbian Orthodox Church source), that is at issue. On the contrary, through the mechanisms of traumatization, transference, and "primitive hatred,"[13] the nature of the discomfort is generalized beyond the possibility even of outlining the conditions for redress or satisfaction. As Kernberg notes, "regardless of its origin and the concrete unconscious fantasies encompassed by such hatred, its most impressive characteristic is . . . the intolerance of reality on the part of the patient controlled by such hatred."[14]

It would be difficult to argue that the Serbs and their Church had "always" been traumatized by their history, let alone by the Battle of Kosovo standing by itself. What I shall argue, on the contrary, is that this "traumatic nationalism" is a new phenomenon, dating, in its present incarnation, from 1986.

World War Two certainly prepared the ground for this latest nationalist surge. Driven from Croatia, persecuted, its ranks decimated by forced conversions, the Serbian Orthodox Church had plenty to rue as a result of World War Two. A 1943 publication of the Serbian Orthodox Church captures the Church's mood at that point in time:

> The enemies of the Serbs have relentlessly persecuted them through centuries. They have persecuted their leaders, their patriarchs, their bishops, their priests and their monks, killing them, hanging them and thrusting them alive upon sharp pointed posts, while at the same time, Serbian churches and monasteries have been plundered and then razed or burned. The Turks hanged the Serbian Patriarch John [Jovan] because of a national Serbian movement for liberation, while Bishop Theodore of Vrshac was skinned alive for the same reason. During those dark days, Sinan-Pasha, a ruthless Turkish governor in Serbia, burned the holy remains of Saint Sava. In the latter part of the XVII century, the Serbian Patriarch Gavrilo was strangled to death by the Turks because he was seeking for his people aid from Russia. In the beginning of the XVIII century much suffering from persecution was endured by the Serbian Church and its people in Dalmatia. . . . Similar tribulations appeared in the heroic struggle of the Serbs for their liberation from the Turks in the beginning of the XIX century, when many of the noblest Serbian priests and clergy were either thrust upon sharp pointed oak posts in the fields of Kalimegdan [sic] in Belgrade, or killed outright in the prison camps. . . . The atrocities which have been visited upon the Serbian people and the persecutions of the Serbian Or-

thodox Church cannot even be compared with those committed against the Armenians in the time of Abdul Hamid, a ruthless Turkish emperor, but only with those wild massacres and barbarous annihilations of ancient Carthage and the extermination of Christians in Nubia, North Africa, by the Vandals.[15]

Under Tito's rule (1945–80), the Serbian Orthodox Church was prohibited from addressing nationalist issues publicly. And in Tito's time, it seemed that Serbian nationalism had shaken itself of some of the trauma experienced during World War Two.

An important turning point came in April 1981—only a year after Tito's death—when Albanian riots in the province of Kosovo stirred resentment and bitterness among Serbs, ultimately galvanizing the armed mobilization of Serbian civilians in local ethnically pure militias. Symptomatically, the backlash began among local Serbs in Kosovo who drew up petitions in 1982, 1985, and early 1986, charging that Albanians were perpetrating violence against local Serbs and buying up their property. Initially inchoate and lacking leadership, the Serbian nationalist backlash received its earliest articulation in the "Appeal for the Protection of the Serbian Inhabitants and Their Holy Places in Kosovo," prepared by several Serbian Orthodox priests in 1982 and in the famous 1986 Memorandum of the Serbian Academy of Sciences. In this memorandum, the Academy charged that Serbia was the "true" underdog of the Yugoslav federation (hence, not Kosovo), and that in Titoist and post-Tito Yugoslavia, Serbs had been the victims of systematic discrimination.

The Memorandum became the manifesto of the Serbian nationalist opposition, at a time when Serbian leader Ivan Stambolić was trying to steer a moderate course that avoided the shoals of chauvinistic nationalism. The memorandum was a product of Serbian intellectuals, but it quickly had effects far beyond intellectual circles. It became a matter of creed for a diverse set of people including the Serbian Writers' Association, certain media, an assortment of cultural figures (such as rock singer Bora Djordjević), key figures in the Serbian Orthodox Church (and most notably the editorial council of *Pravoslavlje*), and, most significantly, the older generation in the Serbian countryside. It was this last group which has always been Milošević's greatest support, which enabled Milošević to destabilize the governments of Vojvodina, Kosovo, and Montenegro (through large street demonstrations), and which remains loyal to him even today. Significantly, the anti-Milošević demonstrations of March 1991, March 1992, and June 1992 were all urban-based protests, involving a larger percentage of young people and a more visible representation of women.

Where Stambolić was the master of communist double-talk, Milošević gained fame early in his career as a straight-talker: this reputation was

The Serbian Church and the Serbian Nation

especially helpful to him in the countryside. And Milošević's message was that the Serbian nation should reclaim its soul, its history, its nationalism, its land. The Serbian political landscape was transformed—one could even say inverted—in December 1987, when Slobodan Milošević, an erstwhile colleague of Stambolić's, ejected the Serbian leader from office and seized power for himself. It was, in a way, the triumph of the countryside over the city. Overnight, Serbian nationalism became government policy in Belgrade, and positions critical of Serbian nationalism were shunted into opposition.

The Serbian nationalist program, as it has unfolded under Milošević, embraces the following points:

1. Serbia has always been "entitled" to incorporate Vojvodina, Kosovo, Montenegro, and most of Bosnia, and it is only because Tito, a Croat (as Serbian nationalists like to think) wanted to weaken Serbia, that separate republics of Bosnia and Montenegro, as well as the autonomous provinces of Vojvodina and Kosovo, were created in the first place. All of these regions are rightfully parts of Serbia. "The borders were planned by the Communist International, carried out by Nazi-Fascist and Ustasha occupation and reinforced and extended by Tito's communist dictatorship," according to a statement issued by the Serbian Orthodox Church synod, "through his extremely anti-Serbian Anti-fascist Council of New Yugoslavia (AVNOJ), contrary to the will of the Serbian people . . . This is why neither the Serbian Orthodox Church nor the Serbian people have ever acknowledged the artificial and illegal 'AVNOJ' internal borders, which have no historical or ethnic foundations."[16]

2. Serbia was "milked" by the other republics of Yugoslavia under Tito and the immediate post-Tito leadership. The relocation of certain enterprises from Serbia to Croatia and Slovenia during the period when Tito feared a Soviet invasion (i.e., 1949–50) has often been cited by angry Serbs as an example of such exploitation.

3. All Serbs are entitled to live in a united Serbia; and hence, the Serbs, who constituted 20 percent of the population of Eastern Slavonia (prior to the outbreak of war in June 1991), are entitled to attach that region to Serbia, while the Croats, who constituted 60 percent of the population of that region, are not entitled to seek to attach that region to Croatia.

4. Serbs share a common fate, a common lot, and the ties of blood and race and history that bind the Serbian people are stronger than any ties which might have developed between Serbs and their non-Serbian neighbors in Slavonia, in Bosnia, in Kosovo, or anywhere else.

108 Sabrina Petra Ramet

5. The Serbian state must be a unitary state with a centralized government. Notions of federation and autonomous zones are designed to weaken and divide Serbia.

This program has been repeatedly stated and restated in very explicit terms, including in the speeches of Milošević.

The Serbian Church's View of the World

The foregoing discussion of Serbian nationalism no doubt invites questions about how Milošević mobilized the Serbs for war, why the Serbian opposition failed to mount an effective resistance to his program, why Serbs have been prepared to pay the high costs of internecine war in order to achieve territorial aims integrally centered on notions of nation and blood, etc. My purpose here is not, however, to probe these and related questions, but to use this brief analysis as a springboard to a discussion of the Serbian Orthodox Church more specifically.

This Church, which many observers (including the present writer[17] have interpreted as less important for many Serbs as a religious body than as a cultural bastion, and hence as a political phenomenon, has often epitomized, in many ways, "the Serbian experience." Just as Serbs have often felt embattled, exploited, victimized, so too, the Serbian Church has come (at least since 1981) to see itself as *victim par excellence*. After all—Church clerics remember now—did not the Serbian Church have to suffer first the suppression of the Patriarchate of Skopje in 1459 and then, after the restoration of the patriarchate at Peć in 1557, the suppression of the Patriarchate of Peć in 1766? And did it not share in the suffering of the Serbs under more than four centuries of Ottoman domination? And did not the Serbian Church have to defend itself against Catholic efforts to obtain a concordat with Belgrade in the 1920s? And did not the Serbian Church suffer terribly in the course of World War Two, being forced to witness the forced conversion of many of its believers to Catholicism?[18] Lately, the Serbian Church publication, *Pravoslavlje*, has even compared the Serbian nation with Job[19]—righteous but compelled to suffer without warrant.

Students of psychology know that self-perceived "victims" have three basic courses open to them: to identify with the oppressor and assume the posture of guilt and sinfulness; to disengage from the perceived wrong and come to terms with it, without becoming dependent on revenge to redress the balance; or to seek the reverse the relationship, transforming the erstwhile perceived oppressor into the victim, but in the process remaining entrapped within the "victim complex." This third option (which we shall call the "Kernberg syndrome," in view of Kernberg's study of

The Serbian Church and the Serbian Nation 109

hatred as pleasure) rivets on the desire to exact "just" revenge for past pain. The first two options attempt to overcome psychological pain: the first by transforming pain into pleasure (by interpreting sufferings as just and appropriate); the second by attempting to move beyond preoccupation with pain. The Kernberg syndrome recalls the plot of Alexandre Dumas's *The Count of Monte Cristo*, in which an unjustly imprisoned man spent his years of imprisonment plotting his revenge, and upon escape from prison, devoted his life to carrying out that revenge. The Kernberg syndrome amounts to refusing even to try to overcome pain; on the contrary, the actor gives in to his pain, basks in it, converting it into the very meaning of his existence, but apotheosizes his reactive hatred and derives pleasure from that hatred. Pain and suffering may even become noble (as a Serbian bishop told me in 1982, "God has selected two people for special suffering—the Jews and the Serbs"), but the desire to "redress the balance" ("to get even," as colloquial language puts it) is neither forgotten nor expunged.

Churchmen have not been the only representatives of the nation to construe the Serbian experience as one of extreme weakness, isolation, and danger. On the contrary, among the most vocal nationalists of Serbia, this has become the standard approach. For example, Milorad Pavić, a member of the Serbian Association of Writers, told a gathering of that association in early 1989,

> . . . in multinational and multiconfessional communities, some nations happen to enjoy strong international religious protection. Others, like the Serbian nation, have no international religious protection at all.
> This becomes particularly evident at times when instances of aggressiveness appear on the religious plane. Serbia is at the moment in such a position, between two powerful religious internationals. We must not close our eyes to facts. The state is unable to protect our people . . . I believe we should be doing something about this.[20]

The Serbian Orthodox Church's "victim complex" is the psychological reaction of that Church to its own history. Serbian Orthodox remember that their original Church, the Patriarchate of Peć, was suppressed in 1459, at a time when many Serbian eparchies and monasteries had been razed during the Turkish conquest.[21] The Orthodox remember, too, that upon completing their military conquest of medieval Serbia, the Turks "gradually converted all the larger and more beautiful churches and monasteries around the cities into mosques, or alternatively dismantled them and used their stones to build bridges."[22] The Serbian clergy, like the rest of the Serbian population, slid into dire poverty at that time.[23]

The Patriarchate of Peć was restored in 1557, and survived for two hundred years, with an ecclesiastical jurisdiction which, in the north, stretched as far as Croatia, Bačka (Vojvodina), and Baranja. There was a restoration of monastic life. But conditions worsened again in the later years of the seventeenth century, as war broke out once again between Austria and Turkey. Serbian peasants drew courage from this and rose in revolt against their Turkish masters, consequently viewing the Austrians, at first, as allies. In 1688, Austrian forces captured Belgrade, and in 1689, they reached Ipek. But the Austrian forces were accompanied by black-robed Jesuits who tried to force the Latin rites upon the liberated Serbs. As a result, the Serbian auxiliaries disappeared from the Austrian flanks, the Turkish forces regrouped, and soon the Turks retook Belgrade and northern Serbia. Patriarch Arsenije III Carnojević now organized a huge migration of Serbs from Turkish-occupied lands to the relative safety of Austrian-controlled Bačka. Temperley writes, somewhat poetically, that "over 30,000 Serbian families joined the new Moses in this great migration."[24] Meanwhile, the Sublime Porte ordered the execution of a certain number of Serbs for rebellion, abolished almost all the semi-feudal liberties previously established, but then offered to restore intact the religious liberties of the Serbian Church, as granted by the Sultan in 1557, in the hope that the patriarch would persuade the Serbs to give up thought of renewed rebellion. The Serbs, however, held fast to their view of the Turks as "religious persecutors," and came, in time, to interpret the migration northward as the demographic surrender of Kosovo to ethnic Albanians.[25]

The compromise offered by the Sublime Porte did not hold, and the subsequent centralization of Balkan Orthodox life under the Greek Church is remembered today for its constriction of Serbian culture and its elimination of Serbian ecclesiastical autocephaly. As Peter Sugar notes, "everybody noticed the gradual replacement of Church Slavonic by Greek in the services, the steady replacement of Serbian and Bulgarian bishops by Greek nationals, and the increase in church taxes. . . . [Moreover,] the grecification of the church and its educational institutions cut the Slavs off from the sources of their civilization, which was beginning to grow along original lines just when the Turkish attacks on Southeastern Europe began."[26]

The litany of complaints which have entered into the contemporary discourse of Serb clerics is much longer than I can summarize here, reflecting the Serbian Church's construal of its history as the experience of pain and suffering. However, the two wounds which have been the most mythologized and which consequently have come to resonate within the Serbian mind with the greatest force, as already mentioned, were the defeat at the Battle of Kosovo in 1389, and the ravages of World War Two.

The Serbian Church Since 1945

The communist takeover of Yugoslavia at the end of World War Two brought the suppression of the Church press, the confiscation of Church lands, the harassment of clergy, and the relegation of the Church itself to second class status.[27] Construction work on the ambitious St. Sava Cathedral in Belgrade was halted. And Serbian clergy were advised that they had no legitimate role to play in nurturing or defending the Serbian nation and its culture.

The Serbian clergy became accustomed to thinking defensively, and to fearing for its ability to function in society in anything resembling a normal way. Then in April 1981, massive anti-Serbian riots among the Albanian majority-population in Kosovo triggered a reaction from the Church. Serbian clergy complained that local Albanians had set fire to the historic Serbian monastery at Peć and that Serbian Orthodox nuns were being attacked and violated by Albanian men. On 26 February 1982, a group of Orthodox priests from the Raška-Prizren diocese in Kosovo drew up a letter pointing out some of these problems and accusing the patriarchate's organ, *Pravoslavlje*, of ignoring these problems. Finally, on 15 May, *Pravoslavlje* published a lengthy "Appeal for the Protection of the Serbian Inhabitants and Their Holy Places in Kosovo," signed by 21 priests. The appeal charged that the communist regime's policies in the province had failed, even as it underlined the now-*spiritual* importance of Kosovo. "The question of Kosovo"—the appeal said—"is a question of the spiritual, cultural, and historical identity of the Serbian people. . . . Kosovo is our *memory*, our hearth, the focus of our being."[28] It was a cathartic moment: the Serbian Church was not only claiming the moral right and duty to speak for the Serbian nation, it was also adopting a bolder posture generally, identifying itself explicitly with Serbian nationalism and, without realizing it, preparing the way for its own rehabilitation at the point at which Serbian nationalism became official policy in Belgrade.

Already in 1984, the Serbian authorities granted permission for the resumption of work on the Church of St. Sava (begun in 1935, and suspended in 1941). In 1986, the Church obtained permission to reconstruct and restore the historic monastery of Gradac in central Serbia. But it was with the accession of Slobodan Milošević to supremacy within the League of Communists of Serbia in December 1987, that the Church's fortunes took a decided turn for the better. A series of concessions followed, and in July 1990, Milošević received a high-ranking Serbian Orthodox delegation for consultations.[29] Meanwhile, the republication of earlier Serbian Orthodox writings signalled a new attitude toward the Serbian Church. Among the books released at this time, two may be singled out: Bishop Nikodim Milaš's *Pravoslavna Dalmacija*, originally published in 1901, which argued for the

Orthodox character of early Dalmatia;[30] and Radoslav Grujić's *Pravoslavna Srpska Crkva*, originally published in 1921.[31] The latter book, among other things, argued that Serbs, Croats, and Slovenes were originally (in the seventh century)the same people, that eleventh-century Dubrovnik and western Herzegovina were populated by "Roman Catholic Serbs" (who only later came to think of themselves as Croats), and that Macedonia was historically Serbian. The book also recounted the persecution of Serbian Orthodox believers at the hands of the Austrians.[32] That the re-publication of these nationalist outpourings was not without political significance was made clear in September 1990, when the Serbian daily *Politika*, which had become a mouthpiece of Milošević earlier, published an article which overturned the Titoist proscription of a nationalist role for the Church, and, on the contrary, lauded the Serbian Church for its service to the Serbian nation, and pronounced Orthodoxy "the spiritual basis for and most essential component of the national identity [of Serbs]."[33] The Serbian Church has always felt this way anyway, and thus, Bishop Vasilije told a meeting of about 500 Serbian intellectuals from Bosnia-Herzegovina in March 1992 that "Serbism without the holy Orthodox faith is worth nothing."[34]

The Serbian Church was quick to take advantage of the change of political climate, and in late 1990, its elder bishops convened a special meeting, at which they decided to commemorate the fiftieth anniversary of the outbreak of World War Two in Yugoslavia in 1991, with special liturgies and prayers to recall the suffering of the Serbian Church and the Serbian people.[35] That it could have recalled the suffering of *all* of Yugoslavia's people (or even all of Serbia's people, not all of whom are Serbs) did not occur to the Church. The Serbian Church subsequently sent a letter to the Ministry of Education of Serbia to demand the introduction of Orthodox religious education in all elementary and secondary schools, as a regular required subject, beginning in the 1992/93 academic year.[36] A group of parliamentary deputies loyal to the Church subsequently tried to accommodate the Church on this score, but ultimately the parliament rejected the demand for religious instruction in the state schools. In March 1992, Bishop Irenej of Bačka declared at a public forum that the Orthodox Church would no longer tolerate proselytization by other faiths in "Orthodox territory."[37] The stridency apparent in these examples would have been unimaginable in the years prior to Milošević's accession to power. Yet, so completely have the combination of Serbian nationalist rule and civil war changed the entire equation that in March 1992, after 13 years of stoney silence, the Serbian and Macedonian Orthodox Churches, long estranged by their jurisdictional dispute,[38] finally met for talks.[39] A report in *Borba* suggested that this breakthrough came as a result of direct pressure by the Serbian government on the Serbian patriarchate.[40] The talks failed to as-

The Serbian Church and the Serbian Nation 113

sure a meeting of minds, however, and the Holy Synod of the Serbian Orthodox Church responded by issuing a canonical order to the Macedonian Church to "return to the canonical order" and appointed rival administrators for the Skopje diocese and the eparchies of Zletovo-Strumica and Ohrid-Bitolj. Not surprisingly, Metropolitan Gavrilo, head of the Macedonian Orthodox Church, denounced these moves, declaring them "unjust and insulting."[41]

A Field of Blackbirds

In spring 1989, Patriarch German gave an interview to *Politika*. In this interview, the Serbian patriarch maintained that in the 1389 Battle of Kosovo, the Serbian army fought not only to protect the sovereignty of Tsar Lazar's realm, but also to protect Christianity, human freedom, culture, and all of Christian Europe.[42] The implication was clear that there are battles, and wars, which enjoy divine favor—holy wars. Set against the background of the then-incipient escalating chorus of complaints, on the part of the Serbian Orthodox Church, about the treatment of its clergy and other Serbs in Kosovo,[43] Croatia,[44] and elsewhere, this glorification of past struggle appeared to bless the coming struggle which, by that point, had already become a constant topic of conversation.

A memorial outdoor service (in commemoration of the Battle of Kosovo) conducted by the Church in Bosnia in August 1989 was rife with all the nationalist symbols which had crept into Serbian discourse. The service was held in front of the church building in Knezina, a town 70 percent of whose inhabitants were Muslims. Some 150,000 Orthodox gathered for the service, bearing banners of various Orthodox saints; amid these saints were pictures of a new "saint"—Slobodan Milošević. The Croatian daily *Vjesnik* found it "incomprehensible that pictures of a communist like Slobodan Milošević were carried at a religious feast."[45]

The Church press reflected the Church's nostalgia for the past, with references to the fifteenth, eleventh, even ninth centuries presented as if they had obvious contemporary relevance. Inevitably, an irredentist tone crept into Orthodox Church publications, perhaps especially into articles published in its principal newsorgan, *Pravoslavlje*.

Given the emotions wrapped up with the Church's recollection of its past, and given the strength of its yearnings for Dalmatia including Dubrovnik, as well as for parts of Bosnia and Slavonia, the prospects for Serbian expansion that were opened up by the outbreak of civil war in June 1991 could only stir a deeply ambivalent response on the part of the Serbian Church. The Church as religious body sometimes felt that its rightful role was to work for peace. But *Pravoslavlje*, the newsorgan of the patriarchate, often voiced a kind of satisfaction as Serbian forces routed Catholic Croats and expanded the realm controlled by "Orthodox" Belgrade. To the Serbian bishops, it may well have seemed like a just revenge for the Catholic conversions forced on Serbs in fascist Croatia during World War Two. Hence, when Serbian militias, backed by the so-called Yugoslav National Army, laid siege to the Slavonian city of Osijek (population in early 1991, 200,000, of which 30,000 Serbs),[46] *Pravoslavlje* hastened to publish a full-page article devoted to "The Contribution of the Serbian Orthodox Church to the Development of the Culture of the City of Osijek." Among other things, the article highlighted that the presence of Serbs in Osijek could be dated at least as far back as the eighteenth century, noting the erection of an Orthodox cathedral there in 1743.[47] Later, when Serbian militias encircled and bombarded the Croatian coastal city of Zadar, *Pravoslavlje* devoted almost as much space to detailing the historic role of Serbs in Zadar, noting, *inter alia*, the founding of a girls' school by the Serbian Church in 1879 and the establishment of the Serbian Choral Society "Branko" in 1904.[48]

Throughout all of this, the Orthodox press has repeatedly tried to portray the Catholic Church as fascistic and terroristic. In late 1990, for example, Veljko Djurić wrote a series of articles for *Pravoslavlje*, among other things accusing Croatian Catholic writer Tomislav Vuković of saying that the deaths of innocent people in World War Two, among them some 200 Serbian Orthodox priests, were "not important." Vuković's reply, denying the accuracy of this portrayal, was published in *Glas koncila*, and reprinted in *Pravoslavlje*.[49] Or again, in July 1991, *Pravoslavlje* published an article by Milorad Lazic which purported to review Živko Kustić's book, *Stepinac* (Zagreb, 1991). (Kustić, a Greek Catholic priest, has been the chief editor of the Zagreb Catholic newspaper *Glas koncila* for many years.) In this article, Lazić claimed that Kustić's purpose in writing the book was to stoke aggressive impulses among young Croats and to legitimate a clerical dictatorship in Croatia. Kustić denied both allegations.[50] Even in an otherwise receptive reply to Croatian Cardinal Kuharić's invitation to set aside differences and reopen ecumenical dialogue, then-patriarch German could not refrain from dwelling, as ever, on the travails of the Church under the wartime fascist dictatorship in Croatia or from complaining that contributors to *Glas koncila* offered different estimates of the numbers of persons killed during World War Two.[51] This insistence on an exclusive monopoly on truth and the consequent refusal to consider even the most scientifically-based alternative data betray the fact that the sufferings of the Serbian Church (and the Serbian nation) in World War Two had been elevated to the level of mythology. And mythology, like Scripture, is not open to scientific challenge.

A constant refrain, reiterated by the more nationalist media (such as *Politika ekspres*) has been that the Vatican has been waging a systematic "religious war" against Orthodox believers—a theme picked up by some Serbian bishops (such as Irinej, Bishop of Backa).[52]

The Serbian Church and the Serbian Nation   115

Accompanying these attacks on the Catholic Church were constant and repeated recollections of World War Two, complaints about the status of the Serbian Orthodox Church in post-communist Croatia (and, for that matter, also in communist Croatia), and comparisons between the wartime fascist state of Croatia and the present Croatian state. In July 1991, *Pravoslavlje* launched a series of articles on "The Sufferings of the Serbian Nation."[53] By March 1992, 16 installments had been published.[54] Jasenovac was described by one contributor to *Pravoslavlje* as "the spiritual capital of heavenly Serbia"[55]—a phrase that only underlines the importance of *suffering* for the Serbian soul. In another context (published about the same time), *Pravoslavlje* equated Jasenovac with "demonism."[56] This alternation between divination and demonization of a traumatic site is, of course, typical of neurotic patients who have experienced profound trauma.

But if the Serbian Church found plenty to lament where World War Two was concerned, it also complained endlessly of prejudiced treatment in the Tito era. In September 1989, for instance, the Church noted that while there had been some 86 Orthodox priests and 134 churches in the Orthodox Eparchy of Slavonia in 1937, there were only 42 priests and 94 churches in the eparchy as of 1989.[57] Not mentioned in Belgrade was the fact that after the destructive war, the Serbian Orthodox Church was able to restore 64 churches, two monasteries, 15 residential buildings, and nine chapels in Croatia (in the years 1945–85), and to build 25 new churches, alongside four chapels and 16 new residential buildings (in the same period); some of these were located in Slavonia.[58]

With the collapse of communism in Croatia and the election of a nationalist government under retired General Franjo Tudjman in spring 1990, the Serbian Orthodox patriarchate complained that "in this new independent state of Croatia, as in the earlier one, there is no life for Orthodox Serbs."[59] In October 1991, Pravoslavlje even claimed that the Tudjman government was reviving the policies of wartime fascist leader Ante Pavelić.[60] Serbian Orthodox Patriarch Pavle restated the comparison in an open letter to Lord Carrington, chair of the International Peace Conference for Yugoslavia, published in *Pravoslavlje* the following month.[61]

Yet the war could scarcely have been expected to further the integration of Serbian Orthodox into Croatian society. On the contrary, by May 1992, the Orthodox bishopric in Šibenik had been forced to relocate on rocky Mt. Bukovica,[62] and the eparchal seat in Zagreb had been forced to move to Ljubljana.[63]

Waxing Serbian nationalism increasingly laid claim to Montenegro as indigenous Serbian territory, and the Serbian Church was dragged into the controversy. Among Montenegrins, as is well known, there has been a long-standing dispute between those Montenegrins who see themselves as Serbs, and those who believe that Montenegrins are a distinct nation.[64] Now, as some nationalist Serbs have sought to "abolish" the Montenegrin nation and annex the Republic of Montenegro outright, Montenegrin "autonomists" turned to ecclesiastical innovation for defense. By fall 1992, an initiative "Committee for the Restoration of the Montenegrin Autocephalous Orthodox Church" had been established and was characterizing the Serbian Church as a residue "of the Serbian occupation forces of 1918."[65] If, as Orthodox tradition holds, the presence of an autocephalous Orthodox Church is the sign of national distinctiveness, then the creation of a Montenegrin Orthodox Church would provide the ecclesiastical legitimation of the Montenegrin nation and confer religious sanction upon it. To be sure, there had been talk of a Montenegrin schism from time to time up to the early 1970s.[66] But the revival of the question more recently seems to have obvious political motivations. At any rate, *Pravoslavlje* condemned the Montenegrin autocephalists in a front-page article, pointing out that the leading advocates of Montenegrin autocephaly had "practically no connection" with the Church at all, and included a certain Shefket Krčić, whom *Pravoslavlje* described as "a Muslim by origin."[67]

A New Gospel?

The expansion of the war into Bosnia-Herzegovina in March—April 1992 had a profound effect on certain sectors of the Church. Certainly, by May 1992, despite the Serbian Church's enthusiasm for "Greater Serbia," there were increasing misgivings among the hierarchy about the war. In the course of that month, serious disagreements surfaced among the leading hierarchs of the Church, regarding the war. In early May, the patriarch conducted a mass for peace. Later, on 28 May, the Church issued a statement calling on Milošević to step down and endorsing an opposition call for a boycott of parliamentary elections in Serbia and Montenegro, noting that the constitution under which the elections were being held had been adopted without the consent of the governed. The eight-page statement further affirmed, " . . . that the parties in power in Serbia and Montenegro have inherited the structures and organs, the means and principles of the postwar communist system, that even today they do not permit equal, democratic dialogue in society, and that they do not share responsibility and cooperation with all others."[68]

The bishops further criticized Serbian and Croatian authorities alike, blaming both equally for the launching of the Serbian offensive against Croatia and Bosnia. Further, in the bishops' words, "The authorities in Serbia and Montenegro are still unwilling to genuinely accept national reconciliation, to heal the consequences of civil and fratricidal war and create

The Serbian Church and the Serbian Nation   117

the preconditions for the spiritual rebirth and recovery of the nation. This is why the Serbian Church openly disassociates and distances itself from this and any such governments and their standard-bearers."[69] The statement criticized the inability to reach a negotiated settlement prior to June 1991, but glossed over the fact that Serbian intransigence at the negotiating table was directly connected with the Serbs' preparations for a war of territorial expansion (including the purchases of vast amounts of armaments abroad and the illegal arming of the Serbian population in Croatia and Bosnia). This statement on the part of the Church bishops came as a great shock to most of the Serbian public who, regardless of their own attitudes with regard to the war, had come to view the Church as implicitly supportive of the war effort. The statement did not restrict its fire to the Milošević government, however, but also criticized the European Community, blaming the latter for having contributed to the present crisis by its support of the Titoist government.

But even now, in striking an oppositionist pose, the hierarchs of the Serbian Church returned to the theme of the victimization of the Serbian people: "This is not the first time for the Serbian people in their history," the bishops declared, "to have experienced crucifixion."[70] The bishops developed this theme further: "A victim of the cruel Nazi and fascist occupation and of the bloody revolution largely provoked by that experience, the Serbian nation after the war became a victim of communist tyranny, and not without responsibility for that were some of its wartime allies."[71] There is no mention here that any Serbs were involved in the communist regime. On the contrary, the Serbs are portrayed exclusively as victims, and blame is laid on England and the US for Tito's consolidation of power. This fits, of course, with Milošević's tendency to describe Tito ("Broz," as Milošević prefers to call him) as a Croat. The bishops arrived at the inevitable conclusion: " . . . the situation in our country is primarily a consequence of communist tyranny. We have all been its victims, but it is obvious that the greatest victim has been the Serbian nation, which is the only one to have been divided into artificial nations . . . "[72] The reference is to the Montenegrins, ethnic Muslims, and Macedonians.

Two weeks later, on 14 June, Patriarch Pavle led a procession of several thousand Serbs through the streets of Belgrade, bearing a message for Milošević: "Resign!"[73] After reaching the Saborna Church, Patriarch Pavle gave a 10-minute sermon, in which he criticized Milošević obliquely for having spread hatred and conflict in ways "that would shame the devil."[74] After bemoaning recent criticism by "individual people" that the Church was "meddling in politics," the patriarch avowed that "these people . . . do not have eyes or do not wish to see what is actually happening with the Serbian nation today, and in what danger the Serbian nation is from outside and inside."[75]

118   *Sabrina Petra Ramet*

Yet, even as the anti-Milošević opposition began to show new strength and confidence, *New York Times* reporter Michael Kaufman issued a word of caution against making too much of these protests. On the contrary, Kaufman pointed out, even Serbs hostile to Milošević were apt to view their people as the victims of this tragedy, not its villains.[76] And indeed, even if one wanted to assign culpability for the war exclusively to the Serbian leadership (Milošević, et al.), it should be clear enough that the proliferation of voluntary citizens' militias among the Serbs of Bosnia and Croatia was the first decisive step toward war and reflected growing Serbian hatred of everything Croatian, Muslim, or Albanian. Judging from the Serbian press, recent Serbian historiography, recent speeches by Serbian political figures, and conversations with prominent Serbs, it is quite apparent that the Serbs construe themselves as the greatest victims of the present war, even if all of the fighting has taken place outside Serbian borders and even if, as a result of the fighting, the Serbs are ending up in possession of much more land than they had before.

In the months that followed, Patriarch Pavle reestablished contacts with Franjo Cardinal Kuharić, the Catholic archbishop of Zagreb, and collaborated with him in issuing a series of joint statements calling for peace. In a joint statement issued in Geneva on 23 September 1992, Pavle and Kuharić urged the immediate cessation of all hostilities, the freeing of war prisoners and hostages, an end to ethnic cleansing, a facilitation of the return of all refugees to their homes, etc.[77] By the beginning of November 1992, these two Church leaders had issued three such joint statements. Then, on 25 November, they were joined by Reis ul-ulema Jakub Selimoški in a wider joint appeal for peace in Bosnia-Herzegovina.[78] By that point, Pavle had a new line on the war. Said Pavle, "The war benefits only our common enemy—the devil."[79]

Serbian secular propaganda notwithstanding, the Serbian Orthodox Church did suggest that the Serb-Croat war at any rate was not a religious war.[80] But whatever the Belgrade hierarchs of the Church may say about peace and about the war not being religious in nature, for the ordinary clergy, the outlook is rather different. Indeed, the ordinary clergy have given overwhelmingly strong support to the Serbian war effort.[81] Moreover, various bishops from around the country have repeatedly spoken out to denounce the Croats for the destruction of Serbian religious shrines and the expulsion of indigenous Serbian populations. Of these, the most vocal has been Bishop Atanasije Jevtić of Zahumlje-Herzegovina.[82] Other bishops to denounce Croatian military actions have included Bishop Lukijan of Slavonia[83] and Bishop Vasilije of Tuzla.[84]

In the years since 1987, Serbia has been awash with hate propaganda. Often this propaganda takes the form of describing the present Croatian state as nothing more than a resurrection of the *Ustaša* state of 1941–45.[85] Croatia,

The Serbian Church and the Serbian Nation 119

thus, is portrayed as the oppressor, and Serbia, accordingly, as the victim.

Indeed it is characteristic of Serbian nationalism today to complain that "despite all attempts [to correct the situation], Serbia has remained on its knees."[86] Serbia is the wronged party, the universal victim, the martyr, the Jew, the new Job. The Serbian Church, thus, has rebuilt its strength in the past decade by presenting itself as the traditional champion of downtrodden Serbia, by reinforcing, thus, the "victim complex" of Serbs. In this way, despite the occasional criticisms of the war by Serbian clergy and despite the patriarch's liturgy for peace in May 1992, the Serbian Church made a not insignificant contribution to the stoking of inter-ethnic hatred, lust for revenge, and aggressive behavior among Serbs. At the same time, the Church has felt overcome by events, helpless before the furious forces of phenomenal fate, once again cast in that so familiar role as victim of history. Thus the plaintive, hopeless note sounded by Patriarch Pavle in his 1992 Christmas sermon: "How has it come, after the proclamation of democracy and multiparty elections, to so much hatred and violence, to so many crimes and criminals?"[87]

Conclusion

Nationalism is a modern ideology and, as such, has often informed religious movements in modern times. Nationalist goals may change from one era to another, and accordingly, the tools of nationalism must change as well. History is, ultimately, sifted through collective subjectivity, interpreted and reinterpreted according to need.

Nationalism and readings of history also change as a function of the historical epoch, as Ivo Banac has noted. Nationalism, thus, is given a romantic cast in the age of romanticism, a fascist cast in the age of fascism, and even found a meeting ground with communism, despite the latter's original hostility to all manifestations of nationalism (as the examples of Ceauşescu in Romania and Milošević himself make clear).

In endeavoring to distinguish among diverse historical instances of nationalism, one is obliged to bear in mind not only the numerical proportions of given groups (as conceded earlier) and the psychological cast, but also the era in which the given case occurs. To put it concretely, the traumatic nationalism of a newly dominant nationality in the post-communist era should not be expected to look the same as the traumatic nationalism of a minority nationality in the age of romanticism.

That said, I hope that I have succeeded, in this brief chapter, in suggesting how the intellectual and political elite in Serbia evoked a "traumatic nationalism" by reinterpreting past history, how the Serbian Orthodox Church became associated with this traumatic reading of history, and how this traumatization contributed to the desire for a war of "revenge."

Notes

The author wishes to thank Obrad Kesić for sharing research materials that have contributed to the final product.

1. Pedro Ramet, "Christianity and National Heritage among the Czechs and Slovaks," in Pedro Ramet (ed.), *Religion and Nationalism in Soviet and East European Politics*, Revised and expanded ed. (Durham, N.C.: Duke University Press, 1989).

2. Sabrina Ramet, "Politics and religion in Eastern Europe and the Soviet Union," in George Moyser (ed.), *Politics and religion in the modern world* (London and New York: Routledge, 1991), pp. 75–76.

3. In the English case, the precondition for the emergence of this type of nationalism was the removal of the Norman dynasty to England and to fusion of the Norman and Saxon peoples into a single nation. This is why appeals to the "Robin Hood" mythology, with its tales of Norman oppressors and Saxon oppressed, miss the point: in today's England, there are no Normans and no Saxons, only English.

4. Daniel Yankelovich and William Barrett, *Ego and Instinct: The Psychoanalytic View of Human Nature—Revised* (New York: Random House, 1970), p. 72.

5. Clara Thompson with Patrick Mullahy, *Psychoanalysis: Evolution and Development* (New York: Grove Press, 1950), pp. 101–104.

6. Ramet, "Christianity and National Heritage" [note 1], p. 266.

7. *Ibid.*, p. 267.

8. Thompson, *Psychoanalysis* [note 5], p. 48.

9. *Ibid.*, p. 49.

10. *Pravoslavlje* (Belgrade), 15 November 1990, p. 6.

11. Yankelovich and Barrett, *Ego and Instinct*, p. 98.

12. Otto F. Kernberg, "Hatred as Pleasure," in Robert A. Glick and Stanley Bone (eds.), *Pleasure Beyond the Pleasure Principle* (New Haven, Conn.: Yale University Press, 1990), pp. 179–180.

13. Kernberg's term: *Ibid.*, p. 181.

14. *Ibid.*, p. 181.

15. *Martyrdom of the Serbs: Persecutions of the Serbian Orthodox Church and Massacre of the Serbian People*, Prepared and issued by the Serbian Eastern Orthodox Diocese for the United States of America and Canada (Chicago: Palandech's Press, 1943), pp. 5, 6, 7.

16. *Politika—International Weekly* (Belgrade), 25–31 January 1992, p. 13. Actually, AVNOJ is mistranslated. A correct translation is: Anti-fascist Council for the People's Liberation of Yugoslavia.

17. See Pedro Ramet, "Yugoslavia 1987: Stirrings from Below," in *South Slav Journal*, Vol. 10, No. 3 (Autumn 1987).

18. For a development of these themes, see Sabrina Petra Ramet, *Balkan Babel: Politics, Culture, and Religion in Yugoslavia* (Boulder, Colo.: Westview Press, 1992), chapter 8 ("The Serbian Orthodox Church").

19. *Pravoslavlje* (1 December 1989), pp. 1–2.

20. Milorad Pavić, "Between Two Religions," in *Kosovo 1389–1989*, a Special edition of the *Serbian Literary Quarterly* (1989), no. 1–3, p. 50.

21. Radoslav M. Grujić, *Pravoslavna Srpska Crkva* (Belgrade: Izdavačka Knjižarnica Geca Kona, 1921; reissued by Kragujevac: Cvetlost-Kaleríć, 1989), pp. 71–72.

The Serbian Church and the Serbian Nation   121

22. *Ibid.*, p. 74.

23. *Ibid.*, p. 76.

24. Harold W. V. Temperley, *History of Serbia* (London: G. Bell & Sons, 1917; reissued by New York: Howard Fertig, 1969), pp. 128–129.

25. *Ibid.* , pp. 130–133.

26. Peter F. Sugar, *Southeastern Europe under Ottoman Rule 1354–1804* (Seattle: University of Washington Press, 1977), pp. 253–254.

27. Re. the confiscation of land, see *Borba* (Belgrade), 22 August 1953, and *Politika* (Belgrade), 1 June 1982; re. the seizing of the Church presses, see Radomir Rakić, "Izdavačka delatnost crkve od 1945. do 1970. godine," in *Srpska Pravoslavna Crkva 1920–1970: Spomenica o 50-godišnjici vaspostavljanja Srpske Patrijaršije* (Belgrade: Kosmos Publishers, 1971), p. 291n.

28. *Pravoslavlje* (15 May 1982).

29. *Ibid.* (1 July 1990), p. 1.

30. Nikodim Milaš, *Pravoslavna Dalmacija: Istorijski pregled* (Reissued, Belgrade: Sfairos, 1989).

31. Grujić, *Pravoslavna Srpska Crkva* [note 21].

32. *Ibid.*, pp. 2, 12, 154–155, 160–174.

33. *Politika* (2 September 1990), p. 18.

34. Quoted in *Borba* (Belgrade), 30 March 1992, p. 5, trans. in FBIS, *Daily Report* (Eastern Europe), 10 April 1992, p. 36.

35. *Politika—International Weekly* (22–28 June 1991), p. 6.

36. *Pravoslavlje* (15 December 1991), p. 7.

37. *Politika ekspres* (Belgrade), 18 March 1992, p. 4.

38. For details, see Suzanne Gwen Hruby, Leslie Laszlo, and Stevan K. Pavlowitch, "Minor Orthodox Churches of Eastern Europe," in Pedro Ramet (ed), *Eastern Christianity and Politics in the Twentieth Century* (Durham, N.C.: Duke University Press, 1988), pp. 338–346.

39. Reported in *Glas koncila* (Zagreb), 15 March 1992, p. 4.

40. *Borba* (6–7 May 1989), p. 6.

41. *Politika* (18 December 1992), p. 9, trans. in FBIS, *Daily Report* (Eastern Europe), 15 January 1993, pp. 66–67.

42. As reprinted in *Pravoslavlje* (1 June 1989), pp. 3–4, at p. 4.

43. *Ibid.*; and *Nedeljna Borba* (1–2 July 1989), p. 19.

44. *Pravoslavlje* (15 March 1989), p. 5, and (15 April 1989), p. 12; also *Pravoslavlje* (15 March 1991), p. 2.

45. *Vjesnik* (Zagreb), 14 August 1989, pp. 1, 4, trans. in FBIS, *Daily Report* (Eastern Europe), 22 August 1989, p. 61.

46. *Neue Zürcher Zeitung* (10/11 August 1991), p. 7, and (22 August 1991), p. 2.

47. *Pravoslavlje* (15 July 1991), p. 8.

48. *Ibid.* (1-15 August 1991), p. 6.

49. *Ibid.* (15 November 1990).

50. *Ibid.* (1–15 August 1991), p. 15.

51. *Ibid.* (15 November 1990), p. 6.

52. *Politika ekspres* (Belgrade), 20 March 1992, p. 11.

53. *Pravoslavlje* (1 July 1991), p. 9.

54. *Ibid.* (1 March 1992), p. 9.

122

Sabrina Petra Ramet

55. *Ibid.* (15 November 1990), p. 3.

56. *Ibid.* (1 October 1990), p. 10.

57. *Intervju* (Belgrade), 29 September 1989, p. 30.

58. *Nedjeljna Dalmacija* (Split), 17 September 1989, p. 11.

59. Quoted in *Danas* (Zagreb), 17 March 1992, p. 27.

60. *Pravoslavlje* (15 October 1991), p. 3. See also the exchange of letters between Patriarch Pavle and Croatian President Tudjman, as published in *Vjesnik* (20 March 1992), p. 16.

61. *Pravoslavlje* (1 November 1991), p. 1.

62. *Politika—International Weekly* (18–24 January 1992), p. 13.

63. *Politika* (1/2 May 1992), p. 13.

64. For the early history of this controversy, see Ivo Banac, *The National Question in Yugoslavia* (Ithaca, N.Y.: Cornell University Press, 1984).

65. Quoted in *Politika* (8 October 1992), p. 9.

66. See Ramet, *Balkan Babel* [note 18], p. 156.

67. *Pravoslavlje* (15 November 1990), p. 1.

68. Memorandum of the Holy Synod of Bishops of the Serbian Orthodox Church, in *Politika* (29 May 1992), p. 10, trans. in FBIS, *Daily Report* (Eastern Europe), 11 June 1992, p. 56.

69. *Ibid.*

70. Quoted here from an official Church translation of the memorandum, in author's files. The FBIS translation is syntactically awkward.

71. *Politika* (29 May 1992), [note 68], p. 55.

72. *Ibid.*, p. 55.

73. *International Herald Tribune* (Paris), 15 June 1992, p. 1; and *Corriere della Sera* (Milano), 15 June 1992, p. 1.

74. Quoted in *International Herald Tribune* (15 June 1992), p. 7.

75. Radio Belgrade Network (14 June 1992), trans. in FBIS, *Daily Report* (Eastern Europe), 16 June 1992, p. 42.

76. *New York Times* (7 June 1992), p. 6.

77. The statement was published in *Novi Vjesnik* (Zagreb), 26 September 1992, p. 9A; and *Politika—International Weekly* (3-9 October 1992), p. 1.

78. *Politika* (4 November 1992), p. 1; and Tanjug (26 November 1992), in FBIS, *Daily Report* (Eastern Europe), 30 November 1992, p. 41. See also *Srpska reč* (Belgrade), 28 September 1992, pp. 40–41.

79. Quoted in *Church Bulletin* of St. George Serbian Orthodox Church (Schererville), December 1992–January 1993.

80. See, for example, *Pravoslavlje* (1 November 1991), p. 1.

81. See *The Times* (London), 6 January 1993, p. 9.

82. See *NIN* (9 October 1992), pp. 26–28; and *Politika* (29 October 1992), p. 14, trans. in FBIS, *Daily Report* (Eastern Europe), 24 November 1992, pp. 32–33.

83. *Politika* (30 October 1992), p. 9.

84. *Ibid.* (31 October 1992), p. 7.

85. For example, Petar Čačić, *Nova ustaška država*, 3rd expanded ed. (Belgrade: Politika, 1991).

86. *Politika ekspres* (22 March 1992), p. 15.

87. Statement in Serbo-Croatian, as distributed by the Serbian Orthodox Metropolitanate of New Gračanica, Diocese of America and Canada.

6

Democracy and Nationalism in Croatia: The First Three Years

Dijana Pleština

Nowhere in Eastern Europe have the "Terrible Twos"[1] been more terrible than in the countries that used to comprise the former Yugoslavia. For decades known as the maverick who successfully defied Stalin, celebrated for its theoretical contribution to democracy in the workplace through worker management, champion and founding member of a hoped-for alternative to the power blocs through non-alignment, Yugoslavia was long seen as a model socialist experiment which successfully combined economic development with ethno-national integration.

The shock value that these long-accepted truisms now evoke is indicative of just how terrible the past two years have been in this region and how swiftly and totally the once-dominant image of Yugoslav socialism with a human face has been eclipsed by the horror of the war and the bleakness of an uncertain future.

Yet, it is this situation of war, for which it lacked both armaments and an army, that marked Croatia's first six and a half months of independence as well as its first experience of parliamentary democratic rule. Even after recognition by the United Nations (UN) was granted on 15 January 1992, unofficial war waged by the Yugoslav (by then, mostly Serbian) National Army (JNA) along its borders, as well as on its territory in the so-called UN-protected "pink zones" of Krajina, has meant that physical survival has had to take precedence over the socio-political "engineering" used to create a market based democracy. It is this dual imperative, to survive the attempt at annihilation by the JNA and subsequent danger of economic collapse and, simultaneously, to create and set in motion functioning institutions for a liberal democracy, that has placed Croatia in an almost untenable situation of having to accomplish too many equally critical tasks at once. How it set about doing this, and with what result, is the subject of this chapter.

More specifically, this chapter will examine the evolving nature of Croatian democracy since spring 1990. It will do so by focusing on the gap between the democratic nature of the formal institutions which have emerged in the almost three years since the Croatian Democratic Union assumed power and the frequently less than democratic behavior of the government.

The study begins with a brief background to the first post World War Two multi-party elections in Croatia. This is followed by a discussion of the electoral system of 1990, of the results of the first elections (April–May 1990) and of the first days and first tasks of the new regime. Although, as we shall see, the Constitution promulgated in December 1990 is an example of a liberal-democratic document safeguarding the civil liberties of all its citizens, it did not (as, indeed, it could not) stem the tide of recurring and increasing socio-political crises which finally led to Croatia's declaration of independence on 25 June 1991, and, a few days later, to the war launched by the JNA.

Following its recognition as a sovereign state, the Croatian government began to prepare a new electoral system in anticipation of the first elections in a now-independent Croatia. The subsequent section will examine the 1992 electoral system, which is important, as it, along with the Constitution, defines the nature of the state. It will then analyze briefly the results of the August 1992 elections for the Lower House of parliament and of the February 1993 elections for the Upper House. A longer discussion of the three branches of government, the Legislative, the Executive, and the Judiciary will follow. Here, the focus will be on the discrepancy between their formal and actual powers and the institutional mechanisms which, together with specific circumstances, have facilitated the concentration of power in the hands of the government and the President.

The chapter will conclude with a comment on the "paradox of democratic transition" (Attila Agh) and "the dilemma of simultaneity" (Claus Offe), as they apply in Croatia, where the continuing power monopoly of the Croatian Democratic Union (CDU) and its increasing use of that power in a voluntaristic manner is undermining the constitutional system of "checks and balances" and risking derailment of the fragile democracy-in-the-making.

The reader is warned that any conclusion regarding a political system in such early stages of development can only be made with the greatest caution. This is especially true when a large portion of the state is still under virtual occupation by the Serbian militias, with war on its doorstep occasionally spilling over, and a continuing possibility of renewed Serbian aggression. Nevertheless, some observations regarding both the formal nature of key political institutions and their functioning is useful to assess the process of democratization in the first stages of transition as well as to better understand the nature of the obstacles and the range of possibilities open in the pursuit of democracy in Croatia. It is further hoped that this one case study can join others to form a mosaic which may help to illuminate the broader question of transition from authoritarian to democratic rule and, through comparisons with other cases, arrive at a general theory of transformation or at least its regional versions.[2]

Background

The undeclared war within the former Socialist Federal Republic of Yugoslavia began on 27 June 1991, when the Yugoslav National Army (JNA) marched against Slovenia to recapture the international customs and border posts and thus symbolically to rein Slovenia back into the Yugoslav federation. That Yugoslavia, which the JNA claimed to want to preserve, had ceased to function, at least since the 14th Extraordinary Party Congress of January 1990, when a determinedly West European-oriented, democratic, further defederalized Slovenian and Croatian-championed vision of Yugoslavia confronted the centrally dominated, old-style "Bolshevik" Serbian model. Frustrations and recriminations had been accumulating through the 1980s; chief among them, in chronological and ascending order were: the Kosovo Albanian "problem," the 1986 memorandum of the Serbian Academy of Science and Art, Slobodan Milošević's attempt at restructuring Yugoslavia through the overthrow of "disobedient" governments (which, in Montenegro, Vojvodina, and Kosovo, he succeeded in overthrowing), and his calculated creation of ethno-national suspicions and animosities through orchestrated "meetings of truth" held in neighboring republics and regions. The addition of a decade-long, overall economic decline, as well as the sharp increase in regional inequalities, combined with the rise in unemployment and the precipitous hyperinflation in late 1989, ensured that by the time the party congress met, two intractable sides had been created.

It was in this situation of escalating tension and absolute deadlock at the federal center that the League of Communists of Croatia (LCC) held the first democratic multi-party elections. Their result was an astounding victory for the Croatian Democratic Union (CDU) which swept into power capturing 69 percent of parliamentary seats and thus ending, with a flourish, 45 years of communist party rule.[3]

The April 1990 vote was a vote against communism, which was blamed for both suppressing basic civil rights and leading the country to economic ruin. It is important to remember that in December 1989, when the League of Communists of Croatia (LCC) called for open democratic elections, Yugoslavia was in an unprecedented economic and socio-political crisis.

Nationwide, the unemployment rate measured approximately 20 percent, some 60 percent of the population was living at or below the poverty line, and inflation had climbed to a yearly 2,500 percent. Furthermore, with only 25 percent of Yugoslavia's population, Slovenia and Croatia were contributing some 55 percent to the federal budget. Thus, while the economic downturn affected all (and for that matter was felt much less at the existential level in Slovenia and Croatia than in the lesser developed republics and regions[4]), both believed that it was their money which was being syphoned off, resulting in their stagnation while yielding neither political nor economic dividends.

At the socio-political level, fear of Serbian expansionism and, with it, of the return to "Bolshevik Totalitarianism"[5] had been reawakened by the rise of Slobodan Milošević who, over the previous two and a half years, had first purged the liberals within the Serbian Communist Party before turning on the liberals elsewhere. By 1989, he had successfully toppled the leaderships of Montenegro, Vojvodina, and Kosovo and had tried (unsuccessfully) to do the same in Bosnia-Herzegovina (B-H), Slovenia, and Croatia. Slovenia and Croatia's answer was to elect parties which stood above all for political sovereignty (DEMOS in Slovenia and the CDU in Croatia) and were thus seen as committed and able to defend their republic's economic interests and ethno-national integrity.

The April/May 1990, elections in Croatia, as in most countries of Eastern Europe, inaugurated a historic change: one-party monopoly rule was dislodged peacefully and democratically after 45 years of power in a region with little historical experience of either democracy or peace. The democracy that was voted in was without doubt the liberal variant because its main competitor, "socialist democracy," had been totally discredited (for now) and because of the strong desire to emulate the West which Croats so much wanted to join. Thus, the classical liberal freedoms (such as those of speech, association, etc.) and the rule of law were equated with democracy, and it was further assumed that by dislodging communism and voting in a Croatian (national) democratic party, liberal democracy would more or less automatically follow.

Nationalism was running understandably high with the toppling of barriers to "free speech" and, in the euphoric state which followed, expressions of nationalism were for many equated with liberal democracy. In the eagerness to embrace the latter, the fact that in the West the "democratic franchise was not installed until after the liberal society and the liberal state were firmly established," in C. B. McPherson words, was ignored.[6] That specific problems might arise from the attempt to establish them simultaneously did not seem to have occurred to the political leaders at the time; certainly no particular precautions or even major debates on how to ensure the establishment and preservation of a civil society took place. By

Democracy and Nationalism in Croatia: The First Three Years 127

the time they did occur, problems related more directly to physical survival had displaced them and, in the process, delegitimized the much needed debate and political struggle over the definition and implementation of both liberalism and democracy in post-communist Croatia.

The Electoral System of 1990

On 12 December 1989, at its 11th Party Congress, the Croatian League of Communists (LCC) surprised many, both within the party and among the populace, by electing as its new leader the relatively young (45 year old) and definitely liberal and democratically-oriented Ivica Račan. To the further surprise of all (and consternation of many in the party), Račan immediately announced that, within a few months, open democratic elections would be held in Croatia, that the LCC would be only one party among many to vie for the voters' support and that, should it not receive that support, it would peacefully step down from power.

Because of the rapidly deteriorating relations among the republics, as well as the growing threat of army intervention to stop the elections in Croatia,[7] the LCC decided that it was imperative to hold the elections as soon as possible. As a result, there was less than four and a half months between the LCC announcement of the elections and the first round of the first elections which were held on 22 April 1990. During this time, political parties had to be formed, an electoral system appropriate to the new socio-political environment had to be created, and arrangements had to be made for upcoming elections.

The main problem faced by the body of experts chosen for the task[8] was how to ensure free, democratic, multi-party elections in a system which for 45 years had been (and still was) based on and operating through undemocratic political institutions. Moreover, while in the process of change, the system still had to contend with a recalcitrant "Bolshevik" old guard both in the Croatian League of Communists and in the center in Belgrade, which, threatened by the coming changes, was hoping to undermine the process of liberalization and re-establish centralized control. Additionally, the committee of experts felt that as an ad hoc constituted body they lacked both the legitimacy and the time (they had less than three weeks!) to devise a permanent electoral system.

Since the electoral system shapes the nature of the government which emerges, as well as its relationship to the society on behalf of which it rules, it can be seen as the foundation of the entire socio-political structure. As Arendt Lijphart points out,[9] the first choice that needs to be made by the "political engineers" is between the majoritarian and the consensual models of democratic rule. The former, based on plurality elections, favors large parties and tends to lead to a two-party system; the latter bases itself on proportional representation and a coalition government and favors, or at least acknowledges, small parties as well as a greater variety of interests.

The result of the committee's deliberations was the Law on Elections and Recall of Councillors and Representatives[10] which was to apply to the 1990 elections only. The system adopted by the then-ruling Croatian League of Communists (LCC) was that of majority rule with the winning candidate receiving at least 50 percent plus one vote of all registered voters which had to exceed one third of the votes of the electoral roll. If no clear winner emerged in the first round, a second round of voting was to be held for those candidates above the 7 percent cut-off line; then the candidate with the plurality would be declared the winner.[11]

The decision to adopt majority rule rather than proportional representation was explained first by the frequently volatile and unstable nature of the latter and the need to ensure a modicum of stability in Croatia at a time when political parties were mushrooming, as evidenced by the 40-odd parties which registered for the 1990 elections. Whether this fear of "atomized pluralism" or what some have called the "Weimar syndrome,"[12] was so strong as to counteract the obvious advantage that proportional representation would have in terms of government legitimacy in a society highly differentiated along regional, cultural, ethnic and religious lines, is not clear. We can, however, note that in all of Eastern Europe only three cases of pure majority rule were to be found, all in the then still-constituted Yugoslavia: Croatia, Macedonia, and Serbia.[13]

It has been speculated that the LCC chose the majority system for the first democratic elections because the majority system favors large parties and was thus expected to boost the LCC's falling rating. However, according to Ivica Račan, the majority system was adopted because the proportional system made no sense in a situation in which two of the three houses of Parliament had to be voted in by majority rule in any case, while for the third it would have made minimal difference.[14] The two main constitutional experts in Croatia, Smiljko Sokol and Branko Smerdel, were also inclined towards the majority, semi-presidential system and presented arguments of a technical nature. In addition to the stability argument, the simplicity of the majority system, its clarity to citizens and transparency of results, which translated into intelligibility and increased legitimacy of the process, were invoked as especially important at a time of such large and rapid changes.[15] The minimal opportunity for cheating, which this system also provided, was an additional point in its favor.

Indeed, the elections did proceed smoothly, with relatively few irregularities and the results were generally accepted both in Croatia and by the international community as valid.[16]

Democracy and Nationalism in Croatia: The First Three Years 129

The First Elections: April 1990

The results of the first elections were astounding both for the incumbent Croatian League of Communists, renamed the League of Communists of Croatia-Party of Democratic Changes, LCC-PDC, and soon thereafter, Social Democratic Party (SDP), and for the winning Croatian Democratic Union (CDU). The first and most obvious effect of the majority electoral system was that the relative electoral plurality of the CDU of 43 percent was transformed into an absolute mandate of 69 percent in the socio-political chamber, while the coalition of SDP and the former Socialist Alliance with 34 percent of the vote managed to gain only 25 percent of the seats.[17] This very large disproportion of 26 percentile points between the electoral support of the CDU and their parliamentary power clearly illustrates how the bias of the majority system can break the spirit of democracy even as it may formally follow its specific rules.[18]

Furthermore, in addition to the problem of representation that such a large discrepancy between voter support and parliamentary success raises, there is the additional question of how the ruling party interprets this "manufactured parliamentary majority." In the case of the CDU, as Nenad Zakošek points out, it was used to reject compromise and consensus even on some fundamental political issues. Instead, basing itself on the parliamentary rather than the electoral results, the CDU has frequently claimed plebisciterian support[19] which, in turn, it has then used to justify the over-centralization of power of the Executive (both of the President and of the Government) and the marginalization of both the legislative and judicial branches.

The reasons for the seemingly large CDU victory are varied. First, some gerrymandering occurred through the mixing of urban and rural districts, and the electoral units varied in voter eligibility size by as much as 1:3.7 (Susedgrad/Zagreb).[20] However, it is not clear that these affected the results a great deal; in any case, that had been meant to favor the SDP as the incumbent party. Secondly, the unwillingness of the voters to heed the message of the opposition parties and unify behind them against the strong winner in the second round of elections held on 6 April 1990, meant that the expected self-corrective of the second round in a two-round majority system election failed to occur.

The main reason, however, that the CDU won among the electorate and that the voters failed to use the second round as a corrective, is that at that particular moment of history, when communism was being dislodged all over Eastern Europe and nationalism was touted as the path to self-determination, democracy, prosperity and the West, the CDU campaign based on emotional appeals to Croatian nationhood, emphasizing its special historical and exclusive character and favoring minimally the strongest possible autonomy for Croatia within the Yugoslav confederation, or preferably full independence, found deep resonance among the voters. In addition, the CDU's close collaboration or even identification with the Roman Catholic Church which in Croatia, much as in Poland, is seen as guardian and repository of the Croatian nation, had a strong appeal for the substantial religious segment of the population. The historically timely dual appeal of nation and church and their identification with the CDU, as well as the clearly superior organization and financial assets of the CDU, both helped considerably by the large, well organized and generally conservative Croatian diaspora, account for the CDU victory in 1990.

This explanation is backed by Nenad Zakošek in an excellent study which seeks to explain voter behavior in the Croatian elections of 1990.[21] Using Lipset and Rokkan's model of cleavage structures, Zakošek examines the results of the Croatian elections of 1990 in terms of three types of cleavages: the traditional, the post-socialist, and the modern.[22] His findings indicate the dominance of the traditional cleavage especially on the issue of center-periphery relations. More specifically, Zakošek found that sharp differences existed over the issue of Croatian autonomy/ Yugoslav unity, as well as over Croatian unity/Serbian autonomy in terms of regionalism within Croatia. The cleavages were especially pronounced on the question of Croatia's constitutional position with 4/5 of the Croats favoring independence (either within the Yugoslav confederation or outside of it), while most Serbs favored either a re-centralized Yugoslavia or at least the maintenance of the status quo. Those who identified themselves as Yugoslavs also favored a stronger Yugoslavia though less stringently so. In addition, among the electorate, those who voted for the CDU stood out by their pronounced Catholic self-identity so that the CDU was the only party that fit the traditional half of the traditional/modern cleavage. The electorate of all other parties had a predominantly modern and secular self-identification, with the socialists and communists the furthest from the CDU.[23]

Two other notable findings highlight the need for a moderating national policy towards the Serbs in Croatia so as to diffuse an inherently explosive situation. The first is the division between Croats and Serbs (and to a lesser extent between Croats and Yugoslavs) over the acceptability of the multi-party system and over socialist symbols; here, more than 2/3 of the Croats accepted unequivocally the multi-party system, while less than 1/5 of the Serbs and 1/3 of the Yugoslavs did so. A similar rejection of socialist symbols among the vast majority of Croats and a continuing attachment to these by the Serbs and to a lesser extent by the Yugoslavs could, as Zakošek points out, further emotionalize a situation

Democracy and Nationalism in Croatia: The First Three Years　　131

in which polarization along national lines over the key issue of socio-political transformation already existed. Political clashes undermining the possibility for negotiations and compromise necessary to establishing and upholding a liberal democratic order would then easily follow, unless special precautionary and pre-emptive measures were to be taken by the party in power.[24]

First Days and First Tasks

Of the many urgent problems facing the new regime, the two most critical ones were the Yugoslav crisis and the brewing conflict with the Serb population in Croatia. The two were related. While 4/5 of the Croatian electorate wanted either a Yugoslav confederation (64 percent) or full Croatian separation (15 percent), the majority of Serbs living in Croatia wanted either to maintain the status quo (31 percent) or return to a more "unitarist" (23 percent) or centralist (35 percent) model of Yugoslavia.[25] Given that the issue was of such vital importance both to individual and national interests while the positions of the two sides were so diametrically opposed, a compromise would have been difficult to achieve in the best of circumstances.

Parallel to this difference over the nature of the Yugoslav state, there was also a vast difference over the acceptance/rejection of symbols. The Croats massively rejected socialist symbols (87 percent) while Serbs continued to value them (74 percent).[26] This meant that the changes, both concrete and symbolic, that were bound to come with the new regime, were a priori experienced by most Serbs in Croatia as a provocation.

Thus, both in form and in content, differences between Croats, especially those in the ruling CDU and the Serbs, especially those in the main Serbian party, the Serbian Democratic Party (SDP), were large enough to create cleavages between the two groups. The most recent cleavage was a result of Milošević's expansionist policy aimed at "protecting" all "endangered" Serbs throughout Yugoslavia by organizing them at the local levels against their so-called "oppressors." Milošević's interpretation of the Croatian elections as the resurgence of the World War Two Croatian fascist regime, consciously propagated in Belgrade and then re-imported to the regions outside of Serbia where Serbs lived, found fertile ground among some of the local Serb leaders in Croatia like Milan Babić, Jovan Opačić and Jovan Rašković. They, in turn, used this manufactured fear to propel themselves to positions of power in areas of Croatia which have a substantial Serb population.

While these latent cleavages were first becoming externalized, the CDU and Croatia's new president, Franjo Tudjman, were mostly preoccupied

132   Dijana Pleština

with setting up a working government and administration with all the changes that this required after 45 years of one-party rule. Yet, although forming, dissolving, altering and renewing institutions, bureaus and ministries had to be done, much time and energy were also spent (and thus diverted from more important tasks) on post-election triumphalism. While celebrations, parades and new symbols of status and power to affirm Croatian "statehood" may have been an understandable popular reaction to the dislodging of communist rule, the CDU should have concentrated its energies on assuaging the fears which the combination of regime change and the upsurge of Croatian nationalism had evoked in those who felt themselves excluded in this new system, notably the Serb population of Croatia. Their failure to do so in the crucial first six months of power left the door open for Babić, Opačić, Rašković, and others who deftly manipulated symbols to increase fear and thus widen the cleavage between Croats and Serbs in Croatia.

One such example of the symbolic taking on an extraordinary significance to the detriment of the new regime is the crystallization of Croatian triumphant nationalism on the one hand and misguided fears of some Serbs on the other, over the Croatian coat of arms. The model of the coat of arms first adopted in May 1990, was the historic red and white checkboard in which the top left corner square is white. For the Croats, this coat of arms was an affirmation of their 900-year link to their hero-king, Tomislav and thus to their own nationhood. For some Serbs, it was the symbol of World War Two fascist rule and it was exploited as such by Slobodan Milošević to frighten the Croatian Serbs and turn them against the new regime. Although the new Constitution of December 1990 changed the coat of arms so that the top left corner was now red, thus symbolically making a break with the fascist period, by then many Serbs had been radicalized either by local or by Belgrade-imported Milošević supporters as well as by the exclusivist nature of the new Croatian nationalism.

Some energy and effort were directed towards reaching a conciliation with the Serbian Democratic Party by incorporating them into the polity, including offering to Jovan Rašković the position of Vice-President of Parliament. Furthermore, the new Constitution, passed in December 1992 specified the equality of all nationalities and minorities, further stipulating the guarantee of parliamentary representation according to population to the Serbs living in Croatia. However, all this came "too late" to undo the damage that had been done; too many alienated Serbs, led by national ideologues, were no longer interested in being incorporated into the polity.

Nevertheless, some attempts at conciliation were made by the government. Of the meetings, open and secret, held between President Tudjman and key Serbian leaders in Croatia, one with Rašković was published by the weekly *Danas* after differences of opinion surfaced in the Belgrade media

Democracy and Nationalism in Croatia: The First Three Years 133

over Rašković's interpretation of the meeting.[27] The transcript of the meeting shows a conciliatory Tudjman agreeing to Rašković's demands for Serbian language, cultural institutions, newspapers, and other media in regions which have a majority Serb population; promising to think about autonomy for Serb areas within the Croatian state; and once again offering the position of Deputy Prime Minister to a Serb of their choosing.

Despite this meeting and Rašković's unkept promise to resume the dialogue, a portion of the Serb leadership in Croatia continued to radicalize its followers by a call to arms against the supposed Croatian "fascists in power waiting for the opportune moment to slaughter all Serbs." According to this claim (frequently repeated in the Serbian media), the physical safety of Serbs could be insured only by staying within the Yugoslav federation. A move to confederation would, they threatened, lead Serbs to declare autonomy, while Croatia's separation from Yugoslavia would result in their secession from Croatia.

Yet, as Mirjana Kasapović points out,[28] Serbs in Croatia adopted the position of autonomy by August 1990, as demonstrated by the Knin referendum; this was several months before the Croats declared themselves in favor of confederation in October 1990. Similarly, their vote for secession in March 1991 predated by several months the Croatian intention (May 1991) or declaration of independence (June 1991). This gives further weight to the argument that the Serb separatist movement in Croatia was not primarily a reaction to Croatian separation from Yugoslavia; rather, it was a result of the manipulation of an opportunistic Serb leadership, both at the local level in Croatia (Babić, Opačić, Rašković and others) and in Serbia (Milošević), who saw in their alliance the opportunity to create or increase their individual power base.

The Constitution

It was in this atmosphere of growing tension that the preparations for a new Croatian Constitution were begun in July 1990. Once again a Commission for Constitutional Matters formed a task force which, following ten general points of guidance provided by President Tudjman, was requested to submit a draft by the end of August. It is interesting to note that on 12 August, the Presidency decided to form another much broader "Constitution Making Commission" of 229 people from all walks of life "from law professors to farmers and fishermen" to ensure the "widest possible popular participation in the constitution-making process." This commission, formed at the suggestion of President Tudjman, in turn set up an "Editorial Board" with its own task force to formulate a draft of the Constitution. However, by then, the parliamentary task force had already com-

134   *Dijana Pleština*

pleted its draft, and so the two groups were joined and together they presented to the public the draft of the Constitution in mid-September 1990.[29]

This elaborate process of multiple committee formation to supposedly increase the democratic component in the constitution-making process is an uncomfortable reminder of the old "Bolshevik"-style consultation with the masses. It is particularly striking because first, these commissions were formed by the President or at his suggestion; second, the committees were so large and were formed so late that they could not participate effectively in the constitution-making process; and third, key elements, such as the bicameral composition of the Parliament (*Sabor*) were never discussed at all in public. Nevertheless, despite such meaningless populist holdovers from the old days, some discussion and negotiation did take place in the *Sabor* with the Constitution undergoing five or six drafts before it was passed on 22 December 1990.

The most controversy in the discussions regarding the nature and form of the Constitution arose over the question of national sovereignty, specifically over the proposed definition of Croatia as "the national state of all Croatians" which could be interpreted as leaving open the issue of who was Croatian and thus lead to the discrimination against other nationalities. The controversy was resolved by emphasizing the equality of all citizens in Article 1 of the Constitution: "In the Republic of Croatia power derives from the people as a community of free and equal citizens." Croatian nationalist sentiments were also assuaged without doing so at the expense of other groups by declaring in the Preamble of the Constitution that: "The Republic of Croatia is established as a national state of the Croatian nation and the state of members of other nationalities and minorities who are its citizens: Serbs, Muslims, Slovenes, Czechs, Slovaks, Italians, Hungarians, Jews, and others, who are guaranteed equality with citizens of Croatian nationality and the realization of national rights in accordance with the democratic norms of the OUN and the countries of the free world."

Other classically liberal rights are guaranteed by the Constitution such as freedom of thought, of speech, of press and of information (Article 38), freedom of movement (Article 32), the right to strike (Article 60), the guarantee of presumed innocence until proven guilty (Article 28), the equality of all religions and the separation of church and state (Article 41). National equality is emphasized a number of times (Articles 1, 14 and 15), and cultural autonomy along with the right to use one's language and script are also included (Article 15).[30] All these rights were, in turn, to be guaranteed by the independent judiciary, the general principle of separation of powers and the principle of the rule of law, all provided for in the Constitution.

The Constitution also changed the structure of Parliament from tricameral to bicameral—the Chamber of Representatives (*Zastupnički dom*) and the Chamber of Districts (*Županijski dom*, Croatia's historical equivalent of the Upper House). Elaboration of laws regarding the electoral system, including the choice between majority and proportional representation was left to the electoral legislation, which was to be drafted within a year of the proclamation of the Constitution. Because of the war, however, that had to be postponed until April 1992.

Socio-Political Crises: The First Two and a Half Years

It is difficult to evaluate the success of the transition to democracy in Croatia or the nature of the current regime in any definitive way both because they are of such recent origin and, even more so, because throughout this time the situation in Croatia has been one of constant, recurrent crises.

The first year, from early June 1990 to early July 1991, was a period of escalating crises both in terms of Croatia's position within the Yugoslav federation, as well as its position vis-à-vis a small, vocal and radical segment of its own Serbian minority population. The subsequent half year, July–August 1991 to January–February 1992, was the height of internal crises as a result of a war launched by the Yugoslav National Army against a mostly unarmed and army-less Croatia. For the remainder of 1992, though the country was no longer at war, its situation remained critical as one third of its territory remained under occupation with some 750,000 thousand refugees (approximately half from B-H and half from Croatian territory under occupation) flooding Croatian cities and straining to the limit an economy already badly crippled by war. The continuing and ever-present threat of renewed aggression on Croatia, including against civilian targets, especially in UN-protected zones, has meant that this crisis atmosphere has persisted. Although I will not discuss these events at any length because they are outside the focus of this study, it is necessary to remind ourselves briefly of the number and nature of the crises which so rapidly succeeded each other since they form the general context within which the new democratic order had to establish itself and begin to function.

In early July 1990, the Serbian parliament suspended the Kosovo Provincial Assembly and Executive Council, dismissed both the editors of the main Albanian language newspapers, including *"Rilindija,"* the Priština daily, as well as radio and television station managers, and assumed full control of the province.[31] In Croatia, tensions escalated in the Knin area after the local Serb leadership blockaded the road, seized the police station and later, held an illegal referendum (organized by the Serbian Democratic Party, SDS) in which Serbs of that region voted for autonomy. Throughout the summer of 1990, small acts of "terrorism" or "sabotage" occurred, such as puncturing of tires on cars with Croatian license plates in Montenegro,

136

Dijana Pleština

mysterious fires of pine forests on the Dalmatian coast attributed to Serb arson, brawls which suddenly took on nationalist overtones and chauvinist graffiti on walls. All these created increasingly an atmosphere of discomfort and led many people to self-imposed limits in travel.[32] By the end of the year, the Slovenian plebiscite showed that of the 93 percent Slovenian electorate who went to the polls, 88 percent voted for an independent and sovereign Slovenia.[33]

Also in December, 1990, the "robbery of the century" amounting to $1.5 billion U.S. was discovered to have been engineered by Milošević and the Serbian parliament through the printing of money to shore up their collapsing economy.[34] In January 1991, the Špegelj affair over the Croatian government's secret and illegal purchase of arms from Hungary brought Yugoslavia yet again to the edge of an undefined abyss, as did the Belgrade demonstrations in early March. Here, the violent response with which Milošević greeted the peaceful demands for an end to media censorship precipitated the first major internal challenge to Milošević's power. This was immediately followed by Milošević's own attempt to destroy the federal presidency and impose martial law.

In Croatia, tensions with Serb minorities continued to escalate as Milošević-linked Serbian extremist groups infiltrated Serbian regions of Croatia resulting in new incidents and casualties in March, April, and May in the Knin, Pakrac and the Plitvice regions. An agreement reached between the federal presidency and the republic leaders on 9 May over the demands of Serbs in Croatia and over the role of the JNA soon collapsed as Serbia blocked the 15 May ascendance of Stipe Mesić to the post of President, thus setting off another constitutional crisis. In the referendum held later in the month over the question of "disengagement" from the Yugoslav federation, Croatians voted overwhelmingly for independence which was accordingly set for 25 June 1991. On the 27th, the Yugoslav National Army (JNA) marched against Slovenia; a few days later it turned its force on Croatia.

While the open war against Croatia lasted some six months, the war psychosis has continued to dominate everyday life as incidents against unarmed Croatian civilians have continued in UN-protected areas and in the so-called "pink" zones of occupation which still encompass more than one quarter of Croatian territory.[35] In addition, Serbia's offensive against B-H which began in April 1992, and continues unabated has meant war on Croatia's doorstep, frequently crossing over the threshold. The Serbian policy of ethnic-cleansing, aimed at the Croat and Muslim population of B-H has led to Croatian involvement first informally through Croatian volunteers who, with the Croatian government's blessing, are fighting on the side of defenseless, embargoed (mostly Croatian and Muslim) B-H facing the might of the now-Serbian JNA. It has also led to the mostly unac-

Democracy and Nationalism in Croatia: The First Three Years   137

knowledged involvement of the Croatian army in the border areas of Croatia and Bosnia-Herzegovina. Further, the cost of feeding and caring for war refugees, Croatia's own as well as those of B-H, totalling more than 750,000 people, amounts to some $100 million U.S. per month, or 20 percent of Croatia's national budget.[36] This, in addition to the expense of the Croatian army, the housing, and financing of petrol for the UN troops and the loss to the economy through occupation of its territory, is leading to hyper-inflation, a growing absolute impoverishment of the population and a general acceptance that, for Croatia to have a chance at developing into a democracy, first the war must be stopped.

It is this continuing environment of crisis that has shaped the first three years of democratic transition in Croatia. We now turn to an examination of that rule, first by looking at the framework as set up in the new electoral system of 1992, then by analyzing the results of the elections for the Lower House (August 1992) and those of the Upper House (February 1993). Finally, the functioning and interrelationship between the legislature, the executive and the judiciary will be examined before concluding with a brief comment on the nature and the direction of parliamentary rule under the CDU and the outlook for liberal democracy in Croatia.

The Electoral System: 1992

The Legislative and Law Commission of the *sabor* or parliament which formed the group responsible for drafting the new electoral system chose for the task three experts, all CDU party affiliates and members of the government. The members of the group were Zlatko Crnić, Judge of the Supreme Court of the Republic of Croatia; Smiljko Sokol, constitutional expert and professor of law; and Vladimir Šeks, vice-president of the House of Representatives and President of the Legislative and Law Commission, which nominated the three people to the group for the electoral system. Thus, while the expertise of the committee may not have been in dispute, the choice of experts drawn solely from the ranks of CDU, closely affiliated or part of the government and through Vladimir Šeks even self-chosen for the post, fails to inspire confidence to all those for whom some consultation and co-operation are necessary to form and sustain democracy.

That consultation and co-operation with other party representatives is not, unfortunately, high on the list of the CDU priorities was made perfectly clear by Vladimir Šeks: "I want to dispel the illusions of all those who think that electoral laws are passed on the basis of consensus."[37] Smiljko Sokol further clarified this position at a round table held at the faculty of political science in spring 1992, when, to a question regarding the reason why the group had not consulted with other experts or with leaders of major parliamentary parties, as had been done widely in Slovenia, replied that there was no need since he had anticipated their demand and, for that purpose, had built into the electoral process for the House of Representatives the half majority/half representation system.

Thus, what we can call democracy-by-anticipation was responsible for the Law on the Election of Representatives to the *Sabor* (Assembly) of the Republic of Croatia and the Law on the Election of the President of the Republic of Croatia which were passed on 18 April 1992. These two fundamental laws determine the form and thus influence the nature of the electoral system and through it, of the polity; in Croatia this was to be the semi-presidential, mostly majority rule electoral system.

The Second Elections: August 1992

On 24 June 1992, the government announced that elections for both parliamentary and presidential posts would be held on 2 August. The announcement was greeted by criticism from the opposition which pointed out that it is highly questionable whether elections should be held when the country is de facto still at war, when in the more than one quarter of the territory still under occupation elections cannot be held, and when a large percentage of the population, both refugee and other is gravely affected physically, economically, and psychologically by the war. Furthermore, they noted, the Constitution clearly states that elections for the two houses are to be held simultaneously (Article 72) unless a special law on the elections of representatives is passed (Article 141); this was not done. Thus, both the Constitution as well as political wisdom and the spirit of democracy argued against holding elections for the House of Representatives in August 1992.[38]

The government countered with the argument that it was important to hold elections as soon as possible because the President of the Republic had not been elected in general elections and, therefore, did not have the legitimation of the electorate. Although this was true, after 26 months in power, another six without legitimatiom through elections would have hardly undermined the institution or the position of the President. Furthermore, the President is chosen in separate elections, and therefore elections for the House of Representatives could have been postponed until elections for both Houses of Parliament could be held without postponing the Presidential elections.

Rather, the reasons for holding the elections at that particular time were, above all, political in nature. That is, the CDU wanted to capitalize on its still-glowing reputation as the party that was able to stand up to both the Serbian aggression in the defense of the homeland, as well as to the inter-

Democracy and Nationalism in Croatia: The First Three Years 139

national community by insisting on the formation of an independent sovereign Croatian nation-state. It was important to the CDU to call elections while these successes could still rally the people around the emotional appeals to nationalism, homeland and the CDU, and before the difficult reality of a devastated economy and lack of government ability, preparation or courage to devise a serious program for economic reform through privatization and capitalist marketization, became apparent.

The result of the August elections showed that the CDU's political calculations had been correct. With a 75 percent turnout of those eligible to vote, the CDU scored another victory capturing 43.72 percent of the votes and 62 percent of the parliamentary seats. Its closest contender, the Croatian Social Liberal Party (CSLP) won some 17.33 percent of the votes which translated into 10 percent of the seats in the House of Representatives. The right radical Croatian Party of Rights (CPR) became the third strongest party, although its electoral support of 6.91 percent and parliamentary representation of 4 percent of seats ensured that it retained very limited influence. The biggest setback was suffered by the left parties of which only the Social Democratic Party (SDP, the reformed communists) passed the 3 percent electoral threshold. Its 5.4 percent of electoral votes gave it 5 percent of parliamentary seats. The elections were also marked by the emergence of regionalist opposition (Dalmatia, Istra and Rijeka) which won 3.11 percent of the votes and 3 percent of parliamentary seats.[39]

The August 1992 elections for the House of Representatives confirmed that the political system in Croatia continues to be dominated by one party, the CDU, itself more of a national movement or coalition of groups than an ideologically unified whole. The opposition remained highly fragmented, and this fragmentation and consequent lack of electoral strategy benefitted the CDU. The half proportional, half majority, single-round elections favored the CDU which gained most from the plurality half of the House of Representative seats, in the process increasing its parliamentary representation 10.5 percent above its electoral vote.

In the Presidential elections, Franjo Tudjman received an impressively high 56.73 percent of the popular vote while his closest competitor, Dražen Budiša, leader of the liberal CSLP received 21.87 percent. Of the remaining six candidates, none received more than 6 percent of the votes. The Presidential elections thus clearly showed that Franjo Tudjman enjoys broad popularity among the voters, with his support exeeding that of his party by 13 percentage points. It is a support which he has used to keep in line the occasional recalcitrant members of his party, thus further augmenting his power.

Although the continued presence of the war makes certainty impossible, some indications of a shift in voter support which could lead to a shift in the direction of the polity is discernible. Extending his research on

140   Dijana Pleština

the 1990 parliamentary elections to those of 1992, Ivan Grdesić shows that in
the 1992 elections the CDU lost half of its young supporters in relation to the
1990 elections, with most of these turning to the Croatian Socio-Liberal Party
(CSLP). The latter has also made gains among the educated and employed,
both in the industrial sector and in professional circles, while the CDU support remains strongest among the pensioners, administrators and, more generally, among those dependent on the government—the retired, the unemployed and women who do not hold paying jobs. In addition, while the CDU
has continued to attract the more "religous" than average among the population, the CSLP supporters define themselves as less religious than average
or non-religious.

The Elections for the Upper House: February 1993

The shift first apparent in the August 1992 elections for the Lower House
was confirmed in the February 1993 elections for the Upper House. First,
although 43.14 percent of the electorate voted for the CDU, thus ensuring its
victory, the CSLP increased its support among the voters by more than 50
percent. In the process, it became the undisputed major opposition party,
supported by 26.32 percent of the electorate. Furthermore, at the local level,
the CDU lost support in all the major cities except Zagreb, thus confirming
the trend that the educated, urban, and younger electorate is turning to the
liberal parties.

The surprising gain in strength of the Croatian Peasant Party (CPP), which
captured 11.05 percent, of the voter's support, and of the regional parties in
the Istra region (5.54 percent), show that there is a growing viable opposition
at the national and local levels, that the liberal CSLP and to a lesser extent the
CPP possess political strength and that they can be expected to become contenders for power. Thus, the CDU can no longer present itself as a national
movement of all Croatians; Instead, it may soon have to get used to being an
ordinary political party.

Furthermore, the disappearance of the numerous parties from the political scene and the polarization of the electorate around the CDU, CSLP, and
CPP (in addition to the presence of the regional parties of Rijeka, Dalmatia,
and Istria and the SDP), is a positive sign, which, along with this first defeat
of the CDU, shows a political maturation which bodes well for the future.
No major shifts are expected at the national level as a direct result of these
elections, since the Upper House has minimal power and both houses continue to be firmly held by the CDU. But because of the results at the local
levels and the perceptible shift in voter profile, one can be cautiously optimistic that, barring unforeseen disasters (which are possible given the continuing war crisis), a functioning democracy in Croatia may yet emerge.

The Legislature: Formal Powers

The House of Representatives—Zastupnički dom

The Sabor or Parliament of the Republic of Croatia is composed of the House of Representatives or *Zastupnički dom* (Lower House) and of The House of Districts or *Županijski dom* (Upper House) (Article 70), both elected by secret ballot in general elections for four year terms (Article 72). The House of Representatives is composed of 124 members who are elected by a combination of proportional and plurality representation. Approximately one half of the House of Representatives, that is 60 members, are elected from as many precincts of roughly the same size (approximately 50,000 voters) with the whole territory of Croatia considered one constituency. The mandates are distributed proportionally among the parties according to the number of votes won by each party which presents a closed list of candidates for which the voters must vote "en bloc" in Parliament. A minimum of 3 percent of votes is required for representation. The other 64 members are elected in uninominal constituencies on the basis of plurality vote (Article 23).

In addition, national minorities who, according to the 1981 census, make up less than 8 percent of the total population of the Republic of Croatia, have the right to elect at least five representatives to the Sabor. Those who make up more than 8 percent of the population have a right to representation proportional to their population. The Serbs in Croatia, who are the only group to fall in this category, have, as a result of this clause, a guarantee of 13 representatives in Parliament. These can present themselves as candidates on any party list with the guarantee that if the total number of those who win in elections falls under 13, those who were not elected shall be considered elected in order to achieve the required representation in Parliament. Thus the voters have two votes, one for each half of the Parliament with the rules and results of the two halves independent of each other.

The House of Representatives is the more powerful component of the legislative branch and the one which decides on all matters concerning the Constitution, the laws of the land, the state budget, matters of war and peace and changes in international borders. It also has the power to call for a referendum, as well as elections, grants amnesty, oversees the work of the government and generally is responsible for whatever else is decided in the Constitution (Article 80). Legislation in the House of Representatives is divided into three categories. A simple majority is required to pass most legislation; a majority of all representatives is needed to pass electoral legislation as well as legislation which regulates civil rights, establishes state agencies and bodies of local government; and, finally, two

142   *Dijana Pleština*

thirds of all representatives is needed to pass legislation related to all matters of nationality rights (Article 83).

The House of Districts—*Županijski dom*

The House of *Županija* (Upper House) is composed of representatives of local self-government districts, elected by majority rule with three representatives in each *županija*—one for each of the three constituencies. On 19 November 1992, the government finally announced its proposal to divide the Republic of Croatia into 20 *županija* and two *kotari* (the two regions where there is Serb majority population which will have special status), 22 cities as capitals of the *županija* and *kotari* and 383 counties. The first elections for the House of Districts were held on 7 February 1993.

The House of *Županija* has mainly an advisory function and in that capacity can give suggestions and opinions on the laws of the land, the referendum, the Constitution, national and minority rights and others. It can also return legislation to the House of Representatives for further discussion and amendment within 15 days of passage of a new law (Article 81).

The Legislature: Behavior

Two peculiarities related both to "objective" circumstances as well as to the behavior of the ruling party, the CDU, have "conspired" to limit the effectiveness of the legislative branches. The first is "historical-circumstantial"; the second is more "voluntaristic."

When the first democratic elections were held in April 1990, the old Constitution, still in force, mandated that elections be held for all three chambers of parliament, the House of Representatives, the Chamber of Associated Labor and the Chamber of Municipalities—even though the latter two were anachronisms from the old regime. In December 1990, when the new Constitution was promulgated and the latter two Chambers were abolished, the House of Representatives continued to rule alone—taking on itself the powers of both the non-constituted Upper House, the *Županija*—and its own powers. Furthermore, when the new elections were held in August 1992, they were held only for the House of Representatives so that it continued to appropriate the powers of both houses. This "historical-circumstantial" reason for the lack of an institutional check in Parliament is both a consequence of, as well as being augmented by, the "voluntaristic" aspect of the ruling CDU party.

First, in terms of the de facto unicameral parliament, it is important to see that the main reason why there was no Upper House for almost three

Democracy and Nationalism in Croatia: The First Three Years   143

years is not as the CDU claims that the war situation had made it impossible to decide on the regionalization and on the power allocation between Zagreb and the regions "on time" for the August 1992 elections. To this claim one can point out, as the parliamentary opposition did, that there was no pressing reason why elections for the House of Representatives *had* to be held in August rather than, say, in December 1992; the latter date would have given a few more months to work out the definition, nature and powers of the *Županija*.

Rather, as already mentioned, the CDU wanted to hold elections for the Lower House while it could still capitalize on the popularity gained from leading Croatia to independence and international recognition and before the economic and social costs of the war and of less-than-competent government were felt by the population. Additionally, the CDU wanted to create an Upper House which would be a relatively weak rubber stamp rather than a body which could act as a check on its powers. As a result, the creation of the *županija* first entailed the breakup of the historical economic/administrative/geographical regions in order to redraw their boundaries as a prerequisite to enhancing central power at the expense of local autonomy. This, of course, was bound to meet with a great deal of opposition and resistance within the regions, even in the CDU-held territories. This interpretation of the CDU decision not to form the upper house until the CDU was safely back in power with a large enough majority to rein in or override the opposition is backed up by CDU subsequent actions.

In mid-November 1992, the government announced its proposal for the formation of the *županija,* placing the discussion on the agenda of the parliamentary session of 26–28 November. The proposal to form 20 *županija* and two autonomous *kotari* with some 360 *općina* (counties)[40] in a manner which would both break up the natural/historical regions and amalgamate new areas, met indeed with a great deal of opposition, some of it coming in an uncharacteristic manner from within the ranks of the CDU. Clearly this kind of political regionalization before the August 1992 elections would have cost the CDU some and perhaps a lot of popular support. Instead, the 43.72 percent of received electoral votes were translated into 62 percent of the seats in the House of Representatives. This gave the CDU enough political power to ignore arguments and positions different from theirs no matter how rational, democratic or feasible they might be.

This is the point at which the "historical-circumstantial" and the "voluntaristic" factors intersect. Thus, although war, occupation and refugees (especially since they surfaced just as the transition period from one-party monopoly power to a multi-party democracy was beginning), have all constrained the democratization process, the ruling CDU and its leader, Franjo Tudjman, have also shown by their actions that their primary goal is to

144

Dijana Pleština

strengthen and expand their power rather than to create genuinely democratic institutions to represent the plurality of groups and interests in Croatia.

In addition to the issue of timing in the formation of the *županije* and of power distribution between the local *županije* and the central government in Zagreb, even minimal measures of democratization such as the televised sessions of the parliamentary discussions are affected by indirect censorship. Since there is no independent TV station and the state-run stations stop the full broadcasting of parliamentary sessions at 6 pm (and even the highlights of the sessions appear only on the late news), the government routinely raises key, controversial issues late in the afternoon. This ensures that a full discussion of the opposition's arguments is not heard by the larger public—thus de facto censoring the news. This happened in early November over the most contentious question of that parliamentary session, the removal of parliamentary immunity to the 3 members of the Croatian Party of the Right (CPR). It happened again at the session in late November over the issue of the *županije*.

Another example of the weakness of the legislature as a "representative body of citizens" (Article 70) is the frequent usage of accelerated (emergency) procedures. Although these procedures are meant for exceptional circumstances only, in its more than two and a half years in power, the government has passed 70 to 75 percent of the legislation by using these accelerated procedures.[41] As Mirjana Kasapović points out, this is considerably greater usage than the 25–30 percent that the Communist regime had made of it. Although, according to Branko Smerdel, this overuse of accelerated procedures is more a problem of streamlining by creating appropriate government bodies than an indication of the authoritarian nature of the ruling party,[42] nevertheless, after watching three sessions of Parliament, one cannot help but notice the frequency of the arbitrary use of these procedures as well as the glee with which certain members of the CDU inform their colleagues of the opposition that accelerated procedures will be used once again, and that they (the opposition) can't do anything about it.

When we consider that until February 1993 the Parliament consisted only of the Lower House, that the latter is controlled by the Croatian Democratic Union who, with their 62 percent of the seats, have monopoly power and that the government passes 3/4 of the legislation by using accelerated procedures, the conclusion is unavoidable that a Parliament, as an independent legislative body representing the various interests of the citizens, is still waiting to be formed in Croatia.[43]

Democracy and Nationalism in Croatia: The First Three Years 145

The Executive

The President

The President of the Republic of Croatia is elected by majority vote through universal suffrage in direct elections for a period of five years, renewable once. Among the more important duties and prerogatives of the President are the right to appoint and dismiss the Prime Minister (PM) and, on his proposal, the ministers and other members of the Government (Articles 94 to 106). This means that even in terms of formal powers, as decreed by the Constitution, the President has more power than the Government, and the latter is more responsible to him than to Parliament.

The President may also call for the referendum, and may dissolve the House of Representatives if the latter refuses to pass the budget (Article 98).[44] In addition, the President is the supreme commander of the armed forces (Article 100) and has the power to pass emergency ordinances which have the force of law. This can be done not only when the country is at war, but, more problematically, also in a loosely defined situation of "threat to the sovereignty and integrity of the Republic or its constitutional order" (Article 101). This latter clause opens wide the possibility for extending the position of the President into a "super presidency" or "authoritarian presidency" as has indeed happened in Croatia.

The development of the presidency into an authoritarian "super-presidency" has meant that the relations between the Executive and the Legislative branches resemble more those of democratic-centralism than they do those of democracy. This development is the result of four interrelated factors. The first is the formal concentration of power which enables the President to appoint and dismiss the Prime Minister as well as to pass, at his discretion, emergency ordinances which have the force of law. With these two powers, the President is clearly dominant. Secondly, the fact that, in this case, the President of the Republic is also the head of the party in power and, that the latter has such preponderant strength in Parliament that with its 62 percent of seats it can literally ignore the opposition, means that the separation of powers between the Executive and the Legislative branches is seriously impaired. Thirdly, both the socio-political formation and, related to it, the personal style of President Tudjman gravitate towards the authoritarian or autocratic presidency. Like many of his generation, Franjo Tudjman came of age in and was shaped by the hierarchical authoritarian structure of wartime and post-war communist party discipline. This early formation was further emphasized by his position as a general in Tito's army. Finally, the dual political and economic crises of the current war and the overall impoverishment of the population along with the lack of developed civic and democratic culture has led to a kind of calling forth, or at least a ready acceptance of a strong leader, a person who, in the average person's mind, "can make sense of it all and knows what to do."

In addition, both the President and the CDU have consciously and systematically linked all the major successes of the past two and a half years—the end of Communist rule, the "rebirth of democracy" in Croatia, the survival of the new republic through the war, international recognition and affirmation of the Croatian state "after 900 years"—to themselves, equating the CDU and President Tudjman with the formation and survival of the Croatian state and even with Croatian patriotism. This, in turn, has meant that "too much" criticism can be construed as "unpatriotic" and, given the war situation and continuing war psychosis, as bordering on treachery. It is understandable that, in this kind of atmosphere, a certain amount of self-censorship occurs and that, in turn, further augments the space for autocratic rule. As a result, although criticism of President Tudjman and especially of the government is rampant, particularly among the intellectuals, the latter are very conscious that the President (and by extension the CDU as the President's party) has virtual monopoly of power and that their criticism can largely be ignored.

The Government

An additional problem arises from the concentration of power which is creating a new elite of decision-makers, party/state functionaries whose major decisions are made outside the proper government sphere. One result is a fluidity of power which further undermines the development of democracy. The range of examples in this is quite wide. First, there is the extent to which members of the ruling party and of the government hold key positions in the economic, social, cultural and other spheres, all of which in a liberal-democratic society should be independent from government control. Thus, to give but two examples, Anton Vrdoljak, member of Parliament, party affiliation with the CDU is also the general director of CTV (Croatian Television), the state-run and controlled network which thus far has held monopoly; Vrdoljak is also the President of the board for Croatia Air, the state-run airline, once again a monopoly; he is also President of the Olympic Committee of Croatia, and thus controls sports in Croatia. Further, the minister for economic renewal, Slavko Degoricia, is also President of the board of INA, the strong oil and gas company in Croatia, also a monopoly.

Secondly, there is a frequent and flagrant breach of parliamentary rules, procedures and norms both by the President and by the government. For example, after the August 1992 elections, the President failed to present

Democracy and Nationalism in Croatia: The First Three Years	147

the government for approval to the *Sabor* within twenty days as mandated by the Constitution. This inattention to procedure, later rationalized through a judicial re-interpretation of the Constitution to cover for the breach, is behavior not atypical of those holding absolute or near absolute power. Those more directly dependent on an electorate tend to be more responsible and much less arbitrary and willful. Similarly, the President has replaced numerous key ministers in the first two years of his rule without presenting new ones to the *Sabor* for approval.

A third example of the concentration and misuse of power is the President's wide use of emergency measures which, as shown in the previous subsection, has meant that many issues that should have been discussed in Parliament, like those related to employment, social security, old age and accident insurance, as well as those more specifically related to the war, like internal affairs, information and others, were decided by one man alone. This personalization and broadening of the power of the Executive at the expense of the Legislature could be somewhat mitigated by the third branch, the Judiciary. However, as we will see, the Judiciary has also been constrained from becoming an independent actor.

The Judiciary

The major characteristic of the judicial system in Croatia today is that more than two and a half years after the CDU came to power and despite three elections (two for the Upper and one for the Lower House), and overwhelming parliamentary victories, the implementation of an independent judiciary acting as a check on the government to protect civil rights continues to be postponed. The reason for this negligence has at times been understandable. The regime's ambivalence towards a Judiciary inherited from the communist period has meant that the government has had to continue relying on people that it fundamentally mistrusts. Furthermore, the war itself has had a negative effect on the development of an independent Judiciary. A war situation allows all executives to pass extraordinary measures which may (and usually do) limit civil and human rights without making them (at least immediately) accountable to the democratic checks within a system. Even though some of these limitations may be necessary and legitimate, it is not unusual that boundaries of the necessary be expanded to include what is convenient and politically expedient for the government in power.

Three examples, two general and one specific, will be used to illustrate how this broadening of executive power has undermined the independence of the judiciary. The first is the Presidential Decree granting the military court the right to trial of civil cases, broadening its powers from narrowly specified areas of jurisdiction to include a much more open-ended and inclusive definition of "other criminal acts which they commit as . . . accomplices to army personnel."[45] When we look at the powers of the military court in Croatia comparatively, we see that various international declarations of law and human rights state that although military courts may be necessary in extraordinary circumstances, the power of these must be limited to military matters and personnel, specifically stating that civilians must be tried by civil courts. Thus, the presidential decree granting the military court the right to trial of civil cases, has clearly gone beyond the international judicial norms.[46]

A second example of the undermining of judicial independence is the massive purging of judges and public prosecutors—including virtually all of the members of the Constitutional and Supreme Courts—and the reappointment of new ones whose main qualifications often consist of their political suitability to the ruling CDU. The summary dismissals, which continue still, are in direct opposition to the Constitution (Article 120), which states that judicial positions are permanent unless the judge wishes to resign or is found incompetent or guilty of a criminal charge.

Even if we take into account that many of the judges and public prosecutors would have to be phased out in the transition from a "totalitarian" to a "democratic" regime since one would correctly assume that many were given their positions as a result of their "political suitability" to the previous regime rather than on the basis of professional criteria, as Alan Uzelac points out, the method of accomplishing this change matters a great deal. Thus, to break the law while trying to set up a lawful democratic state is certainly one case of the means undermining, rather than serving, the goal.[47] Furthermore, one can surely question how independent a judge is likely to be if he owes both the origin and continuation of his position to the ruling party which has a monopoly of power. Finally, according to the International Bar Association, the United Nation's Universal Declaration of Human Rights, and other International institutions of law, judicial institutions must play the key role in the selection, promotion, and dismissal of judges; in Croatia this standard is not followed.

A third and more specific example of the attempts to undermine the independence of the Judiciary is the dismissal of Vjekoslav Vidović, president of the Supreme Court of Croatia on 4 April 1992. The dismissal came through the Minister of Justice Misetić, who gave as reason for the decision Vidović's age, which was past that of usual retirement. However, when one considers the fact that a year earlier, at the time of his appointment, Vidović, a man of great expertise and proven integrity,[48] had already been past retirement age and that, furthermore, the Constitution makes no mention of age as a factor of eligibility, Misetić's "explanation" for Vidović's dismissal becomes highly suspicious.

Vidović's explanation is more credible. According to him, the dismissal was a result of his refusal to bow to the pressure of the public prosecutor Željko Olujić, Minister of Justice Bosiljko Misetić and ultimately to the pressure of President Tudjman regarding specific judicial cases which were already in the process of criminal investigation by the Supreme Court. Vidović's refusal to break the law and subvert the independence of the Supreme Court to the political will of the ruling CDU cost him his job.[49]

This example of the dismissal of the President of the Supreme Court cannot fail but send a strong signal to the entire Judiciary that the government will not tolerate judicial independence and that, furthermore, it has enough political power to carry out its will. Thus, some judges are cowed into anticipating what an acceptable judicial position might be—thus, effectively, through self-censorship (backed by direct pressure when "necessary") subverting the independence of the Judiciary. As a result, members of the Judiciary are insecure and frightened for their positions and under constant pressure to prove their loyalty to "the nation" which the ruling party equates with the Government and the President. Thus, although a key prerequisite for democracy, an independent Judiciary is guaranteed by the Croatian Constitution (Article 115), once again there is a gap between the formal aspect of the law and the actual practice.

Conclusion

What can we say, then, about the development of democracy in Croatia over the past three years and its outlook for the future?

First, the "paradox of democratic transition" as pointed out by Attila Agh,[50] is that the concentrated political effort needed to successfully restructure the economies of ex-communist countries, while avoiding social unrest, creates a need for power concentration which in turn undermines the democratic process, reproducing instead some form of authoritarian rule. This risk of authoritarianism is increased when the regime is faced with the three-fold "Dilemma of Simultaneity"[51]: (1) the creation or consolidation of a nation-state; (2) the institutionalization of democracy; and (3) the restructuring of economic and property relations. These processes, which in the West occurred more or less sequentially and over a period of centuries, are compressed in the democratizing regimes of "East Europe" by populations for whom notions of democracy and capitalism are derived from a one-dimensional view of the West, too often acquired through movies or in superficial interactions with foreigners.

The unrealistically high expectations for consumer plenty, after decades of deprivation, necessarily create frustration as the cost of restructuring the inefficient, over-planned and mismanaged economies via market systems leads to a competition for resources in which only the best-prepared and/or the best-connected prosper. The increasing number who find themselves backsliding to the edge of subsistence may then pose a threat to social stability, a threat to which the regime will tend to respond with a concentration of power to "restore order." The concentration of power and slide into authoritarianism is especially likely and perhaps (almost) inevitable when the tasks of economic and political restructuring coincide, as they do in Croatia, with the need to defend the very existence of the nation-state because of the external threat posed by the armed aggressor. At that point, the need for power concentration to mobilize for defense of the nation-state risks institutionalizing and, in that sense, normalizing, a response first derived to cope with the "abnormal" crisis of war.

The combination of the nature and the enormity of the task—lack of experience and therefore of a political culture of democracy, the simultaneity and urgency of building a new political system while restructuring the economy and, if the war is successfully completed, of rebuilding the country—along with the non-democratic formation of both the political elites and the people, will almost necessarily bias the political development toward authoritarian rule.

This, as has been shown, is the case in Croatia where the noticeable and growing gap between the democratic nature of the formal institutions and the authoritarian behavior of the regime can be seen, among other places, in the following: 1) the lack of checks on the near-absolute power of a President who is also head of the party in power which, furthermore, has full control of the Legislature; 2) the marginalization of the opposition parties; 3) the political interference in the independence of the Judiciary; 4) the continuing near-monopoly and resulting censorship of the media and; 5) the creation of an atmosphere in which criticism of the party in power is often equated with disloyalty to the nation-state. These are some of the indications of the malfunctioning of the Croatian democracy-in-the making.

On the other side, the institutionalization of liberal democratic principles, guaranteed by the Constitution and operating through Parliament and the formally independent Judiciary is no small achievement given the historical absence of democratic rule for ruler and ruled alike. Furthermore, recent elections indicate a change in the profile of the electorate providing some evidence that a growing number of voters, who represent the future (the younger, educated, urban population), is turning towards liberal principles that give hope for a democratic future in Croatia.

Yet, we can have no illusions regarding that future. For now, it remains both suspended between the still fragile political wisdom of the parties and the electorate and contingent on a peace which they have little power to bring about.

Democracy and Nationalism in Croatia: The First Three Years 151

Notes

I wish to thank the Faculty of Political Science at the University of Zagreb, where I was a Visiting Scholar Autumn 1992—Winter 1993, for providing me with a good working environment, and especially my friend and colleague Ivan Grdesić, Mirjana Kasparović, Ivan Šiber, and Nenad Zakošek, for generously sharing their work with me. I am also grateful to Agan Begić for his research assistance and to Jasna Petrić and Rosalia Uzum for their help in the library. I also wish to thank the College of Wooster for granting me a research leave, for the 1992-93 academic year.

1. The phrase is taken from Joshua Muravchik's comparison of Eastern Europe's pattern of post-communist development entitled "Eastern Europe's 'Terrible Twos'," in *Journal of Democracy*, Vol. 3, No. 1 (January 1992).

2. For more on methodological dilemmas in the comparative approach to the transition processes in Central and Eastern Europe, see Attila Agh, "The Transition to Democracy in Central Europe: A Comparative View," in *Journal of Public Policy*, Vol. 11, No. 2 (April–June 1991).

3. Ivan Grdesić, "1990 Elections in Croatia," in *Croatian Political Science Review*, (*CPSR*) Vol. 1, No. 1, 1992.

4. In post-1965 Yugoslavia, the developed regions were Slovenia, Croatia, Serbia, and Vojvodina, and the less developed Bosnia-Hercegovina, Macedonia, Montenegro, and Kosovo. For more on the causes and effects of increasing economic inequalities in post-World War Two Yugoslavia, see Dijana Pleština, *Regional Development in Communist Yugoslavia: Success, Failure and Consequences* (Boulder, Colo.: Westview Press, 1993).

5. The term was used increasingly from 1988 on by liberals in all the republics and regions of the former Yugoslavia.

6. C. B. McPherson, *The Real World of Democracy* (New York: Oxford University Press, 1972), p. 5.

7. Interview, Ivica Račan, 18 November 1992, Zagreb, Croatia.

8. The group of experts were chosen by the parliamentary committee in charge of the socio-political system and consisted of Branko Horvat, Žarko Puhovski, Branko Smerdel, Smiljko Sokol, Ivan Starčević and Željko Oluić.

9. Arendt Lijphart, "Constitutional Choices for New Democracies," in *Journal of Democracy*, Vol. 2, No. 1 (Winter 1991).

10. *Narodne Novine* (Zagreb), No. 7, 1990.

11. For a full explanation of the electoral system adopted in 1990, see Grdesić, "1990 Elections" [note 3].

12. For more discussion, see Mirjana Kasapović, "Politički učinci hrvatskog izbornog sustava," in *Politička misao*, Vol. 28, No. 3 (1991); and Mirjana Kasapović, "Izborni modeli i politički sustav," in *Politička misao*, Vol. 29, No. 2 (1992).

13. The fact that the same three electoral systems produced very different types of polities alerts us once again to the importance of non-institutional factors, notably political culture—which mitigates and further shapes the institutions. For one analysis of electoral results in the above three-named cases, see Kasapović, "Izborni modeli" [note 12], *passim*.

152   *Dijana Pleština*

14. As Ivica Račan pointed out, both the Chamber of Municipalities and the Chamber of Associated Labor by their very nature of one representative per political or work unit, call for majority rather than proportional rule; reasons for then applying majority to the third house as well outweighed those for proportional representation in this first election: Interview, Ivica Račan, 18 November 1992, Zagreb, Croatia.

15. Branko Smerdel, "The Republic of Croatia: Three Fundamental Constitutional Choices," in *Croatian Political Science Review*, Vol. 1, No. 1 (1992).

16. Ivan Grdesić, "Izbori u hrvatskoj: birači, vrednovanja i preferencije," in Ivan Grdesić, Mirjana Kasapović, Ivan Šiber and Nenad Zakosek (eds.), *Hrvatska u izborima '90* (Zagreb: Naprijed, 1991), pp. 49–95.

17. Grdesić, "1990 Elections" [note 3]; and Kasapović, "Politički učinci" [note 12], *passim*. Following Grdesić, Kasapović, Deren-Antoljak and others, elections of 1990 will be considered on the basis of the results in the Socio-Political Chamber (Chamber of Representatives) which is the only one that met the criteria of democratic parliamentary elections. Additionally, the CDU received majorities in the other two houses so that its parliamentary strength remained unchallenged.

18. A Coalition of Popular Agreement composed, among others, of social democrats, liberals, and greens, received the support of 14 percent of the electorate but gained only 4 percent of the parliamentary seats; the Serbian Democratic Party (SDP) and Independent candidates each gained the remaining 1 percent of parliamentary seats. For more on these results see Grdesic *CPSR*, Vol. 1, No. 1, 1992, and Kasapović, "Politički učinci" [note 12], *passim*.

19. Nenad Zakošek, "Setting up the new Institutional framework for Croatian politics: the role of the legislature," in *Budapest Papers on Democratic Transition*, No. 39, Hungarian Center for Democracy Studies Foundation, 1992.

20. For a comprehensive exposition and analysis of the size and importance of electoral districts in the 1990 elections see Kasapović, "Politički učinci" [note 12], *passim*.

21. Nenad Zakošek, "Polarizacija strukture, obrasci političkih uvjerenja i hrvatski izbori 1990," in Grdesić et al. (eds.), *Hrvatska u Izborima* [note 16], pp. 131–188.

22. Only the traditional cleavage is examined here as it is both the most dominant and the most applicable to this study. For definitions and applications of these, see *Ibid*, pp. 139–146.

23. See Ivan Šiber, "Nacionalna, vrednosna i ideologijska uvjetovanost stranačkog izbora," in Grdesić et al. (eds.), *Hrvatska u Izborima* [note 16], pp. 98–128; and Zakosek, "Polarizacija" [note 21], pp. 150–182.

24. Zakosek, "Polarizacija" [note 21], pp. 182–185.

25. *Ibid.*, p. 152.

26. *Ibid.*, p. 180.

27. For a full transcript of the meeting see *Danas* (Zagreb) 31 July 1990, pp. 12–15.

28. Mirjana Kasapović, "Temeljni politički sukobi u Hrvatskoj nakon izbora," *Encyclopedia Moderna*, God. 13, No. 1 (37), Zagreb: Hrvatska Akademija Znanosti i Umjetnosti (1992).

29. Smerdel, "Republic of Croatia" [note 15], p. 62.

30. *Ustav Republike Hrvatske, (The Constitution of the Republic of Croatia)*, 4th edition, Informator, Zagreb, 1992.

Democracy and Nationalism in Croatia: The First Three Years 153

31. Sabrina P. Ramet, "Serbia's Slobodan Milošević: A Profile," in *Orbis*, Vol. 35, No. 1 (Winter 1991).

32. Dijana Pleština, "From Democratic Centralism to De-Decentralized Democracy? Trials and Tribulations of Yugoslavia's Development," in John B. Allcock, John J. Horton, and Marko Milivojevic (eds.), *Yugoslavia in Transition—Choices and Constraints: Essays in Honour of Fred Singleton* (Oxford: Berg Publishers, 1992).

33. Dennison Rusinow, "Yugoslavia: Balkan Breakup?," *Foreign Policy*, No. 83 (Summer 1991).

34. Bogomil Ferfila, "Yugoslavia: Confederation or Disintegration," in *Problems of Communism*, Vol. 40, No. 4 (July/August 1991).

35. The "pink" zones are the Serb occupied areas outside the UN protected zones.

36. Slavko Matesa and Filip Brekalo, *The Country Privatization Report-1992: Croatia*, Republic of Croatia, p. 7, Agency for Restructuring and Development, Zagreb, Croatia, November 1992. Prepared for Central and Eastern European Network (CEEPN), 1992.

37. Štefica Deren-Antoljak, "The Croatian Electoral Model—The Most Important Elements," in *CPSR*, Vol. 1, No. 1 (1992), p. 106.

38. The above is taken from an internal document of the SDP used as the basis for a discussion with President Tudjman in July 1992. I am grateful to Mate Arlović and Ivica Račan for providing access to this and other material.

39. The Croatian National Party (CNP) with 6.55 percent of the popular vote placed fourth, while the Croatian Peasant Party (CPP) with 4.16 percent of the vote was sixth in popular ranking.

40. By the time of the elections, Croatia was divided into 450 counties.

41. Kasapović, "Izborni modeli" [note 12], p. 26.

42. Smerdel points out that in the U.S. some 80 percent of laws are not discussed in Congress but in the special agencies and committees who make the appropriate recommendations which the Parliament merely approves. Interview with Branko Smerdel, November 1992, Faculty of Law, Zagreb, Croatia.

43. As of this writing, mid-February 1993, the Upper House has not been convened. Thus nothing can be said of its operation. Indeed, according to Dražen Budiša, leader of the liberal CSLP, the main opposition party, it is doubtful that given its very limited powers, the Upper House can serve any function. *Globus*, (Zagreb), 12 February 1993.

44. Smerdel, "Republic of Croatia" [note 15], p. 89.

45. *Narodne Novine* (Zagreb), No. 25 (1992), Article 3, Point 5. This decree is particularly galling since it is against this very question of the right of military tribunals to try civilians that public criticism and debate first mobilized the broader populace in Slovenia and Croatia in 1988–89 leading to the first steps of "revolt" against the "Bolshevik" regime in Belgrade. Furthermore, during the four months that the liberal wing of the Croatian Communist Party ruled (December 1989–April 1990), they had repealed that decree. Thus, its reappearance and further extension by the CDU and President Tudjman was a matter of considerable symbolic, as well as legal, significance.

46. A. Uzelac, "Zavisnost i nezavisnost: neka komparativna iskustva i prijedlozi o položaju sudstva u Hrvatskoj," Manuscript, 1992, pp. 12–18.

154   *Dijana Pleština*

47. *Ibid.*

48. Back in 1971, Vidović had refused to be presiding judge on the political process against the liberals of the "Croatian Spring," choosing instead to resign.

49. *Nedjeljna Dalmacija* (Split), 23 April 1992, p. 30.

50. Agh, "The Transition to Democracy" [note 2], p. 148.

51. Claus Offe, "Capitalism by Democratic Design? Democratic Theory Facing the Triple Transition in East Central Europe," in *Social Research*, Vol. 58, No. 4 (Winter 1991); see also George Schöpflin, "Post-Communism: Constructing New Democracies in Central Europe," in *International Affairs*, Vol. 67, No. 2 (April 1991).

7

The Bosnian Crisis in 1992

Paul Shoup[1]

Are not things already crazy enough in this madhouse? Cannot anyone except Bosnians and Herzegovinians understand that the division of BH along national lines would make this war even worse, and more bestial?
—Zlatan Cabaravdić, *Vreme*, Belgrade, 11 May 1992

In the months since April 1992, the world has borne witness to the agony of a civil war in Bosnia-Herzegovina. Of all the republics of the former Yugoslavia, Bosnia-Herzegovina least deserved this fate. The destruction of Bosnia-Herzegovina, furthermore, marks a point of no return for Yugoslavia, her final demise. The blame for this situation lies above all with the national parties who have sought to carve up Bosnia-Herzegovina into national mini-states. Yet *all* the actors in this tragedy, including the international community, bear responsibility for the present situation, as this chapter will seek to demonstrate.

Before the present crisis, Bosnia-Herzegovina was a society where the three major nationalities—Muslims, Serbs and Croats—lived in apparent harmony. The region's boundaries, with some interruptions, were among the most enduring in the Balkans. Yet, at the same time, Bosnia-Herzegovina was a region which lived under the shadow of her neighbors. The presence in Bosnia of Serbs, Croats, and Muslims of undetermined nationality excited the cupidity of Croatia and Serbia in the nineteenth century, just as it has today. Bosnia's autonomy, stable borders and tradition of tolerance could survive only under the benevolent patronage of others—at one time Austria, at another Yugoslavia. In the absence of such patrons, Bosnia was a nationalist's delight and a statesman's nightmare—a witch's brew of ethnic Slav nationalities, who left alone, might live in peace, but could always be aroused—through fear, cupidity or ignorance—to communal violence and ethnic warfare. These facts conditioned the history of Bosnia: for the most part, united, and at peace, under Austrian and Yugoslav rule; yet

156   *Paul Shoup*

also subject to violent periods of civil war and partition, notably during World War Two.

Fueling the present crisis is the fact that the national composition of the population of Bosnia-Herzegovina has undergone dramatic changes in the last sixty years as a result of demographic trends, changes in census categories, and casualties and outmigrations resulting from World War Two. Since 1971 Muslims have been recorded as a nationality in their own right, rather than as Serbs, Croats, or "Muslims unspecified."[2] The net result of these changes has been favorable to the Muslims, and from the point of view of the Serbs, a disaster.

According to Kocović, out of a total population in 1931 of 2.323 million, Bosnia-Herzegovina, in its present boundaries, was made up of 1.02 million Serbs, 715 thousand Muslims, and 516 thousand Croatians.[3] In 1991, of a total population of 4.124 million, 1.9 million were Muslim, 1.4 million Serb, and 755 thousand Croatian (43.7 percent Muslim, 31.4 percent Serb and 17.3 percent Croatian).[4] In brief, while Serbs were 45 percent of the population of Bosnia-Herzegovina in 1931, and almost double the number of Croats (assuming that the data on religious persuasion reported in 1931 can be equated with nationality), the situation had by 1991 almost reversed itself, with the Muslims the dominant nationality, and the Serbs reduced to less than a third of the total population.

Differential rates of population growth, and outmigration from certain regions, continued to alter the population structure after World War Two. Croats, whose number has fallen absolutely, now base their claims to territory on the census of 1961.[5] Serbs, in order to justify their territorial claims, insist that national boundaries within Bosnia-Herzegovina be established by settlements, not by districts.[6] Finally, the census of 1991 shows a marked decline in the number of Yugoslavs in comparison to the census of 1981, a reflection of the polarization of Bosnian society after 1990. This has rendered the 1991 census suspect by all three national groups, because, somewhat perversely, when the number of Yugoslavs was greater, they could be claimed as one's "own," just as the Muslims, at an earlier time, were claimed to be Serbian, or Croatian.[7]

The history of Bosnia-Herzegovina mirrors that of other parts of Yugoslavia. She had not been an independent state since the middle ages (a point used by the Serbs to throw doubts on Bosnia-Herzegovina's status as a state, although Slovenia did not even enjoy the distinction of independence in medieval times). Yet there may be a lesson for Bosnia-Herzegovina's present leaders in the region's medieval past: King Tomašević was recognized by the Pope, who crowned Tomislav king of Bosnia in 1461. This offered little protection to Tomislav, who was beheaded by the Turks in Jajce two years later. Austrian rule was more benign, and Kálláy, until his death in 1903, nurtured those qualities of traditional Bosnian culture

The Bosnian Crisis in 1992

which we find most appealing today. In the interwar period, Bosnia-Herzegovina was under Serbian tutelage. At the same time the influence of the YMO (Yugoslav Muslim Organization), was not inconsiderable in Belgrade. Mehmed Spaho—who opposed the creation of a Greater Croatia in 1939, and recommended that Bosnia-Herzegovina either be granted autonomy or ally herself with Serbia—assiduously protected the rights of the Muslim landowning class, while not challenging Serbian rule. [8]

In 1939 Bosnia-Herzegovina was partitioned for the first time, following the creation of the Croatian Banovina; then, in 1941, she was absorbed into Independent Croatia. The war was a time of death and rebirth for the region. (If only the same could be said now!). While the Croats, Serbs and Muslims engaged in bloody internecine ethnic warfare, they were also drawn into the struggle against the Germans and Italians through the Partisan movement. Bihać, a Muslim city, became a Partisan shrine, the birthplace of AVNOJ Yugoslavia. The encounters between the Partisans and their foes involved towns and regions which are now flash points in the Bosnian war. While history is not exactly repeating itself, a knowledge of the Partisan campaigns of World War Two is useful in sorting out the conflicts taking place in Bosnia-Herzegovina today. The failure of the Axis powers to subdue the Partisan units operating in Bosnia-Herzegovina during World War Two has influenced calculations of how great an international force would have to be mustered to subdue the Serbs laying siege to Sarajevo.

Bosnia-Herzegovina was the linchpin of the federal system created by the Communists after the war—a republic where three of the six major Yugoslav nationalities co-mingled and shared power. Over time, the Muslims, showing their traditional adaptability, were absorbed into the mainstream of political and economic life in the republic. Economically backward, Bosnia-Herzegovina experienced rapid economic growth in the postwar period, thanks in part to the defense industries which were located in the republic, far from Yugoslavia's vulnerable borders with the rest of Eastern Europe. The turmoil of the late 1980s, triggered by the rise of Milošević and the mobilization of the Serbs outside Serbia in support of Serbian nationalist goals, at first bypassed Bosnia-Herzegovina. Yet Titoism, which seemed so deeply entrenched in the region, succumbed to nationalism as elsewhere in Yugoslavia. In the elections of November and December 1990, the voters gave their overwhelming support to the three national parties. The Party of Democratic Action won 34 percent of the seats; the Serbian Democratic Party, 30 percent; and the Croatian Democratic Union 18 percent. The remaining parties (the two strongest were the Alliance of Reform Forces, led by Nenad Kecmanović, and the former Communists, the Party of Democratic Change, led by Nijaz Duraković) ended up with only 38 of the total of 204 seats.[9]

158

Paul Shoup

The New Government

The elections to the State Presidency, which took place at the same time as the elections to the parliament, in November and December, produced a similar result: Fikret Abdić and Alija Izetbegović of the Party of Democratic Action won the greatest number of votes, followed by two Serb members of the Serbian Democratic Party, Nikola Koljević and Biljana Plavšić, and two Croatians, Stjepan Kljuić and Franjo Boras. Nenad Kecmanović also ran as a candidate for the Alliance of Reform Forces, and received 21 percent of the vote—more than Franjo Boras—but failed to secure a seat on the presidency.

It was against this backdrop that Bosnia-Herzegovina faced the challenge of survival posed by the collapse of Yugoslavia. This challenge had two components: making the coalition of three national parties function, in the best Bosnian tradition, as a model of coexistence and tolerance which the rest of society could emulate; and fashioning an agreement over Bosnia's future, either within a new Yugoslavia, or as an independent state. Even with the best will in the world, these were formidable challenges, bound to test the new Bosnian leadership.

At first, the formation of a coalition government was hailed as an example of the Bosnian skill at compromise. Alija Izetbegović, President of the Party of Democratic Action, was elected by the collective state presidency as President of Bosnia-Herzegovina; Jure Pelivan, a Croat, was chosen Prime Minister; and Momčilo Krajišnik, a Serb, became President of the National Assembly. The arrangement seemed to reflect the need for balance and compromise in government, while the three national parties were represented in equal numbers in the State Presidency.[10]

One gains the impression, nevertheless, that over time the government of Bosnia-Herzegovina became largely a province of the Muslims and the Croats.[11] Izetbegović dominated the scene, thanks to his international prestige and popular support among the Muslims. The two most critical posts in the government apart from the premiership—those of Minister of Foreign Affairs and Minister of the Interior—were in the hands of the Muslims (Haris Silajdžić and Alija Delimustafić). This is not to say that it was not possible for the three parties to cooperate, on occasion, among each other, and with the army as well. Furthermore, the institutions of government, if ineffective, did have a tradition of impartiality to defend. Radio TV Sarajevo did this brilliantly.[12] The Ministry of the Interior tried to remain above national divisions, but was eventually forced by the Serbian Democratic Party to submit to reorganization and parcelization in April of 1992. The absence of consensus in the decisions of the Presidency and other organs—a major complaint of the Serbs—by no means justified the Serbian effort to break down the ministries along national lines, each serving its

The Bosnian Crisis in 1992

own ethnic constituency, unless of course, these institutions were anti-Serb, a point argued vociferously by the Serbian Democratic Party, but yet to be convincingly proven.

At the same time, democratic procedures were for the most part ignored under the impact of repeated crises, both domestic and international. Parliament was largely shut out of the decision-making process, much to the chagrin and anger of the opposition.[13] Most power came to be concentrated in the hands of the Presidency and its Crisis Command (Krizni stab) headed by Ejup Ganić.[14] In this respect, Bosnia-Herzegovina did not differ greatly from the other Yugoslav republics, where concentration of power in the hands of the President was the rule. Informal consultations among the national parties did of course take place behind the scenes, but the practice could hardly be said to have enhanced democracy in Bosnia-Herzegovina following the collapse of communism in 1990.

It was with a divided and largely undemocratic government, then, that Bosnia-Herzegovina faced her second challenge: responding to the collapse of Yugoslavia. While Bosnia-Herzegovina had no territorial disputes with neighboring republics, and had been able to avoid being drawn into the controversies over Kosovo and economic reform (while playing the role of a mediator in the debates over constitutional revisions), she was peculiarly vulnerable on other grounds. This became evident as the Yugoslav crisis deepened, above all, as Slovenia and Croatia pushed for the creation of a confederal Yugoslavia made up of sovereign and independent republics.

The source of this vulnerability lay, as we know, in the need for some type of social contract among the three nationalities if the unity of Bosnia-Herzegovina were to be preserved. The underlying issue was this: on what basis could the three nationalities justify their coexistence? What were the principles that should govern a social contract between them? As the crisis in Yugoslavia deepened, the debate over this question became the focus around which the future of the republic revolved. The fact that the controversy was artificially stimulated by dreams of a greater Serbia and greater Croatia by Serbian and Croatian extremists, respectively, and that the debate finally degenerated into a struggle over territory, does not diminish its significance in understanding the origins of the Bosnian crisis.

That the terms of such cooperation were in dispute was apparent in the argument over whether Bosnia-Herzegovina, after the collapse of communism, was Yugoslavia writ small, or Bosnia writ large. Izetbegović flatly denied the comparison between Bosnia-Herzegovina and Yugoslavia: Bosnia, he argued, had existed longer than Yugoslavia; the relations among her nationalities were more authentic, and so forth. From this it followed that the foundation upon which relationships among the three nationalities was based derived from Bosnian traditions and modern European experience—in brief, the Bosnian (the Serbs would say, spitefully, Muslim) version of a civil society.

On the other hand, Radovan Karadžić, president of the Serbian Democratic Party, favored the analogy between Yugoslavia and Bosnia-Herzegovina: just as Yugoslavia was an artificial state, in which Serbs received short shrift, so too was Bosnia-Herzegovina; just as Yugoslavia was destined to break into its component parts, so too was Bosnia-Herzegovina. From this it followed that the relationship among the nationalities must be based on consensual decision-making (no major decisions should be made without the consent of all three nationalities), and that each nationality should develop its own institutions, including parliaments, police, and media. The unarticulated premise of Karadžić's position was that of the link between ethnicity and territory. Each nation should have, or create, its own territory. If Bosnia-Herzegovina was not Yugoslavia writ small, she would have to be remade in this image. Clearly, if this principle were to be implemented, the Serbs could claim the majority of the land mass of Bosnia-Herzegovina, given their strength in the rural portions of the republic, even though they constituted only one third of the population.

For the opposition parties, on the other hand, the failure of Yugoslavia to democratize was the major point—and Bosnia-Herzegovina ran the risk of making the same error as Yugoslavia by falling under the domination of the nationalist parties. The supporters of this point of view also professed to see a contradiction in the Serbian position, which at one and the same time argued for a confederation in Bosnia-Herzegovina and for a strong federal government in Yugoslavia.

It was the struggle to persuade, or enforce one or another of these views on the Bosnians as Yugoslavia disintegrated and the civil war spread which constituted the heart of the Bosnian crisis up to the time of the outbreak of the civil war. This struggle, in turn, can be broken down into three periods: (i) the spring of 1991, prior to the secession of Croatia and Slovenia in June; (ii) the period between June 1991, and Bosnia-Herzegovina's bid for recognition as an independent state on 20 December 1991; and (iii) the period between December and the recognition of Bosnia-Herzegovina on 6 April. The first two periods will be examined in a somewhat cursory fashion, the third in more detail.

(i) *Spring 1991: Opportunities Foregone*: The period of the spring of 1991 must be considered one of opportunities foregone—the opportunity, that is, to make the three-party nationalist coalition function, and for Bosnia to sort out her relations with the rest of Yugoslavia. Izetbegović, Stjepan Kljuić (President of the Croatian Democratic Community), and Karadžić, were, after all, not the most radical in their respective national parties. All three were at the time prepared, albeit on their own terms, to support the integrity of Bosnia-Herzegovina. Izetbegović and Karadžić agreed that as long

The Bosnian Crisis in 1992

161

as Yugoslavia remained intact, Bosnia should not seek to secede. The Serbs, it is true, were engaged during the spring in "self-organization": that is, creating alternative organizations in case the cooperation of the three parties should break down. These efforts, meanwhile, did not yet pose a threat to the integrity of the republic, assuming that the three national parties could still cooperate at the national level.[15]

It was during this period that Izetbegović played a prominent role in trying to resolve the Yugoslav constitutional crisis by pushing the idea of a "Yugoslav state community." Karadžić may have been dubious about some aspects of this plan, which tried to preserve the international status of the Yugoslav state while devolving most real power to the republics. But as long as Izetbegović showed some receptivity to the notion of an asymetric Yugoslav federation, which would have allowed Bosnia-Herzegovina to remain in a close union with Serbia, Karadžić was willing to give Izetbegović his support in the search for a solution to the constitutional crisis.[16]

Yet a commitment to preserving Yugoslavia on the part of the Serbian Democratic Party and the Party of Democratic Action did not translate itself into a willingness to find a compromise solution over the issue of Bosnia-Herzegovina's internal structures, either as a unitary, "civil" (gradjanska) and sovereign state, as Izetbegović wished, or as Yugoslavia writ small, as Karadžić proposed. The immediate issue was that of Bosnian sovereignty. As Yugoslavia disintegrated in the spring of 1991, Izetbegović pushed for a declaration of sovereignty, claiming that the choice was between "sovereignty and chaos."[17] Karadžić was equally insistent on the right of the Serbs to set up their own organs of government, arguing that this was the only course open to him if the Bosnian government and presidency would not honor the principle of consensus. Izetbegović hardly helped matters by using the office of president for purposes which, if not reflecting purely Muslim political priorities, fell outside the domain of tripartisanship: turning up in Croatia on the occasion of ceremonies for the promulgation of a new Croatian constitution, paying official visits to Libya and Iran, and airing his own views about the future of Bosnia on his trip to the United States and other foreign capitals during the summer of 1991.

In brief, the differences in outlook between the national parties were already too great to be bridged. For the Serbs, the only reality was Yugoslavia, of which Bosnia-Herzegovina was necessarily a part. For the Muslims, and to a lesser degree the Croatians, Bosnia was the reality, while Yugoslavia was fast becoming an anachronism.

(ii) *June 1991 - December 1991*: The second period is that of turmoil and uncertainty following the outbreak of the civil war which, miraculously— it seemed at the time—passed Bosnia by. The incursion of the Montenegrin reservists into Herzegovina (in September) and the destruction these reservists wreaked on the village of Ravno; reports of a Serbian plan, codenamed RAM, for the creation of a Greater Serbia at the expense of Bosnia-Herzegovina;[18] the near lynching of the Minister of Interior of Kninska Krajina, who unwisely ventured onto Bosnian soil; the refusal of the Ministry of Interior to cooperate with the army in mobilizing the male population to fight the war in Croatia; and the threat of civil war which accompanied the Bosnian bid for EC recognition in December—all these events kept Bosnia-Herzegovina in turmoil during the fall months.[19]

These tensions were accompanied by the establishment of Serbian autonomous areas in September,[20] and a growing confrontation between the Serbian Democratic Party and Party of Democratic Action. With Yugoslavia in an advanced state of dissolution, Izetbegović again insisted that Bosnia-Herzegovina adopt a declaration of sovereignty. Such a declaration was pushed through the Bosnian parliament over the strenuous objections of the Serbian Democratic Party on 14 October. In the heat of the debate Karadžić threatened that a war might break out which would threaten the Muslim population with annihilation should Bosnia secede from Yugoslavia;[21] Izetbegović answered that such threats only strengthened his resolve to push ahead with plans for an independent Bosnia.[22] The Serbs reacted with measures of their own, creating an Assembly of the Serbian Nation of Bosnia-Herzegovina on 25 October; declaring that the laws of Bosnia would no longer apply to the Serbian Autonomous Areas; and holding a referendum on 9–10 November, in which the Serbs voted to remain in Yugoslavia (i.e., in association with Serbia and Montenegro).[23] During the fall of 1991 Bosnia-Herzegovina became a divided society in fact if not in name. In the words of the Sarajevo weekly newspaper *Nedjelja*: "two assemblies, two presidencies, two governments and almost no opposition."[24]

Nevertheless, war (for the time being) was avoided, and this was a signal achievement. This success was, at the time, attributed to Izetbegović's willingness to collaborate with the army (which wished to keep Bosnia-Herzegovina intact as a base of operations for the war in Croatia),[25] and because the Muslims were not ready, or willing, to go to war. (In Izetbegović's words, "it takes two to tango")[26]. To quote Tihomir Loza at the time "the crowning incident that [proves] that a common life is impossible has yet to happen."[27]

The reality was more sobering, and less flattering to Izetbegović and the Muslims. By December, Slobodan Milošević, president of Serbia, had decided to push for a cease-fire in the civil war and to request a UN presence in Croatia. A war in Bosnia-Herzegovina clearly did not serve his purposes, until UN forces were in place. The army, although implicated in the transfer of arms to Serbian irregulars, was anxious to keep Bosnia intact, and at peace.[28] This was evident in the agreement between General Kadijević and Izetbegović in October, cited above, in a meeting of the army's

The Bosnian Crisis in 1992   163

top generals with Izetbegović at Christmas, meant to defuse the crisis created by the debate over recognition,[29] and in the efforts of the army to organized joint military-Ministry of Interior police patrols, which helped maintain some semblance of order in those parts of Bosnia under Serbian and Muslim control.[30]

At the same time, Karadžić and the Serbian Democratic Party made it abundantly clear what lay in store for Bosnia if Izetbegović went ahead with his plans to hold a referendum and declare Bosnia's independence. The Serbs would, in turn, assert their own independence. If the division of Bosnia-Herzegovina into national regions had not yet been agreed to, the result would be bloody civil war.

(iii) *December 1991 to April 1992.* The third phase of the Bosnian crisis encompasses the period from the decision of the European Community in December to grant recognition to Slovenia and Croatia to the recognition of Bosnia by the EC on 6 April. During this period the Muslims and Croatians threw their support behind a referendum for Bosnian independence. The declaration of independence which followed, on 3 March, marked the first steps toward war, which broke out on a massive scale after 6 April. Up to December, the focus was on saving Yugoslavia in the hope of saving Bosnia; after December, on saving Bosnia, as a means of stabilizing and rebuilding a loose association of successor states to Yugoslavia.

In assessing this situation, it is necessary to take a step backward and examine the options open to Bosnia as the Yugoslav crises developed. Broadly speaking, five were available.

(i) The best hope for Bosnia-Herzegovina lay in preserving Yugoslavia as a loose confederation, possibly with closer ties among some republics than others (the asymmetric solution). This was the policy advocated by Izetbegović prior to June of 1991.

(ii) If the preservation of Yugoslavia was no longer possible, the safest, if most unpalatable course for the Muslims and Croatians, was to link up Bosnia-Herzegovina with Serbia and Montenegro in a new (rump) Yugoslav federation. This would perhaps have prevented the spread of the civil war to Bosnia-Herzegovina. This option was dangled in front of the Muslims by Milošević in the summer of 1991, but fell through, primarily because of opposition with the ranks of the Party of Democratic Action and Izetbegović's own priorities, which lay elsewhere. The idea was in any case fiercely opposed by the Croatians.[31]

(iii) A third alternative was to form a confederation with Slovenia and Croatia. Zulfikarpašić, one of the leaders of the Muslim Bosnjak Organization, supported this option for Bosnia-Herzegovina before the civil war broke out, and Izetbegović clearly preferred this option to the "Eastern solution," as he called association with Serbia.[32] The idea surfaced again in

164   *Paul Shoup*

talks between the Party of Democratic Action and Croatian Democratic Community in Split in May 1992, but in 1991 could only be achieved at the risk of spreading the civil war to Bosnia-Herzegovina.

(iv) A fourth possibility was to agree to a partition of Bosnia-Herzegovina, as the Serbian and Croatian nationalists wished. Not only was this in principle unacceptable to the Muslims, but it was also a dangerous course for the Muslims to pursue against the express intent of the international community to recognize Bosnia-Herzegovina within its traditional boundaries. Tudjman and Milošević were for their part drawn to this solution (i.e., partition), and on at least two occasions discussed this option as a way of avoiding a civil war between Croatia and Serbia.[33]

(v) The fifth, and remaining alternative, was to internationalize the Bosnian problem, and to push for an independent Bosnia-Herzegovina, not ruling out links with either Serbia or Croatia once hostilities had ceased. This was the course which Izetbegović pursued from June onward, when it became clear that Croatia was bent on a final rupture with Yugoslavia. Even before the elections of 1990, Izetbegović did not hesitate to make it clear that if Croatia and Slovenia were to secede from Yugoslavia, Bosnia would immediately declare its independence.

The Role of the European Community

Three decisions of the EC brought the goal of recognition measurably closer to realization during the summer and fall of 1991. The first was to accept the former republics as participants in the peace process; the second, to recommend that the solution to the Yugoslav crisis entailed the preservation of the republics in their existing boundaries; and the third, the decision that Yugoslavia no longer existed, or, as the Badinter Commission put it, was "in a state of dissolution," a finding that was hotly contested by the Serbian Democratic Party in Bosnia Herzegovina.

Still, international recognition of Bosnia was not assured until the EC could sort out its own internal differences over how and when to recognize the republics as successor states to Yugoslavia. Germany was pressing the other members of the EC to recognize Slovenia and Croatia. Bosnia-Herzegovina, in concert with Macedonia, urged recognition of all the republics simultaneously, arguing that the early and uncoordinated recognition of individual republics would lead to a spread of the war.

The decision of the EC on 17 December to recognize those republics which met certain criteria, including support for the provisions of the 4 November Hague Conference recommendations for a solution to the Yugoslav conflict, set the stage for the campaign in Bosnia-Herzegovina for recognition. On 20 December the Bosnian presidency, over the opposition of its two Serbian members, requested recognition from the EC.[34] (This followed the re-election of Izetbegović to a second one year term of office on the same day.) After an exchange of correspondence with Serbia, on the one hand, and Bosnia on the other, the Badinter commission agreed that Bosnia-Herzegovina met EC criteria for recognition, on condition that she hold a referendum which would confirm that the majority of the population were in favor of independence.[35] The decision, referred to the Serbs in Bosnia-Herzegovina as a "minority," rather than using the traditional formula that the Serbs were one of three constituent nationalities of Bosnia-Herzegovina—a point to which this account shall return.

The decisions of the Badinter Commission polarized the political situation in Bosnia-Herzegovina still further. Izetbegović was now given the green light to hold the referendum for independence which he had so long desired. The Serbs reacted predictably. On 18 December the Serbian autonomous region of Bosanska Krajina declared that it was part of Yugoslavia, not Bosnia-Herzegovina, and that the EC decisions on Bosnia-Herzegovina did not therefore apply to its territory.[36] On 21 December the Serbian Assembly announced the formation of the Serbian Republic of Bosnia and Herzegovina, and on 9 January, declared the republic's independence. (The Serbian Republic of Bosnia and Herzegovina was recognized by the Republic of Serbian Krajina just before Christmas.)[37]

The crisis could have led to civil war, but for reasons noted above, was contained. Belgrade, hoping to end the fighting in Croatia, was eager to avoid a conflict in Bosnia-Herzegovina, and developed the idea of a new Yugoslavia made up of Serbia and Montenegro within their existing ("AVNOJ") borders. The possibility was left open for other Serbian regions in Yugoslavia to join the federation, but it was left unclear when and how this might be accomplished.[38]

This new line permitted the Serbian Democratic Party in Bosnia-Herzegovina to take a more flexible approach on the question of Bosnian independence. This was already apparent in December when Karadžić addressed the opening session of the Serbian assembly. While asserting that, as a result of the decision to apply for recognition, "in a constitutional and legal sense Bosnia-Herzegovina has ceased to exist," Karadžić suggested that Bosnia-Herzegovina might be transformed into a confederation. The Serbs would have the right to be "federally" tied to Serbia and Sarajevo would have the status of an extraterritorial city.[39]

After the December crisis, the tensions in Yugoslavia eased as the cease fire in Croatia went into effect. The campaign to gain international recognition for Bosnia-Herzegovina, which Izetbegović and his Foreign Minister, Haris Silajdžić, pursued with great skill, also began to pay off. The United States was drawn back into the Yugoslav crisis on the side of the Bosnian government, perhaps at the urging of Cyrus Vance, who had become increasingly concerned over the situation in Bosnia. The surfacing of a new proposal for a "Community of Independent Former Yugoslav Republics," purportedly raised in conversations between Izetbegović and Vance in early January (and later somewhat sensationally described as the "Vance Plan"), seemed part of this effort to reconstruct Yugoslavia, at Izetbegović's urging, with Bosnia-Herzegovina as its linchpin.[40] (It bears remembering, in light of subsequent criticisms of the decision to recognize Bosnia, that the policy of support for Bosnian independence had the unanimous approval of the European nations, as well as the United States, in contrast to the differences of opinion which surfaced over the question of the recognition of Croatia.)

But the closer that Bosnia-Herzegovina came to holding a referendum on independence, the more the internal divisions in Bosnia-Herzegovina came to the surface. The Serbian Democratic Party made it clear that the Serbs of Bosnia-Herzegovina would launch an armed secession if Bosnia-Herzegovina declared her independence. Although it was inopportune for the Serbs to propose the union of Serbian Bosnia with Yugoslavia, it was still possible to push for the formation of a confederation, so loosely constructed that it would leave the Serbian portions of Bosnia free to merge with the new Yugoslavia, made up of Serbia and Montenegro, at some future date.

Such a solution to the Bosnian question was also attractive to the extreme elements in the Croatian Democratic Union, if not to Stjepan Kljuić. Tudjman was repeatedly drawn to the idea of the partitioning of Bosnia between Serbia and Croatia, as we have noted earlier.[41] In July 1991, Mario Nobilo, a senior advisor to Tudjman, in an interview with the London *Times*, suggested that the partitioning of Bosnia was the "only peaceful solution" to the Yugoslav conflict.[42] A key part of the deal would be the creation of a Muslim state in the center of Bosnia-Herzegovina and a voluntary population exchange, according to this *Times* account. In the middle of January, talks were held between Tudjman and Nikola Koljevic (joined by Franjo Borac, one of the two Croatian members of the Bosnian Presidency), signaling a rapprochement between the Serbian Democratic Party and the Croatian Democratic Community.[43] Koljević came forth with a plan for a confederal Bosnia-Herzegovina shortly thereafter—a reasonable proposal, in fact, which could have formed the basis of an agreement over regionalization if it had been embraced by the remaining leaders of the Serbian Democratic Party.[44]

The real bombshell fell with the adoption of the "Livno Declaration" by the Croatian Democratic Union in early February. The document suggested that the referendum be reworded, and that it affirm that Bosnia-Herzegovina was a state built on the sovereignty of its three nationalities.[45] This was followed by the resignation of Stjepan Kljuić as president of the

The Bosnian Crisis in 1992

Croatian Democratic Community in late January,[46] and secret talks between Karadžić and Josip Manolić the end of February.[47] The Croatian position that emerged was not, on the surface, greatly different from that of the Serbian Democratic Party, calling for a Bosnia-Herzegovina made up of "sovereign" constituent nations linked together in a confederal relationship. In the event, the version of the referendum placed before the voters was that adopted by the Bosnian national assembly reflecting the position of the Party of Democratic Action and the opposition that Bosnia-Herzegovina should declare her independence as a sovereign state of its citizens, not its constituent national groups.[48]

These events were paralleled by a shift in the position of the EC. The EC Conference on Bosnia had been set up by Lord Carrington in early February. At the second session of the conference in Lisbon 22–23 February, the EC mediator, José Cutilheiro, put forth a proposal for a settlement which for the first time called for a Bosnia-Herzegovina of national regions, while requiring the three national parties' leaders to pledge to accept the independence of Bosnia-Herzegovina.[49] Judging from the intense consultations with the Yugoslavs that preceded the Lisbon meeting,[50] the EC and the US considered the proposal as the key to reaching a Bosnian settlement.

The agreement of all three national parties to this proposal was, in turn, widely viewed in the Western press as a breakthrough in the talks on Bosnia-Herzegovina.[51] The agreement was a bitter disappointment to Izetbegović, however, who was forced to accept the regionalization of Bosnia-Herzegovina along national lines as the price for gaining the support of the Serbs for the independence of that republic.[52] Željko Vuković, writing for *Borba*, commented that "the maximum that can be hoped for is that the idiotic and devastating parcelization and democratization of [these] 'national totalitarianisms' be accomplished—in peace."[53]

Karadžić, on the other hand, was triumphant, sensing that the parcelization of Bosnia had begun, although the powers of the Bosnian government as set out in the Lisbon document far exceeded those which Serbs were ready to accept in practice. The Croatian representative to the talks kept a low profile, but had every reason to be satisfied with the Lisbon proposals, which balanced the Croatian desire for regionalization with the need to preserve a Bosnian government, if only to prevent Serbian Krajina in Croatia from seceding and uniting with Bosanska Krajina.

The Lisbon agreement did not, as we know now, produce the hoped-for breakthrough in the negotiations over Bosnia. Most important, no attempt was apparently made to resolve the issue of where the ethnic regions, or cantons, would be located. In the follow-up in Sarajevo at Villa Konak the end of February, a number of maps were circulated in greatest secrecy, the beginning of the "battle of the maps," about which more will be said below.[54] On 9 March, after strenuous negotiations in Brussels, a

168   *Paul Shoup*

second version of the Lisbon agreement was produced, which placed greater stress on confederal relations among the national units.[55] While the agreement offered a great deal to the Serbs, Karadžić found the proposals inadequate, insisting that the Serbs of Bosnia would accept nothing less than their own state, linked with the two other nations through a loose confederal arrangement.

Karadžić's refusal to approve the new agreement was ominous, coming as it did shortly after the declaration of Bosnia-Herzegovina's independence in early March.[56] One possible explanation was that the radical wing of the Serbian Democratic Party, with its strongholds in the Serbian autonomous regions, had grown in power after the events of 2–3 March (discussed below). In any case, contrary to the position of the Yugoslav rump presidency, which had come out in favor of the Brussels accords, the Serbian assembly of the Serbian Republic of Bosnia and Herzegovina voted to reject them on 11 March, arguing that the proposals placed too much power in the hands of the central authorities.[57]

A Final Effort

One final effort was made to settle the question of Bosnia-Herzegovina's internal structure, prior to recognition, at the meeting of the Conference on Bosnia-Herzegovina which took place in the third week in March at the Villa Konak in Sarajevo. The negotiations produced proposals for the restructuring of Bosnia-Herzegovina similar to those suggested at Brussels. The one novelty was the appearance of a map prepared by the EC and distributed to the press at the end of the conference, the first attempt on the part of the EC to delineate the national regions, or cantons, on which the EC plan was based.

If one is to understand the difficulties that these negotiations were encountering, it is necessary to return events within Bosnia-Herzegovina. In retrospect, it appears that the referendum for Bosnian independence on 29 February–1 March was a turning point in the Bosnian crisis. Although the Serbian Democratic Party did not attempt to block the referendum, the Serbs refused to participate, and remained adamantly opposed to any declaration of independence made before Bosnia's internal transformation— into some kind of confederation—had been accomplished. The referendum, by setting in motion the procedures which would result in independence and recognition, was, from the Serbian point of view, a step toward civil war.

This is suggested by the events of early March. The referendum was held largely without incident. The official results showed a victory for those

The Bosnian Crisis in 1992 169

who favored an independent Bosnia-Herzegovina: 62.68 percent of the total number of voters in Bosnia-Herzegovina voted in favor of independence, almost precisely the outcome one would expect if all the Muslims and Croatians supported the referendum, and the Serbs, staged a boycott and failed to vote.[58] With an additional 200,000 Serbian votes, the referendum would have had the support of approximately 70 percent of the registered voters—an outcome that must be considered within the realm of possibility if the Serbian population had not been in fact under pressure to stay away from the polls.[59]

The day following the referendum Serbian barricades went up in Sarajevo, accompanied by Karadžić's now familiar threats.[60] (The ostensible reason was the shooting of several Serbs at a wedding over the weekend.) The Serbs demanded that the negotiations over the future of Bosnia-Herzegovina be brought to a conclusion before the declaration of independence was adopted; that independent Sarajevo TV be replaced by national television channels; and that the Ministry of Interior be reorganized along national lines. These demands were first accepted by Izetbegović, then repudiated after the army stepped in and the people of Sarajevo took to the streets to protest the terror. Encouraged by the support of the masses, and convinced that the Serbian side had suffered a major defeat, Izetbegović went ahead and declared the independence of Bosnia-Herzegovina on 3 March 1992. His actions were ratified by parliament (in the absence of the Serbs) the same night.

The motives of the Serbs in setting up the barricades on 2 March have been debated; most commentators saw it as a dry run for an eventual Serbian takeover. It is also possible that the Serbs were seeking to paralyze the Bosnian government at this crucial juncture (in effect, to stage a coup), but were deterred by the actions of the army[61] and the peace demonstrators, setting the stage for the "rural war" and the siege of Sarajevo that followed. It is possible to speculate, therefore, that if the Serbian demands had been met, and the central government had fallen under Serbian control or been paralyzed, the Lisbon "formula" for Bosnia-Herzegovina might have received a warmer reception from the Serbian assembly.

Be this as it may, the terrorist actions of the Serbs were a blunt warning aimed at dissuading the Bosnian government from declaring independence prior to the end of negotiations with the EC. If this was the intent of the Serbian Democratic Party, it failed, for on 3 March Izetbegović declared Bosnia-Herzegovina independent. On 6 March, the same day a large rally for peace was held in Sarajevo, Karadžić made a call for an army takeover, and warned that if the EC were to recognize Bosnia-Herzegovina before it transformed, there would be civil war.[62] The army refused—just as it had turned down the offer of the Milošević forces to take power in Yugoslavia on 9 March the previous year.

It was against this backdrop that the meeting of the conference on Bosnia took place in Brussels over the weekend of 8–9 March, and that the EC met on 10 March, amid some confusion, to issue a joint declaration with the United States reiterating the Western position against threats to the integrity of Bosnia-Herzegovina, but delaying recognition.[63] The meeting of the Conference on Bosnia at Villa Konak on 18 March was, as we have seen, unable to reach agreement over the boundaries of the national units. This meeting was followed by another session of the conference (its sixth), on 31 March in Brussels, which proved equally futile.

Meanwhile, during the month of March, all three national camps prepared for war. Fighting broke out in the Croatian area of Bosanska Posavina in the city of Bosanski Brod in the middle of March. The conflict then spread to Herzegovina, where Croatian forces engaged the army and Serbian reservists in the area of Mostar. The first engagement of Serbian forces on any scale occurred in Bijeljina around 1 April, when what started as a local dispute between extremist Serbs and Muslims sparked the intervention of the forces of the Serbian Guard, under the command of Željko Raznjatović (Arkan).[64] This first phase of the struggle was characterized by the breakdown of law and order, the takeover of power throughout the republic by the national parties and their "crisis staffs" (krizni stabovi), and local struggles between Serbs and Croatians in anticipation of major battles to come.

By 6 April, when the EC granted recognition (followed by the US the next day), Bosnia-Herzegovina was on the brink of full-scale war, and panic had seized the population.[65] Western hopes that recognition would head off the civil war had clearly not been realized. Under these conditions, recognition became gamble, a move which would hopefully bolster the Sarajevo government and deter the Serbian extremists.[66] In the event, recognition did not halt the fighting, but precipitated (or at least was coterminous with) a full scale attack on Muslim areas of Eastern Bosnia by Serbian irregulars, Arkan's national guard, and Yugoslav army reservists from Serbia. Fighting broke out in Sarajevo on 7 April, and on 8 April the Yugoslav army entered the fray. Instead of slowing or halting the war, as in Croatia, recognition had apparently accelerated the pace of Bosnia's decline and destruction. The Bosnian crisis had become the Bosnian tragedy.

Shared Responsibility

At this point it is necessary to take a step back and to comment on the role of the main actors in the drama, closing with some comments on what form a solution to the problem of Bosnia might take, if it is agreed that the present state of affairs must not be allowed to continue.

The Bosnian Crisis in 1992

First, it is appropriate to comment on Izetbegović's role in the crisis. It is apparent from this account that Izetbegović was not without blame for what transpired. From the beginning, he pushed for the creation of a sovereign, "civil" Bosnian state, utilizing his not inconsiderable influence in the West to gain support for this end. This led him to support the referendum for Bosnian independence, a suicidal policy, given the conditions that prevailed in Bosnia in the spring of 1992. Furthermore, Izetbegović was not concerned with working by consensus, despite his reputation as a politician skilled at compromise. While his optimism that war would not come to Bosnia was calculated to soothe tensions, Izetbegović at times seemed to misread the situation badly. (For example, in an interview with *Der Spiegel* in January, he predicted that the Serbs were exhausted from the civil war with Croatia, and would have to return Vukovar and Baranja to Croatia.)[67]

Yet one cannot, for these reasons, lay the responsibility for the civil war on Izetbegović's shoulders. While the Serbs were justified in complaining that the Bosnian government failed to act by consensus, the Serbian resort to violence was a gross violation of that very same principle. Karadžić needed only the flimsiest of excuses to go to war, and was determined to divide and polarize Bosnian society into warring national communities, a situation which he apparently thought would work to the Serbian advantage. Whether Izetbegović could have achieved more by adopting a more conciliatory attitude toward the Serbs is therefore an open question.

The Serbs, for their part, stated clearly and unequivocally that they would go to war if Bosnia declared its independence prior to restructuring, which in effect meant the creation of Serbian, Muslim and Croatian states within the old republic's boundaries. (We have seen that there was disagreement over whether to accept the Brussel's accords within the Serbian camp, in mid-March; yet there was no sign that Karadžić was committed to accepting the Lisbon formula, subsequent claims to the contrary notwithstanding.) This stand was perfectly in keeping with the Serbian position that they would not allow themselves to be treated as a "minority" in Bosnia.

On the other hand, it is unclear what role Karadžić played in the events which led to the emergence and spread of the civil war in March. The attempted coup in Sarajevo was clearly his affair; but the fighting that followed began in a a number of different areas, and was, as we have seen, not at first the work of the Belgrade government.

It is also unclear whether the Serbian incursions into Bosnia after 6 April were premeditated, or a response to Croatian moves and the general disintegration that was taking place in Bosnia at the time (although the former seems more likely). In the last analysis, it is not certain that Milošević wanted the war to break out when it did. Unlike the situation in December, when he was able to negotiate a cease-fire in Croatia, Milošević was not in full control of events in Bosnia. Paradoxically, the army proved to be a serious obstacle to the gameplan Milošević and Karadžić had worked out for the dismantling of the Sarajevo government in early March. Throughout March, the army acted as a damper on the fighting in Sarajevo. Unfortunately, this only shifted the scene of the fighting to the rural areas, where Serbian forces from Eastern Herzegovina and Bosanska Krajina took the offensive, joining in the siege of Sarajevo in the first week in April, now with the support of the army.

The Serbian role in precipitating the civil war is beyond dispute. The attitude of Karadžić, supported by Milošević, was throughout that of a reckless, violent man, who came to believe his own propaganda about the danger that Bosnia-Herzegovina was facing Islamization under Izetbegović, a claim for which there is no evidence in the record of the period from 1990 to the spring of 1991. Indeed, the constant harping by the Serbs on Izetbegović's 1970 work, *The Islamic Declaration*, was a tacit admission that no better evidence for the Islamization of Bosnia-Herzegovina was at hand.

There is less to say about the role of the Croats and the Croatian Democratic Union in Bosnia-Herzegovina, simply because it was the Croatian policy to keep a low profile during the disputes over the future of Bosnia. The triumph of the radical (Herzegovinan) wing of the Croatian Democratic Union in the spring of 1992 has been noted. The initially favorable reception of the Croatians to the Lisbon and Villa Konak proposals for restructuring Bosnia was replaced, toward the end of March, by a hard line, evident when Miljenko Brkic repudiated the EC "Konak" map, insisting that the borders between the three national units would have to be drawn on the basis of the 1961 census.[68] It became abundantly clear that the Croats had lost interest in an independent Bosnia when they struck the first blows in the civil war, in the middle of March, and subsequently, when they agreed to partition most of Bosnia-Herzegovina with the Serbs, in the Graz accords of May.[69] One can only add that the motives of the hard-line Croatians (not the moderates, like Kljuić) were essentially no different from those of the Serb radicals, with the difference that the Croats had to give some consideration to the need for a central government in Sarajevo, for reasons suggested earlier.

Finally, some observations are in order on the role of the international community in bringing about the crisis in Bosnia. A common argument in Belgrade, after all, is that recognition of Bosnia by the EC and the United States was mistakenly made before the negotiations over Bosnia had been completed, thus precipitating the civil war. The Western press has made the same criticism of the recognition decision.[70]

There is a great deal of truth to this charge in one sense: with the best of intentions, the negotiations conducted by Cutilheiro were not handled well. It is difficult to know who was at fault: the EC, which seemed more inter-

The Bosnian Crisis in 1992 173

ested in the appearance rather than the reality of agreement, or the Yugoslav participants, with their constant dissimulating. One had the strong impression that the EC was inhabiting one world, the delegates of the national parties from Bosnia, another.

As an example, one can point to the Brussels negotiations of 31 March, when the three delegations from Bosnia declared that they were in complete agreement with the Villa Konak agreements which they had been busily denouncing several days earlier. The expert commission set up at Brussels to determine the final boundaries of the national units was then instructed to report back to the conference on 15 May—six weeks—as fighting was breaking out all over Bosnia! [71]

Furthermore, the EC negotiators seemed slow to grasp that the central issue was territory—where the boundaries of the national units would be drawn. Perhaps because the issue of regional boundaries was so intractable (and because Izetbegović would not tolerate a discussion of the issue), the problem of boundaries kept being put off. The first maps demarcating national boundaries within Bosnia were circulated, it appears, at the Villa Konak meeting at the end of February. The map drawn up by the EC negotiators on 18 March was apparently handed out to the press before getting the reaction of the national parties, setting the stage for a wholesale attack on the EC plan in the weeks that followed.

The absence of any agreement on where the regional boundaries were to be drawn in turn gave the green light to Serbs to push ahead with their claims to over half the territory of Bosnia. This fact may explain the despair felt by Izetbegović at the Lisbon meetings 22–23 February, since in lieu of an agreement over the boundaries of the national units, consenting even in principle to the regionalization of Bosnia was an extremely dangerous move, opening the door for a deal between the Croats and Serbs to divide up Bosnia-Herzegovina at the expense of the Muslims.

On the other hand, it is misleading to suggest that the EC and the US, simply by recognizing Bosnia, ignited the Bosnian civil war, as is implied in those accounts critical of the EC's actions. This is true for three reasons. First, there was no indication, prior to recognition in April, that the three national parties were near agreement on where the boundaries of their respective national units were to be drawn. (Making recognition conditional upon such an agreement, furthermore, while it might have spurred the Muslims and Croats to compromise, would have had precisely the opposite effect on the Serbs.) Second, by the middle of March, the radical (rural) factions of the Serbian Democratic Party were in control, and Belgrade seemed unwilling, or unable, to place pressure on them, as it had in dealing with Milan Babić in the Serbian Republic of Krajina (in Croatia) in December.

Third, by the beginning of April, Bosnia was already at war. While it is

174   *Paul Shoup*

true that the major incursions from Serbia came a few days after 7 April, it must be remembered that the local conflicts which began as early as the middle of March had important strategic ramifications, especially in respect to the ability of the Serb autonomous regions to link up in a common front against the Croatians and Muslims. Once the war broke out, Belgrade's intervention was just a matter of time. It might have come sooner but for the desire on the Serbian side to give the appearance of being provoked into action by the EC decision on recognition.

What is often overlooked in the debate over recognition is that by 6 April the situation in Bosnia had deteriorated to the point that the EC *had* to act. Failing to recognize the Sarajevo government at this point would have given the green light to violence and anarchy, for which the EC would certainly have been held responsible. Recognition was granted Bosnia not because it was a state, in the legal sense, but because it was fast losing all the attributes of a state; not because Bosnia was stable, but because it was weak and fragmenting. And the EC had no other means at its disposal to prop it up.

Mistakes by the West

An argument can be made, thus, that the recognition of Bosnia should have been approached differently by the EC and the United States. To make the case requires that we look at the Bosnian problem in its entirety.

If the goal of Western policy was to preserve an independent Bosnia-Herzegovina, the means were, in their totality, self-defeating. The Western powers did not take the utterances of the Serbs seriously enough—that is, at their face value. At times, it seemed that the West did not even understand what the Serbs were saying about the need for consensual decision-making, restructuring of the Bosnian government, and the importance of the territorial issue.

This was already obvious in the approach taken by the Badinter Commission to the issue of the recognition of Bosnia-Herzegovina The objections to the recognition of Bosnia-Herzegovina submitted to the EC by the Serbian government were acknowledged but dismissed by the commission with the assurance that the Serbs would be guaranteed their national and cultural rights. Having offered the Serbs this assurance, the Commission suggested that Bosnia-Herzegovina could be recognized if she were to carry out a referendum, and if the results would confirm that the majority of the population favored independence. The suggestion that all three nationalities should give their approval before Bosnia-Herzegovina declared independence was rejected, in effect, perhaps because international law provided no precedent for making recognition dependent upon the

The Bosnian Crisis in 1992

175

consent of any but the majority nationality.

Indeed, how and where the Badinter Commission hit upon the notion of a referendum is something of a mystery. Perhaps Izetbegović planted the idea in the minds of the EC officials, who passed it on to the commission. It is interesting to note, in this connection, that the Serbian reply to the original EC decision of 17 December, which contested the conditions laid down for recognition by the EC, placed emphasis on the right of self-determination of nations (not republics), and pointed to the referenda that had been held in the two Krajina in support of this principle. One suspects that the Badinter Commission, unversed in the affairs of the Balkans but sensitive to legal arguments (and with hardly enough time to read anything but the briefs placed before it by the republics), may have concluded that a referendum in Bosnia would satisfy the Serbian government or at least counter Belgrade's arguments about the right of the Serbs outside Serbia to national self-determination. All speculation aside, it is important to emphasize that the Badinter Commission's insistence on the holding of a referendum, without specifying that it be approved by each of the three nationalities, pushed the republic further toward civil war.

If, however, the West was mistaken in pushing for Bosnian independence—assuming that we are right that such a move was bound to provoke the Serbs—what might have the West done to preserve Bosnia-Herzegovina? It must be admitted that there is no obvious answer to this question.

The solution did not lie in withholding recognition from all the republics until a peace settlement was reached. This approach was tried and failed during the period September—November 1991, when the Yugoslav peace conference was attempting to end the civil war in Croatia. While there are many reasons why the peace conference on Yugoslavia failed, one contributing factor was the virtual absence of any discussion of the question of altering republic borders. At the time, and perhaps properly so, such a discussion was seen as complicating the peace talks, and possibly delaying recognition of Croatia and Slovenia, as well as being against the spirit and letter of the CSCE principles to which the EC was bound.

Nor did it seem that raising the issue of drawing dividing lines among the ethnic groups in Bosnia-Herzegovina would serve any other purpose but to complicate matters immensely, and invite the partition of Bosnia-Herzegovina. One can assume that Vance argued this position, as well as the US ambassador, Warren Zimmerman, in discussions with Serbian and Bosnian leaders.

Yet with the benefit of hindsight one can suggest that the key to avoiding a civil war in Bosnia-Herzegovina was to have acknowledged that the republic had become fragmented into national regions by the spring of 1992, and that Bosnia-Herzegovina could not be saved unless an agreement could be reached over where these borders were to be drawn. Understandably, the EC was reluctant to raise the issue of ethnic regions. The disappointment, even bitterness, of the Party of Democratic Action and the opposition parties over the Lisbon accords is also easy to grasp. Be this as it may, at some point the negotiations over Bosnia-Herzegovina had to take into account the fact that the partition of Bosnia-Herzegovina was already well underway. The error, it would seem in hindsight, was not to draw the necessary conclusions and focus the negotiations on where the boundaries of these national regions would lie (as well as their number), before the matter was taken into the hands of the Croatian Defense League (Paraga's paramilitary force), the Serbian National Guard, and local nationalists with visions of grandeur and scores to settle.

The events surrounding the Bosnian tragedy will be long debated. As documents become available, it may be possible to provide answers to the many questions raised in this essay. One would like to know more about Serbian intentions, and whether the existence of operation "RAM" meant that the Serbs were, from the first, bent on the forceful partition of Bosnia-Herzegovina. Much remains unclear about the role of the army in blocking Serbian moves to stage a coup in March. Not enough is known about the strength of those within the Serbian community who were opposed to the partition of Bosnia-Herzegovina.

Still, the major events surrounding the outbreak of the civil war are known. The difficulties that must be overcome if Bosnia-Herzegovina is to resolve her present crisis are also painfully evident. In the remainder of this chapter, I propose to consider the options that have been debated as means of ending the crisis. The first issue is whether Bosnia-Herzegovina should be divided along ethnic lines (cantonization), or restructured along regional lines, relying on economic and other criteria to determine where provincial boundaries should be drawn.

The debate over regionalization or cantonization of Bosnia-Herzegovina goes back to the time of the formation of the Serbian Autonomous Regions in the fall of 1991. It was renewed at the London Conference on Yugoslavia in August 1992 when the U.S. delegation charged that the cantonization of Bosnia-Herzegovina was a cover for Serbian aggression.[72] This position was reiterated by UN spokesperson at the follow-up conference on Bosnia-Herzegovina in Geneva in September 1992, when cantonization was ruled out as one of the alternatives for a solution of the Bosnian question.[73] The Serbian side, for its part, remained wedded to the idea of cantonization, although frequently issuing contradictory statements about where the boundaries of the cantons were to be drawn.

The government of Bosnia-Herzegovina, for its part has insisted on the restructuring of the republic along regional lines. This has also been the

The Bosnian Crisis in 1992   177

position of the intellectuals in Sarajevo who have decried the parcelization
and ethnicization of Bosnia-Herzegovina. A study on Bosnia-Herzegovina
prepared by the Belgrade-based Ethnic Forum, a group which has been
attempting to bridge national differences in Yugoslavia, recommended creating natural regions in Bosnia-Herzegovina which would take into account economic and historical factors, as well as the ethnic composition of
the population. According to this plan, the republic boundaries would be
preserved and the Bosnian government in Sarajevo would retain sufficient
powers to govern Bosnia-Herzegovina, rather than serving as a figleaf for
independent Serbian, Croatian, and Muslim states.[74]

There are a number of reasons for arguing that Bosnia-Herzegovina
should be divided into natural regions rather than cantons. First, it is a
solution which avoids creating ethnically-based territorial units in areas
where the indigenous population (those in the majority before the civil
war began) has been driven out. For example, "cantonization" of the formerly Muslim inhabited regions in northeast Bosnia would seem to require the creation of a Muslim region in an area where the Muslims are no
longer present, and may be slow to return. Serbs would have to surrender
the area to Muslims, or claim the canton as "Serbian," an unacceptable
solution in the light of the manner in which Muslims were driven from the
area. More or less the same problem, if in less acute form, would emerge in
other regions where the population balance has been altered by policies of
"ethnic cleansing."

Second, regionalization would make possible the creation of a central
government organized along federal lines. Under plans for cantonization,
on the other hand, a central government would be the captive of the ethnic
parties and governments. Such a situation could prolong the anarchy and
eventually lead to the *de facto* partition of Bosnia-Herzegovina between
Croatia and Serbia.

Finally, and perhaps most important, the regional formula provides a
mechanism for weakening the hold of the national extremists in Bosnia-
Herzegovina. Unless steps are taken to undercut the power base of these
groups (and the best way to begin, it could be argued, is through organization of the internal administrative boundaries of the republic along non-
ethnic lines) there can be no democracy in Bosnia-Herzegovina, and the
anarchy and excesses of ethnic strife will continue. To state the argument
in another way, a long-term solution to the Bosnian question involves a set
of mutually reenforcing policies: preservation of the republic's boundaries;
breaking up the territorial power base of the ethnic extremists; demilitarization; protecting the rights of nationalities in areas where they are a minority; democratization; and the return to law and order. These steps should
culminate with free elections which are not dominated by the extremists.
All this could be summed up under the rubric "DDI"—Demilitarization,

Democratization, and International Guarantees. If a peace settlement for Bosnia-Herzegovina were to adopt a scheme of ethnic cantons, it would appear that these goals would be placed in jeopardy.

The case for cantonization, on the other hand, rests first and foremost on the argument that—as this essay has suggested—the civil war in Bosnia-Herzegovina is being fought for territory and therefore must take the territorial interests of the parties to the conflict into account; that the boundaries of regions or cantons in Bosnia-Herzegovina, in lieu of foreign intervention, will have to be established by negotiations among the national leaders themselves; and that in the last analysis, the borders of the territorial units established in Bosnia-Herzegovina will be based primarily on ethnic criteria, rather than economic or other considerations, regardless of what these units may be called (regions, cantons, provinces). The primary objective of a peace conference on Bosnia-Herzegovina, according to this argument, is to gain equitable borders for each of the three ethnic groups, and thereby anchor the regional structures of Bosnia-Herzegovina in the territorial imperatives which have motivated the Serbian and Croatian—if not the Muslim—actors in this Balkan tragedy. The role of the international community, in this case, would be to assure that an emergent Muslim republic had sufficient territory to survive as an independent state under UN protection.

Conclusion

Writing at a time when the civil war is still raging, it is difficult to know whether either of these two proposed solutions could be realized in practice. It would appear that the temptation will be great to "meld" the two— to try to create a Bosnia-Herzegovina divided into regions with features of ethnic cantons, while at the same time trying to create a viable government for Bosnia-Herzegovina along federal lines. Such an approach—which was that suggested by the Conference on Bosnia-Herzegovina in its proposals at Lisbon and Brussels in the spring of 1992—would seem bound to fail, if only because it would repeat the formula which proved unworkable in the case of Yugoslavia. If the Bosnian state is to play a significant role in the future, it must rest on a solid foundation. Cantons—or cantons masked as regions—would look to the outside for support (this would be true of a Muslim canton as well). They would almost certainly oppose efforts to create a common currency, police force, or army under federal control. In brief, strong and stable central government and even a modified form of ethnic regionalization are likely to prove incompatible.

The problems just alluded to were apparent when the International Conference on Former Yugoslavia (ICFY) convened in September of 1992,

The Bosnian Crisis in 1992

under United Nations and European Community sponsorship. Under the leadership of its two co-chairman, Lord Owen and Cyrus Vance, the conference produced a proposal for a solution to the Bosnian crisis which was put before the warring parties the end of January 1993. The plan called for the creation of 10 provinces, a highly decentralized governmental structure which would vest all effective power in the provinces, and the demilitarization of the republic.[75] Without elements of an international force capable of implementing the agreement, the Vance-Owen plan would seem to have invited further civil war among the provinces, which would have received a designation as either Serbian, Croatian or Muslim, and to which the armies of the respective sides would have retreated, prior to their disarming. Mate Boban, representing the Croatian Democratic Union, agreed to the plan; neither Karadžić or Izetbegović accepted it, the latter on constitutional grounds; the former because of differences over the drawing of the boundaries of the provinces which would have been considered Serbian.

In the last analysis, the choice between different methods of restructuring Bosnia-Herzegovina hinges on the willingness of the international community to play a major role in support of a Bosnian government regardless of how the territorial units are formed. It is on the role of the international community, and its future in resolving the conflict in Bosnia-Herzegovina, that I propose to end this chapter.

The role of the international community and the West in the conflict seems to confirm the adage that the road to hell is paved with good intentions. By recognizing Bosnia-Herzegovina in order to save it, the United States and the EC helped to create the present tragic situation, and then to sustain it. This is true in two respects: first, the West failed to grasp that the Serbs would refuse to accept the independence of Bosnia-Herzegovina without going to war.[76] This was not an error committed by a single government, or even only by the EC, whose record in handling the Yugoslav crisis was generally spotty. Rather, this tragic oversight was committed by politicians of the entire international community—a puzzle for future historians to explain.

Second, the West, by insisting on the sanctity of the borders of Bosnia-Herzegovina, ruled out direct intervention by Croatia and Serbia. While this was laudable in one sense—it may have prevented a war between the two countries—the policy left the field open to local forces responsible to no one, although heavily armed by both Serbia and Croatia. What resulted was the worst of all possible worlds. Unwittingly, Western governments created a situation in which the most extreme nationalist elements in Bosnia-Herzegovina were free to act at will, since the Bosnian government was too weak to enforce its rule, Serbian and Croatian governments were barred from entering the fray, and the West, after much agonizing, declined to undertake military intervention.

180   *Paul Shoup*

This is not to accuse the West of creating the Bosnian tragedy or trying to exploit it for selfish ends, as those nationalists—both Serbian and Croatian—who criticize the West's "new order" assert. Rather, it would seem, the basic miscalculation of the West was to rely on the peaceful settlement of ethnic disputes in a region where the resort to violence was not only a tradition, but appeared, in the short term, to pay off handsomely. It was the inability of the West, prior to the imposition of sanctions on Serbia, to develop a method to make violence counter-productive, that was at the root of the West's failure to deal with the Bosnian situation. Even the sanctions could prove counter-productive if they should lead to the spread of the civil war to Serbia and thence to Kosovo, a strong possibility in light of the rapid decline in living standards in Serbia and the failure of both Serbia and the West to resolve their differences over Bosnia-Herzegovina.

Meanwhile, the resolution of the Bosnian tragedy will not be accomplished without the presence of a stabilizing force from outside the area. This is the basic lesson of the history of the region. This in turn suggests, as argued above, that the crucial variable in the future of the Bosnian question is the degree of international supervision and control exercised over Bosnia-Herzegovina. Without an international presence it is doubtful that peace can come to the region. At a minimum, it would appear, Sarajevo must be placed under international control[77], and it may be that other regions of Bosnia-Herzegovina should receive protectorate status as well.[78] This would be a step toward saving Bosnia-Herzegovina for which the urban intellectuals of Sarajevo have pleaded and fought. In the absence of such intervention, the future of the republic looks dark, and peace might be best assured by outright partition between Serbia, Croatia and a Muslim state with its capital in Sarajevo, or at least the "pealing off" of areas from the republic which are Croatian or Serbian and contiguous to Croatia and Serbia, respectively. Since the future of a peaceful Europe is at stake, the commitment of international forces to the region, in an effort to reconstruct Bosnia-Herzegovina, would not seem too great a price to pay.

With hindsight, it is likely that the outbreak of the civil war in Bosnia-Herzegovina will be considered one of two major turning points in the disintegration of Yugoslavia (the first being the secession of Slovenia). Even as the civil war raged in Croatia, it was possible to hope for an outcome which would permit the Yugoslav republics to emerge essentially unscathed, each independent, and still linked by economic and other ties. The fact that civil war was avoided in Bosnia-Herzegovina even as the violence spread to Dubrovnik and other parts of Croatia gave reason to hope for this relatively favorable resolution of the crisis resulting from the breakup of Yugoslavia. The descent of Bosnia-Herzegovina into civil war and anarchy during the spring of 1992 dashed such hopes, leaving it profoundly unclear what fate awaits the former Yugoslav republics. The out-

The Bosnian Crisis in 1992

181

look appears especially grim if it proves impossible to establish an international protectorate over all or part of Bosnia-Herzegovina, and lift the sanctions against Serbia.

Ideal solutions may not be possible, for as this chapter is being completed, time would appear to be running out. If the war continues in Bosnia-Herzegovina, and Serbia fragments under the impact of sanctions, all the Balkans may be in flames. The alternative would seem to be either a massive international commitment to reconstruct Bosnia-Herzegovina along non-ethnic lines, or a quick and dirty solution focusing on drawing up cantonal boundaries, backed up by steps to demilitarize the region, reintroduce law and order, and encourage democracy, assuming such steps are possible in the lawless and brutal world of the new ethnic homelands which have been formed in Bosnia-Herzegovina. It is a grim picture, although still not a completely hopeless one, if the international community, and especially the West, is willing to take on the responsibilities for finding a way out of the crisis for which they are in part responsible.

Notes

1. The author would like to acknowledge the support of the Council for Soviet and East European Research in carrying out the research on this paper, and to express his thanks to Radio Free Europe, which put its facilities at his disposal.

2. In the 1948 census, Muslim Slavs were identified as Muslim-Serb, Croat, or Unspecified; in 1953, as "Muslims unspecified," in 1961 "Muslims in the ethnic sense," and in 1971, 1981, and 1991, "Muslims." For the Muslims in Bosnia, see Zachary Irwin, "The Islamic Revival and the Muslims of Bosnia-Herzegovina," in *East European Quarterly*, Vol. 17, No. 4 (January 1984), pp. 437–58 and Irena Reuter-Hendrichs, "Jugoslawiens Muslime,"in *Südost Europa Mitteilungen*, Vol 29, No. 2 (1989), pp. 105–115.

3. Bogoljub Kocović, *Žrtve drugog svetskog rata u Jugoslaviji* (London: Naše delo, 1985), p. 143. The *Enciklopedija Jugoslavije*, Vol. 2, p. 35, gives the number of Muslims in Bosnia-Herzegovina as follows: 1910 - 606,306 (31.9 percent); 1921 - 587,316 (31.1 percent); 1948 - 788,403 (30.7 percent).

4. "The National Composition of Yugoslavia's Population, 1991," in *Yugoslav Survey* (Belgrade), Vol. 33 (1992), No. 1, p. 4.

5. The Croatian preference for the 1961 census may lie in the fact that, as in the 1971 census, no count was taken of religion, but unlike the 1971 census, Muslims were not considered a nationality.

6. Serb claims to over 60 percent of the territory of Bosnia-Herzegovina are based on these settlement maps, whose nature has been the source of considerable confusion. Some sources have attributed these maps to Serb claims to land *owned* by Serbs. The proper explanation appears to be that these maps are based on the ethnic composition of subdivisions of districts called "cadastral opštinas," whose boundaries were established over time on the basis of landowning patterns. Em-

182

Paul Shoup

ploying these smaller units on balance probably renders a more accurate picture of which nationality is in the majority in any given part of the republic, but obvio sly works to the disadvantage of the Muslims if a balance between territory and population is one's measure of ethnic equality when drawing boundaries. For a professionally prepared map of the distribution of the nationalities of Bosnia and Herzegovina according to cadastral opštinas, see David Atlagić (ed.), *Bosna i Hercegovina: Ogledalo razuma* (Belgrade: Borba, 1992), insert.

7. In 1981, 326,280 persons, or 7.9 percent of the population of the republic, declared themselves Yugoslavs; in 1991, 239,845, or 5.5 percent, a decline of 26.5 percent. See "National Composition" [note 4], p. 4.

8. Wayne Vucinich, "Yugoslavs of Moslem Faith," in R. J. Kerner (ed.), *Yugoslavia* (Berkeley: University of California Press, 1949), chapter 15, esp. p. 271.

9. For the election results, see John B. Allcock, "Yugoslavia," in Bogdan Szajkowski (ed.), *New Political Parties of Eastern Europe and The Soviet Union* (Harlow: Longman Group, 1991), pp. 311–319.

10. Milan Andrejevich, "Moslem Leader Elected President of Bosnia and Herzegovina," in *Radio Free Europe, Report on Eastern Europe* (18 January 1991), pp. 30–34. Note also by the same author, "Bosnia-Herzegovina: Yugoslavia's Linchpin," in *Ibid.*, 7 December 1990, pp. 20-27; "The Future of Bosnia-Herzegovina: A Sovereign Republic or Cantonization," in *Ibid.*, 5 July 1991, pp. 28-34; "Bosnia and Herzegovina Moves toward Independence," in *Ibid.*, 25 October 1991, pp. 22-26; and "Bosnia and Herzegovina: A Precarious Peace," in *Ibid.*, 28 February 1992, pp. 6-14.

11. For a negative assessment of the work of the government of Bosnia, stressing the absence of cooperation among the national parties, see Mensur Camo, "Saz, gusle, tamburica," in *Nedjelja* (Sarajevo), 24 November 1991, pp. 11–12. According to one critic, Jure Pelivan only appeared three times before parliament after his appointment and late November 1991. See Zdravka Latal, "Politička kriza—ekonomska katastrofa," in *Nedjelja*, 24 November 1991, p. 13.

12. For the work of RTSA and its director, Nenad Pejić, see *Vreme* (Belgrade), 13 April 1992, pp. 8–9. Note that every day RTSA broadcast three news programs on TV: Croatian HTV; Serbian TVS; Yutel, and of course, RTSA news.

13. For a biting critique of the system by one of the leaders of the opposition Muslim Bosniak Organization, see the interview with Professor Muhamed Filipović, "Alija je zakasnio," *Nedjeljna Dalmacija* (Split), 30 January 1992, p. 6.

14. *Ibid.*

15. A Serbian National Council was formed in October 1990, and a "Regional Community of Communes" in Bosanska Krajina in April of 1991. See *Borba* (Belgrade), 15 April 1991, p. 5.

16. Izetbegović met with Tudjman, Milošević, Bulatović and Kučan in the spring of 1991 to persuade them of his plan for a loose union of the republics, the "Yugoslav state community." In early February, Izetbegović had talks with Kučan in Sarajevo which produced agreement over principles of self-determination and sovereignty for the republics. This agreement appears to have contemplated some elements of an "asymmetric federation," which would have made his plan for a Yugoslav state community more acceptable to Karadžić. All this appeared to be encouraging to Karadžić, whose interview with *Borba*, 26 February 1991, was remarkably tolerant toward Izetbegović, although also containing references to the creation of a greater

Serbia. The notion of an asymmetric federation met with shock and consternation among the ranks of the SDA and other Muslim politicians, however. For this issue, see Foreign Broadcast Information Service *Daily Report* (Eastern Europe), for February 1991 and especially Karadžić interview in *Borba* (26 February 1991), translated in FBIS, *Daily Report* (Eastern Europe), 6 March 1991, p. 54. Izetbegović's scheme for a Yugoslav state community was modified, becoming more "confederal" with the passing months; the final version, presented as a joint proposal of Izetbegović and Macedonian President Kiro Gligorov, called for an "alliance" of the republics which would have some characteristics of a state community.

17. Tanjug Domestic Service, 21 February 1991, translated in FBIS, *Daily Report* (Eastern Europe), 22 February 1991, p. 45.

18. For operation RAM, see *Vreme*, 30 September 1991, pp. 4–5, which gave excerpts of a taped conversation between Milošević and Karadžić, giving the impression that the two were closely coordinating the arming of the Serbs. *Vreme* claimed that confidential sources had revealed that operation RAM was a plan for redrawing the Western boundaries of Serbia so that all Serbs could live in one state. Whether RAM served as a blueprint for Serbian actions in Bosnia-Herzegovina is unclear; Serb plans for the the creation of a Greater Serbia, evident in August and September, were scaled back as the civil war in Croatia dragged on.

19. For analyses of the Bosnian situation in the fall of 1991, see "Drina bez Ćuprije," in *Vreme*, 21 October 1991, pp. 20–25, and Tihomir Loza, "Igra Živača," in *Nedjelja*, 24 November 1991, pp. 14–15.

20. The Serbian Autonomous Area, of Eastern and Old Herzegovina was founded on 12 September, followed by the Serbian Autonomous Area of Bosanska Krajina on 16 September, the Serbian Autonomous Area of Romanija on 18 September, and the Serbian Autonomous Area of Northeastern Bosnia on 20 September. Andrejevich, "Bosnia and Herzegovina moves toward . . . " [note 10], p. 25. The Croatian region of Herceg-Bosna was established later in the fall.

21. Radio Sarajevo quoted Karadžić to the effect that the Serbs would not consent to leave Yugoslavia, and that "Do not think that you will not lead Bosnia-Herzegovina into hell, and do not think that you will perhaps lead the Muslim people into annihilation, because the Muslim people cannot defend themselves if there is war . . . How will you prevent everyone from being killed in Bosnia-Herzegovina?" Radio Sarajevo, 14 October 1991, translated in FBIS, *Daily Report* (Eastern Europe), 16 October 1991, p. 44.

22. Izetbegović replied that "His manner and his messages perhaps explain why others also refuse to stay in such a Yugoslavia. Nobody else wants the kind of Yugoslavia that Mr Karadžić wants any more, no one except perhaps the Serbian people. Such a Yugoslavia and such a manner of Karadžić are simply hated by the people of Yugoslavia...and I then say to the people of Bosnia-Herzegovina that there will not be war, that is my prediction based on the facts, on some confirmed facts. Therefore sleep peacefully, there is no need to fear, because it takes two to tango." *Ibid.*

23. For a good account of the referendum, see Nedim Šarac and Tihomir Loza, "Zabranićemo otcjepljenje," in *Nedjelja* (17 November 1991), pp. 12–14. Three different ballots were available, one of them a yellow ballot for non-Serbs. The yellow ballot used for non-Serbs asked if the voter wished Bosnia to remain in Yugoslavia;

184   Paul Shoup

the ballots for Serbs, whether the Serbian people wished to remain in Yugoslavia, suggesting that the Serbs were prepared to secede from Bosnia-Herzegovina. The article notes the threats of Radoslav Brdjanin, Vice-President of the AR Bosanska Krajina, that all directors in Bosanska Krajina who did not vote would lose their jobs.

24. *Nedjelja* (24 November 1991), p. 13.

25. On 15 October, Izetbegović and General Kadijević, Minister of Defense, met in Sarajevo, immediately after the crisis occasioned by the adoption of the sovereignty declaration. They pledged that they would attempt to keep the war from spreading to Bosnia. See Andrejevich, "Bosnia and Herzegovina moves toward . . ." [note 10], p. 24.

26. "Drina bez Ćuprije" [note 19]; and "Igra Živača" [note 19].

27. *Nedjelja* (22 December 1991), p. 9.

28. In fact, the army's behavior was at times hard to fathom. Under Operation RAM the army was distributing weapons to Serbian irregulars. At the same time, it is known that the army was attempting to get back weapons stolen from weapons depots by Serbian recruits.

29. *Vjesnik* (Zagreb), 27 December 1991.

30. Joint patrols operated in the fall of 1991, and were again set up in Sarajevo after the 2 March events described below, functioning until the outbreak of fighting in Sarajevo in April.

31. For an analysis of the negotiations, which involved the Muslim Bosnjak Organization and Belgrade, see *Danas* (Zagreb), 13 August 1991, pp. 28–29. According to this account, Izetbegović participated in some of the discussions, but later repudiated them after knowledge of the talks became known. On this occasion it was the turn of the Croats to feel left out, and Kljuić threatened an armed rebellion if the talks were not carried out through government channels.

32. *Danas* (16 July 1991), trans. in FBIS, *Daily Report* (Eastern Europe), 13 February 1992, p. 55.

33. See Željko Vuković, "Da li su Tudjman i Milošević delili BiH," in *Vreme* (10 June 1991), pp. 22–23.

34. *Borba* (23 December 1991), pp 1–2.

35. *Politika* (Belgrade), 17 January 1991, pp. 6–7.

36. *Politika* (18 December 1991), p. 2.

37. *Vjesnik* (25 December 1991), p 8

38. This line was most fully articulated in the conclusions of the convention for a new Yugoslavia, which met in late December in Belgrade. See *Politika* (31 December 1991 and 1–2 January 1992), for the "Conclusions of the Convention for New Yugoslavia."

39. *Borba* (23 December 1991), pp. 1–2.

40. For a good analysis of US policy as this time, see the article by Vladimir Drobnjak, in *Vjesnik* (17 January 1991). Note also *Politika* (30 January 1991), which suggested that the US position made a certain allowance for cantonization prior to recognition.

41. It has been suggested that Tudjman always raised the territorial issue when faced with a loss of territory in Croatia. T. Šutalo, *Borba* (11 February 1992), p. 5. Šutalo cites the example of Herceg-Bosna, formed a day after the loss of Vukovar.

42. *Times* (London), 12 July 1991.

The Bosnian Crisis in 1992

43. According to one account, the participants agreed that Bosnia was a "Turkish creation." See *Nedjelja* (26 January 1992).

44. The plan is described in *Borba* (16 January 1992), p. 8.

45. The wording for the referendum suggested at Livno began as follows: "Should sovereign and independent Bosnia-Herzegovina, a state community of its constituent and sovereign nations, Croatians, Muslims, and Serbs, on their national territories . . ." *Borba* (11 February 1992), p. 5.

46. The struggle against Kljuic was led by Mate Boban and the radicals in the Croatian Democratic Community from Western Herzegovina, especially Jozo Marić, President of the Grude opština. For an excellent account of the Kljuić affair, see *Politika* (5 February 1992), p. 8 by I. Stojković.

47. *Borba* (29 February–1 March 1992), p. 3.

48. The wording of the referendum was as follows: "Are you for a sovereign and independent state of Bosnia and Herzegovina, a state of equal citizens and the peoples of Bosnia-Herzegovina—Muslims, Serbs, Croatians and persons of other nationalities (naroda) who live there?" *Politika* (5 February 1992).

49. *Vjesnik* (27 February 1992), p. 7.

50. Genscher was in Croatia several days before the Lisbon meeting, and Izetbegović met with Eagleburger on 20 February. Carrington met with Milošević on 27 February, after the conference.

51. See *Frankfurter Allgemeine* (24 February 1992).

52. See "Lisabonski teferić," in *Vreme* (2 March 1992).

53. *Borba* (25 February 1992), p. 5.

54. *Slobodni tjednik* (Zagreb), 11 March 1992, p. 9. ST published one version showing seven cantons divided among the three nationalities.

55. *Vjesnik* (12 March 1992). The proposal permitted the constituent units to have ties with neighboring states and a virtual veto power over the actions of the central government, through an upper house which would require 4/5th vote to approve legislation.

56. *Borba* (10 March 1992).

57. *Vjesnik* (13 March 1992), p. 7. While Karadžić said that borders were not a question, it appears that the boundaries of the national regions, or cantons, were not settled at this meeting. *Borba* (7–8 March 1992) reported that Karadžić offered Cutilheiro a map of BH divided into mini-units with "corridors" joining them into some sort of archipelago, which Cutilheiro apparently rejected out of hand.

58. *Borba* (4 March 1992), p.1.

59. The number of Serbs that voted cannot be known, and it may well be that those who favored independence did vote. For the charge that the referendum was marked by pressure against the Serbs by the Serbian Democratic Party to boycott the referendum, see Commission on Security and Cooperation in Europe, US Congress, *The Referendum on Independence in Bosnia-Herzegovina*, 12 March 1992.

60. The events of 2 and 3 March are very well covered in the Western press. See *The Guardian, Frankfurter Allgemeine* and *Süddeutsche Zeitung* (Munich) for 3 and 4 March. Karadžić, speaking on Belgrade TV, said that "I am afraid we cannot avoid an interethnic war on the same scale as the Indo-Pakistan war."

186 Paul Shoup

61. The *Guardian* of 3 March quotes the commander of the Sarajevo military district (this would be General Kukanjac) that what the Serb militants were doing was "sheer madness."

62. *Borba* (6 March 1992), and AP dispatch of this date.

63. See *The Guardian* and the *New York Times* for 11 March 1992.

64. Željko Raznjatović, alias "Arkan," was born in Slovenia to an army colonel. He first built his reputation as one of the best bank robbers in Europe, and he is wanted in Italy in connection with the killing of a restaurant owner. After Croatian authorities released him from prison in September 1991, he formed his own militia to fight in Bosnia. Arkan's incursion into Bosnia was a major factor in escalating tensions, and was accompanied by the reports of the massacre of Muslims, which provoked an agonized appeal from Izetbegović. A list of his victims in Bijeljina is given in *Borba* on 7 April 1992; they are all Muslims.

65. See *Borba* (6 April 1992), "Teror, smrt, anarhija," reads the headline on page 1.

66. See the *Financial Times* for 7 April 1992, which notes the feelings of Joao de Deus Pinhiero, Portugese PM, that EC should not give support to the radicals in the Serbian camp by withholding recognition.

67. *Der Spiegel* (Hamburg), 13 January 1992, p. 124.

68. *Borba* (23 March 1992), p. 7.

69. The agreement was signed on 6 May in Graz by Mate Boban (for the Croatians) and Karadžić for the Serbs. The agreement disingenuously purports to be a spin off of the EC conference, and calls for the rapid reconvening of the conference, while in actual fact providing for the partitioning of Bosnia. Three points in the agreement deal with areas in dispute between the two sides: the region of central Bosnia, around Kupres; Mostar; and the north central region of Bosanska Posavina. See *Novi Vjesnik* (Zagreb), 8 May 1992.

70. See, for example, Viktor Meier's analysis of Western mistakes in dealing with Bosnia, *Frankfurter Allgemeine* (25 April 1992). In earlier dispatches, Meier had favored recognition of Bosnia.

71. The 18 March conference was also something of a fiasco—the final communique was never signed by the three national parties, and an SDA spokesman said later that the party was opposed to the agreement but did not wish to take this stand publicly, for fear that it would be blamed for blocking the accord!

72. This position was put forth by Lawrence Eagleburger, Acting US Secretary of State, and head of the American delegation.

73. *Washington Post* (19 September 1992).

74. Srdjan Bogosavljević et al., *Bosna izmedju rata i mira* (Belgrade: Institut društvenih nauka, 1992).

75. See International Conference on the Former Yugoslavia, *Report of the Co-Chairmen on Progress in Developing a Constitution for Bosnia-Herzegovina*, STC/2/2, 27 October 1992.

76. Whether Serbia misled the West by giving assurances that she would not go to war if the independence of Bosnia-Herzegovina was recognized before the cantonization of the country and a confederal system was established remains unclear. The United States has repeatedly claimed that Milošević lied to it. Whether

The Bosnian Crisis in 1992 187

such charges refer to promises by Milošević to respect the integrity of Bosnia-Herzegovina, or related to other matters (the presence of Serbian troops in Bosnia-Herzegovina, for example) requires further clarification.

77. The case for international administration of Bosnia-Herzegovina is given by Zoran Pajić, in "UN Trusteeship Can Halt Ethnic Ghettoes," in *Yugofax*, No. 11, 7 May 1992, p. 1.

78. Elements of such a solution were proposed by a workshop on peace in Bosnia-Herzegovina which met in Washington D.C., 10-11 February 1993, under the sponsorship of IREX and the Woodrow Wilson Center.

8

Slovenia's Road to Democracy

Sabrina Petra Ramet

I

With less than two million inhabitants and no history of independent statehood in the last millennium, Slovenia seemed to many in the West to be an unlikely candidate for independence. Advocates of large states warned in vain that Slovenia was "too small" to be viable and suggested that if the republic separated from Yugoslavia, it would inevitably find it necessary to join a federal or confederal union with one of its neighbors—whether Austria, Italy, Croatia, or—in the most fanciful rendition—combining with Austria, Hungary, and Croatia to form an entirely new state.

Yet despite all this skepticism, Slovenia, which had been a part of Yugoslavia from 1918 to 1941 and again from 1945 on, declared its independence on 25 June 1991. Almost two years later, Slovenia's economy has been strained by the influx of Bosnian refugees, and recovery has been delayed by the long delay in passing a bill of privatization. That said, Slovenia appears to be roughly in a class with Poland, Hungary, and the Czech Republic in terms of its prospects for carrying out the transition to pluralism successfully.

Slovenia has had several important advantages in this regard. First, Slovenia's per capita social product, while lower than Austria's or Italy's, has nonetheless ranked as the highest in Eastern Europe, more than twice as high, for example, as that in Hungary or Poland. Second, the transition to pluralism was begun by the Slovenian communists themselves, for reasons having nothing to do with broader processes in Eastern Europe. Indeed, for reasons quite specific to Slovenia, pluralization was undertaken (in the late 1980s) by the local communists and local dissidents jointly and cooperatively. Third, the population of Slovenia remains, despite the recent immigration of people from other parts of then-Yugoslavia, largely homogeneous: about 90 percent of the population is Slovenian. Fourth, none of Slovenia's neighbors has either active or inactive claims on its territory. Compared to the uncertainties associated with most of the rest of ex-Yugoslavia, let alone Transylvania, Sub-Carpathian Ruthenia, and the Kaliningrad district, there is little to trouble Slovenian authorities here. Their most difficult "border" problem has related to free access to the sea through Croatian territorial waters—a problem which might be resolved by trading some territory west of Zagreb in exchange for Cape Savudrija.[1] And fifth, Slovenia's transport infrastructure, a critical element in calculating the prospects of economic success, is on a par with other Central and West European states. On the other hand, Slovenia has, since the Serbian side launched its war against Bosnia-Hercegovina at the end of beginning of April 1992, been faced with a large influx of refugees from Bosnia, straining Slovenia's absorptive capacities.

Just two years into independence, Slovenia has a new constitution, a politically pluralist landscape with ten parties in parliament, a free press, an independent judiciary, and an informed citizenry. And yet, there are problems, the chief ones being the unrelieved controversies about how to privatize the economy, and the temptations experienced by the new authorities to use surviving communist mechanisms of control for their own purposes.

II

Slovenia's drive toward independence must be dated to 1986, when the liberal wing within the League of Communists of Slovenia triumphed over the conservative wing, and ousted the conservatives from the party leadership. Party liberal Milan Kučan became president of the party and the de facto arbiter of Slovenian political life. The Kučan leadership pursued a more liberal path, and in the succeeding years, public debate became steadily more lively. Ljubljana's independent Radio Student and *Mladina*, officially (at the time) the organ of the Socialist Youth Organization of Slovenia contributed to the more relaxed atmosphere by opening up discussion of long-taboo subjects. *Mladina's* circulation tripled between 1984 and 1987, reaching a level of 28,000 by mid-1987. *Delo*, the leading daily newspaper in Ljubljana, also began to chart a more independent course.[2]

In February 1987, the Slovenian journal *Nova revija* published a special issue devoted to the "Slovenian national program." This issue contained articles protesting the second-class status of the Slovenian language in Yugoslavia and affirming Slovenes' right to greater self-determination. The issue sparked widespread public controversy and helped to fuel rising

Slovenia's Road to Democracy 191

Slovenian nationalist consciousness. A year later, amid rumors of an impending military move to quash Slovenian liberalism, a young Slovenian recruit (Sgt. Ivan Borstner) purloined some incriminating military documents and passed them on to *Mladina*, which published them. The documents substantiated fears that a military *putsch* had been in preparation, and helped to scotch the military's plans. In response, the military arrested Borstner, together with Franci Zavrl (the editor of *Mladina*) and two other *Mladina* journalists (Janez Janša and David Tasić).

The subsequent trial of "the Four" electrified the Slovenian public, who were outraged at the military plan and still more outraged that the four young men were being put on trial. Slovenian sensitivities were further aggravated by the fact that the military chose to conduct the trial in Serbo-Croatian, even though it was taking place on Slovenian soil. Large public protests followed, including a dramatic demonstration by at least 40,000 people on Ljubljana's Liberation Square on 22 June 1988. It was the largest public gathering of Slovenes since the end of the Second World War.

Overnight the political landscape of Slovenia was transformed. An independent Committee for the Protection of Human Rights was established in Ljubljana and gathered more than 100,000 signatures on its protest petitions. Under the influence of this example, several alternative political parties were launched, including the Social Democratic Alliance, the Slovenian Democratic Union, the Slovenian Christian Socialist Movement, and the Green Party. A previously established Peasant Union grew rapidly and claimed some 25,000 members by September 1989.[3]

Thus was born the "Slovenian Spring," a pluralizing current which ultimately gave birth to Slovenia's nascent multi-party system. Voices started to be raised calling for change. In October 1988, for example, France Bucar, a retired professor of law and one of the most important spokespersons of the Slovenian opposition, called for the urgent introduction of a market economy and underlined that this in turn required political pluralism.[4] Marko Hren, editor of the opposition bulletin, *Independent Voices from Slovenia*, warned that proponents of the communist status quo were having ever greater recourse to repressive measures, violating human rights, in their effort to block change. Hren warned that hardliners were laying the groundwork for an eventual "state of emergency" in Yugoslavia.[5] And the Slovenian Democratic Union and other opposition parties called for passage of a new constitution, establishing a Western-style parliamentary system and sanctioning political pluralism.

Within the League of Communists of Slovenia there were signs of growing support for the establishment of a multi-party system, coupled with a realization that such a solution necessarily entailed a redefinition of Slovenia's relationship to the Yugoslav federation. One solution, briefly advanced in 1989 by Slovenian autonomists within the communist party, was to reorganize Yugoslavia as an "asymmetric federation," in effect allowing Slovenia special prerogatives and more autonomy than the other federal units.[6] This idea found little support outside Slovenia, however, and died within a matter of two or three months.

But it was the growing tensions with Serbia that finally pushed Slovenia toward secession. Serbia's Slobodan Milošević was demanding the recentralization of the Yugoslav political system—at the very time when Slovenia and Croatia were proposing its reorganization as a confederation. Moreover, Milošević's tactics, which have included the provocation of mob disturbances, the illegal arming of Serbian civilian militias with arms purchased with federal funds, the unauthorized printing of Yugoslav money for use by the Serbian government (in effect stealing from the other republics), the dispatch of Serbian agents to gather intelligence in other republics (specifically Bosnia), and the effort to replace locally elected leaders with his own cronies—all of these things alienated the Slovenes and contributed to a deterioration of ties between Slovenia and Serbia.

In September 1989, the Slovenian parliament passed a series of amendments which underlined Slovenian sovereignty, and declared that only the Slovenian parliament itself could authorize the declaration of a state of emergency in Slovenia, or the movement of Yugoslav military forces into the republic. Serbian politicians raised a clamor of protest and tried to organize a mass demonstration by Serbs in the Slovenian capital. When Slovenia's leaders banned the demonstration and prevented the Serbs from entering their republic, the Serbian Socialist Alliance of Working People (an arm of Milošević's communist party) called on Serbian businesses to sever cooperative ties with businesses and enterprises in Slovenia. By the end of the year, there was little traffic between the two republics. Meanwhile, the Slovenian communists decided to approve the introduction of a multi-party system in their republic, and on 27 December 1989, the delegates of the Slovenian parliament adopted a package of new laws on elections and on political association. Their adoption effectively legalized political pluralism in Slovenia.[7]

Slovenia's first democratic elections in more than 40 years were held in April 1990. About 20 political parties contested the elections. Milan Kučan, who had just stepped down as head of the communist party, easily won election as president of Slovenia. But the communists (who had, in the interim, renamed themselves the Party for Democratic Renewal) were unable to ride to victory on Kučan's coattails, and a broad anti-communist coalition, calling itself "Demos," won a majority and took power. The Demos coalition embraced seven parties: the Slovenian Democratic Union (which obtained 25 deputies in the new assembly), the Social Democratic Party of Slovenia (18 deputies), the Slovenian Christian Democrats (26),

Slovenia's Road to Democracy 193

the Slovenian People's Party (formerly the Peasants' Union, 34), the Green Party (17), and the Liberal Party (4), as well as three affiliated deputies without specific party membership. In all, Demos controlled 127 seats out of 240.[8] The opposition consisted of the Liberal Democratic Party (40 deputies), the Party of Democratic Renewal (35), and the Socialist Party of Slovenia (12). In October 1991, the nominally left-of-center Slovenian Democratic Union split in two. The formal successor to the SDU was a right-of-center party calling itself the National Democratic Party (led by Minister of Justic Rajko Pirnat). Most of the historic founders of the SDU were associated with the other offspring of this divorce: the left-of-center Democratic Party.[9]

On 25 June 1990, the newly elected Presidium of the Republic of Slovenia announced that a new constitution for Slovenia would be written, in which Slovenia would be constituted as an independent state; and on 2 July, the Slovenian parliament issued a formal declaration of independence. Later that same month, the three chambers of the Slovenian parliament adopted three amendments to the constitution of Slovenia which, *inter alia*, invalidated all federal laws and acts of federal organs which were contrary to the Constitution and laws of the Republic of Slovenia.[10] Independence, as Slovenian politicians understood it then, was not incompatible with a *confederal* union with the other Yugoslav republics. Indeed, Slovenia's new post-communist leadership made it clear that confederation was their preferred alternative. In early October, the Slovenian and Croatian presidencies presented a joint proposal for the reorganization of Yugoslavia as a confederation. Among other things, the draft proposal called for union members to have their own armed forces and foreign ministries, but to coordinate military action and foreign policy through confederal agencies to be established.[11] As late as November 1990, Slovenian Foreign Minister Dimitrij Rupel insisted that Slovenia wanted to be part of a new Yugoslav confederation.[12]

In September 1990, the Socialist Party proposed calling a referendum on independence. Two months later, the Demos coalition accepted this proposal and announced that a referendum would indeed be held on 23 December. The result was an overwhelming majority of 88.2 percent of votes in favor of independence. The following month, the Slovenian parliament adopted an Action Program for the Realization of the Goals of the Referendum. The Slovenian government also set a deadline of 26 June 1991 for the conclusion of a confederal agreement with the other republics. In the absence of an agreement, Slovenia intended to secede.

As 1990 drew to a close, Slovenian Prime Minister Lojze Peterle issued a call for international mediation to solve the crisis in Yugoslavia.[13] The call went unheeded.

III

By the dawn of 1991, Slovenia was already behaving as an independent state. It began withholding the federal customs duties and other payments from Belgrade, set up independent institutions for the conduct of its foreign policy (including a number of quasi-diplomatic offices abroad), and began preparations for the establishment of a Slovenian army and the introduction of a separate Slovenian currency.

In February, the Slovenian parliament adopted a resolution calling for a "consentaneous separation of the Republic of Slovenia and the SFRY," and sent the Yugoslav Assembly a note proposing mutual recognition and the preservation of institutionalized forms of cooperation.[14] Subsequently, on 9 May, the Slovenian parliament approved the transmission of a letter to Yugoslav Prime Minister Ante Marković and to the respective prime ministers of the other five Yugoslav republics. This letter gave official notification of Slovenia's intentions to secede from Yugoslavia "by 26 June 1991 at the latest," but underlined the Slovenian parliament's continued willingness to discuss possible forms of future cooperation or association in economic, defense, diplomatic, and other spheres, including—even at that late date—a formula for confederal union.[15] And in fact, during the early months of 1991, the presidents of the six republics held a series of summit talks, nominally in the hope of finding a last minute solution. But in the acrimonious and tense atmosphere that prevailed at these talks, nothing could be accomplished, and as June approached, it was clear that Slovenia's only acceptable option was unilateral secession.

Ironically, these summit talks were conducted under the premises of a legal fiction: the Yugoslav federation was no longer intact, and the Yugoslav federal government, stripped lean by the withholding of payments by *all* the republics, was no longer an effective actor. Moreover, the Serbian republic had passed a new constitution on 28 September 1990, which in fact had already terminated Serbia's subordination to the federal government. There is no trace in the Serbian constitution of any institutional connection between the organs of the republic and those of the federation, and among its 136 articles, it is only in Article 135 that there is a brief reference to Serbia's being a constituent part of Yugoslavia. This figleaf can scarcely conceal the fact that in legal-constitutional terms, Serbia had actually been the first republic, thus, to constitute itself as an independent state.[16] Serbia's unilateral move was closely linked with Milošević's determination to dictate the political framework for a new Yugoslavia. In meeting after meeting, Milošević rejected any confederal arrangement, and come June, the Slovenes did the inevitable—they seceded. They were joined, in this, by the Republic of Croatia.

As of June 1991, the Slovenian armed forces consisted of something less than 20,000 troops, although Slovenian Defense Minister Janez Janša boasted that Slovenia could mobilize up to 200,000 troops on short order.[17] Facing the Slovenes was a Yugoslav army (JNA) with 138,000 troops on active duty, some 30,000 of them actually stationed in Slovenia at the time, and nominally, at least, another 400,000 troops in reserves. Hence, when the Yugoslav army struck against Slovenia on 27 June, two days after Slovenia's declaration of independence, there was room for doubt regarding the outcome. But despite the unfavorable odds, the Slovenes held their own, and captured large numbers of JNA recruits, many of them confused as to why they were fighting the Slovenes in the first place. By the beginning of July, the JNA had agreed to pull its forces out of Slovenia. And by October 1991, the withdrawal of the JNA from Slovenia was completed. Slovenian independence had become an accomplished fact.

IV

The withdrawal by the JNA first to their bases and subsequently out of Slovenia gave birth to a brief euphoric moment, as Slovenes realized that they were finally on their own. But the new state was confronted with a number of pressing tasks, including the normalization of its foreign relations, the revival of the economy, the execution of a program of reprivatization, the writing of a new constitution, and the development of effective political institutions suitable for democracy.

Foreign relations. In spite of the delays in obtaining international recognition, Slovenia's foreign policy notched some early successes. From a diplomatic point of view, the most important of these was the successful courtship of Germany, Austria, and Italy, resulting in those countries' support for more general European recognition of Slovenia.

But a combination of skepticism and disinterest in many Western capitals—most notably in Washington DC, London, and Paris—complicated Slovenia's quest for recognition. US Secretary of State James Baker visited Belgrade on the eve of Slovenian/Croatian secession and made a public declaration that the US endorsed the preservation of a unified Yugoslavia. Slovenian Prime Minister Lojze Peterle told me in March 1992, "I did not expect quick American recognition of Slovenia, especially because Belgrade was very convincing when explaining the situation. Belgrade told Baker, just give us a few hours and we will suppress all of this."[18] Several EC countries, including Britain, France, and Spain warned against any unilateral recognition of the breakaway republics of Slovenia and Croatia. France, in particular, exerted strong pressure on Bonn, not to recognize Slovenia or Croatia,[19] joining Britain and the Netherlands in urging restraint and "evenhandedness" in the conflict. Greek Prime Minister Mitsotakis visited Belgrade in late November for talks with Milošević and urged the Serbian president to consider a confederal arrangement for Yugoslavia[20]—an overture that seemed out of touch with the reality of Slovenian/Croatian secession and Serb-Croat war.

In November 1991, the European Community and the US imposed economic sanctions on "Yugoslavia," thus injuring Slovenia and Croatia equally with Serbia. The US cancelled the trade advantages it had given to Yugoslavia earlier and suspended the bilateral agreement on export permits for Yugoslav textiles. The US has lately ranked as Slovenia's sixth most important trading partner, after Germany, Italy, the Soviet Union/Russia, France, and Austria. The combined European/American sanctions had their effect on the Slovenian economy, as well as on the economies of the other ex-Yugoslav republics.[21] Finally, in mid-December, the European Community foreign ministers agreed to recognize the breakaway republics upon receiving assurances that the successor governments were committed to the rule of law, human rights, and ethnic/minority rights. The European Community set 15 January 1992 as the date on which recognition would be forthcoming. But Germany formalized its recognition of Slovenia and Croatia already on 23 December, and other European states quickly followed suit. By the end of January, both Slovenia and Croatia had been recognized by virtually all other European states, though not yet by the United States. On 18 March came word that the US would shortly announce diplomatic recognition.[22] This followed on 7 April.

Some of Slovenia's initial contacts have been with other former-communist states in the region. Thus, Slovenia quickly signed three agreements with Hungary: a five-year agreement on cultural, educational, and scientific cooperation in September 1992, a protocol on the mutual protection of each other's minorities two months later, and a free trade agreement likewise in November.[23] Later, in January 1993, the Slovenian and Hungarian defense ministries signed a protocol on cooperation in security and military affairs.[24] About the same time, Slovenia concluded economic agreements with Poland (for a free trade zone) and with the Czech Republic.[25]

Although the partial loss of the Yugoslav market (as a result of the war) has hurt the Slovenian economy, an increase in direct investments from Austria has helped to compensate. Slovenian-Russian relations have also chalked up progress, with the appointment of Yuri Stepanovich Girenko as Moscow's charges d'affaires to Ljubljana in early October 1992.[26]

Of all Slovenia's neighbors, Croatia has been the most difficult partner, with frictions over fishing rights, Slovenian access to international waters, uncertainties about borders, and concerns about the status and rights of the 54,000 Croats officially recorded as living in Slovenia.[27] Negotiations

Slovenia's Road to Democracy

between the two former republics of Yugoslavia have been long and difficult, but have begun to bear fruit. Already in March 1992, a joint Croatian-Slovenian Chamber of Commerce was established and began work, and the following month, officials announced the conclusion of a draft agreement on fishing rights.[28] In February 1993, the foreign ministers of the two republics (at that point: Zdenko Škrabalo for Croatia, and Lojze Peterle for Slovenia) met and announced "great satisfaction and a great similarity of views," promising "the beginning of a new period in the development of mutual Croat-Slovene relations."[29]

Other economic relations. Between the Serb-Croat war and the EC sanctions, Slovenia's foreign trade has been seriously disrupted. Economic trade agreements with Croatia and with Russia[30] were first steps toward normalizing Slovenia's foreign trade activity, although the republic has experienced some problems in obtaining payments on time from Croatia.[31] Slovenia also expressed interest that enterprises in foreign countries would invest in the Slovenia economy; aside from Austria and Germany, Italy is among the countries seen as most likely to do so.[32] In April 1992, Slovenia and France agreed to form a joint economic council to foster ties; meanwhile, trade with the Benelux countries has blossomed.[33] In May, an agreement was signed with EFTA,[34] and preparations were made for Slovenia's admission into the IMF. Beyond this, Slovenia signed a now largely obsolete trade agreement with Bosnia and signalled clear interest in the resumption of trade with both Serbia and Macedonia.

By the end of 1992, Slovenian authorities could report that Slovenia's trade with foreign countries (not counting other former republics of Yugoslavia) had increased. More specifically, during the months January-October 1992, Slovenian enterprises exported 8.2 percent more goods to countries outside former Yugoslavia than during the same period the previous year; exports to EC countries specifically increased 15.6 percent in that period. And after recording foreign trade deficits in July and August 1992, Slovenia tallied a tangible foreign trade surplus (of $76.5 million) in September, followed by an equivalent foreign trade surplus in October 1992 ($73.3 million). These trends bode well for the long term. In the short term, however, Slovenian enterprises have had to cope with some reverses in trade with markets in former Yugoslav republics. In early 1992, trade with Croatia, Serbia, and other ex-Yugoslav republics reached a low, but by the end of October 1992, these trade connections had been substantially restored and trade with these republics for the period January–October 1992 stood at 96.4 percent of the total for the same period in the previous year, and trade with Croatia and Serbia in particular was said to be reviving and expanding with each passing month.[35]

Privatization and economic reconstruction. Coping with the present economic slowdown while engineering simultaneous recovery and reconstruction as a market economy is a far thornier issue than normalizing foreign economic relations, however, not least because of prolonged conflicts over alternative views about privatization. Passage of a law on denationalization, taking effect 7 December 1991, was an important step. But that law pertains only to the regulation of conditions under which citizens may apply for the return of property forcibly nationalized between 1945 and 1963. And while authorities expected that some 60,000 demands would be tendered, involving property worth some 4.5 billion DM, about 70 percent of the property in question is said to involve wooded areas and agricultural land.[36] Much of the Slovenian economy, including many of the most important enterprises, are not covered under this law. As a result, Slovenian politicians were forced to prepare a separate law on privatization. There has been, of course, nothing to prevent the establishment of new enterprises. There is even a Slovenian Private Enterprise Association, which functions as a kind of lobby group for private entrepreneurs. But in the absence of some legal mechanism for privatizing the "socially owned" sector, Slovenia has, for the time being, combined political pluralism with a state-run economy. This commixture has been, of course, the norm throughout post-communist Eastern Europe during the region's transition to free enterprise.

The earliest effort to set forth a concrete plan for privatization came in early 1991, when Jože Mencinger, the then Deputy Prime Minister, offered a draft law on privatization to the parliament. Under Mencinger's plan, 10 percent of the stock in each company would have been put up for immediate sale, as preferred shares, with the remaining 90 percent entrusted to a government fund. Each succeeding year, the fund would have put another 10 percent of the stock up for sale, thus enabling would-be investors to buy their stock in increments. The left-of-center Liberal Democrats were among those supporting the plan. Critics of this plan, on the other hand, warned of the danger that only the communist-appointed managers and foreigners would be in a position to buy stock. In April 1991, Harvard economist Jeffrey Sachs visited Ljubljana and joined Dušan Plesković, the prime minister's adviser on privatization, in criticizing the plan. Mencinger's proposal was scuttled, Mencinger resigned his office, and the government entrusted Igor Umek, Minister of Planning, with the responsibility to draft an alternative plan. This plan was ready by late summer 1991. Where the larger companies were concerned, this second plan allowed for the distribution of 10 percent of stock free to the employees at the respective enterprises, with another 20 percent reserved for purchase by the employees (both managers and workers). Yet another 20 percent was to go into pension funds, 35 percent to be distributed free of charge to all voters, male and female, and 15 percent to be used as compensation for people from whom property had been confiscated. For smaller compa-

Slovenia's Road to Democracy

199

nies, the plan called for a somewhat different distribution scheme.[37]

This second plan was submitted to the parliament on 8 August and was immediately accepted by Demos. It subsequently passed in two of the three chambers of the parliament. However, it failed to garner support in the Chamber of Associated Labor (a relic of socialism), whose deputies represented the interests of enterprise managers. As a result of this setback, Professor Ivan Ribnikar of the Faculty of Economics was asked to undertake to develop a third plan for privatization. This third plan eliminates any concept of free distribution (which had been a point stressed by Sachs) and would set aside 60 percent of stock for purchase by employees of the given enterprise.

But this third plan, favored by Pleskovič and Peterle, came under fire from parties left of Peterle's Christian Democratic Party. For example, Spomenka Hribar, a leading functionary in the Democratic Party and a parliamentary deputy, accused Prime Minister Peterle of surrounding himself with an emigre lobby and with pursuing policies that would have returned Slovenia to what it had been 50 years ago.[38] Hribar charged that under this approach to privatization, the Catholic Church, which had been a major landowner prior to the communist takeover, would have been able to regain the extensive properties that had been confiscated, including forest lands and schools. "I believe it would be catastrophic to destroy the entire system set up by the communists at one blow," Hribar told me in March 1992. "Privatization must be slow and gradual. We in the Democratic Party are working on an alternative plan."[39]

Under these conditions, there developed a rising tide of criticism of the Peterle government, culminating in the calling of an ultimately unsuccessful vote of no confidence in December. Opposition politicians charged the government with failing to appreciate the urgency of privatization, and the general controversy over this issue contributed to the eventual collapse of the Demos coalition in December 1991.

Rastko Močnik, head of the Social Democratic Union, told *Delo* in November,

> The present government is not successful by its own standards. It has not carried out privatization, and it has not even begun to reconstruct the economy. That alone would be enough to make the statement that it is unsuccessful, and [that] it should leave the leadership to more effective people. The postponement of privatization, and the economic collapse resulting from it, were caused by the government itself... It has not acted in accordance with economic considerations, but rather party interests. That is why this government has also lost human confidence and moral credibility.[40]

200
Sabrina Petra Ramet

Viktor Zakelj, president of the Socialist Party, echoed these sentiments, and expressed concern that "the social and economic situation in Slovenia is becoming more serious. A number of reasons for this are objective in nature, but at the same time, it is also true that the present government underestimated certain problems, did not even react to them, sometimes reacted too late, and in some cases, reacted incorrectly."[41] Prominent figures from other parties also criticized the government's approach to privatization.

But while politicians debated over which medicine was best, the Slovenian economy continued to show clear signs of illness. Industrial production declined an average of 1.1 percent between November 1990 and January 1992, registering its first modest growth (1.072 percent) in February 1992. One study, conducted in November 1991, found that industrial production the preceding month was the lowest since 1978, and only 0.6 percent higher than in 1977; that put it about 26 percent below the peak year in 1985.[42] Meanwhile, unemployment has risen steadily in Slovenia. As of mid-1991, some 75,430 persons were out of work.[43]

Finally, as a culmination of many factors, including the controversy over privatization, Peterle was ousted from the prime ministership by a party coalition in mid-April, and replaced by Janez Drnovšek, the recently elected head of the Liberal Democratic Party.[44] Just over a month later, a new privatization plan, worked out in consultation with Ljubljana economist Ivan Ribnikar, was accepted by the government with only a few amendments and submitted to the Assembly. The Drnovšek government confidently predicted that the latest privatization plan would be adopted by the end of June.

Meanwhile, in the three months from March to June, an entirely new factor was added to the economic equation: the massive influx of refugees from wartorn Bosnia-Herzegovina. By mid-June, some 60,000 Bosnian refugees had come to Slovenia—representing 3 percent of Slovenia's population. And refugees continued to arrive at a rate of 1,500 per day. The Slovenian government and the Catholic archbishop of Ljubljana, Alojzij Šuštar, issued separate calls for international assitance to cope with the refugee problem.[45] Slovenian authorities expressed concern that the republic would have been hard pressed to handle even 10,000 refugees, let alone 60,000, and in July 1992, took administrative steps to dam the flow.[46]

Debate on the privatization bill dragged on until November 1992. Meanwhile, in the absence of legal regulation, there were reports of "runaway privatization," as enterprises were disinvested and sold off cheaply through "bypass enterprises" designed to skirt the spirit of the law.[47] Finally, on 11 November, the Slovenian Assembly adopted a bill on privatization. For months, the Assembly had tried to agree on a universal formula on property transformation. The final bill reflected a compromise,

Slovenia's Road to Democracy

combining sales of 40 percent of stock with free distribution of 20 percent. At the same time, however, the Assembly promised to issue investment credit certificates to citizens, under which they might invest in the enterprises where they work.[48]

V

Politics: the constitution. The tasks Slovenia has confronted in the political sphere can be divided into three broad areas: drafting of the constitution, the construction of effective democratic institutions, and the development of attitudes and behaviors compatible with democracy.

As might be expected, the simplest of these three has been the drafting of a new constitution. A constitutional commission was appointed to produce a draft document, under the chairmanship of Miro Cerar, otherwise a professor at the Faculty of Law. Cerar and his colleagues studied a number of foreign constitutions (especially the German, Italian, and Austrian constitutions) in order to arrive at some sense of what a democratic constitution should include, and also consulted with foreign constitutional experts. The Cerar Commission also looked carefully at the Hungarian constitution, the Serbian constitution of 1990, and the Croatian draft of 1991, viewing these three as countries with similar problems and challenges, studied the Spanish, Greek, and Portuguese constitutions because those countries were former dictatorships, and looked at several other constitutions (such as those of Sweden and Libya) regarding specific points they were considering. Finally, the commission studied two alternative European political models: the presidential model (associated with France, and otherwise adopted only in Croatia and Serbia) and the parliamentary model (adpted in all other European countries). Members of the parliament felt that in Croatia and Serbia, the "French" model had proven conducive to presidential *diktat*, and therefore voted for a parliamentary formula.[49]

Ultimately, there were only two points which aroused intense controversy: abortion, and the structure of the parliament itself. On the question of abortion, there was a sharp left-right split. Parties of the left and center (center to left: the Democratic Party, the Green Party, Social Democratic Party, Liberal Democratic Party, Socialist Party, and Party of Democratic Renewal) wanted a clause guaranteeing a woman's right to abortion incorporated directly into the constitution. Parties right of center (the People's Party, Christian Democratic Party, Liberal Party, and National Democratic Party) fought this constitutional guarantee and wanted ultimately to impose a legal ban on any abortions on the territory of Slovenia, except when the woman's life was endangered by the pregnancy. Parties on the left won this point and the constitution includes an explicit guarantee of the right to abortion.

The second question was more complex, and involved a choice between a unicameral and a bicameral parliament. But here again, alignment followed a clear, left-right divide. The four parties furthest to the left (Social Democrats, Liberal Democrats, Socialists, and Party of Democratic Renewal) urged the establishment of a bicameral legislature, with one chamber elected through republic-wide elections, and the second chamber to consist of deputies elected at the local level and thus reflecting the heterogeneity of regional interests in Slovenia. The center parties joined the parties right of center in opposing this solution. The National Liberal Party and the Green Party preferred a strict unicameral system, but joined the Christian Democratic, Democratic, and People's Parties in sponsoring the compromise that was eventually adopted: a 90-member Assembly with legislative power, alongside a 40-member Council of State having no legislative power but possessing the authority to review decisions taken by the Assembly and to return them to the Assembly for reconsideration. The Green Party agreed with this compromise, but not without registering its belief that the mixed solution would prove unstable. The other parties ultimately endorsed the mixed solution as well.

Political institutions. The Demos coalition inherited a network of institutions designed by the communists to serve communist policies. Inevitably, it has been necessary to change both personnel and the institutions themselves. Immediately after the April 1990 elections, thus, there was virtually a complete turnover of police authorities.[50] But this was only the first change. Ultimately, the present authorities intend to remake the entire system—a process which is expected to take another two years at a minimum and to entail the passage of at least 300 new laws. Among the tasks with which the new authorities have been confronted: establishing rules ensuring a truly independent judiciary, the reduction of the number of ministries from 27 (the current level, inherited from the communists) to about 15–17 as the economy is marketized, the elimination of agencies set up to regulate production and distribution, and the establishment of a Slovenian diplomatic corps. There are also vestiges of the old system embedded in the educational system. At the university level, for example, students are still required to take a course on "Socialism and the Modern World," chiefly because the professor teaching it has played on his seniority to demand that it remain a general university requirement.[51] In addition, the University of Ljubljana also still teaches a course on the "Sociology of Work," which includes a section on the structure of self-management in the enterprises.

Institutional changes in the Slovenian establishment have included the establishment of an Agency for the Financial Rehabilitation of Banks, passage of a Law on Investments, the establishment of a new press agency, and the reorganization of the intelligence service.[52]

Political behavior. As institutions change and as laws change, behavior is also supposed to change. But in two areas, there have been sharp frictions and acerbic exchanges. These two areas are education and the broadcast media.

Controversy in the educational sphere focuses on the Christian Democratic Party's insistence that the schools reflect Christian values. After the electoral victory by the Demos coalition in spring 1990, the Christian Democrats took control of the ministries of education and culture. With these ministries in their pocket, the Christian Democrats have pushed for the inclusion of religious instruction in the schools, opened discussions about prayer in the schools, and—anticipating the second issue—have suggested that the media should not offend "Christian values." The Catholic Church now displayed a new self-confidence and in fall 1992, the Bishops' Conference of Slovenia even called for the dissolution of the parliament, on the grounds that it embodied "nondemocratic principles." The bishops emphasized that " . . . the people should place their trust in those who have a correct stand regarding Christian values and the Catholic Church."[53] The Christian Democrats' sympathy for the Church's positions increasingly alienated that party's erstwhile coalition allies, who now charged that Prime Minister Peterle was "...spending too much time reopening churches and not enough [time] mending the economy."[54] In fact, other parties were strongly opposed to this tendency and the Liberal Democrats promised that once a new coalition had been formed, the Christian Democrats would have to give up their control of these ministries—a promise that the Liberal Democrats were able to keep.

Where the broadcast media are concerned, there have been two problems. First, the non-communist government has inherited a system structured in such a way as to assure government control when so desired. Above all, this relates to the retention by the government television station (RTV Slovenia) of a monopoly control of broadcast frequencies—which means, in practice, that Kanal A, Slovenia's only private television station, remains beholden to RTV Slovenia, its competitor. As a result of this monopoly, Kanal A had failed, as of January 1993, to be granted permission for a large transmitter reaching all of Slovenia and could, therefore, be received only in the Ljubljana area. In fact, RTV Slovenia's monopolization of broadcast frequencies remained a heated topic of debate throughout 1992,[55] and even in 1993, the Administration for Telecommunications (a branch of the Ministry for Transportation and Communications) continued to reject Kanal A's pressure for a demonopolization of frequencies, despite charges that this reinforced the "monopolistic" position of RTV Slovenia.[56] The Ljubljana daily newspaper *Dnevnik* continued that this struggle for frequencies had broader political implications:

... frequencies represent the foundation and necessary condition for establishing new radio or television stations, which, of course, can become an important factor in the struggle for dominance in the Slovene political or economic sphere. Whoever owns or at least controls the media thus also has an opportunity to increase her or his political or economic power, and consequently the struggle for frequencies at this moment, in a Slovenia divided by politics, parties, and interests, represents one of the most subtle means of fighting for power.[57]

Second, the post-communist politicians have repeatedly given in to the temptation to exert subtle pressure on both television stations to prevent stories they have not liked from being aired. Soon after coming to power, the ruling coalition simply imposed a supervisory board on RTV Slovenia, filling its seats with party appointees, despite widespread public opposition to the selection of political appointees, rather than professionals, for these seats. Subsequently, the coalition also tried to prepare a new law on information which would have effectively brought the principal news media under state ownership and control; this would have entailed, *inter alia*, a renationalization of the daily newspaper, *Delo*.[58] But opposition from among journalists succeeded in derailing this scheme, at least for the time being. That victory notwithstanding, the noncommunist politicians continued to exert subtle pressure on the media in order to influence programming. "The politicians think they have a natural right to control everything, to plan everything," complained Andrej Poznic, chief editor of Kanal A. "The notion of liberalism has almost no roots here."[59]

VI

In late April 1992, after withstanding two votes of no confidence, the Peterle government fell, as a result of a third vote, with 126 negative votes out of 208 cast. Janez Drnovšek, at one time Slovenia's (communist) member of the federal collective presidency and now head of the Liberal Democratic Party, was elected prime minister. Drnovšek invited parties on both the left and right sides of the spectrum to join him in a "unity coalition," but the Christian Democrats and the Slovenian People's Party (formerly Peasant Party) declined.[60] Drnovšek therefore put together a left-oriented government, forging a coalition with Igor Bavčar's Democratic Party, the Socialist Party, and the ex-communist Party of Democratic Renewal (PDR). The PDR members named to ministerial posts were Anka Osterman, proposed to head the Ministry for Veterans Affairs and War Disabled,[61] and Hermann Rigelnik, named Deputy Minister for Economic Affairs.[62]

Slovenia's Road to Democracy

In the wake of this swing to the left, Ivan Oman, founder-president of the Slovenian People's Party (SPP), abandoned his own party to join Peterle's Christian Democrats. Oman's abandonment of the party he created drove the SPP down in the polls, and as of July 1992, the once-vigorous SPP commanded the loyalty of only 4 percent of the electorate.[63] Jože Pučnik's Social Democratic Party was also sliding in the polls, as desertions from the party's ranks mounted.[64]

The coalition government put together by Drnovšek in April 1992 was only an interim government, pending elections scheduled for later that year. The elections, held on 6 December 1992, included both the election of the President of the Republic and the election of the now-bicameral Assembly, whose available seats were contested by 23 political parties. Incumbent President Milan Kučan easily won reelection, garnering a landslide 64 percent of votes.[65] With these elections, the tri-cameral legislature inherited from the communist era (with 240 deputies total) was abolished and replaced with a bicameral legislature, consisting of a 90-member Chamber of Representatives and a 40-member Council of State. All 90 seats in the first chamber were to be filled through the December elections, but only 22 seats in the Council of State.[66]

Voter turnout was high, with some 1.4 million citizens taking part in the vote.[67] The Liberal Democrats captured 23.3 percent of the vote—easily the largest slice. But the Christian Democrats placed second with 14.5 percent. In third place was the Party of Democratic Renewal, with 13.6 percent, followed by the radical-right Slovenian National Party (SNP), with 9.9 percent. The SNP is headed by Zmago Jelinčič, a rowdy politician whom an Italian newspaper has compared to Hitler,[68] and who agitated against the presence of Gastarbeiter and refugees in Slovenia, during the election campaign.[69] SNP members had earlier stirred controversy by refusing to return firearms issued to citizens during the JNA invasion of July 1992. The Slovenian People's Party placed fifth, with 8.8 percent of the vote, while the Democratic Party of Bavcar and Rupel, which had played so important a role in the initial months of transition, received only 5 percent of the vote.[70]

As a result of these votes, the Liberal Democrats won 22 seats in the 90-member Chamber of Representatives; the Christian Democrats took 15; the left-wing United List (comprising the PDR and three other left-oriented parties), 14; the Slovenian National Party, 12; the Slovenian People's Party, 10; the Democrats, 6; the Greens, five; and the SDP, four. In the Council of State, of the 40 members (22 elected at these elections), 17 are members of the Liberal Democratic Party.[71] Rajko Pirnat's National Democratic Party received too few votes (2.35 percent) to obtain any seats in the Assembly.

The resultant coalition government brought together the Liberal Democratic Party, the PDR, the Democrats, the Social Democrats, and the Chris-

206   Sabrina Petra Ramet

tian Democrats. This unlikely coalition was achieved by giving the Christian Democrats the post of Minister of Foreign Affairs and excluding them from any involvement in cultural, educational, or social questions.[72]

VII

Slovenia's first two years of transition have been rocky and strewn with obstacles. Its record in transcending these obstacles has been mixed. Slovenia has done well in terms of redesigning the institutions of the political landscape, striking a reasoned balance between reckless haste, on the one hand, and undue slowness, on the other. Its achievements in creating a functioning parliamentary system are obvious and impressive. And while its slowness in passing a privatization bill has been harmful to the Slovenian economy, now that a law is in effect, privatization can presumably proceed, giving additional energy to Slovenian economic recovery. On the negative side, however, the continued controversies over the media reflect the allure of power and the danger that restrictions on the media might serve as a tool for the ambitions of less than democratic forces.

The economy remains the top priority on Slovenia's agenda. In the months from January to July 1992, industrial production dropped 16 percent, with the greatest losses in the steel industry.[73] Unemployment stood at 13.6 percent in September 1992—on a par with Poland (also 13.6) and Bulgaria (13.8), marginally behind Hungary (11.4), but tangibly better off than Croatia's rate of unemployment (17.4 percent).[74] Altogether, Slovenia's standard of living was said to have sunk by a third between December 1990 and December 1992.[75]

But as I have emphasized throughout this chapter, whatever the short-term difficulties, Slovenia's long-term economic prospects are good. Slovenia's resumption of payments on its foreign debt and an EC agreement to extend some $12.5 million in additional credits to assist the restructuring of Slovenian businesses are symptoms of those good prospects.[76]

Finally, where nationalism is concerned, Slovenia seemed to have little to fear. Nationalism, which has been the bane of Serbia and Croatia alike, scarcely animates the Slovenian public. In a poll conducted in August 1992, more than 25 percent of respondents had not noticed *any* signs of nationalism in Slovenia, while another 25 percent saw nationalism as a normal reaction in conditions of perceived threat. Some 17.8 percent viewed nationalism as "an isolated phenomenon, which a democratic society should be able to tolerate," while only 10.7 percent believed that rising Slovenian nationalism was damaging the democratization process or Slovenia's image abroad or both.[77]

Successful democratization presumes economic recovery. And for Slovenia's post-communist authorities to steer a course to economic recovery, they must successfully carry out their rather laissez faire program of privatization, make progress with the construction of a stable market economy, reverse the continued decline in industrial production, build on the favorable trends in foreign trade with the EC, and find a way to cope with the hefty number of refugees from Bosnia and from the Serbian Krajina. Despite these serious challenges, Slovenia's prospects for stabilizing a functioning parliamentary democracy and for restoring economic vitality appear to me to be good to excellent.

Notes

The author was in Ljubljana, Slovenia, from 17 to 27 March 1992, thanks to a grant from IREX. While in Slovenia, she interviewed some of the leading political figures, as well as important persons in the media. This chapter was originally published in *Europe-Asia Studies* in September 1993 and is gratefully reprinted by permission of the journal's editors.

1. *Business Europa* (May/June 1992), p. 48; see also *Vjesnik* (Zagreb) 26 March 1992, p. 12.

2. This paragraph summarizes some of the information contained in Sabrina Petra Ramet, *Balkan Babel: Politics, Culture, and Religion in Yugoslavia* (Boulder, Colo.: Westview Press, 1992), chapter 4 ("The Press").

3. For further discussion of the events of this period, see *Ibid.*, chapter 2 ("The Gathering Storm, 1987–1989").

4. France Bučar, "Towards democracy or authoritarian rule," in *Independent Voices from Slovenia*, Special edition: "Slovenian Spring—Centralism or Democracy" (October 1988), pp. 24–25.

5. *Independent Voices from Slovenia*, Vol. 5, No. 1 (January 1989), p. 3.

6. *Borba* (Belgrade), 1 June 1989, p. 7.

7. Tanjug (Belgrade), 24 December 1989, in Foreign Broadcast Information Service (FBIS), *Daily Report* (Eastern Europe), 28 December 1989, p. 83; and Tanjug (27 December 1989), trans. in FBIS, *Daily Report* (Eastern Europe), 28 December 1989, p. 84.

8. Miro Cerar, "Die verfassungsrechtlichen Grundlagen der Konstituierung des Staates Slowenien," in Joseph Marko and Tomislav Borić (eds.), *Slowenien— Kroatien—Serbien: Die neuen Verfassungen* (Vienna: Böhlau Verlag, 1991), p. 105.

9. See Ali Žerdin, "Slovenia: Alone at Last," in *East European Reporter*, Vol. 5, No. 3 (May–June 1992), p. 54.

10. *Delo* (Ljubljana), 3 August 1990, p. 4, trans. in FBIS, *Daily Report* (Eastern Europe), 13 August 1990, p. 55.

11. Zagreb Domestic Service (11 October 1990), trans. in FBIS, *Daily Report* (Eastern Europe), 12 October 1990, pp. 551–52. The full text of the proposal was published in *Delo* (6 October 1990), p. 20.

12. *Borba* (10/11 November 1990), p. 5.

208   *Sabrina Petra Ramet*

13. *Süddeutsche Zeitung* (Munich), 13/14 October 1990, p. 7.

14. *Delo* (15 February 1991), p. 2, trans. in FBIS, *Daily Report* (Eastern Europe), 20 February 1991, pp. 70–71.

15. *Neodvisni Dnevnik* (Ljubljana), 9 May 1991, p. 4, trans. in FBIS, *Daily Report* (Eastern Europe), 23 May 1991, p. 27.

16. Joseph Marko, "Die neuen Verfassungen: Slowenien—Kroatien—Serbien. Ein Vergleich," in Marko and Borić (eds.), *Slowenien—Kroatien—Serbien* [note 8], p. 24.

17. *Neue Zürcher Zeitung* (4 June 1991), p. 2.

18. Lojze Peterle, Prime Minister of Slovenia, in interview with the author, Ljubljana, 23 March 1992.

19. *Los Angeles Times* (15 September 1991), p. M6.

20. *Neue Zürcher Zeitung* (3 December 1991), p. 4.

21. *Delo* (10 December 1991), p. 3, trans. in FBIS, *Daily Report* (Eastern Europe), 2 January 1992, pp. 35–37.

22. *Dnevnik* (Ljubljana), 19 March 1992, p. 9.

23. MTI (Budapest), 2 September 1992, in FBIS, *Daily Report* (Eastern Europe), 3 September 1992, p. 13; Radio Slovenia Network (6 November 1992), trans. in FBIS, *Daily Report* (Eastern Europe), 9 November 1992, p. 47; and MTI (1 December 1992), in FBIS, *Daily Report* (Eastern Europe), 2 December 1992, p. 15.

24. MTI (21 January 1993), in FBIS, *Daily Report* (Eastern Europe), 22 January 1993, p. 31.

25. Re. Poland: PAP (Warsaw), 29 October 1992, in FBIS, *Daily Report* (Eastern Europe), 2 November 1992, p. 18; and PAP (22 November 1992), in FBIS, *Daily Report* (Eastern Europe), 23 November 1992, pp. 27, 46. Re. the Czech Republic: Radio Slovenia Network (16 November 1992), trans. in FBIS, *Daily Report* (Eastern Europe), 18 November 1992, p. 38.

26. *Delo* (3 October 1992), p. 2.

27. *Slobodna Dalmacija* (Split), 13 March 1992, p. 17; *Dnevnik* (Ljubljana), 3 September 1992, p. 24; *Dnevnik* (Ljubljana), 15 September 1992, p. 8; and Tanjug (6 October 1992), trans. in FBIS, *Daily Report* (Eastern Europe), 7 October 1992, p. 25.

28. *Dnevnik* (Ljubljana), 28 March 1992, p. 2, and 15 April 1992, p. 24.

29. Radio Croatian Network (3 February 1993), trans. in FBIS, *Daily Report* (Eastern Europe), 4 February 1993, p. ?

30. Re. Russia, see Tanjug (12 December 1991), in FBIS, *Daily Report* (Eastern Europe), 13 December 1991, p. 23.

31. *Dnevnik* (Ljubljana), 7 January 1992, p. 3, trans. in FBIS, *Daily Report* (Eastern Europe), 28 January 1992, p. 44.

32. *Delo* (9 December 1991), p. 4, trans. in FBIS, *Daily Report* (Eastern Europe), 24 December 1991, pp. 29–30.

33. *Dnevnik* (Ljubljana), 30 April 1992, p. 3, trans. in FBIS, *Daily Report* (Eastern Europe), 18 May 1992, p. 34; and *Informacije iz Slovenije* (Ljubljana), 2 March 1992, pp. 2–7, trans. in FBIS, *Daily Report* (Eastern Europe), 1 May 1992, pp. 35–39.

34. Radio Slovenia Network (21 May 1992), trans. in FBIS, *Daily Report* (Eastern Europe), 22 May 1992, p. 26.

35. *Dnevnik* (Ljubljana), 21 December 1992, p. 4, trans. in FBIS, *Daily Report* (Eastern Europe), 7 January 1993, pp. 17–18. See also *Dnevnik* (Ljubljana), 25 De-

Slovenia's Road to Democracy 209

cember 1992, p. 3, trans. in FBIS, *Daily Report* (Eastern Europe), 13 January 1993, p. 56.

36. Tanjug (7 December 1991), in FBIS, *Daily Report* (Eastern Europe), 10 December 1991, p. 42.

37. This account is based on the author's interview with Dr. Boris Pleskovic, adviser to the prime minister on privatization, Ljubljana, 23 March 1992; and *Neue Zürcher Zeitung* (8 January 1992), pp. 9–10.

38. Spomenka Hribar, Democratic Party deputy in parliament, in interview with the author, Ljubljana, 24 March 1992.

39. *Ibid.*

40. Quoted in *Delo* (23 November 1991), pp. 20, 21, trans. in FBIS, *Daily Report* (Eastern Europe), 10 December 1991, pp. 42–43.

41. *Ibid.*, p. 42.

42. *Neodvisni Dnevnik* (26 November 1991), p. 5, trans. in FBIS, *Daily Report* (Eastern Europe), 10 December 1991, p. 47.

43. Radio Slovenia Network (17 September 1991), trans. in FBIS, *Daily Report* (Eastern Europe), 18 September 1991, p. 30.

44. *Dnevnik* (Ljubljana), 20 March 1992, p. 3; *Neue Zürcher Zeitung* (25 April 1992), p. 2; and *Novi Vjesnik* (Zagreb), 16 June 1992, p. 15B.

45. *Die Presse* (Vienna), 16 June 1992, p. 3; *Die Furche* (Vienna), 18 June 1992, p. 1; and *Delo* (25 April 1992), p. 2, trans. in FBIS, *Daily Report* (Eastern Europe), 8 May 1992, p. 24.

46. Radio Slovenia Network (15 April 1992), trans. in FBIS, *Daily Report* (Eastern Europe), 16 April 1992, p. 39; *Delo* (25 April 1992), p. 2, trans. in FBIS, *Daily Report* (Eastern Europe), 8 May 1992, p. 24; *Neue Zürcher Zeitung* (3 July 1992), p. 2; and *Delo* (3 October 1992), p. 2.

47. *Delo* (29 September 1992), p. 3, trans. in FBIS, Daily Report (Eastern Europe), 20 October 1992, p. 35.

48. *Neue Zürcher Zeitung* (29/30 November 1992), p. 16.

49. Miro Cerar, Secretary of the Constitutional Commission of the Republic of Slovenia, in interview with the author, Ljubljana, 18 March 1992.

50. Interview with Igor Bavcar, president of the Assembly, in *Vreme* (Belgrade), 3 February 1992, p. 22.

51. Ali Zerdin, chief editor of *Mladina*, in interview with the author, Ljubljana, 20 March 1992.

52. Re. the press agency, see *Delo* (25 April 1992), p. 2, trans. in FBIS, *Daily Report* (Eastern Europe), 7 May 1992, pp. 38–40. Re. the reorganization of the intelligence service, see *Delo* (9 January 1993), p. 2, trans. in FBIS, *Daily Report* (Eastern Europe), 26 January 1993, pp. 57–59.

53. Tanjug (26 November 1992), in FBIS, *Daily Report* (Eastern Europe), 30 November 1992, p. 48.

54. *International Herald Tribune* (Paris), 15 July 1992, p. 4.

55. *Delo* (7 October 1992), p. 2.

56. *Dnevnik* (Ljubljana), 7 January 1993, p. 4, trans. in FBIS, *Daily Report* (Eastern Europe), 26 January 1993, p. 59.

57. *Ibid.* ("her or" added by author).

58. Boris Bergant, member of the Board of Directors of RTV Slovenia, in inter-

210   *Sabrina Petra Ramet*

view with the author, Ljubljana, 26 March 1992.

59. Andrej Poznić, chief editor of Kanal A, in interview with the author, Ljubljana, 20 March 1992.

60. *Eastern Europe Newsletter*, Vol. 6, No. 9 (27 April 1992), p. 6.

61. *Delo* (8 May 1992), p. 3, trans. in FBIS, *Daily Report* (Eastern Europe), 24 May 1992, p. 37.

62. *Neue Zürcher Zeitung* (7 May 1992), p. 1.

63. *Eastern Europe Newsletter*, Vol. 6. No. 14 (6 July 1992), pp. 3–4.

64. *Dnevnik* (Ljubljana), 11 May 1992, p. 1, trans. in FBIS, *Daily Report* (Eastern Europe), 15 May 1992, p. 47.

65. *Süddeutsche Zeitung* (Munich), 5–6 December 1992, p. 10; and *Neue Zürcher Zeitung* (9 December 1992), p. 1.

66. *Neue Zürcher Zeitung* (5 December 1992), p. 5.

67. *Ibid.* (8 December 1992), p. 2.

68. *Il Messaggero* (Rome), 6 December 1992, p. 6.

69. *Süddeutsche Zeitung* (9/10 January 1993), p. 5.

70. *Neue Zürcher Zeitung* (10 December 1992), p. 2; re. Jelinčič's party's withholding weapons, see *Delo* (1 September 1992), p. 2, trans. in FBIS, *Daily Report* (Eastern Europe), 22 September 1992, p. 38.

71. Figures as reported by Radio Slovenia Network (9 December 1992), trans. in FBIS, *Daily Report* (Eastern Europe), 10 December 1992, p. 32.

72. See *Süddeutsche Zeitung* (9/10 January 1993), p. 5.

73. Tanjug (27 August 1992), trans. in FBIS, *Daily Report* (Eastern Europe), 1 September 1992, p. 44.

74. *Neue Zürcher Zeitung* (3 March 1993), p. 18.

75. *Ibid.* (5 December 1992), p. 5.

76. Tanjug (11 May 1992), in FBIS, *Daily Report* (Eastern Europe), 12 May 1992, p. 35; and *Wall Street Journal* (12 August 1992), p. A8.

77. *Delo* (29 August 1992), p. 1, trans. in FBIS, *Daily Report* (Eastern Europe), 16 September 1992, p. 26.

9

The Macedonian Enigma

Sabrina Petra Ramet

I

Concerning the existence of a territory known as Macedonia there is no dispute. Nor is there particular debate as to its borders (with the sole exception of its southern border, with Greece). But concerning the existence of a Macedonian people, there has long been dispute. And now, in a post-communist Eastern Europe highly charged with revived nationalism and irredentism, Serbia, Greece, and Bulgaria have all issued statements denying the existence of a Macedonian people and affirming their interest in the region, while some political figures among Kosovo's Albanian community, implicitly supported by Albania, have demanded the reassignment of territories in western Macedonia to Kosovo.

The Macedonian government in Skopje claims that there are Slavophone Macedonians living in Greece and Bulgaria. Athens and Sofia deny this, however. The Greek government claims that all persons living in Greece are Greeks and that there are no Slavophones in the country. The Bulgarian government claims that all Slavophones living in Bulgaria are Bulgarians, adding, for good measure, that all Slavophones residing in Macedonia are likewise Bulgarians. As for the Serbian government, its stance here is less explicitly formulated, but it is known that influential elites in Serbia (including senior figures in the Serbian Orthodox Church) cling to the idea (widespread in interwar Serbia) that Macedonians are merely "south Serbs," while both Serbian President Slobodan Milošević and Serbian Radical Party leader Vojislav Šešelj have demanded the retention of Macedonia in a Serb-dominated new "Yugoslavia."

In these circumstances, it is clear why, beginning in the summer of 1992, there developed a growing sense of urgency in Macedonia—an urgency which was only deepened by the long refusal of American and European Community leaders to extend diplomatic recognition, thus implicitly legitimating Greek, Serbian, Bulgarian, and Albanian claims against this troubled, if enigmatic, nation.

I shall argue, in what follows, that Macedonia's situation is precarious and fragile, and the republic remains vulnerable to destabilization, whether by ethnic Albanians or by the possible polarization of Macedonians themselves, or perhaps through other channels. By late summer 1992, the danger of a Serb-Montenegrin invasion seemed to be receding, partly because Skopje seemed to have succeeded in working out a tentative modus vivendi with Belgrade, partly because there have been so few Serbs living in Macedonia to begin with, and partly because Serbian forces have increasingly been bogged down on the Croatian and Bosnian fronts. Yet the Greek economic embargo and the virtually complete diplomatic isolation of Macedonia had devastating effects on the republic's economy and fueled political extremism in a republic hitherto renowned for its moderation and openness to negotiation. By February 1993 it appeared conceivable that the prolongation of Macedonia's economic and diplomatic isolation might yet succeed in sowing the seeds of social disintegration, thus opening the doors to foreign intervention. Indeed, the political and economic outlook within Macedonia was markedly gloomier in 1993 than just two years earlier, and this has the potential to be destabilizing, even given a belated Western diplomatic recognition of Macedonia.

II

Macedonia never intended to seek independence. Of postwar Yugoslavia's six constituent republics, Macedonia was, in terms of social product per capita, consistently one of the two poorest republics (alongside Bosnia-Herzegovina),[1] and was heavily dependent on special federal funding to sustain its developmental programs. In 1990, Macedonia accounted for 10.1 percent of the territory of Yugoslavia, 7.7 percent of its population, 5.7 percent of its overall social product, 6.7 percent of industrial social product, 6.6 percent of agricultural social product, 9.2 percent of agricultural population, 4.9 percent of investments, 4.0 percent of total exports to the convertible area, and 5.6 percent of imports.[2] By every measure, Macedonia was an economic backwater.

Macedonia was also a political backwater, condemned to play a reactive role, while political elites in Serbia, Croatia, and Slovenia set both the agenda and the framework for discussion. No one in Macedonia ever imagined that Macedonia could survive as an independent state, let alone prosper. Association with Yugoslavia was Macedonia's best chance for economic and political stability.

The Macedonian Enigma

Habitually fearful of Serbian nationalism, wary of their own Albanian minority (officially estimated at 21 percent of the Macedonian population in 1991),[3] and unwilling to hitch their wagon to Bulgaria, regardless of ethnic affinity, Macedonians were the last of Yugoslavia's peoples to become infected with the nationalist frenzy that started to blaze in 1986[4]—first among the Serbs, and later among the Croats, Slovenes, and other peoples of Yugoslavia. The Macedonians were, one might say, the last Titoists. Indeed, even today, Tito's portrait still hangs in shops and offices in Skopje, alongside portraits of Goce Delchev, an insurrectionary leader who led a revolt against Ottoman rule in 1903.[5]

The region inhabited by today's Slavophone Macedonians has been called "Macedonia" for at least 3,500 years.[6] The population was largely Grecophone until the sixth century A.D., when large numbers of Slavs migrated into the area. During the nineteenth century, the "Macedonian question"—as it was called in acknowledgement of the historic name of the region—preoccupied European diplomats. When the Slavs of Macedonia formed a revolutionary organization in 1893, they called it the Internal *Macedonian* Revolutionary Organization, taking as their rallying cry, the motto "Macedonia to the Macedonians!" In 1903, IMRO staged the Ilinden Uprising, with the goal of driving the Ottomans out of Macedonia.[7] The uprising gave birth to an independent Macedonian state—the Krushevo Republic—which survived for 11 days before being crushed by Ottoman authorities.

Yet, when Tito created a Socialist Republic of Macedonia at the end of World War Two, as a constituent republic in federalized Yugoslavia, some observers claimed that the name was "artificial" and that Tito was "inventing" a Macedonian nation. It is conceded by all observers that Macedonians are closely related to Bulgarians, perhaps even linguistically and culturally indistinguishable from Bulgarians. But nations arise not only on the basis of objective differences, but also as a result of subjective perceptions (as in the case of the Austrian nation, and, should their sense of identity continue to develop, the Moravians). In a concession to this principle, and acknowledging the political climate of the time, the Bulgarian regime itself recognized the existence of a separate Macedonian nationality after World War Two and even required Bulgarian citizens residing in Pirin Macedonia (western Bulgaria) to declare their nationality as "Macedonian."[8] Indeed, in the Bulgarian census of 1956, some 180,000 Macedonians were reported to be residing in Bulgaria, although the census of 1960 found only 9,000 Macedonians in Bulgaria.[9]

Ironically, the subsequent Soviet-Yugoslav rift, and concomitant Bulgaro-Yugoslav rift, by feeding the flames of anti-Bulgarian propaganda in Macedonia, probably helped to strengthen the sense of Macedonian national identity.[10]

During the Tito and early post-Tito eras, Macedonia was the most quiescent of Yugoslavia's six republics. But as the pressures for political and economic demonopolization grew in Yugoslavia, they sent out ripples that eventually reached Macedonia. By April 1989, the Macedonian Assembly had proclaimed 32 amendments to the republic's constitution, effectively introducing multi-candidate elections and laying the legal groundwork for eventual privatization.[11] At first, Macedonian politicians hoped to preserve the federation—though they decisively rejected a Bosnian initiative to introduce an asymmetric model which would have given greater autonomy to Slovenia and Croatia than to the other units.[12] But gradually, voices could be heard calling for Macedonian independence. In August 1990, the Movement for All-Macedonian Action endorsed Macedonian secession;[13] six months later, the leadership of the Internal Macedonian Revolutionary Organization—Democratic Party for Macedonian National Unity (hereafter, IMRO Democratic Party) seconded this call and urged the Macedonian legislature to adopt a resolution in favor of Macedonian independence.[14]

On 25 January 1991, the Macedonian Assembly adopted a declaration of sovereignty, following similar declarations by Slovenia and Croatia. The declarations pointedly left the door open to continued association with other Yugoslav republics. Article 4, in particular, noted that "the Socialist Republic of Macedonia, as a sovereign state, shall independently decide about [its] future relations with the states of the other peoples of Yugoslavia, in accordance with its interests, in a peaceful and democratic manner."[15]

Yet as late as spring 1991, as Slovenia and Croatia were preparing to declare their independence and as Serbia was stockpiling huge quantities of arms in preparation for its impending campaigns against those two republics, Macedonia still hoped for a compromise formula that would reconcile Yugoslavia's squabbling republics. Together with the Bosnian leadership, Macedonia's political elite tried, in Yugoslavia's waning months, to fashion a compromise formula that contained elements of both the Slovene-Croatian confederalist proposal, and the Serbian centralist draft for a new Yugoslavia. As late as 25 June 1991, the virtually defunct "Yugoslav" Federal Assembly was scrutinizing the Bosnian-Macedonian draft and concluded that it offered "a solid basis for [the] continuation of negotiations on Yugoslavia's future organization."[16]

But that same day, tanks and units of the Yugoslav People's Army (JNA) mounted an assault against Slovenia. A month later, the JNA withdrew from Slovenia and, in coordination with local Serbian militias, opened hostilities against Croatia. In early April 1992, Serbian militias, well armed with hardware from JNA stocks, opened hostilities against Bosnia, quickly capturing 70 percent of the territory of the republic, and driving some 1.5 million Bosnians from their homes by early June.[17] Serbian militias laid

The Macedonian Enigma

siege to Sarajevo and by February 1993, the defenders of Sarajevo were running out of ammunition and, with only foodstuffs coming in from outside, started to appear more like targets than defenders. The eventual fall of Sarajevo, whether accompanied by the wholesale slaughter of its defenders or not, would effectively eliminate Bosnia as a player and permit Serbia to turn its attention to new fronts. Already in 1992 it began harnessing its armed force to drive the non-Serbian population of Vojvodina—about one-third of the population of the province—out of the country. Vojvodina's local Hungarians have begun fleeing, in large numbers, across the border to Hungary.

Serbia's program of territorial expansion and subsequent "ethnic cleansing" is not, however, confined to the northern and western fronts. Serbia also has ambitions where Kosovo is concerned, but its attitude toward Macedonia has been tinged with ambiguity. As early as 26 June 1991, the Macedonian Assembly took up the question of possible independence for Macedonia. Divided between nationalist elements impatient for an immediate proclamation of independence and elements urging restraint, the Assembly decided to postpone the question for the time being.[18] Although Macedonian President Kiro Gligorov personally was reluctant to let go of the Yugoslav idea, he, like other Macedonian politicians, had to face the fact that the old structures and realities no longer existed. On 6 July, the Macedonian Assembly decided that "if no agreement can be reached in a peaceful and democratic way on a union of sovereign states on Yugoslav territory, the government must put before the assembly a constitutional law whereby the Republic of Macedonia, as an independent and sovereign state, will assume and carry out its sovereign rights."[19]

On 8 September, Macedonia carried out a republic-wide referendum on the future of the republic. Some 74 percent of the returns supported Macedonian independence.[20] Scarcely over a week later, the Macedonian Assembly drew the inevitable conclusion and declared the republic an independent state. Article 4 committed Macedonia to respect "the principle of inviolability of the borders, as a guarantee for peace and security in the region," and in the same breath, confirmed "its policy of not expressing territorial claims against any . . . neighboring country."[21]

A new constitution was adopted on 29 November, and in December, the republic applied for recognition by the European Community. At that time, the EC Arbitration Commission determined that of the four ex-Yugoslav republics seeking recognition, only Slovenia and Macedonia met EC criteria for recognition, including those related to human rights.[22] Croatia and Bosnia-Herzegovina were found to fall short on EC criteria. Yet the EC now moved with dispatch to recognize not only Slovenia, but also Croatia and Bosnia, but shelved any recognition of Macedonia for, as it turned out, more than a year (at this writing). It took until 15 January 1992,

216   *Sabrina Petra Ramet*

before neighboring Bulgaria became the first state to recognize Macedonian statehood. Slovenia, Croatia, and Russia soon followed.[23] In June 1992, Macedonian President Kiro Gligorov held talks in Tirana with Albanian President Sali Berisha, regarding mutual recognition and economic cooperation, but the Albanian government declined to agree to such recognition for the time being, pending Macedonia's making concessions to its Albanian minority.[24]

III

In January 1992, Macedonia formally declined a Serbian invitation to associate with the new "Federal Republic of Yugoslavia" (essentially a Serb-Montenegrin federation). Macedonia withdrew its members from the diplomatic and consular staff of the Yugoslav Foreign Secretariat, recalled Macedonian officers from the Yugoslav People's Army, and recalled its representatives from the impotent Yugoslav Assembly and the largely defunct Yugoslav Presidency.[25]

Within Macedonia there was a debate between Macedonian nationalists, who wanted to define the new republic as "the national state of the Macedonian people," and moderates, who wanted to define the republic as a civil state of all its citizens. Unable to resolve their differences, the two sides finally agreed on a mixed formula: in the preamble to the Macedonian constitution, the republic is indeed described as "the national state of the Macedonian people,"[26] while in the body of the constitution itself, reference is to "an independent, sovereign, democratic, and welfare state of equal citizens."[27]

Macedonia subsequently established a separate Macedonian News Agency,[28] introduced a separate Macedonian currency,[29] and initiated deliberations regarding a new flag, coat of arms, and national anthem.[30] In April 1992, the Macedonian government approved a law authorizing the privatization of up to 85 percent of the enterprises in the republic, and the transfer of 15 percent of the stock to the republic's Pension and Disability Insurance Fund.[31] By September 1992, 85 percent of all firms (accounting for 17–20 percent of total capital) were in private hands.[32]

Meanwhile, the Macedonian government concluded an agreement with a delegation of the Federal Secretariat for National Defense, led by Colonel-General Blagoje Adžić, under which the JNA was to withdraw all units from Macedonian territory by 15 April 1992 at the latest. Under this agreement, the JNA agreed to leave behind all its radio communications equipment with the exception of digital centers at Kičevo and Kumanovo, and of weapons and equipment belonging to Macedonian Territorial Defense forces.[33] Macedonian Defense Minister Traian Gočevski commented,

If we were to start from nothing, we would need around $2 billion for the Macedonian defense system, which, logically speaking, is unreasonable. Because Macedonia has allocated funding for the JNA in the past, our republic has the right to demand part of the inheritance of the JNA in a division of military equipment, weaponry, and systems, within the framework of its participation in financing the army. For the model that has been decided on, this would be quite adequate for the intitial equipping of the armed forces.[34]

Even so, a Macedonian army in the range of 25,000–30,000 troops (1 percent of the population) was expected to cost about $9,000 per troop per year for sustenance, not counting weaponry and other resources needed for maintaining the armed forces.

In actual fact, the JNA completed its withdrawal from Macedonia ahead of schedule—by 26 March.[35] But contrary to Macedonian expectations, the JNA did its best to strip its installations bare. Almost all of the military technical material and equipment had been taken out of Macedonia by early February already, and (contrary to agreement) the JNA attempted to remove communications and radar equipment from the Petrovac airport. Macedonian authorities objected to the latter step and placed special units of the Macedonian Ministry of Internal Affairs in the highest state of alert.[36] "There were also attempts to take away [other] equipment that is of vital importance for the functioning of the republic," Radio Belgrade reported.[37] At the 4 July Barracks in Stip, contrary to point 10 of the Gligorov-Adžić agreement, military authorities tried to dismantle the automatic telephone exchange—an attempt sharply resisted by ethnic Macedonian officers and civilians working there.[38]

Despite all of this uncertainty, the Macedonian Territorial Defense forces assumed control of all of the republic's borders by mid-March, along with the military airport in Skopje and other installations. In mid-April, the fledgling Macedonian army began recruiting young men.[39] But the JNA had withdrawn all large weapons, leaving Macedonian military authorities to confront the dilemma as to how to build an army from scratch given the UN-imposed arms embargo on all ex-Yugoslav republics. Macedonia made some attempts to purchase arms on the black market, including in Poland,[40] but in the Polish case, these attempts were not successful. On the other hand, the conclusion of a security treaty with Turkey in May 1992 and repeated references to the friendliness of Macedonian-Turkish relations may be accompanied and reinforced by arms supplies.[41]

218   *Sabrina Petra Ramet*

IV

But even as Macedonia took these and other steps to assume responsibility for its own affairs, the European Community and the United States balked at extending diplomatic recognition to the new state. To Macedonia's request for recognition, the EC decided, on 16 December 1991, that Skopje first needed to provide constitutional guarantees of its respect for its neighbors' borders as of its respect for the principle of noninterference in the internal affairs of its neighbors, and an unambiguous renunciation of any territorial ambitions (i.e., above and beyond the renunciation already provided in its declaration of independence).[42] Since Macedonia did not have any such ambitions to begin with, this was only a question of providing its neighbors (specifically Greece) with unreciprocated guarantees. Accordingly, the Macedonian Assembly met the following month and, with evident dispatch, passed two amendments, affecting articles 3 and 49 of the republic's constitution. These amendments were tailored to satisfy the EC conditions.[43] Macedonia's politicians seemed, at first, to believe that this would resolve the dispute.

It quickly became clear, however, that much more was involved than mere assurances to neighbors. Greece, in fact, was Macedonia's sole antagonist within the European Community, but succeeeded, singlehandedly, in persuading its EC fellow-members and the US to postpone diplomatic recognition of Macedonia from one month to the next. In April 1992, for example, British Foreign Secretary Douglas Hurd declared, after consultations with Greek Prime Minister Konstantin Mitsotakis, that Macedonia had not complied with the EC conditions of 16 December.[44] What the Greeks now demanded, as the price of EC recognition, was that Macedonia change its name. Athens claimed that the name "Macedonia" was the exclusive property of Greece and denied that the 3,500-year association of the name with the region of present-day Macedonia gave its present inhabitants any right to continue to call the region by its established name. The Greeks suggested that the Macedonians rename their republic "the Republic of Skopje." The US, which at first seemed to show favor toward the Macedonians,[45] later hardened its position in deference to the powerful Greek lobby[46] and fearing that an American recognition of Macedonia might destabilize the Mitsotakis regime and return the more anti-American Papandreou to the helm of power.

As the EC and the United States gradually extended recognition to Slovenia, Croatia, and Bosnia-Herzegovina, it became quite obvious that Macedonia was being singled out for discriminatory treatment. The Macedonian Assembly took a grave view of the situation, and in June 1992, Macedonian President Kiro Gligorov paid a short visit to Paris, to try, in vain, to persuade the French government to change its stance. The con-

The Macedonian Enigma   219

tinuing refusal to normalize relations, Gligorov argued with his French hosts, posed "very great dangers and very great threats" for the entire Balkan region.[47] The French, like other members of the EC, showed no sign of budging.

As the people of Macedonia gradually realized that the EC and the United States actually expected them to change their nation's name, disbelief and resolute optimism gave way to horror, frustration, outrage, and defiance. In mid-July, 50–100,000 people protested, in downtown Skopje, against the EC refusal to recognize their nation.[48] The moderate government of Nikola Kljusev fell under the pressure of EC repudiation, producing a political void which it was to take more than two months to fill.

The Greeks claimed that they were only asserting a "copyright" on the Macedonian name. But the argument is clearly specious, because the broader region known as Macedonia includes the area of the Republic of Macedonia. So what are Greece's *real* interests in the matter?

To begin with, Greece has always denied that there are any ethnic Macedonians living within its borders. Skopje claims, on the contrary, that there are some 230,000 ethnic Macedonians living in northern Greece (in the region known as Aegean Macedonia).[49] The Macedonian government, whether under Tito, under the post-Tito communists, or under the post-communist coalition, has consistently criticized Greek treatment of its Macedonian minority, documenting a systematic policy of forced Hellenization of geographic and personal names, proscription of the use of the Macedonian language, and the denial to Greek citizens of permission to study abroad at the Cyril and Methodius University of Skopje.[50] Even before Macedonia's own declaration of independence, Gligorov had promised to put the question of the human rights of Macedonians living in Greece on the agenda of various international organizations.[51] In this way, an internationally recognized Macedonia promised to be a painful thorn in Greece's side. It is even conceivable that Greece feared that recognition of an independent Macedonia would stir separatist feeling among its Macedonian minority.[52]

Second, Greece may entertain irredentist notions in connection with Macedonia. It is not without some interest, for example, that Athens conducted talks with Belgrade about a "joint Serbian-Greek border"[53] or that Branko Kostić, vice president of rump Yugoslavia, spoke (in March 1992) of the possibility of partitioning Macedonia (even though he did not specify with whom).[54] In October 1992, *Time* magazine reported that "several European governments have relayed to Washington reports that Mitsotakis has secretly discussed the partition of Macedonia with Serbia and perhaps with Albania and Bulgaria as well."[55] The Bulgarian Foreign Ministry immediately issued a denial,[56] but Serbian President Milošević's openly admitted proposal to Greece to form a "Serbian-Greek" confederation[57] and the persistent reports of Serbian-Greek rapport[58] made the notion of Serbian-Greek discussions about Macedonia's fate seem quite plausible.

Third, thanks in part to elite manipulation, the Macedonian controversy had, by now, inflamed the Greek public, making it increasingly difficult for Athens to back away from its anti-Macedonian position even if it had wanted to. Mass protests involving up to 200,000 persons in Salonika provided a dramatic stage for demands that Macedonia be recognized as Greek,[59] while six prominent Greek intellectuals, including Nobel Prize winner Odysseus Elytis and former Minister of Culture Melina Mercouri, sent an open letter to the EC in April, setting forth their conviction that any recognition of Macedonia, under that name, would call into question the very territorial integrity of Greece.[60] In early December 1992, an estimated 1.3 million persons were said to have massed on the streets of Athens to demonstrate their opposition to any recognition of Macedonia under its historic name[61]—a dramatic testament to the frenzy which had seized the Greek populace by then. The political mood in Greece seemed to be captured by a decision, taken in January 1993, requiring all Greek citizens to declare their religion in their passports.[62]

At first, Greece attempted to deny the reality of Macedonian independence, and urged the ex-Yugoslav republics—in December 1991—to patch up their differences and set up a loose confederation.[63] This would have been a sensible proposal two years earlier, but seemed utterly out of touch with reality, coming five months after the outbreak of war between Serbia and Croatia and more than two months after Macedonia's formal secession.

Athens then insisted that the name "Macedonia" belongs exclusively to Greece, and insinuated that the Skopje government's insistence on this name betrayed irredentist and expansionist aspirations—a notion hard to reconcile with Greece's overwhelming military and economic superiority. Athens urged Macedonia to accept the name "Republic of Skopje." When the EC accepted Athens' reservations and withheld recognition from Macedonia, Macedonian President Kiro Gligorov sent an official reply to the EC Arbitration Commission, noting *inter alia* that "bargaining over the name of a state as a condition for its international recognition is contrary to all the standards of international law and to the practice that applies when a state's independence is recognized.[64] In a follow-up message to the foreign ministers of the EC, Gligorov argued that "to comply with the Greek demand that Macedonia change its name would mean that the people of that republic would also lose their name, from which it would further stem that this people have no right to a state at all.[65] While Macedonians held fast to the principle that they were entitled to retain the name associated with their land for more than three millennia,[66] and lashed out at Athens' repression of Slavophone Macedonians living in Greece,[67] Athens mocked

The Macedonian Enigma 221

Macedonia as a "Titoist invention"[68] and began blocking fuel shipments to Macedonia.[69]

By September 1992, Macedonia had been recognized by only a handful of countries: Bulgaria, Turkey, Russia, Belarus, Lithuania, Croatia, Slovenia, and the Philippines.[70] In addition, Germany agreed in April 1992 to open a consulate in Skopje, economic contacts with Albania have been intensified, and in October 1992, the Bulgarian and Macedonian Ministries of the Interior signed a cooperation agreement covering the combat of terrorism, drug trafficking, organized crime, and other related matters.[71]

As early as January 1991, Greek authorities closed their border to Macedonians.[72] Greece imposed a blockade on Macedonia, delaying or halting the importation of food, oil, medicine, and other staples. In January 1992, this led to a protest by Macedonian Prime Minister Kljusev when Greece held up 97 tons of medicine and children's food in the port of Piraeus, while Macedonia was coping with a serious flu epidemic.[73] At the same time, the Greeks have maintained their ire by rebaptizing several warships and northern airports. Salonika's airport was, for example, renamed "Macedonia Airport," while Kavalla's airport was renamed for Alexander the Great. In April 1992 alone, Athenian museums put on two displays of Macedonian artifacts.[74]

But Greek policy has provoked serious concern not just in Macedonia, but also in Bulgaria, where politicians expressed concern that Greece's obstruction of EC recognition might facilitate an eventual destablization first of Macedonia and from there of the entire Balkan peninsula.[75]

V

The Serbian connection is, in some ways, even more interesting, and certainly more intricate, than the Greek. To begin with, it is clear that Belgrade hoped to keep Macedonia within the new federation it was setting up. It is much less clear whether anyone in the Belgrade government has ever intended to employ force to compel Macedonian adherence, let alone to engage in "ethnic cleansing" in that republic. Compared with the noisy polemics over Croatia and Bosnia, which built up over months to a crescendo long before open warfare broke out in either republic, polemics over Macedonia have been confined to a whisper, a hint. If Macedonia should slide into chaos, it is apt to be set in motion by factors internal to Macedonia (the most likely candidates for this being the right-wing IMRO-Democratic Party and the ethnic Albanians), rather than by a front assault by Serbian militias and regular forces on the Croatian or Bosnian model.

And yet, Macedonian authorities claim to have evidence of a plan developed by the Counterintelligence Service of the JNA to destabilize Macedonia by manipulating its ethnic divisions. Code-named "Operation Opera," the plan involved 30 trained officers, but was allegedly scrapped after the breakup of the Service's network in ex-Yugoslavia.[76]

For that matter, there are Serbian interests in Macedonia. Official Macedonian census figures record that there were some 44,000 Serbs living in Macedonia as of 1991, accounting thus for about 2.2 percent of the population. Since most of them were said to be army officers and their families, it appears that the number of Serbs living in Macedonia today would be even smaller.[77] But some Serbs estimate a much larger number, claiming as many as 300–400,000 Serbs.[78]

Relations between post-communist Macedonia and Serbia got off to a rocky start, as Macedonian politicians spoke of "threats made by the Serbian chauvinists to occupy Macedonia and turn it into southern Serbia,"[79] and Serbian politicians replied with condemnations of "primitive political posturing and strongly orchestrated Serbophobia" in Macedonia.[80] Distrust colored both sides. The Democratic Union of Bulgarians was, thus, the only sociopolitical minority formation in Serbia to be denied registration in Serbia's 1990 elections,[81] while there were complaints from Serbs of a lengthy delay in the registration of the Skopje-based Democratic Party of Serbs in Macedonia[82] and of the continued proscription of a Macedonian-Serbian-Montenegrin Friendship Society, seeking to register in Gostivar.[83]

When Macedonia adopted a new constitution in 1991, it made some provisions for the protection of minority nationalities, listing, by name, some of the more numerous. The Serbs are not one of the more numerous nationality groups within Macedonia. But all the same, some Serbs were outraged not to be mentioned by name in the Macedonian constitution, and Milan Paroški, a deputy in the Serbian Assembly, declared in November 1991, "The separatist Macedonians have adopted a VMRO [Internal Macedonian Revolutionary Organization] constitution that has suspended Serbs as a state-creating people, putting them in the position of a nonexistent people in Macedonia, a historical Serbian territory in the SFRY or southern Serbia."[84]

Within Macedonia itself, the newly registered Democratic Party of Serbs in Macedonia declared, upon registration, its frustration that "the new Macedonian constitution does not even mention Serbs, but elaborates on some marginal ethnic groups [such] as 'ethnic Egyptians'."[85] Zoran Andjelković, a Serbian deputy in the Federal Assembly, raised the issue of significant Serbian historical monuments in the territory of Macedonia.[86] Still others pledged that "Serbia will not abandon the Serbs who live in other republics,"[87] while Vukašin Jokanović, vice president of the Serbian Assembly, pointedly noted, in February 1992, that "Serbia is strategically

The Macedonian Enigma

interested in *the area that is currently being called Macedonia.*[88] Jokanović added on the same occasion that Serbia "cannot allow an artificial state to interrupt the historical and religious bonds between Serbia and Greece."[89] Placed in this context, it is scarcely surprising that there have been reports that Milošević offered to divide Macedonia with Greece.[90]

Serbs claimed that their rights were not being respected in postcommunist Macedonia, and in particular that they were denied primary education in Serbian and freedom to practice their own religion (Serbian Orthodoxy as opposed to Macedonian Orthodoxy).[91] As early as September 1991, a so-called Party of Yugoslavs in Macedonia registered a protest against Macedonian independence on behalf of the small Serbian and Montenegrin minorities living in Macedonia. In an unveiled plea for union with Belgrade, the party issued a statement averring: "the Party of Yugoslavs particularly criticizes the commitment of the proponents of the new Macedonian Constitution to the effect that 'the sovereignty of the Republic of Macedonia is untransferable,' which is contrary to the decision in the referendum which established the 'right of the Republic of Macedonia to enter into an alliance of sovereign Yugoslav states,' which also means the right to transfer a part of the sovereignty of Macedonia to Yugoslavia."[92]

A still more ominous note was struck by the Serbian National Assembly in November 1991, as its deputies discussed the situation of the Serbs living in Macedonia. As *Politika* reported, " . . . the separatist Macedonian constitution is carrying out a political genocidal operation against the Serbian and other peoples in Macedonia. Among other things, there is a desire . . . to carry out the complete assimilation of Serbs, Montenegrins, and others."[93]

By December 1991, Serbian newspapers were accusing Macedonian President Kiro Gligorov of being involved in a "Vatican conspiracy"[94]—a propaganda line used earlier against Tudjman in preparation for the Serbian attack on Croatia—and that same month, there started to be speculations about possible scenarios for a Serbian military intervention in Macedonia.[95] In March 1992, the Association of Serbs and Montenegrins in Kumanovo, which had staged a 10,000-strong anti-independence protest the preceding month, demanded the establishment of a Serbian autonomous zone in the Kumanovo region. The association complained of discriminatory military recruitment, harassment at the workplace, transfers to lower posts and dismissals from work on ethnic criteria, and other forms of discrimination.[96]

Since then, there have been pointed remarks (from the Serbian side) about "unresolved" borders between Serbia and Macedonia,[97] and demands for a license to operate a Serbian-language radio station in Macedonia,[98] as well as more ambiguous statements to the effect that Macedonia's Serbian minority could serve as a "bridge of cooperation" between the two republics.[99] In October 1992, the Belgrade daily *Politika*, which generally reflects the policy of the Milošević regime, wrote of damage allegedly done by Macedonian "nationalist-chauvinist euphoria" and reported calls for assistance to "socially threatened Serbs and Montenegrins" in the republic.[100] Then, on New Year's Eve, an incident occurred in the Serb-inhabited village of Kučeviste, in which Macedonian police allegedly roughed up Serbian young people, reportedly in connection with the display of pictures of Slobodan Milošević at a New Year's party. Within days, local Serbs scheduled a meeting "to inform the public about the truth"[101]—as the euphemistic phrase has it. Locals remembered that similar meetings had been used earlier to mobilize Serbs in other republics and to whip up aggressive nationalism.

Since summer 1992, signals between Belgrade and Skopje have become more mixed, as both sides have come to appreciate the importance of future bilateral economic ties.[102] In March 1992, for example, Serbian Prime Minister Radoman Bozović received Macedonian Prime Minister Nikola Kljusev in Belgrade for talks concerning economic cooperation, the settling of mutual liabilities, and questions of tariffs and protectionism.[103] Subsequently, however, when the UN Security Council called for trade sanctions against rump Yugoslavia, Macedonia felt obliged to follow suit, as a demonstration of good faith as it pursued its quest for EC and US recognition.[104]

At the same time, however, the Serbian and Greek governments maintained a regular schedule of high-level reciprocal visits, conducting bilateral talks in November 1991 (Belgrade), March 1992 (Athens), April 1992 (Belgrade), June 1992 (Belgrade), and October 1992 (Korfu).[105] Greece violated the UN embargo and continued to tranship oil and war materiel to Serbia, and to export Greek foodstuffs to Serbia. Various subterfuges were employed in order to get shipments past the UN troops, including false claims that the shipments were destined for troops of the Bosnian government.

Serbia and Greece also offered each other broad diplomatic support. Milošević, for example, told Greek Prime Minister Mitsotakis (in April) that he "understood" Greece's political stand concerning Macedonia and promised that he "certainly will not make any moves that could harm Greece's interests."[106] In reciprocation, Mitsotakis offered Milošević an endorsement of Serbian policy in Kosovo. Said Mitsotakis: "We do not recognize that the Albanians in Kosovo have an absolute right to self-determination. The borders of former Yugoslavia, foreign and internal, must be respected. They [the Albanians] have a right to autonomy, as all minorities have the same rights."[107] Interestingly enough, three months earlier, the Albanian Foreign Ministry in Tirana summoned Greek Ambassador Stylianos Mallikurtis and handed him a formal protest, accusing Greece of flagrant interference in Albania's recent elections, including the illegal distribution of materials expressing "chauvinist and nationalist sentiments."[108]

The Macedonian Enigma 225

June brought Milošević's aforementioned astonishing proposal to the Greek government to form a Serbian-Greek confederation[109]—a proposal which, despite its utterly fanciful character, could only reinforce such Macedonian uncertainties as may have been kindled by repeated rumors of Serbian-Greek discussions about a partition of their republic. About this time, reflecting his uncertainty about the proclivities of his northern neighbor, Macedonian President Gligorov told a newsreporter that in Serbia, anything was possible, "all scenarios are possible."[110]

VI

Uncertainty is, of course, not equanimity. After all, Macedonia's two chief trade routes were traditionally through Greece and Serbia. Now, with a Greek embargo of Macedonia and Macedonian participation in the UN embargo against Serbia, the Macedonian economy is pinched. As a result of the rupture in its trade with Serbia, Macedonia will lose $2.5 billion per year.[111] Rather than remain dependent on Serbia and Greece, Macedonian authorities have decided to begin joint construction with Bulgaria of a 600-km. highway or an 800-km. railroad to connect the two countries and by-pass Greece. They also agreed to connect the Macedonian gas pipeline near Kriva Palanka, on the Macedonian-Bulgarian border.[112] Bulgaria also began deliveries of oil to Macedonia in September 1992, but Bulgaria has not been able to compensate fully for the effects of the Greek embargo, with ramifications for industry, the transport sector, and even for the fall harvest.[113]

But there are also political ramifications for Macedonia of these uncertainties, including those connected with the lengthy Western procrastination with regard to recognition. Gligorov has not minced words, and in June 1992, warned that "The EC's tendency to take a wait-and-see attitude regarding recognition . . . encourages all those who are interested in exploiting the unclear situation in that region or even turning to open aggression."[114] In an open letter, that same month, to Joao de Deus Pinheiro, President of the EC Council of Ministers, Gligorov asked, "Is it necessary for a war to break out in Macedonia and then to settle its international recognition under summary proceedings?"[115]

Meanwhile, the economic situation in Macedonia continues to deteriorate. This, combined with general frustration at Macedonia's inability to break out of diplomatic isolation, resulted in the collapse of Nikola Kljusev's government in early July 1992, and by September 1992, authorities were warning of the risk of total economic collapse, if the Greek embargo were not lifted soon.[116]

As of February 1993, inflation in Macedonia was running at 2,000 percent, while production was 40 percent lower than in June 1991. The loss

226   *Sabrina Petra Ramet*

from sanctions against Serbia amounted to almost $2.9 billion at that time, while the Greek embargo had cost Macedonia another $1.5 billion. But for all that, there were some positive signs too. Specifically, between April 1992 and February 1993, Macedonia succeeded in *increasing* its foreign currency reserves from only $20 million to about $50 million, and Macedonian authorities expressed hope that they could reduce the inflation rate to 100 percent by the end of 1993.[117]

The government crisis lasted for two months, and only in early September was Branko Crvenkovski, the 30-year old chair of the Social Democratic Party, able to put together a left-of-center coalition. His coalition included generous representation for members of the Albanian parties in terms of ministerial portfolios, but pointedly excluded the nationalist IMRO which, with 37 seats in the 120-seat Assembly, commanded the largest single bloc of deputies. (There are 23 Albanian deputies in the Assembly.)

VII

At first Macedonian parliamentarians found it difficult to believe that the EC would support Greece for long. The Greek argument seemed to defy all logic. But as days wore into weeks and weeks into months, the Macedonian politicians came to realize that the drama over their name was all too real. At one point, the Macedonian Assembly passed over from anguish to inanity as one parliamentarian proposed that Macedonia could declare itself the Republic of Coca Cola—a choice which, as he noted, would immediately assure it of a state emblem and a national anthem, and perhaps also the generous support of the Coca Cola company itself.[118]

In November 1992, almost a year since Macedonia first filed for diplomatic recognition, the EC devised a compromise formula under which the word "Macedonia" might be used as an adjective in the republic's official name, but not as a noun. The EC now pressed Athens and Skopje to accept this half-measure.[119] Skopje returned with a counter-proposal and suggested that it would agree to call itself "the Republic of Macedonia (Skopje)," offering the paranthetical insertion as its olive branch to Athens.[120] This solution was rejected by Athens. A subsequent French offer to submit the dispute to an international tribunal was rebuffed by Macedonia as giving too much honor to the Greek position.[121] But in January 1993, Danish Foreign Minister Uffe Ellemann-Jensen sharply reproved the Greek government for holding up recognition of Macedonia and declared the Greek arguments about historical claims and irredentist possibilities utterly specious.[122] This led directly to the surprising announcement the following month that Greek Prime Minister Konstantin Mitsotakis would accept a formula under which "Macedonia" would not be the sole name of the re-

The Macedonian Enigma

public.[123] Mitsotakis' policy about-face led to demands for his resignation in the Athens daily, *Kathimerini*. The socialist opposition backed these demands, condemning Mitsotakis for being prepared to accept what they called a "humiliating diplomatic defeat." Meanwhile, the New Democracy Party (of which Mitsotakis was the chair, at this writing) seemed to be in danger of splitting in two over the issue of Macedonia.[124] But regardless of the strength of Greek sentiments, it seemed clear that Macedonia was winning increasing support in West European capitals. But Mitsotakis held fast to his new position, and intimated that the Macedonian Republic might call itself "Northern Macedonia." Macedonian President Gligorov rejected this suggestion out of hand: "We have chosen a name, and it is not negotiable."[125] By then it also appeared that Macedonia would be offered admission to the UN, albeit under the rather anomalous name, "Former Yugoslav Republic of Macedonia"—a solution favored by Greece and by the US, but viewed with dismay in Macedonia.[126]

The international community also adopted other measures designed to address some of Macedonia's *political* dilemmas. Thus, in early December 1992, CSCE spokespersons in Geneva announced that a new census would be conducted in Macedonia under international auspices, in an effort to ascertain the veracity of Albanian claims to comprise as much as 40 percent of the republic's population,[127] and a week later, the UN Security Council agreed to a Macedonian request to dispatch peacekeeping forces to the republic, pledging 700 soldiers, 35 military observers, and 26 civilian police.[128]

By mid-February 1993, there was growing pressure on Greece to give in. EC ministers hinted that full recognition was no longer far off,[129] and Italian Prime Minister Giulano Amato announced that Rome would not wait much longer, and in the absence of a broad international agreement, would proceed with unilateral recognition of Macedonia.[130] Meanwhile, Turkey began to offer Macedonia concrete assistance, pledging wide-ranging political and economic support, as well as the dispatch of military trainers to train Macedonia's 14,000-man army, and war materiel appropriate to Macedonia's needs.[131] And in October 1992, Russia offered to send oil to Macedonia.[132]

Throughout 1992 and early 1993, there had been repeated Greek violations of Macedonian air space, as well as systematic jamming of the working frequencies of Macedonia's access flight control wavelength.[133] Then, abruptly, in early February 1993, just a few weeks after the arrival of the first contingent of the UN Protection Force in Macedonia, Greece and Macedonia reached an agreement to reopen access routes to landlocked Macedonia, and as a result, the government in Skopje announced, on 2 February, that it was ending a seven-month old gasoline rationing scheme.[134]

228   Sabrina Petra Ramet

Meanwhile, the Greek government continued to harass the Macedonians in sundry petty ways, for example by pressuring the European Film Industry (largely unsuccessfully) to declare Macedonia's 1992 film entry ("Tattooing") ineligible,[135] by pressuring the publishers of *The World Almanac* (unsuccessfully) not to include an entry on Macedonia,[136] and by massing Greek army forces along the border with Macedonia and placing them in a state of "high alert."[137]

Despite the growing acceptance of Macedonian passports (e.g., in the course of February 1993, by Canada and Norway), Greek Foreign Minister Michalis Papakonstantinou sounded positively cocky when he declared, on 25 February 1993, that the "problem" of Macedonia's name would be "resolved within 10 days or so, regardless of what the Skopjans wanted."[138]

VIII

The prolonged diplomatic imbroglio has had an unhealthy effect on Macedonia's political landscape. In mid-1991, Macedonia's prospects to build a stable pluralistic system appeared reasonably good, and at the end of the year, as already noted, the European Community gave Macedonia high marks for the protection of human rights and the assurance of civil liberties. As of early 1993, the prognosis no longer looks very bright for Macedonia, and at least part of the credit for that must be laid at the feet of Western diplomats, especially those of Greece.

In a word, the Western repression of Macedonia's name had such an electrifying effect on the Macedonian public and on its politicians, that much of the energy that was needed to resolve other issues of post-communist transition is being drained away in this diplomatic fight with Greece. As of the end of December 1992, there were more than 50 officially recognized political parties and associations in Macedonia. Surveying this gallimaufry, the Skopje daily *Nova Makedonija* bemoaned tendencies of " . . . political disorientation, changes in political coloring and definitions, no follow up or uninvolvement in the implementation of their own political programs, frequent reactions changing on a daily basis, [and] confrontation (for the sake of confrontation) with politically opposing parties."[139] With Macedonia's politicians distracted in this way, state-owned enterprises have stopped keeping accurate accounts, have withheld taxes from the government, and became involved in illegal foreign currency speculation. *Nova Makedonija* concluded that Macedonia's legal and economic systems were "in a state of chaos."[140] Add to this the growing politicization of the Macedonian Orthodox Church, which now concludes that its time has come and that it can push its own social agenda onto a confessionally mixed society.

The Macedonian Enigma 229

Yet despite the chaos, despite the escalating nationalist polemics, despite the economic troubles, and despite even calls for a suspension of party politics and a working consensus on "the vital interests of Macedonia,"[141] it has been hard to focus on domestic agendas in the midst of controversy with Greece. On 1 March 1993, Macedonian President Kiro Gligorov told a Bulgarian newspaper that Serbian President Slobodan Milošević and Greek Prime Minister Mitsotakis had met and had "agreed to invade and divide up Macedonia."[142] When the President of the country fears foreign invasion and partition, it is difficult to give priority to other items on the political agenda.

IX

Macedonia has not been without its advocates in the West. The *Financial Times*, for example, argued (in an editorial published in its 1 July 1992 edition), that "of all the ex-Yugoslav republics, except Slovenia, Macedonia is the one that best qualifies for international recognition. Its government controls its territory, and has won the support of the ethnic Albanian minority. Yet if not helped to consolidate itself rapidly, it is vulnerable to destabilisation and even partition, especially if fighting breaks out between Serbs and Albanians in neighboring Kosovo."[143] Or again, US Senator Dennis DeConcini and Representative Frank McCloskey, returning home from an official visit to Macedonia in November 1992, issued a joint statement, recommending that "international recognition of that country would be the right thing to do, and . . . it should be done immediately."[144]

Macedonia's situation as of 1993 is complicated. Albania, its neighbor to the west, is concerned about the status and rights of Macedonia's substantial Albanian minority. Serbia, its neighbor to the north, continues to utter dark phrases open to alarming interpretations. Greece, its neighbor to the south, expects the Macedonians to renounce a name they have borne for 1,300 years, ever since they migrated into the area, even though they have no other name (unless, of course, they are Bulgarians). And Bulgaria, its neighbor to the east, is all too friendly, insisting all the while that Macedonians are just Bulgarians,[145] and the Macedonian government cannot help wondering whether Bulgaria has more in mind, in the long run, than mere friendly relations. Small, landlocked, covered with rugged mountains, and poor, Macedonia is still, as it has perennially been, "the Balkan apple of discord."

Postscript (August 1994)

In December 1993, Macedonia belatedly obtained diplomatic recognition from Germany, France, Britain, Norway, and other west European powers, as well as from Japan. On 9 February 1994, the American White House

230   *Sabrina Petra Ramet*

released a statement announcing the extension of formal recognition to the Republic of Macedonia.[146] Immediately after this, US Senator Paul Sarbanes of Maryland, Representative Michael Bilirakis of Florida, and several other prominent Greek-Americans began to exert pressure on the White House to withdraw its statement. The White House bowed to the pressure and cancelled its recognition of Macedonia. Meanwhile, Representative Bilirakis began promoting a bill to "bar the United States from ever establishing diplomatic relations with Macedonia." [147]

Notes

1. See Sabrina Petra Ramet, *Nationalism and Federalism in Yugoslavia, 1962-1991*, 2nd ed. (Bloomington, Ind.: Indiana University Press, 1992), pp. 142-143.

2. *Statistički godišnjak Jugoslavije 1991* (Belgrade: Savezni Zavod za Statistiku, 1991), p. 410; and *Danas* (Zagreb), no. 459 (4 December 1990), p. 18.

3. *Broj i struktura na naselenieto vo Republika Makedonija po opštini i nacionalna pripadnost* (Skopje: Republički zavod za statistika, 1991), p. 6.

4. I am dating this from the issuance, that year, of a plaintive "memorandum" by the Serbian Academy of Sciences and Arts. For discussion, see Sabrina Petra Ramet, "War in the Balkans," in *Foreign Affairs*, Vol. 71, No. 4 (Fall 1992).

5. *The Economist* (London), 8 February 1992, p. 48.

6. N. G. L. Hammond, *A History of Macedonia*, Vol. 1 (Oxford: Clarendon Press, 1972), p. 276.

7. Charles and Barbara Jelavich, *The Establishment of the Balkan National States, 1804-1920* (Seattle: University of Washington Press, 1977), p. 202.

8. Theodore Zang, Jr., "Destroying Ethnic Identity: Selective Persecution of Macedonians in Bulgaria," in *Macedonian Review*, Vol. 21 (1991), nos. 1–2, pp. 71–72.

9. *Nedeljne informativne novine* (NIN), Belgrade, 5 January 1975. For further discussion, see Dimitrije Kulić, *Makedonija i socijalistička revolucija u Jugoslaviji* (Belgrade: Savremena administracija, 1979).

10. *Večernji list* (Zagreb), 20 June 1992, p. 52. Re. the Soviet link in this equation, see Pedro Ramet, "The Soviet Factor in the Macedonian Dispute," in *Survey*, Vol. 24, No. 3 (Summer 1979).

11. Tanjug (14 April 1989), in FBIS, *Daily Report* (Eastern Europe), 24 April 1989, p. 58.

12. *Borba* (Belgrade), 8 November 1990, p. 3.

13. *Ibid.* (3 August 1990), p. 3.

14. Tanjug (23 February 1991), in FBIS, *Daily Report* (Eastern Europe), 25 February 1991, p. 55.

15. "Declaration on the Sovereignty of the Republic of Macedonia," in *Yugoslav Survey* (Belgrade), Vol. 32 (1991), No. 3, p. 58.

16. Tanjug (25 June 1991), in FBIS, *Daily Report* (Eastern Europe), 26 June 1991, p. 46.

17. *Financial Times* (London), 3 June 1992, p. 14; and *Neue Zürcher Zeitung* (24 June 1992), p. 2.

The Macedonian Enigma 231

18. Radio Belgrade Network (26 June 1991), trans. in FBIS, *Daily Report* (Eastern Europe), 27 June 1991, p. 56.

19. Radio Slovenia Network (Ljubljana), 6 July 1991, trans. in FBIS, *Daily Report* (Eastern Europe), 8 July 1991, p. 56.

20. *Los Angeles Times* (10 September 1991), p. A12.

21. This declaration was dated 17 September 1991. "Declaration on the Sovereignty," p. 59.

22. *Report on the U.S. Helsinki Commission Delegation to Hungary, Greece, Macedonia, and Croatia (Codel DeConcini), November 11–17, 1992,* Prepared by the Staff of the Commission on Security and Cooperation in Europe, Helsinki Commission (Washington D.C.: Commission on Security and Cooperation in Europe, December 1992), p. 8.

23. Re. Bulgaria, see *The Independent* (London), 17 January 1992, p. 11; and *Borba* (24 March 1992), p. 13; re. Slovenia, see Tanjug (12 February 1992), trans. in FBIS, *Daily Report* (Eastern Europe), 13 February 1992, p. 29; re. Croatia, see Tanjug (30 March 1992), trans. in FBIS, *Daily Report* (Eastern Europe), 31 March 1992, p. 29; and re. Russia, see Tanjug (15 May 1992), in FBIS, *Daily Report* (Eastern Europe), 18 May 1992, p. 44.

24. Tanjug (3 June 1992), two reports of same date, trans. in FBIS, *Daily Report* (Eastern Europe), 4 June 1992, pp. 6 and 73; and Tirana ATA (4 June 1992), in *Ibid.*, pp. 6–7.

25. Tanjug (24 January 1992), in FBIS, *Daily Report* (Eastern Europe), 31 January 1992, p. 40.

26. *Nova Makedonija* (Skopje), 4 January 1992, p. 12, trans. in FBIS, *Daily Report* (Eastern Europe), 29 January 1992, p. 39.

27. Radio Belgrade Network (Belgrade), 18 November 1991, trans. in FBIS, *Daily Report* (Eastern Europe), 18 November 1991, p. 53. See also "Constitutions of the Republics," in *Yugoslav Survey*, Vol. 33 (1992), No. 1, pp. 33–36.

28. Tanjug (24 December 1991), in FBIS, *Daily Report* (Eastern Europe), 30 December 1991, p. 44.

29. *Politika ekspres* (Belgrade), 18 March 1992, p. 3.

30. *Vjesnik* (Zagreb), 26 March 1992, p. 7.

31. *Nova Makedonija* (12 April 1992), p. 2, trans. in FBIS, *Daily Report* (Eastern Europe), 6 May 1992, p. 44.

32. "Interview with Jane Miljovski, minister for privatization," in *East European Reporter* (Budapest), Vol. 5, No. 5 (September–October 1992), p. 51.

33. Tanjug (21 February 1992), trans. in FBIS, *Daily Report* (Eastern Europe), 24 February 1992, p. 37.

34. Quoted in *Borba* (28 January 1992), p. 8, trans. in FBIS, *Daily Report* (Eastern Europe), 7 February 1992, p. 39.

35. Tanjug (26 March 1992), trans. in FBIS, *Daily Report* (Eastern Europe), 27 March 1992, pp. 49–50.

36. Radio Belgrade Network (5 February 1992), trans. in FBIS, *Daily Report* (Eastern Europe), 6 February 1992, p. 25; and Tanjug (13 February 1992), trans. in FBIS, *Daily Report* (Eastern Europe), 14 February 1992, p. 41.

37. Radio Belgrade Network (7 February 1992), trans. in FBIS, *Daily Report* (Eastern Europe), 10 February 1992, pp. 36–37.

232   *Sabrina Petra Ramet*

38. Radio Macedonia Network (Skopje), 24 February 1992, trans. in FBIS, *Daily Report* (Eastern Europe), 24 February 1992, p. 47. See also Radio Macedonia Network (Skopje), 26 January 1992, trans. in FBIS, *Daily Report* (Eastern Europe), 28 January 1992, p. 39.

39. Tanjug (13 April 1992), in FBIS, *Daily Report* (Eastern Europe), 14 April 1992, p. 48.

40. Radio Warszawa Network (Warsaw), 30 December 1991, trans. in FBIS, *Daily Report* (Eastern Europe), 30 December 1991, p. 21.

41. Tanjug (18 May 1992), in FBIS, *Daily Report* (Eastern Europe), 19 May 1992, p. 28; *Nova Makedonija* (7 July 1992), p. 2; and *Nova Makedonija* (24 September 1992), p. 1.

42. *Neue Zürcher Zeitung* (28 April 1992), p. 4, and (21/22 June 1992), p. 6.

43. *Politika—International Weekly* (Belgrade), 11–17 January 1992, p. 4.

44. *Neue Zürcher Zeitung* (28 April 1992), p. 4.

45. See, for example, the report in *Nova Makedonija* (21 April 1992), pp. 1, 7, trans. in FBIS, *Daily Report* (Eastern Europe), 11 May 1992, pp. 42-43.

46. *Neue Zürcher Zeitung* (3 April 1992), p. 2, and (26 June 1992), p. 2.

47. Quoted in *Le Monde* (Paris), 20 June 1992, p. 3, trans. in FBIS, *Daily Report* (Eastern Europe), 24 June 1992, p. 30.

48. Radio Belgrade Network (12 July 1992), trans. in FBIS, *Daily Report* (Eastern Europe), 13 July 1992, p. 58.

49. Tanjug (24 September 1991), in FBIS, *Daily Report* (Eastern Europe), 25 September 1991, p. 30.

50. Petre Nakovski, "Evidence of the Repression of the Macedonians in Greece," in *Macedonian Review*, Vol. 21 (1991), No. 3, pp. 203, 205. See also *Nova Makedonija* (15 May 1992), pp. 1–2, trans. in FBIS, *Daily Report* (Eastern Europe), 3 June 1992, pp. 60–61.

51. Tanjug (17 June 1991), trans. in FBIS, *Daily Report* (Eastern Europe), 18 June 1991, p. 30.

52. As suggested in *Financial Times* (16 June 1992), p. 3.

53. Radio Belgrade Network (19 January 1992), trans. in FBIS, *Daily Report* (Eastern Europe), 21 January 1992, p. 58.

54. *Politika* (Belgrade), 6 March 1992, pp. 1, 6, trans. in FBIS, *Daily Report* (Eastern Europe), 17 March 1992, p. 17.

55. *Time* (12 October 1992), reprinted in MAK-NEWS (9 October 1992). MAK-NEWS is a wire service distributed by the Macedonian Information and Liaison Service, with offices in Brussels. At the end of 1992, MAK-NEWS was renamed MILS-NEWS, *Dnevi Vesti*.

56. *Kontinent* (Sofia), 10-11 October 1992, p. 2, trans. in FBIS, *Daily Report* (Eastern Europe), 14 October 1992, p. 3.

57. Admitted by Milošević on Greek Television (23 June 1992), as summarized in Tanjug (25 June 1992), in FBIS, *Daily Report* (Eastern Europe), 25 June 1992, p. 26.

58. E.g. *Politika* (18 October 1992), p. 1, and 1 November 1992, p. 2.

59. ORF Television Network (Vienna), 25 March 1992, trans. in FBIS, *Daily Report* (Eastern Europe), 26 March 1992, p. 29; and *New York Times* (15 February 1992), p. 4.

60. *Neue Zürcher Zeitung* (2 April 1992), p. 4.

The Macedonian Enigma   233

61. *Ibid.* (12 December 1992), p. 3.
62. *Süddeutsche Zeitung* (Munich), 9/10 January 1993, p. 5.
63. *Neue Zürcher Zeitung* (3 December 1991), p. 4.
64. Tanjug version (3 May 1992), trans. in FBIS, *Daily Report* (Eastern Europe), 4 May 1992, p. 54.
65. Tanjug (10 May 1992), in FBIS, *Daily Report* (Eastern Europe), 11 May 1992, p. 40.
66. *Nova Makedonija* (1 July 1992), p. 4, and 4 July 1992, p. 3.
67. *Ibid.* (7 July 1992), p. 2.
68. *Ibid.* (22 July 1992), p. 2.
69. *Ibid.* (16 September 1992), p. 1, and (24 September 1992), p. 1.
70. Tanjug (15 September 1992), in FBIS, *Daily Report* (Eastern Europe), 16 September 1992, p. 30; CSTK (Prague), 16 September 1992, in FBIS, *Daily Report* (Eastern Europe), 18 September 1992, p. 30; and *Nova Makedonija* (24 September 1992), p. 2.
71. *Nova Makedonija* (9 April 1992), p. 3, trans. in FBIS, *Daily Report* (Eastern Europe), 6 May 1992, p. 43; ATA (Tirana), 18 June 1992, in FBIS, *Daily Report* (Eastern Europe), 19 June 1992, p. 27; and BTA (Sofia), 19 October 1992, in FBIS, *Daily Report* (Eastern Europe), 20 October 1992, p. 4.
72. Tanjug (13 January 1991), in FBIS, *Daily Report* (Eastern Europe), 14 January 1991, p. 58.
73. Radio Belgrade Network (24 January 1992), trans. in FBIS, *Daily Report* (Eastern Europe), 27 January 1992, p. 42.
74. *New York Times* (17 April 1992), p. A8.
75. See the comments by Bulgarian Foreign Minister Stojan Ganev, as reported in *Süddeutsche Zeitung* (13/14 June 1992), p. 9.
76. "Interview with Ljubomir Danailov-Frčkovski, minister of interior," in *East European Reporter*, Vol. 5, No. 5 (September–October 1992), p. 50.
77. *Delo* (Ljubljana), 22 February 1992, p. 22, trans. in FBIS, *Daily Report* (Eastern Europe), 6 March 1992, p. 40; *Uj Magyarorszag* (Budapest), 21 February 1992, pp. 1, 2, trans. in FBIS, *Daily Report* (Eastern Europe), 26 February 1992, p. 36; and Tanjug (30 March 1992), in FBIS, *Daily Report* (Eastern Europe), 31 March 1992, p. 40.
78. *Neue Zürcher Zeitung* (27 June 1992), p. 5; these Serbian figures are also cited by Macedonian President Kiro Gligorov in an interview with *NIN* (22 January 1993), pp. 50–53, trans. in FBIS, *Daily Report* (Eastern Europe), 2 February 1993, p. 70.
79. A statement by the IMRO-Union of Macedonian Societies on 8 October 1991, as quoted in Sofia BTA (8 October 1991), in FBIS, *Daily Report* (Eastern Europe), 9 October 1991, p. 4.
80. *Politika* (2 February 1992), p. 7, trans. in FBIS, *Daily Report* (19 February 1992), p. 27.
81. *Demokratsiya* (Sofia), 4 October 1991, p. 5, trans. in FBIS, *Daily Report* (10 October 1991), p. 4.
82. Tanjug (18 March 1992), in FBIS, *Daily Report* (Eastern Europe), 19 March 1992, p. 27.
83. *Intervju* (Belgrade), 20 March 1992, p. 15.
84. Quoted in *Borba* (27 November 1991), p. 7, trans. in FBIS, *Daily Report* (Eastern Europe), 13 December 1991, p. 34.

234   *Sabrina Petra Ramet*

85. Tanjug (19 March 1992), in FBIS, *Daily Report* (Eastern Europe), 20 March 1992, p. 36.

86. *Borba* (13 January 1992), p. 19.

87. Radio Belgrade Network (22 February 1992), trans. in FBIS, *Daily Report* (Eastern Europe), 24 February 1992, p. 40.

88. *Ibid.*, my emphasis.

89. *Ibid.*

90. *International Herald Tribune* (Paris), 13/14 June 1992, p. 6.

91. Tanjug (30 March 1992), in FBIS, *Daily Report* (Eastern Europe), 31 March 1992, p. 39.

92. *Politika* (26 September 1991), p. 17, trans. in Joint Publications Research Service, *JPRS Report* EER-91-154 (15 October 1991), p. 57.

93. *Politika* (28/30 November 1991), p. 8, trans. in FBIS, *Daily Report* (Eastern Europe), 17 December 1991, p. 57.

94. *Borba* (4 December 1991), p. 9, trans. in FBIS, *Daily Report* (Eastern Europe), 18 December 1991, p. 44.

95. *Republika*, a Macedonian independent news daily, as cited in Radio Croatia Network (Zagreb), 30 December 1991, trans. in FBIS, *Daily Report* (Eastern Europe), 31 December 1991, pp. 44–45.

96. Radio Belgrade Network (8 February 1992), trans. in FBIS, *Daily Report* (Eastern Europe), 10 February 1992, p. 37; and Tanjug (30 March 1992), in FBIS, *Daily Report* (Eastern Europe), 31 March 1992, p. 40.

97. *Politika* (7 May 1992), p. 11.

98. Tanjug (20 November 1992), trans. in FBIS, *Daily Report* (Eastern Europe), 23 November 1992, p. 58.

99. *Politika* (13 October 1992), p. 7.

100. *Ibid.* (5 October 1992), p. 5.

101. TVP Television Network (Priština), in Serbo-Croatian, 2 January 1993, trans. in FBIS, *Daily Report* (Eastern Europe), 4 January 1993, p. 74; Radio Belgrade Network (13 January 1993), trans. in FBIS, *Daily Report* (Eastern Europe), 14 January 1993, p. 58; and Radio Belgrade Network (15 January 1993), trans. in FBIS, *Daily Report* (Eastern Europe), 19 January 1993, p. 59.

102. *Borba* (12 May 1992), p. 9, trans. in FBIS, *Daily Report* (Eastern Europe), 21 May 1992, p. 43.

103. Radio Macedonia Network (3 March 1992), trans. in FBIS, *Daily Report* (Eastern Europe), 5 March 1992, p. 21.

104. Tanjug (31 May 1992), trans. in FBIS, *Daily Report* (Eastern Europe), 2 June 1992, p. 44.

105. Milošević's 3-day visit to Athens in March was described as a "private" visit; all the others were described as official visits.

106. Quoted in editorial report based on Belgrade RTB Television Network (30 April 1992), in FBIS, *Daily Report* (Eastern Europe), 1 May 1992, p. 40.

107. Quoted in *Politika ekspres* (18 June 1992), p. 7. See also *Politika ekspres* (16 June 1992), p. 9.

108. Radio Tirana (Tirana), 10 March 1992, trans. in FBIS, *Daily Report* (Eastern Europe), 11 March 1992, p. 2.

The Macedonian Enigma 235

109. Confirmed in Tanjug (25 June 1992), in FBIS, *Daily Report* (Eastern Europe), 26 June 1992, p. 26.

110. Quoted in *Novi Vjesnik* (Zagreb), 20 June 1992, p. 24A.

111. *Frankfurter Allgemeine* (15 June 1992), p. 6, trans. in FBIS, *Daily Report* (Eastern Europe), 19 June 1992, p. 27.

112. *Politika* (18 April 1992), p. 10, trans. in FBIS, *Daily Report* (Eastern Europe), 4 May 1992, p. 54.

113. Tanjug (21 September 1992), trans. in FBIS, *Daily Report* (Eastern Europe), 22 September 1992, p. 43; and *New York Times* (4 October 1992), p. 6.

114. *Frankfurter Allgemeine* (15 June 1992), p. 6.

115. Quoted in Tanjug (14 June 1992), in FBIS, *Daily Report* (Eastern Europe), 15 June 1992, p. 45.

116. See Radio Croatia Network (Zagreb), 7 September 1992, trans. in FBIS, *Daily Report* (Eastern Europe), 10 September 1992, p. 45.

117. *The European* (London), 18-21 February 1993, p. 39.

118. There is a brief allusion to this proposal in Vladimir Milčin, "A Little Miracle in the Balkans," in *Balkan War Report*, No. 14 (September 1992), p. 13.

119. *Financial Times* (24 November 1992), p. 4.

120. Radio Belgrade Network (Belgrade), 9 December 1992, trans. in FBIS, *Daily Report* (Eastern Europe), 10 December 1992, p. 50. This is also reported in *Neue Zürcher Zeitung* (12 December 1992), p. 3.

121. Tanjug (9 January 1993), trans. in FBIS, *Daily Report* (Eastern Europe), 11 January 1993, p. 57.

122. *Neue Zürcher Zeitung* (22 January 1993), p. 3; and *Süddeutsche Zeitung* (23/24 January 1993), p. 8.

123. *New York Times* (15 February 1993), p. A5.

124. *The European* (18-21 February 1993), p. 13.

125. AFP (Paris), 26 January 1993, in FBIS, *Daily Report* (Eastern Europe), 27 January 1993, p. 60.

126. *New York Times* (26 January 1993), p. A7; and MILS-NEWS, *Dnevni Vesti* (24 February 1993).

127. *Süddeutsche Zeitung* (5/6 December 1992), p. 10.

128. *Neue Zürcher Zeitung* (15 December 1992), p. 2.

129. See *Ibid.* (29 January 1993), p. 4, and (14/15 February 1993), p. 2.

130. *Ibid.* (7/8 February 1993), p. 3.

131. *Süddeutsche Zeitung* (20/21 February 1993), p. 7.

132. MILS-NEWS, *Dnevni Vesti* (12 October 1992).

133. See, for example, the reports in *Nova Makedonija* (29 December 1992), p. 2; and Tanjug (11 January 1993), trans. in FBIS, *Daily Report* (Eastern Europe), 13 January 1993, p. 59.

134. AFP (Paris), 3 February 1993, in FBIS, *Daily Report* (Eastern Europe), 3 February 1993, p. 74.

135. As a concession to Greece, the Academy agreed not to fly the Macedonian flag at the festival. See MAK-NEWS (10 October 1992).

136. MILS-NEWS, *Dnevni Vesti* (2 December 1992).

137. *Ibid.* (4 December 1992).

236   Sabrina Petra Ramet

138. *Ibid.* (25 February 1993).
139. *Nova Makedonija* (26 December 1992), p. 13, trans. in FBIS, *Daily Report* (Eastern Europe), 4 February 1993, p. 58.
140. MILS-NEWS, *Dnevni Vesti* (2 March 1993).
141. Proposed by the Social Democratic Party of Macedonia in December 1992. See MILS-NEWS, *Dnevni Vesti* (1 December 1992).
142. Reported in *Ibid.* (1 March 1993).
143. *Financial Times* (1 July 1992), p. 16.
144. Quoted in *New York Times* (23 November 1992), p. A12.
145. Confirmed again in Sofia BTA (10 February 1992), in FBIS, *Daily Report* (Eastern Europe), 11 February 1992, p. 2. See also *Neue Zürcher Zeitung* (27 June 1992), p. 5. Bulgaria has a long history of interest in Macedonia. See, for example, Nadežda Cvetkovska, *Politićkata aktivnost na Makedonskata emigracija vo Bugarija od 1918 do 1929 godina* (Skopje: Institut za nacionalna istorija, 1990); and Taško Mamurovski, *Bugarskata propaganda vo jugozapadna i centralna egejska Makedonija (1941–1944)* (Skopje: Institut za nacionalna istorija, 1989). For materials relating to contemporary relations, see "Bulgarien: Die Anerkennung Makedoniens," in *Südost Europa*, Vol. 41, No. 3/4 (March–April 1992).
146. "U.S. Recognition of the Former Yugoslav Republic of Macedonia", in *U.S. Department of State Dispatch*, Vol. 5, No. 8 (21 February 1994), p. 98.
147. Hanna Rosen, "Why we flip-flopped on Macedonia—Greek pique", in *New Republic* (13 June 1994), p. 12.

10

Politics in Montenegro

Milan Andrejevich

Developments in the fall of 1991 in the Yugoslav republic of Montenegro suggested that leaders there were engaged in a power struggle over the republic's future status. And in the process of this struggle, speculation arose that there were cracks in the relationship between Montenegro and Serbia. At the end of October, the Montenegrin leadership affirmed the republic's sovereignty and approved a peace plan brokered by the European Community whereby a new Yugoslav state based on an association of sovereign republics would be created. The latter action raised much discussion that Montenegro was reconsidering its close relations with Serbia in a federal Yugoslav state and that in affirming its sovereignty the republic was seeking independence from the truncated Yugoslav federation. However, it is important to remember that in the past, Montenegrin moves toward independence from Yugoslavia have resulted in civil wars and interclan fighting between pro-Serbian and pro-Montenegrin nationalists. Nevertheless, Montenegro's actions suggested that for the first time since 1989, the republic's politicians placed themselves at some distance from Serbia. Also of relative significance at the time was the fact that some key opposition leaders openly criticized the Yugoslav People's Army (YPA) for having involved Montenegro in the war in Croatia.

As a nation, Montenegrins have long prided themselves on their reputation as warriors and liberators; their sense of independence; and their tradition of clan rule, which has continued well into the twentieth century and still has some influence on Montenegrin politics. This tradition has frequently led to blood feuds among the larger and more powerful Montenegrin families, even as recently as 1945. Since then the League of Communists and its successor, the Democratic Party of Socialists (DPS), have skillfully, and with far less violence, manipulated interclan antagonism to their advantage. Many of the old Montenegrin attitudes persist; according to the prominent writer and critic of the current Montenegrin

238   *Milan Andrejevich*

government, Jevrem Brković, these attitudes include placing great value on a pastoral life style, preferring to give orders rather than to work, and tending toward anti-intellectualism.[1]

Background

Most of Montenegro is situated on one of Yugoslavia's highest mountain plateaus, running from the Adriatic to the continental hinterland. During the early fifteenth century it emerged as a distinct political unit on what had been the Serbian territory of Zeta. Over the centuries Montenegro was unable to remain entirely autonomous; but its inaccessible rugged mountain areas saved it from being completely overrun first by the Venetians, in the late fifteenth and throughout the sixteenth century, and then by the Ottomans. Montenegro resisted Ottoman rule even after becoming part of the empire in 1499 as a frontier province. That same year Venice took over part of the Montenegrin coastline, and Kotor became its main port in the region. After 1700 the Turks led several military campaigns aimed at subjugating the Montenegrins but never succeeded in fully conquering the country. In 1878 Montenegro's formal independence was confirmed by the Great Powers at the Congress of Berlin.

According to the last census, taken in April 1991, Montenegro's ethnically mixed population totals 616,327. Preliminary figures show there are 380,484 Montenegrins (accounting for 61.5 percent of the total population), 90,000 Moslems (17.4 percent), 57,176 Serbs (9.29 percent), 41,000 Albanians (8.5 percent), 25,854 Yugoslavs (4.3 percent), and 6,249 Croats (1 percent).[2] Some estimates indicate that Montenegro, which covers only 5.4 percent of the country's territory, is the poorest of the six Yugoslav republics. Unemployment has reached almost 27 percent; and in 1990 some 12 percent of the work force were employed by firms facing bankruptcy, mainly because of mismanagement, low productivity, and a lack of demand from outside the republic for Montenegrin industrial products (which are not able to compete against those of the wealthier republics of Slovenia, Croatia, and Serbia). The average monthly wage in September 1991 was the equivalent of $400, compared with the national average of $470. In the first three months of 1991, some 121 firms registered losses, six of which subsequently declared bankruptcy. More than 20 percent of Montenegrins live below the poverty line and are on social welfare. Montenegro's share of Yugoslavia's $14 billion foreign debt is about $1 billion, a sum that exceeds the republic's annual revenue.[3]

Relations between the republic's Montenegrin and Serbian majority, on the one hand, and its Muslim and Albanian minorities, on the other, have traditionally been antagonistic, owing to the centuries-old animosity

Politics in Montenegro 239

between those professing the Orthodox and the Islamic faiths. But since the multiparty elections in December 1990, when Muslim and Albanian parties won 13 of the 125 seats in the republican National Assembly, interethnic relations have improved. In fact, Muslim leaders are now saying they are better able to solve their problems through local government and the National Assembly as a result of increased dialogue. While some Muslim politicians are of the opinion that ethnic relations in the republic remain poor, Montenegrin leaders argue that they have improved significantly over the past year because of greater interaction between political forces in government institutions.[4] However, concern has been expressed by Montenegrins and Serbs over some of the consequences of the nascent democratic process in neighboring Albania. Although encouraged by the democratization of Albanian society and politics, Montenegrins fear that Albania's recent recognition of the self-proclaimed Republic of Kosovo's independence will incite Albanian nationalists in Montenegro, Kosovo, and Albania proper, who are keen to unite all Albanians in one state.[5]

Montenegrin-Serbian Relations

In the past, relations between Montenegro and Serbia have, for the most part, been very good. Montenegrins and Serbs speak the same language and are both followers of the Eastern Orthodox Church. But during the Turkish occupation, the two peoples were separated from each other and developed their own political institutions. In the course of the nineteenth and twentieth centuries, Montenegrin-Serbian relations have been marred largely owing to sharp differences over how to establish and maintain an alliance without compromising the independent nature of both republics.

Disputes between Montenegro and Serbia have not only significantly affected the former's political evolution but were also one of the principal causes of interclan violence before 1945. (Serbian politics have largely remained unaffected by these disputes.) Owing to the Montenegrins' strong sense of identity, the actions of some Montenegrin politicians are often regarded by others as a betrayal of the republic's interests. In defining the extent of its loyalty to Serbia, Montenegro will have to take care not to compromise its status as a distinct nation. Attempts to change Montenegro's status to that of a fully independent state could quickly lead to civil war, as was the case in both World Wars One and Two (when the pro-Serbian "Whites" clashed with the pro-Montenegrin "Green" independence movement). Thus, it seems unlikely that Montenegro will follow Slovenia and Croatia in declaring its independence in the near future.

In 1918 the Montenegrin National Assembly overthrew the Petrović-Njegoš dynasty and voted for union with Serbia. A Montenegrin uprising

240   *Milan Andrejevich*

followed, its leaders demanding foreign intervention and free elections. The uprising, however, was crushed; and in the spring of 1919 a Serbian civilian governor assumed power. In 1922 the Montenegrin National Assembly approved the republic's incorporation into the Kingdom of Serbs, Croats, and Slovenes. This close affinity with the Serbs resulted in the Montenegrins being classified as Serbs in interwar censuses. But Montenegrin ambivalence vis-à-vis Serbia continued throughout this period and beyond.

The Yugoslav Constitution of 1946 recognized Montenegro as a distinct Yugoslav republic and Montenegrins as a nation, justifying these statuses on historical and political grounds rather than ethnic ones. This suggests that creating a sovereign Montenegrin republic, rather than incorporating it into Serbia, was intended to allay fears among the other Yugoslav republics of Serbian hegemony. Close relations between Montenegro and Serbia continued and were for the most part economically advantageous to Montenegro. Per capita investment in the republic was well above the national average. And Montenegro had a disproportionate share of seats in the Central Committee of the formerly ruling League of Communists of Yugoslavia and of officers in the YPA.

Montenegrins are generally pro-Serbian but have traditionally resented the administration of their republic by a non-Montenegrin. Although cultural ties and economic interests have drawn Serbs and Montenegrins together, there have been forces intent on defining what is to be regarded as Montenegrin. In the 1960s nationalist movements became part of the Yugoslav political mainstream; and in Montenegro a campaign was launched to promote a Montenegrin national culture as well as a separate Montenegrin language and Orthodox Church. Local leaders emphasized the uniqueness of Montenegrin culture, and clan leaders from the past were glorified for their exploits against the Turks. Although the constitutional amendments of 1971 granted the republic broad powers, one consequence was the emergence of nationalist movements throughout most of the country. As the purge of the Croatian nationalist mass movement in 1971 extended to Montenegro, as well as other republics, a large number of Montenegrin politicians and academics accused of promoting extremist nationalist views were systematically removed from office.

The Montenegrin Renaissance

Signs of Montenegrin assertiveness began to reappear in the fall of 1988. On 10 and 11 January 1989, after the leadership of the formerly ruling League of Communists of Montenegro (LCM) had made a bleak assessment of the economic and social situation in the republic and Montenegrins had been

Politics in Montenegro 241

advised to prepare for "harder times," some 150,000 Montenegrin workers, young rank-and-file Communists, and students held protests in several towns and cities. Angry at the leadership's failure to introduce reforms and blaming them for the economic mess in the republic, the protesters succeeded in securing the resignation of LCM leaders and the government through what they called an "act in the name of democracy." The overthrow of the Montenegrin government reflected the younger generation's support for what was perceived at the time as the "antibureaucratic revolution" engineered by Slobodan Milošević, at the time President of Serbia's League of Communists. (This was the second manifestation of popular discontent in Montenegro at the end of the 1980s, the first having occurred in October 1988.) By April 1989 the LCM had installed a new leadership and was pledging its commitment to a more democratic way of life, which was referred to as the "Montenegrin Renaissance" and regarded as a revival of the Montenegrin national movement of the late 1960s (which had come to an abrupt end in 1971). However, the new leadership—the average age of which was 40, making it the youngest of any in Yugoslavia—promised no immediate solutions to the republic's most pressing problems.

After a year in power, it became clear to the Montenegrin leadership that critical issues at home had to be tackled by Montenegrins rather than Serbia. On 10 January 1990, the first anniversary of what is now commonly referred to as the Montenegrin Uprising of January 1989, members of the State Presidency of Montenegro and the Presidium of the LCM proposed that a multiparty system be introduced not only in the republic but throughout Yugoslavia. The Serbian Communists were strongly opposed to this proposal, which came after round-table talks between Montenegrin party and state leaders, on the one hand, and representatives of alternative political parties and associations, on the other. In fact, the Montenegrin leadership was the first in Yugoslavia to engage in such talks with the opposition. After months of paying lip service to political pluralism, on 3 October 1990, the Montenegrin National Assembly finally passed a law legalizing multiparty elections.

On 9 December 1990, the first multiparty elections in Montenegro since 1938 took place. The fact that the LCM won convincingly and that Momir Bulatović, at the time President of the LCM, was elected State President suggested a clear vote of confidence in the relatively young leadership. The Montenegrin voters were apparently of the opinion that the new LCM leadership could not be held responsible for the republic's worsening economic situation. Opposition parties have persistently complained, however, that the LCM's strict control over both the media and the police prevented them from running effective election campaigns and that this control has remained in force to the present day.

The 125 seats in the National Assembly were distributed among eight parties: the LCM, which in June 1991 changed its name to the Democratic Party of Socialists, won 86; federal Prime Minister Ante Markovic's Alliance of Reform Forces, in coalition with two other parties, 17; the Democratic Coalition, composed of the Albanian Democratic Alliance, the Muslim Party for Democratic Action, and another Muslim party called the Party for Equality, 13; and the pro-Serbian Peoples' Party, which is the second largest single party in the assembly, 12. During the 1990 election campaign the eight major parties focused on three issues that are still explosive: the need to save the failing Montenegrin economy by instituting programs that would reduce unemployment, prevent enterprises from going bankrupt, modernize the agricultural sector, and promote tourism; the reestablishment of a federal Yugoslavia; and, in the event that a federal Yugoslavia not be reestablished, the development of alternative solutions for Yugoslavia's future that would best serve Montenegrin interests.

Today, the major parties in Montenegro agree that the republic would be better off in a united Yugoslavia. All support the idea of a sovereign republic within a united Yugoslavia; and most favor a sovereign republic with a government and assembly whose powers would be strictly defined. All parties advocate a market-oriented economy; some favor mixed ownership (the coexistence of state and private sectors), while others advocate the privatization of the economy as a whole and the complete rejection of socialism. All parties support integration into the European Community (EC); and several have emphasized the need to address environmental issues as one way of drawing international attention to the natural beauty of the republic.

Only two parties expressed different views. The Albanian Democratic Alliance of Montenegro stated in its platform that Montenegro's Albanians had the right to determine that republic's future in either a confederation or a federation.[6] The People's Party, on the other hand, said that if Yugoslavia had become a confederation, Montenegro's borders would have needed to be redrawn to provide for the republic's unification with Serbia. In fact, the party advocates the "spiritual unification and moral renaissance of Serbianism." A few smaller, less significant groups have also opted for this formula.

Cracks in the Montenegrin-Serbian Alliance?

With the escalation of the war in Croatia in the early fall of 1991, renewed signs that relations between Serbia and Montenegro had become strained appeared. On 17 October 1991, the Montenegrin National Assembly took steps toward affirming its sovereignty, which is written into its

Politics in Montenegro 243

constitution. Bulatović explained that the affirmation did not mean a declaration of independence but rather a statement regarding Montenegro's position as an internationally recognized sovereign part of a Yugoslav state. However, on 20 October the Zagreb media reported that two days previously the Montenegrin National Assembly had, in fact, voted in favor of sovereignty; and it suggested that the republic, like Bosnia and Herzegovina and Macedonia, was preparing to leave the Yugoslav federation. The Zagreb media also claimed that 612 Montenegrin reservists in the federal army had joined Croatian forces in the resort village of Slano, near Dubrovnik, and that this was a sign of growing opposition to Montenegro's "undeclared" war with Croatia.[7] The Montenegrin and Serbian press did not comment on these reports.

The Montenegrin National Assembly also instructed its representatives to the EC-sponsored peace conference on Yugoslavia at The Hague to declare the republic in favor of the fundamental proposals of a document drawn up by the United Kingdom's Lord Carrington calling for the creation of an association of sovereign republics; Serbia was opposed to this document. The majority of Montenegrin lawmakers were clearly agreed that "an urgent compromise was necessary" to prevent an escalation of the fighting in Yugoslavia.[8] But they also realized that blocking the peace initiative would result in economic sanctions that Montenegro could ill-afford.

Indeed, on 18 October Bulatović voted to accept Lord Carrington's document, which Serbia rejected. This move caught many people by surprise, since the republic had been considered Serbia's most loyal ally. Many Yugoslav and Western reports spoke of a rift between Bulatović and Serbian President Slobodan Milošević, who are both Serbs of Montenegrin origin and have largely the same political philosophy. The former's decision, however, did not mean that both he and Montenegro had changed political direction overnight. Bulatović explained that the Montenegrin National Assembly had recommended that he accept the basic components of Lord Carrington's plan, which, in effect, defined Montenegro as "nominally a sovereign state."[9] He added that no one had signed the document, because the negotiations had not been concluded, and that he had accepted the document so that the negotiations could be continued. He also pointed out that Serbia had not totally rejected the document but rather had objected to "certain formulations and interpretations." According to Bulatović, Montenegro and Serbia did not differ over strategic interests and goals but over how to achieve those goals.

Bulatović also said he was convinced that as the talks continued at The Hague, "all these illusions existing in the public's mind—that there is some kind of a quarrel, that we do not wish to talk to each other—will be quickly dispersed, leaving no room for doubt."[10] Both leaders favored forming a federation of republics that wished to remain in a Yugoslav state.

244   Milan Andrejevich

Fireworks in the Montenegrin Assembly

The long-standing divisions between pro-Serbian and pro-Montenegrin forces may help explain why criticism of Bulatović was most vocal in Montenegro. By and large, both he and those legislators who voted to recommend Montenegro's approval of the Carrington document were labeled "traitors." Critics described the document as the "legalization of the final destruction of Yugoslavia." The sharpest response came from the poet Ranko Jovović, a leader of the pro-Serbian Peoples' Party: "Why should we sign a document with those who want a confederation? Why should we think we can live in a confederation with people who decorate themselves with the [amputated] fingers of our children?"[11]

President of the People's Party Nikola Kilibarda said that his party was not out to destroy Bulatović; but he stressed that all Serbs—including those in Serbia, the self-proclaimed governments of the Serbian Autonomous Regions of Krajina (in Croatia and Bosnia), and Montenegro—should be represented by a single delegation at The Hague and not by separate ones. Asked what would happen if Bulatović did not heed such advice, Kilibarda answered: "Then let the protest meetings, if he wishes, destroy those who voted for him" (a reference to the January 1989 mass demonstrations that toppled the old guard regime and replaced it by those currently holding top government positions). Kilibarda's critics assumed that the party leader was proposing that new protests be mounted to unseat Bulatović and the government.[12]

Montenegrin Foreign Minister Nikola Samardžić responded on behalf of the government, explaining that not only did Montenegro differ with Serbia on how to establish a new Yugoslav state but also that Montenegrins did not consider the war in Croatia and the sporadic fighting in Bosnia and Herzegovina to be "Montenegro's war but rather the federal army's war." (This mood prevails among many Serbs as well.) He added that by agreeing to accept the EC document in principle, Montenegro was opting for peace. The Hague document would not destroy Yugoslavia, Samardžić commented; rather, it was "the politicians and the will of individual nations within Yugoslavia" who had destroyed the country.[13] Bulatović responded to his critics by saying "if the criterion for good government in Montenegro is absolute obedience to Belgrade, then [we] need neither a government nor elections."[14]

Showing deep concern over Montenegro's growing involvement in Croatia, the seven-member Presidency of the Republic of Montenegro decided on 24 October that two YPA units composed of Montenegrin reservists sent to battlefields in Croatia on 20 October "should be returned in an organized and military fashion to their barracks in Titograd and Danilovgrad."[15] The Montenegrin Presidency said it had had no other

Politics in Montenegro 245

choice after federal army officials had failed to respond quickly to Montenegrin demands to withdraw from war-stricken parts of Croatia those reservists who had not volunteered to remain on the battlefields.

The decision to return the reservists to their barracks was in response to widespread public concern over the mobilization of Montenegrin reservists in Slavonia, southern Dalmatia, and southeastern Herzegovina, which, relative to population size, was much more extensive in Montenegro than in Serbia. In late September, Bulatović and other Montenegrin leaders had not been opposed to sending reservists into battle and had decided that it was important to increase their presence along the Croatian-Montenegrin border in the strategically located Prevlaka peninsula, at the opening of the Bay of Kotor. (Montenegro and Croatia were, by mid–1992 engaged in high-level negotiations aimed at settling a dispute over the peninsula, which Croatia claims as its territory. For its part, the Peoples' Party said the negotiations were tantamount to treason.) Shortly after heated battles with Croatian forces had resulted in heavy losses and a large number of casualties, many reservists said they were being forced to fight against their will; Bulatović subsequently had second thoughts about Montenegro's involvement in the war.[16] This partly explains why Bulatović and the ruling DPS decided to accept the peace terms at The Hague.

Charting a Clearer Course

On 24 and 25 October the Montenegrin National Assembly convened once again. After a debate that lasted nearly nine hours, 81 of the 125 deputies in the assembly upheld the stand taken by the republic's delegation on October 18 at the Hague conference on Yugoslavia. Only two deputies were opposed to the Hague document, and the remaining forty-two boycotted the vote. The strongest criticism came from the 12 deputies of the People's Party, who were among those who refused to vote. The assembly concluded that the delegation had acted in line with the recommendations it had received from the assembly on 17 October stressing the need to find a peaceful and democratic settlement of the Yugoslav crisis. But opposition leaders persisted in their criticism of Bulatović, claiming that the Montenegrin delegation's stance had surprised and angered many Montenegrins, "traditionally the closest friends of the Serbs, with whom they share the same language, religion, and flag."[17]

Yugoslav State Vice President Branko Kostić had tried to persuade the National Assembly to recommend that the Montenegrin delegates at The Hague not sign the document until Montenegrins had had an opportunity to vote on the issue in a plebiscite. Deputies opposed to Kostić's proposal had said there was no time to organize such a plebiscite. Some deputies from opposition parties had supported Kostić's proposal, saying that Bulatović was carrying out decisions of the Communist-dominated republican State Presidency and not of the people or the assembly. Kostić argued that signing the document would lead to the dissolution of Yugoslavia and that such an act could only be decided upon by the people, not politicians. Montenegrin Prime Minister Milo Djukanović opposed the idea that Yugoslavia would be abolished if the Hague document were approved: "The abolition and dissociation of Yugoslavia started a long time before the Hague conference. The Hague conference calls for a loose association—and this is more than what we have today. Between war and the hypothetical peace that The Hague is offering, one should choose the latter."[18]

Prior to traveling to The Hague on 25 October, Bulatović noted that there was concern in the National Assembly over alterations to Lord Carrington's document. He told the assembly that he would ask for an explanation at the very opening of the session and that if the explanation were unsatisfactory, it would be unlikely that the altered part of the document would be accepted.

Still defending the document as a whole, Bulatović said that "The Hague document will not create a state but neither does it prohibit the creation of a state by those who wish it."[19] He added that there were absolutely no differences between the Hague declaration; the so-called Belgrade Initiative for Settling the Yugoslav Crisis, issued in August by Serbia, Montenegro, and Serbian leaders in Bosnia and Herzegovina; and the Yugoslav State Presidency's proposals of October. Both the initiative and the rump State Presidency's proposals call for Yugoslavia to be transformed into several state communities organized in loose political and economic associations. One such community would be a federation of those republics and autonomous regions that have opted to remain in Yugoslavia (namely, Serbia and its two provinces of Kosovo and Vojvodina, Montenegro, and the self-proclaimed Serbian autonomous regions in Croatia and Bosnia and Herzegovina). The other state communities would be composed of independent republics that have already declared their sovereignty or are about to do so in referendums (Croatia, Macedonia, Slovenia, and non-Serbian regions in Bosnia and Herzegovina).

An EC session at The Hague late on 25 October 1991 produced mixed responses to Lord Carrington's document; Serbia and Slovenia rejected the proposal to turn Yugoslavia into a loose association of independent republics. Slovenia said it wanted complete independence and that "talk of some form of a united Yugoslavia is a waste of time and energy." Serbia argued that a federation should be maintained for those who wanted it, while the four remaining republics opted for independence within a "customs union." Another stumbling block was the rejection by Serbia, Macedonia, and Montenegro of an EC document detailing the status of ethnic minorities in

Politics in Montenegro

Yugoslavia. Five of the republics agreed in principle to continue discussing the document for the sake of achieving peace. Serbia, while underscoring its desire for a peaceful settlement of the crisis, continued to argue that parts of the document were unrealistic and unacceptable to Serbs living in republics outside Serbia.[20]

Sovereignty, Montenegrin Style

Before clarifying Montenegro's position on how to resolve the Yugoslav crisis and affirming Montenegrin sovereignty by accepting Lord Carrington's peace proposals, the Montenegrin National Assembly had already taken small steps toward redefining the republic's sovereign status. On 20 September, acknowledging long-standing public concern over environmental issues, the assembly proclaimed Montenegro the world's first "ecological state."[21] Although this move can hardly be regarded as a genuine expression of sovereignty, Montenegrin lawmakers have argued that the declaration is indicative of the republic's "commitment to peace and a healthy environment," which, it is hoped, will improve the prospects for increased foreign investment in Montenegro's tourist industry and transportation system. But the sad irony is that Montenegro is slowly losing its reputation as "an ecological oasis." The large aluminum enterprise in Podgorica and the large steel and iron works in Nikšić, both located on the banks of the River Zeta (one of the most beautiful areas in the republic) have destroyed the flora and fauna in much of the river valley. Small factories near Lake Skadar have been dumping chemicals into the lake, killing fish and wildlife. Moreover, the Bay of Kotor and its fjord, which is regarded as one of the most beautiful in the world, is endangered by pollutants from a detergent factory.[22]

A different, somewhat muddled vision of Montenegrin sovereignty was offered by Djukanović at a press conference on 22 September 1991, the day on which the proclamation was signed. The Montenegrin Prime Minister said that lately the republic had been considering becoming independent and that the Montenegrin leadership was preparing to declare the republic's sovereignty.[23] He described the insistence that Yugoslavia maintain its territorial integrity as counterproductive and argued that it should first be established which of the six Yugoslav republics wanted to remain in a common state and only then should negotiations on determining the nature of that state be begun. "Divorce proceedings should be initiated against those in the Federal Assembly who do not wish to remain in Yugoslavia," he commented. According to Djukanović, the future state should maintain control over three areas: defense, the economy, and foreign policy. He recalled that Montenegro's "thousand-year tradition as a state could

248 Milan Andrejevich

not be called into question," adding that Montenegro was the 27th state in the world to be recognized as having such a tradition.

Further steps toward defining sovereignty came on 18 January 1992 when Bulatović proposed to the national assembly that a referendum be held, saying that he feels it is time to consult the Montenegrin people on what "degree of sovereignty" they wanted.[24] As politicians haggled over the timing and wording of the referendum, opposition parties organized protest rallies. On 1 February, about 10,000 people in Cetinje demonstrated for Montenegrin independence; shortly after the protest, Bulatović made it clear that Montenegro would not accept junior-partner status in relation to Serbia.[25] Finally on 22 February Montenegro's Democratic Socialist-dominated national assembly adopted a decision that a referendum be held on 1 March. On 23 February two rallies were held over the issue of the republic's future as a sovereign state. In the republic's capital Titograd a rally organized by the United Opposition and the Democratic Coalition was attended by more than 10,000 people. Protesters described the referendum as unconstitutional and as an act of "a one-party dictatorship," and demanded that Montenegro be declared an independent state. In Cetinje, a rally attended by some 5,000 backed the referendum.[26]

Results of the turnout for the referendum was 66 percent of the eligible voters (410,000 were eligible to vote) and 96 percent responded in the affirmative to the question: "Are you in favor of Montenegro continuing to live in a common state of Yugoslavia as a sovereign republic and as an equal with other republics wishing to remain in Yugoslavia?" A total of 63 percent of the electorate circled the answer "for." Also residents of the republic's capital Titograd voted in favor of the city government's proposal that the city be given its pre-1945 appellation Podgorica; in mid-March, the republican national assembly finalized the change.[27]

Finally, on 27 April, the national assemblies of Serbia and Montenegro, the two remaining republics of the former Socialist Federal Republic of Yugoslavia, declared themselves the legitimate successors of that state. In late December both republics began talks on creating the new smaller federation commonly referred to as "the third but smaller Yugoslavia." The new state calling itself the Federal Republic of Yugoslavia (FRY) comprises two-fifths of the former Yugoslav territory and less than half its population. The assemblies also adopted a new constitution joining the two republics in a federation based on parliamentary democracy and a free-market economy. The main opposition parties in the two republics as well as most ethnic Albanians boycotted the ceremonies and oppose the new constitution.[28] Federal parliamentary elections for a new bicameral parliament were also announced and took place on May 30. The results gave the clear majority to the ruling Socialists. The main opposition parties boycotted

Politics in Montenegro

the elections and described the elections as a farce and convoluted vision of parliamentary democracy.

Assessment

Prior to the political developments in Montenegro since October 1991, President Bulatović had been widely regarded as responsible for enforcing the pro-Serbian line in Montenegrin politics. Both times the Democratic Coalition had proposed a vote on affirming Montenegrin sovereignty and declaring its neutrality. Bulatović's DPS, as well as the People's Party, had flatly rejected the motion. By approving Lord Carrington's proposal that an association of sovereign republics be created and by recalling several armed units of reservists, the President made known his tacit support for Montenegrin sovereignty (already defined in its constitution) and neutrality. In the past, Montenegro had repeatedly disregarded its neutral status to assist Serbia when the latter had been threatened by outside forces. This explains why Bulatović's call for the withdrawal of Montenegrin reservists from the Slavonian front was sharply criticized by some leaders of the pro-Serbian parties, who claimed that it was Montenegro's duty to come to the aid of Serbia.

The apparent split within the pro-Serbian forces in Montenegro will undoubtedly spell trouble for the future of Montenegro. The republic will have to decide whether it wants to remain subservient to Serbia or become a truly sovereign state and equal partner with Serbia. For the time being, it appears that the republic's leaders would prefer the latter option, but only on the condition that Montenegro become part of an association of sovereign states that includes Serbia.

Notes

1. *Osimca* (Belgrade), 15 November 1990, p. 12.

2. *Oslobodjenje* (Sarajevo), 27 June 1991, p. 5; "Stanovništvo Jugoslavije" in *Jugoslovenski Pregled* (Belgrade), Vol. 35 (1991), Nos. 5–6, pp. 331–340.

3. *Oslobodjenje*, 1 September 1991.

4. *Pobjeda* (Titograd), 14 and 18 September 1991, p. 6, and 28 October 1991, p. 7.

5. *Ibid.*, 16 August 1991, p. 4.

6. Muslims in the Serbia's southeastern region of the Sandzak held a three day referendum on political and cultural autonomy on 27 October 1991. Results showed that Muslims in five municipalities in the Sandžak overwhelmingly voted in favor of autonomy. The Sandžak is located in Serbia and Montenegro. Muslims in the Montenegrin part seemed to have largely ignored the referendum. Muslims leaders there said they could resolve their problems through local government negotia-

250   Milan Andrejevich

tions and because relations with Montenegrins were good. Sandžak Muslim leaders, however, emphasized that their citizens feel threatened by Serbs and that as a nationality Muslims have the right to declare themselves for autonomy just like Serbs have done in Croatia. Local Serbs described the referendum as "illegal and unnecessary and senseless." Though Belgrade said it would take tough measures to prevent the balloting, no clashes were reported. The referendum was organized by numerous Muslim political and cultural groups. Both the Serbs and Muslims claim to have an absolute majority in the Sandžak.

7. *Večernji list* (Zagreb), 21 and 22 October 1991, p. 6.

8. *Ibid.*, 18–19 October 1991, p. 8; and *Večernje novosti* (Belgrade), 17 October 1991, p. 7.

9. *Pobjeda* (Titograd) 20–24 October 1991, pp. 1–4.

10. *Ibid.*

11. *Večernje novosti* (19 October 1991), p. 4.

12. *Ibid.* (21 October 1991), p. 6.

13. *Pobjeda* (19 October 1991), pp. 1–6.

14. *Ibid.*

15. *Pobjeda* (25 October 1991), p. 1.

16. *Slobodna Dalmacija* (Split), 4 October 1991, p. 8; and *Vjesnik* (Zagreb), 17 October 1991, p. 5.

17. *Pobjeda* (25 October 1991), pp. 1–6.

18. *Ibid.*

19. *Ibid.*

20. *Večernje novosti* (26 October 1991), pp. 2, 6.

21. *Pobjeda* (21 September 1991), p. 1.

22. *Vjesnik* (2 October 1991), p. 7.

23. *Pobjeda* (24 September 1991), p. 5.

24. *Ibid.* (19 January 1992), p. 1.

25. *Ibid.* (8 February 1992), p. 1.

26. *Ibid.* (24 and 25 February 1992), pp. 1, 3; and *Vjesnik* (24–25 February 1992), p. 7.

27. *Pobjeda* (4–5 March 1992), pp. 1, 5.

28. *Borba* (28 April 1992) , p. 1; and (5 June 1992), p. 1.

PART THREE

Economics

11

Economic Transformation in Former Yugoslavia, with Special Regard to Privatization

Ljubiša Adamovich

Privatization, one of the most important factors of the transition process, is taking place in former Yugoslavia under conditions which are far from what is usually considered "normal." This is due to the fact that not long after the Law on Privatization was accepted in the Yugoslav Parliament in December 1989, the process of privatization began to face unfavorable conditions caused by ethnic tensions, armed struggle, damage to property, and bloodshed. After June 1991, Yugoslavia started to disintegrate. Various "new" entities have been created with their own regional legislation and ways of implementing these regulations as well as those elements of Federal legislation acceptable to the leaders of the new states. That is why it has become extremely difficult—and is sometimes even impossible—to follow the privatization trends in Yugoslavia as a whole.

Privatization Issues in Yugoslavia

The process of transition in Yugoslavia started under very unfavorable conditions as the preexisting state structure shattered under the weight of inter-republican feuds, which in turn culminated in interethnic war. At a time when there was the greatest need to provide a stable socio-economic framework for the normal functioning of the macroeconomic policy of the federal government, Yugoslavia as a federation was facing collapse. This is why it is very hard to draw a general picture of the privatization process in what used to be Yugoslavia. Since there is no longer a unified state in the territory of what was socialist Yugoslavia, the patterns and specific challenges of privatization will inevitably differ to some extent from republic to republic. In addition, there is a second challenge for the analyst, viz., it is technically impossible to get basic information. What used to be a single Yugoslav market is now fractured into several mini-states and, even worse, these states do not have normal functional economic, technological, or information networks.

On the basis of the federal regulations accepted by the weak but still functioning federal government, a social consensus was achieved that the new property structure had to be revised in order to prepare conditions for the introduction of the market economy. In other words, the privatization process is the backbone of the transition process, a term used particularly since the fall of the Berlin Wall for the process of transformation of the relatively less developed and less efficient former socialist economies into market-oriented and efficient economies.

It is readily understood that there is no way to achieve an absolute degree of privatization. Private property is a conditio sine qua non for having an efficient economy. At the same time, for reasons of efficiency on a macro level, it is unavoidable that there be some forms of public property, particularly in infrastructural and service sectors. Considering the transition process as a process of changes at both the macro and micro levels in the case of those states developed on the territory of the former Yugoslavia, it is hardly realistic to hope to achieve successful privatization without assuring a relatively stable macroeconomic framework—which is missing in all parts of the former Yugoslavia except, possibly, in Slovenia. At the same time, there is no way to have successful privatization without structural changes in the economy. Privatization is expected to bring new winds and new elements in economic behavior on the part of the decision makers.

Privatization means several things, but the most important elements of that process could be stated as follows:

- the owner has the right to receive a share of the profit (in the form of dividends) in proportion to the value of his or her share in a particular property;
- the right to participate in the process of decision making with voting power in accordance with one's share in the property;
- the right to sell partially or fully one's share in a particular enterprise or any other form of private property.

Experience in privatizing public (i.e., governmental) property has been accumulated in Western countries, but that experience was not a good precedent for the necessary changes in former socialist countries. Sometimes privatization is accomplished by selling the enterprise to the employees. Another type of privatization deals with the privatization of management

Economic Transformation in Former Yugoslavia

when the management runs a publicly owned enterprise by the rules and criteria of a privately owned firm. But in this case there are no property changes involved. The firm is still owned by the government, but managed in a more efficient way when the management has been privatized. The property of the firm owned by the government could be transferred to the holding trusts or to the financial institutions (insurance, investment trusts, pension funds, etc.). This type of change is not perfect privatization either, because very often government agencies have an important role in running the aforementioned institutions. Therefore, it is necessary to take into account the fact that any type of property changes transferring the property out of the governmental sector, or in the ex-Yugoslav case, out of the social sector, does not necessarily mean full privatization.

By the same token, real privatization means that a certain portion of existing resources or properties becomes the property of a private owner who may decide independently and at his or her own risk to maximize the value of that property any way the owner sees fit, taking advantages of all three basic features of property rights: usus, usus fructus, as well as abusus.

The transition process in the former socialist countries, including former Yugoslavia, has been based on experiences from the capitalist economies with the goal of minimizing the differences in functioning of the economic system which existed during the socialist experience and to enable those countries to have basic common denominators with the rest of the world. Therefore, in the territories of what was socialist Yugoslavia, one can identify the presence of various models of the privatization process already known in the West:

a. privatization from the "bottom" as the process of the growth of private property on the basis of already existing private firms (either large or small ones) as well as on the basis of creation of the new private firms;

b. privatization from the "top" as the process of sale of shares of the publicly owned enterprises (governmental property or social property). Along this way, an increased number of individual and/or institutional new owners (shareholders) is developing and the social strata of property owners is increasing its share in the total population;

c. "spontaneous" privatization is taking place when individuals are able to buy smaller public firms which are sold at auctions. Compared with the other two types of privatization process, the "spontaneous" one is of relatively limited size.

Among many issues dealing with the privatization process are certain social preferences about the structure of the new shareholders which means

256   *Ljubiša Adamovich*

a policy of encouraging certain social categories to become new owners, while discouraging the other categories of the population. Also, in some countries there is a special policy as far as the share of foreigners is concerned both in terms of the size of foreign ownership in particular sectors and in terms of the share of foreigners in particular enterprises.

In the former socialist countries—ex-Yugoslavia included—it is to be expected that as experience is being accumulated, it will be necessary to introduce further changes in laws and regulations in this area. It is important, however, that certain basic principles about the protection of private property are respected to minimize the risk of potential investors.

In this respect, the experience over even a relatively short time which is modest from the point of view of the social property being privatized—as the case of former Yugoslavia is concerned—already shows some elements which are making the privatization process less smooth than expected by many analysts. Some of these elements are:

- armed struggles in various parts of former Yugoslavia with the economic, social and political consequences much broader than geographic areas of turmoil;
- the process of privatization is taking place in times of deep recession combined with heavy inflationary pressures in many parts of former Yugoslavia;
- there is no convertible currency which among other things is keeping many potential foreign investors away from investing in former Yugoslav territory;
- in conditions of high unemployment and recession personal incomes and the propensity to save is low and therefore relatively low demand by the potential domestic investors for purchasing the shares and becoming private owners;
- the methods and technical aspects of privatization are relatively unknown to those who are supposed to push the program of privatization through;
- the majority of potentially privatized enterprises are in the red and therefore not very attractive for potential buyers of shares issued by those firms;
- there is a relatively justified fear that if the vouchers for share purchases are distributed free of charge, that many receivers of vouchers are going to sell them cheaply for cash and use the cash to buy consumers goods. In that case, instead of promoting the capital formation process, a free distribution of share-vouchers would increase the propensity to consume, which might have disastrous effects in already inflationary conditions;

Economic Transformation in Former Yugoslavia

- due to the underdeveloped institutional framework necessary for the normal functioning of the market type economy, there is a risk that while breaking down former state monopolies, a new type of private monopoly could be created and that favorable conditions for creation of a mafia-type economy might bring into play new, highly speculation-oriented marketeers. Among the underdeveloped institutions, private banking could be considered as the most important one and the one with potentially the largest negative effect upon the economy in transition;
- last but not least is the persistence of the old scale of values which have had enough time to become rooted among the population during the period after 1945. A large majority of the population (at various levels of education and income) became used to living under noncompetitive conditions and, for many of them, lack of competition has been a nice excuse for their own mediocrity and personal failures. These values and habits from the "socialist way of life" cannot be easily discarded in the years to come.

The Concept of Privatization in Serbia

The Republic of Serbia has created its platform of privatization in the law on conditions and the procedures of transformation of the social into other forms of property.[1] One of the most important features of that law, as well as of the process of property transformation in Serbia, is the voluntary character of the changes of property structure. This means that the socially owned enterprises may decide to preserve the current status of social property and not take part in the transition process at all. That would be in accordance with the Constitution of Serbia, where the principle of the equal position of all types of property has been underlined.[2]

Another important principle of the law is the principle of public notification of one's intentions to change the property structure. Once the enterprise as the entity via its competent managerial structure decides to change its property structure, that decision has to be made public in order that all potential buyers of shares and all partners of the firm—both creditors and debtors—are aware of coming changes and are able to protect their interests and make necessary adjustments.

The third important principle is the principle of autonomy of the firm to make decision on property transformation and the sale of shares so that it can change both the legal status of the firm and the property structure.

The fourth principle deals with protection of the integrity of social property. This means that certified institutions are in charge of making assessments of property in order to avoid the undervaluation and very cheap sale of public (social) property during the process of transformation towards privatization. A special governmental agency has the right to control the financial aspects of property transformation.

As far as the models of transformation of social property is concerned, there are several possibilities and forms of transformation: issuing and sales of shares in order to promote the sale of social property, issuing of shares in order to increase the capital portfolio of the socially owned firm, sale of the enterprise or of part of the enterprise, renting the enterprise, or contracting the running and control of the enterprise with a special managerial group.

According to the first model of issuing and selling the shares, they could be sold to the employees, retired and/or former employees as well as to domestic and foreign natural and legal persons. The transformation and privatization of property include net business assets minus uncovered losses, short-run and long-run debts of the firm as well as the assets owned by known owners. Publicly owned housing can be maintained even if socially owned firms are being privatized in accordance with the different legal solutions and legal regulations. Such housing need not be included in the process of privatization. If shares are being bought by the employees, they are able to take advantage of the 20 percent discount plus 1 percent discount of the nominal price of the share for each year of work in that particular enterprise. One upper limit, however, has been established: buyers of shares using a discount price cannot make purchases above a 20,000 German Marks per person limit (in Dinars) or up to 1/3 of the total value of the purchase. There is no limit for buying shares if the domestic or foreign buyer purchases the shares at full value. If this model of privatization is adopted, the value of real properties would have to be assessed by the appropriate government agency or certified institution. If the sale has been processed without any discounts, the income on the sale is distributed to the different funds. However, if the sale of shares has been done using various discount models, the income on the sale is distributed in such a way that 50 percent is transferred to the funds (or holding) and 50 percent to the business fund of the firm. These shares could be paid for over a period of 5 years (20 percent a year) and they are not transferable unless fully paid for.

The functioning of the second model—issuing and selling shares in order to mobilize fresh capital for the firm—is basically very similar to the conditions of the previous model and includes the participation of both domestic and foreign natural and legal persons. In the case of the sale of shares without decision-making rights (the right to manage), only the real estate type of property has to be evaluated. But in the case of shares with managerial rights (or voting rights), the property of the enterprise as a whole has to be evaluated. In cases where, instead of payment in money, purchases of shares are made by physical goods or certain rights, these specific forms of payment also have to be evaluated.

In case the model covers the sale of an enterprise or of part of an enterprise, regulations provide the possibility that the sale could be made either to a domestic or foreign natural or legal person. This could be done either through public auction or by collecting the submitted offers. The use of payments and the distribution of income received is similar to the conditions from the previous models.

The model of renting an enterprise and contracting new management as a model of property transformation could be done both with domestic and foreign partners. It is necessary, however, to hold an auction and collect offers as well as to evaluate the socially owned capital which is entering the process of transition. In the case that the purchase of shares is taking place simultaneously with the rental, the contract has to get the approval of the agency for the evaluation of capital.

Comparative analysis of the legal regulations of the privatization process in the Republic of Serbia leads to the conclusion that there are no basic differences between the rules of the game in Serbia and the former Federal Law on the Transformation of Social Capital.[3] The basic difference, however, is that the Federal Law is more liberal in the sense that the discounts offered are higher and there is no type of control over the privatization process. It might be expected that the model developed in Serbia will tend to increase the value of social capital on two bases: first, because of the compulsory evaluation, and second, due to high inflationary pressure.

At the same time, the federal regulations and the regulations in Serbia have some similarities. One of them is the principle of voluntary decision to change the property structure of the firm or not to change. Since many firms are in the red and not attractive to potential purchasers of shares, they will tend to stay in the realm of social property. In practical terms, that means a postponement of the process of transformation and the need to pay higher prices due to a time lag, during which the same firms will fall deeper in debt. Furthermore, both sets of regulations (federal and Serbian) allow for the survival of social property through the revalorization process. Both models accept a grey zone and do not provide a clear cut line when it comes to property division. Public interests and private interests are not separated in a crystal clear way.

Another interesting similarity between the federal and Serbian models of privatization is that in both models there is a strong tendency to grant workers shares in the firm of their employment.

As with many other important changes in property structure in Yugoslavia since 1945, it was hard to put all the workers into a similar, let alone equal, position. The current transformation of property does not include the denationalization factor, or the transfer of formerly nationalized property into governmental hands. Therefore, the workers employed in the nationalized enterprises are in a privileged position compared with the workers who had to invest large parts of potential take-home money into the improvement of socially owned enterprises.

The experiences with privatization gained in former SFRY and particularly in Serbia show that many questions have been raised but not all of them answered in a satisfactory way. The lack of proper answers is a result of the fact that privatization is a much more complex, new and difficult process on many grounds than, for example, the process of nationalization. Many rules of the game developed during the period of the development of the market economy in Western countries, where that process has been uninterrupted from the medieval period onward, cannot be applied to the former socialist countries, former Yugoslavia included. It is difficult to coordinate the interests of the various social groups which are directly involved in the process of privatization and being either favored or discriminated against. These groups include employed labor, retired labor, the unemployed labor force, and (last but not least) the state.

Opening this problem does not mean that the author considers that the Western market economy and society are functioning in a harmonious and non-controversial way. But the discrepancy of interests and different position of various social groups there have been developed over centuries and through the transformation of a feudal economy into a market economy. Simultaneously with the development of a competitive economic society, a competitive political system has developed and the mechanism of countervailing powers helps ensure that from time to time serious and controversial issues are dealt with on the basis of a multiparty system and democratic procedures. In former Yugoslavia, as in all other former socialist countries, the privatization process has started abruptly. The current reality in the former socialist countries is that the elites still expect to reach the level of a working and efficient democratic political system, while at the same time the process of privatization is being brought about through decree. Since the decision is the result of an abrupt legal change, all social strata expect to see their interests properly protected—which does not seem to be happening in either the federal or Serbian system of transformation of public into private property. It remains to be seen how many of these inadequate solutions are the result of lack of information and knowledge and professional expertise on the part of law makers and their teams of experts, and how much is the result of the objective situation and the fact that there have been no precedents from which to learn.

Economic Transformation in Former Yugoslavia

Another interesting set of problems is associated with ranking the goals of privatization. What are or should be the priorities of the transition process? Is the main goal to assign via the privatization process as many resources as possible to the known owners, who should via facti be engaged in better use of property and thus promoting development of a more efficient and rational national economy, as well as increased rationality and efficiency on the enterprise level? Another goal may be to use the privatization process to mobilize new capital and bring new fuel to the economy, transferring some of the potentially consumed income into fresh money and new investments, providing an injection for revitalization of the slow growing and even stagnating economies in the former socialist countries? Or should the main goal of privatization be to change the legal position of property and create a new basis for the development of a more efficient organizational and managerial structure for the formerly public enterprises?

As far as the timing is concerned, one of the important questions to be asked is: should the privatization process take place as quickly as possible (almost like another shock-therapy) or should it be a gradual process, which would leave enough time for adjustment and learning—both for the newly created managerial elite and those who will become unemployed, as well as for those who are expected to improve their skills and performance and survive in a more competitive climate? Whatever the answer to these questions, it is certainly not an easy decision. If the verdict is cast in favor of shock therapy, there may be in the field of privatization, as in many other fields before, shock only, but with the therapy missing. If it is decided that the adjustment process should be longer, then the problem is to determine how long, since it seems to be a fact that in many areas human beings tend to perform better under a certain level of pressure than when at ease and under no pressure at all. Many of these, as well as other questions, can hardly be answered in an academic and theoretical way. But not having any established guidance or paradigms against which to judge the privatization process makes it more difficult to use objective criteria either in positive or negative criticism in analyzing the issue.

Privatization in Montenegro

The case of the Republic of Montenegro is of particular interest because it seems to offer various relatively flexible solutions with the one basic common denominator: instead of the loose notion of socially owned firms, the basic concern of the new legislation is to get a clear-cut picture about the property structure of the firm. Among the various possibilities provided by the legislator in Montenegro, some elements deserve to be particularly underlined:

262   Ljubiša Adamovich

- the firm can make the choice of the model of transformation;
- the model of transformation of the firm facing bankruptcy;
- the distribution of shares of the firm in the form of vouchers with no charge (free distribution);
- special programs of privatization.

The legal regulations in Montenegro offer the possibility of various types of transformation of property as well as various types of managerial structure. The most important feature of the regulations dealing with the transformation process is that firms can make free decisions about the model of transformation, taking care primarily of the interests of the persons on the payroll but also considering the potential attractiveness of a particular approach to potential outsiders who might have an interest in joining the firm and bringing fresh money into the transformation process. As a matter of fact, the main intention of the regulations is to stimulate the firms in transition to reach out to the capital market and attract new investors. The existence of a certain amount of capital in the hands of individual and institutional investors and a successful attempt to make them new partners of the firm in transition are two of the best tests of the validity of both internal organizational production and personnel structure of the firm as well as of its public image. If the firm is ready to enter the process of transformation of both property structure and the management structure, there are various ways it can do so:

- sales of shares in order to sell publicly owned capital under special and favorable conditions for potential buyers;
- sale of shares in order to mobilize new capital (fresh money) to improve the firm's portfolio;
- sale of the firm either as a whole or in parts under more or less standard market conditions;
- sale of the firm as a whole or of an ideal part of the firm to the person(s) who intend to take over the management functions in that enterprise;
- investment of capital by domestic and/or foreign natural and legal persons without any privileges or discounts;
- transformation of debt into investments (making co-owners out of creditors);
- transfer of shares to the Development fund of the Republic, or to the Pension funds and other institutional investors with no charge;
- exchange of shares among various firms;
- identification of the state share in the total value of the firm;
- contracting certain activities in the form of franchising and time-sharing.

Economic Transformation in Former Yugoslavia   263

By the same regulations both the employed and the citizens at large are invited to join the process of property transformation. In order to make the offer more attractive, there is a 30 percent discount and in addition a discount of 1 percent per year of employment (all based on the nominal value of the shares).

The role of government in the process of transformation is coming to the fore along the following lines:

- taking care of the transformation of the firm facing bankruptcy;
- taking over the management of some firms;
- providing special programs of privatization by the government of Montenegro.

This is a way to provide another opportunity to the firms which are facing difficulties and where the workers and managers running the socially owned firm have not been able to survive. The government's involvement, however, does not by definition mean that the process of transformation will be successful. It means that before letting the firm down the drain, the government is trying once more to use public funds to bring the firm back on its feet. This type of intervention should be considered as a social cost of the process of transformation. A similar approach entails the distribution of publicly owned capital in the form of vouchers distributed free of charge, particularly to those workers who may lose their jobs during the transformation process, so that they would be able to start a business of their own (private small business) or buy the shares from the State Development Fund. The main conclusion by both legislators and citizenry on the basis of legislation on the transition of property structure in Montenegro is that there is no way the economy can be improved by amending the existing system of social property. Instead of trying further to rationalize the model of social property, that type of property is going to be totally eliminated from the business sector in Montenegro. The firm has to have recognizable proprietors with their vested interests to protect their property by promoting rational criteria for the operation of the enterprise.[4]

Privatization Dilemmas in Macedonia

The process of property transformation in Macedonia is hard to follow not only because more general information for the state as a whole is not available, but also because even such information as may exist within Macedonia is not easy to obtain outside the state. While in the case of Croatia, one could accept the lack of available sources on privatization on the basis of war operations as the most important preoccupation of society

264   *Ljubiša Adamovich*

at large, such a strong excuse, fortunately, does not exist in the Macedonian case. Therefore, the Macedonian experience will be discussed on the basis of a case study well analyzed in the weekly review *Ekonomska politika*.[5]

According to the aforementioned analysis, similarly to the experience in Croatia, Serbia and Slovenia, there is also a threat to privatization in Macedonia such that the privatization process may degenerate into a process of an increased role of the government in the economy. At the same time, like in other parts of former Yugoslavia, the privatization process in Macedonia is burdened with the danger of possible creation of new monopolies replacing the old ones. In order to understand the climate and dilemmas of privatization in Macedonia, the case study of the enterprise "OTEX" from the city of Ohrid could be very instructive. This firm belongs to the small group of efficient and successful enterprises in Macedonia. According to the general manager, the privatization process is long overdue, because from the mid-1960's onward there has not been strong enough motivation for efficient performance. This is why "OTEX" belonged to the small group in Yugoslavia which started adjustments towards privatization as soon as the first draft of the federal law on that subject became available. Social property did not provide a large enough framework or sufficient incentives for efficient performance, while, on the other hand, that type of property system has overemphasized the elements of social solidarity and some fundamental features of the standard of living as far as the basic needs of the firm were concerned. The firm "OTEX," however, even in conditions of social property, was capable of achieving above average results. The average growth of physical volume of production reached a level of about 10 percent a year, and the firm has been hiring about 200 new workers a year, with personal incomes remaining above the average in Macedonia. Being a firm which was aware of the growing competition by new private and mixed owned firms, "OTEX" managers decided to use a large part of the profit gained in 1989 for the purchase of internal shares. The alternative was to use these funds to increase the personal incomes of the employees by the amount of about 4 monthly take-home wages and salaries. That was the way to create about 12 percent additional capital as seen from the balance sheet of "OTEX" for the year 1989. This decision was perfectly in accordance with the legal system. It was up to the firm to decide either to use the earned profits for the increase of personal take-home incomes, or to use it as investment capital to improve the financial position of the firm on the basis of issuing internal shares. A similar policy was followed by "OTEX" in 1990. This was to increase the share of shareholders capital in "OTEX" from 12 percent in 1989 to 35 percent in 1990. In other words, this percentage shows the amount of social capital bought by the shareholders, or the additional capital for "OTEX" received from its own employees, as well as by banks and other outsiders. By the same

Economic Transformation in Former Yugoslavia 265

token, the sale of shares to physical and legal persons outside of "OTEX" meant the possibility of creating a mixed ownership rather than merely of changing the status of a socially owned firm into a firm eventually owned by its own employees. The firm planned to sell more shares to outsiders, but external demand has been very low compared to the number of issued shares. Still, out of the total capital of "OTEX," 97 percent has the status of shareholders' capital and about 35 percent of that amount has been already sold and paid for. Another, larger part of the capital will be paid for either on the basis of personal incomes, or out of dividends.

The firm "OTEX" tried to reach out for the participation of foreign investors and for a while several potential foreign partners showed serious business interest. It came close to the signing of the contract to develop a lady's garment factory. According to that arrangement, "OTEX'"s part of the investment would have been made out of fixed investments (buildings and capital equipment) while the foreign partner would make its share of 51 percent in the form of the fresh money and with its engagement in the marketing of the factory products mainly on the West European market. It is clear that political turbulence in Yugoslavia, including in Macedonia, was a very strong reason for the foreign partner to postpone the arrangement without any hint of the timing of an eventual reopening of negotiations.

The case of the firm "OTEX" shows that there are business units and relatively sophisticated managers who are doing their best to speed up the process of privatization using various models of property transformation, from internal shares to public sale of shares and engagement of foreign investors too. However, regulations in the state of Macedonia do not provide incentives to treat dividends as a form of additional income for shareholders. Various forms of taxation are increased by about six times if the profit of the plant is distributed in the form of dividends as compared to the fiscal treatment of profit if it were ploughed back into investments. This is why the managers of the firm have decided to postpone payments of dividends after the regulations change and after more favorable fiscal treatment for dividends is provided. In many other ways, the firm "OTEX" is promoting new ways of doing things. One of the most important steps taken by this firm is the development of steeper wage and salary differentials between the management and employees of the firm. The managers receive a salary six times as high as the average income in the firm and they also receive a 5 percent commission for the amount of profit which they make above the expected profit.

Another important policy decision by the management of "OTEX" is that those who have managerial rank cannot enjoy the privilege of so-called "double ownership"—to be high-ranking managers in "OTEX" and at the same time to own their own businesses. This is the way to avoid the risk of double loyalty, which, as a rule, means super loyalty to the personally owned firm and neglect of the interests of "OTEX."

Institutional Ownership—Preservation of Public Ownership?

The process of transformation of ownership, at least in the case of the republic of Serbia, has shown a strong tendency to preserve the importance of the public sector by the use of institutional ownership. Due to the fact that banks and insurance institutions are not privatized and that a Republican Fund for Restructuring is the most important factor in the growth of institutional ownership, one reaches the conclusion that by developing institutional ownership, authorities are showing that in very important areas they are not ready to see real privatization.

Institutional ownership based on the role of parastatal or directly governmental financial intervention does not contribute to the growth of the private sector with all of its positive and negative consequences. Just the opposite: it helps preserve both an organizational and, even more important, a general attitude towards such issues as cost-consciousness, economic efficiency, profitability, etc., as it has been the case in the system of social property in former Yugoslavia and/or the system of state property in other former socialist countries.

The "new" institutional owner composed of the various subjects of social property (or even more precisely of social non-property) caretakers is equally behaving like its predecessors—caretakers of social property. Even the best managed non-privately owned property, as it has been known as an axiomatic truth, is not a good substitute for private property. If nothing else, then at least public and/or semi-public owned and managed firms are mainly concerned with broad interests in the long run, and not with the interests of particular owners over both the short term and the long term. The model of behavior by all relevant standards in institutional-owned firms in the case of Serbia is different from the standard model of behavior in a privately owned firm and therefore the results are different. Maximization of general interests is the main concern of the state or parastatal and in the case of Serbia of privately-owned firms. While as a principle it could be accepted, it becomes unacceptable when compared with the privatization process.

As a matter of fact, institutional ownership in Serbia could be explained as a hidden form of growth of state ownership. By the sale of socially owned capital, there is a process of accumulation of funds in the hands of the Republican Fund for Restructuring (Republički fond za prestruktuiranje). These funds then are being used to join with banks and insurance systems in order to become partners and/or buy shares of other

Economic Transformation in Former Yugoslavia

socially owned firms. It is also possible to use the funding ear-marked in the state budget for increasing the share of the government in the ownership of particular firms. On the assumption that budgetary funds are based on tax collection and that before the taxes have been paid most of that money belonged to individuals and many private businesses, many people have decided not to invest in the private sector but to use their funds via the state budget for the enhancement of public property! The fact that this type of property by its legal position and by name is not considered public, does not change the basic economic behavior of these businesses. This type of transformation of property looks more like transformation from socially owned firms to governmentally owned firms than like a transformation from socially owned firms to privately owned firms.

There is more than one reason for the concern of the government to keep its hands in the economy. One of the most often quoted in Serbia and in other countries—because Serbia does not have a monopolistic position and is far from being a unique case for such a behavior of government—is that the ruling party likes to be close to the sources of income creation. But that argument could easily be considered flawed, since many of the firms which have undergone the transformation from socially owned to institutionally owned are far from being profit-creating centers. Instead, many of them, being in the red, are deficit-creating centers and they need government involvement in the firm in the hope that with the government participating in the firm's management they may be able to postpone bankruptcy.

This brings the analysis to the second, equally important, possible explanation of governmental involvement. As a rule, most of the firms which are now institutionally owned employ a large number of people. Whichever party or government is in power cannot close its eyes to the fact that a shock therapy in the privatization process might lead to social turmoil. Such a price for the more intensive privatization process may be too risky to accept. Therefore, it seems to be simpler and safer, at least in the short run, to create conditions for social harmony in misery than to expose the economy of Serbia to the great opportunities (and great risks) of an abruptly privatized economy. The fact that this attitude seems to be applicable in Serbia's case became clear after the process of democratization and a multiparty political system were introduced. For Serbia, for the first time since 1941, the government has to be concerned with the results it achieves. Another reason may be that due to the almost half-century long experience marked with the strong and interwoven connections between economic policy and social policy, it becomes first mentally and then organizationally very hard to divorce the functioning of the enterprises from the needs of social policy and the social protective network. Sooner or later, it has to be done, but the current government is obviously opting for the postponement of this issue for the time being.

268   Ljubiša Adamovich

Getting government more and more involved in the everyday functioning of the economy as a co-owner via institutional ownership could be understood on political grounds but hardly accepted on economic grounds. From the latter point of view, the growth of institutionalized property in the conditions of the Serbian economy looks more like a new grand effort to save social property from bankruptcy by the use of more public funding and more direct governmental intervention. This type of therapy is not new and, more importantly, there are too many proofs that in the long-run the therapy applied is lethal. Whether the policy is based on ideological prejudices or on the best knowledge of the decision-makers involved is beside the point. This policy is tantamount to the already known scheme of nationalization of losses and socialization of gains.

Opponents of Privatization

Privatization is one of the most important features of the process of transition from a command economy and public ownership toward a market economy in Yugoslavia. Perhaps that is the main reason why the ruling elites in all mini-states made from former Yugoslavia are slow to introduce the process of privatization. Even less dynamic, throughout this whole territory, from Slovenia to Macedonia, is the introduction of private property as the leading and most important form of property. Why is this? Is it a result of ideological preferences, the remnants of leftist dogmatism, or a logical consequence of the objective conditions in the economic, social, and legal domains in various parts of former Yugoslavia? Another question deserving exploration is associated with the eventual vested interests of one or more social strata in postponing or slowing down the process of privatization.

Change in the structure of property rights represents in many ways a revolutionary act even when it takes place in the absence of bloodshed. In order to make it possible, it is necessary to create conditions in the political, legal, social, business, and economic areas, similar to the conditions already existing in the international environment. Unfortunately, on the whole territory of former Yugoslavia these conditions are missing—not only one or two, but almost all of them. Although the analysis could be made only for Serbia, whose data is at hand—it could be said with certainty that the situation is not very different in other states of the former SFRY.

In the analysis of current conditions in Serbia, it is not an exaggeration to claim that most of the business firms face a lack of the state of law and a lack of power of the managerial elite not only in some but in too many firms. Many enterprises have been scourged by overemployment for decades. It is hard to face the process of privatization in the firms where

Economic Transformation in Former Yugoslavia 269

managers are mediocre and with employees whose marginal productivity is zero. They are afraid that they might become unemployed once privatization and competition take place in their firms. The majority of these firms are also marked by a relatively low level of technology. To this picture of the firm it should be added that an unsophisticated and inadequate fiscal system does not make the position of the firms any easier, particularly those which might become more competitive and eventually leaders in their branches of activities. To complete the current picture of the state of firms in Serbia it should be noted that most of them are overindebted. Some analysts estimate internal debts in a number of firms to be ten times higher than their net revenues.

The current experience of privatization shows that large groups of the population seem to be less enthusiastic about the process of privatization than expected. When this transition must take place in a relatively short period of time and be introduced via legal changes, it is almost inevitable to find that large groups of the population are at least disturbed if not even scared. These groups are important in creating the general climate pro or against the process of privatization, and the political leaders have to take this attitude as a very important and relevant factor in shaping and timing the privatization process.

On the other hand, the most capable and most competitive individuals of this society are pushing toward a quicker pace of transition, including privatization. The role of this group in shaping the social climate is much more important than its size might suggest; still it is hard to claim that they may be able to win the support of the majority who still seem to prefer the security of an income at a lower level to the opportunity and chances of competitive society.

Equally important in discouraging the process of privatization and transition in Serbia are some negative features of the general socio-economic conditions. One of the most important of these is the current easy money policy leading toward hyperinflation in conditions of recession and heavy unemployment. The political theater in Serbia, which is marked by a high level of animosity among various political parties, is also an unfavorable factor.

It is of the greatest importance that in what was Yugoslavia, as in other former socialist countries, the energy, talents, and efforts of various social groups are not dissipated in the process of transition of public into private economy, but instead are channeled toward the creation of favorable conditions for development of new business activities which will generate new sources of income and employment. Privatization will hopefully bring new chances for more efficient use of the existing factors of production. For the economic advancement of those countries, however, it is even more important to help the creation of the new lines of economic activities.

Trying to develop a "fair" system of privatizing public property may be an almost endless job, and the participants in that process may find themselves in the position of "waiting for Godot." That is why the process of privatization has to be coupled with efforts to create legal, institutional, economic, and psychological conditions—a macroeconomic entourage, in general—in order to promote the entrepreneurial activity of vairous social and business groups at various levels of income and investment potential. This is especially important due to the fact that a large part of the existing assets that were publicly owned within the framework of the socialist system may turn into liabilities once exposed to the "judgment day" of the market economy.

The further expansion of the process of privatization not only in a legal but also in a functional sense, demands some serious changes in current economic and business conditions in Serbia. The first step should be to put an end to the almost uncontrollable money supply which is the main source of hyperinflation. The second area of necessary changes of condition is fiscal policy. Currently, both publicly and privately owned firms are faced with very high taxes. The publicly owned firms are able to find an easier way out through tax evasion, at the same time calling to government attention the fact that high taxation could lead to the bankruptcy of firms and to the growth of serious unemployment. However, the public authorities do not accept such excuses from the private owners. Therefore, it is not impossible to find cases where small private firms pay more taxes in absolute terms than much larger publicly owned firms. With lower taxation, government could better stimulate the creation of new private firms and receive more revenue.

The achievement of at least a grosso modo consensus about the main trends of future economic, social, and political development in Serbia would be a very important factor in stimulating the process of future privatization and starting up new firms.

Having in mind the difficulties analyzed in the current socio-economic climate for privatization in Serbia, it is easily understandable that the very process carried on currently shows some deficiencies. One of them is that the process of transformation from public to private property is mainly taking the form of a legal change. Formerly socially owned enterprises are changing their legal status by becoming corporations based on internal sales of shares. Legally the enterprises are transferred into corporations, but everything else stays as before—without any change in the essence of the functioning of the firm. This type of transformation of property rights is no more than a nominal change.

The second type of change of property rights is marked by strong elements of etatization, replacing formerly socially owned property with mixed ownership that involves the strong participation of the state as a co-owner.

Economic Transformation in Former Yugoslavia 271

This type of property change is also more nominal than real. It seems to be just a form to preserve the status quo. All the basic features of the firms are unchanged, from production program and technological structure to the structure of management personnel.

The most successful change in property structure is carried on, at least in Serbia, through the so-called "capillary"—individual size, but at relatively large scale, process of creation of new private mainly small business type firms.

Very important changes in property structures took place during 1991. The main feature of these changes could be summarized as a pro private property trend. The number of privately owned firms during 1991 in Serbia has increased from 21,567 to 42,697. Since in 1991 the total number of enterprises in Serbia was 83,452, this means that the share of private firms has been almost 50 percent.[6] Yet, the number of socially owned firms has barely declined during the same year: from 5,040 to 4,955. This means that most of the new private business firms are newly created and as a rule are the small firms. At the same time—during 1991—the number of cooperatively owned and mixed firms has also increased from 1,532 to 5,090. The process of new private firm formation was most intensive in Belgrade, where the number of private firms during 1990 and 1991 rose by a factor of almost 30—from 754 in 1989 to 21,182 at the end of 1991.[7] These firms represent a solid economic basis in the economy of the capital city. In 1991 they made around 11.5 percent of total revenue, about 16.2 percent of gross income, and 31.5 percent of capital formation. Private firms in Belgrade employed 14,848 workers in 1991.

A more detailed analysis of the structure of private firms in Serbia, particularly from the point of view of their financial abilities and technological capacities, shows that the largest number of private firms are the small ones, mainly owned by a single owner. Only 30 percent are formed as a corporation. The retail trade and service sector in general seem to be the most preferred areas for small businesses in Serbia. In Belgrade, for example, about 53 percent of all private firms today are in retail trade.

It should be stressed that foreign capital has also made a contribution to the process of structural transformation of the Serbian economy in the direction of privatization. In 1991, there were 370 private businesses fully owned by foreigners. The total value of invested foreign capital in these 370 firms reached only 141.7 million DM.

The foregoing analysis leads to the conclusion that the privatization process is carried on mostly through new small firms. There is no doubt that this is a positive sign of economic transformation but carrying in itself many known and unknown risks characteristic for new small businesses.

It is of particular importance that in the process of privatization, not all the important large enterprises in Serbia have been included. Their number is only about 5 percent of the total number of enterprises, but they provide about 60 percent of the jobs and create about 60 percent of the total revenues from sales. Unfortunately, this relatively small group of enterprises creates about 73 percent of the total business losses in Serbia.

Some of these big socially owned enterprises have been recently transformed, but in the opposite direction from privatization. Instead of being transformed into private or mixed ownership, they have become state owned firms. The importance of this group of firms owned by the state can be seen from the fact that they provide 15 percent of employment and income in Serbia.

On the basis of the foregoing analysis, it is more than appropriate to ask the question who is trying to limit the process of the transformation of property structure and why. Some persons clearly want to subject the economy to mainly "cosmetic" changes instead of a more energetic introduction of privatization not only at the level of small firms but also at the level of large socially owned firms. The answer to this question is in the hands of all those who are trying to preserve their status and privilege. Namely, a majority of members of the political establishment, members of the existing managerial strata, and a majority of the employees who have vested interests in preserving the status quo. Among these three groups, the political establishment, more than the other two groups, is mainly interested in accepting legal changes in the status of property, without serious changes in the economic area. Therefore, with the already mentioned "cosmetic" adjustments, the political establishment is postponing the termination of its direct involvement in controlling the use and movements of capital. It is fully aware that once control over the movements and use of capital are lost, it will be deprived of the basis of its political power as well as monetary and non-monetary privileges. Being deprived of this commanding position over the economy, the ruling elite in all former republics would be forced to limit its activities in the area reserved for the governments in market economies. That would still leave significant responsibility in the areas of social welfare policy, culture, and defense, as well as in the main issues associated with macroeconomic policy, but no direct control over capital, and hence much reduced political and economic power. At the same time, the decentralized ownership of economic resources in the hands of thousands and millions of people is the best precondition for political democratization and therefore smaller opportunities for the practice of monopolistic political power. By slowing down the process of transformation of social property into various forms of private and mixed property, the political elites in all former Yugoslav republics are trying to preserve their domination over economic resources and economic performance which have made possible the financing of various activities which fit the policy platform of the ruling parties. Therefore, it is possible to claim that in both Serbia and Croatia,

Economic Transformation in Former Yugoslavia 273

there is a new danger of centralization on the horizon, despite nominal legal changes and the use of particular terms, like "Croatization."

Another important group which is trying to postpone the process of privatization is the existing managerial strata. Most of them have been given their jobs as a result of the involvement of the political leadership, either on the basis of total and undisputable loyalty to the political bosses and/or on the basis of corruption, nepotism, political favoritism, and similar criteria rather than on the basis of their professional qualities. This does not mean that within professional management, there are no capable individuals who could be accepted by any owner and/or political party, but they are a definite minority. The majority of the members of the managerial strata prefer to keep the process of transition only within the framework of nominal changes. Between now and the day when they can no longer stop real changes, they are doing their best to diminish the value of the enterprises so that when the time for real privatization comes, there will be hardly anything to privatize! In many firms, shares are being sold to the employees at a discount rate reaching as much as 30 percent with a possible payment time of 10 years. The main buyers of these shares are members of the management team in those plants, as they have the highest incomes and purchasing power. This is one way that many managers of enterprises not only avoid responsibility for the mismanagement of socially owned enterprises, but—from the very start of the transformation process—gain special privileges both as managers and often as the most important shareholders of the "transformed" firms. Many of them at the same time found new individual private firms, taking away customers and suppliers and using important information received on their jobs as managers of the "transformed" enterprise and transferring this specific type of resources into their privately owned firm. In some cases, managers buy machinery and equipment or buildings from the "transformed" firms cheaply and improve the structure of their privately owned firms. In case that the "transformed" firm is facing financial troubles, the only people who were on the payroll and who know what to do relatively easily as far as the adjustment problem is concerned are the former managers. They could easily leave the firm they have been running for years and get busy full time in their own private firms. In conditions such as those described, it is more often than not the case that many shareholders each having a small number of shares, are at a strong disadvantage when compared with those who own a large numbers of shares and are also the decision-makers regarding the survival, profit making, and bankruptcy of the "transformed" firm. This is the way the new category of property owners is being created in the process of transition or transformation of property structure. Those who have been privileged during the period of the command economy seem to have the greatest chance to once again become privileged, at least under the current conditions of the market economy. There is a big difference, however, where the durability of privileges is concerned. In conditions of command economy and the one-party political system, privileges have been directly connected with the political position and political rating of the members of nomenclature, while in conditions of market economy these privileges are an excellent starting point. There is no guarantee that those who became rich quickly during the period of transition will be able to preserve their wealth using it under the rules of the game of the market economy. Some of them will without doubt be able to multiply their wealth, while some of them will lose it.

Many workers also show a lack of enthusiasm about the process of transformation of social property into private property. Their attitude expresses itself in two ways: either they try to block totally the process of transformation of property, or they try to at least slow down the process of privatization. Once the sale of "internal shares" (sale of shares to the employees) is over, regardless of the fact that workers also own a certain number of shares, they tacitly, and sometimes openly, slow down the process of further adjustment of the firm to market conditions. In other words, they do not push for the transformation of the financial, organizational structure of the firm, or for changes of the personnel and/or developmental goals of the firm. The main attitude among much of the rank and file is not to rock the boat. This type of development could have been avoided if the potential buyers of the shares had been sought not only among the employees of a particular enterprise but among a larger circle of potential customers. One of the most important principles of the market economy—the separation of property functions from the managerial function—seems not to have been respected in Serbia, or in many other parts of former Yugoslavia and the former socialist countries in general. If most of the shareholders of the privatized public enterprises are the employees of those enterprises, then the result of such a privatization is a specific form of shareholders' self-management.

Comparing this situation as result of transformation of property with the conditions in the Western economies, it is not difficult to see that in enterprises in Serbia and not only in Serbia, there is almost no chance to develop positive tensions between the managerial group in the firm and the interests of the shareholders. Instead, there is almost a visible presence of equality between the managerial function and the property or function of ownership. Further development of the privatization process, therefore, could hardly be achieved without the transformation of the workers from their traditional self-managerial position into a position of hired labor in a society where there is mobility of labor and where the free market economy includes the free movement of both labor and capital and more opportunity than security. But it is the impression of this

Economic Transformation in Former Yugoslavia 275

analyst that this is exactly what much of the rank and file labor do not like to have. They prefer security to opportunity. The closer the economy gets to the model of free market economy, the stronger the competition will be and the higher the risk, so that many so far "happily employed" may lose their jobs. Buying some shares of the firm by whom they are employed, the workers feel as if they had bought their jobs. In enterprises which have been transformed in this way, labor in general—and now the shareholders in particular—are able to press management for higher wages and the preservation of the status quo. Managers of these firms are partially under pressure from the workers and partially looking for their future in the privately owned firms anyway, and are not ready to counter the position of workers. Having the attitude of running the firm with soft budget constraints actually helps the firm to get closer to bankruptcy. The lack of mass bankruptcy may be explained, however, by the fact that many firms are in the same position and, instead of strong competition, all of them are surviving at a declining level of profits and personal incomes. This type of social climate is not the monopoly of the Serbian and Balkan area. The former system of command economy in Eastern Europe and the U.S.S.R. has developed industrial peace at the cost of acceptance of low income by the working class and low productivity by the owners (government). The former Yugoslav system of self-management developed a relatively comfortable position for all employees, enhancing their human rights, personal freedom, and chances to own limited private property. This is why in order to get workers' support for a transition of the economy along the lines of privatization and the development of a market economy, it is inevitable in the areas of former SFRY to provide more "carrots" and less "sticks" to win popular support for transition.

The process of the disintegration of Yugoslavia and the development of four new states has been, among other things, followed with different approaches and results in the process of transition from publicly owned to privately owned market-oriented economy. What used to be a unified market and single monetary system is becoming a diversified picture of five independent states and sooner or later five monetary systems. The disintegration of federal power has meant also the disintegration of the federal legal system, including the laws and regulations dealing with the process of transition. All the new states show an interest in preserving only those parts of the federal regulations which fit directly the interests of a particular state because there is no need any more for making compromises as a price for the existence of the federation. At the same time, each new state is trying to develop its own legislation in general, including the legislation and regulations dealing with the process of transition and particularly of privatization. It was to be expected that each new state would

276   *Ljubiša Adamovich*

design its own path for the transformation of property both timewise and formwise in accordance with its own socio-political conditions.

Underground Economy—Important Source of Privatization and Softening of Social Tensions

The stagnation of the Yugoslav economy can be traced to the time of the second oil shock in 1979. From then on, the Yugoslav economy was exposed to heavy recessionary pressures. The years of political turbulence in the country during the eighties certainly did not help its economic performance. On the contrary, growing political disintegrative forces contributed greatly to the already pre-existing economic disintegration. In fact, the processes of political and economic disintegration played a mutually reinforcing role.

Stagnation and the negative rate of growth during the decade of 1980's had many negative effects upon the performance of the economy. One of the most important indicators of the negative trends has been the decline of personal income. According to the assessments made by experts in the Federal Office of Statistics, the purchasing power of the Yugoslav population has been cut to the level of the early 1960s. A recent comparison (April 1992) shows that the real personal income had been cut in half compared with the conditions of 1990![8] One of the inevitable questions associated with the disastrous position of the consumers relates to the lack of social turmoils and upheavals. That fact can only partially be explained by the growing nationalistic homogenization and ethnic unity—factors which at least for a short while could act as compensation for the economic losses and the falling trends of the standard of living. The more important factor is the growth of an illegal and/or underground economy in Yugoslavia, a growth which has been intensified since 1965.

The very existence and growth of the underground economy in Yugoslavia and its analysis has methodological and statistical features similar to those in many other countries. The specific feature of that economic sector in Yugoslavia compared with its existence in other former socialist countries, is that, for several decades, the Yugoslav economy and society have been more open and less dictatorial. Both factors contributed to the growth of the underground economy.

Beginning in the mid-1960s, many activities in Yugoslavia associated with the flourishing tourist industry, became a real "El Dorado" for the participants in the underground economy. Several experts have claimed that for years, income from tourism has reached a level of 4 to 4.5 billion of U.S. dollars, while the official data from the National Bank of Yugoslavia has shown for years only an amount of 1 to 1.5 billion dollars. The difference in these estimates is due to the underground economy. Other areas of

Economic Transformation in Former Yugoslavia

underground economy in Yugoslavia include activities such as various services which could be offered in private apartments, the construction of summer homes, reconstruction and adaptation of existing private apartments and office spaces, middlemen activities in the distribution and sale of agricultural produce, transportation services, illegal dealings with foreign exchange, subletting of apartments, various forms of educational and health services, stealing of spare parts from publicly owned enterprises, the "use" (stealing) of time paid by the public sector to employees who use that time for their private deals, etc.

A more general approach to the notion of underground economy would include any form of unregistered economic activity, including all household work. Using the broader notion, according to the estimates done by the Federal Office of Statistics of Yugoslavia, the share of underground economy of the GNP grew from a level of 8 percent in the 1960s, to approximately 15 percent in the 1970s and to around 31 percent in the 1980s. The methodological differences between the Western concept of GNP and the Yugoslav concept of GDP are important. One must take into account both the contribution of the tertiary sector (almost 20 percent of the GNP) and the contribution of workers remittances from abroad (4 percent). The GNP of Yugoslavia in 1986 was about 55 percent larger than expressed in the official statistical publications.[9] According to the same source, the structure of the underground economy includes performance within households, manufacturing, workers' remittances from abroad and performance in the service sector. The important role of the underground economy could explain why the economic situation in Yugoslavia, even when near collapse, did not develop social explosions—or at least has not yet. Both production and income are heavily undervalued in the official sources. By the same token, figures on unemployment seem to be exaggerated due to the fact that a large group of officially unemployed are active in various forms of the underground economy. On the other hand, the lack of realistic data on the economic and social position of various strata of the population represents a serious barrier against the formulation of a realistic social policy network. At the same time, the very existence of an underground economy is proof of the inadequate performance of the legal and "regular" economic system. During the early period of transition in the Yugoslav economy (the first 6 months of 1990), many of the activities included in the underground economy came to the fore and many new individual private firms were founded. However, the deterioration of the economic situation in the second half of 1990 and particularly the ethnic warfare since June 1991 contributed to the revival and expansion of the underground economy not so much in its "classical" form, but more in terms of speculation with contraband in armaments and ammunition as well as other activities.

278

Ljubiša Adamovich

Conclusion

It is a very risky task to prescribe the methods, timing and speed of privatization, but on the basis of experiences in former socialist countries, not only in former Yugoslavia, it is possible to take the position and risk of suggesting certain steps:

- start the privatization process using the leading firms as the best case group in order to achieve as soon as possible very positive results and to be able to stimulate the population to participate in the process;
- in promoting the process of privatization, it is important to insist that it is the best way to get rid of those enterprises which have been artificially supported for decades at the expense of efficient firms and the taxpayers at large;
- buyers of newly privatized property must have serious guarantees that all their ownership rights will be honored by the economic system and by the government;
- there should be no limitations on the relationship between foreign and domestic owners of a particular enterprise;
- it seems more rational to sell shares than to distribute them with no charge. In Serbia, for example, there has for centuries been a deep feeling that if something has value, no intelligent person would give it up for free, if there is a chance to earn compensation. If something is given "for nothing," then, the value of that "something" is simply, nothing;
- special attention should be given to potential foreign investors. In order to provide a more secure investment framework, it is necessary to promote the program of economic stabilization, to provide relatively favorable working conditions from the point of view of the owners and managers of the enterprises, re-align the fiscal system with those in countries from which potential foreign capital might come. It is also extremely important to eliminate all barriers which could seriously slow down development of free enterprise activities and which may have a tendency to isolate the country in transition from the positive impacts and impulses of the world market.

Finally, like any other type of economic reform, the transition process is followed by "social costs," so that in order to earn the support of the public, the government has to make the "security network" a priority issue. This will diminish the fear that the new, more competitive society may develop in a brutal climate of social insecurity, which would pose a risk to

Economic Transformation in Former Yugoslavia   279

the promoters of privatization of finding themselves in the position of a "general without an Army."[10]

Notes

1. *Ekonomska politika*, no. 2073, Belgrade, 23 December 1992, p.9.
2. *Ustav Republike Srbije* (Belgrade, 1990).
3. *Ekonomska politika*, no. 2073, 23 December 1992, p.9.
4. *Ekonomska politika*, no. 2078, 27 January 1992, p.9
5. *Ekonomska politika*, no. 2068, 18 November 1991, p.16
6. *Politika*, Belgrade, 31 March 1992, p. 5.
7. *Politika*, 6 May 1992, p.11.
8. *Ekonomska politika*, no. 2088, 6 April 1992, p.29.
9. *Ekonomska politika*, no. 2088, 6 April 1992, p.3.
10. For further information, see Srdjan Bogosavljević, "Siva Jugoslavija," in *Ekonomska Politika*, no. 2088 (6 April 1992); Vladimir Grličkov, "Uspesnost kao smetnja," in *Ekonomska politika*, no. 2068 (18 November 1991; Srdjan Petrovic, "Institucionalno vlasništvo—stara logika," in *Ekonomska politika*, no. 2088 (6 April 1992); Tomislav Popović, "Rezultati dosadašnje privatizacije u Srbiji" (unpublished paper, 1992); "Tranzicija privrede Srbije," in *Ekonomska politika*, no. 2086 (23 March 1992); Paul Starr, *The Limits of Privatization* (Washington, D.C.: Economic Policy Institute, 1987); P. Uri, "Privatizacija—olako obecana bržina," in *Ekonomska politika*, no. 2078 (27 January 1992); Slobodan Vidaković, "Ko sputava privatizaciju?," in *Ekonomska politika*, no. 2090 (20 April 1992); Miodrag Žeć, "Crnogorski koncept privatizacije," in *Ekonomska politika*, no. 2078 (27 January 1992); and Miodrag Žeć, "Srpski koncept privatizacije," in *Ekonomska politika*, no. 2073 (23 December 1991).

12

Foreign Economic Relations

Oskar Kovač

It is certainly very difficult to write a well balanced, consistent, and comprehensive chapter on any aspect of a so unfortunately fragmented country as Yugoslavia. This chapter will inevitably have to follow the different stages of development and fragmentation of the Yugoslav economy and of the foreign economic relations of the country.

Therefore, the chapter has three fairly different parts. The first one gives a standard presentation of Yugoslavia's foreign economic relations covering the period of real functioning of the federal state. The second part deals with recent features of Yugoslav foreign trade, up to the stage of acute fragmentation and the outbreak of war. The third part addresses the question: how are the Yugo-Slavs and other citizens of former Yugoslavia going to live within and outside Yugoslavia in the future as their mutual economic relations become external economic relations?

The Structure of the Economic System

An Indian diplomat once remarked that Yugoslavia was one country with two alphabets, three religions, four languages, five nations, and six states.[1] People usually added to that that Yugoslavia was a federation which bordered seven European countries and consisted of eight federal units. The country had to live through four different social and economic systems in the lifetime of one generation: (1) inefficient capitalism before the Second World War; (2) etatism immediately after the war; (3) self-management until 1965; and (4) a period of new polycentric etatism ending with national chauvinism.[2] Those different institutional systems have shown different economic performance. Foreign economic transactions naturally reflected those developments.

282

Etatism or command-economy (1945–1951) was, of course, nothing specific to Yugoslavia. It achieved a GNP growth rate of slightly above 2 percent per year, with negative growth in agriculture and commodities export volume.

Worker management was, according to Horvat, the golden age of Yugoslavia from 1952 to 1965. The rate of growth of real GNP was around 9 percent yearly with similar rates of export volume growth and slightly lower rates of growth of imports (volume). Labor-managed firms and their independence in decision making implied the development of a market economy; self-management was economic democracy. As long as it was possible to develop the institutional structure of a market economy and economic democracy, the Yugoslav economy was highly successful. The Yugoslav economy was one of the fastest growing economies in the world. The per capita real rates of growth of GNP (1950–1985) were higher only in Taiwan (6.64 percent), Japan (6.26 percent), and China (5.10 percent) than in Yugoslavia (4.46 percent).[3] There was also a significant and continuous improvement in the welfare of the population, since real wages increased almost three times by the beginning of the seventies.

After the 1965 attempt to introduce economic reform which failed and brought some years of very slow growth with increasing inflation, the attitude of economic policy became that of laissez faire, of liberalization, with non-existing preconditions for it. Liberalization of an economy without factor markets could not succeed. The rate of growth of GNP slowed down to some 5 percent, but the real growth of wages continued, setting thereby the stage for lower national savings and even slower rates of GDP growth.

The reaction of the political establishment was the worst possible. In some federal units (republics) which never intended to remain in Yugoslavia, nationalism and economic egocentrism became the main determinants of behavior. Since any nationalism induces nationalism in others, Yugoslavia entered the stage of polycentric etatism by 1971. At that time the federal constitution was amended and by 1974 completely changed to admit the new reality: Yugoslavia became a loose confederation of primitively nationalistic small republics. The otherwise incomplete labor-managed market economy was replaced by a politically dominated, newly invented system of "agreement" economy. Market signals were replaced by parameters set by agreement among governments, firms, and banks, reflecting ill-conceived national priorities. Of course, all performance indicators of the economy turned down. In the eighties there was no real per capita GNP growth, and real wages returned to the 1966 level. Strangely enough, the national bureaucracies succeeded in convincing their people that the other peoples of Yugoslavia are to blame for that. Yugoslavia or Yugo-Slavia is now experiencing the results of such national chauvinistic policies.

Foreign Economic Relations 283

Foreign economic relations of Yugoslavia reflected those general economic and institutional changes.

With the exception of the decentralization period (1953–1960) when liberation from the monopoly of foreign trade resulted in a rapid increase and imports, in the major part of the subsequent period there is a tendency toward slowdown in the growth of exports and in recent years of imports as well. Such a development of foreign trade resulted in an increased trade deficit and in a deficit of the balance of payments.

Table 12-1

Basic foreign trade indicators

	1947	1952	1965	1979	1984
Share in GNP					
exports (in %)	5.9	7.8	23.3	11.1	18.8
imports (in %)	6.0	11.7	27.5	22.8	22.0
Degree of coverage of					
Import by export (%)	99.0	66.0	84.7	48.5	85.0
Exports per capita (US$)	10.4	14.7	56.2	306.5	445.3
Imports per capita (US$)	10.6	22.2	66.2	632.4	520.9
The balance of payments (% of GNP)	-1.3	-0.0	1.6	-6.0	0.9
The balance of payments (million US$)	-37	-1	73	-3661	504

Source: Federal Institute of Statistic (FIS), *Yugoslavia 1945–1964*, Belgrade, 1965, and FIS, *Statistical Yearbook of Yugoslavia*, (SYY), 1984., p. 81.

It was true, especially in the 1960s, that the deficit in commodities trade was largely covered by the surplus from transport, tourism, and other services, and especially by unilateral transfers, where the key role was played by remittances from temporary workers abroad. However, time has shown that this factor favored the postponement of the required structural adaptations in production and export, and did not represent a stable source of improvement of the balance of payment. In the seventies, a deceleration in the growth rate also characterized foreign currency earnings through invisibles.

284   Oskar Kovač

The commodity pattern of exports and imports did not change rapidly. They represent the consequences of structural changes in the economy and, partly, in foreign trade policy. In Yugoslavia, the basic changes, in comparison with the situation in 1952, were achieved already in the early seventies. In lieu of food and basic raw materials, Yugoslavia's exports for a long time consisted of processed products, industrial products, machinery, and equipment. Imports show an increase in fuel, in various semi-finished products of industrial origin, as well as very high importance of equipment. The changes which occurred in the pattern of imports in the late seventies and in the early eighties—an increase in the share of primary products in export and a decrease in the share of equipment and finished consumer goods in import—cannot be considered lasting and normal, but represent, in a certain sense, the consequences of the adaptation of the balance of payment to a crisis situation.

The regional pattern of trade in Yugoslavia until 1954 was almost exclusively under the influence of exogenous factors.

The initial orientation of Yugoslavia's trade to Eastern Europe was drastically curtailed, after 1948, by the total rupture of relations between those countries and Yugoslavia. Only after 1954–56 did the regional structure of exports and imports start to reflect the influence of economic factors (see Annex Table 12-1). In principle, the regional distribution of exports and imports should be determined by the demand and supply realtions on the world market and by the structure of Yugoslav output. The problem is, however, that—among other factors—differences in forms of payment and other commercial mechanisms resulted in the accumulation of trade deficits, current account deficits in the balance of payments, and external debt, predominantly with countries with convertible currencies. (The major part of trade with Eastern European countries was done on the basis of bilateral clearing.)

The unsatisfactory development of exports, expressed by the long-term deceleration in growth, the regional imbalances, the culmination of the deficit of the balance of payments and of foreign debt in 1979 and 1983 respectively, can be considered the consequences of the system of foreign trade. The exchange rate policy, the system of export incentives and the system of protection of domestic production from imports favored the substitution of imports more than the development of export-oriented production.

The exchange rate policy, which was also subject to a number of important reforms, influenced very much the development of foreign trade and the entire system of resource allocation in Yugoslavia.

When in 1952 the decentralization, as the beginning of self-management, started with the liberalization of prices, i.e., with the acceptance of the laws of the market, a new exchange rate was introduced—300 old dinars

Foreign Economic Relations

for one U.S. dollar. Since the domestic price structure differed considerably from the structure of relative prices in foreign economies, these big price distortions made it impossible for the new exchange rate to perform its economic function properly. Therefore, interventions were introduced in the foreign trade and payments systems, creating a system of multiple exchange rates which was in force until 1961.

All subsequent reforms of the foreign trade system in Yugoslavia had, among their objectives, the elimination of multiple and unrealistic exchange rates. As early as the 1965 reform, it was expected that a single, realistic exchange rate would: (1) establish a link between the general levels of domestic and world prices; (2) improve the balance of payments; and (3) allow a unique and realistic pricing of exports and imports for the allocation of investment projects.

In the implementation of such an exchange policy rate, the dinar was significantly devalued in 1965 and in 1971. Since May 1973, there has existed in Yugoslavia an interbank foreign exchange market where the National Bank of Yugoslavia, through its interventions (buying and selling), forms the floating exchange rate of the dinar in relation to a basket of convertible currencies. The accounting exchange rate for clearing payments—with some oscillations and lags—followed the exchange rate of the dinar in relation to convertible currencies. In its exchange rate policy, the National Bank uses a certain system of indicators which takes into account the weighted average of the producer price index in the foreign trade partner countries which form the currencies basket, and the price trends of producers in the Yugoslav industry. This results in the nominal depreciation of the dinar which neutralizes the differences of inflation rates and maintains the price competitiveness of Yugoslav exports. Periodically, as for instance in 1983, a real depreciation is resorted to in order to improve in a more substantial way the competitive position of Yugoslav producers.

Recent Trends

The confederal period of Yugoslav, including the stages of polycentric etatism and national chauvinism, was highly inefficient in its economic and even more controversial in its social and political aspects. In the eighties, there was virtually no per capita economic growth. At the beginning of the nineties there is the deepest economic recession and crisis (with negative rates of growth of GNP and industrial output of more than 10–15 percent) in all Yugoslav economic history.

Strangely enough, but probably right because of the slow-down of investment and growth, after the worst balance of payments and foreign indebtedness crisis at the end of the seventies, there were significant improvements in Yugoslavia's foreign economic relations in the eighties.

Partly because of import restrictions, but also as a result of a more active exchange rate policy including some real depreciation of the national currency, the balance of payments turned into a surplus in 1983, which kept increasing until 1989. After two partial reschedulings of the foreign debt, Yugoslavia normalized its debt-service ratio and ceased to belong to the group of highly indebted countries.

During the eighties, Yugoslavia improved the competitiveness of her exports and achieved good access to the markets of EEC, EFTA, USA, and other OECD countries. This helped to redirect the regional pattern of Yugoslav foreign trade.

The share of OECD countries in Yugoslav exports increased from 35.6 percent in 1975 to 51.0 percent in 1988. The corresponding share of the EEC increased from 24.0 percent to 36.8 percent. Accordingly the share of COMECON countries fell from 46.1 percent to only 33.8 percent.

The Yugoslav economy was always highly import dependent. Imports of fuel and semi-finished products as inputs into the manufacturing industries took between 2/3 and 3/4 of total Yugoslav imports. According to one of the most recent econometric estimations of import functions of 26 branches of the Yugoslav manufacturing industry, although most of the import dependence is technologically determined, the firms behaved logically in their import decisions, taking into account the variations in the real rate of exchange of the national currency. The whole manufacturing industry falls into three distinctively different groups. The first group of industrial branches has an input dependence which is in equal proportion determined by variations in output and the real rate of exchange. Such branches are: ferrous metallurgy, final products of the furniture industry, intermediate and final products of the textiles industry.

In the second group of branches, imports depend much more on the variations of production than on changes in the real rate of exchange. Those branches are: basic chemicals, paper, footwear, and rubber products.

The third group of industrial branches reveals the opposite situation; imports depend much more on the variations of the rate of exchange than on the variation of their output. Such branches are: metal products, mechanical engineering, transport equipment, electrical equipment, and final products of the chemical industry.[4]

The improvement in the balance of payments was not only the result of measures restraining imports but also of significant real growth of exports. The relationship between exports and economic growth in Yugoslavia was not always the same. According to the study of Kovačic and Djukić,[5] exports at the level of the whole economy were indeed the engine of growth.

Foreign Economic Relations

It was the other way round in manufacturing industries. There, domestic demand used to be the main source of growth.

A team of researchers, including this author, produced some interesting results concerning the international competitiveness and effective protection of the Yugoslav economy. The constant-market-share analysis of Yugoslav exports to the EEC and EFTA countries covered the period 1965–1988. The results show a significant difference in the determinants of export performance of the Yugoslav economy up to and following 1986. This holds true both in regard to EC and EFTA. In the first period, the poor relative export performance of Yugoslavia (compared with the growth of EC trade) was mainly explained by slowness to adapt the pattern of supply of exports to the changes in the commodity pattern of EC import demand and by the worsening of competitiveness of Yugoslav exports. In 1987 and 1988, there was a high positive export differential in favor of Yugoslavia, which was mainly explained by enormously improved export competitiveness.[6]

Table 12-2

Export performance annual percentage change

EEC					
EEC trade	Yugoslav exports to EEC	Export growth differential	Regional effect	Commodity effect	Competitive effect
1	2	3 (2-1)	4	5	6 (3-4-5)
1965–1980	16.9	14.4	-2.5	2.0	-1.5	-3.0
1980–1986	0.4	-0.1	-0.5	0.4	1.4	-2.3
1987	22.3	52.3	30.0	1.1	1.6	27.3
1988	-7.5	16.6	24.1	-28.2	3.3	49.0

EFTA					
EEC trade	Yugoslav exports to EEC	Export growth differential	Regional effect	Commodity effect	Competitive effect
1	2	3 (2-1)	4	5	6 (3-4-5)
1965–1980	15.8	14.7	-1.1	1.3	1.0	-3.4
1980–1986	1.2	-0.9	-2.1	0.7	-0.6	-2.2
1987	22.3	64.6	42.3	-0.5	-0.3	43.2
1988	-25.8	10.6	36.4	-36.0	-0.6	72.9

Note: Export performance on the basis of constant market share analysis.
Source: Institute's calculation based on OECD Trade Statistics.

The fact that the residual competitive effect explains most of the export performance is even more clearly shown in Annex diagram 1A. Annex diagram 1B shows the relatively low influence of the market and product pattern effects. This leads to the question as to what the determinants of the variations in the competitive effect might be. From Diagram 1, it is clear that there was a strong relationship between relative unit labor costs and export performance. Diagram 2, on the other hand, shows that increases in the real effective exchange rate of the dinar always leads to worsening competitiveness of exports and vice versa.

Diagram 1. International competitiveness

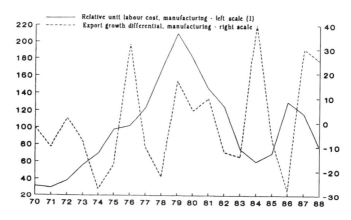

1. 1970-1988 = 100
Source: OECD National Accounts and IES estimates

Diagram 2. Exchange-rate developments and competitiveness

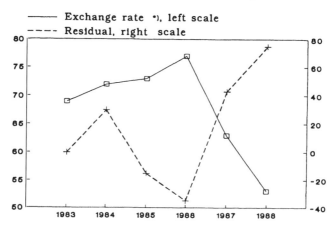

*) Effective exchange rate deflated by inflation differentials against major trading partners, December 1982 = 100.
Source: National Bank of Yugoslavia and IES estimates.

Foreign Economic Relations 289

Towards the end of the eighties, the Yugoslav economy started to respond to market signals and approached a stage of structural adjustment. The need to open up the economy in order to increase competition within the relatively small domestic market necessitated a study of the effective protection of the Yugoslav economy.[7]

The nominal customs tariffs listed in Yugoslavia's current Customs Tariff do not provide the information needed for this type of analysis, for there are other protectionist measures in effect in addition to the nominal customs duties. It must also be born in mind that there are many exemptions from payment of customs duties. In order to gauge the real level of nominal protection afforded to the final product of various sectors of the Yugoslav economy, the effect of all protectionist intruments must be taken into account.

The real effect of protection is the combined protection of the final product and of production inputs in the various sectors of the economy. The indicator of it is the effective rate of protection. It shows how much greater the value added is in individual sectors thanks to the present level and structure of protection than it would have been otherwise. The level and structure of effective protection are important to know when negotiating a reduction in protectionist barriers and when establishing the order in which nominal tariffs are to be abolished when free trade areas are created.

The analysis of effective rates of protection was made on the basis of information collected in a survey of a large number of enterprises in all the Yugoslav republics and most of the sectors of the Yugoslav economy.

The nominal rate of protection is the rate of departure of the domestic price of output from its world price, resulting from protectionist measures. Positive nominal rates of protection show that the domestic prices of output are above world prices, suggesting that domestic production is not competitive. Negative nominal rates of protection would therefore single out the sectors which are competitive.

Nominal rates of protection obtained for the Yugoslav economy in this study, fluctuating between -55 percent and +41 percent, are generally in line with the figures obtained in similar studies of other developing countries.

Industries enjoying the highest nominal rates of protection are (113) fabricated metal products, (13) food products, (118) manufacture of chemicals, (105) crude petroleum refineries, (125) yarns and fabrics, (124) manufacture of paper, (117) electrical appliances, and (128) leather footwear and fancy goods (more information in the enclosed diagrams and tables).

These are obviously products with a high degree of finalization, having positive nominal rates of protection (NRP); this fact indicates that the structure of nominal protection in Yugoslavia follows a "cascade" principle of protection.

290

Oskar Kovač

If levels of nominal protection in Yugoslavia were to be compared with the nominal rates of protection in the Community, these industries would come under the greatest pressure to lower levels of protection for their final products and would require the longest period of adjustment.

A medium level of nominal protection in Yugoslavia has been recorded for (11) non-ferrous metal refineries, (12) construction materials, (127) leather & fur products, (107) iron and steel industry, (129) rubber products, (134) printing & publishing, (201) agricultural products, (122) sawmills and wood boards, and (112) non-metallic mineral products.

These industries have very low either positive or negative nominal rates of protection, suggesting that their domestic prices are at the same level as world prices or lower, so that they are competitive in the world market.

This group of industries might in tariff negotiations face the greatest reductions of nominal custom tariffs within a provisional period of adjustment.

There is another group of activities where the nominal rates of protection are highly negative and which have already been exposed to the impact of liberalized imports. These are (126) finished textile products, (119) chemicals processing, (123) finished wood products, (109) non-ferrous metal industry, (115) transport equipment, (114) machinery manufacture, (133) tobacco manufacture, and (131) beverage industries.

In these activities, domestic prices are lower than world prices.

The effective rate of protection is the difference between value added calculated at domestic prices and the same value added calculated at "world" prices, which is the result of the application of protectionist measures. The amount of value added is calculated for a fixed quantity of goods as the difference between the values of output and input, in the first instance according to domestic prices and in the second according to world prices. In this way, the quantities are fixed, and only the prices change. Given the above postulates, protectionist measures affect both the prices of outputs and the prices of inputs. The result of their effect should be expressed in effective rates of protection, ERP.

The effective rates of protection are most often taken as indicators of the protection provided by a government to various industries, but they are also useful in designing tariff and other reforms. Furthermore, it is widely accepted that the ERP provide a preliminary guide for identifying those industries which are economically efficient and those which are not, because economic activities enjoying the highest ERP are most often the least efficient, and vice versa.

Generally speaking, positive rates of protection indicate that thanks to protectionist measures, manufacturers have higher levels of value added than they would otherwise have had in the conditions prevailing in the

Foreign Economic Relations

world market. The effective rates of protection show how far domestic manufacturers are from the point at which they could hope to compete successfully on the world market. Manufacturers with negative effective rates of protection, on the other hand, are operating in conditions which are less favorable than those in the rest of the world. They manage to produce the same product with less value added. The order of economic activities in terms of competitiveness is thus the reverse. It is also possible to look at effective rates of protection as a measure of the "attractiveness" of various industries: industry groups with higher rates of ERP attract resources, and vice versa.

The results of the calculation of effective rates of protection of the Yugoslav economy reached in this study range from -72 percent to +151 percent and are similar to those reached in studies on effective protection in other developing countries; they are in line with the theoretical postulate that dispersion of effective rates of protection should be greater than the dispersion of nominal rates of protection.

The highest effective rates of protection in the Yugoslav economy are enjoyed by (118) manufacture of chemicals, (130) food products, and (105) crude petroleum refineries.

Other industries with positive effective rates of protection were (113) fabricated metal products, (117) manufacture of electrical machinery and appliances, (125) yarns and fabrics, (122) sawmills and wood boards, (110) non-ferrous refineries, and (124) manufacture of paper. All these industry groups had positive nominal rates of protection. According to our interpetation, these are industry groups with higher levels of value added than in the rest of the world; they attract resources and are farther away from the point of being able to compete successfully in the world market.

Negative effective rates of protection in 1988 were noted for the following activities: (121) construction materials, (107) iron and steel industry, (134) printing & publishing, (127) leather & fur products, (112) non-metals, (128) leather footwear and fancy goods, (129) rubber products, (123) finished wood products, (201) agricultural products, (115) transport equipment, (126) finished textile products, (119) chemical processing, (114) machinery manufacture, (109) non-ferrous metal industry, (131) beverage industries, and (133) tobacco manufacture. These industry groups with negative effective rates of protection are potentially competitive in the world market.

There is no sign of a cascade pattern here as had been noted in the case of nominal rates of protection. It was not possible to establish any link between the degree of finish of products and effective rates of protection. Whereas the nominal rates of protection to some extent reflected a link between the degree of finish and level of NRP, there was no such connection between the ERP and degree of finish. This finding lends weight to argu-

292   *Oskar Kovač*

ments against protectionist policies and shows that not enough attention is being paid to the complex effects that protection may have on individual economic activities. Nominal rates of protection most often, and Yugoslavia is no exception, are the result on the one hand of development policy and on the other of administrative decisions adopted under pressure from interest groups demanding protection of specific industries. As in decision-making governments are most often guided by nominal rates of protection, which are easier to calculate, the final result of their impact on inputs and output is not clear until the effective rates of protection have been determined.

Industry groups with negative effective rates of protection in 1989 were (117) electrical machinery and appliances, (129) rubber products, (110) non-ferrous metal refineries, (112) non-metals, (107) iron and steel industry, (115) manufacture of transport equipment, (126) finished textile products, (105) crude petroleum refineries, (133) tobacco manufacture, (109) non-ferrous metal industry, (119) chemicals processing, (131) beverage industries, and (114) machinery manufacture.

The crude petroleum refineries (105) was found to be highly protected in 1988, but in 1989 this sector was barely in 20th place, with a negative rate of protection. Such a change can be explained by increases in the price of crude oil. The share of inputs in the value of production in 1988 was 61.9 percent, while domestic value added was therefore relatively higher than in the following year, so that effective rates of protection were higher. The increased prices of raw materials in the world market and the uncompetitive domestic market in finished products owing to administrative price control caused value added in 1989 to fall below value added calculated at world prices.

As regards (110), non-ferrous metal refineries, the NRP of output fell much more than that of inputs, bringing about such a drop in value added that the effective rates of protection became negative instead of positive. The NRP of output in the industry group of (117), electrical machinery and appliances, fell from 8 percent in 1988 to -1 percent in 1989, while the NRP of inputs rose; these trends in nominal protection led to a drop in the effective rates of protection.

The calculated effective rates of protection can be used as guidelines for conducting the policy of restructuring Yugoslav industry and for improving the global efficiency of resource allocation.

The policy of liberalizing imports and reducing effective protection, which postulates a balance of final and intermediate goods, should be tailored to fit economic activities with medium levels of effective protection. Those with high negative effective rates of protection are already competitive and will remain viable with the average level of protection in the EEC. The longest period of transition will be required by those industries presently enjoying the highest effective rates of protection.

The Future of Foreign Economic Relations

It is certainly a bitter irony that the foreign economic relations of Yugoslavia, after significant improvements during the years 1983–1989, took a bad turn from which there can be no full recovery. Even if the individual republics improve their economies and their foreign economic relations, it will not be the Yugoslavia we have known for almost fifty years. Some of the republics seceded from Yugoslavia. It will take years to negotiate fair solutions of many economic issues among them and the remaining new Yugoslavia. What is even more serious, problems of ethnic incompatibility in certain regions require changes of borders. Without that, there will be no lasting peace between those who leave and who remain in Yugoslavia.

Part of hitherto domestic trade among Yugoslav republics will become international trade. The new countries and the new federal Yugoslavia will still belong to what will in terms of geography and ethnicity remain Yugo-Slavia, the part of Europe where the South Slavs live.

The question is what kind of economic relations will be negotiated and developed among states in the area of South-Slavia.

At the beginning of fragmentation of the second Yugoslavia, it seemed that, after separation of states for ethnic and other political reasons, it will still make a lot of sense to negotiate a certain type of economic integration agreement among all of them. Assuming this position, all republics, except Slovenia, agreed, in the framework of the EEC-sponsored Yugoslav peace conference, to establish a customs union with other institutional arrangements leading possibly to an economic union.[1]

The customs union was considered the minimum requirement for building any successful economic cooperation agreement. The customs union would enable the parties to the agreement to maintain a common internal market for the movement of goods without either tariffs or quantitative restrictions. The customs union should have had a common external tariff, a common foreign trade policy, and appropriate arrangements for sharing customs receipts. The common external tariff should have been based on that applied for imports into Yugoslavia at 1 July 1991. The common external trade policy should have included the continued implementation of external regimes and external agreements as applied by Yugoslavia at 1 July 1991.

It was agreed upon that the republics may establish also, between all or some of them, a single internal market. It would consist of a customs union and appropriate arrangements for full freedom of movement of factors of production, including the right of establishment of firms, common policies in agriculture, transport, energy and regional development, including a compensation mechanism aimed at fostering the development of less developed regions.

This first-best, maximum solution to the Yugo-Slav economic cooperation issue included also a necessary degree of harmonization of macroeconomic, including fiscal and social, policies. Common economic and harmonized social policies should have been backed by the establishment of appropriate structural funds.

It had been expected that the republics would cooperate to limit the adverse effects of other obstacles impending the free movement of goods (and for those republics entering into an economic union, of services and of factors of production) such as technical standards, subsidies, and regulations affecting trade, by taking flanking measures, such as sharing information, concerning policy objectives and, if necessary, harmonizing rules and regulations which restrict competition.

It was also envisaged that the republics would maintain existing arrangements in the fields of transport and infrastructure, and take measures to maintain competition, especially for the protection of the common or single internal market.

Certain possible monetary arrangements were also discussed. It was expected that republics would cooperate in monetary matters with a view to maintaining or achieving monetary stability and the highest possible degree of convertibility as the best support for the market economy. It was understood that the appropriate monetary mechanisms for those republics entering into economic union should be built on the basis of a common currency, or of the experiences of the European Monetary System.

As a minimum, in the absence of a common currency and currency convertibility, republics could have established a common payments system, based upon a multilateral clearing mechanism and a reserve fund.

In the meantime, although the described arrangements still make a part of the main document of the Yugoslav Peace Conference, developments in the field have made the real acceptance of this first-best solution less and less likely. Some republics have declared that they are no longer interested in economic cooperation agreements with other subjects in the region of South-Slavia, while Serbia and Montenegro started to build their common federal state, the new Yugoslavia.

Some of the republics are expecting to complete their separation from Yugoslavia. At the same time the Federal Parliament is preparing to adopt a new constitution for the Federal State of Yugoslavia to become the common state of Serbia and Montenegro, as well as of others who care to join. Serbia and Montenegro have 44.2 percent of the population and 41.3 percent of the territory of Yugoslavia.

Rump Yugoslavia is a federal state, as a parliamentary democracy based upon the division of power between the legislative and executive branch and with independent courts of law. The federal parliament consists of

Foreign Economic Relations

two chambers: the Chamber of Republics and the Chamber of Citizens. The Chamber of Republics is composed of an equal number of representatives elected in the republics (Serbia and Montenegro). The Chamber of Citizens consists of deputies elected by the population on a proportional basis. The parliament decides by majority vote in each of the chambers. Prerogatives of the chambers are defined according to the principle of equality of republics and citizens.

The federal state guarantees human rights of citizens throughout the country. The federation defines by law the monetary, banking, foreign exchange, foreign trade and customs tariff system, the foundation of the fiscal system, the functioning and development of large technical and technological networks, the foundation of social and employment legislation as well as the protection of the environment. The federal state also represents Yugoslavia in international relations.

The federal state is responsible for the functioning of the single domestic market, and the economic and monetary union. Such an economic system is compatible and convergent with the economic system of most European countries. What kind of economic arrangements could exist between this remaining Yugoslavia and the other states of South-Slavia?

Taking into account that Bosnia-Herzegovina will be a composite, confederate state divided along ethnic (and religious) lines, it is only realistic to expect that part of Bosnia-Herzegovina will seek some ties and closer economic arrangements with the Federal Republic of Yugoslavia (Serbia and Montenegro). It is also important to estimate what kind of arrangements might be suitable between Macedonia, Slovenia, Croatia, and the Federal Republic of Yugoslavia.

After the latest developments, it is largely unclear how economic cooperation between Slovenia, Croatia, Macedonia, and the Federal Republic of Yugoslavia might be arranged, especially taking into account the shift in the balance of their mutual economic interests. It is clear that Slovenia and Croatia will propose only mutual agreements trying to secure their easy access to the largest part of the Yugoslav market. On the other hand, the less developed republics and the remaining Yugoslavia will not have interest for such a truncated solution. Within such an arrangement, the differences in the level of economic development of the participants would cause income redistribution from the less to the more developed regions. In the second Yugoslavia, there were compensations for such flows of income through the federal fund for financing the development of the less developed republics and province. Without such compensation mechanisms, the remaining Yugoslavia does not have the same interest in the relatively small markets of Slovenia, Croatia, and Macedonia. If it has to grant concessions to gain access to markets, those could be the markets of

296   *Oskar Kovač*

Hungary, Poland, and of the Czech and Slovak states. They are already planning a free-trade zone among themselves.

Rump Yugoslavia and the other South Slav countries will have to build links to their European surroundings. Compatibility with the European surroundings will be more important than they have been up to now, because the states of South Slavia are of a very sub-optimal size.

The war and truncation of Yugoslavia, not without a significant role of some EEC countries, greatly damaged rump Yugoslavia's relations with the EC. Now, it would be necessary for all parts of former Yugoslavia to reestablish the functioning of the 1980 cooperation agreement. At the same time, the remaining Yugoslavia should ask for the continuation of the negotiation of an association agreement with the EC. It should also continue talks to join OECD after more than 25 years of fruitful cooperation.

However, rump Yugoslavia should not hesitate to show its interest for different economic cooperation mechanisms which, sooner or later, will have to be created among the countries of Central and Eastern Europe. Although they would all like to join the EEC, that will by no means happen soon. In the meantime, it is only natural that they try mutually to exploit their own market potential and potential for economic growth.

Notes

1. Branko Horvat, *The Economic System and Economic Policy of Yugoslavia* (Belgrade: Institut ekonomskih nauka, 1970), p. 5.

2. Branko Horvat, *The Paradox of Yugoslav Economic Success* (distributed at the conference of the European Policy Unit of the European University Institute, Florence (24–25 January 1992), p. 30.

3. *Ibid*, p. 30.

4. Rasto Ovin, "Estimation of Import Functions: Yugoslav Industry Case," in *Economic Analysis and Workers' Management*, Vol. 25, No. 2 (1991), pp. 108–109.

5. Zlatko Kovačić and Djordje Djukić, "Export Expansion and Economic Growth in Yugoslav—Some Empirical Evidence," in *Economic Analysis and Workers' Management*, Vol. 25, No. 2 (1991), pp. 108–109.

6. Miša Jandrić, "Export Performance and Competitiveness of the Yugoslav Economy Relative to EEC and EFTA Markets," in Oskar Kovač (ed.), *Effective Protection and Competitiveness of the Yugoslav Economy* (Belgrade: Institute of Economic Sciences, 1991), pp. 182–201.

7. Kovač (ed.), *Effective Protection and Competitiveness*, pp. 42–62.

8. Conference on Yugoslavia, *Treaty Provisions for the Convention* (The Hague, 4 November 1991), pp. 6–7.

Annex diagram 1. Decomposition of the growth differential (1)

A. Growth of Competitiveness

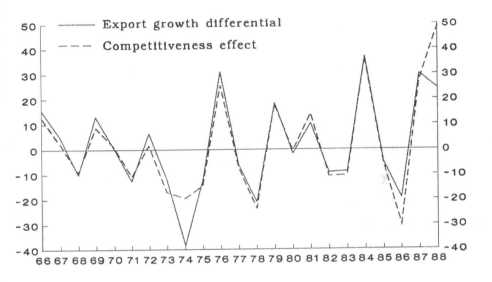

B. Market and Product effect

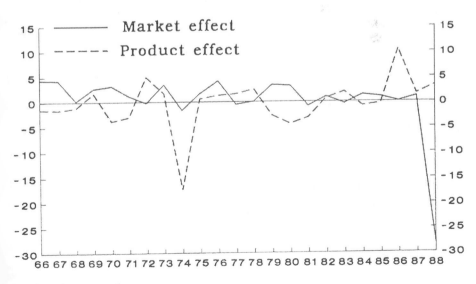

1. Annual percentage change.
Source: IES estimates.

Annex diagram 2.

Nominal rates of protection 1989
(industrial classification)

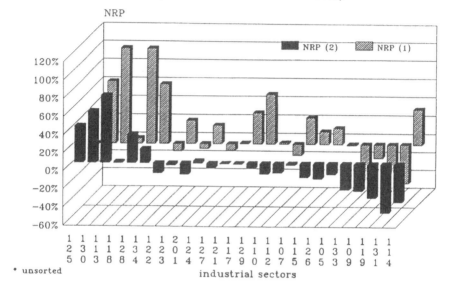

* unsorted

Annex diagram 3.

Effective rates of protection 1989
(industrial classification)

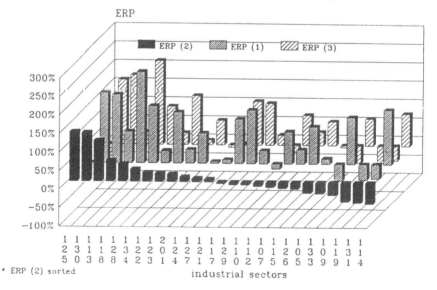

* ERP (2) sorted

Annex table 1. Geographical distribution of foreign trade

Per cent of total

	Exports						Imports					
	1988 $ million	1970	1975	1980	1985	1988	1988 $ million	1970	1975	1980	1985	1988
OECD countries	6413	56.1	35.6	37.1	35.0	51.0	7330	68.9	60.7	52.6	46.1	55.7
EEC countries of which:	4630	41.2	24.0	26.6	24.7	36.8	5099	48.5	42.6	35.2	30.9	38.8
France	491	3.8	2.1	2.7	2.5	3.9	555	3.8	4.6	4.5	3.1	4.2
Germany	1428	11.8	7.8	8.7	8.2	11.4	2256	19.7	18.7	16.6	13.0	17.2
Greece	170	1.9	1.0	1.8	1.4	1.5	95	1.5	1.0	0.5	0.9	0.4
Italy	1887	15.2	9.1	9.3	9.2	15.0	1371	13.2	11.3	7.4	8.5	10.4
United Kingdom	322	5.8	1.6	1.0	1.7	2.6	297	6.2	3.1	2.6	1.9	2.3
EFTA countries of which:	773	8.3	3.8	4.7	4.4	6.2	1148	11.5	8.7	8.1	6.2	8.7
Austria	432	3.0	1.8	2.2	2.5	3.5	600	5.3	4.1	3.6	3.2	4.6
Switzerland	108	3.1	1.0	1.2	1.1	0.9	276	4.5	2.6	2.2	1.7	2.1
Other OECD countries of which:	1010	6.6	7.8	5.8	5.9	8.0	1083	8.9	9.4	9.3	9.0	8.2
United States	708	5.3	6.5	4.4	4.4	5.6	728	5.6	5.4	6.7	6.4	5.5
Comecon countries	4249	32.2	46.1	44.4	49.6	33.8	3574	20.5	24.1	29.3	31.7	27.2
Developing countries	1917	11.7	18.3	18.5	15.4	15.2	2248	10.6	15.2	18.1	22.2	17.1
Total (US$ million)	12579	1679	4072	9718	10642	12579	13152	2847	7699	16476	12164	13152

Sources: OECD, Foreign Trade by Commodities, 1988 and data submitted by national authorities.

Annex table 2. Rates of protection and domestic resource costs 1989

Code	Industry	NRP (industrial classification)			ERP			Short run DRC			Long run DRC Percent		
		(A)	(B)	(C)	(A)	(B)	(C)	(A)	(B)	(C)	(A)	(B)	(C)
125	Textl. yarns & fabrics	-20.6	40.9	-20.6	-33.5	133.4	-29.8	42.1	147.6	44.4	179.1	628.3	189.1
130	Food products	68.0	57.1	68.0	189.2	131.2	174.1	82.8	66.2	78.5	152.3	121.8	144.4
113	Fabricated metal prod.	104.4	74.6	104.4	184.1	110.3	187.0	56.4	41.8	57.0	132.8	98.3	134.1
118	Manufact. of chemicals	5.9	1.4	5.9	83.7	57.1	32.6	21.8	18.7	15.8	118.3	101.2	85.4
128	Leather footwear,goods	104.1	32.2	104.1	246.3	47.6	226.8	69.5	29.6	65.6	257.2	109.6	242.7
134	Printing & publishing	65.4	16.0	65.4	154.0	33.6	102.5	45.4	23.9	36.2	112.6	59.2	89.8
122	Sawmills & wood boards	-8.4	-11.2	-8.4	33.8	24.8	31.6	17.3	16.2	17.0	63.9	59.6	62.9
123	Finished wood products	25.5	-2.5	25.5	138.0	23.7	131.7	50.8	26.4	49.4	101.5	52.7	98.8
201	Agricultural products	-5.4	-12.6	-5.4	37.3	20.4	11.7	17.2	15.1	14.0	296.1	259.9	241.0
124	Manufacture of paper	20.3	2.5	20.3	81.4	13.4	65.6	18.4	11.5	16.8	56.0	35.0	51.2
127	Leather & fur prod.	-7.3	-5.2	-7.3	5.2	10.2	-6.2	26.3	27.6	23.5	67.7	70.9	60.4
121	Construction materials	0.7	-0.6	0.7	11.2	8.0	2.5	16.9	16.4	15.6	70.0	68.0	64.5
117	Electrical appliances	34.0	-1.0	34.0	119.9	-4.7	117.7	44.5	19.3	44.1	177.0	76.7	175.2
129	Rubber products	54.5	-5.7	54.5	145.1	-7.0	112.6	46.7	17.7	40.5	159.1	60.4	138.1
110	Non-ferrous metal ref.	1.4	-11.9	1.4	36.1	-7.0	26.9	17.4	11.9	16.2	63.6	43.5	59.3
112	Non metallic min. prod.	-12.5	-10.3	-12.5	-14.2	-10.5	-17.9	21.9	22.8	20.9	63.1	65.8	60.3
107	Iron & steel industry	28.8	-1.8	28.8	86.7	-13.5	81.1	18.4	8.5	17.8	163.7	75.9	158.8
115	Transport equipment	13.9	-15.1	13.9	38.7	-16.6	35.8	26.9	16.2	26.3	64.2	38.6	62.8
126	Finished textile prod.	17.6	-16.9	17.6	100.7	-17.6	64.3	61.1	25.1	50.0	174.3	71.6	142.7
105	Crude petr. refineries	-1.4	-11.8	-1.4	14.9	-28.8	-4.9	25.3	15.7	21.0	176.8	109.5	146.3
133	Tobacco manufactures	-39.0	-28.9	-39.0	-44.5	-30.0	-46.5	5.6	7.0	5.4	11.5	14.6	11.1
109	Non-ferrous metal ind.	-15.2	-30.2	-15.2	126.5	-34.5	72.6	67.0	19.4	51.0	111.0	32.1	84.6
119	Chemicals processing	-30.1	-37.9	-30.1	-41.8	-52.0	-45.7	8.9	7.3	8.3	55.5	45.7	51.8
131	Manufact. of beverages	-43.0	-53.9	-43.0	-39.3	-54.6	-39.3	5.6	4.2	5.6	34.1	25.5	34.1
114	Machinery manufacture	38.5	-42.2	38.5	147.6	-57.1	86.8	67.0	11.6	50.6	186.8	32.4	140.9

13

Environmental Issues and Policies, with Special Attention to Montenegro

Svetlana Adamović and Vukašin Pavlović

The encounter, or more precisely, the conflict between ecology and politics, is a universal phenomena in the twentieth century. It became especially obvious during the 1970s and 1980s in the most developed countries of the West, when ecology entered the field of social controversies and became an inevitable item on political agendas. At the same time when numerous new social activists, ecological movements, and green parties appeared on the political scene, placing environmental issues in the center of social attention.

The battle between ecology and politics was fierce in the so-called socialist countries, with ecological issues arousing, as a rule, hostility toward the government. The spectrum of social conflicts, of course, varied from country to country. Bulgaria is an illustrative example: The process of democratic changes began in the ecological field, with the formation and activity of the "Ecoglasnost" movement.

The appearance of ecological movements in Yugoslavia was slow, as it was in other East European countries. The first important initiatives in Yugoslavia did not emerge until the 1980s in the disputes that surrounded the proposal to build a hydroelectrical power plant in the canyon of the River Tara, one of the most beautiful in Europe. Protests from experts and the public managed to stop the plan of the governments of three republics (Serbia, Bosnia-Herzegovina, and Montenegro). Another major environmental conflict erupted in the mid-1980s, when the federal government developed a proposal to build four new nuclear power plants. The country witnessed a complete reversal from the early 1980s, when the first nuclear power plant in Krško (on the border between Slovenia and Croatia) was constructed, virtually without a protest. The public was so hostile that the government had to scuttle its plans.

302   *Svetlana Adamović and Vukašin Pavlović*

If we compare the new environmental forces in Yugoslavia with those in Western countries, we see an important difference. The social importance of ecology and its entrance into the political sphere had three distinct phases in the West:

a) the appearance of wide-ranging initiatives of citizens and grassroots local ecological movements;
b) the formation of ecological movements on a national level;
c) finally, the entrance of ecology into the political arena through the formation of green parties.

It would be extremely difficult to differentiate between these three phases in Yugoslavia. We could rather say that they were intertwined, or simultaneous. The second, and perhaps the most important, phase of creating a wide and strong environmental movement was missing. A partial exception was Slovenia, where a relatively wide and influential ecological movement arose. In the first multi-party elections in Slovenia the Green Party was more successful than any other Green party in Europe (about 9 percent of the members of the Parliament). Indeed, several ministers, the vice president and a member of the Presidency (the collective leadership), had also joined the Greens. This level of success was not replicated elsewhere in the country, where results were far worse than expected.

Generally speaking, in ex-Yugoslavia as well as in other socialist countries, ecological issues were far more prominent before and during the course of radical political changes than in the period following them. If we extrapolate this phenomenon to the introduction of the multi-party system, we can see that environmental issues were present in the programs of other political parties in addition to the Greens. All parties determined that support for ecological programs was essential for electoral success, but the political uses and abuses of the environmental plank became apparent after the first multi-party elections. The parties that scored well, as well as those that lost in the elections, quickly and conveniently forgot their pre-election promises and any political treatment of environmental concerns became marginal again.

Toward Ecological Development in Yugoslavia

Socialist Yugoslavia lagged behind many countries in forming an ecological strategy despite the fact that its representatives have taken part in many international conferences on the environment, starting with the First UN Conference on the Environment held in 1972 in Stockholm and including the Rio de Janeiro conference of 1992.

Environmental Issues and Policies, with Special Attention to Montenegro 303

Yugoslavia's slowness has been the result of complex factors—from the socioeconomic structure and policy of the country to the lack of funds as well as inadequate knowledge and understanding of global and regional ecological issues.

Of course, this lag does not mean that socialist Yugoslavia ignored environmental problems entirely. On the contrary, roughly 400 laws were passed mostly on the republic level,[1] while national and international environmental issues were regulated by federal laws.

Despite this rather extensive legislation activity, genuine protection and development in the environmental sphere were unsatisfactory, often as a result of legislative shortcomings. Specifically, the laws dealing with protection and development of the environment were restrictive by their nature. They could have been more effective if they had taken a more positive approach: for example, offering temporary release from taxation or some other economic incentives to those who must take steps to protect the environment. Also, the provisions of these laws very often were contradictory and environmental problems were treated in a fragmentary fashion. Thus, environmental protection efforts were primarily concentrated on short-term results, while long-term goals were neglected.

Some analysts found that the fragmentation of environmental policy was aggravated by the adoption of a new Federal Constitution in 1974, which allowed the republics more power and autonomy in relation to the center. Rivalry among the republics grew, leading to virtual paralysis in solving even the most vital inter-republic environmental problems.

In this respect, an illustrative example is the case of the Sava River, Yugoslavia's major tributary of the Danube.[2] Its headwaters in Slovenia and subsequent path through Croatia create a natural border between Croatia and Bosnia before the river flows through Serbia to join the Danube near Belgrade. The water of the Sava River has been visibly deteriorating primarily from wastewater and other pollutants discharged from industrial plants situated upstream on its banks. The heavily polluted river represents a health hazard for residential settlements along the river. Hoping to tackle the problems together, endangered communities signed "The Sava River Compact" in 1980, but the republican governments did not commit to the document. Unfortunately, the federal government could not help the implementation of this compact because it had neither the influence nor the power to pressure the governments of the republics to act. So the Sava River Compact became more of a symbol of good intentions than a working document. The same fate befell many other valuable projects that logically came under federal jurisdiction; yet the federal government failed to intervene.

In the meantime, many environmental problems in Yugoslavia became worse during the 1980s and in some areas reached near-crisis. A research paper released by the Federal Environment Division details the magnitude of these problems: From the status of a "net importer" of sulphur dioxide (SO_2), Yugoslavia became "net exporter" of it. The emission of SO_2 has become the number one pollutant in Yugoslavia. Acid rain comprises 10 to 40 percent of all precipitation with the result that one third of all forests (46 percent of all coniferous and 28 percent of all deciduous trees) have been damaged by pollution.[3] Generally air pollution is one of the most critical environmental problems facing Yugoslavia.

Waters in former Yugoslavia are particularly threatened. The 170 water control stations on the Adriatic show a disturbing state of affairs. Also of concern is the supply of potable water, especially considering that 74 percent of the total (and 91 percent of the urban) population is dependent on urban water supplies. The water of the Sava River falls mostly in the third or fourth quality category. The same is true of the Danube and Morava rivers and their Yugoslav tributaries.

Around 2 million tons of waste materials were collected annually in socialist Yugoslavia, but only a small amount of that was recycled. The problem of the disposal of toxic waste materials was particularly acute.[4] This environmental degradation has negatively affected the quality of life and generated serious concerns among the citizenry, increasing their level of environmental consciousness.

The Chernobyl accident of 26 April 1986 had a tremendous global impact providing inspiration to mass environmental movements in many parts of the world, including in Europe, and particularly in Yugoslavia. The anti-nuclear movement started first in Slovenia and then spread to other parts of the country. High pressure from these anti-nuclear groups forced federal legislators in November 1987 to place a moratorium until the year 2000 on the planned construction of four nuclear plants in Yugoslavia.

This success gave renewed strength to environmental movements and emphasized a new dimension in the treatment of ecological issues. All developmental acts and laws adopted in Yugoslavia between 1987 and 1990 (a strategy of technological development, the development of energy and tourist sector, the economic plan for 1990, etc.) recognized environmental protection and promotion as one of the prerequisites for long-term development and as an inseparable part of social and economic prosperity.[5]

This was a time when Yugoslav society faced serious difficulties and reforms aimed at restructuring the economy and introducing elements of the free market. At the same time, the Communist Party monopoly disintegrated and multi-party systems were introduced in the republics.

It should be emphasized that until recently there was no special institution in Yugoslavia devoted to environmental problems. Environmental concerns were handled by different governmental bodies at local, republic, and federal levels together with other issues.[6] It was only at the end of 1989 that a new Federal Secretariat for Development was formed, and inside it a special Environmental Division.

The Environmental Division was responsible for developing a framework system of environmental protection and promotion[7] and it formulated environmental policy on the federal level that emphasized common Yugoslav goals.[8] This division prepared a paper entitled "The Policy of Environmental Protection and Promotion in Yugoslavia with Measures for Implementation," (March 1991)[9] based on the previously elaborated "Strategy of Environmental Protection" commissioned by the Secretariat from the Rudjer Bošković Institute in Zagreb. This report provided a selective and very systematic overview of general environmental issues for the country as a whole and offered a program with 52 specific measures.[10] The paper stressed specifically the need for scientific evaluation of both the problems and the measures for their solution in the area of ecology. It underlined that Yugoslavia did not have a research institution specialized in environmental problems. Instead, some research institutes were doing this job as an adjunct to their main tasks. The most important of these institutes have been the: "Boris Kidrić" Institute (Beograd), the "Rudjer Bošković" Institute (Zagreb), the "Jozef Stefan" Institute (Ljubljana), the "Hasan Brkić" Institute (Zenica), as well as some institutes within different universities of the country. The Environmental Division also made a priority list of environmental problems that demanded further research and that affected more than one republic:[11]

- the Sava River basin;
- the protection of the Danube and Tisa against pollution;
- the Adriatic Sea, coastal areas and islands;
- the protection of lakes cut by a state border (the lakes of Scutari, Ohrid, Prespa and Dojran);
- the protection of the atmosphere in the largest industrial centers;
- the protection of rivers divided by a state border;
- the erosion of soil;
- the management of dangerous wastes.

Of the 52 specific measures for environmental protection and improvement outlined, five dealt with the importance of international cooperation. The Environmental Division insisted on the fulfillment of all of Yugoslavia's international obligations arising out of 49 ratified conventions, numerous protocols, declarations, and agreements, on global, regional, subregional, and bilateral levels.

The Environmental Division also stressed the following international obligations:[12]

- the protection of international rivers that flow into Yugoslavia from other countries (Danube, Tisa, Drava, Mura, etc.);
- the protection of the Adriatic and Mediterranean Seas, and shared lakes (Ohrid, Scutari, Dojran, Prespa);
- issues related to energy and the environment, the protection of the atmosphere, human settlements, the work environment, the natural and architectural heritage, territorial planning and management, management of natural resources, issues of technology and environment, turnover of chemical compounds, environmental monitoring, integration with international systems, the complex of environment-and-development issues, and the inclusion of economic aspects in environmental protection, as part of the efforts to achieve sustainable development and the New International Economic Order.

Needless to say, the division paid special attention to the country's obligations in regard to the protection of the Earth's ozone layer. This worldwide problem involves wide cooperation with many international programs both in scientific and practical fields, including the United Nations financial agencies, in order to receive from them the financial aid for their research programs and their implementation.

The "Policy of Environmental Protection and Promotion in Yugoslavia with Measures for their Implementation" was elaborated primarily on the basis of common Yugoslav interests and objectives. Yet, full respect was given to traditional, economic, and rational differences and value judgments in the various republics and provinces in setting priorities. This opened up the possibility that the Federal Environmental Program would not come in serious collision with plans of the republics and local governments. Indeed, the federal Environmental Division suggested the formation of special independent administrative bodies at the republic level that would formulate their own comprehensive environmental program complementary to some degree with the federal mandate.

However, it seems that this body was organized only in the Republic of Serbia. The parliament and the government of Serbia adopted two important documents related to the policy of environmental protection in Serbia: "The Resolution on Environmental Protection of Serbia," adopted by the Assembly in 1986,[13] and the "Law on Environmental Protection" adopted by the National Assembly in Serbia in 1992[14] when the special independent body on the environment was formed. Despite this legislative action, the strategy developed and proclaimed in Serbia by the political authorities is poorly formulated, lacking both political and scientific foundation.

Environmental Issues and Policies, with Special Attention to Montenegro 307

The scientific groundwork for a strategy of ecological development of Serbia should include:

- an ecological study of Yugoslav historical heritage, i.e., a reaffirmation of the ecological ideas from the cultural heritage of the nation;
- a review of past and ongoing ecological studies;
- making as complete as possible a survey and diagnosis of the present state of affairs and the level of ecological danger in the territory of Serbia, with appropriate projections based on past and current trends;
- the development of a general strategy (or, possibly, strategies) and specialized ones (regional and landscape-oriented, or strategies suited to individual activities);
- taking into account comparative analyses of the ecological strategies of Serbia's neighbors: the former Yugoslav republics, the Balkan region, the countries of Eastern and Central Europe, countries in the Danube basin, the Euro-Mediterranean countries, and the industrially developed European countries.

The fact that apart from the Republic of Serbia, the other republics have not yet formed special independent bodies does not mean that their work on environmental problems is inferior. In fact, in the late 1980s environmental protection initiatives in all parts of SFR Yugoslavia were seriously intensified. Unfortunately, with the ongoing war, most of these programs have fallen dormant, but they could become the least painful basis for future cooperation among different parts of ex-Yugoslavia when the fighting ceases.

The Ecological Critique of the Titoist Political System

It is quite reasonable to suppose that a democratic political system provides more fertile ground for nurturing an ecologically acceptable and healthy attitude toward nature. One can justifiably expect that the exploitative and destructive attitude of humankind toward the environment goes hand in hand with authoritarian relations in social organization and in political life. Conquering nature and establishing new forms of power and dominance in society are—as it frequently happens—only two sides of the same process. It gives us the right to state that, generally speaking, ecology and democracy are natural allies.

Socialism and ecology were, unfortunately, everywhere in very serious conflict. The Yugoslav variant of socialism (self-management) saw in

Marx a forerunner of Stakhanov and nature as the enemy that should be conquered. Nothing remained of Marx's reform-minded concept of the reconciliation of humankind with nature.

If we analyze Tito's political model, (especially its last variant, based on the 1974 Constitution), we can observe that many characteristics of the system cannot sustain ecological criticism. We will single out only those with the strongest negative effects for the preservation of the environment.

1) Autarky, disunity, fragmentation and the polarization of interests, were not only inimical to an ecological attitude—which is integral and unifying by its very nature—but led to the disintegration of Yugoslav society.

2) The system had a wasteful attitude toward all important national resources, from economic to intellectual. A high level of spending in various areas multiplied negative ecological consequences. For example, with up to 17 different licenses granted for manufacturing the same new products, it is understandable that there were fewer funds and opportunities for solving environmental problems.

3) The practical inefficiency of the political system and the low level of ability of the political and the state institutions to regulate environmental protection proved very destructive. To illustrate, one should mention that the state and other bodies in charge very often were able neither to realize their functions of control nor to enforce sanctions on violators of adopted standards and norms of behavior.

4) Technological dependence, economic inequality, and non-competitiveness, as well as indebtedness in relation to other countries, lessened the practical possibilities and capabilities of the political system to protect itself and stop the importation of negative environmental effects from all over the world (as in the case of dirty technologies), as well as from neighboring countries. (Well-known examples include: the construction of the nuclear power plant modelled after the Chernobyl in Hungary, which was carried out without Yugoslav protest; a Bulgarian nuclear power plant in Kozloduj; and several ecological incidents and cases of pollution in Romania.)

5) A low level of ecological culture, an insufficiently developed democratic public, and a relatively low level of ecological awareness led to an extremely low level of practical engagement by the most important political forces in environmental concerns. One could say that environmental problems were very rarely present in the decision making process of a one-party political system.

6) A low level of motivation on the part of the political, economic, and military elite in solving environmental problems brought about a constant political marginalization of ecology, along with the marginalization of all other quality-of-life dimensions.

Environmental Issues and Policies, with Special Attention to Montenegro   309

7) The resistance of Tito's political system toward alternative interests lessened the possibility of citizen mobilization in environmental projects and in practical actions at the local or regional level.

8) The generally poor capacity of the old political system to forecast led to strikingly inaccurate forecasts of the environmental consequences of various political decisions and economic, technological, and developmental investments.

Generally speaking, the interest structure of social and political power in the Titoist model of politics was not unsympathetic to environmental issues. The political system did not offer appropriate answers to the frequent, justified, and clear-minded requests of the citizens and left no chance for a democratic transformation of the country.

Why Did the Process of Democratic Transformation Fail?

Despite many Yugoslav and foreign critiques of Tito's regime in Yugoslavia, many eminent analysts predicted that Yugoslavia would be the frontrunner in the process of democratic transformation. Not only was it not a leader it was not even a follower when the wave of democratic transformation began in other socialist countries at the end of 1980s. The following set of factors was responsible for decreasing Yugoslavia's chances for real democratic transformation:

First, the social pressure for quicker and more radical changes in ex-Yugoslavia was not as strong as in other East European countries after the fall of the Berlin Wall. Tito's Yugoslavia had always outstripped its socialist neighbors in all changes, which softened the social and political pressure from below. So ex-Yugoslavia became a paradoxical case. The country that had been ahead of other socialist countries in many dimensions of social openness and development (thanks to the introduction of the self-management system in the 1950s) quite unexpectedly found itself in last place for all those changes at the end of 1980s.

Second, post-Tito Yugoslavia failed to make radical democratic changes. Both the internal and international conditions for such changes were far more favorable for Yugoslavia in the late 1960s and early 1970s, or even in the early 1980s, after Tito's death. As each opportunity for pluralization was missed, the chances for successful radical changes in Yugoslavia decreased.

Third, due to Tito's skillful balancing between the two blocs, and between the superpowers, Yugoslavia long had a privileged status in the international community. Yet, its reputation and political influence were much greater than its actual economic and political capacities, and Tito's successors proved unable to retain that status after his death. Blinded by its perception of privileged and enduring status, the country and its post-Tito leadership were slow to understand the implications of the changing international order.

Fourth, the long-term and virtually unquestioned rule of one party and one person, together with other negative effects, destroyed the capacity of the society to create competent political elites and sub-elites. The political incompetence of some of the elites in the ten years after Tito's death was legendary and brought the country to the point of crisis. At the same time, the absence of viable sub-elites made the situation even more difficult and left Yugoslavia's people at the mercy of manipulative and aggressive politicians. The presence of a developed managerial sub-elite would have softened the forms and ways in which conflicts were handled.

Everywhere in the world, as was the case in Yugoslavia, socialism destroyed or considerably retarded the development of civil society. The realization of civil society is not possible without freedom of the press, academic autonomy, independent trade unions, developed and guaranteed freedoms and rights for its citizens, and a market economy. Yugoslavia lagged behind very seriously in many of these areas, with a double negative effect: On one hand, the low level of political culture brought about the formation of many new political parties, which instead of leading into democratic political pluralism, revived Balkan political tribalism; on the other hand, the formation of a multi-party political system in which the majority of the parties—those with the most political influence—assumed a nationalist orientation, created a condition of "pre-politics" in which all economic and political problems were portrayed as ethnic problems, thus contributing to the current ethnic war.

Amid the massive destruction produced by civil war, the environment could be one of the biggest victims. Of course, the loss of an estimated 400,000 human lives (by the end of January 1993), as well as a large number of wounded and disabled persons and more than three million refugees, represents the most tragic aspect of the war. But another grim consequence of the fighting is the enormous damage to flora and fauna, including destruction of the National Park of Plitvice Lakes and oil leaks into the Sava River during the war in Croatia. In addition the economic infrastructure (buildings, roads and railroads, bridges, electrical lines, and oil and gas pipelines) of many regions has been damaged to an even greater extent than during the Second World War.

There have been many threats of environmental terrorism too. For example, during the conflict in Slovenia, an officer threatened to blow up an enormous storehouse of petrol and during the war in Bosnia-Herzegovina, there were threats to blow up the dam of the reservoir in Višegrad, which would have caused catastrophic flooding and threats to destroy the chemical complex SODA-SO in Tuzla.

It should be emphasized that the war effectively shelved serious policy addressing many environmental issues that had been publicly recognized in all parts of Yugoslavia as vital problems. Only the Republic of Montenegro took a different, unique course in that respect—in September 1991 it proclaimed itself an "ecological state."

The Ecological State of Montenegro

The Republic of Montenegro has adopted a modern strategy of environmental development. Since this republic was relatively less developed than other parts of Yugoslavia, its strategy of ecological development had to take into account at least two specific features:

First, as a less developed area industrially, Montenegro saved many of its natural beauties and avoided many of the negative environmental consequences of industrialization that plagued relatively more advanced areas.

Second, in order to maintain an active environmental policy—both for current improvements and to avoid future damage, considerable funding is necessary. As a less developed area, the Republic of Montenegro cannot allocate funds in the standard way; i.e., by introducing special taxation or by pressing existing producers and polluters to introduce technological changes that would diminish the negative consequences of economic development on the natural environment.

Taking into account both sets of factors, the government and the Parliament of Montenegro have opted for a genuine environmental policy. The Montenegrin parliament adopted a declaration on the environment at a special session held in the Durmitor National Park in the town of Zabljak on 20 September 1991, declaring Montenegro an "environment-conscious state"[15] or "ecological state."[16] To issue a Declaration on Montenegro as an "ecological state" in the midst of war may not seem very impressive to a western observer. But bearing in mind that until recently the idea of environmental costs and dangers has been rather strange both to the government planners and to the Montenegrin population at large gives this "Statement of Intent" a higher significance than in many other countries where "environmental consciousness" has been developed for decades. By proclaiming the republic an ecological state, the Parliament of Montenegro imposed the ecological factor on any future policymakers as a criterion for regulating all kinds of economic activities both in production and in the service sector.

In the declaration, several basic ideas were outlined:

(1) Due to the dangers threatening the natural environment, the protection of the quality and identity of the environment has become an important social obligation;

(2) The natural environment is the source of health and the "inspiration of freedom and culture." Therefore, it is important to protect the environment for the wellbeing of current and future generations;

(3) Regardless of the national, religious, political, and various other differences, the dignity and the sanctity of human life are directly connected with the preservation of the sanctity and purity of nature;

(4) The misuse of nature is usually connected with the misuse of human beings. Therefore, fighting for the dignity of people has to be coupled with the fight for the dignity and preservation of nature.[17] In this respect the Republic of Montenegro represents the first case of a whole state proclaiming itself an "ecological state."

It would be hard to accept that this proclamation of an "ecological state" is the result only of rapidly growing environmental consciousness among the people of Montenegro and their representatives. This proclamation was also an effort and political challenge of the new young Montenegrin leaders seeking to find a way for their country's survival at the time when SFR Yugoslavia was in the tragic process of disintegration.

The notion of the "ecological state" is not fully defined, due to the fact that this policy step is new in both theory and practice. But considering the fact that the Republic of Montenegro has about 0.6 million inhabitants, the proclamation of an "ecological state" means, among other things, that the economic and social development of this small country is part of the world process. It has become almost impossible to consider today any economic and social action without taking into account the fact that the atmosphere is being shared with the rest of the world, or, more narrowly, for example, that the Adriatic Sea is shared with five other states. In that respect, the decision to proclaim Montenegro an ecological state means that its leadership has become more conscious of environmental concerns and thus better integrated into the global network.

The fact that Montenegro belongs to the less developed regions of Europe and is in a relatively early stage of development offers unique opportunities in the theory and practice of economic development. Are these opportunities to be put into practice or will this political platform on ecology, approved in 1991 by the Parliament of Montenegro, be only a memento of strong wording without practical consequences? This will be more clear when the war in the former Yugoslav republics ends.

The Republic of Montenegro now offers a laboratory for studying the problem of a balanced use of the most important components of growth: the size and quality of population, natural resources, the level of technology and production, and last but not least, environmental goals and concerns. Needless to say, it is not easy to balance properly all these elements of economic growth and the standard of living, either from the point of view of consumerism or of general quality of life. By proclaiming itself an ecological state, the Republic of Montenegro has pledged itself to pursue a policy of strict protection of the natural environment so that economic development should not be allowed to pollute the environment. At the same time it is hard to expect any economic improvements without the promotion of production in various fields of goods and services. Therefore, at every level of government (local, regional, and national), it will be important in years to come to provide for a close cooperation between the population at large and the economic, technical, and ecological experts in coordinating a policy of economic and social development in accordance with the goals of the ecological state.

Reasons for the "Ecological State"

The most important reasons for proclaiming Montenegro an "ecological state" could be summarized along the following lines:

1) The high pressure of many environmental problems identified and analyzed in Montenegro especially between 1987 and 1989 when environmental research was being conducted in the framework of a broader program in Yugoslavia. Some of Montenegro's environmental problems were very serious and some already had come to the critical point of demanding urgent resolution if the further development of Montenegro was to be expected. One of the most acute, from the government's point of view, is the disposal of waste materials.

One contradictory problem for Montenegro is its abundance of national parks. About 8 percent of Montenegro's land surface is covered by national parks, compared to socialist Yugoslavia's 2.2 percent.[18] This relatively high percentage has two conflicting effects on the Republic. On the one hand, national parks create pressure on scarce governmental funds given the high cost of protection. But, on the other hand, the abundance of national parks is a great resource, opening up possibilities for the intensification and diversification of tourism.

2) The economic crisis, characterized by a high rate of unemployment, has been deepening in Montenegro during the last several years. In 1990, there were around 48,684 people unemployed or around 20 percent more than in 1986.[19] In 1991, the crisis became critical when the relatively small Yugoslav national market was convulsed by political secessions—disrupting all economic ties among the former federal republics. This development has had an especially negative effect on the Montenegrin economy since a

population base of 0.6 million inhabitants with modest incomes represents an inadequate market for any serious increase of production and productivity on the basis of an economy of scale.

3) The political reforms that were initiated in the late 1980s brought to Montenegro a multi-party system and a multi-party parliament as a result of general elections held in 1990. This gave strength to the new government and the new parliament for a more nuanced reconsideration of the existing unbalanced structure of the economy and of the policies which led to this imbalance. The parliament concluded that the implementation of a policy of "fast economic growth" was especially harmful because it often neglected the value of natural and human resources and thus permitted their degradation and often destruction. A very instructive example of this one-sided economic policy was expressed in the old government's decisions to build large-scale power stations on the Morača River (Montenegro) and the Drina River (Bosnia and partly Serbia). That decision became law on 29 May 1984. There is no doubt that the construction and exploitation of the hydroelectric potential of these rivers and their tributaries would play a very important role in the further fast economic growth of Montenegro, Bosnia, and Serbia.

But these projects included the dam construction across the Tara River, which would flood 52 kilometers of the Tara River Canyon, listed by UNESCO as one of the most beautiful places in the world and internationally protected since 1977. However, this fact stopped neither the dam's constructors nor the governments. But the aforementioned law (passed in May 1984) contributed to very intense public pressure on government as well as to protests led by environmentalists and members of the Serbian Academy of Science. The law was reconsidered and changed before the end of 1984. The Tara Canyon was saved and environmentalists gained momentum for their activities in environmental protection, especially in Montenegro.[20]

4) The more objective analyses of Montenegro's current stage of development and of its economic, social, and political structure gave the first multi-party government an important basis for discussing short- and long-term projections for future development. Also, specific geomorphological and environmental conditions in Montenegro at the beginning of 1990 were taken into consideration. The government's vision of future development was summarized succinctly in 1991 with the equation: Montenegro = an ecological state.

Basic Features of the Ecological State

In order to justify its ambition to call itself an ecological state, the Republic of Montenegro has to provide some of the basic characteristics of an

Environmental Issues and Policies, with Special Attention to Montenegro   315

ecologically well-managed state. Only, in Montenegro's case, those features must be visible throughout the system. That means that it would not be possible to consider one region ecologically at the expense of another. It also would not be possible to concentrate production based on "dirty technology" in one part of the state while the rest of the state could draw "ecological compliments." Therefore, in opting for an "ecological state," the Republic of Montenegro has to overhaul its total economy, including its existing manufacturing capability. This could be achieved with relatively large investments and an infusion of fresh capital in a relatively short period of time. This alternative, however, does not seem to be viable for the time being. Another alternative would be to extend the timeframe for achieving the government's goals. However, this approach could dilute the momentum and desire for change thereby subtly diminishing the process even before it has begun. In the case of Montenegro, this alternative has the added burden of contending with a population that has many features of a Slavic-Mediterranean style in attitude and action: a high level of enthusiasm in the beginning of the process, but often a lack of consistency and perseverance as time goes by.

Clearly, before Montenegro's potential can be realized, the war in the former SFRY must be put to an end, and the economic sanctions against rump Yugoslavia (including Montenegro) must be lifted.

Important features of the ecological state must include not only well-preserved natural landscapes and natural resources, but also the use of appropriate technology in the production of goods and services, the availability of "natural" food and drink, the use of biodegradable packaging and wrapping materials, etc. In other words, the ecological state must use its potential in accordance with the principles of environmental protection, while not diminishing economic activity, production, and employment.

One challenge that Montenegro faces is the fetish of economic growth—and of maintaining impressive growth rates specifically—an important psychological factor here, as in many other less-developed countries. Besides, for several decades Montenegro, as the rest of former Yugoslavia, has been open to foreigners wishing to visit while allowing local citizens to travel abroad, creating conditions for the "demonstration effect." So it is to be expected in Montenegro that there will be permanent social pressure toward higher economic performance, even at the expense of ecological priorities.

To assess the resources that could provide a healthy economic basis for the development of the "ecological state" of Montenegro, we must consider several important sectors:

- energy: Montenegro should give priority to the development of hydro-electric power plants as well as to other under-researched sources of energy (wind, solar, geothermal, etc.).

- minerals: Mainly non-ferrous metals like bauxite, as well as granite, decorative stones, coal, lignite, and offshore oil deposits.
- woods: Forty-four percent of Montenegro's territory is covered with forests, including-low quality woods and maquia. One of the largest wood potentials in Europe, its abundance is a key factor in Montenegro's success as an "ecological state" by improving landscape and air quality and by providing employment in logging, lumbering, and in the production of a variety of finished wooden products from furniture to tourist souvenirs.
- agriculture: Montenegro is almost a symbol of a mountainous area, but since it is not overpopulated, there are relatively favorable conditions for the development of agriculture. However, in some regions, there is a real danger of soil depletion and erosion caused by overuse. The Zeta valley, for example, is a prime candidate, with its fertile soil and Mediterranean climate providing strong commercial and marketing advantages to its farmers. Montenegro's farmers were able to deliver agricultural produce to the market several weeks earlier than any other producer of former Yugoslavia, skimming top profits from the high prices commanded by early fruit and vegetables. Agricultural production in Montenegro includes cereals, fruit, vegetables, and herbs for pharmaceuticals. In the coastal area, high-quality grapes, olives, and citrus are grown, and Montenegro has an international reputation for the quality of its wines, brandy, and beer. Dairy farming has been underdeveloped in Montenegro, despite the availability of large tracts of pasture land as well as the conditions to produce organic food using cow manure instead of chemical fertilizers. Conditions are ideal for harvesting a variety of fish, whether from the sea or from fresh water.
- tourism: Tourism seems to be the most important sector for future development. The natural beauties of the country combine mountains, valleys, and coastal terrain; low population density; and minimal general industrial pollution. All are important assets for the development of tourism and which has been providing conditions for increased employment income, without high pressure on manufacturing, which tends to be less concerned about negative environmental impacts than the tourist industry. Montenegro has opportunities both to develop standard-type commercial tourism, and to offer health and convalescent services. On the littoral of Montenegro there are several deposits of radioactive mud and sand (Igalo, Ulcinj), which provides the basis for a successful year-round sale of services—from accommodations to highly special-

ized medical and convalescent treatment—to domestic and foreign guests alike. Winter tourism, skiing for example, is also developing. Although overshadowed by coastal tourism, it has the potential to grow in years to come.

- Other tourist activities could be provided in Montenegro, e.g., nautical tourism, hunting tourism, congressional tourism, sporting tourism, and eventually village tourism. Village tourism is a relatively new trend, particularly in Serbia, but the latter could lead to numerous activities in villages where farmers are offering their homes to individuals and their families from cities to spend from one week to one month as paying guests. It is a type of "Retour à la Nature" that brings additional income to farmers and cuts vacation expenses for many city dwellers compared with conventional hotel costs.

- transportation and communication: This sector could contribute to economic development without negative environmental effects. Montenegro provides an opening to the Adriatic sea both for itself and for Serbia. The Belgrade-Bar railway and the port of Bar will allow Montenegro after the end of the war, to capitalize on transit transportation of cargo not only from Serbia, but also from parts of Romania, Hungary, Bulgaria, Macedonia, Ukraine, and Russia.

With its manufacturing enterprises, Montenegro faces the challenge of effecting structural change, particularly by introducing less-polluting technologies and producing ecologically acceptable products. Certain existing plants for aluminum production, metal processing, machine tooling, the production of electrical equipment, and shipbuilding, although polluters, cannot be overhauled all at once. It would be impossible for financial and capital budgetary reasons, as well as on the grounds that these enterprises are sources of income and employment for the population and of taxes for the government.

In these early stages of action, there is a growing social consensus that a register of polluters has to be made. Polluters must not only be identified, but also described, classified, and marked, depending upon the nature and intensity of the pollution (e.g., from automobiles, quarries, thermoelectric power stations, asphalt producers, mining, tourism, ferrous and non-ferrous metallurgy, or of paper mills, food processing, textiles, artificial fertilizers, herbicides, pesticides, farms, slaughterhouses, and garbage depositories).[21] It is the law that all new investments or modifications of existing capacities from now on must be undertaken in accordance with the principles of the development of the ecological state. In fact, Montenegro

318   Svetlana Adamović and Vukašin Pavlović

is facing a need for a double transition: its economy must continue its transition toward a market economy and at the same time oversee a set of changes in accordance with its ambition to make this small state the first "ecological state" in the world. In order to mobilize necessary funding it must marshal several categories of sources:

a) domestic private sources engaged in private business activities;
b) foreign capital, which is expected to respect the demands and laws of the "ecological state." This fact may deter some potential foreign private investors, but most serious corporations and long-term oriented business projects could hardly be discouraged by the concern of Montenegro to provide a healthy environment;
c) public funding both of national and foreign origin, including regional and global international institutions.

But, as in many other areas, human input and human awareness of the problem will serve as the most important resources in providing both financial and nonfinancial resources for achieving that goal.

Development and Environment

With the proclamation of Montenegro as an ecological state, its authorities provided a framework for the country's main orientation in development:

Tourism

Tourism was chosen to become the catalyst for economic development. However, some very influential economists strongly opposed this general reorientation of the economy, arguing that the production of goods must always be the backbone of any sound economy. Tourism cannot be respectable in this sense because, according to their views, tourism is strictly a service industry. But, in spite of this strong opposition, the first multi-party authorities of Montenegro (the government and the parliament) gave full support to the concept that tourism in the future has to become the pivot of the Montenegrin economy.

Sustainable Developement

Montenegro's new leaders have accepted some very progressive concepts of economic development. Instead of the traditional developmental formula insisting on a high rate of economic growth, which in developing countries, including Montenegro, led in many cases to the degradation of

Environmental Issues and Policies, with Special Attention to Montenegro 319

natural and human resources, the new government accepted the concept of "sustainable development," as defined in the Report of the Federal Secretariat for Development.[22] This concept is based on development that leads to an improvement in the standard of living, but at the same time considers the protection of natural and human resources.

In fact, the concept of sustainable development was introduced into common use by the World Commission on the Environment and Development in 1987. The term means that sound economic development must "meet the needs of the present generation without compromising the needs of future generations."[23] This became a powerful theme for raising public awareness by focusing on the need for better environmental managment care for resources.

It is clear that the very acceptance of sustainable development cannot immediately stop the negative consequences of earlier economic policies that neglected the protection of natural resources and therefore often led to their degradation. However, it would be realistic to expect that the future economic policy of Montenegro will be oriented toward the protection and improvement of natural resources in the republic. Some steps in this direction were undertaken during 1991 and 1992.

Environmental Impact Assessment

The current government also has recently accepted an idea enthusiastically promoted by the World Bank that the costs of environmental protection should be considered equally with the costs of other factors of production: labor and capital. The Montenegrin authorities accepted this concept, which is also found in "The Long-term Policy of Environmental Protection and Promotion in Yugoslavia" program.[24] This program underlined the need for the introduction of environmental impact assessment for all new investments. It is expected that the cost-benefit evaluation of environmental effects as an important economic criterion for new investment decisions should be introduced in Montenegro.

Family Planning

The family planning concept—highly recommended by World Bank experts as a factor in sustainable development—already represents a part of Montenegrin policy. This concept holds that human reproduction has to be in balance with the production of goods and services, if sustainable development is the policy aim. The government has applied this concept in recently enacted laws, including a progressive rise of benefits for families having up to three children. For families with more than three children, the benefits decrease, also progressively. The application of this concept was made on the basis of the current birth rate of the nation and on prospects for future economic growth.

320   *Svetlana Adamović and Vukašin Pavlović*

International Orientation

An intensive international orientation represents an indispensable component of Montenegrin policy for sustainable growth. It stems from Montenegro's recognition of its international obligations as a successor state of the SFRY as well as of numerous regional and bilateral agreements such as the South Adriatic Development plan, The Italian-Yugoslav Agreement on Cooperation in the South Adriatic Region, and the OECD Rural Development Program.

Montenegro's international engagement also is related to the fact that more and more environmental problems are coming to be treated as global world problems (e.g., the greenhouse effect, and the protection of the ozone layer), the solution of which has to become the obligation of all nations. In this framework, the new Montenegrin government is paying needed attention to its obligation on the basis of Montreal Protocol.[25]

Pushing the government toward an intensification of its international orientation are many other factors: the need for foreign investment, financial aid, improvement of technology, and common research programs. But the most important factor is the selection of tourism as the top priority in the development of the economy. Naturally, foreign tourists are the alpha and omega of such a developmental orientation, not only as a potential source of income in general but, even more important, of foreign exchange earnings. However, this pattern of development presents many difficulties. First of all, there is severe competition to capture the international tourist market, supply is much higher than demand, especially in the early 1990's, which marked a general trend of decreasing incomes in the developed countries from which most tourists come. In the short run, Montenegro's ability to attract tourists will most certainly be hurt by the war. In the long run, Montenegro has to become a more market-oriented economy able to offer better goods and services to foreign tourists. On top of that, Montenegro also has to offer to the foreign tourists something new, attractive, widely accepted, and very different from what other tourist destinations offer. Today, the enticements of a clean environment and healthy food are very attractive on the international tourist market. The proclamation of Montenegro as an ecological state is a great challenge as well as a guarantee that the government is commited to protecting the diverse beauties of Montenegro: the Southern littoral of the Adriatic coast, the mountainous region of Durmitor with its national park, and the Tara River Canyon.

This ecological dimension of Montenegrin government policy implies that the government has not only embraced direct action in support and improvement of environmental protection, but also movement toward healthy, organic food production. The availability of health food has to become an important part of the republic's unique attraction to foreign tourists.

Environmental Issues and Policies, with Special Attention to Montenegro 321

In a broader sense, the term "Montenegro—the ecological state" represents a long-term commitment to environmental protection. This policy is an essential component of the economic, social, and political development of the republic. The implementation of this policy is expected to be done through a series of programs, measures, and activities on the local and national levels of government. In many cases, international cooperation and help will be crucial.

The physical geography of Montenegro is heterogeneous, with several ecologically sensitive regions: the littoral (the southern part of the Adriatic coast); some plain regions (around Skadar Lake and some larger river basin—Zeta, for example); mountainous regions (especially the Durmitor National Park and the Tara Canyon) and in the north the Pljevlja Valley region. Such a variety suggests that programs and strategies must become highly diversified when it comes to putting into practice the promise of an "ecological state."

Environmental Projects in Montenegro

Montenegro's environmental programs and projects are mostly oriented toward the coastal region, which has generated the greatest part of Montenegro's national income during the last 30 years from the intensive development of tourism. The most important places of this region are Budva, Tivat, Kotor, and Cetinje with an urban population of about 60,000 that swells to 400,000 during the summer period with incoming tourists.[26] The greatest increase in population during the summer can be found in Budva (around 900 percent) and Tivat (400 percent). With such tremendous periodic imbalances of population, many environmental problems arise, including inadequate clean drinking water and communal waste disposal. The pressure for their urgent solution is very high and during the early 1990s, about 15 projects of very high priority were identified and sent to international financial institutions.[27]

Among these projects whose aim is to protect the Adriatic Sea and especially the southern costal region, the most important are:

1) The integral protection and development of the Boka Kotor Bay. The position of this bay in the Adriatic is such that it has a very narrow passage to the open sea, with a very specific abiotic and biotic element, very different from living conditions in the open sea. Studies undertaken so far indicate that environmental conditions and the development of the bay are progressively worsening. If protective measures are not implemented soon, the basis for the future development and even life of many maritime species could be endangered.

A considerable part of the pollution of the Boka Kotor Bay comes from the settlements situated along its shoreline. Even more serious pollutants come from several industrial plants, two shipyards, several hospitals and sanatoriums, children's resorts and rest homes, as well as a number of tourist settlements, located in the municipalities of Kotor, Herceg-Novi, and Tivat. Although each of the three communities has some environmental programs, an integrated effort is essential if the bay is to be saved. The construction and regulation of a new sewage system has been assigned priority to correct the most serious contaminators and landslides.

International environmental experts and institutions recently concluded that any further pollution in even one has disastrous consequences regionwide. This realization offers hope that the World Bank and other international institutions will give the financial and practical help essential to the integral protection and development of Boka Kotor Bay.

2) The collection and separation of solid waste in the territory of the Budva, Tivat, Kotor, and Cetinje communes. Solid waste collection and its permanent disposal represents the most difficult environmental problem facing the government.

3) The construction and erection of a water treatment plant in Budva. The existing water supply system exploits karst spring water resources of limited capacity during the summer period. With the development of tourism in Budva during the 1980–1990 period, the population of this city increased ninefold during the summer months. Although some improvement of the drinking water supply has been made through the Master Project Plan for Water Supply (1985), the inadequate water supply may limit the further development of tourism in Budva. With the completion of Budva's water treatment plant, the city will receive additional water from Cetinje's supply. According to the project director, the water surplus from Cetinje will be stored until the summer period and delivered on demand.

4) Among 15 Montenegrin environmental programs and projects submitted during 1990 and 1991 to international organizations for financial aid, two are based on Yugoslavia's obligation as one of the signatories of the Montreal Protocol. One is the Project for Ozone Layer Protection by Reducing and Replacing CFC.[28] The Henkel Riviera Chemistry and Cosmetics Plant, jointly owned by Henkel, Vienna, (51 percent) and Riviera Kotor (49 percent) is elaborated very similarly to the first project.[29] The main goal of both programs is to contribute to the protection of the ozone layer, which has been alarmingly endangered by harmful gases. Both projects were submitted to WB, UNDP, and UNEP in 1991.

The first project was undertaken by one of the biggest refrigeration equipment manufacturers in Yugoslavia, "OBOD," situated in the city of Cetinje. The plant was founded in 1953 and currently employs around 3,800 workers. The detailed plan calls for the reduction and replacement of the refrigerant CFC-12 in the production and servicing of their products (refrigerators, freezers, etc.).[30] The program also encompasses the reduction

Environmental Issues and Policies, with Special Attention to Montenegro 323

and replacement of CFC-11 polyurethane foam. The program will be carried out in stages, with the expectation that by the year 2000, CFC-12 and CFC-11 will be eliminated or replaced by non-ozone-depleting substances.

5) The Program of Environmental Protection in the Valley of Pljevlja is another attempt to solve a very urgent problem. This program differs from most others in a Montenegro by the very nature of the Valley and by the irrational and irresponsible exploitation of its natural resources in the course of economic development since the World War II.

Pljevlja Valley, about 9 km in length, is situated in the northern part of Montenegro in highly mountainous region at about 700 meters above sea level. The valley is encircled by the famous Tara River Canyon, by the Lim River Valley, and by several mountain ranges. In this relatively small and enclosed valley is situated the town of Pljevlja, with about 18,000 inhabitants (in 1990), a coal mine, a cement plant, and a power plant.

In the span of the last 50 years the economic development of the region was based primarily on the extensive exploitation of natural resources. This activity did not provide the capital for investments in new industries, i.e., for the diversification of the economic structure of the town or for the modernization of the already old and obsolete capacities of the existing plants. This led to serious environmental degradation and devastation in the region, diminishing the possibilities for its further economic development. It should be emphasized that today all the elements of the environment in the Pljevlja Valley—air, water, and soil—are degraded to a level considerably below the standards prescribed by laws. Air pollution is especially serious in Pljevlja. Today respiratory tract diseases in all age groups in Pljevlja are on the top of the list of diseases in the region. In order to halt these negative tendencies in the Pljevlja Valley it is crucial to prevent further pollution.

An analysis of water quality in the Pljevlja Valley basin during 1990 showed that the concentration of heavy metal is considerable, but still below the maximum level allowed by the law. But, lately there has been a tendency for the concentration of heavy metal to increase quickly. The quality of water declines seriously as the water level lowers at the change of seasons.[31]

It has to be emphasized that the level of environmental pollution in Pljevlja Valley is damaging the flora and fauna of the region. Beyond that, it represents a danger for the surrounding woods and even for the the forests in Durmitor National Park. Experts have already noticed the appearance of diseases caused by the fungus *Fommes Anasus* which is attacking some of Durmitor National Park's trees. This attack is connected with the long-term exposure of the trees to high concentrations of SO2 coming from the Pljevlja's power plant.

Because the endangered National Park of Durmitor is on the UNESCO's list of World Heritages, there is hope that the solution of the acute environmental problems in the Pljevlja Valley will be given serious priority, despite the existing economic sanctions against the Federal Republic of Yugoslavia.

6) Montenegro's Environmental Programs and Projects, submitted in 1992 to international organizations for financial aid and other help, reflect the idea that environmental protection is and must be understood as a component of the economic, social, and political development of this state. This new orientation is clearly underlined in the title of this program: "Program for the Integrated Development of the Durmitor Region with a Basic Orientation on the Protection of the Natural Environment, its Healthy Surroundings and Employment on the Mountainous and on the Hilly Area (Durmitor National Park, Tourist Development and Organic Food Production)."

The Durmitor region is situated in the northwestern part of Montenegro and is dominated by Mt. Durmitor with its highest peak at 2,523 meters above sea level. The region is well-known for its natural beauties: Durmitor National Park, the Tara River Canyon (both are recognized by UNESCO), 18 mountainous lakes with clear water, dramatic landscape, and an abundance of flora and fauna.

The program proposes to establish the Durmitor Development Center for the promotion and development of the region through tourist development; organic food production; the establishment of small and medium sized firms and service industries, the consolidation of individual farms, an increase in the standard of living by maintaining current levels of employment in the region. This should create a "sound basis for the optimal development of the Durmitor area as zone in line with the intention of inaugurating Montenegro as an ecological state."[32]

Even in conditions of economic prosperity, Montenegro's proclamation of itself as an "ecological state" would demand the earmarking of considerable funds for environmental purposes instead of current consumption. Therefore, it is unrealistic to expect significant changes in the near future given the ethnic warfare raging nearby. When the deterioration of their already modest standard of living is so striking, it is doubtful the voters and the population at large will be willing to sacrifice a part of their already low current income in order to deal with long-range environmental problems. Also, it is difficult to expect support for a policy of protection of the environment while people are mired in poverty, while the cost of helping tens of thousands refugees is enormous, and while there is a high level of general uncertainty about the future. It is in the interest of Montenegro as well as all the other states created after the disintegration of the SFRY to come to some compromise and to accept solutions that will bring a state of peace to the region, a necessary precondition for any improvements, environmental and otherwise.

Possible Strategies for Environmental Development

All global strategies for FRY ecological development would have to include a revision of past and current strategies of economic and technological development, urban development and planning, development of the energy sector and, first of all, an end to the war. And just as ecology reflects interdependence and interlinkage, thus each ecological strategy implies a variety of interwined dimensions of social progress and their interdependence and interaction. The 1992 UN Conference held in Rio de Janeiro also recognized the essential connection between issues of ecology and development.[33]

In contemporary literature in this area, as well as in the practice of ecologically advanced societies, the possible strategies of ecological development that have emerged differ widely from one another. We shall mention only some of them:

The "zero growth" initiative was launched and most strongly championed in the mid-seventies by the Club of Rome, but, because of its advocacy of maintaining the status quo in the relations between North and South, the developed and the underdeveloped, it was seen to be unfair, unrealistic, and unacceptable by many, especially the less-developed countries.

The strategy of coercion has proven ineffective, even in regimes with centrally planned economies, with the result that former socialist countries were among the most polluted. Even the strategy of changing political elites, turbulently practiced in recent years in such countries as Bulgaria, where "Ecoglasnost" was an important political lever in democratization and the introduction of political pluralism, has shown weaknesses. The oppositionist zeal and the democratic potential of ecological movements in these countries lost their edge very soon after the arrival into power of new political elites, while environmentalism was pushed back to the margins of social interest.

The strategy of rehabilitating sources of pollution has fueled the propulsive growth of so-called eco-industry (filters and ecological equipment), but it has not provided for the successful removal of sources of environmental degradation. The principle that the "polluter pays penalties" can only partially compensate for pollution or endangered or devastated ecological resources. Indeed, in many cases, ecological damage cannot be repaid or compensated. Similar to the above is the strategy of economic motivation, which calculates that market laws and the promotion of private interest will stimulate economic agents to behave more reasonably, from the ecological point of view. The problem with this strategy is that environmental categories and values cannot easily be translated into economic categories, especially not through the market alone, although there have been attempts to determine the so-called ecological profit, ecological rent, ecological loss, and calculations of ecological risk.

There are also some important untapped potentials for savings in Yugoslavia, for instance, in the sphere of energy consumption, which can yield important ecological results.

The strategy of conserving and restoring nature relies on self-regulatory protective mechanisms of ecosystems, but overlooks the fact that, today, even the wildest oasis of nature cannot protect itself against easily transportable air pollution, radiation, the contamination of groundwater, and other hazards.

Strategies of the substitution of non-renewable resources by renewable ones envisage the development and use of alternative sources of energy, and a high level of scientific and technological development.

The strategy of tightening normative and legal sanctions has some effect, at least in the short run, but even that has not yielded long-term results, not even in societies with more advanced ecological legislation and regulation and, in general, with a true rule of law. Important normative strategies include, above all, strategies of regulating and prescribing technical and other standards and norms for the production of various goods to protect both consumers and nature.

The group of "trivial strategies" includes the following: the strategy of fire-fighting, i.e., reacting to ecological accidents; the strategy of postponing confrontation with negative effects (a typical example of this is the appearance of problems that are difficult to resolve, such as the disposal of nuclear waste, which is more or less being left to future generations to deal with); the strategy nicknamed NIMBY (Not-in-my-backyard), as well as the strategy of "Russian roulette," which gambles by opening ecologically dangerous industrial plants in the hope that accidents will not happen. A typical example is "Prva iskra" of Barić. At the opening ceremony of the plant it was stated that this factory would be as hazardous to the environment as a fruit pro cessing factory. Later on, it was discovered that the factory operated without a licence and without other technical documents required by law.

From the standpoint of the humanities, the educational dimension is particularly important. Under this heading we would place, first of all, the empirico-rational approach, to which scientific research is naturally inclined, believing that it is sufficient to establish facts and present arguments in order to bring about actual changes and improve the ecological situation. Experience tells us that this is not the case.

The strategy of promoting social invention and creativity is an ecological strategy of great capacity. It means, inter alia, an ecological rechannelling of scientific research, discovering new, cleaner technologies and technical devices.

Environmental Issues and Policies, with Special Attention to Montenegro   327

A separate, very important group involves ecological strategies that dedicate the greatest attention to ecological education, raising the level of ecological awareness and the readiness of citizens to participate in efforts to deal with ecological problems, to bring together expertise and the public at large (where the mass media play a crucial part), to develop ecological activism through initiatives of citizens, and ecological movements.

Bearing in mind Yugoslavia's recent performance, as a general recommendation, it will be vital to avoid trivial strategies and to stress the strategies of social changes, environmental education, and social invention and creativity in the field of environmental protection and development.

Conclusion

The democratic transformation of Yugoslavia's society during the last years of the eighties encountered serious difficulties in the form of an absence of the necessary prerequisites for multi-party political democracy. This could be explained by the low level of political culture and the destroyed or undermined elements of civic society. It refers also to the absence of larger and autonomous activities in different social fields such as the economy, science, a free press, independent trade unions, grassroots environmentalism, and other dimensions of civil society.

Instead of democratic transformation during the late 1980s and early 1990s, socialist Yugoslavia became an area torn with conflicts that resulted in the secession of some former republics and the country's final disintegration. Unfortunately, some of the international community's well-intended measures actually multiplied these conflicts and accelerated the war. Difficulties arose also from the international endorsement of an economic blockade of Montenegro and Serbia, with the heaviest impact on those civilians with an already very low standard of living and on the part of the environment, which represents non-replaceable resources and beauties of nature.

Notes

1. *National Report to United Nations Conference on Environment & Development 1992* (Belgrade: Federal Secretariat for Development, 1992), p. 9.

2. *Statistički Godišnjak Jugoslavije 1991* (Belgrade: Savezni Zavod za Statistiku, 1991), p. 81.

3. *The Policy of Protection and Enhancement of the Environment in Yugoslavia with the Program of Measures for its Realization* (Belgrade: Federal Secretariat for Development, 1991), p. 4.

4. *Ibid*, pp. 4–5.

5. *Ibid* p. 89.

6. *National Report* [note 1], p. 90.

328   *Svetlana Adamović and Vukašin Pavlović*

7. *Ibid*, pp. 90–100.
8. *Ibid*, p. 95.
9. *Ibid*, p. 95.
10. *Policy of Protection* [note 3], p. 36.
11. *National Report* [note 1], p. 97.
12. *Ibid*, p. 112.
13. The Assembly of the SR Serbia, *Resolution on Environmental Protection* (Belgrade: P.N.A., 1986).
14. The National Assembly of Serbia, *Law on Environmental Protection* (Belgrade, 1991).
15. *National Report* [note 1], p. 92.
16. *Pobjeda* (Podgorica), 21 September 1991, p. 1.
17. *Politika* (Belgrade), 21 September 1991, p. 1.
18. *National Report* [note 1], pp. 4–5.
19. *Statistički Godišnjak* [note 2], p. 471.
20. Barbara Jancar, "Environmental Protection: "The Tragedy of the Republics," in Pedro Ramet (ed.), *Yugoslavia in the 1980s* (Boulder, Colo.: Westview Press, 1985), p. 238, 239, quoting *Politika*, 26 August and 24 September 1984.
21. *Ibid*, p. 21.
22. *Policy of Protection* [note 3], p. 10.
23. The World Bank, *World Development Report 1992* (Washington, D.C., 1992), p. 8.
24. *Long-Term Policy of Environmental Protection and Promotion in Yugoslavia* (Belgrade: Federal Secretariat for Development, November 1990), p. 2.
25. This Protocol, signed in 1987, committed all signatories (by early 1991 there were 67) to reduce by half their consumption of five CFC (chlorofluorocarbon) compounds by 1998 and by the end of the century to eliminate their use.
26. *Environmental Program: Project for Communal Waste Management in the Montenegro Littoral Commune of Budva, Kotor, Tivat and Cetinje* (Belgrade: SFRY Federal Secretariat for Development, August 1991), B-002-1.
27. The Survey of Projects was prepared in November 1990 and sent to all international financial institutions.
28. CFC - Chlorofluorocarbons
29. Henkel, Riviera, Kotor: *Reference Recommendation of the Montreal Protocol* (Kotor: February 1991), pp. 1, 3.
30. Obod, Elektroindustrija Cetinje: *Project for Ozone Layer Protection by Reducing and Replacing CFC* (Cetinje: January 1991), pp. 1, 2.
31. *Long term Policy of Environmental Protection and Promotion in Yugoslavia* (Belgrade: Federal Secretariat for Development, November 1991), p. 259.
32. Ministry for Environmental Protection of Montenegro: *Project submitted to the World Bank* (Podgorica, 1992), p. 3.
33. The link between ecology and development is considered in: *The World Commission on Environment and Development: Our Common Future* (New York: Oxford University Press, 1987).

PART FOUR

Foreign Relations

14

Relations with the Superpowers

Branko Pribićević

Post-World War Two Yugoslavia—the "second" Yugoslavia, given the dismantlement of the interwar kingdom in 1941—was an important factor not only in the Balkan and East European regions, but on the world stage as well. Its international position was, in some respects, quite unique. It was certainly almost without precedent that a country of this size and with such modest economic potential could play such an active and salient role in international politics. An American expert recently said that Tito's Yugoslavia had enjoyed "a singular role in the balance of East-West relations."[1] One might add that Yugoslavia, beginning in the mid-fifties, was also very present in the political processes in some parts of the Third World. This international position of Yugoslavia was also manifested in its relations with the two superpowers. Both of them often paid special attention to their relations with Yugoslavia, which they viewed as an important factor in the relations between the two blocs. This was the case particularly in the late forties and early fifties, and again in the late sixties and seventies.

There are a number of reasons for this specific international position and role of Yugoslavia. The most important ones are the following:

The Soviet-Yugoslav Rift in 1948

This was the first case in the history of international communism that a communist party had had the guts to say no to Moscow's diktat, and not only to defy Moscow but also to be strong enough to survive almost seven years of confrontation with Moscow and the entire communist world. During the conflict, Moscow used all sorts of pressure short of direct military intervention. As is well known, the instruments of pressure used against Yugoslavia were really drastic and brutal, but in spite of that, this was the first battle (in the history of the communist movement) that Moscow had lost. The official ending of the conflict was also without prece-

332   *Branko Pribićević*

dent. The new post-Stalin Soviet leadership made a journey of repentance to Belgrade in May 1955 and publicly admitted that the conflict had been due to the "mistakes" of the former Soviet leadership (i.e., Stalin). Thus, the Soviet Union had lost this battle, and Yugoslavia had won. As a result, Yugoslavia's international position improved enormously.

Yugoslavia's Geopolitical Position

Yugoslavia was located on the territory which, for quite some time, has been very important for the balance of power in Europe. Furthermore, Yugoslavia occupied the borderzone between different cultures, even civilizations, with its Western-oriented, Catholic cultures in Slovenia and Croatia, and its Eastern-oriented, Orthodox cultures in Serbia, Montenegro, and Macedonia. In antiquity, this region had been divided between the West and East Roman empires, and later between the Austro-Hungarian and Ottoman Turkish empires. Moreover, Bosnia (together with parts of Serbia and Macedonia) was the only part of Europe where Islam penetrated (after 1463). The geopolitical position of this country became particularly important after the Soviet-Yugoslav split and the Cold War confrontation between the East and the West. Robin Alison Remington, one of the best known American experts in the field of Yugoslav studies, stresses the importance of this factor: " . . . although Yugoslavia is roughly the size of Wyoming, geography magnifies the strategic importance of the area it covers. Yugoslavia is the heart of the Balkans . . . Physically, ideologically, even economically, it has been the dividing line between East and West."[2] One should keep in mind also the fact that World War One was ignited here (in Sarajevo).

The Yugoslav Model of Socialism

Within the context of the Soviet-Yugoslav confrontation, this country rejected not only Soviet dominance but also the Soviet model of socialism.[3] Step by step, it shaped and asserted a new model of socialist society which, in spite of all the inconsistencies in its implementation, was in some respects really very different from the Soviet one. Thus, while the Soviet model provided for the most centralized type of political system available, the Yugoslav model represented, in some respects, the very opposite—viz., extensive decentralization. In the sphere of civil and political rights, there were also considerable differences. If nothing else, the Yugoslav system was no doubt far less repressive than the Soviet system, and Yugoslavia was, for more than 30 years, a relatively open country—(its citizens enjoyed, for example, freedom of travel)—as against the Soviet bloc countries which were, to varying degrees, much more closed. That is particu-

Relations with the Superpowers

larly important. Yugoslavia opted for self-management (workers' participation in decision-making at the enterprise level, as a form of direct democracy); Yugoslav socialism did not concentrate decision-making in the hands of bureaucratic structures, in fact, but developed a system which was neither Western nor Soviet-inspired. Yugoslavia was indeed a maverick state. Thus, for a number of reasons, the Yugoslav political system attracted a lot of attention in many parts of the world, both in the East and in the West, and again both in the North and in the South.

The Role of Yugoslavia in the Nonaligned Movement

At the time of escalating Cold War confrontations, when it seemed that the world was heading toward total bipolarization, and that all countries would sooner or later have to side with either one side or the other, Yugoslavia had a really important, even central, role in launching this new policy and movement. It was obviously not an accident that the founding conference of the nonaligned movement was in Belgrade (in 1961). This movement was, one way or the other, joined by a very large number of developing countries, including almost all of the African countries, the majority of the countries in South and Southeast Asia, and a large number of Latin American countries. The movement did play quite an important role in the development of international relations, particularly in the sixties and seventies. As Yugoslavia had one of the key roles in this grouping, it further strengthened its international position.

A Triangular Relationship

In my analysis and assessment of the development of interactions in this triangular relationship (Yugoslavia, US, USSR), it would be useful to keep in mind the following propositions and characteristics:

First, these relations were marked, to a large extent, by frequent fluctuations, including sometimes really dramatic and sudden changes. There was not much stability and continuity. This was the case particularly in the first 25–30 postwar years.

Second, the relations in the triangle were very much interrelated. The relations with one of the superpowers had a direct bearing on the relations with the other; specifically, any improvement in the relations with one had negative implications for the relations with the other, and vice versa. At the same time, one should stress that this was not the only determining factor. In some cases, oscillations in these relations reflected Yugoslav responses to some other international policy moves of the two superpowers (for example, the war in Vietnam and the Soviet military intervention in Czechoslovakia in August 1968 caused problems in the relations between Yugoslavia and the two superpowers although these military operations did not directly affect Yugoslavia). This is closely related to the active role Yugoslavia had in the world arena.

Third, changes in the relations between Yugoslavia and the two superpowers were not important only for Yugoslavia and the corresponding superpower. In some cases, Yugoslavia was an important issue in the relations between the two superpowers themselves.

Fourth, these relations were often asymmetric.[4] This was the case even in the periods when the policy of equidistance was officially proclaimed by the Yugoslav leadership. Thus, Yugoslavia several times was restrained in criticizing some Soviet moves and actions although they were in disagreement with them (e.g., in the connection with the Soviet invasion of Hungary in 1956, or with regard to the Soviet military presence in some African countries in the 1970s and 1980s).

Fifth, these inconsistencies in Yugoslav policy are to be explained not only by reference to political interests and considerations, although the Yugoslav leadership was basically motivated by the real interests of the country; ideological considerations were also present. In spite of all criticisms they had with respect to the Soviet model of socialism and their resolve to distance themselves from this model, it was, after all, a socialist country. Therefore, the feeling was widespread, not only among the ruling strata but also in some sections of the society at large, that Yugoslavia and the USSR had some basic values in common, as well as common principles of social organization. After all, Yugoslavia had not defected from the world of socialism, only from the Soviet bloc. This traditional socialist orientation also presupposed, at the same time, a critical stance toward the other ("capitalist") system. In 1963, Tito said that Yugoslavia's " . . . independent foreign policy must not be detrimental to the socialist countries and workers' movement. . . . We must always keep in mind that we are part of that [revolutionary left] movement."[5]

Sixth, the Soviet Union was geographically closer than the United States, and hence its presence was more closely felt. Indeed, until the end of World War Two, the US had no special interests in this area. But after the war, the US, as a superpower with global interests, became steadily more concerned about and involved in this part of Europe. Much later, in the course of the 1980s, the Soviet Union was obviously losing ground. The eventual collapse of the Soviet system in Russia left only one superpower for the time being.

Relations with the Superpowers 335

Historical Stages

Three main stages can be identified in the development of Yugoslav relations with the two superpowers. The first covers the years 1943–1948, from the establishment of a federal Yugoslavia ("second" Yugoslavia) under communist rule, to its emergence as an important political factor with its expulsion from the Moscow-controlled Cominform on 28 June 1948. The second stage is the era of intense Soviet-Yugoslav conflict and tension, ending with Khruschchev's visit to Belgrade on 13 May 1955. A third stage ran from that landmark to the end of the 1980s, when this "second" Yugoslavia broke down. Tito's death in May 1980 divides the third stage into two subphases.

In the first period, the relations with the two superpowers were very different. Tito's Yugoslavia, formed and led by a communist party, was at this time very closely aligned with the Soviet Union. Many observers believed that the two countries were the best of friends, perhaps even that the Yugoslav leaders were the special darlings of the Kremlin, among all the new communist leaderships in Eastern Europe. In my view, this interpretation does not tell us the whole truth. The Soviet-Yugoslav relationship was not as simple as that. There is no doubt that the bonds were very strong, that the Yugoslav leadership identified the interests of the country with those of the Soviet Union. At the same time, even in this period, there were some differences and disagreements concerning both domestic and foreign policy issues. As is well known, Moscow was very critical, for example, of some of Belgrade's attitude about its anti-fascist liberation struggle. The Soviet leadership criticized Tito (albeit not publicly), saying that he was going too far, that he should slow down and make more concessions to the Yugoslav government in exile (in London), that the social and political dimensions of Yugoslavia's liberation struggle should be, for the time being, set aside, and that Tito's people should avoid using the words "socialism," "class struggle," and "proletariat." Moscow strongly criticized Tito when he formed the National Liberation Committee (29 November 1943) as the provisional Yugoslav government. There were also disagreements concerning the civil war in Greece. Moscow also opposed Yugoslav initiatives to form the Balkan Federation, and even more so Tito's ideas of a Balkan-Danubian Federation. The reasons for opposing these moves were obvious: Stalin was afraid that it might further strengthen Tito's position. It was very difficult to control him as the leader of Yugoslavia. It would have been even more difficult had Tito become head of a much larger state. Moscow also refused to support Tito's territorial claims against Italy (for Trieste and additional parts of Istria), and against Austria (for Carinthia). Tito reacted, for the first time publicly, when he said in his speech in Ljubljana (in May 1945): "We have no wish to be dependent on

336   *Branko Pribičević*

anyone . . . We do not want to be small change, we do not want to be involved in any policy of spheres of influence."[6] The next day, the Soviet ambassador informed the Yugoslav leaders that his government regarded this speech as an act of hostility toward the Soviet Union.[7] There were also disagreements concerning the economic relations between the two countries, concerning Yugoslavia's strategy of economic development, the scope of Soviet economic assistance, and the Soviet offer to form joint enterprises. To put it briefly, the problems appeared because the Yugoslav leadership, even in this period, was not prepared to "tow the line" completely or to accept the position of obedient satellite regime.

In the Yugoslav-American relationship, one can identify two phases in this period. In 1943/44, the relationship was reasonably good. The US government realized the importance of the Yugoslav contribution to the anti-fascist coalition and decided in 1943 to establish direct contact with Tito and to give the Partisans military assistance. The US was not, however, very much involved in these contacts. Washington agreed that Great Britain should have the central role in this area in representing the interests of the West. By the end of the war, the policy of cooperation was more and more pushed out by various problems, differences, and disagreements. Very soon the relationship between the two countries became very tense and bad in general. In summer 1945, when the US and Great Britain demanded that the Yugoslav army should leave Trieste, the Yugoslavs backed off and direct armed conflict was averted at the last minute.[8] The following year, two American Air Force planes were shot down as they were flying over Yugoslav territory without permission. There were three main reasons for this negative turn. First, the US government was very critical of Tito's policy of eliminating all noncommunist political groups and parties and establishing single party communist rule. (Yugoslavia was the first East European country in which this was done.) Second, it was believed in Washington that Yugoslavia went too far in aligning itself with the rival superpower. Third, Yugoslav territorial claims against Italy and Austria, involvement in the Greek civil war, and military presence in Albania were resented in Washington. All this contributed to bringing Yugoslav-American relations to the lowest point in the whole postwar period.

The second period brought radical and dramatic changes in the relationship within the "triangle." Yesterday's best friends and allies (the Soviet Union and Yugoslavia) became the worst of enemies. The Yugoslav-American relationship moved in the opposite direction, quickly forging very friendly relations. The Yugoslav-Soviet relationship was marked by total confrontation.[9] The Yugoslav party was expelled from the international communist movement and the people's democracies terminated all friendly ties with Yugoslavia. The Yugoslav leadership was accused not only of various ideological and political "deviations" (nationalism, petit

Relations with the Superpowers　　　　337

bourgeois liberalism) but also of being "imperialist stooges." Tito was accused of having collaborated with Hitler and of having later become an "imperialist" spy. Following through in economic relations, an economic blockade was imposed on Yugoslavia. Large numbers of Soviet armed forces were positioned close to the border, as the armed forces of Hungary, Romania, and Bulgaria were suddenly (and without explanation) strengthened and expanded. Soviet intelligence also tried to organize popular uprisings against Tito's government, and to recruit agents within Yugoslavia. For nearly five years, Yugoslavia faced the threat of direct Soviet military intervention.

The US and the whole world were really taken aback by these developments. No one had anticipated the conflict, which " . . . had an effect everywhere nothing short of a bomb."[10] One analyst said that "the condemnation of Tito and his party caused a stir for which we have to go back to the excommunication of Luther to find a parallel."[11] This is the explanation why the US and the West in general were restrained and very cautious in their first reactions to this sudden change. There was a lot of disbelief with respect to this change. The idea was widespread that the conflict was "fake," reflecting a Soviet gameplan to insert a "Trojan horse" into the Western camp. It took the US almost a year to realize that the conflict was not fake. Once this was realized, the US changed its policy toward Yugoslavia. Within a short period of time (half a year or so), the relationship between the two countries improved enormously. The US realized that it should support the Yugoslav side in this new conflict, as this suited the interests of the West. This approach was founded on a correct assumption that the survival of an independent Yugoslavia, not under Soviet domination, would be a very serious defeat for the Soviet Union. As Warren Zimmermann has noted, "US support for Yugoslavia has been founded on a bedrock of US national interest: (a) to encourage socialist countries to assert and maintain their independence; (b) to encourage the development of alternative non-Soviet models of socialist development; and (c) to promote stability in this historically turbulent area."[12]

The US decided to give full support to Yugoslav resistance to Soviet pressures. One might say that this was the first time in its history that the US had come to have such an important role in political developments in this part of the world. It is also beyond doubt that American support was an important factor that affected the final outcome, viz., the Yugoslav victory in this conflict. The US and its Western allies offered Yugoslavia not only large quantities of economic assistance but, what is even more important, also badly needed military assistance. As the Yugoslav economy reached the point of collapse, as a result of the total blockade on the part of the East, the West stepped in with its direct economic assistance. It is estimated that this economic and military assistance was worth about $15 bil-

338 *Branko Pribićević*

lion (in 1992 prices). The US share in this was almost 90 percent. Military support was of critical importance too, and here the US helped to modernize the Yugoslav army, by supplying it with all sorts of modern armaments. Not a small number of Yugoslav army officers went to the US to attend army training schools and centers. US army officers were even sent to Yugoslavia to help in modernizing the Yugoslav army.[13] At the peak of the Soviet-Yugoslav confrontation, the American government warned the Soviets that in case of their direct intervention, the US and the West in general would not be in the role of passive observers, and that this intervention might have very serious implications for global international realities. There is no doubt that these warnings from Washington were a central reason why the Kremlin finally called off plans to launch direct war against Tito's Yugoslavia.[14]

Under the circumstances, Yugoslavia had to change its international policy. Although it was in principle against switching from one bloc to the other, it had to establish, in this tense period, close linkages with the US and other Western powers. As a result, the Tito regime signed a "Treaty of Alliance, Political Cooperation, and Mutual Assistance" with Greece and Turkey in 1954; this treaty became known as the Balkan Pact. The Pact provided that in case any of the three countries should be attacked, the other two would immediately step in with their full support; since Greece and Turkey were already members of NATO, the security implications of this pact were clear. Not a few analysts were in fact convinced that this was a step in the direction of direct Yugoslav affiliation with NATO. Some said that by signing this pact, Yugoslavia was already semi-affiliated with NATO. General Dwight D. Eisenhower, the future US President, told the US Senate Foreign Relations Committee in May 1951, "You do not have to be a great soldier to know the great value which would accrue to freedom by including [in NATO] these countries: Spain, Turkey, Greece, and Yugoslavia."[15] It seems that it was not only General Eisenhower's idea at the moment—it had some support also in the US administration. The idea was not realized, first, because Tito and his leadership were not yet ready to affiliate directly with NATO. Also important was opposition from the British and French governments. The Yugoslav leadership, no doubt, wanted and needed close contacts and cooperation with the US and NATO, but at the same time, they realized that joining the pact would be too risky for them, for both political and "ideological" reasons. They thought that joining NATO would be incompatible with their resolve to preserve their version of communism ("self-managing socialism"). They looked at their close political cooperation with the West, at their policy of "semi-affiliation" with it as a marriage of convenience. It is quite possible that this policy was also largely influenced by changes in Moscow which followed Stalin's death. On the other hand, there is no doubt that if Stalin had lived

Relations with the Superpowers

for a few more years and the Soviet Union had persisted with its aggressive policy vis-à-vis Yugoslavia, the Yugoslav leadership would have moved closer yet to the West.

The third stage (from 1955 until the end of "second Yugoslavia") was characterized by the assertion and long-term stabilization of Yugoslavia's policy of equidistance, its nonalignment, and its resolve to develop and maintain good political and economic relations with both superpowers. At the same time, this was a period when the relationship with both superpowers was marked by frequent fluctuations. This was the case particularly in the Soviet-Yugoslav relationship. In spite of these fluctuations, Yugoslavia did stick to its basic strategy of equidistance, consolidated its position of a buffer zone, a dividing line between the two blocs.

The central problem in the Yugoslav-Soviet relationship throughout almost the whole of this period was their fundamental disagreement as to the purpose and scope of the "normalization" of their relations which had been initiated in 1955. The Soviet Union had, for years, tried to persuade the Yugoslav leaders to return their country to the socialist bloc. They tried very hard to bring it back to the fold. On the other hand, the Yugoslav leadership was strongly opposed to it. The Yugoslavs considered it essential that the Soviets accept their nonaligned status, and neither challenge it nor try to subvert it. The Soviets found this easy to concede in theory, and more difficult in practice, and this gave rise to many problems and disagreements over the years. At the same time, one should keep in mind the fact that the Yugoslav leadership several times did make some concessions to the Soviet Union, that were, to some extent, at variance with its longterm strategy of nonalignment.

Here I shall briefly present the most important trends and junctures in the Soviet-Yugoslav relationship in this period. To begin with, Khrushchev's "Canossa" visit of May 1955 obviously ushered in a dramatic change for the better, and within a year or so, the relationship between the two countries was largely normalized both in political and economic terms. But this proved shortlived. By the end of 1957, the two countries were again engaged in serious political controversy, provoked, in part, by growing realization on the part of the Soviets, and hence also by growing Soviet disappointment, that the Yugoslavs were not intending to rejoin the Soviet bloc as such. When the Yugoslav communist party published a draft party program in Autumn 1957, the CPSU responded with brutal criticism. Within a few weeks, relations were almost as tense as they had been in the preceding years. The Kremlin accused the Yugoslavs of various political "deviations" and denied that the Yugoslavs were good Marxist-Leninists. The Soviets now boycotted the Seventh Congress of the League of Communists of Yugoslavia (LCY) in spring 1958, and compelled the other bloc parties to do likewise. The Soviets also canceled some eco-

340

nomic agreements. The Yugoslav party had, for its part, refused even earlier to sign the declaration adopted at the 1957 conference of ruling communist parties. After that, the LCY was to refuse to attend international conferences organized by Moscow. In the early sixties again, the two sides reached a compromise and there was a transient improvement in relations in the years 1961–1968. This improvement was canceled and reversed by the Soviet military intervention in Czechoslovakia in August 1968. But the pendulum soon swung the other direction, and there was yet another rapprochement in the early 1970s. The relations between the two countries improved so much that some people even speculated that Yugoslavia was about to join the Warsaw Pact. Yugoslavia supported some Soviet foreign policy initiatives in this period. The two sides, for instance, took very similar stands on the Arab-Israeli war of October 1973. Yugoslavia even opened its air space to the Soviets to airlift weaponry to the Arabs.

Relations soured once more beginning in late December 1979, when Soviet forces were sent into Afghanistan, a member state of the nonaligned movement. But this time the disagreement did not take the dimensions and forms characteristic of the earlier years. Moreover, the Soviets seemed to be prepared to accept the Yugoslav view that friendly relations did not require an identity of views or monolithic unity.

Fluctuations in the Yugoslav-American relationship reflected, to a large extent, changes in Yugoslavia's relations with the Soviets. Thus, for example, when the rapprochement of 1955 was achieved (via Khrushchev's "Belgrade Declaration") and it seemed that the two communist states were about to consolidate reasonably good relations, the US reacted by reducing and cooling its relations with Yugoslavia. American military advisers were withdrawn from Yugoslavia. Economic assistance was radically reduced, military assistance even more so. There were, however, a few cases in which changes in American-Yugoslav relations were not directly correlated with changes in Soviet-Yugoslav relations. Thus, in 1953 and early 1954, while Soviet-Yugoslav relations were still bad, serious problems appeared in the American-Yugoslav relationship as a result of Yugoslav-Italian territorial disputes in which the US quite understandably sided with Italy. Serious problems appeared again in the early 1970s, when Washington's appraisal was that Yugoslavia had gone too far in its cooperation with Moscow.[16] But in spite of these fluctuations, one might say that American-Yugoslav relations in this period were more stable than was the case with Soviet-Yugoslav relations. Nor did occasional political disagreements impose barriers on bilateral cooperation in other spheres (such as the cultural and economic).

Relations with the Superpowers 341

Disintegrative Tendencies

The 1980s and early 1990s represent the last stage in the history of "second" Yugoslavia. These were the years of crises affecting practically all the components of its political and economic system. The problems that had been simmering below the surface for some time during the 1980s erupted and assumed really dramatic dimensions.[17] These developments within the country had direct bearing on its international position. Within a short period of time, the country had lost much of its international prestige and position. Yugoslavia had lost its credentials as an important positive factor in the world arena. The country that had, in the preceding three decades, been widely recognized and respected as an important factor of stability not only in the Balkan region, but also in Europe and the world at large, had turned into an important source of instability. Indeed, with the total collapse of the system 1989–91, the disintegration of the federation, and the rise of ethnic tensions and internecine armed conflict, Yugoslavia became, by 1990–91, the most dangerous powderkeg in all Europe.

Yet another factor contributed to these disintegrative trends, viz., the collapse of the communist order throughout what had been the Soviet bloc and the disappearance of the Warsaw Pact. As a result of these developments, Yugoslavia lost one of the most important credentials it had to justify its specific international position, as a buffer zone between the two blocs. The end of the Cold War also had serious ramifications for the nonaligned movement.

The crises and processes of disintegration in Yugoslavia produced important changes in the relationship within the triangle. First, important changes emerged with respect to the strategic interests of the two superpowers in this region. While their interests had been divergent and conflicting in the past, now their interests converged to the point of being almost identical. More specifically, while it had been the US interest since 1948 to support independent Yugoslavia, the Soviet Union, until the mid-1980s, was preoccupied with the thought of bringing Yugoslavia back into the bloc. The independent position and role of Yugoslavia were incompatible with the longterm strategic interests of the Soviet Union as they were conceived in that period. Now, however, both superpowers had the same basic strategic interest of keeping Yugoslavia together, to prevent its total disintegration. Second, this stage was also characterized by important changes with respect to the presence of the two superpowers in the area. In the past, the Yugoslav regime had taken care to keep the Soviet and American presence, such as it was, in some kind of balance. But as time went on, the Soviet Union was becoming less and less important as a factor on the international scene, while the US gained much more weight. The reasons for this change are obvious—at the time when the Soviet Union was facing escalating crises in the country, the crises that would lead to its ultimate disintegration and the breakdown of the entire system. The Soviet Union was so preoccupied with its problems that it had no chance to take a more active role with respect to developments in Yugoslavia.

Third, as time went on, Yugoslavia was rapidly losing its position as an important partner of the two superpowers. Both of them were by now assessing the unfolding Yugoslav drama primarily as a regional (i.e., not continental) problem. Although they were publicly supporting the preservation of Yugoslavia, they were either not able (as in the Soviet case) or not willing (in the American case) to get too directly involved in the sundry international initiatives and actions undertaken after June 1991 to try to bring the warring sides in ex-Yugoslavia to the negotiating table. This change is particularly important in the case of the US. While in the preceding decades (between the early 1950s and the late 1980s), the US had been by far the most active state in shaping Western policy toward Yugoslavia (and was more active in its relations with Yugoslavia than any other Western state except perhaps Germany), this was not the case in the final stage of the process of disintegration and disappearance of "second" Yugoslavia. The burden of this role was now handed over to the European community and Western Europe in general. It seems that it was agreed among them that the European Community should take over the role of mediator between Serbia and Croatia, Serbia and Bosnia.

It is still an open question why the US handed over this key role to the European Community, why it partly retreated from its earlier position of central Western actor in confronting major problems in this part of Europe. It seems that two reasons were most important. The first was the US government's assessment that the Yugoslav crisis was basically local and regional in character, and that, under the new circumstances entailed in the disappearance of the Soviet bloc, it could not seriously threaten the balance of power in Europe and the world at large. It seems that the view prevailed in Washington that the US need not be as directly involved in European affairs as hitherto. This did not mean, however, that the US was willing to "withdraw" from Europe. Though the main role (with respect to the Yugoslav crisis) was handed over to the EC, the US has not been just a passive observer. Washington has been quite active, 1990–92, in negotiations and initiatives affecting Yugoslavia. Until April 1992, in fact, the US remained opposed to the idea of recognition that Yugoslavia had disintegrated and steadfastly refused to extend diplomatic recognition to the new states of Slovenia, Croatia, Bosnia-Herzegovina, and Macedonia. On a number of occasions, the US government made it clear that it supported the preservation of unified Yugoslavia. As late as October 1989, President Bush had said (during a meeting with Yugoslav Prime Minister Ante Marković) that the US was " . . . committed to support for Yugoslav inde-

Relations with the Superpowers 343

pendence, unity, and sovereignty."[18] That these were not just statements of intention is clear from the US refusal to follow the EC lead in recognizing Slovenia and Croatia in December 1991. When the EC finally decided to accord recognition to these two new states, that month, setting the expected date of recognition for the following month, the US' first reaction was critical. The US refused to follow suit, and only three months later, after the escalation of interethnic conflicts, did the US belatedly extend recognition to the republics of Slovenia, Croatia, and Bosnia-Herzegovina.

The decision of the US to recognize those three republics (in April 1992) reflected a shift in the American approach. It seems that, in the meantime, the US government had realized that the Yugoslav crisis had assumed such serious dimensions that it could no longer be seen as a purely local or regional problem, but that it could have very dangerous implications for Europe as a whole, even to the supposed "new world order" proclaimed by President Bush. As a result of this new assessment, the US became once again more active in numerous initiatives to stop further escalation of the Balkan war. Once it became clear that the EC and the West European Union could not successfully handle this problem alone, the US strongly supported and to some extent initiated the idea that the Council on Security and Cooperation in Europe (CSCE) and the United Nations should be directly engaged in tackling the problem of the Serb-Croat (and Serb-Muslim) war. Serbia has been particularly blamed for spreading the war to Bosnia-Herzegovina, and was warned (on 15 April 1992) that if it did not cease its "aggressive policy" in Bosnia-Herzegovina, it would have to face very serious sanctions. It seems that Washington, with its allies, was planning not only economic sanctions but some other forms of direct pressure—political and even (so it seemed at the time) military.

The Soviet Union was not able to become more involved in the final stages of the Yugoslav drama. Apart from making some general statements in support of continuation of a unified Yugoslavia, it was not in a position to do anything in practice. It abandoned its traditional view that the Balkan peninsula was of strategic interest to Moscow, and failed to play any substantive role in the emerging Western debate about the Yugoslav crisis. Russia not only had nothing to say against the West's involvement but even supported some Western initiatives and steps. This Russian stand implied that Moscow was prepared to accept the central role of its recent Western rivals in attempting to defuse the Yugoslav crisis. As time went on, the Russian role actually became more and more marginal. Moscow undertook no initiatives of its own, and simply endorsed various initiatives coming from the major Western powers. How much things have changed in the Russian approach to Yugoslavia was clear from Moscow's decision to recognize the independence of Croatia and Slovenia even before the US did. This was a shock for the Serbs, who had seen Russia as a traditional Serbian friend. Russia's recognition of Croatia and Slovenia was no doubt of great importance for these two new states and they welcomed it publicly. At the same time, this was a great blow for Serbia, where it was received as a "betrayal" of a centuries-long friendship. It seems that this switch in Russia's policy with respect to the Yugoslav crisis was not the result of a reassessment of developments in former Yugoslavia, but rather of more general strategic considerations. Russia badly needs economic assistance, and the West is the only part of the world that could provide such assistance.

The War in Bosnia

America's and Russia's responses to the latest developments in the region that once comprised Yugoslavia continued in the same direction through much of summer 1992. The tragic events in Bosnia-Herzegovina, where the escalation of war helped to bring the total number of war-related deaths to 60,000 by August 1992, made it clear that all international efforts to stop the war were failing utterly, and that the sundry diplomatic and economic pressures exerted by the UN, the European Community, the CSCE, and some individual states have not been strong enough to compel the chief antagonists to change their policies and thus bring about the restoration of peace in the region. The US played perhaps the key role in the preparation of UN Security Council resolutions 752 and 757 that imposed drastic sanctions on "third" Yugoslavia,[19] total economic blockade (which did not prove entirely effective), a transport and communication blockade, the withdrawal of ambassadors from Belgrade, the reduction of the number of diplomatic representatives assigned to Belgrade, a cessation in cultural cooperation, etc.[20] While some Western countries were advocating milder sanctions, the US insisted on a more rigorous stance. Thus, the US was the first Western state to close a number of "Yugoslav" diplomatic outposts, including, for example, the Consulate-General and Cultural Center in New York. In addition, the US asked the Belgrade's ambassador in Washington to leave the country. All (more than 270) branches and agencies representing Yugoslav companies in the US have also been closed. Washington was also very active in the CSCE discussions that led to the temporary exclusion of "third" Yugoslavia. Washington insisted on the complete exclusion of Belgrade, but the majority opted for a temporary exclusion, until mid-October 1992.[21] The US government refused to recognize "third" Yugoslavia as the (sole) successor to "second" Yugoslavia, insisting that all five new states (i.e., also Slovenia, Croatia, Bosnia-Herzegovina, and Macedonia) must have the same rights as far as succession status is concerned. The US has played a very important role in vari-

Relations with the Superpowers   345

ous international initiatives to restore peace in Bosnia and to establish humanitarian aid corridors to Sarajevo, and in August 1992 also to some other parts of Bosnia. Perhaps the most indicative of this new approach is the fact that the US seemed to be ready now to consider the possibility of military intervention to stop the war in Bosnia. President Bush said in August 1992 that the US would do "everything necessary to restore peace in Bosnia." The message to Belgrade was obvious—if the Serbian side did not stop the war, i.e., if the UN sanctions were not enough, military intervention might be considered. At this writing, the US was still debating the intervention option, and seemed reluctant to make a final decision. Typical of American hesitation was George Bush's comment in early August: "Before I'd commit American forces to a battle," President Bush said in reference to the Yugoslav crisis, "I want to know what's the beginning, what's the objective, how is the objective going to be achieved, and what's the end . . . I don't see the answers to my questions."[22] Administration spokesmen stated on several occasions that Washington was, at the given moment, ready to use only its air force and naval units, not ground forces. The reason for hesitation is obvious: the commitment of ground forces in Bosnia could be very costly in terms of human lives. Washington has "offered" this commitment to its West European allies.

In early July 1992, the US revised its stand vis-à-vis the war in a potentially significant way. While in May and June, Washington had held exclusively Belgrade, the Serbian side, responsible for these developments, Washington now criticized the Croatian Republic as well, for its involvement in Bosnia.[23] Washington was beginning to face the fact that Zagreb had also contributed to spreading the civil war in Bosnia-Herzegovina.

Russia was largely, and in some respects completely, supportive of America's new approach to the Yugoslav crisis. Shortly after the US recognized Slovenia, Croatia, and Bosnia-Herzegovina (on 7 April), Russia also recognized Bosnia as an independent and sovereign state. What was an even greater surprise and shock for Belgrade, and not only for Belgrade but also for a large part of the Russian public, was that Moscow fully supported the UN sanctions against "third" Yugoslavia; indeed, the Russian representatives in the UN voted for the sanctions. Moscow not only voted for the sanctions but declared its willingness to impose a complete economic blockade on "third" Yugoslavia. In July 1992, Moscow addressed some stinging criticisms at Belgrade, that seemed to represent a radical shift in Russia's approach to Belgrade. Russia's Foreign Minister stated that he had been disappointed by the results of his talks with Serbian President Slobodan Milošević.[24] He even said that the Serbian leadership had been pursuing an "aggressive policy" toward some of its neighbors, particularly Bosnia-Herzegovina. In his opinion, Serbia had made a big mistake when it refused to recognize all the newly formed states on former

346   Branko Pribićević

Yugoslavia's territory, i.e., to do what Russia did when it recognized all the ex-Soviet republics as independent and sovereign states. The Russians also accused the Belgrade regime of being a national-communist and even "national Bolshevik" regime, for its blend of traditional bolshevism with aggressive nationalism.

The only aspect in which Moscow did not support the new policy of the West was the proposal to exclude "third" Yugoslavia from the CSCE. When the initiative was launched, Russia voted against it and blocked the American/EC proposal. Instead of complete expulsion, Russia proposed the "empty chair" option which was ultimately adopted.[25] As the CSCE decisions presupposed unanimous support, all the other member states had no other option but to accept this compromise proposed by Moscow. With regard to the war in Bosnia-Herzegovina, Moscow took the position that Serbia was not the only culprit, and that the Muslims and the Croats must also share some blame.

The Yugoslav drama gradually assumed the characteristics and dimensions of a major policy problem for the Russian government. Moscow's support for the policy of the US and the EC was no doubt well received in the West, and might have positive implications with respect to Western policy toward Russian problems, including financial support. At the same time, this policy has not been well received within Russia itself. Quite a number of important political organizations and groups have already strongly criticized President Yeltsin and his government for his "betrayal" of fellow-Orthodox states, Serbia and Montenegro, and for subordinating Russian policy to the interests of the West. In the Russian parliament, a special session was held at which opposition groups strongly criticized Russia's support for the UN sanctions against Yugoslavia and asked that Russia should reject these sanctions or delay its own adherence. Yeltsin's government experienced the worst defeat since it was formed—only seven MPs voted for the government, while 130 voted against it (with a few abstentions). The same groups and organizations mentioned above have been demanding that Foreign Minister Andrei V. Kozyrev and some of his associates resign.[26] It is also interesting to note that this "pro-Serbian lobby" in Moscow has support both from the left and from the right (i.e., from old-style communists and right-wing nationalists alike).

But as the months went by, the Russian government has come under increasing domestic pressure to break ranks with the West and to assist Serbia openly and energetically. Russians taking this view speak of Russia's "national shame" in letting down the Serbs and call Russia's cooperation with the sanctions "capitulation."[27] Various intelligence services have indicated, beginning in November 1992 if not earlier, that Russia was shipping oil to Serbia in violation of the embargo. In late February, the Russian parliament returned to the issue once again and called for lifting the

Relations with the Superpowers

sanctions against Serbia and Montenegro and for imposing them against Croatia. And on 1 March 1993, British defense analysts issued a statement claiming that Russia had signed "a secret deal to supply Serbs in Bosnia and Croatia with tanks and anti-aircraft missiles."[28] Meanwhile, there have been repeated reports of Russian mercenaries fighting on the Serbian side in Bosnia.[29]

In January 1993, Governor Bill Clinton of Arkansas took office as the new American president and immediately announced a serious review of the Balkan situation. A month later, President Clinton and his Secretary of State, Warren Christopher, gave a qualified endorsement to the Vance-Owen peace plan (discussed in the following chapter), and the Russian government declared its satisfaction and concurrence with the Clinton administration's stance.[30] Meanwhile, Russian President Boris Yeltsin faced a growing challenge from the Russian parliament, a struggle which could have wide implications for Russia's foreign policy, in the Balkans and elsewhere.

"Second" Yugoslavia is no doubt finished. But this is not the end of this historic drama. Not a single one of the problems that led to the disintegration of the country and the present interethnic war have been solved. On the contrary, the problems and conflicts are still escalating, assuming more dangerous forms and dimensions. The territory of former Yugoslavia will unfortunately remain one of the central problems for the international community for quite some time. The country is in the process of radical "Lebanonization." There is also the threat that the Yugoslav powderkeg could eventually threaten regional and international security. For this reason, the US and all other important states have to pay special attention to developments in the territory of former Yugoslavia.

Notes

1. David Anderson, "Europe in the 1990s," in P. Simić, W. Richy, and M. Stojčević (eds.), *American and Yugoslav Views on the 1990s* (Belgrade: Institute of International Politics and Economics, 1990), p. 64.

2. Robin Alison Remington, "Yugoslavia and Foreign Affairs," in Gary K. Bertsch and T. W. Ganschow (eds.), *Comparative Communism* (San Francisco, Calif.: W. H. Freeman & Co., 1976), p. 421.

3. For discussion, see Dennison I. Rusinow, *The Yugoslav Experiment, 1948–1977* (London: C. Hurst Co., 1977).

4. Anton Bebler, "The US Strategy and Yugoslavia's Security," in Simić et al. (eds.), *American and Yugoslav Views*, pp. 183–185.

5. Josip Broz Tito (13 May 1963), quoted in *Savez komunista Jugoslavije u medjunarodnom radničkom pokretu, 1948-1968* (Belgrade: Sedma sila, 1968), pp. 98, 103.

348   *Branko Pribičević*

6. Quoted in Fernando Claudin, *The Communist Movement from Comintern to Cominform* (London: Penguin Books, 1975), p. 489.

7. Francois Fejto, *History of People's Democracies* (New York: Praeger, 1971), p. 85.

8. Bebler, "The US Strategy and Yugoslavia's," pp. 173–176.

9. Radovan Radonjić, *Sukob KPJ sa Kominformom* (Zagreb: Globus, 1975); Adam B. Ulam, *Titoism and the Cominform* (Cambridge, Mass.: Harvard University Press, 1952); and Robert Bass and Elisabeth Marbury (eds.), *The Soviet-Yugoslav Controversy, 1948–58, Documentary Record* (New York: Prospect Books, 1959).

10. Claudin, *The Communist Movement from Comintern to Cominform* , p. 486.

11. R. N. Carew Hunt, *The Theory and Practice of Communism* (Harmondsworth, Middlesex, Great Britain: Penguin Books, 1973), p. 251.

12. Warren Zimmermann, "American-Yugoslav Relations in the Light of Current Changes in East-West Relations," in Simić et al. (eds.), *American and Yugoslav Views*, p. 156.

13. Bebler, "The US Strategy and Yugoslavia's Security," p. 176.

14. See Bela Király, "The Aborted Soviet Military Plans Against Tito's Yugoslavia", in Wayne S. Vucinich (ed.). *At the Brink of War and Peace: The Tito–Stalin Split in a Historic Perspective* (New York: Brooklyn College Press, 1982).

15. *Eisenhower Public Record Office*, CAB 125/45 CP(51), 17 May 1951.

16. See Laurence Silberman, "Yugoslavia's 'Old' Communism: Europe's Fiddler on the Roof," in *Foreign Policy*, No. 26 (Spring 1977).

17. See Marijan Korošić, *Jugoslavenska kriza*, 2nd ed. (Zagreb: Naprijed, 1989).

18. Quoted in Zimmermann, "American-Yugoslav Bilateral Relations," p. 156.

19. By "third" Yugoslavia, the author means the rump Yugoslavia consisting of Serbia and Montenegro.—Eds.

20. *Politika* (Belgrade), 1 June 1992, p. 3.

21. *NIN* (10 July 1992), p. 50.

22. Quoted in *Wall Street Journal* (5 August 1992), p. A16.

23. *NIN* (10 July 1992), pp. 52–53.

24. *Izvestiia* (Moscow), 8 June 1992, pp. 1, 4.

25. *Borba* (Belgrade), 11 July 1992. pp. 2–3.

26. *Ibid.* (1 July 1992), p. 17.

27. *Neue Zürcher Zeitung* (3 February 1993), p. 3.

28. *The Times* (London), 2 March 1993, p. 14.

29. See, for example, Radio Bosnia-Herzegovina (Sarajevo), 26 January 1993, trans. in FBIS, *Daily Report* (Eastern Europe), 27 January 1993, p. 37.

30. *Neue Zürcher Zeitung* (14/15 February 1993, p. 3; and 16 February 1993, p. 1).

15

Yugoslavia's Relations with European States

Zachary T. Irwin[1]

There are good reasons for attempting to better understand relations between Europe and the former Yugoslav republic.[2] Several recent studies of the Federation's disintegration interpret the event as a consequence of institutional failure, nationalist separatism, and economic crisis, and, understandably, place their emphasis on internal dynamics.[3] An appraisal of socialist Yugoslavia's relations with Europe may help to place European involvement in the crisis within a broader context. A clearer sense of socialist Yugoslav diplomacy can point out policy dilemmas confronting the country's successor states. Second, an emphasis on former Yugoslavia's interaction with Europe may have theoretical significance in view of the interconnection of Yugoslav foreign and domestic policy.[4] Finally, a study of Yugoslav-European relations can address the assertion that nonalignment retarded Yugoslavia's association with European integration.[5]

Before discussing Yugoslavia's relations with specific European states or organizations, I wish to consider briefly what was socialist Yugoslavia's overall position in Europe. Foreign Minister Budimir Lončar spoke about the country's place within "concentric and mutually connected circles [of Europe]" and as a "link and a balance vis-à-vis the European Community (EC)."[6] At the time, he stressed the importance of Belgrade's closer association with the EC, the European Free Trade Association (EFTA), the Organization of Economic Cooperation and Development (OECD), the Council of Europe, as well as the Council of Mutual Economic Cooperation (CMEA), "quadrilateral cooperation" with Italy, Austria, and Hungary, and multilateral cooperation with other Balkan states. Lončar wished to enumerate the diplomatic arenas of activity of activity, to depict opportunity for Yugoslavia in a rapidly changing Europe, and to recommend support for the economic reforms of the government of Ante Marković.

350   *Zachary T. Irwin*

Lončar's views about "concentric circles" were contingent on policy choices which proved beyond the power of the federal government to implement. But the geographic basis of the "circles" was plausible. For much of its postwar history, a nonaligned Yugoslavia was generally perceived to be central to maintaining equilibrium between NATO and the Warsaw Pact. Standing outside either alliance, Yugoslavia did not threaten any of its seven neighbors; yet in view of its geostrategic position, its importance to both superpowers was indisputable. Had Moscow fundamentally compromised Yugoslavia's position, the result would have gravely complicated the security of NATO's southern flank, and, conversely, had NATO stationed forces in (a presumably receptive) Yugoslavia, the Warsaw Pact would have probably redeployed forces in Bulgaria and Romania. Albanian isolation and Austrian neutrality have been no less dependent on Yugoslavia's remaining nonaligned. Thus, Yugoslavia, regional states, and both alliance systems shared a common interest in "nonalignment" as a foreign policy choice.

Nonaligned Yugoslavia's self-perception as a "bridge" or "link" was evident particularly during the Arab-Israeli wars when the Soviet Union depended on Yugoslav air space and base facilities to resupply Arab clients. Yugoslavia's position has been no less valuable to the West. As I hope to show, European diplomacy, on occasion, looked to Belgrade as a mediator with certain Arab states. Within the context of the East-West European balance, Western states supported Yugoslavia through the mid-1980s, partially owing to its geopolitical position. Apart from any exaggerated sense of importance Yugoslav officials may have attributed to their country's role, Belgrade's policy appears to have encouraged two misperceptions that shaped policy towards Europe.

The first might be called the "myth of equivalence," that is a conviction of approximate symmetry between the two "blocs." For example, Ranko Petković, editor of the semi-official *Review of International Affairs*, forecast in early 1990 the disintegration of both NATO and the Warsaw Pact and a corollary decline in American and Soviet influence in Europe, in proportion to the blossoming of "all European [integrative] processes."[7] The argument assumed the preservation of nonalignment and socialism by denying socialism's exclusive failure and Yugoslavia's necessary adjustment.

The second, a "myth of Balkan vulnerability," insisted that threats to the region's security came wholly from outside the region, whether in the form of "active measures" to destabilize regimes or as a new Yalta Accord designed to satisfy superpower interests.[8] Official opinion in Belgrade denied the existence of a threat from within the region. In 1989, a Yugoslav commentator observed that Albania had never renounced its bilateral treaty of friendship with Bulgaria, despite its 1968 repudiation of the Warsaw

Yugoslavia's Relations with European States

Pact. He considered Albania's decision to retain its treaty with Bulgaria a reflection of groundless fear of Yugoslavia, and opined that "dangers to peace and security in this region have always come from outside, and not from inside, regardless of borders, minorities, ideas, economies, or policies."[9] One consequence of this view was an insistence that nonalignment was not only the most relevant response to the region's security dilemmas, but also that Yugoslavia's closer association with Western Europe would compromise nonalignment, socialism, and by implication Yugoslav security.[10] During the mid-1980s, partisans of "nonalignment," or a more "Eurocentric" foreign policy, were a persistent, if muted, element in the country's political life.[11] Only the collapse of the Warsaw Pact and CMEA appears to have settled the question in favor of closer association with Western Europe and rapid economic reform. By that time, secession may have been irrevocable.

The point bears repeating that debates about "nonalignment" were closely connected with Yugoslavia's European policy, although some might have found the debate confusing. No one suggested the renunciation of nonalignment. Those in favor of accelerating Yugoslav association with European integration, such as Foreign Minister Lončar, pointed out the advantage of "nonalignment" in the sense of a common diplomatic status with the Middle East and other developing countries. As I hope to show, Yugoslavia's mediation with certain Arab states or in "North-South" economic questions was valued by West Europeans. However, when "nonalignment" was discussed as a consequence of attitudes about "bloc equivalence" or "Balkan vulnerability," the concept became a pretext for resisting change. As a result of the situation, Yugoslav adjustment to the decline of polarization in Europe was relatively slow despite the country's "nonbloc" status.

The problem of adjustment was compounded by the uncertainty of Western Europe's evolution and its consequence for Yugoslavia. First, the government feared becoming a marginal actor in the new Europe. In his January 1991 report to the Presidency, Prime Minister Ante Marković spoke of the dangers of the country's being drawn into a new West European "cordon sanitaire" to contain westward migration from the East.[12] Marginalization in the rush to Europe might follow from falling behind the more evenly developed East European economics, such as Hungary and Czechoslovakia, with their lighter political baggage. Foreign Minister Lončar was keenly aware of the many obstacles that hindered Yugoslavia's adjustment to the emerging Europe. He spoke of the need to "free ourselves from the burdens we [have] imposed on ourselves," especially the "ideological criminal code [as] . . . contrary to elementary European conventions," and of the need for "closer relations with emigrants who left [Yugoslavia] for political reasons." He recommended a simple prescrip-

352   Zachary T. Irwin

tion for the delicate relations with Albania and in regards to Kosovo, i.e., "the more complex the situation the more effort one needs to invest."[13] Perhaps the most challenging problem was the general expectation that closer affiliation with Europe also implied a multiparty system. Meeting the criteria for West European integration required political democracy, and while some republics such as Slovenia and Croatia, quickly introduced multiparty systems, authentic elections were unlikely in others or in the federation as a whole.

Yugoslavia's position in the "concentric and mutually connected circles" of Europe is summarized in Table 15.1. In mid-1990, Yugoslavia sought affiliation or was involved with about ten European entities.

Table 15.1

Yugoslavia and European Organizations—1990*

Association	Affiliation	Membership
European Community (EC)	Seeks Associate Status	Bel, DK, D, Gr, Sp, Fr, Ire It, Lux, NL, P, UK
European Free Trade Assoc. (EFTA)	Seeks full membership	Au, Fin, I, N, Sw, Ch
(Org. of Economic Cooperation & Development (OECD)	Special Status, Seeks membership	Twenty-four states includes all major economies
Council of Europe	Seeks membership	Twenty-three members include most West European states
Conference on Security and Cooperation, in Europe (CSCE)	Member	Thirty-four members include all European states, US, USSR
CSCE Neutral and Non-aligned Group	Founder-member	Au, CH, Cyp, Fin, Malta, Yu
Alpine Adriatic Group	Founder-member	Eleven Subnational State Units and Au, Cz, H, It, Yu
Pentagonale-Hexagonale	Founder-member	Au, Cz, H, It, P, Yu
Quadrilateral Group	Founder-member	Au, It, H, Yu
Danube Commission	Founder-member	Au, BL, H, Rom, Cz, USSR, Yu
Balkan Foreign Minister Group	Founder-member	Al, Bl, Gr, Rom, Tur, Yu

* This list is not exclusive.

Yugoslavia's Relations with European States 353

Obviously, not all of these associations are equivalent in any sense. What is called the "Quadrilateral Group" of Italy, Austria, Hungary and Yugoslavia appears to have represented no more than meetings of foreign ministers. The "Pentagonal Group," adding Czechoslovakia to the previous four states, worked through a number of functional committees in such areas as migration, the environment, and industrial cooperation. Poland's admission in July 1991 made the group "hexagonal." The Pentagonal Group had evolved from the Alpine-Adriatic Group that had included some twelve republics, provinces, or regions of the five member states. However valuable, the importance and consequences of diplomatic cooperation at this level paled in comparison with Yugoslav Associate Membership in the EC. Associate and eventual full membership in the European Community would have left few areas of Yugoslav economic and political life unchanged. Similarly, admission to the Council of Europe implied a functioning pluralistic democracy and eventual accession to more than 100 multilateral treaties. In 1990, the federation was a party only to three Council treaties.[14] Foreign Minister Lončar's reference to the "ideological" Yugoslav Criminal Code was not only accurate but appropriate given the Presidency's expressed wish for Council Membership. Council Members were parties to the European Convention on Human Rights and the Statute of the European Court of Justice.

Some observations follow from this overview. First, it is inadequate to consider Yugoslavia's European relations from a strictly bilateral viewpoint. For example, relations with Austria involved four distinct organizational arenas, direct contacts between Slovenia and certain Austrian Länder, as well as bilateral commercial ties. In 1987, Yugoslav President Lazar Mojsov acknowledged Italian support for Yugoslav participation in the EC Eureka project of scientific research.[15] Second, Yugoslavia's overall position between the collapse of East European communism and the promise of West European integration involved many domestic actors. As the number of actors increased with the domestic impact of foreign policy decisions, the power of the federal government diminished. For example, the Chairman of the Foreign Affairs Committee of the Federal Assembly referred to "ever more frequent occurrences where individual republics or their highest officials . . . have been transgressing the competencies and provisions of the federal constitution, *inter alia*, in the field of foreign policy. . . . [16] Different republican perspectives compounded the problem of reaching a consensus about political democratization and economic reform.

Finally, an account of Yugoslav relations with Europe confirms the cumulative tension between social and economic trends and residual political practices. In 1983, Yugoslav exports to the EC area stood at $2.3 billion, less than half its exports to CMEA at $4.7 billion, but by 1989, EC exports reached $5.2 billion, while CMEA exports remained virtually stag-

354   Zachary T. Irwin

nant.[17] At that time, EC-EFTA exports reached 46 percent and imports 49 percent. The promise of these trends and threat of a single integrated EC market by the end of 1992 implied that previous *ad hoc* treaty arrangements with Europe were insufficient. As Boran Karadžol, Deputy Minister for Foreign Economic Relations, explained, "Yugoslavia does not wish to *cooperate* with the European economic space, because it is far too important an area for us merely to *cooperate* with. We need to find mutually acceptable ways of including ourselves in the process known as Europe 1992."[18] While the viewpoint may not have been universal throughout Yugoslavia, it was common in federal circles and was well founded. Reforms in federal investment laws in 1984 and 1989 had a desirable effect in promoting foreign investment. Although the registry of joint investment ventures in Yugoslavia has been closed since 1974, about 56 percent of personal and institutional investors after 1989 were domiciled in the European Community, with capital from the area constituting 59 percent of the total investment value of $1.2 billion.[19] West Germany, Italy and Austria were the largest investors, while total United States' investment reached only 14 percent. About 80 percent of all foreign investment was concentrated in Serbia, Slovenia, and Croatia. Nevertheless, as of 1990, Yugoslavia lagged behind Hungary, the Soviet Union, and Czechoslovakia with respect to the total number of joint ventures.

About a third of all "foreign" investors in 1989 in joint ventures were, in fact, Yugoslavs working abroad with convertible savings.[20] The number of Yugoslavs who were employed abroad is difficult to estimate, and the most recent official data provided by Yugoslavia is now a decade old. Nevertheless, in 1981, of 751,617 Yugoslavs employed in Western Europe, 60 percent were resident in West Germany.[21] West German sources cited a total of "slightly under 700,000" Yugoslavs in Germany in 1991, exclusive of those who fled the war.[22] Similarly, the number of foreign tourists increased substantially in the 1980s, and between 1985 and 1990, "registered revenue" from tourism approximately tripled from slightly over $1 billion to about $3 billion, or 2.9 percent of the social product and 8 percent of total exports of goods and services.[23] About 80 percent of tourism originated within the EC. Information on trade, workers abroad and tourism is summarized in Tables 15.2–15.5. While the implications of the overall trends are controversial, several conclusions are plausible. Traditional Yugoslav treaty arrangements with the EC were no longer appropriate or effective, since further unilateral EC concessions were likely. Second, Yugoslav workers in Europe could not increase without a closer form of EC association in view of new visa requirements for France and Germany. Finally, a newfound willingness of Yugoslavs abroad to invest at home recommended eventual reconciliation with political emigres.

Table 15.2

Destination of Exports*

Percent of Total	
USSR	21.7
Italy	15.1
West Germany	11.5
USA	4.7
OECD	51.4
Developing Countries	13.6
EC	36.9

Table 15.3

Main Origin of Imports

Percent of Total	
West Germany	16.9
USSR	14.5
Italy	10.6
USA	4.8
OECD	54.8
Developing Countries	18.8
EC	38.9

* *Yugoslavia: Country Report* (Economist Intelligence Unit), No. 4, 1990, p.3.

Table 15.4

Yugoslavs "Temporarily" Employed in Europe: 1981*

Total in Europe of all abroad	85.9	(751,617)
Austria	16.3	(122,247)
France	6.5	(49,134)
FR Germany	60.0	(451,607)
Switzerland	9.3	(70,178)
Sweden	3.5	(26,650)
Others	4.2	(31,801)

* *Statisticki Godisnjak Jugoslavije*, Vol. 37, 1990 Savezni zavod za statistiku, Belgrade: 1990, p. 131.

Table 15.5

Number of Tourists in Yugoslavia, 1989*

Total of All Tourists (in thousands)		(8,644)
FR Germany	28.5%	(2,462)
Italy	16.4%	(1,424)
Austria	8.6%	(746)
UK	7.5%	(650)
USSR	4.7%	(408)
France	3.6%	(315)
Other	30.7%	(2,639)

* "Tourism in Yugoslavia," *Yugoslav Survey*, No. 3, 1990, p. 160.

356   Zachary T. Irwin

Yugoslavia in the Balkans and Central Europe

Before briefly discussing Yugoslavia's relations with its bordering neighbors, I wish to comment on the general character of interstate relations in the Balkans. In March 1990, Foreign Minister Lončar commented on the "autochthonous nature of Balkan cooperation" and the region's tendency to resist European trends of integration. He observed that "the historical wall between the Balkans and other parts of Europe [had still] not been destroyed."[24] Lončar acknowledged frustration in finding "consensus" within Yugoslavia to pursue the goal of Balkan multilateralism. The apparent achievement of Balkan Foreign Ministers' Conferences in 1988 and 1990, as well as other meetings, did not survive Yugoslavia. Although I do not wish to imply that the region's overall situation predetermined the policy choices of the member states, the differences between Yugoslavia's relations with other Balkan states, and, let us say, its relations with Austria and Hungary, are unmistakable.

Like certain other less developed regions, Balkan states trade relatively little with one another. Yugoslavia's combined trade with Albania, Bulgaria, Greece, Romania, and Turkey amounted to only 4 percent of its total turnover (in 1988).[25] The absence of institutionalized economic relations reflected a lack of industrial complementarity and the absence of a political pluralism supportive of commercial interests. The postwar political division of Europe clearly discouraged economic and political contact across bloc lines; yet the sources of the underdevelopment of Balkan cooperation run deeper. Historical conflict attending the creation of each state became socialized in successive generations' experience of war or official hostility and could be rekindled in the form of national irredentism. Normal relations remained stagnant. Indeed, after more than forty years, Greece and Albania ended a formal state of war only in 1987.[26] In the mid-1970s, a Yugoslav official conceded to me that Yugoslavia's diplomatic relations remained fundamentally as they had been in the interwar period, i.e., relatively good with Romania and Greece but poor with Albania and Bulgaria. One may interpret the foreign policy of each state as a particular consequence of the Balkans' place as a buffer between hostile empires or modern alliances, but it is perhaps the problem of the Balkan nationalism and political development that is most distinctive.

Despite the fervor of Balkan national movements, Balkan identity has traditionally emphasized the role of language as a more fundamental focus of loyalty than any political institutions, which were always relatively weak. A Yugoslav Albanian expressed the problem nicely in criticizing equally Albanians who wished to make Kosovo an Albanian republic and Macedonians who denied Albanians official use of their language in the Slavic republic. Both instances, he said, reflected the attitude that "jeopardizing the state language means jeopardizing the state."[27] It might be added that the same could be argued for other Balkan states as well, and that a fear of "jeopardizing" the state reflected less an attachment to language than a well-founded fear of the state's weakness. Of course, such generalizations are impressionistic; yet their importance for diplomacy is illustrated by a 1989 interview with the Chairman of the Commission on International Relations of the Republic of Serbia, published in *Borba*. In this interview, he contrasted the lack of language rights for the Serbian minority in Albania and Romania compared with the favorable conditions in Hungary.[28] Serbia's complaint about the behavior of the two states and the "passive attitude" of Yugoslavia's Foreign Ministry in regard to the situation was a recurrent feature in Yugoslavia's relations with each Balkan state.

Historical and demographic burdens encumbered Yugoslav-Albanian relations. The symbolic importance of Kosovo for Serbia has been described at length.[29] The province's political significance is suggested by the response to Serbian President Slobodan Milošević's 1989 speech to some hundreds of thousands of Serbs at the 500th anniversary of the Battle of Kosovo Polje. Milošević evoked thunderous applause in asserting that "after many decades Serbia's national and spiritual integrity" had been restored with the constitutional restriction of the "autonomy" enjoyed by Kosovo and Vojvodina.[30] Ironically, the previous year, Albanian Foreign Minister Reis Malile had made a remarkable concession (for Albania) at the Balkan Foreign Ministers Conference in describing "minority problems" as an "internal question of each [Balkan] country."[31] Apart from Milošević's personal responsibility in squelching an Albanian gesture to normalize relations with Belgrade, the obstacle to reconciliation between the two states could not have been more formidable. Between 1948 and 1981, the Albanian population of Yugoslavia increased from 4.76 percent to 7.71 percent of the total, and the percentage of Albanians living in Kosovo approached 80 percent. During the next decade, the trend intensified. The overall percentage of Albanians in Serbia increased from 14% in 1981 to 17.2% of the total in 1991, and the absolute number increased by 29.4%.[32] In 1981, riots in Priština spread throughout the province, and the fragile dialogue between Albania and Yugoslavia, which had developed in the 1970s, seemed to have ended.[33] Many Serbs considered the protesters' demands for Kosovo to become a republic a mere pretext for secession and union with Albania, especially since about 43 percent of all Albanians lived in Yugoslavia.

In fact, the issue of Kosovo's constitutional status was raised in 1968 by former minister Mehmet Hodža, who asked why more than a million Albanians in Yugoslavia could not live in a republic, while 370,000 Montenegrins were able to do so.[34] Until 1981, Kosovo was able to increase its autonomy through direct ties with federal organs; yet no formal change occurred. To have granted Kosovo republican status could have involved the creation of Albanian "irredenta" in Macedonia, Montenegro, and Serbia proper. Unfortunately, Albanians and Serbs alike often remained dissatisfied. Albanians considered it unfair that they should be subjected to Serbian rule regardless of any "rights" their rulers granted them. Albanian migration to the area had been promoted at the height of Ottoman power. Most Albanians could claim residency for many generations, but alleged Albanian harassment of Serbs and pressure on Serbs to migrate from Kosovo made harsh repression popular in Serbia. By 1989, the repressive situation had worsened.

The importance of the riots for Yugoslav relations with Europe exceeded the matter of relations with Albania. After the European Parliament passed a resolution criticizing Yugoslavia for its human rights violations in Kosovo, a visiting delegation from Strasbourg expressed "great disappointment" that the government had not "insured the necessary conditions" for an inquiry.[35] Despite the condemnation both of the European Parliament and the United States Senate, Yugoslavia had been able to realize limited, but significant, cooperation with Albania after the death of its dictator Enver Hoxha in 1985. In November, a new trade protocol for five years was signed as well as mutual provisions for a 476-km railroad line from Shkoder to the Montenegrin capital of Titograd.[36] Yugoslavia and Albania continued bitter polemics at a lower level; yet both sides found the 1988 Balkan Foreign Ministers Conference the occasion for a discussion.

Ranko Petković criticized past policy towards Albania. Instead of demanding the same human rights standards towards Slavic minorities expected of Austria and Italy, the government had tolerated "non- reciprocity" for its [pre-1981] policy towards Albania. Petković objected that Yugoslavia had ignored the "non-bloc" character of Albanian foreign policy in pursuit of an "ideological-party strategy."[37] The relevance of that "strategy" to Yugoslav interests had disappeared with the Cold War, and surely neglecting the fate of Albanian Slavs did nothing to diminish criticism of Serbia's policy towards Albanians. In May 1989, a Yugoslav representative to the UN Economic and Social Council challenged Albania on the issue, a challenge the Albanians rejected as "absurd" and a "slander" intended to deflect criticism of Yugoslavia's policy.[38] In fact, the event followed the resumption of bitter polemics. An Albanian spokesman defended claims for a republic of Kosovo, condemning Serbian "persecution," and affirming the "duty to defend the Albanians no matter where they live."[39] A Yugoslav official rejected the "interference" in internal affairs and acknowledged that relations had "deteriorated."[40] Conditions in Kosovo had also deteriorated. Several years earlier, in 1986, Slovenian President Milan Kučan had demanded a policy of conciliation in the province, but in 1989, a general strike and the death of many protesters signaled a return to repression.

Relations between Yugoslavia and Romania differed fundamentally from those with Albania. During the interwar period, Romania and Yugoslavia had been allied in the Balkan Entente, while the Albanian-Yugoslav boundary was unsettled until 1926. Yugoslav President Josip Broz Tito and Romanian President Nicolae Ceauşescu professed common aims and personal friendship; Tito and Secretary Enver Hoxha elevated personal animosity to the center of relations. If Albania had been the object of an "ideological-party strategy," Romania was the beneficiary of such a strategy. Bucharest and Belgrade shared an interest in diminishing regional Soviet influence, and Romania had long affiliated with the nonaligned movement as an "observer." Years after Tito's death, Ceauşescu continued to visit Yugoslavia almost annually, e.g., a December 1985 communique pledged "to collaborate ever more closely in the world arena."[41] Bilateral collaboration on a jet fighter, the Orao (Eagle), supplemented a large joint hydroelectric project at the Iron Gates on the Danube. At the same time, Yugoslavia was less than enthusiastic about the prospect of seeing expansive Romanian ideas for joint economic collaboration "put into concrete terms."[42]

In fact, Romanian industrial autarky made industrial collaboration unlikely. A commentator took the risk of offending the Ceauşescu regime by comparing Yugoslavia's relations with Romania and Hungary. Though half the size of Romania, Hungarian trade with Yugoslavia was twice as great, and while Hungary sought to address Yugoslav concerns about Slavic minorities in its borders, Romanian officials rejected such "interference" out of hand.[43] The implicit criticism continued through the late 1980s, and though high-level meetings were frequent, neither side offered approval of one another's "socialism." A commentator in *Politika*, remarking on the strikes in Braşov in late 1987, considered that Romania's "economic crisis is assuming more and more of a political character."[44] But before 1989, there was little change in relations.

At their first meeting after the overthrow of the Ceauşescu regime, Yugoslav Prime Minister Ante Marković and Romanian Prime Minister Petre Roman called for "new foundations for the two countries' relations in keeping with the political, social and economic changes that have taken place in the last two months."[45] More specifically, Romania would bring the position of its Yugoslav minorities "into line with the democratic processes taking place in the country." Ministers of Energy and Industry reconsidered a possible expansion of the Iron Gates Project and other joint ventures that had emerged after the Balkan Foreign Ministers' Conference. They judged "all aspects of bilateral cooperation to be 'unsatisfactory,' far removed from reality, and [therefore] should be abandoned." More limited goals might be sought. Greater candor now brought Romanian objections to compulsory currency exchange for citizens crossing the border.

360   Zachary T. Irwin

The following September, relations took on a further dimension with a three-day visit of Romanian President Ion Illiescu to Belgrade. Serbian President Milošević and Croatian President Franjo Tudjman joined talks that reportedly discussed the possibility of settling Serbs and Croats from Romania respectively in Kosovo and Istria.[46]

In less than a year after Illiescu's visit, Yugoslavia would no longer exist, and Balkan interstate relations would be transformed. Romania's absorption in its domestic affairs made the Yugoslav tragedy somewhat less urgent for Bucharest than for Sofia or Athens. For both of these states, the question of a distinct Macedonian nation state became the centerpiece of relations with Yugoslavia. Well into the late 1980s, the Yugoslav press continued to imply that Bulgaria's alleged attachment to the short-lived San Stefano Treaty (1878) and its claim that the anti-Ottoman 1903 Ilinden Uprising had been a Bulgarian nationalist event expressed territorial designs on the Socialist Republic of Macedonia. The history of the question and its place in relations with Bulgaria has been studied extensively.[47] Nevertheless, the problem continued through Yugoslavia's disintegration.

The significant fact about Bulgarian-Yugoslav relations was that most of the goals declared in joint statements were achieved. Macedonia's Premier was received by high Bulgarian officials; Sofia became an openly enthusiastic supporter of Balkan multilateralism; the Foreign Ministers opened a new border crossing; and an Intergovernmental Committee for Technical and Scientific Cooperation was created.[48] A more detailed study of bilateral relations would leave little doubt that the level and quality of Bulgarian-Yugoslav relations between 1988 and 1989 was unprecedented. By mid-1990, it appeared that the ouster of Todor Zhivkov would not jeopardize progress. A new Premier, Andrey Lukanov, met with Ante Marković and proclaimed that democratization had set the two states on "identical paths" and that their "comprehensive expansion of cooperation" would lead to the "Europeanization of the Balkans rather than the Balkanization of Europe."[49] The phrase had expressed Lončar's aspiration to extend the idea of European cooperation to the Balkans rather than that of the further division of existing states. Implicitly, the "Balkanization of Europe," which would have involved public disagreement about the Macedonian issue, was now "no obstacle to agreement."

Unfortunately, foreign policy could not be left to the two governments. Early in 1989, after Marko Orlandić had led a League delegation to Sofia, the LCY Commission on International Cooperation resolved, "In all contacts with Bulgaria, Yugoslavia will insist that Sofia change its position towards the Macedonian national minority in that country."[50] The resolution exceeded the demand that Bulgaria deal with the Macedonian republic, for it sought a change in Bulgaria's domestic policy. At this point, Greece became a factor. Yugoslavia had avoided involvement in Bulgaria's con-

Yugoslavia's Relations with European States

flict with Turkey, as it had avoided Romania's conflict with Hungary. Nevertheless, Turkish refugees from Bulgaria attracted much sympathy, and it appeared that Athens would only overlook the Turkish exodus from Bulgaria by criticizing Turkey.[51] An implicit alliance on the minority issue between Sofia and Athens now became active.

Yugoslavia encouraged Greece's independence from NATO and the two states had actively opposed the Turkish occupation of parts of Cyprus. Yet, Greek Prime Minister Andreas Papandreou denied that any Macedonian minority existed in Greece.[52] Papandreou's conservative successor Konstantine Mitsotakis went a step further in 1990 adding that Greece could never have such a minority because "the Macedonian nation does not exist and has never existed."[53] Some years earlier the comment would have elicited a routine protest by the Yugoslav Foreign Ministry and been forgotten, but now a more vigorous Macedonian organization forced the issue. From Skopje, the Movement for All Macedonian Action (MAAK) demanded a "unified" Yugoslav response to the Greek Prime Minister and attacked Lončar's passivity.[54] MAAK found a sympathetic response on the issue from the LCY presidium whose resolution on Macedonia was already mentioned. Belgrade protested sharply and closed border crossings with Greece. A detour through Bulgaria left traffic in miles long queues for several days.[55] Lukanov now was compelled to deny the existence of a Macedonian minority in Bulgaria, and more seriously from Yugoslavia's viewpoint, to join with Greek officials in a Sofia press conference to do so.[56] Belgrade could only express its "surprise and regret" at the matter, for it mocked Lončar's phase of "Europeanization of the Balkans," much as the border closings negated the efforts of cooperation among Balkan transport ministers.[57]

The Macedonian issue also affected other bilateral issues. According to Yugoslav sources, Greece's refusal to sign an agreement with Macedonia had brought about the suspension of United Nations Funds to study the feasibility of a navigable canal linking the Danube and the Aegean Sea.[58] Belgrade had also sought unsuccessfully to change Greece's requirement that all Yugoslavs obtain visas before traveling to Greece. Use of water from the border Lake Dojran had been a problem apparently resolved.[59] In fact, Greek-Yugoslav tensions came to a climax late in 1987 during talks between Foreign Ministers Karolos Papoulias and Raif Dizdarević. The two affirmed the "historical significance" of the planned Balkan Foreign Ministers Conference and the "strategic" value of bilateral relations[60] Like similar meetings between the Bulgarian and Yugoslav Foreign Ministers, the two emphasized the role of "small scale border cooperation." The two sides agreed on the need for scientific cooperation through the European Community's Eureka Project. Yet the communique expressed no agreement about a way to "overcome unresolved problems."

362   Zachary T. Irwin

Compared with the four Balkan states, Yugoslavia's relations with Austria and Hungary showed little of the same idiosyncrasy. First, both states had been prepared to deal respectively with bordering Yugoslav republics. Although Slavic minority rights had been guaranteed in the 1955 Austrian State Treaty, Vienna exceeded the letter of requirements by dealing directly with Slovenian officials.[61] Similarly, Hungary accepted the involvement both from the Republic of Serbia and the Province of Vojvodina, where the predominant share of the Hungarian minority was settled. Second, relations with the two central European states were responsive to the decay of Soviet power after 1986. Austria accelerated its involvement with Western Europe, and Hungary moved most rapidly towards political pluralism and a multiparty system. In both cases, relations with Yugoslavia adapted flexibly and positively to the change. Finally, neither of the two states bore the same historical legacies. Both Hungary and Bulgaria had occupied parts of Yugoslavia during the Second World War as Axis allies, but unlike relations with Bulgaria, "historical debates" played no part in relations with Hungary. Even so tangible a "legacy" as the Presidency of Kurt Waldheim, whose Nazi past in Yugoslavia was discussed in the country's press, did not become a disputed issue in relations with Austria.[62]

Among the more important features of Yugoslavia's relations with Hungary was the durable interparty relationship between President Tito and Hungarian General Secretary János Kádár. Unlike the case of Romania, the question of "socialism" was a subject of mutual approval. In 1986, a Hungarian commentary recognized the "determining importance" of interparty contact for overall relations between the two countries; for example, a 1984 communique on the occasion of General Secretary Kádár's visit to Belgrade spoke of the "respect for the peculiarities, experiences and practice of socialist development and the differences in the two countries' international situation."[63] The ties survived Hungarian communism in the Kádár era! In 1989, Yugoslavia provided Hungarian officials with requested party archives concerning Yugoslav involvement in the 1956 Hungarian revolution, Imre Nagy's flight to the Yugoslav Embassy, and subsequent execution.[64]

Hungary's early efforts at economic reform made possible a 50 percent increase in commercial exchange between 1986 and 1989 and a relatively high level of trade compared with the rest of Eastern Europe. Delegations at all levels of government visited each country frequently. When Hungarian Premier György Lázár visited Belgrade in 1985, he met separately with Serbian President Dušan Čkrebić, who acknowledged the "substantial cooperation" of Hungary with the Province of Vojvodina.[65] Lázár's visit led to agreements for the joint construction of electric and natural gas lines as well as exploration for coal and oil in the border area and common energy

Yugoslavia's Relations with European States   363

research. By mid-1989, the level of relations brought the Hungarian Foreign Minister to recognize an "exceptionally close, stable, and friendly" relationship.[66] Cooperation through the "Pentagonal Group" and the Alpine-Adriatic Group was mentioned.

The collapse of the Yugoslav Federation and the new non-communist government of József Antall in Hungary fundamentally ended most of the goodwill that had accumulated, at least as far as Serbia was concerned. Initially, Hungary identified itself with the position of the European Community, but after an early report, Croatia's Premier in March 1991 acknowledged purchase of arms from "several countries" including Hungary.[67] Some interpreted Antall's remarks about the situation in mid-1991 to mean that since Vojvodina had been ceded to Yugoslavia in 1920, it could be reclaimed from an independent Serbia.[68] In any case, it is unlikely that the cordial relations that had existed could survive Serbia's 1989 reassertion of control over the Autonomous Provinces. Antall warned that it was "not possible to uphold good relations with a neighboring country that does not treat the Hungarian minority in an honest manner from a human rights and minority standpoint."[69] Nationality problems would become a centerpiece of relations.

Austria's attitude towards the crisis in Yugoslavia was decidedly more cautious than Hungary's. Antall had approved the principle of "self-determination" in describing the situation, but in May 1991, a month before war, Chancellor Vranitzky, meeting with Prime Minister Marković, remarked that the "Federation was the only competent partner" for Austria.[70] Although Vice-Chancellor Alois Mock was more encouraging of Slovenian aspirations in supporting "self-determination," the government initially avoided direct involvement with Slovenia.[71] Austrian policy traditionally had been accommodating of Yugoslav interests, and throughout the 1980s, the two states enjoyed excellent relations. A 1989 analysis of bilateral relations by the Yugoslav political scientist Radovan Vukadinović, in fact, could find few questions of controversy: the interpretation of Article 7 of the Austrian State Treaty that guaranteed the rights of Yugoslav workers, the problem of unemployment among Yugoslav workers in Austria, and "negative" presentation of Yugoslav events in the mass media.[72]

Interpretation of the Treaty, according to Vukadinović, was an "open question" in "individual situations" where "goodwill" was required. In 1987, one of those "situations" occurred. The government announced its eventual intention to eliminate bilingual education for Slovene children in primary school. Instruction would still be provided in the Slovene language, but Yugoslav commentators spoke of the danger of "ghettoization" and a violation of the "spirit" of Article 7, if not its letter.[73] Apparently Foreign Minister Raif Dizdarević won a commitment to delay the measure from the Austrian government, but what was especially significant had been the

364   Zachary T. Irwin

attitude of the Vice Chancellor. In an interview with the Zagreb newspaper, Večernji list, Mock remarked that the talks on the issue had been "very proper" despite "criticism" and that "among good friends criticism is possible."[74] Talks further included commercial relations, problems affecting Yugoslav workers, and industrial cooperation. Austria was the third largest foreign investor in Yugoslavia. The frequency of high-level talks and the number of international fora requiring Yugoslav-Austrian collaboration were unequaled with any other state. Some officials were displeased with the way Austria depicted Yugoslav events in the mass media; yet criticism was not expressed formally. Finally, official discussions often included Yugoslav relations with EFTA and the Conference on European Security and Cooperation (CSCE).

Relations with Western Europe and the Community

Yugoslavia's relations with Western Europe differed from those with Austria or the Balkan states in obvious ways: Yugoslavia has always been peripheral to Western Europe, but central to the Balkans and part of Central Europe. Tourists and Gastarbeiter, not national minorities, constituted the major elements of diplomatic intercourse between Yugoslavia and the countries of Western Europe; political relations were shaped by commercial and financial incentives, while in the Balkans relations were subordinate to political questions. Recognizing the impact of diminished Soviet-American rivalry in the Balkans could be prompt and obvious, but adjusting to changes in Europe was far more complex, for it involved at once a response to European integration, a response to the end of Soviet hegemony, and an uneven response to the failure of East European communism.

Before 1988, Yugoslav foreign policy had demonstrated a capacity for adjustment to changes in Europe. Belgrade advanced proposals for disarmament in the Mediterranean, organized a group of "neutral and non-aligned" states within the CSCE process, and negotiated commercial pref erences for its goals with the European Community. However, the failure of East European communism and the impending consequences of an integrated Europe far exceeded Yugoslavia's ability to adjust. In retrospect, Yugoslavia's descent into civil war appears to have seldom been considered a likely outcome in public discussion before early 1991.

The problem of adjusting to the international system included a series of perceived challenges that Belgrade could scarcely confront. The danger of becoming a marginal actor in Eastern Europe has been mentioned. Similarly attaining a consensus among the Yugoslav republics on necessary foreign policy decisions required rewards for cooperation that the federal

Yugoslavia's Relations with European States 365

government lacked; yet the requirements were recognized. In an interview in December 1987, Raif Dizdarević anticipated the need for Yugoslavia "to adapt much more quickly to the standards that will prevail in a European market in order for us to be able to survive and participate."[75] Republican leaderships understood that an active foreign policy would encroach on republican prerogatives. Most, but perhaps not all, West European governments were supportive of Yugoslav efforts. According to a Yugoslav source, poor relations with Greece over the Macedonian issue had brought Athens to argue that Yugoslavia had "not fulfilled political conditions" necessary for the OECD program for Central and Eastern Europe.[76]

The question of Yugoslavia's joining the Council of Europe illustrates that the problem of relations with Europe was political rather than economic. Janez Drnovšek, President of the Federal Presidency between 1989 and 1990, remarked that multiparty elections in Croatia and Slovenia, lifting the state of emergency in Kosovo and acquittal of Albanian politician Azem Vllasi would be useful in improving Yugoslavia's "image" in Europe.[77] Concurrently, the Secretary General of the Council of Europe, then in Belgrade, agreed, but he felt it necessary for the country to achieve "more [in the way of] pluralism and human rights" to meet Drnovšek's goal of Council membership in 1991.[78] Subsequently, Drnovšek addressed the Council affirming that Yugoslavia had "no more urgent interest than its involvement in the democratic processes of general European integration." Logically, the goal would require extensive reform, e.g., "federal multiparty elections . . . by the end of the year, an independent judiciary . . . and accession to the European Convention on Human Rights . . . once we become a member of the Council of Europe."[79] The step would coincide with full membership in EFTA, the OECD, and within "two or three years full membership in the European Community."

In retrospect, was the optimism at all justified? To be sure, Drnovšek had acknowledged in his speech the rise of "distrust," "nationalism," and the "great autonomy and sovereignty of the republics"; yet it was exactly these conditions which made the "dynamics" of Yugoslavia's involvement in Europe all the more significant. Before leaving office to his successor Borislav Jović, Drnovšek claimed the collective presidency had achieved a "true breakthrough" in the question of relations with Europe, for the body no longer gave "absolute priority" to relations with the nonaligned states. Lacking a more detailed account, I cannot be certain of the extent of support Drnovšek's viewpoint enjoyed, but his strategy was analogous to Lončar's wish to "Europeanize the Balkans." The President believed that "quick integration" would "facilitate the relaxation of internal pressures and disputes." Furthermore, "once such a prospect [of integration] had been made clear there will be no reason for us to disintegrate first, only to unite at a later point."[80] An article in the party theoretical organ *Socijalizam* by Aleksandar Sekulovic, LCY Chair for the Commission on International Relations, objected to the sacrifice of "nonalignment" and "self-management" for European integration. Sekulović also wrote against the "utilitarian" ideology of pro-EC forces in Yugoslavia and their desire "to absolutely suffocate the possibility of any other viewpoint or critical reflection."[81]

Borislav Jović succeeded Drnovšek as chair of the collective presidency in May 1990. The new President expressed a viewpoint consistent with Sekulović's. Although he did not revise Drnovšek's foreign policy, Jović warned against "pluralism in contravention to the SFRY Constitution." Instead of rapid reform to appease Western Europe, the "world" should see a Yugoslavia enjoying "conditions of stability without traumas or shocks."[82] In place of future change, Jović spoke of consolidating the economy, e.g., maintaining the stature of convertible reserves, the low level of inflation, and the convertibility of the dinar. Arguably, the de-emphasis on relations with Europe reflected less an oscillation back towards "nonalignment" and more a caution consistent with impending republican developments.

Multiparty elections in Slovenia and Croatia brought parties to power which questioned the idea of a single foreign policy. Shortly after the election of the Slovenian Democratic Opposition Party (Demos), Dimitrij Rupel, President of the Republican Committee for International Cooperation and later Foreign Minister, committed Slovenia to seek membership in several European regional associations, observing that Slovenia "did not wish to enter Europe via Belgrade."[83] Speaking at the 1990 meeting in Winchester (U.K.) of the Standing Committee for European Regions, Rupel expressed an interesting approach to foreign policy in which regional relations would "serve as a kind of substitute for cooperation between states"; here lies "the future of Europe [which] would respect all differences which are culturally and politically productive." Croatia's President Tudjman expressed a distinct but analogous position in rejecting any drive towards a "renewed centralism" on the part of the Marković government, since it was "up to us to regulate relations with our neighbors."[84] Tudjman went on to reject the idea that an independent or confederal Croatia would become "anybody's client" or that it might join some kind of "small entente" against Germany which, through unification, would become "the main European power." Tudjman criticized the United States and European officials who nurtured "oversimplified views" and objected to internal Yugoslav boundary adjustments.[85] The Italian Foreign Ministry was singled out for its "great inclination . . . that sought joint interests with Belgrade against Croatia."[86] Consensus in Yugoslavia's foreign policy would clearly be impossible without a negotiated confederation.

Yugoslavia's Relations with European States 367

Croatia and Slovenia had previously pursued an autonomous foreign policy through the Alps-Adriatic Work Community, a regional association encouraging functional cooperation among Italy, Austria, Switzerland, Bavaria, and the two Yugoslav republics.[87] Croatia's and Slovenia's leadership now conceived a foreign policy far exceeding regional functionalism. Their conception of an emerging Central European identity differed from Belgrade's, whose high-level Central European contacts were absent or infrequent between 1988 and 1991. The new government in Prague waited more than five months to name an ambassador to Belgrade.[88] By contrast, Croatia and Slovenia immediately sought contacts with Austria; Slovakia's premier was perhaps the first foreign official to support Slovenian independence, and, as I have mentioned, Hungary sold weapons to Croatia.[89]

A republican foreign policy viewpoint became an alternative either to "Eurocentrism" or "nonalignment." Serbian President Milošević seemed to be hostile to Yugoslavia's European orientation, and he was especially "sorry to see that in some of our republics representatives of foreign states are supervising and 'guarding' democracy and freedom."[90] Serbia sought to develop ties with Greece and Romania, while both Presidents Tudjman and Milošević visited France. "Very positive" talks between the Greek and Serbian Foreign Ministers in mid-1991 coincided with Macedonia's impending announcement of independence.[91]

In February 1991, Serbia's newly appointed Foreign Minister cautiously explained the Republic's goals. Branko Mikasinović vowed to defend Serbian interests and devote his efforts to establishing "the best possible links with [Serbia's] old traditional allies."[92] In the meantime, Serbia would not follow the example of the federation because " . . . we cannot enter Europe with everyone." Instead, Belgrade would develop relations with other states by virtue of its "geopolitical position" along the "Europe-Middle East Axis" and the "great role in the future" of the Danube between East and West Europe. The end of the Cold War, some would argue, had diminished the intrinsic value of the link with the Middle East. While Belgrade had given its name to the primary Convention on Danubian Navigation, the overall regime remained relatively undeveloped and the promise of a Rhine-Main-Danube canal was still unrealized.[93]

Mikasinović had complained about Serbia's "lost years" apparently when the republic's interests had been neglected. As I hope to show, a major commitment on the part of the European Community to finance Yugoslavia's transportation infrastructure might have helped compensate Serbia along with additional advantages from Balkan multilateralism. Slovenia and Croatia were able to express their interests within the Federation, not only through the Alps-Adriatic Work Community, but also through the "Pentagonal Initiative" and, for Croatia, through the growing functional basis of the nonaligned Mediterranean group. In June 1990, the

Mediterranean group among nonaligned states had started to emphasize regional cooperation along with its usual themes of security and disarmament.[94] The "Pentagonal Initiative" had created nine cooperation committees at the first meeting in 1989 and, in addition to Yugoslavia, included Austria, Italy, Czechoslovakia, and Hungary. Austrian Prime Minister Franz Vranitzky regarded the group's potential value to be one of regulating migratory labor and common environmental concern.[95]

Despite the complexity of Yugoslavia's regional involvement and the apparent independence of republican foreign policy activity, the central government continued to achieve a high level of flexibility before the latter part of 1990. In fact, as late as January 1991, Foreign Minister Lončar sought to enhance Yugoslavia's European status through his reputation among the nonaligned. Lončar undertook two missions to Baghdad during the Gulf crisis on behalf of the European Community, reporting directly to Foreign Ministers Gianni de Michelis of Italy and Hans-Dietrich Genscher of Germany.[96] Yugoslav authorities had succeeded in winning loans, renegotiating payment schedules and interest rates throughout the 1980s. Despite the threats of republican secession, foreign support continued. In 1990, following talks between Lončar and Foreign Minister Taro Nakayama, the Japanese government promised unspecified amounts of technical assistance, financial aid, and joint investments within the IMF, IBRD, the Paris Club of major lenders, and the full members of the OECD (G-24).[97]

The Japanese were interested in shipping arrangements through Adriatic ports and a projected "customs free zone" in Belgrade. In view of Japanese caution towards economic involvement with Eastern Europe and the USSR, Nakayama's commitment was significant. Generally the government of Ante Marković and its pragmatic position won the confidence of foreign governments, not only for its refusal to identify with the variety of desired alternative Yugoslav futures, but also for its economic performance. From December 1989 to May 1990, retail inflation had fallen from 64.3 percent to .2 percent; trade with the convertible area increased 3.5 percent; 300M. of debt had been retired; convertibility was established, and foreign reserves stood at 8.1 billion.[98] The World Bank rewarded these achievements by one of the largest loans it would grant a single country. Bank President Barbara Conable announced a fifteen-year loan of $400 M. at 7.7 percent with five-year grace periods for general economic restructuring and infrastructure.[99]

The World Bank loan, Conable announced, included provision for additional credits for such purposes as "environment protection within the World Bank's Mediterranean Project." The statement provides an example of the Yugoslavs "successfully translating activity among bilateral, multilateral, and economic arenas of diplomacy. As I have mentioned, Belgrade sought to bridge its relations with Europe and the nonaligned movement.

Yugoslavia's Relations with European States 369

Regular ministerial meetings of the "Mediterranean Non-Aligned Countries" were one example, for they included Cyprus and Malta, along with Arab littoral states, and routinely advanced disarmament and "collective security" proposals for consideration by the Conference on Security and Cooperation in Europe (CSCE). At its third Ministerial Conference in late June 1990, the group noted the "alarming proportions" of recent Mediterranean pollution and affiliated with a CSCE meeting on Mediterranean protection scheduled for the fall in Palma de Majorca.[100] Yugoslavia had been involved with the problems since 1975 when Ambassador Živorad Kovačević chaired the first United Nations Environmental Program (UNEP) for Mediterranean Protection. The 1975 Barcelona meeting adopted the Mediterranean Action Plan (MAP) which included all littoral states except Albania. The four major MAP protocols were supplemented in 1985 by the "Genoa Declaration on the Second Mediterranean Decade," again chaired by Kovačević.[101] As a consequence of the Genoa Declaration, the Prime Ministers of Yugoslavia and Italy signed a joint "Adriatic Initiative" intended to implement specific targets of the MAP.[102]

The agreement with Italy was an example of the general character of Yugoslavia's bilateral relations with West European states. At an earlier time, bilateral relations with most European states had involved major political conflicts with Belgrade, e.g., issues of decolonization in the 1950s and early 1960s with Britain and France, recognition of East Germany in 1958 and a decade-long rupture with the Federal Republic, and, in 1974, the so-called "Zone B" incident concerning the status of the Italian-Slovenian border.[103] From the mid-1970s through 1990, relations had come to embrace a variety of functional, consular, and multilateral issues. Relations between Yugoslavia and individual European states were increasingly rationalized in economic terms and merged with EC relations.

The British Ambassador in Belgrade, Andrew Wood, took pride in the fact that Anglo-Yugoslav trade had tripled between 1982 and 1986, while Britain supported the "Long Term Economic Stabilization Program."[104] As European "partners," Britain would now "play an increasing role" in Yugoslav affairs through the European Community and through British help for the economy's adaptation "to market oriented mechanisms."

Wood's view reflected accurately the priorities of the Thatcher government. In successive meetings with Foreign Minister Gordon Howe and Prime Minister Margaret Thatcher, Yugoslav officials had been encouraged to follow IMF austerity conditions and attain a basis for long-term debt rescheduling.[105] Thatcher, no doubt, might have seemed patronizing to Presidency member Veselin Djuranović. After praising the "more modern approach" to economic questions of the promised reform in 1990, Thatcher expressed her "surprise" that a country "with such human and material potential had been in crisis so long."[106] Like other European states, the

British demanded an account of Yugoslavia's policy in Kosovo, encouraging Yugoslavia to work as a mediator on "North-South" economic issues among the nonaligned, perhaps since the movement included most Commonwealth members.

Apart from the linked questions of economic reform, the Kosovo crisis, and relations with the European Community, Europeans consistently raised the delicate issue of terrorism. The French appear to have been the most concerned. Reportedly after the terrorist Illich Ramirez (Carlos) had killed several French security officials, he obtained safe passage in 1976 through Yugoslavia. A similar opportunity was accorded Mohammed Abbas, who was involved with the 1985 hijacking of the Achille Lauro cruiseship.[107] By the mid-1980s, Yugoslavia's tolerance of terrorists had become too costly, and the policy was abandoned. In July 1986, the French Interior Minister signed an unpublished accord for "new forms of cooperation [with the purpose] of combatting international terrorists."[108] For the first time, the Yugoslav press asserted that Yugoslavia "must try to prevent its territory from becoming a transit route for the movement of terrorists."[109] The result of the agreement apparently satisfied the French, for the same meeting brought promised French cooperation against émigré Yugoslav terrorists, improved social security conditions in France for Yugoslav workers, and promises of expanded scientific cooperation.

In discussing bilateral relations, both French and Yugoslav spokespersons referred to the "special quality" of their historic ties and common ideals.[110] Nevertheless, the French and British pursued similar goals regarding Yugoslavia in the late 1980s, i.e., to promote rapid economic reform, to encourage political liberalization, and to seek Yugoslav mediation among the nonaligned. Late in 1989, French Prime Minister Michel Rocard visited Belgrade, exchanging an earlier trip of Ante Marković to Paris. Rocard encouraged Yugoslavia to seek membership in the Council of Europe, as Marković sought French support in seeking associate membership in the EC.[111] Rocard also brought officials who were interested in specific investment projects, e.g., nuclear power plants, a high-speed TGV train, and an underground metro in Belgrade. A "Mediterranean Cultural Project" to increase tourist facilities in Yugoslavia was broached in the talks as a joint effort with Spain and Italy.

The French were reluctant to loan Yugoslavia additional money until the results of the reform had been established. Rocard spoke of "contradictions" between the economic imperatives of change and "state" institutions of power.[112] The Italian government was more forthcoming. In January 1988, Italian Foreign Ministers Giulio Andreotti and Budimir Lončar signed an accord for $60 million in outright grants and $325 million of credits to finance joint investment projects.[113] The loan was repayable at 1.75 percent over 20 years. The same meeting provided the forum for di-

Yugoslavia's Relations with European States   371

rect talks between Yugoslav industrialists and over 100 Italian businessmen. A new agreement on joint ventures became the occasion for remarks by the President of the Italian economic association *Confindustria*. He praised the new agreement as the "most important agreement since the Osimo Accords," but added somewhat cryptically, "If there is a question mark hanging over the industrial zone in Trieste . . . I am in favor of the two governments discussing alternatives."[114] Precisely what was meant is not obvious, since the status of "Zone B" south of Trieste had been resolved. It is, nevertheless, possible that Croats objected to additional investment in highly developed areas so close to Italy, or that not all Italians were satisfied with the 1975 Osimo Accords. According to the agreement, Rome surrendered any claim to Zone B, whose final status was left unresolved in the 1954 London Agreement. Italian Prime Minister Aldo Moro recognized that Osimo had "resolved multiple problems of cooperation between the two countries."[115]

Other areas of bilateral relations indicated the centrality of the Mediterranean and the Adriatic for the two states. Not surprisingly, permissible fishing harvests were disputed, but more importantly, a series of accords concerned the use of the two seas and port development. During a 1989 visit to Yugoslavia, Italian Foreign Minister Gianni De Michelis coined the phrase "Beyond Osimo" to depict a new level of cooperation. The benefit for Yugoslavia included enthusiastic support for Balkan multilateralism and recognition by the Italians that cooperation was "significant" for Yugoslavia's involvement with the European Community.[116]

With regard to Yugoslavia's leading financial and commercial partner, bilateral relations with Germany were of particular interest. Relations have involved about a half-million Yugoslav workers in the Federal Republic, the issue of indemnity for wartime losses, and about a third of Yugoslavia's foreign tourists.[117] After Chancellor Helmut Kohl's visit to Yugoslavia in mid-1985, German officials stressed support for Yugoslav stability along with closer rapprochement with the EC.[118] An active mixed Yugoslav-German Committee for Economic Cooperation enjoyed co-chairmanship at the cabinet level. Scientific and cultural exchanges were highly developed. In 1990, relations became somewhat strained owing to Germany's attitude towards East European migration. Germany required that all arriving Yugoslavs first acquire visas and banned the activities of Yugoslav parties on German soil.[119] However, concurrently, Yugoslavia ratified a new agreement on the "Mutual Protection and Stimulation of Investments" with Germany. The details of the agreement were intended to guarantee repatriation of profits and indemnification for non-commercial risks.[120] Between 1968 and 1989, some 117 joint ventures had been undertaken, 306 agreements on long-term cooperation, and 282 agreements on technology transfer, and by 1989, the Federal Republic had become

Yugoslavia's largest trade partner with a turnover of 13.4 billion D.M.[121] Understandably, Yugoslav officials were cautious about criticizing possible outcomes after unification. Jović remarked that the change was a "problem for the German people. . . . We have [had] excellent economic and political cooperation with both German states and we want to continue in the same way with the United Germany."[122] German economic interest in Yugoslavia in all likelihood would have declined with the emerging promise of investment elsewhere in Eastern Europe, but, sadly, by mid-1991, the question had become moot.

Yugoslav relations with the European Community were the centerpiece of the efforts to "join Europe." I have mentioned the absence of "consensus" about the future of Yugoslav-European relations without mentioning the attitude of Ante Marković. Marković was careful to avoid the enthusiasm of Drnovšek or unqualified commitments to self-management and nonalignment. Although he refused to consider removing "socialist" from the country's name, the end of East European communism for Marković was, instead, a philosophic matter, i.e., the result of a "natural law." When " . . . these countries were unable to solve the problems brought about by modern development . . . the system was unable to attain an efficient economy and a political democracy. When the system started to disintegrate, logically, because of internal relations . . . the thinking of people must change since those who lived in one system must now live in another."[123]

Thus, it was logical that political opinion should "shift to the right." Marković's interpretation of political change served as the main reason for Yugoslavia to realize membership in the European Community as an "Associate Member" or a full member of EFTA. Each was a "specific and symmetrical form of relations" involving "free trade" and certain mutual protection such as patent policy. In any case, Yugoslavia must not delay because of the danger of capital diversion to other Eastern European states, i e, "a larger number of people is more inconvenient[!]"[124] In short, Yugoslavia would soon confront rivalry from other East European states in attracting Western capital.

The decision of the LCY undertaken in December 1988 to realize associate membership in the EC by 1992 preceded talks between Foreign Minister Lončar and the Greek Foreign Minister, representing the EC and the EC-Yugoslav Council for Cooperation. The talks affirmed Yugoslavia's unique treaty status with the EC, acknowledged the significance of the country's reform efforts and its aspirations for a "market economy and wider inclusion in the contemporary world, and, in particular, the European Community."[125] The EC delegation sought the passage of laws which would make more attractive foreign investment in Yugoslavia and would apply to all republics and provinces.[126] The 1990 agreement with Germany

Yugoslavia's Relations with European States 373

seems to have been approximately the type of law which the EC delegation envisioned. Finally, the EC-Yugoslav talks included major areas of foreign policy, including Middle East peace and North-South economic cooperation. The status of nonalignment and Yugoslav human rights practices, both especially controversial within Yugoslavia, were left unmentioned in the final communique, although a committee was formed the following year to investigate cases of individual human rights abuse.[127]

Reasons for the timing of the EC-Yugoslav talks were not entirely clear, but the progress of the economic reform and the growing volume of trade are plausible explanations. EC-Yugoslav trade had increased consistently, by as much as 17 percent between 1987 and 1988 for a total of 38 percent of all Yugoslav exports.[128] Expansion of Yugoslav-EFTA trade also improved in Yugoslavia's favor; the share of imports covered by exports increased from 34 percent to 57 percent between 1980 and 1985 exclusive of tourism and workers' remittances.[129] During the same period, the overall level of imports fell 20 percent, as did the overall share of Yugoslav exports to developing countries, i.e., from 20.8 percent to 14.5 percent from 1982 to 1987.

These commercial trends coincided with loans from the IMF and other sources for the purpose of restructuring. Initial assistance from the EC was somewhat disappointing. In October 1989, the EC Secretariat announced that Yugoslavia would take part in "Operation Phare," a program intended to promote East European economic transformation. In 1989, a total of 200 million ECU had been appropriated for projects in Hungary and Poland, but of the 300 million ECU set aside for all projects in 1990, Yugoslavia would receive only 35 million ECU mostly for developing revenue collection, banking procedures, and data collection.[130] Likely reservations for the limited EC response include disagreement within Yugoslavia about approaches to privatization, uncertainty about which enterprises to assist or privatize, and, the least likely, EC doubts about the wisdom of assisting a doomed state.

Instead of being reluctant to assist Yugoslavia, the EC signed a protocol in May 1991 for financial assistance for some 730 million ECU shortly before Yugoslavia's crisis would descend into civil war. By mid-1996, the European Investment Bank would have committed 580 million ECU to the construction of the "Trans-Yugoslav Motorway" and rail links connecting north/west and south/east routes from Greece to Austria.[131] The additional 150 million ECU would have been devoted to "industrial, environmental, telecommunication and energy projects." The protocol emphasized the importance of "mutually coordinated measures to develop [Yugoslavia's] transport infrastructure." Unlike potentially divisive assistance to specific projects, the Community evidently wished to offer the republics an incentive to remain together.

The overall economic challenge to Yugoslavia was more complex than enforcing austerity in public expenditure, achieving convertibility of the dinar, and negotiating a treaty with the EC. The core problem remained profitability of many firms, and, more specifically, what Will Bartlett calls a condition of "domestic viability," i.e., a condition in which domestic costs are sufficient to cover fixed costs of production.[132] As long as a firm remains "domestically viable," the depreciation of a currency will increase profitability by shifting resources to exports. But if the firm is not viable, depreciation will not be effective because the firm can reduce employment and cover costs by raising prices at a lower level of output. Macroeconomic trends threatened domestic "viability" owing to depressed consumption standards. Retail sales fell 14 percent between 1980 and 1985; net personal income fell 26 percent and per capita consumption by 11 percent. These trends had cut profitability to a point that some 7000 firms employing 1.6 million people had ceased to be profitable by 1987,[133] and by 1989, despite the efforts of the Marković government, the lack of fiscal and monetary control, hyperinflation, and the dinar's collapse threatened overall viability. To be sure, there had been major gains. Convertibility, along with privatization of ownership, and abolition of import quotas had improved the trade balance, ended inflation, and increased currency reserves.

But by 1991, trends were no longer so promising. Bankruptcy loomed as a commonplace occurrence and production fell. In fact, arguably, the first major economic crisis of 1991 started a process leading directly to secession. In January, the Serbian National bank made an unauthorized loan of more than 18 billion dinars to the Serbian government reportedly for needed imports.[134] The Federal Executive Council immediately suspended foreign currency dealings and sharply criticized the Serbian Bank for threatening the "stability and convertibility of the dinar which are of key importance for preserving the country's unity."[135] The effect of the decision of the Serbian Bank on those republics which earned more foreign currency than they consumed came at a bad time. Slovenia had held a referendum on her future status in Yugoslavia not quite two weeks before the Serbian loan.

The Serbian loan episode precipitated unsuccessful interrepublican talks, but by 1991 the process of "refeudalization" of the economy, as Zagorka Golubović-Pešić calls it, was far advanced.[136] Notwithstanding the respect accorded the Marković government abroad, the government's weakness was apparent. The basic problem arose from the foreign policy consequences of domestic republican decisions. The examples precede Marković's government. In 1988, the Mikulić government had ignored a new set of restrictive demands set by the IMF by providing striking Borovo workers a 70 percent pay increase and a promise none would be discharged.[137] The next year striking miners at Stari Trg in Kosovo broadened wage demands to include reinstatement of the province's ousted political leadership, a de-

Yugoslavia's Relations with European States

mand that the Federation could not satisfy. For many non-Serbs, the strike came to represent Serbia's polarizing repression in Kosovo. The blend of economic and political demands coupled with conflicting republican and federal authority tore at the fabric of consensus in all areas of policy, and foreign economic policy, in particular.

The Collapse of the Federation

I consider that the general Yugoslav crisis by 1988 was one that dwarfed any question of a "Nonaligned" or "Eurocentric" foreign policy. But, the Yugoslav foreign policy establishment perceptively and consistently sought to obtain, through association with Western Europe, certain "payoffs" for republican leaderships in exchange for foreign policy "consensus." Unfortunately, the state of the economy would have required a level of industrial subsidy incompatible with the entire rationale of economic reform and closer integration.

Slovenia's referendum of 23 December 1990, provided the legal basis for the republic's "division" from Yugoslavia after six months of negotiation. The 99th amendment to the Slovenian Republic constitution proclaimed the "permanent and inalienable right of the Slovene people to self-determination."[138] Just prior to the failure of interrepublican talks and the amendment, the European Commission adopted its first statement on the Yugoslav crisis promising to "closely watch developments" in the country and support for "unity, territorial integrity and need for dialogue . . . [that will] facilitate establishing a new Yugoslavia on the basis of freedom and democracy."[139] In the meantime, all parties should "intensify their efforts" on behalf of a "peaceful and democratic resolution" and "carefully avoid" the use of force. The EC statement called for a settlement on the basis of the Paris Charter of the Conference on Security and Cooperation in Europe (ECSC). Thirty-four countries, including Yugoslavia, had endorsed this eloquent document in November 1990.[140] Ironically its affirmation of human rights, economic liberty and peaceful relations would be invoked by all sides, as well as by the EC during Yugoslavia's crisis. Unfortunately, the ECSC, as the Paris Charter itself, lacked an effective mechanism to enforce its affirmation of common values in a "post cold war" European order. Surely nothing in the Charter was inimical to self-determination. The principles of independence could be justified as Croatian President Tudjman had, by references to the American Declaration of Independence, or as Slovenian President Kučan had by reference to the Helsinki Final Act. The Slovenian President expressed himself as if it were a self-evident proposition for the Republic "to enter Europe in a European manner [assuming] democracy, respect for the rights and interests of others, and peace."[141]

376   Zachary T. Irwin

In February 1991, Secretary Lončar attended the Council of Europe meeting in Madrid, acknowledging the members' "common concern."[142] Initially, no member of the European Community was willing to undermine a common stance in support of an integral Yugoslavia. Thus, Slovenian Prime Minister Lojze Peterle traveling in the Benelux region was unable to win an official reception or breach the community's "conservative" attitude.[143] Croatia's President Tudjman appeared somewhat more successful in Austria. Although no elected official received Tudjman, he could claim Austria's support for a "democratic resolution of the political crisis."[144] Otherwise, the international response was unanimously opposed to recognition of the republics. Lončar met with republican foreign policy officials in early March 1991 in what was probably the last such meeting. He reminded them that during the "transitional period of [interrepublican] negotiation," Yugoslavia's priority goal remained securing support for economic reform through the "coordination and mutual responsibility . . . of all entities that make up our complex community."[145] Events would belie Lončar's request that republican officials avoid "negative descriptions" of the situation.

In March 1991, the first phase of the war started in Croatia when Serbs seized control of a police station in the town of Pakrac. Although cooperation between local police and federal troops prevented immediate escalation of the incident, Pakrac, like other towns in Croatia, became a center of Serbian insurgency. Elsewhere, in a village north of Split, Serbs blockaded an area, while Croatians demonstrated against the failure of the armed forces to support the police. Instead, the Army warned that it would take action unless martial law were declared throughout Croatia.[146] The presidency deadlocked on the measure. After the announcement of future independence referenda in Slovenia and Croatia, Serbs in the Krajina declared a "Serbian Autonomous region"; "Serbian People's Assemblies" organized in Slavonia, Baranja and Srem.[147] The resignation of President Jović in mid-March left the Presidency paralyzed.[148]

The escalating violence did not elicit a forceful European response. The Commission affirmed Slovenia's self-determination "in a peaceful and democratic manner." A mid-May 1991 statement suggested the dilemma. "While reiterating the preference of the European Community and the international community more generally for the maintenance of one federal Yugoslavia, [the EC] insists that this cannot and must not be seen as a willingness to countenance the suppression of democracy and human rights."[149] The statement could alternatively justify the proclamation of local "Peoples' Assemblies" in Serbian populated areas of Croatia, holding referenda for the secession of Slovenia and Croatia, as well as an EC-monitored ceasefire between these republics and the federal army. A critical view could argue that such EC temporizing only served to promote greater violence.

Conversely, the Community had not intended to enforce the principles it espoused, and were it to attempt to do so, Community members could not have agreed on the intrinsic merits of either federation or secession.

The armed forces moved against Slovenia on the grounds that its alteration of the Republic's boundaries, i.e., declaring sovereignty, constituted an unconstitutional and unilateral act. The EC Council of Ministers promptly dispatched the foreign ministers of Luxembourg, the Netherlands, and Italy to mediate, while Italy and Austria proposed bringing the crisis before the ECSC secretariat in Prague. Since Jović's resignation, Yugoslavia had been without a head of state because of Serbian opposition to the supposedly routine election of the Croatian Stipe Mesić. As negotiations progressed, the Slovenes agreed to suspend, but not repeal, their declaration of independence for several months and retain control of the border crossings, but not the disposition of the customs levies. Serbia would withdraw its opposition to Mesić, and Yugoslav forces would return to their barracks. The resulting "Brioni Resolution" endorsed the right of self- determination, army withdrawal, civilian control of the armed forces, and negotiations about Yugoslavia's future.[150] Despite European efforts, their involvement may not have been decisive. The army was at first inexperienced, confronted a hostile population, and suffered morale problems. Geography favored the Slovenes, for supply lines through Croatia were hard to maintain. Meanwhile events in Croatia recommended against further involvement in Slovenia, for the armed forces could not both defend Serbian autonomy in Croatia and occupy territory in Slovenia. In Belgrade itself, war with Slovenia was unpopular.

In July large-scale violence broke out in Croatia, as well-armed Serbian militias began to seize control of portions of that republic, destroying villages and towns and driving indigenous Croats out. Backed by the supposedly neutral JNA, these militias laid siege to Osijek and Vinkovci, took control of Petrinja, and completely destroyed the once-bustling town of Vukovar (pre-war population, about 45–50,000). By October 1991, the Serbian insurgents controlled about 30 percent of Croatia's territory.[151]

By then it seemed clear to many that Serbia's generals under Chief of Staff Blagoje Adžić intended to annex outright parts of Croatia.[152] Some voices spoke of Zadar and Dubrovnik as "Serbian" towns, and the ports of Zadar and Dubrovnik were shelled despite the absence of local Serbs to hold them. With the expiration of the three-month suspension of independence on 7 October, Croatia and Slovenia asserted their complete separation from the old Yugoslavia. The EC Hague Declaration threatened sanctions against Serbia should it attempt to annex parts of Croatia, or against any republic found violating the flimsy cease-fire. Lord Carrington's efforts to bring about a cease-fire included attempts to win endorsement of a "loose association of sovereign republics," no internal border adjustments, a "Court of Appeal" for human rights, within each republic, and a new arrangement between Serbia and the Autonomous Provinces.[153] Ultimately by the year's end, thousands of dead, more than a half-million refugees, and vast destruction brought only limited sanctions (an arms embargo) against all the Yugoslav successor states without distinction, as well as German, and shortly Community, recognition of Croatia and Slovenia.

From the time civil war had started in Croatia, there had been more agreement on what not to do than what measures were best. As Christopher Cviić from *The Economist* explained in mid-October, "The Germans and Danes wanted to recognize Croatia and Slovenia. The French have been reluctant to do that, but have suggested sending a large peace-keeping force. The British are against recognition or intervention. The Italians still hope the various republics will agree to form a loose new confederation."[154] In fact, a closer look at debates in the European parliament revealed a fragmented political spectrum about Yugoslavia's future.

Critics of European efforts to stop the Yugoslav Civil War are understandably impatient in view of the enthusiastic claims on behalf of a common European identity. However, it is useful to remember that the EC "troika" and Lord Carrington's efforts were constrained not only by the intransigence of the combatants and disagreements among EC members, but also by partisan differences within the Community itself. Commission and Council activity regarding Yugoslavia confronted disagreements within the European parliament both about peacemaking strategy and the desirability of Yugoslavia itself. Generally, the West was sympathetic to Croatia and Slovenia. A member of Jean Marie LePen's "National Front" dismissed the EC's "disastrous policy" and "complete lack of understanding . . . There was no awareness of the generous desire for independence of those two peoples [Slovenes and Croats]."[155] Instead, the EC had implicitly encouraged the "federalist and cosmopolitan excess" of communist Serbia. Speaking for the Liberal, Democratic and Reformist Group, Giscard D'Estaing also rejected the EC's "false priority" of unity but demanded action in support for a "clear statement to the effect that we shall not accept the use of force to resolve political problems arising in Europe."[156] A French Socialist insisted on the goal of a new Yugoslavia bound by "cooperative sovereignty leading later to associational sovereignty including a necessary pooling by the liberated republics of all elements of their sovereignty that none of them [i.e. the republics] can exercise alone. . . ."[157] The effect of such division was to produce a distinct resolution for each of nine separately organized political groups within the Parliament.[158]

Yugoslavia's Relations with European States

Conclusion

The effect of Europe's indecision and America's inaction shifted the locus of diplomatic activity to the United Nations. Several months after a painfully negotiated ceasefire in Croatia in January 1992, war began in Bosnia between Serbian forces and Bosnian government forces. By September, Serbian units controlled about 2/3 of Bosnian territory; major cities were subject to siege or blockade, and all sides routinely flouted a United Nations resolution demanding a "no-fly zone" over Bosnia.[159] Reports of systematic rape, terroristic "ethnic cleansing," and other atrocities brought Acting Secretary of State Lawrence Eagleburger to accuse President Milošević and Radovan Karadžić, Bosnia's Serbian leader, of complicity in war crimes.[160] By February 1993, the government in Sarajevo claimed that in that city alone more than 8,000 had died as a result of the siege and about 63,000 were wounded.[161] Serbian objectives in Bosnia appeared to center on territorial enclaves and establishing a corridor in northern Bosnia connecting Serbia proper and Serbian inhabited parts of the Republic of Croatia.[162]

As destruction continued in Bosnia-Herzegovina, the United Nations sponsored ceasefire in Croatia collapsed, threatening a renewed war between Serbia and Croatia. The 1992 agreement left about a third of Croatia's territory in control of indigenous Serbs, while four demilitarized zones were patrolled by a 23,000-man United Nations force. In the opinion of the *Economist*'s correspondent, the arrangement represented "temporary Serb and UN occupancy" of Croatian territory from Zagreb's viewpoint, but for Croatia's Serbs it marked the "frontier of a self-proclaimed republic."[163] On 22 January 1993, Croatia's army advanced south of the Krajina region, known as the "pink zone," including a strategic airport and a bridge connecting the city of Zadar and the Croatian mainland. As of mid-February, fighting continued sporadically. Serbs in Krajina demanded recognition of their "republic," while Croatia sought to reassert authority. The event suggests some generalizations for peace throughout the Balkans. Establishing peace requires an unambiguous military ceasefire attentive to antagonistic territorial objectives; an enlarged mandate for United Nations forces must extend beyond truce supervision and redefine the "rules of engagement"; and settlement in one theater of conflict requires the clear support of neighboring regimes. Arguably, only the logistics of supply through Bosnia has prevented a full scale war between Croatia and Serbia-Montenegro.

The example of the unstable truce in Croatia provides points of contrast with the objectives of peacemakers in Bosnia. Early in January 1993, the conference on Bosnia opened in Geneva following talks between President Milošević and the team of Cyrus Vance and Lord David Owen, representing respectively the United Nations and the European Community.

380   Zachary T. Irwin

Attention centered on the "Vance-Owen plan" consisting of provisions for ceasefire and disengagement, a statement on Bosnia's future constitutional and political principles, and a map delineating the republic's ten autonomous cantons.[164] Although nine of the cantons would be designated as Serb, Muslim, or Croat, the cantons were not intended to be homogenous. Sarajevo and its hinterlands (the tenth canton) would remain an "open" and demilitarized city. Key provisions included the diplomatic recognition of Bosnia by Serbia-Montenegro and Croatia, as well as the significant provision that the cantons "shall not have any legal personality and may not enter into agreements with foreign states."[165] Criticism of the plan concerns whether or not such provisions are enforceable, whether the plan legitimized "ethnic cleansing," and the tenuous relation of Sarajevo with the cantons and their interconnection by UN patrolled "thoroughfares."[166] As of late February, only Bosnia's Croat representatives had accepted all parts of the plan; Serbs rejected certain aspects of the map, and Muslims had rejected both the map and the ceasefire provisions. In early February, the talks moved to New York under the supervision of the Security Council. But on 4 March, Radovan Karadžić rejected the plan altogether, on behalf of the Serbs.

Following the European Community's "full and unqualified support" for the plan and Lord Owen's criticism of American reluctance, pressure intensified on the Clinton administration to declare its support.[167] Secretary of State Warren Christopher enunciated six points that qualified American involvement: appointment of special envoy Reginald Bartholemew; that sanctions against Serbia-Montenegro be tightened; that a war crimes tribunal be created; an offer of American forces for United Nations' purposes; and a pledge of cooperation with Russia, "our ally."[168] At this time, it cannot be said whether American support can promote agreement, much less an enforceable settlement. Apparently, the statement qualified certain aspects of the plan favored by Sarajevo, while dispelling lingering hopes that the United States would furnish arms to the Muslims.

Secretary of State Christopher's solicitous attitude towards Russia may help the Russian Foreign Minister Andrei Kozyrev to deal with opponents to his support for the embargo against Serbia-Montenegro. Russian involvement in efforts to settle the war are certain. Kozyrev appointed his special envoy to the talks and implicitly warned that an effective embargo required Russian support, i.e., that "any actions" involving Western ships in the "Black Sea or adjacent Danube basin" be approved by Moscow in advance.[169] In mid-February 1993, the Russian Parliament voted 162-4 in support of a resolution demanding sanctions on Croatia and their removal from Serbia-Montenegro.[170] Should President Boris Yeltsin be removed or his influence weakened, his primary rival, the parliamentary speaker, would be an unlikely partner with the United States and Western Europe. Sanc-

Yugoslavia's Relations with European States 381

tions' enforcement is a basic condition of diplomatic cooperation in the Balkans. In late January, the Security Council formally urged Bulgaria, Romania, and Ukraine to respect the embargo and especially that Sofia and Bucharest intercept vessels carrying oil to Serbia on the Danube.[171] The countries met on 18 February to coordinate cooperation.

An effective regime of sanctions implied that Serbia's fighting ability could be crippled by material deprivation, diplomatic isolation, and possibly domestic opposition. The question of sanctions is controversial and, at the least, demands careful qualification about the length of time effective sanctions require. In any case, many feared that a ceasefire in Bosnia would occasion new fighting in Kosovo. President Bush warned Milošević explicitly: "In the event of conflict in Kosovo caused by Serbian action, the United States will be prepared to employ military force against the Serbians in Kosovo and Serbia proper."[172] The danger, among others, was that widespread fighting in Kosovo would involve Albanians in both Macedonia and Albania proper. A Turkish alliance with Albania could lead to war with Serbia and a Greek attack on Turkey.[173] Active Turkish diplomacy sought support for Albania and Macedonia. On 14 February 1993, Bulgarian President Zhelev and Albanian President Berisha signed a treaty of cooperation; on the same day, Greece and Romania signed a similar accord.[174]

It is both tempting and premature to speculate about future developments in the Balkans. However, in my judgment an independent and internationally recognized Macedonia is central to regional security. Such a state limits the effects of aspirations for territorial redivision and war. Unlike the territory of Kosovo, Macedonia's independence has permitted the stationing of a contingent of United Nations forces and observers from the CSCE. The presence of the UN and CSCE is intended to promote peaceful relations between Slavs and Albanians, while insuring that diplomatic nonrecognition does not marginalize Macedonia's security. As of early 1993, the issue of Greek opposition to the name "Macedonia" still obstructed EC recognition. A mutually acceptable accord was jeopardized by vigorous nationalist opposition both in Greece and Macedonia, as well as by the sudden resignation of the Macedonian Foreign Minister.

What are we to decide about Yugoslavia's relations with Europe? I consider it important to recognize the flexibility and perceptive understanding that federal officials have shown Yugoslavia so that it might adjust its place in Western, Central, and Southeastern Europe with the changing post-1988 situation.

More than twenty years ago, Wolfram Hanrieder proposed two concepts for foreign policy analysis, which, I believe, provide greater descriptive refinement for Yugoslavia's situation than any version of "linkages." Hanrieder proposed to relate the external and internal dimensions of foreign policy through the concepts of "compatibility" and "consensus." The former "is intended to assess the degree of feasibility of various foreign policy goals, given the structures and opportunities of the *international* system; ["consensus"] . . . assesses the measure of agreement on the ends and means of foreign policy on the *domestic* scene."[175] The concepts offer certain advantages. First, they help explain the changes Yugoslavia confronted after 1987. "Compatibility" highlights the altered international system created by the dispersal of Soviet power in East Europe and the rapprochement between Moscow and Washington. As these changes devalued the diplomatic significance of nonalignment, Yugoslavia placed priority on relations with Europe but did not enjoy its earlier advantages as a nonaligned leader. The problem of "compatibility" between the altered international environment and traditional Yugoslav thinking created problems of "consensus" in foreign policy. Second, bilateral relations with European states became subordinate to multilateral goals. The change raised problems of "consensus" because of differing perceptions of "compatibility" among domestic actors.

The EC's sympathetic response to this adaptive process does not alter Yugoslavia's consistent level of energy and imagination in framing a conceptual basis "compatible" with the international environment in Hanrieder's sense. Unfortunately, the question of "consensus" in Yugoslav foreign policy was undermined fundamentally in two ways. Elected leaderships in Slovenia and Croatia insisted on notions of republican sovereignty incompatible with a strong federal policy necessary for "compatibility" with Europe. Quite apart from disagreements about the place of nationality, e.g., Macedonia, in foreign policy, the "confederal" Yugoslavia envisioned by some would have made impossible the type of decisions necessary. Second, consensus was undermined by the debate about "nonalignment" before 1990. In fact, the debate, I believe, did not concern the nonaligned movement as much as Yugoslavia's position outside of the EC. For certain republics, e.g., Montenegro, whose foreign trade was highly dependent on Eastern Europe and the former U.S.S.R., the reforms implied by "Associate Membership" in the EC struck at their industrial basis and their local political structure by threatening economic insolvency. Only the fall of communism made such change inevitable, and it was hardly welcomed.

A second conclusion about the future of the post-communist Balkans is in order, however risky. At the time of writing, the tragedy of the Serbian government's aggression in Bosnia-Herzegovina threatens to traumatize generations of the area's peoples as surely as the genocidal slaughter of Serbs by Nazis and the Ustasha during World War Two. The outcome of this violence is difficult to predict. I believe that independent post-Yugoslav states will inherit none of the advantages in foreign policy enjoyed by the former Yugoslavia. As the 1991 EC-Yugoslav Agreement on Transportation demonstrated, federal Yugoslavia enjoyed important geopolitical advantages that could have substituted for its lost geopolitical status during the Cold War. Republican officials have referred to the geopolitics of their states as though it could be an intact inheritance. I do not think so. Serbia's hostility towards Hungary and Austria, as well as the attitude of Croatia towards Italy, are not encouraging. No matter how few or numerous are the Slovenes and Croats in Austria and Italy, or Hungarians in Vojvodina, and Albanians in Kosovo, they are likely to occasion future and continuing conflict.

The problem of nationality relations highlights a deeper deficiency of political legitimacy. In the absence of established procedural traditions for democracy or confidence in their outcome, symbolic claims on behalf of identity fill a political void. The region demonstrates several patterns. First, some leaderships, including Serbs and Croats, depict their nation as a historical victim. Recently, certain Hungarian politicians have attacked the 1920 Treaty of Trianon. Second, certain leaders find support in warning about a specific enemy. The opposition party Macedonian Internal Revolutionary Organization (VMRO) has sponsored demonstrations against Muslim refugees in that country. Third, in extreme cases (Krajina and Kosovo), a national group may declare its own "republic."

Politically the results are less obvious. Despite resistance to the war and to Milošević in Serbia, the Serbian opposition has had little apparent impact on the war. Serbian forces have flouted negotiated ceasefires, international law, and Security Council Resolutions. Neither the United Nations, nor NATO, nor European forces have been willing to guarantee the security of food deliveries to Sarajevo or the enforcement of the "no-fly zone" over Bosnia. Many have come to question the value of the arms embargo or the presence of UN truce supervision in Croatia. And, for that matter, it is uncertain how much longer the war may be contained. The presence of some hundreds of Arab volunteer soldiers in Bosnia,[176] understates the threat of a religious dimension to Balkan conflict. The dimensions of the tragedy will extend to those who seek redemption or revenge through "ethnic cleansing" or territorial division. No other issue represents as great a challenge to cooperation between European governments and the new American administration.

Notes

1. The author wishes to thank Sabrina Ramet, Monica Irwin, and Wendy Eidenmuller for their patient, helpful comments with the manuscript. The assistance of reference librarians Patty Mrozowski, Helen Sheehy and Margaret Smith was no less valuable.

384   *Zachary T. Irwin*

2. Unless qualified, "Yugoslavia" refers to the Socialist Federated Republic of Yugoslavia.

3. Sabrina P. Ramet, "The Breakup of Yugoslavia," in *Global Affairs*, Vol. 6, No. 1 (Spring 1991), pp. 93–110; Dennison Rusinow, "Yugoslavia-Balkan Breakup?" in *Foreign Policy*, No. 83 (Summer 1991), pp. 143–159; Christopher Cviić, "Yugoslavia I: New Shapes from Old," in *The World Today* Vol. 47, Nos. 8–9 (August/September 1991), pp. 125–127; and Michele Ledic, "Yugoslavia II: the Costs of Divorce," in *The World Today*, Vol. 47, Nos. 8–9 (August/September 1991), pp. 126–129.

4. For excellent examples of this question, see William Zimmerman, "Issue Area and Foreign Policy Process: A Research Note in Search of a General Theory," in *American Political Science Review*, Vol. 67, No. 4 (December 1973), pp. 1204–1213; and William Zimmerman, *Open Borders, Nonalignment, and the Political Evolution of Yugoslavia*, (Princeton, NJ: Princeton University Press, 1987).

5. Bogdan Denitch, *Limits and Possibilities: The Crisis of Yugoslav Socialism and State Socialist Systems*, (Minneapolis: University of Minnesota Press, 1990), p. 94. Milan Sahović writes, "The sharp criticism of Yugoslavia's non-aligned policy voiced during recent years is mainly to the effect that the country's state interests have been subordinated to the global interests of nonalignment, this resulting in neglect of neighborly relations and Balkan cooperation, the minority question, interests in Europe, especially cooperation with the Common Market." See Sahović, "The Question of Continuity in Yugoslav Foreign Policy," in *Review of International Affairs* (Belgrade), No. 970, (September 5, 1990), p. 14.

6. Budimir Lončar, "Yugoslavia and the World," in *Review of International Affairs* (Belgrade), No. 956, 5 February 1990, p. 4.

7. Ranko Petković, "Requiem for the Warsaw Treaty and NATO," in *Review of International Affairs*, No. 954, (5 January 1990), p. 10.

8. For a discussion of the general problem of "Yalta" among East European intellectuals, see Ferenc Feher, "East Europe's Long Revolution Against Yalta," in *East European Politics and Societies* Vol. 2, No. 1 (Winter 1988), p. 8. See also the remarks of former Foreign Minister Josip Vrhovec about the danger of the Balkans becoming "a special 'grey zone' in which foreign countries would try to demonstrate their presence," in *Borba* (Belgrade), 1 November 1979, p. 7.

9. *Borba* (14–15 November 1987), p. 13, trans. in FBIS *Daily Report* (Eastern Europe), 23 November 1987, p. 43.

10. Aleksandar Sekulović, "Jugoslavija i evropska zajednica," in *Socijalizam* Vol. 32, Nos. 9–10 (July-August 1989), p. 66.

11. Robin Alison Remington, "Foreign Policy," in Dennison Rusinow (ed.), *Yugoslavia: A Fractured Federalism*, (Washington, DC: The Wilson Center Press, 1988), p. 161–166.

12. Tanjug, (11 January 1991), trans. in FBIS, *Daily Report* (Eastern Europe), 14 January 1991, p. 55.

13. *Borba* (23–24 June 1990), pp. 1, 4–6, 10, trans. in FBIS, *Daily Report* (Eastern Europe), 5 July 1990, p. 86.

14. For a list of 135 treaties that bind Council members and those three of which Yugoslavia is a member, see *European Yearbook/Annuaire European, 1989*, Vol. 37 (Dordrecht: Martinus Nijhoff, 1991), pp. 81–86.

Yugoslavia's Relations with European States

15. Tanjug (12 September 1987), trans. in FBIS *Daily Report* (Eastern Europe), 15 September 1987, p. 35.

16. Aleksandar Simović, "New Dynamics of Yugoslav Foreign Policy," in *Review of International Affairs*, No. 973 (20 October 1990), p. 21.

17. "Yugoslavia"(special supplement), *Euromoney* (London), September 1990, p.8.

18. *Ibid*, emphasis in original.

19. This and the following information is from "Yugoslavia," *Business International: Doing Business with Eastern Europe*, No. 112, 1990, pp. 1–10.

20. *Ibid*.

21. *Statistički Godišnjak Jugoslavije 1990*, v. 37 (Belgrade: Savezni zavod za statistiku, 1990), p. 131.

22. "Foreigners in Germany," in *Focus on Germany* (New York: German Information Center), November 1991, p. 3.

23. "Yugoslavia" (Special supplement), *Euromoney* (London), September 1990, p. 3.

24. Tanjug (9 March 1991), trans. in FBIS *Daily Report* (Eastern Europe), 11 March 1991, p. 54.

25. Tanjug (31 January 1988), trans. in FBIS *Daily Report* (Eastern Europe), 1 February 1988, p. 39.

26. ATA (Tirana), (30 August 1987), trans. in FBIS *Daily Report* (Eastern Europe), 1 September 1987, p. 3.

27. *Rilindja* (Priština), (27 December 1987), p. 7, trans. in FBIS, *Daily Report* (Eastern Europe), 6 January 1988, p. 56.

28. *Borba* (6–7 May 1989), p. 4 trans. in FBIS *Daily Report* (Eastern Europe), 12 May 1989, p. 54.

29. Alex N. Dragnich and Slavko Todorovich, *The Saga of Kosovo: Focus on Serbian-Albanian Relations*, (Boulder, CO: East European Monographs, 1984), pp. 4–45.

30. Tanjug (28 June 1989), trans. in FBIS *Daily Report* (Eastern Europe), 29 June 1989, p. 62.

31. "Documentation," in *Review of International Affairs*, No. 910, (5 March 1988), p. 19.

32. The data is drawn from *Statistički Godišnjak Jugoslavije 1990*, v. 37, (Belgrade: Savezni zavod za statistiku, 1990), pp. 129, 441, and "The National Composition of Yugoslavia's Population," *Yugoslav Survey*, No. 1, 1992, p. 11.

33. Elez Biberaj, "Albanian-Yugoslav Relations and the Question of Kosovë," in *East European Quarterly*, Vol. 16, No. 4, (January 1983), pp. 485–510.

34. Jens Reuter, *Die Albaner in Jugoslawien* (Munich: R. Oldenbourg Verlag, 1982), as cited in Sabrina P. Ramet, *Social Currents in Eastern Europe: The Sources and Meaning of the Great Transformation* (Durham: Duke University Press, 1991), p. 177.

35. AFP (Paris) (1 June 1989), trans. in FBIS, *Daily Report* (Eastern Europe), 2 June 1989, p. 63.

36. ATA (17 November 1985), trans. in FBIS *Daily Report* (Eastern Europe), 18 November 1985, p. B1 and Tanjug (23 November 1985), trans. in FBIS *Daily Report* (Eastern Europe), 25 November 1985, p. B4.

37. Ranko Petković, "Jugoslavija i Albanija," in *Socijalizam* Vol. 32, No. 3 (March 1989), p. 105.

38. ATA (20 May 1989), trans. in FBIS *Daily Report* (Eastern Europe), 22 May 1989, p. 3.

386   Zachary T. Irwin

39. Tanjug (29 June 1989), trans. in FBIS *Daily Report* (Eastern Europe), 30 June 1989, p. 66.

40. Tanjug (6 May 1989), trans. in FBIS *Daily Report* (Eastern Europe), 8 May 1989, p. 55.

41. Agerpress (Bucharest), (13 December 1985), trans. in FBIS, *Daily Report* (Eastern Europe), 16 December 1985, p. I3.

42. *Ibid.*

43. Belgrade Domestic Service, (15 December 1985), trans. in FBIS, *Daily Report* (Eastern Europe), 16 December 1985, p. I10.

44. *Politika* (Belgrade), (18 December 1987), p. 3, trans. in FBIS, *Daily Report* (Eastern Europe), 6 January 1988, p. 48.

45. Tanjug (5 May 1990), trans. in FBIS *Daily Report* (Eastern Europe), 10 May 1990, p. 74.

46. Milan Andrejevich, "Illiescu's Visit: The Issue of Romania's Minorities," in *RFE Research* (21 September 1990), pp. 29–31.

47. Alan J. Day (ed.), *Border and Territorial Disputes*, (Essex: Longmans, 1987), pp. 79-84. Other works include Elisabeth Barker, *Macedonia: Its Place in Balkan Power Politics*, (London: Royal Institute of International Affairs, 1950); and Robert R. King and Stephen E. Palmer, *Yugoslav Communism and the Macedonian Question* (Hamden, CT: Archon Books, 1971).

48. BTA (29 October 1988), trans. in FBIS *Daily Report* (Eastern Europe), 28 October 1988, p. 6; BTA (6 May 1989), trans. in FBIS, *Daily Report* (Eastern Europe), 16 May 1989, p. 10; and BTA (20 June 1989), trans. in FBIS, *Daily Report* (Eastern Europe), 27 June 1989, p. 74.

49. Tanjug (30 May 1990), trans. in FBIS, *Daily Report* (Eastern Europe), 1 June 1990, p. 56.

50. Tanjug (6 February 1989), trans. in FBIS, *Daily Report* (Eastern Europe), 8 February 1989, p. 76.

51. BTA (15 June 1989), trans. in FBIS, *Daily Report* (Eastern Europe), 16 June 1989, p. 13.

52. *Politika* (19 June 1986), p. 4, trans. in FBIS *Daily Report* (Eastern Europe), 19 June 1986, p. I3.

53. Tanjug (23 May 1990), trans. in FBIS, *Daily Report* (Eastern Europe), 1 June 1990, p. 57.

54. *Borba* (30 May 1990), p. 4, trans. in FBIS, *Daily Report* (Eastern Europe), 5 June 1990, p. 92.

55. BTA (9 June 1990), trans. in FBIS, *Daily Report* (Eastern Europe), 19 June 1990, p. 15.

56. *Borba* (12 June 1990), trans. in FBIS, *Daily Report* (Eastern Europe), 20 June 1990, p. 62.

57. Tanjug (16 January 1991), trans. in FBIS, *Daily Report* (Eastern Europe), 17 January 1991, p. 43.

58. Radio Belgrade (17 January 1986), trans. in FBIS, *Daily Report* (Eastern Europe), 21 January 1986, p. I6.

59. *Ibid.*; and Tanjug (29 August 1988), trans. in FBIS, *Daily Report* (Eastern Europe) 30 August 1988, p. 70.

Yugoslavia's Relations with European States   387

60. Tanjug (19 October 1987), trans. in FBIS, *Daily Report* (Eastern Europe), 21 October 1987, p. 51.

61. A background of the Slovene question from the Yugoslav viewpoint is provided in Bogdan Osolnik (ed.), *Problem manjina u jugoslovensko-austrijskim odnosima* (Belgrade 1977). Also Thomas M. Barker, *The Slovene Minority of Carinthia* (Boulder, CO: East European Monographs, 1984).

62. For example, *Borba's* treatment of the Waldheim incident spoke about Austria's wish to "rehabilitate" the past and its reaction to "interference" from abroad. The extraordinary work by historian Dušan Plenca in establishing Waldheim's guilt was reported first by Swedish radio, not by the Yugoslav media. See *Borba* (14–15 June 1986), p. 13, trans. in FBIS, *Daily Report* (Eastern Europe), 19 June 1986, p. I4; and Stockholm Domestic Service (31 January 1987), trans. in FBIS, *Daily Report* (Eastern Europe), 1 February 1988, p. 39.

63. MTI (6 December 1985), trans. in FBIS, *Daily Report* (Eastern Europe), 9 December 1985, p. F1.

64. Tanjug (24 May 1989), trans. in FBIS, *Daily Report* (Eastern Europe), 25 May 1989, p. 41.

65. Tanjug (11 December 1985), trans. in FBIS, *Daily Report* (Eastern Europe), 12 December 1985, p. I1.

66. Tanjug (24 May 1989), trans. in FBIS, *Daily Report* (Eastern Europe), 25 May 1989, p. 41.

67. MTI (30 January 1991), trans. in FBIS, *Daily Report* (Eastern Europe), 1 February 1991, p. 23, and *Nepszabadsag*, (Budapest) 20 March 1991, trans. in FBIS, *Daily Report* (Eastern Europe), 26 March 1991, p. 52.

68. For background to Antall's remarks, see Patrick Moore, "Yugoslavia's Neighbors and the Crisis," in *Radio Free Europe Research*, (9 August 1991), p. 47.

69. MTI (25 July 1990), trans. in FBIS, *Daily Report* (Eastern Europe), 25 July 1990, p. 40.

70. Vienna Domestic Service (6 May 1991), trans. in FBIS, *Daily Report* (Eastern Europe), 7 May 1991, p. 2.

71. *Die Presse* (Vienna) (14 March 1991), p. 4, trans. in FBIS, *Daily Report* (Eastern Europe), 15 March 1991, p. 3.

72. Radovan Vukadinović, "Jugoslavensko-austrijski odnosi: od napetnosti do razumijevanja," in *Politička misao*, Vol. 36, No.4, (1989), pp. 125–126.

73. Tanjug (19 November 1987), trans. in FBIS, *Daily Report* (Eastern Europe), 20 November 1987, p. 41.

74. Tanjug (29 January 1988), trans. in FBIS, *Daily Report* (Eastern Europe), 1 February 1988, p. 41.

75. *Politika* (22 December 1987), p. 2, trans. in FBIS, *Daily Report* (Eastern Europe), 6 January 1988, p. 54.

76. Belgrade Domestic Service (19 June 1990), trans. in FBIS, *Daily Report* (Eastern Europe), 20 June 1990, p. 61.

77. *Borba* (30 March 1990), p. 15, trans. in FBIS, *Daily Report* (Eastern Europe), 4 May 1990, p. 71.

78. Tanjug (2 May 1990), trans. in FBIS, *Daily Report* (Eastern Europe), 3 May 1990, p. 63.

388   Zachary T. Irwin

79. Tanjug (8 May 1990), trans. in FBIS, *Daily Report* (Eastern Europe), 9 May 1990, p. 58.

80. Tanjug (14 May 1990), trans. in FBIS, *Daily Report* (Eastern Europe), 15 May 1990, p. 78.

81. Sekulović, "Jugoslavija i evropska zajednica" [note 10], p. 65.

82. Tanjug (14 May 1990), trans. in FBIS, *Daily Report* (Eastern Europe), 15 May 1990, p. 78.

83. *Borba* (11 June 1990), p. 5, trans. in FBIS, *Daily Report* (Eastern Europe), 27 June 1990, p. 68.

84. *Danas* (Zagreb) 1 May 1990, trans. in FBIS, *Daily Report* (Eastern Europe), 7 May 1990, p. 67.

85. *Vjesnik* (Zagreb), 29/30 April-1 May 1990, p. 7, trans. in FBIS, *Daily Report* (Eastern Europe), 8 May 1990, p. 57.

86. *Ibid.*, p. 56.

87. For background material on the Alps-Adriatic Work Community, see Patrick Moore, "New Dimensions for the Alpine-Adria Project," in Radio Free Europe, *Report on Eastern Europe*, (2 March 1990), pp. 53–56.

88. Tanjug (4 May 1990), trans. in FBIS, *Daily Report* (Eastern Europe), 7 May 1990, p. 67. For the Czechoslovak reaction to Yugoslavia's crisis, see Jan Obrman, "Yugoslav Crisis Has Little Impact on Czechoslovak Domestic Policy," in *Radio Free Europe Research*, (9 August 1991), pp. 29–34.

89. Alfred A. Reisch, "Hungary's Policy on the Yugoslav Conflict: A Delicate Balance," in *Ibid*, (9 August 1991), pp. 34–43.

90. *Borba*, (10 May 1990), p. 5, trans. in FBIS, *Daily Report* (Eastern Europe), 11 May 1990, p. 49.

91. Tanjug (4 July 1991), trans. in FBIS, *Daily Report* (Eastern Europe), 5 July 1991, p. 27.

92. *NIN* (22 February 1991), pp. 100, 111, trans. in FBIS, *Daily Report* (Eastern Europe), 7 March 1991, p. 39.

93. Vera Rich, "The Future of the Danube," in *The World Today*, Vol. 47, Nos. 8–9 (August–September 1991), pp. 142–144.

94. "Third Ministerial Conference of the Mediterranean Non-Aligned Countries," in *Review of International Affairs*, No. 966–967 (5 July 1990), p. 17.

95. Franz Vranitzky, "Pentagonale," in *Review of International Affairs*, No. 977 (20 December 1990), p. 2.

96. Tanjug (31 December 1990), trans. in FBIS, *Daily Report* (Eastern Europe), 2 January 1991, p. 37.

97. Tanjug (4 May 1990), trans. in FBIS, *Daily Report* (Eastern Europe), 4 May 1990, p. 65.

98. Tanjug (4 May 1990), trans. in *Ibid.*, p. 75; and Tanjug (11 May 1990), trans. in FBIS, *Daily Report* (Eastern Europe), 15 May 1990, p. 78.

99. Tanjug (5 May 1990), trans. in FBIS, *Daily Report* (Eastern Europe), 7 May 1990, p. 65.

100. "Documentation of the Third Ministerial Conference of the Mediterranean Non-Aligned Countries," in *Review of International Affairs*, No. 966–967 (5 July 1990), p. 18.

Yugoslavia's Relations with European States 389

101. Živorad Kovačević, "The Environmental Problems Facing the Mediterranean Basin," in *Mediterranean Quarterly*, Vol. 1, No. 3 (Summer 1990), p. 8.

102. *Ibid*, p. 10.

103. Yugoslav attitudes on these questions were regularly reported in the *Review of International Affairs* and summaries of bilateral relations in *Yugoslav Survey*. The matter of the Italian boundary is treated in "Italy-Yugoslavia (Trieste)" in *Border and Territorial Disputes*, (Essex: Longmans, 1987), pp. 73–79; and Iva Mihailović, *Nema više zoni B*, (Belgrade: Mladost, 1974).

104. Andrew Wood, "Relations between Britain and Yugoslavia, 1945–1987," in John B. Allcock, John J. Horton, and Marko Milivojević (eds.), *Yugoslavia in Transition: Choices and Constraints—Essays in Honour of Fred Singleton* (Oxford: Berg, 1992), p. 275.

105. Tanjug (23 March 1986), trans. in FBIS, *Daily Report* (Eastern Europe), 25 March 1986, p. 12; Tanjug (23 March 1988), trans. in FBIS, *Daily Report* (Eastern Europe), 24 March 1988, p. 54; and Tanjug (21 April 1989), trans. in FBIS, *Daily Report* (Eastern Europe), 25 April 1989, p. 54.

106. Tanjug (22 April 1989), trans. in FBIS, *Daily Report* (Eastern Europe), 25 April 1989, p. 54.

107. *New York Times*, (19 December 1985), p. 14.

108. Tanjug (17 July 1986), trans. in FBIS, *Daily Report* (Eastern Europe), 18 July 1986, p. I1.

109. Belgrade Domestic Service (20 July 1986), trans. in FBIS, *Daily Report* (Eastern Europe), 21 July 1986, p. I5.

110. "Relations Between France and Yugoslavia," in *Yugoslav Survey*, Vol., No. 3 (1990), p. 113.

111. Tanjug (6 December 1989), trans. in FBIS, *Daily Report* (Eastern Europe), 11 December 1989, p. 91.

112. Tanjug (7 December 1989), trans. in FBIS, *Daily Report* (Eastern Europe), 11 December 1989, p. 93.

113. Tanjug (29 January 1988), trans. in FBIS, *Daily Report* (Eastern Europe), 29 January 1988, p. 35.

114. *Politika* (30 January 1988), p. 1, trans. in FBIS, *Daily Report* (Eastern Europe), 3 February 1988, p. 28.

115. *New York Times*, October 2, 1975, p. A16.

116. *Borba* (19 September 1989), p. 1, trans. in FBIS, *Daily Report* (Eastern Europe), 6 October 1989, p. 78; and Tanjug (30 January 1989), trans. in FBIS, *Daily Report* (Eastern Europe), 7 February 1989, p. 68.

117. This paragraph is drawn freely from Sabrina Ramet's "Yugoslavia and the Two Germanys," in Dirk Verheyen and Christian Soe (eds.), *The Germans and Their Neighbors*, (Boulder, CO: Westview, 1993).

118. Jansjorg Eiff, "German-Jugoslav Relations," in *Review of International Affairs*, No. 916 (5 June 1988), p. 4.

119. Tanjug (26 May 1990), trans. in FBIS, *Daily Report* (Eastern Europe), 1 June 1990, p. 57.

120. Tanjug (11 May 1990), trans. in FBIS, *Daily Report* (Eastern Europe), 14 May 1990, p. 67.

390   Zachary T. Irwin

121. *Ibid.*

122. *Politika* (4 May 1990), p. 3, trans. in FBIS, *Daily Report* (Eastern Europe), 11 May 1990, p. 58.

123. *Excelsior* (Mexico City), 28 April 1990, p. 4, trans. in *Ibid.*, p. 54.

124. *Ibid.*, p. 55.

125. Milodrag Trajković, "Nova etapa u odnosima Jugoslavije i Evropska zajednica," in *Medjunarodna Politika*, No. 931 (January 1989), p. 5.

126. *Danas* (21 February 1989), p. 56.

127. Tanjug (13 June 1990), trans. in FBIS, *Daily Report* (Eastern Europe), 14 June 1990, p. 60.

128. Trajkovic, "Nova etapa," p. 6.

129. Ante Gavranović, "EFTA-Yugoslav Relations: The Long Search for Cooperation," in *EFTA Bulletin* (January 1987), p. 13.

130. *Information Memo*, Commission of the European Economic Community (Brussels), EC 1.31 1990/P91 (28 November 1990), p. 2.

131. "Third Protocol in Financial Cooperation between the European Community and SFRY," in *Official Journal of the European Community*, C134/6-8 (24 May 1991); and "Council Decision COM 91/223," in *Official Journal of the European Community*, NOC 181/7–12 (12 July 1991).

132. Will Bartlett, "Foreign Trade and Stabilization Policy," in Allcock et al. (eds.), *Yugoslavia in Transition* [note 104], p. 250.

133. Harold Lydall, *Yugoslavia in Crisis* (London: Oxford University Press, 1989), p. 87, as cited in *Ibid.*, p. 254.

134. Tanjug (7 January 1991), trans. in FBIS *Daily Report* (Eastern Europe), 8 January 1991, p. 48.

135. *Ibid.*

136. Zagorka Golubović, "Contemporary Yugoslav Society: A Brief Outline of its Genesis and Characteristics," in Allcock, et al. (eds.), *Yugoslavia in Transition* [note 104], p. 105.

137. Dijana Pleština, "From 'Democratic Centralism' to Decentralized Democracy? Trials and Tribulations of Yugoslavia's Development," in *Ibid.*, p. 152.

138. *Delo* (Ljubljana), 21 February 1991, p. 3, trans. in FBIS, *Daily Report* (Eastern Europe), 27 February 1991, p. 53.

139. Tanjug (5 February 1991), trans. in FBIS, *Daily Report* (Eastern Europe), 7 February 1991, p. 39.

140. *New York Times* (22 November 1990), p. 16.

141. Radio Ljubljana (25 June 1991), trans. in FBIS, *Daily Report* (Eastern Europe), 27 June 1990, p. 40.

142. Tanjug (26 February 1991), trans. in FBIS, *Daily Report* (Eastern Europe), 27 February 1991, p. 8.

143. *Vjesnik* (19 February 1991), trans. in FBIS, *Daily Report* (Eastern Europe), 1 March 1991, p. 35.

144. *Borba* (1 February 1991), trans. in FBIS, *Daily Report* (Eastern Europe), 7 February 1991, p. 40.

145. Tanjug (4 March 1991), trans. in FBIS, *Daily Report* (Eastern Europe), 5 March 1991, p. 45.

Yugoslavia's Relations with European States

146. *The Economist* (11 May 1991), p. 45).

147. *Tanjug* (26 June 1991), trans. in FBIS, *Daily Report* (Eastern Europe), 26 June 1991, p. 40.

148. *The Economist* (London), 11 May 1991, p. 45.

149. *Official Journal of the European Communities*, N.O.C. 158/243, (16 May 1991).

150. *Tanjug* (7 July 1991), trans. in FBIS, *Daily Report* (Eastern Europe), 8 July 1991, p. 38.

151. This paragraph is based on Sabrina Petra Ramet, *Balkan Babel: Politics, Culture, and Religion* (Boulder, Colo: Westview Press, 1992), pp. 178–179.

152. *The Economist* (12 October 1991), p. 49.

153. *The Economist* (9 November 1991), p. 48. The EC Resolution detailing a desired future is in *Official Journal of European Communities*, c267/100–103, (14 October 1991).

154. *The Economist* (12 October 1991), p. 49.

155. *Debates of the European Parliament*, No. 3-407/77, (7 September 1991); No. 3-407/75 (7 September 1991).

156. *Ibid.*

157. *Ibid.*, No. 3, 408/97, (10 September 1991).

158. *Ibid.*, No. 3, 409/161–162, (10 September 1991).

159. *New York Times* (10 October 1992), p. A3.

160. *Ibid.* (7 October 1992), p. A1.

161. *Ibid.* (26 February 1993), p. A16.

162. *The Economist* (16 January 1993), p. 8.

163. *Ibid.* (30 January 1993), p. 8.

164. *New York Times* (9 January 1993), p. 41, and *New York Times* (3 January 1993), pp. A1, A6.

165. *The Economist* (9 January 1993), p. 41.

166. Former National Security Advisor Zbigniew Brzezinski objects that the plan is doomed because it "abjures the use of military force to compel compliance"; that it "propitiates the 'ethnic cleansers'"; and because three of the "Croat cantons or provinces and two of the three Serb ones are contiguous to Croatia and Serbia respectively . . . [that therefore] their absorption is . . . almost inevitable." *Washington Times* (25 February 1993), p. G1, 4.(163)

167. *Financial Times* (16 February 1993), p. 2.

168. *New York Times* (11 February 1993), pp. A1, A6.

169. Radio Free Europe, *RFE/RL Daily Report* research fax service, no. 35 (22 February 1993), p. 2.

170. *Ibid.* No. 34 (19 February 1993), p. 1.

171. *Ibid.*, No. 20 (1 February 1993), p. 4.

172. *The Economist* (9 January 1993), p. 23.

173. On 20 November 1992, Albania and Turkey signed agreements on defense technology and military cooperation.Albania'sDefenseMinister Safet Zhulali remarked about the "danger of the extension of the conflict to Kosovo and beyond, so we might be on the verge of a Balkan war."*Philadelphia Inquirer* (21 November 1992), p. A3.

174. Radio Free Europe, *RFE/RL Daily Report*, research fax service, no. 30 (15 February 1993), p. 5.

175. Wolfram Hanrieder, "Compatibility and Consensus: A Proposal for the Conceptual Linkage of External and Internal Dimensions of Foreign Policy," in Wolfram Hanrieder (ed.), *Comparative Foreign Policy: Theoretical Essays* (New York: David McKay Co., Inc., 1971), p. 253 (ital. in orig). This essay appeared originally in the *American Political Science Review*, Vol. 61, No. 4 (December 1967), pp. 971–82 (italics in original).

176. *New York Times* (5 December 1992), pp. A1, A6.

PART FIVE

Culture and Society

16

The New Democracy—With Women or Without Them?

Rada Iveković

No political system in recorded history has included women in its mechanisms or even ensured their participation in more than minimal numbers. The situation is best in Scandinavia,[1] but even here women still confront the structures of male domination. It so happens that the non-participation or minimal participation of women is the staunchest common trait of all political systems. Leftist parties are no exception: it has been the historical mistake of leftist parties to neglect the position of women. This is true both of ruling parties and of leftist parties in opposition, including after 1968, both in the West and in Eastern Europe.

The only explanation for this phenomenon is that all known political systems and social arrangements have been *built on the exclusion of women*. The exclusion of women from public life—there have been some exceptions but not nearly enough to contradict the basic rule—has been the *basis* and not the consequence of existing political systems. This is also true of male-dominated party life. This has been confirmed again in the pluralist conditions developing in the ex-Yugoslav republics. The former one-party system had at least some minimal egalitarian idea which included women also as a matter of principle, if not on purpose. (The late Association of Reformist Forces which appeared as the last hope for the maintenance of a common Yugoslav political space, just before its disintegration, behaved in much the same way: as not explicitly or sufficiently engaged *for* women, but "including them" in a general sense. The same applies also to what has remained of the leftist forces after the collapse of the Yugoslav federation.)

But among the present nationalist parties in the former-Yugoslav republics, there is no question even of an abstract egalitarian attitude with regard to women; the picture is the same whether one speaks of ruling

396
Rada Iveković

nationalist parties or nationalist parties in opposition. Many of them have actually embraced postures favoring negative discrimination against women. Some smaller parties or organizations have a more radical positive attitude or program regarding women, although it may not be very explicit (for example, in Serbia, the Social Democratic Party, The Association for a Yugoslav Democratic Initiative (AYDI), and the Reformist Party of Serbia. But this had been made easier for them insofar as they were and remained far from any chance of winning any elections. The examples from Serbia were particularly conspicuous at the time of the short electoral campaign in November 1990, while the feminist movement visibly resisted the nationalists' tendency to treat women purely as objects and instruments of politics, not as subjects. Politically more active women understood the dialectics of nationalist discourse. This was true of sundry women's groups, such as Feminism, Woman and Society, The Women's Lobby, SOS-Telephone, the Women's Parliament, the Women's Party, and Lesbians—all of them located in Belgrade—as well as of feminist activists and groups in Novi Sad, of the then-Democratic Movement of Women from Kragujevac, and probably of many others as well.

With the collapse of the socialist system, public life and public political discourse came to dominated by aggressive nationalist ideologies, and a new conservatism often reinforced and inspired by religious interests. Feminist groups reacted in a similar way in the three republics in which they had built up some strength (i.e., Croatia, Slovenia, and Serbia): faced with nationalists' glorification of war and the subordination of social interests to the interests of nation, the feminists channeled their energies into pacifist and anti-nationalist activities. This involved, to be sure, chiefly urban feminists, otherwise insignificant in numbers. But the war in ex-Yugoslavia has had at least that to its "credit": it mobilized women beyond traditionally feminist concerns, and brought many passive feminists out into the open. In sum, what is at issue here is the real quality and scope of the idea of democracy which is being cherished by the modest anti-nationalist opposition. I shall make the link between the feminists and the pacifists later.

Nobody has thought of testing the now popular "democracy" according to criteria of gender. Unfortunately, all known forms of democracy would fail at this examination. Democracy without the participation of half the population (women in this case) is no democracy. Yet this is what is being offered under the rubric of "democracy." It is, after all, the tradition of Western "democracy" to be exclusively male.

But women are potential voters (*biračice*, female voters, and not *birači*, male voters). In a more hypothetical sense, women are also candidates (*kandidatkinje*, and not *kandidati*). Their specificity is always covered and forgotten in the abstract universality of "man" and "candidate." As long

The New Democracy—With Women or Without Them? 397

as the normative, repressive dimension of the humanity of women (conformed with the male, supposedly neutral model) remains veiled, democracy will always stay male. In the current situation, democracy is "open" to those who will/can/know how to get involved in the dominant social structure and hierarchy of values, the latter signifying the acceptance, in advance and even unconsciously, social inequality camouflaged as equality. Nor should we forget that all are *not* equal to start with, all do not have the same chances. And "equality" applied to those who are not equal from the start results in inequality and injustice. This is true of minorities and of women, the latter being analogous to but not identical with the first, since they represent a little over half the population. What they need is a complete rewriting of the law, mechanisms of positive discrimination, affirmative action (but not privilege), and a systematic restructuring the political-social system to allow women to become the subjects of law and politics, and not merely their objects.

A party thinking along this line in any of the former republics of Yugoslavia would have stood some good chances before the war: had the project been sufficiently elaborated and carried out, a truly universal party, having women in mind, could have gained more in female votes than it would have lost in male conservative votes. Even leftist parties have always calculated, fearing women's conservative vote while refusing at the same time to *prepare* conditions for a massive progressive vote of women—which would mean giving them concessions. That one could count on women's progressive voices cannot be demonstrated, since this is an untrodden path. No party has ever ventured down this path, which is a result, quite obviously, of the fact that it is men, after all, and not women, who make politics in the traditional sense. In the case of ex-Yugoslavia, even the most decent parties could think of women only functionally (and at the last minute) in order to get voices, but none thought of them in planning a policy of reciprocity and awakening, and of raising and developing *women's public opinion* as part of the common public opinion. A progressive, non-nationalistic party which would want to count also on the votes of women would have to have: (1) a concrete and specific program for women besides a good general program; and (2) a program to encourage the political articulation of female public opinion. In times of social and existential insecurity, of aggressive nationalism and ethnic warfare, this could be achieved relatively rapidly because the dissatisfaction and impatience of women is great and growing, and because an important part of the female population basically did not support nationalist and militarist policies; yet they have no organization to which they can turn. Instead, nationalist, war-mongering parties and Churches have urged women to assume their traditional role. After the elections in the sundry republics, these forces have been busy trying to get the legislation to abolish the modest "women's rights" attained under socialism.

But these rights should be maintained, as a minimum, and even expanded. Just how precarious women's rights are is now shown by the development, in ex-socialist countries: they are historically never safe, they can be threatened and done away with by the arbitrary decision of men (males). The law is, after all, not divine or neutral. There is, behind it, a human subject and author: historically, he is masculine. Women and minorities appear only as the objects of law, *in* the framework construed by the historically dominant subject. Unless we develop and put into action a concept of plural co-subjectivity, that is, unless we dismantle and reconstruct the framework of law itself (with all the practical, political, social, and other implications), women (or others in an analogous situation) will remain subordinated to men.

Nobody is addressing women, and historically established channels for women to communicate reciprocally do not exist. There is no such thing as a women's public opinion (as part of the general and common public opinion), while what is understood as public opinion in general is undoubtedly male dominated. The women's movement is the only one paying attention to this problem. Communication, information, and disinformation are processes which exist for *men*. Women are at most the stake, the object, or the instrumentality in men's battles among themselves. They are not participants in these battles, to which they are, however, subordinated. As a result, these battles are not women's battles, not the concern of women—at least not until they (women) are accepted as co-equal subjects of politics. Not until the rules of the game are changed can women have any stake in men's wars and men's agendas.

But no party in the Balkans is prepared to rewrite the rules of the political game, except of course for the women's organizations and a scattering of small anarchist parties in Bulgaria, and thus, for example, the Women's Party in Serbia. But this latter party clearly had a mission of attracting attention to women's concerns. It is necessary, as a civilization, that we reach the point of no-return where the *feminine* as well as the masculine can be thought of as universal (but of course not imposed as a model). Man is, after all, a woman like any other, isn't he?

Women do not feel responsible for the scandalous war between the former Yugoslav republics, because they have been made historically irresponsible, that is, powerless. Compared to their status just after World War Two, women have suffered a severe setback already prior to the current ethnic war: their number in politics was ever decreasing even during the later years of socialism, and is of course nonexistent in military action. At the time of the first post-socialist elections in Croatia, there were only 6 percent women candidates, and altogether hardly over 4 percent women sat in the first Croatian *Sabor* (parliament) after the elections. The Women's List in Zagreb failed at the first elections, and it did not fare much better in

The New Democracy—With Women or Without Them?

the Slovenian elections, although at least in Slovenia, women would account for 10 percent of the resultant parliament. In Serbia, the numbers were more extreme, however, with only 1 percent of parliamentary deputies being women after the 1990 elections. Whether it be a coalition of nationalist and right-centered parties, as was the case in Slovenia until spring 1992 or the dominance of a single conservative-nationalist party as in Croatia and Serbia after the first elections, the governments in these three former Yugoslav republics soon showed themselves to be hostile to programs of women's rights and made common cause with conservative voices in the Catholic and Orthodox Churches.

Nationalist and conservative parties see women, in the best of cases, in a protectionist legal perspective, in the function of protecting and promoting motherhood, so that as many babies might be born to "us" as possible, ideally while ensuring that there are fewer of "their" babies. Thus, in Serbia abortion has been encouraged for "their" women (Albanian women), with taxes for a fourth child introduced for "them," with conspicuously different policies thus for Albanian and Serbian women in Serbia.[2] At the same time, there has been a clear tendency to limit or forbid abortion and contraception to "our women," to encourage a fourth child (as for example, in the official benediction of families with many children in the Zagreb Cathedral in 1990, after the first free elections). There would also be attempts to introduce taxes for not having children for "our people" lest we consider ourselves "demographically endangered." This was attempted in Croatia after the first pluralist elections, when women's organizations reacted very negatively (especially the Independent Association of Women, and Women's Help Today, both feminist groups in Zagreb), and also in Serbia even before the elections (provoking sharp criticism from the Women's Lobby, especially in connection with a proposed Resolution regarding the Renewal of the Population, which enjoyed official favor in Belgrade). All this was accompanied by an insistent patriarchal propaganda fostering traditional values which limit the few "women's rights" which had actually been won, through an open (and new) condemnation of concubinage and extra-marital children, which sent women back to their families because of the economic crisis and the jobs wanted preferably for the refugees (men), the military and the mutilated, who have come back from the front. There is an explicit tendency for these conservative ideologies to be translated into new legislation and constitutions. Women should, among other things, be able to maintain their right to dispose of their own bodies and minds as they wish, they should be entitled to and be able to decide whether they wish or don't wish to to have children, before and regardless of any national interest. The individual right must always remain prior to any "national" right. But clearly, women's rights are not considered to be elementary human rights.

A good example to illustrate the conservative turn in policy toward women is the case of the tendency now rampant in Croatia, but this does not mean that the new regimes in the other states of ex-Yugoslavia would necessarily make better choices. The vice minister for Reconstruction, Ante Baković, issued a preliminary *Concept for the Demographic and Moral Renewal of Croatia* in May 1992. This program reads as follows:

The program will comprise work on the transformation of today's family into the family of the Croatian future with three or four children. The battle against abortion means the medical, ethical, and humane education of the people, as well as the creation of economic and social living conditions for women not to have any reason for abortion.

The battle against the anti-life mentality. It is urgent to cleanse out of medicine, school books, television, the press, and acts of dating from the times of communist singlemindedness, all elements of anti-life attitudes.

Pro-natalist activity of this Ministry: Producing popular films, video and audio cassettes, stickers, maps with demographic stimulation.

The new family policy: Croatia has to make adequate laws and guarantee the conditions for the supreme of all vocations in the Republic to be the vocation of a mother-breeder.

Working mothers with children should be withdrawn from factories and other heavy and unsuitable jobs. This would provide thousands of vacancies.

Celibacy should be repressed, because the new demographic situation is made worse by a new evil—late marriages contracted at the age between 35 and 50, which have only one child or remain childless.

The new tax policy will not encourage celibacy, but marriages with children.

The moral protection of the family: the Republic must fight, through laws and political influence, anything that is against marriage and the family.

Fighting against pornography, child prostitution and proselytism, and the control of private cinema-halls and video clubs.

The dignity of motherhood should be publicly emphasized, respected and propagated, and a new holiday should be introduced: the Day of the Croatian Mother.

The criteria for permission to divorce should become much stricter in the case of marriages with children.

The social care for children: Nurseries should be limited to a minimum and then gradually discontinued, allowing children to be the first two years with their mothers.

A project of founding children's cooperatives for children from two to six years of age should be worked out.

The ethical renewal of the society: Croatia is free, but today's Croatian society is a social patient, so that the soul of the nation suffers from many injuries from past regimes: asocial behavior, reluctance to work, irrespon-

The New Democracy—With Women or Without Them? 401

sibility, bribery and corruption, a negative attitude toward the State and state property, cursing, bad words and the poisoning of people's ethics through the press and other mass media.

After so much material and spiritual destruction and wandering, Croatian society is entering Europe free and sovereign. It is necessary to organize a Croatian Social Week, when a hundred or so "wise, honest, and patriotic Croats" would meet to give a vision of our future and in so doing, help the government, parliament, and the leaders in the ethical renewal of the Croatian people and of other citizens of the Republic.[3]

Complementary to the overtly clerical attitude of the Vice Minister is the attitude of Franjo Cardinal Kuharić himself. In a letter to the President of the *Sabor*, he writes,

It is urgently necessary either to abolish the law on health measures required for the free decision on giving birth, or replace it with a new law. For us believers, that law is against God and against men. It is contrary to the new Constitution of the Republic of Croatia, according to which "every human being has the right to live." That law is the expression of a materialistic concept of man and therefore of a thoroughly mistaken understanding of human life, of the human person and of sexuality. That law came out of a mentality which is nowadays widespread in the world, and which leads to a civilization of death. Since such a mentality is deeply rooted in Croatia as well, firmly supported also in the mass media, we find it necessary to explain our request in more detail and propose it for consideration to all people of good will.

. . . We find it our duty to stand clearly and with determination for the defense of the right of conceived human beings to be born. The tragic destiny of tens of thousands of unborn children in Croatia, killed by abortion, must not leave the minds of people of good will indifferent. That fact is being passed over in silence, or it is even being justified by claiming different grounds for a decision, or the right to abortion is held to be a personal right of a woman. Abortion is the negation of woman's dignity and the denial of motherly love: evil is evil, and it can never become a right to act.

. . . We consider that the new Croatian legislation should sharply distinguish between the right for free and responsible parenthood from the problem of abortion. The method used by responsible parenthood (in family planning) is the respect of the rhythm of fertile and non-fertile days, which means abstention from marital life in fertile days.

. . . That is how human dignity, and the dignity of sexuality are preserved. Unnatural contraception, be it chemical or mechanical, even with abortive results, is a hard offense against dignity and transforms the human person into an object of selfish satisfaction. Authentic love is against it. Purposely inflicted abortion is an objective evil both in a personal and in a social sense, and should be approached in this perspective by the legislation.

Dear Mister President of the Croatian *Sabor*, I am entrusting this request and explanation of the Croatian bishops, as the Shepherd of the Church in Croatia, to your attention and to the conscience of the *Sabor*. I believe that such a serious topic as this will be examined in the *Sabor* with responsibility to God, to history, and to the nation, that appropriate conclusions will be drawn, and a new law will be passed which will indeed mean the protection of life and of any human being from conception to death.[4]

As a result of this tendency to abolish the elementary rights of women, women and young people have been gripped by profound stress. Indeed, the entire Croatian society is currently feeling the influence of the Catholic Church. The Church's influence has already had baneful influence in the spheres of education, culture, mass media, and national politics, not to mention the debate about abortion rights and divorce. Whatever gains women made under the communists will probably be scuttled. The two long quotations provided above require no comment. They are characteristic of what the official tendencies in the new states are. It is doubtful to what extent women's movements will be able to fight back. Decisions of a general interest and at the same time of a specific female interest are made by a tiny minority of *men* who sit in the *Sabor*. They are also much older, on the average, than the women whose fate they decide.

The new democratization of political life through the activity of many parties is very slow to come and indeed very limited and feeble. It is so, for different reasons, in all parts of what was once Yugoslavia, but all the more in the parts stricken by the war, as well as on the side inflicting the war. There are no more nuances, different views are not allowed, every different and especially non-nationalist attitude is stigmatized. But, more than anything else, what seems, when viewed from the distance, to be the democratization of once totalitarian regimes in Eastern Europe, *is no democracy for women*. This is confirmed by the recent experience of other former socialist countries, where women are threatened to be deprived of two of their few and elementary "women's rights"—specifically, the right to choose whether to give birth, and the right to equally paid work.

To return to a theme adumbrated earlier, a political party which would count on the female half of the population would have to guarantee these rights, however modest and self-evident they may seem, as well as ensure new and far wider rights. It is amazing that no political party has shown even the slightest interest in such a program. Anything else, including silence, is de facto manipulation, because of the false universality of political discourse in general. The drawback of all the other parties could have been transformed into the advantage of the party which would have thought of it, knowing that all parties have failed to address women as a target group. A party which would take women into account would have to tell

The New Democracy—With Women or Without Them? 403

them what it is ready to do for them, aware that the economic crunch has struck women first, that the burden of everyday life is above all on them, and above all, the burden of the war. There should be no question of economic policy without taking into account its impact on women in relation to the whole. Political and economic uncertainty and war are particularly hard on women and affect them in a specific way. They could be mobilized, and are mobilizing themselves—against the war. But no new political discourse is in sight.

The situation of women is equally unenviable—for different reasons—in the republics concerned by war as well as in those spared by it for the time being. There are also specificities and differences which should be taken into account in a closer look. Some of the specificities are due to the small yet significant differences in the legal treatment of women across the republics of pre-civil war Yugoslavia: for example, only Slovenia recognized the possibility of a wife being raped by her husband, and treated it as a crime. More important differences have been due to the huge differences in the general development and life standards. It is women who bear the greatest part of the social, psychological, and material burden of everyday life, more than anything else because of the fact of the double-working day (at home and at work)—which is a fact in all parts of former Yugoslavia. But in the underdeveloped republics and regions of what was socialist Yugoslavia, the pressure on women is much greater, because of general material misery and social backwardness. Women there are really fighting for the elementary survival of the family, or of what is left of it after the menfolk went to war, by guaranteeing material and psychological renewal.

Let's take the example of the evening presentation of political parties on Serbian television during the 1990 elections. The similarity of the set-up in all cases was striking, and only the Social Democrats, the Association for a Yugoslav Democratic Initiative, and to a certain extent, the Green Party, were exceptions to the general rule of male monopoly on the political podium and on the airwaves. Only a few parties had even one or two women representing them on television, and these, as a rule, spoke at the end of the broadcast, usually about culture, and often interrupted or hushed by their male colleagues as broadcast time ran short. Most Serbian parties never speak about women and have no programs concerning them, and those which do mention them (with the exception of the three mentioned above) think of women only as mothers, in contradiction to the general assertion that women are considered as equal in rights with men.

But it is not any better in any of the other Yugoslav successor states. Misogynous ideology has great chances of getting legal consecration and is largely at work in the sway of nationalist revival and "integrism" (or fundamentalism). If we fight for the basic human rights of women, are we paternalistically warned in Croatia that we are in fact joining hands in "their plot against Croatia" and find ourselves, of course, on the side of Serbian nationalists?[5] Or, on the other hand, if we support equal treatment of both married and non-married couples, are we charged with taking part "in the specific war against Serbia?"[6] At the same time, the constitutions of Slovenia and Croatia, both in the draft stage and in the final stage, ghettoize women by mentioning them only in their maternal function (Articles 51, 75 in the Slovenian constitution). The Croatian draft of 1990 (Article 62) spoke about "marriage and family as the moral and natural basis of society"! In its final form, the Croatian constitution deleted this passage, declaring only, "The family is under the special protection of the Republic. Marriage and legal relationships within marriage, concubinage and family are governed by the law" (Article 61). As in the case of abortion, the matter is left to the law. In this respect, the Croatian constitution is purposely ambiguous, introducing the possibility of the abrogation of the communist-era law on abortion, which guaranteed the right to choose one's own parenting freely. In specific, Article 21 of the new Croatian constitution reads: "Every human being has the right to live. There is no capital punishment in the Republic of Croatia." The attitude of the law will clearly depend on the interpretation as to what "human being" means. As illustrated by Cardinal Kuharic's remarks, it is clear that some quarters interpret human life to extend "from conception to death," with all guarantees of civil rights attached "from conception to death." The ambiguity of the Croatian constitution with regard to abortion reflects, in fact, a strong tendency among the ruling elite to limit or forbid contraception and abortion some day (and thus to abolish the right of women to decide for themselves). The limitation will come later, in due time and through legislation, always to be rationalized with the explanation that the laws must be consonant with the Constitution. Thus, Article 56 of the Croatian constitution says that the "rights concerning childbirth, maternity, and the care for children will be governed by law." There is space here for a whole campaign to drive women back to total dependence on men. The fact that there are more general paragraphs claiming to assure the equality of the sexes, nationalities, and religious beliefs before the law, is simply misleading. It is clear, even from them (for example, from Article 14) that the "universality" ("all") does not apply to women, even when it is expressly stated: it speaks of "citizens" in the masculine form only (*gradjani*), while saying that all citizens are to be considered equal genderwise, racewise, etc. At least genderwise, the phrasing makes semantic nonsense, and shows again that the female is never really meant as universal or as simply human; the female is interpreted always as the "exception."

Meanwhile, the Slovenian constitution praises the "sacredness of life" and is imprecise about the right to abortion (Article 52), which was in-

The New Democracy—With Women or Without Them? 405

tended, by the Christian Democrats and their ideological allies, to prove useful in subsequently abolishing the legal right to abortion, especially as it allows "refusal for reasons of conscience" (Article 45), which could be interpreted as the right of the surgeon to refuse to perform it. Article 63 of the Croatian constitution, further, says that "Children have the duty to care for their elderly and disabled parents," while we all know that such care is in any case always left to women. What is even more alarming here, is the manifest intention of the state to wash its hands of any duty toward the welfare of its elderly citizens and of social care. And finally, the Croatian constitution says that "military service and the defense of the Republic is the duty of all able citizens," using again the masculine form, although the language possesses both forms. Are only men citizens, and not women? If so, the constitution is not applicable to women.[7] In fact, the woman-citizen is mentioned for the first time out of context (which shows that it was not meant seriously) in the so-called Constitutional Law Concerning the Amendments in the Constitutional Law for Passing the Constitution of the Republic of Croatia (published on 14 November 1991), in Article 6, paragraph E, where it is said that the he- or she- citizen has the right to decide to which ethnic, national group or minority he or she wishes to belong.

After World War Two, women accounted for 30 percent of the posts in the state and governmental bodies in Yugoslavia, owing partly to a quota, but also to the authority of their significant role in the liberation war. In the post-Yugoslav republics today, they have again completely disappeared from the scene (a few token women being allowed as figleafs): there are practically no women in the governments, and hardly any in any of the parliaments. And this situation is being reinforced by unwritten rules and sheer stereotyping.

The market economy and economic competition, which were supposed to save first Yugoslavia and now its successor states from the crisis, have not really come into their own, except in part in Slovenia. There is no economy whatsoever where war is being waged, where no exchange is possible, and where the markets close down. But should peace be restored, we would soon be able to see that the market economy does not, of its own accord, favor women and their rights or progress. The reverse is the case. And yet, political figures say again, as they have always said, "It is not the right moment" to take up women's rights and claims for equality. Many things are given precedence before women's interests. Right now, the "national interest" comes first. Are women, then, not part of the nation?

The women of former Yugoslavia fall now far behind where they stood during the socialist period, with regard to their status in the political, economic, legal, and cultural spheres. In their everyday life, the women of the post-Yugoslav republics are driven step by step further back into the no "man's" land of national phantasms where they are inflicted real and not phantasmic suffering: the war at large, violence in the family, rape, battering of women and children, child abuse, forced incest, sexual harassment, generalized violence, plunder, misery, migrations, destroyed houses and cities, death. This is only the visible part of the iceberg. There is a general sense of license, that anything is permitted, fueling a rise in various forms of aggression against others, whether as war against "the other" nation or as random violence within one's own community, violence all too often directed against women, and certainly against anyone with different ideas or ways of expressing herself. One may even speak of processes of "ideological cleansing."

Unfortunately, public opinion continues to trivialize these problems of violence and spread negative stereotypes about activists in these organizations, so that women volunteering for such activity have never received encouragement from society or the media. A link has to be made between the very widespread "petty" violence to women (and to the weak, in general), and the outbreak of war in ex-Yugoslavia. It is no mere coincidence that the former has become more widespread since the war began.

A new legislative bill drafted in May 1992 in Croatia addresses this problem in the following way: it endeavors to classify violence within the family as lying outside public concern. Of course, this can only contribute to concealing domestic violence. Women would prefer to see these cases discussed in public. Croatian feminists, for example, have demanded that the state play a role in combatting violence within the family, and argue that it is precisely the state that should guarantee the respect and dignity of the public image of women. This latter issue goes far beyond the rather narrow question of pornography. But far from adopting such protective measures vis-à-vis women, the Croatian and Serbian states have turned a blind eye as local men feel increasingly at liberty to express sexist, hostile, and offensive views about or violence to women, paralleling the license recently given to the expression of racist and chauvinist viewpoints.

In Croatia and Serbia there is today an undeclared "state of emergency" as a result of which morality and legality are suspended. The Nation is taken to have absolute priority over its citizens, whether female or male. The recurrent witch-hunts in Tudjman's Croatia, involving media attacks against intellectuals suspected of not conforming to the general nationalist sentiment, have in fact been chiefly directed against women.[8] There is no parallel for such media attacks on women specifically in Serbia, although that is probably related to the lower political profile enjoyed by Serbian women. But the witch-hunting (for example through massive dismissals of non-Serbs or of the ideologically "unreliable" is there).

The civic state (founded on the principle of the primacy of law) can be contrasted with the national state (founded on the principle of the primacy

The New Democracy—With Women or Without Them? 407

of the interest of the nation); in a choice between these two political configurations, women are much better served by the former. It is in consonance with this concept of the state that a feminist group in Zagreb issued a "Declaration of Reproductive Rights" in 1991, insisting on women's rights to decide about their own bodies and minds, and whether to give birth or not.

There have been three broad stages in the treatment of women by the law. Historically, the first stage was *negative legal discrimination*, and most advanced societies today, whether capitalist or ex-socialist, passed through this stage at one time or another. The second stage is *abstract equality as a matter of principle* (de jure, but not de facto), with legal assurances of equal rights and equal treatment. Most Western and East European societies are currently in this stage, although some of the latter seem to be sliding back into the first stage. It is important to note that in this second stage, guarantees are mostly of a normative order, while the real, effective rights and possibilities of the sexes differ; put bluntly, women, even when equal in rights and in principle, do not have the same chances as men, among other things because their starting point is lower. Across Eastern Europe generally, the new pluralist systems have taken any but a progressive attitude regarding women's rights.

The third stage is *positive discrimination and affirmative action*, and this should now be the goal of women everywhere, indeed of all progressive and anti-nationalist forces.[9] Positive discrimination does not require the renunciation of the legal state, but, on the contrary, its refinement. But to make this feasible, it is essential that this claim not be limited merely to *women's* rights but to the rights of citizens under the law. From the beginning of the 1970s, a modest but determined women's movement began working in Yugoslavia, arguing that women must constitute themselves as political subjects and also as the subjects of law.[10] This movement, now more splintered than ever, continues to work in the post-Yugoslav republics, eclipsed by the present war, but with good reason to continue its work. Its maximal target would be a *cultural choice* as yet unprecedented in recorded history. A "women's parliament" was, in fact, convoked in Zagreb, by various women's and feminist groups to discuss just these questions, in December 1990.[11] But its minimal and most immediate target in the current situation can only be to end this most literally *man*-made war.

After the outbreak of war, first involving the JNA in Slovenia and subsequently involving Serbian militias (backed by the JNA) in Croatia and Bosnia, the existing network of women's organizations continued to maintain contacts across otherwise hostile, even impassable, interrepublican borders for as long as possible. Inevitably, the women's network grew into an anti-war movement, and was joined and supported by those men who could or dared to support it. In Belgrade, the modest pacifist movement was composed essentially of women. They were the only ones who could travel freely (the men requiring military permission to do so). It was, quite understandably, more difficult to articulate pacifist sentiments in Croatia, since Croatia was the victim in this war, but even there, especially as tension eased in Zagreb, pacifist and anti-nationalist groups managed to make their presence felt—again with the prominent participation of women. Women have also been prominent in the anti-war demonstrations in Slovenia. The story of the pacifist resistance in Bosnia is yet to be written.

The resistance to the ruthless war (daily conquests of new territories, siege and famine in the cities, bombings, shellings, rape, murder, ethnic cleansing, etc.) is made by the entire Bosnian population—all ethnicities and religions combined—and not solely by Muslims, as it may appear in some news reports. Muslims, Croats, and Serbs, men and women together in the famine-stricken towns and villages of Bosnia and Herzegovina, as Bosnians, *resist the Nation(s), the idea of an ethnic Nation*. Although the Serbs have taken a disproportionate part of the pie (the biggest), the Croats have also taken as much as their appetites wanted, and as the Geneva conference fails (on 30 January 1993), these two fighting parties have more or less agreed over the partition of Bosnia. It is the Bosnians and, among them, the Muslims (but not only they) who cannot accept the deal which all but erases them from the map of their country. Here is where Bosnia's mostly pacifist resistance gets the signal to turn to guerilla tactics. It is because only a very small part of the news coming out of Bosnia and Herzegovina is given by women themselves, that we still know so little (as the war goes on) about the role of women in the pacifist movement, which, out of despair, is turning into defensive warfare.

But we have all heard about the terrible and undeniable feature of the *mass rape of women*. The numbers are not clear, although figures ranging from 3,000 to 60,000 raped women have been cited in the news. *Whatever the number, be it but one woman, the crime is terrible and should be treated not only as a war crime, but as a crime against humanity.* What is certain is that women are *being raped* in great numbers by *advancing and conquering armies* (witnesses say that an army doesn't rape when retreating) and especially by the bigger aggressor. The bigger aggressor in the Bosnian war is the Serbian side (both from Bosnia-Herzegovina and from Serbia), and the smaller aggressor, but still an aggressor, is the Croatian side (both local and from Croatia). There has been more destruction from the Serbian side, and also more Serbian-held camps, as the Mazowiecki Report shows. So there have also probably been more raped women from that side (more destroyed cities also, and all the rest). But the disproportion does not absolve the other side in proportion to its crimes. Unfortunately, there is nothing unusual about women being raped (and also killed after having been raped) at war, so the claim of originality in this case does not hold. Susan Brownmiller writes: "When German

The New Democracy—With Women or Without Them? 409

soldiers marched through Belgium in the first months of World War I, rape was so extensive and the Franco-Belgian propaganda machine so deft, that the Rape of the Hun became a ruling metaphor. Afterward, the actual cases were dismissed by propaganda analysts as rhetoric designed to whip up British and American support, but if the rapes had not had propaganda value, they wouldn't have surfaced. ... During World War II, when the Germans were on the march again, atrocious rapes were committed on the bodies of Russian and Jewish women in the occupied villages and cities while still more women were dragged off to forcible brothels, or to death. When the tide reversed and the Soviet Army began advancing into German territory on the road to Berlin, it was the turn of German women to experience the use of their bodies as an extracurricular battlefield.... The plight of raped women as casualties of war is given credence only at the emotional moment when the side in danger of annihilation cries out for world attention."[12] Or, as Rossana Rossanda puts it: "Rape accompanies all wars and civil wars, because the female body is considered one of the goods of the enemy to be destroyed and at the same time a way of offending the enemy by invading his area of sexual dominion."[13] In war, women are destroyed as the *enemy's property*, but also, unconsciously, as the "Other" incarnated, as "evil" in itself (and as an extrapolation, a projection of the "evil part of ourselves"). In peacetime, it was very difficult, if not impossible, to draw attention to the problem of rape in former Yugoslavia. Neither the public opinion nor the authorities were interested. But when rape as a topic can serve as nationalistic propaganda (which is interested in the "Nation," and not in women as such), it is gladly being made use of. It is always "they" who rape "our" women (the discourse is actually the same on all sides, and regardless of the disproportion which, however, cannot and must not be dismissed in the reality of concrete women's lives and in humanitarian help). What is being questioned in this approach is not the deplorable fact that unbearable numbers of women are being raped, nor is the urgency questioned of needing to help them. What is being rejected here is the nationalistic manipulation of the horrible crime of mass rape of women (but also girls, boys, and men). That the new element here should be that rape is performed on a mass basis in connection with ethnic cleansing does not really show where the line goes between rape and other methods of terrorizing, such as expulsion from homes, keeping cities under siege, etc.—all these are performed in order to acquire territory and domination (it is the same with women, including impregnated women, who are not treated differently from other property).

Clearly, women cannot come out with their maximal claims in conditions of war. Clearly, like the men, women have been driven some decades back, in social and cultural terms, by the war. But once again, as was the case during World War Two, women shall emerge from this tragedy with more awareness, and possibly with more collective strength.

410

It is, somehow, never the "right moment" for women's claims. In our patriarchal traditions, other problems are always more "urgent." But, from our socialist and post-socialist experiences,[14] we know that "priorities" are not established by us, but by those who govern us, and they manage to find endless excuses not to take women's issues into account. Women of ex-Yugoslavia would repeat their earlier mistake should they allow their dignity and equality to be, once again, pushed aside as "non-priority."

Notes

1. See Gisela Kaplan, *Contemporary Western European Feminism* (New York: New York University Press, 1992), Chapter 3.

2. Slavenka Drakulić, "Šta hoće ginekolozi," in *NIN* (Belgrade), 30 September 1984, pp. 18–19; Slavenka Drakulic, "Patriotizam u krevetu," in *NIN* (10 November 1985), p. 28; "Kosovo: dva nataliteta," documentation prepared by Petar Ignja, in *NIN* (6 March 1988), pp. 6–12; and Slavenka Drakulić, "Silovanje kao politički ispad," in *Danas* (Zagreb), 4 November 1986, pp. 61–63.

3. *Novi Vjesnik* (17 May 1992), p. 17B.

4. *Ibid.*

5. *Vjesnik* (9 November 1990).

6. *Vreme* (Belgrade), 12 November 1990.

7. See Vesna Pusić, "Gradjanin bez zastite," in *Danas* (30 October 1990); and Slavenka Drakulić, "Women and the New Democracy in Yugoslavia," Paper presented at the Women's CSCE Meeting in Berlin (15 November 1990). For the Croatian Constitution, as well as its constitutional law, see *Ustav Republike Hrvatske*, 2nd ed. (Zagreb: Narodne novine, 1992).

8. It is impossible to list all such articles, which would include: Tanja Torbarina, "Tito je bio stonoga," in *Globus* (31 October 1991), p. 48; Dubravko Horvatić, "Petokolonaški dnevnik," in *Vjesnik* (7 November 1991); Tanja Torbarina, "Sred pusaka i bajoneta," in *Globus* (6 December 1991), p. 48; Radovan Stipetić, "Dan za danom," in *Neddjeljni Vjesnik* (Zagreb), 8 December 1991; Tomislav Wruss, "Jagoda Dukić traži predaju Dubrovnika Srbima!," in *Slobodni Tjednik*, no. 90 (December 1991), pp. 19–20; Branimir Donat, "Razapela se Slavenka Drakulić," in *Globus* (24 January 1992), pp. 58–59; and Tanja Torbarina, "Shvatiš Nabijar," in *Globus* (24 April 1992), p. 48. There have been particularly virulent and vulgar attacks on an actress from Zagreb (Mira Furlan), who found herself playing theater in Belgrade at the time of the beginning of the war against Croatia. Three unsigned articles were among the most offensive ones: "Tragična sudbina velike hrvatske glumice—Težak život lake žene," in *Globus* (31 January 1991), p. 29; "Nespremna za životnu ulogu," in *Globus* (7 February 1991), p. 29; and "Priča o dva grada. Da li je `Globusov' Feuilleton a Necrlogue for the Actress?" in *Globus* (14 February 1992), p. 35. Other articles targetting Furlan included: Ladislav Šever, "Sisama na Hrvatsku," in *Top* (Zagreb), 11 November 1991, p. 3; Zvonko Maković, "Razlozi," in *Danas* (15 October 1991), p. 5; Ružica Gabriel, "Otkazi," in *Danas* (12 November 1991), p. 6; and Igor Sprajc, "Pismo Miri Furlan—2," in *Danas* (19 November 1991), p. 6. Another of the ongo-

The New Democracy—With Women or Without Them?   411

ing witch-hunting pieces of journalism, labeled as "the freedom of the press" and supported if not instigated by the official culture and institutions, against five prominent women intellectuals is the one (unsigned again) by the title "The Witches from Rio: Croatian Feminists Rape Croatia!," in *Globus* (11 December 1992), after which an avalanche of attacks followed from all sides. This is not to say that men intellectuals or public figures are not also the target, such as Predrag Matvejević, Rade Serbedzija, and others. But women are at the same time an easier target because they are socially weaker and a "double" target: both as women (the eternal "evil") and as oppositionaries.

9. For an elaboration, see Rada Iveković, "Nastavlja se borba za 'ženska prava'," in *Demokratija danas* (Belgrade), nos. 4–5 (1990), pp. 12–13.

10. For elaboration, see Rada Iveković, "Pravo na prava: Muškarac i ništa više, žena i ništa manje," in *Dar*, no. 1 (6 November 1990), pp. 32–33.

11. See Nadežda Cetković, "Prvi ženski Sabor," in *Vreme* (31 December 1990), p. 64; and Jasmina Kuzmanović, "Ženski sabor pred Saborom," in *Nedjeljna Dalmacija* (23 December 1990), p. 21.

12. Susan Brownmiller, "Making Female Bodies the Battlefield: Alas for women, there is nothing unprecedented about mass rape in war," in *Newsweek*, January 4, 1993, p. 37.

13. Rossana Rossanda, "Stupro finalizzato" ("Finalized rape"), in *Il Manifesto*, January 20, 1993, p. 11.

14. Re. the former, see Blaženka Despot, *Žensko pitanje i socijalističko samoupravljanje* (Zagreb: Čekade, 1987).

17

"Only Crooks Can Get Ahead": Post-Yugoslav Cinema/TV/Video in the 1990s

Andrew Horton

A walrus faced old grandfather silently watches his drunken son and relatives fight bitterly at a large outdoor wedding reception in Sarajevo. The fight is over politics as they have affected their personal lives. The grandfather can take no more. He stands up and announces to the group, "Fuck you all and your politics," and storms out, leaving his family behind, headed for the old folks home to live in peace without warring relatives. A 1992 CNN newscast from the ongoing war in Bosnia? The scene echoes the current chaos in post-Yugoslavia. But the line is actually delivered at the end of Emir Kusturica's Bosnian made film, *When Father Was Away On Business*, voted the Best Film in the world at the 1985 Cannes Film Festival.

The line has much of the hard biting humor we came to expect from Yugoslav cinema from the 1960s to the late 1980s. Filmmakers such as Rajko Grlić, Želimir Zilnik, Dušan Makavejev, Aleksandar Petrović, and Živojin Pavlović first caught the world's attention with startling and innovative works. Furthermore, the line speaks to the present as Yugoslavia has ceased to exist as anything but a shadowy presence, and war, strife, political chaos, and random death have been the price paid by far too many as one republic after another has struck out on its own from the original Yugoslav federation. A very uncertain future faces what was once "Yugoslav cinema" and which now has become a "cinema without a name" as the various republics strive to carve out their own identities and spheres of influence and as television, documentaries, and black market videos replace the more central role cinema once played in Yugoslav popular culture.

A decade ago, an overview of Yugoslav cinema would have done well to focus on individual directors and the importance of particular films. Not so today. As I survey the territory in 1992, it is far more pressing to spotlight the shape and significance of changes within the total image making and distribution system in a desperately uncertain situation as republics strive to redefine their relationship to each other and as a wartime reality and mentality continue to rule in Croatia, Serbia and most tragically in Bosnia. Recognizing that currently this cinema is "without a name," I will, for the sake of clarity, refer to "post-Yugoslav cinema" to cover the collective cinemas of the republics embraced by the former (pre-1991) Yugoslavia while acknowledging the particular backgrounds of the filmmakers as they are relevant.

If Yugoslav cinema, like Yugoslavia itself in the past since 1948, was always "something in between" capitalist and socialist models, it is even more "in between" since the wars for independence broke out in 1991. On one hand filmmakers such as Emir Kusturica continue to pile up international awards and critical applause. Yet on the other, as we shall see, post-Yugoslav cinema has all but ceased to exist in any previously recognizable form.

In part, post-Yugoslav cinema shares the general fate of the now "ex-communist" Eastern and Central European cinemas and, to a degree, the cinema of the Soviet Union. In brief, largely subsidized film industries must now fend for themselves not only on the open market but also against the onslaught of video and the beginnings of expanded television. Granted, Yugoslav cinema has always been an "in-between" model which balanced elements of an American model of independent studios and producers with a socialist form of arts subsidy from various sources. Thus the fall of the Berlin wall did not catch Yugoslav filmmakers totally by surprise. But the rapidity of technological change coupled with the socio-ethnic-political dimensions which have led to the death of Yugoslavia as it previously existed, have led both to a period of cinematic instability and, conversely, fascinating experimentation.

What do the post-Yugoslav '90s hold in store once the shooting stops? Cinema within the former republics of Yugoslavia in the 1990s will share most or all of the following characteristics:

1. The proliferation of smaller production companies, many consisting of only a few filmmakers, which work in conjunction with larger studios/backers on a film-by-film basis (the reverse is true as well: that large companies are in trouble. By 1991 Avala Film of Belgrade, for example, which used to be one of the top three companies in the country had sold out to a non-film manufacturing company and had no films in production);

Post-Yugoslav Cinema/TV/Video in the 1990s   415

2. The increased commerce between film and television production both in made-for-television films and also films partially financed by television for post theatrical airings;

3. The development of a made-for-video film market of cheap, swiftly shot genre movies as in Greece, for instance.

4. An increased number of Yugoslav co-productions with companies from other nations and with many of these films being shot in English;

5. An increasing domination of the Yugoslav film/video/tv market by Hollywood and foreign product;

6. At the same time, a stronger emphasis on ethnic themes and stories as the concept of "Yugoslav cinema," like that of a Yugoslav nation continues to be deconstructed;

7. The flight of filmmakers to Western countries. As I write this in the spring of 1992, over a dozen of the most respected filmmakers from all over the former Yugoslav federation are living in Europe or the United States.

All in all, these indications add up to the merging and blurring of distinctions between film/video/television as well as between the conventional divisions separating what is a "Yugoslav" and "international" film.

Back to the Future: From Black Cinema to a Cinema with no Name

Yugoslav cinema since 1945 established an admirable international reputation for daring innovation in film language as well as in highly personalized narrative visions with critical socio-political implications (Horton "The Whole Story"; Goulding "Cinema of Liberation"). Films such as Petrovic's *I Even Met Happy Gypsies (Skupjači perja,* 1967), Krsto Papić's *Handcuffs (Lisice,* 1969), Bostjan Hladnik's *Dance in the Rain (Ples na Kiši,* 1961), Pavlovic's *The Rats Wake Up (Budjenje pacova,* 1967) and *The Ambush (Zaseda,* 1969), as well as Makavejev's *The Loves of a Switchboard Operator (Ljubavni slučaji ili tragedije službenice ptt,* 1967) among others, put Yugoslav cinema squarely on the world cinema map. Both in terms of strong realism (Petrović, Papić and Pavlović) and surrealistic elements growing out of realism (Makavejev), the Yugoslav cinema of the 1960s became clearly one of the most vibrantly liberated cinemas anywhere, especially respected for reflecting in critical and/or joyful terms, the realities and spirit of Yugoslav society with all its problems, contradictions, and strengths.

Much of the energy of this period, however, was cut short by the general crackdown everywhere in the socialist countries as a reaction to the Soviet invasion of Czechoslovakia in 1969. But a new generation formed in the 1970s. For roughly a decade from 1976 to 1986, Yugoslav filmmakers, especially the so-called "Prague Group" who came into prominence in the

416

Andrew Horton

1970s (Rajko Grlić, Goran Marković, Srdjan Karanović, Lordan Zafronović, etc.), were able to successfully combat the import of Hollywood product at the box office and still bring home international festival awards. To a much greater degree than was true in other countries such as France, Italy, Germany, and Japan, Yugoslavs tended to see Yugoslav films at a rate above the appeal of most Hollywood films shown at the time. This fact made Yugoslavia virtually unique in the world, for almost every other corner of the globe was and is dominated by Hollywood's endless stream of films. These young Yugoslav filmmakers succeeded because they were able to combine something of the irreverent realism and surrealism of the 1960s with a highly professional flair (especially in cinematography) for filmmaking working within a more traditional narrative structure of story telling.

Since the mid-1980s, however, Yugoslav cinema's outlook became far less optimistic. While a number of talented younger directors and writers have emerged with promising debut films (Slobodan Pesić with his imaginative and brilliantly shot film about the Russian surrealist poet of the 1920s, *Harm's Way [Slučaj Harms]*, 1988, for instance), the opportunities for filmmaking have become much more problematic. In 1988, Srdjan Karanović made a film with the timely title of *A Film With No Name (Za Sada Bez Dobrog Naslova)* which, with bitter humor, explored ethnic conflict between Serbs and Albanians through an ironic Romeo and Juliet story. Thus by analogy, in a real sense, the post-Yugoslav film industry in the 1990s might best be, as noted earlier, called a Cinema With No Name.

Why? The increased "videoization" of post-Yugoslavia will be discussed. But three other major factors have appeared. First, there is the uncertainty of the times—that is the forefronting of political problems associated with the breaking apart of "Yugoslavia" has meant a lessening of the desire to go out to the movies; second, the growth of television; and, finally, the further deterioration of the Yugoslav cinemas themselves.

To take the latter first, even when worthy post-Yugoslav films are made, those who enjoy movies are depressed by the poor quality of the cinemas (no heat in winter, no air conditioning in summer in most theaters), and the antiquated projecting equipment which means very poor image quality on the screen and terrible sound systems (there are no cinemas in the country set up with a Dolby system). "This extends to our filmmaking equipment as well," said one film maker. "Now you know why many films from Zagreb and Belgrade are completed in Hungary, Bulgaria, Germany, France and England!' ' Clearly there is a need for the establishment of modern "multiplex" cinemas in the urban areas particularly, perhaps in co-operation with foreign distributors as seen in the Warner Brothers-Soviet Union contract to build multiplex theaters in Moscow and Leningrad. To this list we should also mention the lack of funding to adequately pre-

Post-Yugoslav Cinema/TV/Video in the 1990s 417

serve Yugoslavia's film heritage. Film maker Slobodan Sijan who is presently Director of the Yugoslav Film Archive (Kinoteka) states that if funding is not found soon, many older films will simply disappear.[1]

In terms of television, the tube now exists in practically every post-Yugoslav household. "There are 4.5 million registered sets and probably another million 'illegal' ones today," states Louis Todorović, General Secretary of the Yugoslav Television Association.[2] And in Belgrade, viewers are offered five channels including the popular "independent" CHANNEL B which has practically no government control (or financing) and often expresses an independent viewpoint and alternative programming. With cable tv beginning to be set up, today's viewers already have access to hours of CNN news and British SKY NEWS reports (full coverage of the Iraq-Gulf War, for instance) as well as everything from hard core pornography to American sit coms such as *CHEERS*, and seemingly endless hours of Yugoslav talks shows on every issue imaginable.

Sex, Socialism, and Videotape

The rise of video has been in evidence since the mid 1980s. The advent of home VCR machines which began as a trickle around 1985 has now become a flood. "Many Yugoslavs may not have an apartment of their own," mused the Director of Yugoslavija Film, V. Vučinić in 1991, "But almost all have a VCR."[3] If there are roughly 5.5 million tv sets, there are estimated to be 2.3 million home video machines, or about 30–40 percent of the television viewers (Todorovic), a figure which suggests that Yugoslavia has almost caught up with the European average of 50 percent of all television viewers.

Legalized and black market (far more numerous) video clubs throughout the country have spelled disaster for box office ticket sales, of course. The appearance of black market videos, especially in the cheap sex and violence and music/concert tape category, and continual political/social unrest help explain why audiences have stayed at home around their VCRs and television sets instead of heading for the rundown neighborhood theaters. Yugoslav films, for instance, that could often draw 250,000 first run viewers in Belgrade alone in the early 1980s now pull in fewer than 30,000. While Yugoslav film producers were never able to make much of a profit even from a "hit," the possibilities of regaining one's investments have decreased drastically today so that only the most openly commercial efforts such as Lepa Brena's musical romantic comedies (to be discussed later) can hope to pile up a few extra dinars in dwindling bank accounts.

In 1990 German movie screens were dominated 80 percent by foreign (mostly Hollywood) productions: Post-Yugoslavia in early 1992 is closely

418   Andrew Horton

in line with such figures. During late February of 1991, for instance, not a single Yugoslav film was playing in the central district of Belgrade, as David Lynch's *Wild At Heart* and other foreign films crowded out the home product.

The video revolution has meant that many new small companies have been formed to make and distribute video films. Furthermore, legislation, for the first time, has begun to define the limits of legal vs. black market video practices in Yugoslavia beginning in September 1990. Thus, as in the United States, videos now appear for sale and rental in a variety of shops besides those which are dedicated to video sales and rentals.

But while many post-Yugoslav films are available on tape (and it is a healthy spinoff of the videoization of the country that many classics which were not seen in the cinemas for years are now easy to find), Hollywood films overwhelming make up the video lists in each shop. "The video market is changing, however," comments Mikan Marinović, an executive at Avala Film in Belgrade.[4] He notes that video audiences have now worked their way through many cheap American and foreign films and, especially including an older (thirtysomething and beyond) more educated Yugoslav audience, are "eager for programming in Serbo-Croatian, Slovenian, Albanian or whatever," comments Marinović. The potential for made-for-video films, therefore, is great.

The Age of the Producer

While the Yugoslav film industry was in effect highly decentralized for several decades and thus did not go through the sudden clashes and changes that Soviet cinema experienced in its rapid decentralization, an important shift in all formally socialist-communist countries has been that from a "director driven" industry to a "producer driven" era. Or perhaps to be more accurate we should mention the new compromise: the producer-director. During the mid 1980s there were more than twenty production companies scattered throughout the various republics and provinces. Now that number has more than tripled with many smaller companies being established by filmmakers themselves.

Rajko Grlić of Zagreb, for instance, has formed his own company, Maestro Film, which, until the end of 1991, financed and handled his productions and those of several other Yugoslav filmmakers including Goran Marković and Srdjan Karanović in imaginative cooperation with other agencies and more traditional companies such as Centar Film and Avala Film of Belgrade as well as with companies in France and England. Grlić's 1989 "Maestro" film, *That Summer of White Roses* which won the Grand Prix and Best Director award at the 1989 Tokyo Film Festival, was based on a Croatian

Post-Yugoslav Cinema/TV/Video in the 1990s   419

story about a sympathetic simple fisherman/lifeguard (well played by Tom Conti) during World War II whose life changes as he enters a marriage of convenience to save a refugee (Susan George) and her son from the Nazis and was shot in English with English and Yugoslav financing (Susan George was one of the producers). In 1991, however, he released *Charuga*, based on an outlaw tale somewhere between "Lenin and Al Capone" in Serbo-Croatian and financed through Maestro in coordination with Viba Film of Slovenia and TV Zagreb in Croatia.

Grlić's Maestro Film has also acted as co-producer for Srdjan Karanović's 1991 film, *Virgina*, a moving story of a young girl at the turn of the century raised as a boy according to a peculiar ancient custom in the countryside, with financing and support from a French company as well as Centar Film, the last of the large remaining producers in Belgrade.[5]

Such new freedoms impose new limitations, however. At a recent conference devoted to Soviet and East European Filmmakers Working in the West (Petrie) held at McMasters University many participants pointed to the difficulty of filmmakers used to being somewhat "pampered" and left with what amounted to almost complete artistic autonomy under socialist regimes, now finding it extremely difficult to become "team players" in a producer- driven system. Obviously becoming a producer-director allows the director his or her own control. But unlike the "socialist autonomy" of the past in which certain "prize" directors were able to devote full attention to their projects, now the new producer-director, like his American counterpart, must spend an increasing amount of time in fund raising, "taking" meetings, and dealing with distribution and non artistic worries. "When filming, I used to think mostly about my film—story, cinematography, acting—but now I have to think about money, money, money all the time," remarks director Srdjan Karanović.[6]

In the short run, such a further fragmentation of the post- Yugoslav film industry has led to even less income from, for instance, foreign sales. While in the past, the formerly state supported agency "Yugoslavija Film" used to negotiate foreign sales for most of the Yugoslav producers (as well as handle foreign festivals and much of the import business) with something like a million dollars a year in export sales to over forty countries negotiated at the Cannes Festival each year, the 1989 Cannes market brought in only about $300,000 for Yugoslav films as individual studios and production houses attempted to close their own deals (Vucinić).

Close Up: Emir Kusturica on an Artistic Business Trip

If the overall film and video view is confusing, individual directors continue to cut a distinguished path for image making in the Balkans. And

420

Andrew Horton

no former-Yugoslav film maker in recent years has received more critical and popular attention at home and abroad than Bosnian director Emir Kusturica. A brief consideration of his career is not only to detail a particular success story but also to indicate trends and directions within post-Yugoslav cinema in the 1990s as Bosnia, Kusturica's home republic, has emerged as the most imaginative and energetic filmmaking center in the country.

American Film magazine pointed out that given the fact that he has only made three feature films, each of which has been showered with awards, he can be considered, at age thirty five in 1990, the most celebrated film maker in history (Pachasa). Among many important honors, he has won the following: for *Do You Remember Dolly Bell? (Sjećas li se Dolly Bell?)* the 1981 Golden Lion for a first film at the Venice Film Festival; and at Cannes, for *When Father Was Away On Business (Otac Na Službenom Putu)* the coveted Palme d'Or of 1985 for Best Film; and in 1989, also at Cannes, for *Time of the Gypsies (Dom za Vesanje)*, the Best Director Award.

Already it is possible to speak of Kusturica's career as falling into two camps: his early work including television films and his first two features made entirely as Yugoslav productions and then, beginning with *Time of the Gypsies*, his international production phase. A third stage yet to come will be to work on an international scale *in English*, beginning with his 1991 production to be shot in Arizona and Alaska.

Educated at FAMU, the famed film academy in Prague like the generation ten years his senior known as the Prague Group, Kusturica has absorbed influences of both the quality humanistic film tradition of the Czech new wave of the 1960s (and, subsequently of the Prague Group in Yugoslavia) and Western influences including everything from John Ford and genre pictures in filmmaking and rock'n'roll in music (he still plays with a rock group from time to time in his native city of Sarajevo).

Kusturica is an important force in the "novi" (new) Yugoslav cinema in part because he is a Bosnian film maker and therefore outside the three major filmmaking centers: Belgrade (Serbia), Zagreb (Croatia), and Ljubljana (Slovenia). *When Father Was Away On Business*, for instance, was produced by a tiny company, Forum Film of Sarajevo. While on one level Kusturica reflects the kind of international rock music and Hollywood movie influences felt around the world, on a deeper level he is also a reflection of and spokesperson for a particular Muslim based Bosnian culture. Kusturica's worldwide success, therefore, was "read" by many in post-Yugoslavia as a hopeful sign that one does not have to live and work in one of the three major centers to gain a personal, national, and international voice and audience. The "Bosnian movement" was due not only to talented young directors including Zlatko Lavanić, Miroslav Mandić, Zoran Gospić, Mirza Idrizović, and, as we shall see, Ademir Kenović, but to the

Post-Yugoslav Cinema/TV/Video in the 1990s 421

strong organizational and financial support given these filmmakers. Much of this support came both from the "cultural fund" of the Bosnian state and the resources of Forum Film, a production company based within a larger company controlling the cinema theaters throughout the republic.

Time of the Gypsies marks an unusual new development for Kusturica and, perhaps, for future filmmaking in the former Yugoslavia. Rather than a co-production as such, that is, a joint financing of a film through a Yugoslav based company and a foreign producer, *Gypsies* was a Columbia Pictures Release encouraged by the then-President, David Puttnam. With a budget of under two million dollars, Kusturica felt he had freedoms he had never had on his highly restricted Yugoslav film budgets, yet, in a Hollywood marketplace with average budgets of twenty six million dollars and climbing, the cost to Columbia was negligible.

Almost every case of a foreign director working for a Hollywood or British producer—say Bertolucci when making *The Last Emperor*—has meant the need to work with an international cast in English. David Puttnam provided Kusturica the rare chance to not only NOT film in English and without stars, but to make a feature film entirely in GYPSY with a largely Gypsy cast of non professionals. Furthermore, working conditions for the young director were almost ideal: nine months allowed for shooting followed by a year and a half of editing.

The film is a remarkable epic of gypsy life today in Yugoslavia and Italy, based on the actual illegal practice that has gone on for years in which gypsies sell their own children to "godfathers" who in turn use or sell these children into slavery, prostitution, or crime in Italy. With a script by Yugoslavia's leading scriptwriter, Goran Mihić (a prolific writer who somehow manages to write what seems like half the films made in Yugoslavia!), *The Time of the Gypsies* has the stark dramatic power of, once again, John Ford's *Grapes of Wrath* (a study of dignity within poverty of an entire people) and the hints at "magical" transformation of a crushing reality found in South American fiction such as Gabriel Garcia Marquez's *One Hundred Years of Solitude*. Furthermore, the film is a loving and knowing homage to Yugoslav cinema (I counted direct allusions to over seventeen important Yugoslav films of the past thirty years), most especially to the best celebrated Yugoslav film of all time, Aleksandar Petrović's *I Have Even Met Happy Gypsies* (1967), which, like Kusturica's film, chose to focus on that ethnic-socio class which was at the bottom of Yugoslav culture and which was both within Yugoslavia but always separate.

Starring Davor Dujmović as Perhan, a grandson of a proud, funny, and powerful Gypsy matriarch, Hatidza (Ljubica Adžović), who grows to become a Gypsy godfather himself (and Coppola's *Godfather* is also a blatant model here), the narrative also works in moments of "magic realism" since Perhan is born with certain powers to "make things move." No simple

422   *Andrew Horton*

plot summary can do justice to the powerful effect the film has had on audiences around the world (I personally have seen it in crowded theaters in Moscow—a standing ovation— and New Orleans). What needs to be stressed, however, is that while Kusturica deserves credit as the overall architect of the project, part of his architecture is in gathering an extremely talented group of film workers around him.

Several Yugoslav critics prefer Kusturica's earlier films and in particular the controlled simplicity of *Do You Remember Dolly Bell?* But no one denies Kusturica's ability to evoke a full range of human emotions in *Gypsies.* There is absurdist humor (the scene in which the no-good gambling Uncle Merdzan lifts Perhan's house clean off its foundations by a simple rope tied to his scooter), lyricism (the coming-of-age ceremony in the river as Perhan views his lovely girlfriend Azra naked and joins with her), magical realism (Perhan's ability to make simple objects move around by concentrating on them, an ability which leads to the unexpected death of the Gypsy Don by the film's end), mystical beauty (the haunting movement of Perhan's mother's veil following his car through the countryside evening), violent shabbiness (drunken dance sequences in a Gypsy dive), and heart wrenching sadness (Perhan's final departure from his son in an Italian train station, for instance). As *The Washington Post* wrote, "This is a movie full of hauntingly beautiful moments" (Hinson).

Yet for all of Kusturica's talent, opportunities and awards, his career remains perhaps even more "in between" than before. Consider the fate of his films in the United States. *When Father* played briefly in a handful of major cities and then closed without ever appearing on video. *Time of the Gypsies* also appeared in only a few cities months after its Cannes success and then went direct to video, more or less "dropped" by Columbia which did not know how to market a film in Gypsy.

The major barrier, of course, is linguistic. Thus Kusturica, like other Yugoslav directors, is faced with the necessity of rethinking their approach to cinema: if they shoot in English, they have a crack at the international market, especially with the enlarged Euromarket beginning in 1992. But in doing so, they lose something of the flavor and accomplishment they have built up as native artists.

Kusturica is more fortunate than most: he had the chance to teach for several years at Columbia University in New York and has recently released *American Dreaming* (1992) shot in Arizona and starring Jerry Lewis, Johnny Dep and Faye Dunaway.

Middle Distance Shots: A Period of Adjustment

Much of Yugoslav cinema of the late 1980's and early 1990's bears the same trademark of quality productions about important issues that have

Post-Yugoslav Cinema/TV/Video in the 1990s 423

long appeared on Yugoslav screens. Antun Vrdoljak's *The Glembays* (*Glembajevi*, 1988), for instance, is a lavish 19th century aristocratic family melodrama full of glum corruption, "murders and cheats," as an old woman in the film says, and a melancholy search for a dead mother by a lost son. Bato Cengić, on the otherhand, who had offered such innovative works as *The Role of My Family in the World Revolution* (*Uloga moje porodice u sujetskoj revoluciji, 1971*) *and Portraits From the Shock Workers' Life* (*Slike iz života udarnika*, 1972) returned in 1989 with a war tale set in 1941, *Silent Gunpowder* (*Gluvi Barut*) which openly and directly confronts the clash during World War II between the Chetniks (non-Communist Yugoslav forces) and the Communists. And Carpo Godina who has worked in Slovenian cinema since 1969 as a cinematographer and director, ended the 1980s with *Artificial Paradise* (*Umjetni raj*) which primarily traces the few months spent by a young Fritz Lang in Slovenia as a soldier in World War One. Scenes of sterile life during this ending period of the Austro-Hungarian empire are intercut with what became Lang's "Artificial Paradise" in *Metropolis*.

Using these three recent productions from three different republics— Godina (Slovenia), Cengić (Bosnia), and Vrdoljak (Croatia)—as examples, we detect something of the malaise that currently inhabits and inhibits post-Yugoslav cinema. Each film is an award winning production (*Paradise* played at Cannes, for instance, and *Gunpowder* at Montreal and other festivals). Yet none attracted much interest from Yugoslav audiences and certainly not from foreign customers. Quite frankly, many critics felt there was something of the smell of the museum about all of these and many more being produced throughout the country.

The Glembeys plays like a BBC historical production without a BBC script (that is, without wit and subtle cynicism). *Silent Gunpowder* in suggesting the ambiguous nature of the early Communist movement during the War would have been an explosive work twenty years ago, but current newspapers, books and magazines as well as current events have outstripped the edge such a film might have had and, even today, a film such as Pavlovic's *Ambush* already handled such themes more effectively.

Finally in a year that gave the world the emotionally charged self reflexive *Cinema Paradiso* as a meditation on life and cinema, *Artificial Paradise* had the potential to enter the same ring, but even with a script by Branko Vučićević who has penned many of Makavejev's best works as well as those of other Yugoslav directors, this film suggests that the Austro-Hungarian Empire died of boredom rather than Revolution, cinematic or actual. That the film has one of the most telling exchanges in recent Yugoslav cinema was not enough to pull in an audience which is lured by other distractions: says one character about the formation of modern Yugoslavia, "We have a new state of Serbs, Croats and Slovenes in which everyone is dissatisfied."

424   *Andrew Horton*

If we briefly compare the Yugoslav film situation, for instance, with that of the Soviet Union we can detect a telling contrast. Because Soviet filmmakers did not have the freedom to make "black" films that were politically, socially, sexually open as did the Yugoslavs, the period of *glasnost* beginning in 1985 has led to a true revolution of experimentation and exploration in the arts, most especially in cinema. Thus despite what these films lack in artistic quality, Soviet movies such as *Little Vera, Zerograd and The Fountain* have succeeded in connecting with large audiences hungry to experience new forms and subject matter on the screen.

No such revolution has occurred in recent Yugoslav cinema. Many directors who appeared revolutionary years ago such as Cengic and Godina as well as others such as Lordan Zafronovic (a disappointing attempt to explore sexuality and political themes in *Whore's Holiday [Praznik kurvi]*, 1988 or Živko Nikolić's exploration of the same territory in *The Provocation*, 1989) and others now appear as status quo. This point is underscored all the more by the re-release of films from the 1960s and 70s not seen since their initial release. Centar Films in Belgrade, for instance, has embarked on a valuable program to bring back many of these films including, in 1989, the late Ivica Matić's *A Woman in A Landscape* (*Žena s krajolikom*) completed as a television film in 1976. A Bosnian film about a naive painter in a mountain landscape, the film, made before the Soviet Georgian film *Pirismani* on a similar theme, is shot as "naive cinema" (cinematography by Karpo Godina who directed *Artificial Paradise*). The still fresh clarity and simplicity of the film has reminded worldwide audiences who have now seen the film how startling and vibrant Yugoslav cinema was during that period.

New Trends: Novi Realism vs Novi Spiritualism

Two dominant trends are emerging among filmmakers who care to go beyond the level of pure entertainment. On the one hand there is a return to a harsh realism first explored by Pavlović and others in the 1960s in films such as Ademir Kenović's admirable first effort, *Kuduz* (1989) which won more than twenty Yugoslav awards including Best Director, Actor, Actress and Screenplay as well as a strong popular following (the most successful first film since Slobodan Sijan's *Who's Singing Over There?*) and praise at international festivals including Montreal. And almost diametrically opposed would be a cinema that with the collapse of socialism (and its emphasis on a materialist ideology) represents a new interest in spiritualism and "another reality," as seen in films such as Goran Paskalević's *Time of Miracles* (*Vreme čuda*, 1989) and Goran Marković's *Meeting Place* (*Sabirni Centar*, 1989).

Post-Yugoslav Cinema/TV/Video in the 1990s 425

Kuduz is impressive for its hard hitting simplicity as a tale taken from a newspaper story about a Bosnian man who is released from prison, attempts to lead a "normal" life, but is crushed by "life" and winds up murdering the one he loves, saved only by his love for his five year-old daughter. While Hollywood has been busy offering fantasy escapism from the harsh realities of urban crime and the rise of drug and AIDs related epidemics in such films as *Batman, Ghostbusters, Pretty Woman* and even the "yuppie comic realism" of *Home Alone*, Ademir Kenović represents a younger generation of Yugoslav filmmakers who wish to get back to basics and to a more direct style of filmmaking.

A Bosnian, Kenović is influenced by Kusturica and in fact wrote the script for *Kuduz* with Abdulah Sidran who did the script for Kusturica's *Do You Remember Dolly Bell?* and *When Father Was Away On Business*. An English major at the university in Sarajevo, he did a thesis on Shakespeare and film before working for television where he learned to do, "Everything! I made commercials and documentaries. That was my true education," he comments (personal interview. Montreal: August, 1990).

The film is narrated by the author, Sidran, who plays the character of a train station employee within the film. An edge of irony is added to the text finally as this narrative framing device is put into question when a young man comments to Abdulah at the end, "You're lying." Narrative or literal truth? In a feature documentary on the making of the film, *Kuduz, Lies and Truth*, the real-life character who is still serving time for the murder of his ex-wife comments having seen the film, "Nothing in this film happened in my life but this film is my life."

This form of truth is what Kenović feels drew in such large audiences. "People could identify with the reality in the film which is not urban or the village, but a rough kind of suburb on the edge of the city, neither one nor the other," he states; *Kuduz* catches a no-win reality of people (Muslim in this case), with meaningless jobs caught in a vicious cycle of conflicting traditional and modern ideologies, customs, temptations. Kuduz wants a good life. Yet both his environment and his hot-blooded temperament make such a life a dream, not a reality. Only with his young daughter do we really see moments of happiness with a motif which reminds us of the innocent passages found in *When Father Was Away On Business*.

Time of Miracles offers a very different subject and style. Goran Paskaljević helped launch "the Prague Group" in the mid 1970's with such winningly realistic films as *The Beach Guard in Winter* (*Čuvar plaže u zimskom*, 1976) and *The Dog Who Loved Trains* (*Pas koji je voleo vozove*, 1977). But with *Time of Miracles*, he touches on the dangers of, as he has noted, "moving from ideology to fanaticism" (*Time of Miracle* press kit) in a narrative about 1945 when a simple country church taken over by Communist partisans

426   *Andrew Horton*

becomes the site for a miracle: the icons of the church which had been whitewashed over to convert the church into a Partisan led school house, suddenly reappear through the whitewash, not once but several times, to the despair of the "true believers" of Communism. Parallel to this main plot is a subplot involving a Christ figure, a holy fool, who is ultimately "crucified" in yet another reworking of the Christ narrative.

Paskaljević has been at pains to claim his film is not religious, but "spiritual," that is, concerned with both the dangers of communist fanaticism and with the much longer sense of Yugoslav tradition which embraces a strong sense of spiritualism. Written by Borislav Pekić who spent seven years in prison for "anti-Communist" activity, the script and the film reflected a long-standing interest for many in Yugoslavia for exploring the spiritual side of life which was so long discouraged. It seems no accident that such a film appeared at a time when the village of Medjugorje a short distance inland from the Coast has for recent years received millions of religious visitors from around the world because of the alleged appearance of the Virgin to several teenagers there. "The orthodox faith protected many Yugoslavs for over 500 years under Turkish domination," comments Paskaljević (personal interview. Montreal: August, 1990), "So it is a big mistake for the Communists to have said that history and culture began when they came into power."

Goran Marković takes a transcendental bittersweet ride beyond the grave in *Meeting Place* which we could term the Yugoslav *Ghost*, that extremely popular Hollywood embodiment of American interest in life after death. In fact, we would say that Markovic, who has for a number of years now been interested in genre films, has combined *Raiders of the Lost Arc* with a *Ghost* like theme in a story about an archeologist who discovers a Roman passage into "the other world." Comedy and a moving depth mix as the archeologist suffers a heart attack and enters the in between zone, neither dead nor alive, in which he is in contact with both.

Ms. Yugoslavia: Leaping for Lepa

A consideration of the present and future of films from the former Yugoslavia would be incomplete without a mention of the most impressive box office success of recent years: the well managed phenomenon of pop singer turned actress (of sorts), Lepa Brena.

Imagine something of a blending of Madonna, Marilyn Monroe, Dolly Parton and a dash of Doris Day for good measure and you have some idea of the polyphonic appeal of this Balkan bombshell. Her tapes and records and concerts have sold millions and made millions as she dishes up a variety of "novi" folk styles that have captured a broad popular following. In

Post-Yugoslav Cinema/TV/Video in the 1990s   427

a 1990 sold out concert in a packed football stadium in Bulgaria, for instance, her extravagant sound and light show involved her entrance via
the ex-communist leader's personal helicopter lowering her to the stage in
a sexy, shimmering outfit to the thunderous applause of tens of thousands
of fans.

A Muslim from Bosnia by culture and Fahreta Jahić by name before
her astute manager/producer Raiko Djokic packaged her as Lepa, she has
been the star of a highly profitable series of films called *Let Us Love Each
Other* (*Hajde Da Se Volimo*), parts one (1988), II (1990) and III (1991), directed
by Aleksandar Djordjević. Part two, for instance, not only sold several
million cinema tickets but racked up an outstanding 35,000 video tapes
sold. The films are cleverly constructed entertainment vehicles that nevertheless satisfy audience expectations for political/topical themes as well.

In *Let Us Love Each Other II*, the plot is hung on the simple premise that
Lepa needs a "new look" for her musical show. That's it. Thus over ten
songs, each in a different style from pop rock sung in English and shot in
London, to Turkish belly dancing "I am a slave to love," to numerous
Adriatic bikini numbers gloriously lit and shot, and ending in a clearly
symbolic grand finale with Lepa singing "I am a Yugoslav" as the song
cross cuts between Lepa as a wholesome peasant woman ("My hair is
wheat!") and as a sexy beach siren ("Is the free sunshine shining on you?")
and, finally, with seemingly all of Yugoslavia dancing and singing behind
her, "My soul is Yugoslav!"

The formula is foolproof. She is the virtuous Yugoslav virgin Earth
Goddess and the seductive Circe who nevertheless chooses no single man
of the hundreds she comes in contact throughout the films. That she is all
things to all men and the true embodiment of Yugoslavia herself, is seen in
the third version in which the plot hinges on recognition of Lepa as a national treasure who is in danger of marrying a rich Australian. Thus the
Yugoslavs must save her from foreign domination and keep Yugoslavia
whole!

To talk of Lepa's films is not to speak of Cannes Festival prize winners.
But perhaps more important for Yugoslavs as a whole, Lepa offers both
entertainment and hope as well, as we have seen, embodied in the title as
well, a dream of a unified and happy Yugoslavia. Film scholars will note,
of course, the similarities of the "Lepa phenomenon" in Yugoslav cinema
and the importance of musicals to America and the Soviet Union in the
1930's when the Big Screen offered up fantasies that did not exist in reality
but which audiences eagerly devoured.

Finally those involved have added a political dimension as two drunken
characters, one Serb and one Croatian, taken from a popular stage play,
trade insults mirroring the uneasiness of the times pumped up to wry humor and slapstick farce. It seems safe to say that Lepa may last longer than

428

Andrew Horton

Yugoslavia itself. And she will do so as a multi-media myth. By the time that civil war broke out during the summer of 1991, however, not even Lepa was able to sell many movie tickets. The public had basically given up on movie going all together.

New Kids on the Block: The Fall of Rock and Roll

Good news. Promising new talent with a healthy irreverent streak built in is emerging and will bear fruit in the 1990s. Three young directors made their debut in a three-storied "thesis film" romp for their graduation from the Academy of Dramatic Arts in Belgrade: *The Fall of Rock and Roll (Kako Je Propao Rokenrol* 1989). Zoran Pezo crosses a zany farce that blends a "Yugo-Ninja" plot with that of a Yugo country and western record company (you can imagine the music!), while Vladimir Slavica captures some of the youthful sex and playfulness of Godard's short, "All The Boys Are Named Patrick," in his bedroom vampire sex farce which features a witty script with lines such as, (she to him) "You're a sexual terrorist" and (he to her) "I would sell my soul for a good fuck." A post modern sense of absurdity reigns here as the toilet handle is attached to a cassette player and references to movies, vampires, rock'n'roll saturate each frame. Goran Gajić from Zagreb deftly etches a sex triangle farce worthy of a Balkan Boccaccio entitled "Send Me No Letters." His joyful, fun-loving cinematic celebration suggests that one way or another, new voices are rising and will be heard, often combing, like Lepa, music, movement, movies.

Freeze Frame: Beyond Ethnic Borders

All experts seem to agree: the future of the republics of the former Yugoslavia will rise or fall not so much on economic issues as on those of ethnic and nationalistic disputes.

We should end with a parting shot at three films that address this most pressing of divisive topics.

A first film by Zoran Nasirević, *The Border (Granica*, 1990), written by veteran film maker Z. Pavlović and Ferenc Deak and originally meant for Pavlović as a project, treats the post War period of 1945–48 on the Yugoslav-Hungarian border. As in D.W. Griffith's *Birth of a Nation, The Border* depicts the destruction of two families, one Serbian and the other Hungarian, by the erection of "borders" between nations. The film is in many ways another "running in place" effort that has been done much better in the past, especially by Pavlović himself. Yet the message of the film is certainly timely enough: near the end when in spite of love and much coop-

Post-Yugoslav Cinema/TV/Video in the 1990s

eration at times between the two families, most of the family members have been killed off in one way or another, the two fathers meet and talk about the possible marriage between the Hungarian daughter and Serbian son. Is the Hungarian afraid that the marriage will dilute their Hungarian blood? The father gets angry and says, "First of all they are human beings, damn it. The only way for us all is to stop trying to preserve our race and tear down the borders within ourselves." Noble words, of course, yet in 1991, there appears little likelihood of such a message being seriously heeded as over a thousand people have died as of this writing as national troops clash with Croats over disputed boundaries.

And Srdjan Karanović's *A Film With No Name* concerns a documentary film maker's effort to film the truth about the tragic love story, Romeo and Juliet style, between a Serbian man and an Albanian woman in the troubled predominantly Muslim area of Kosovo. The marriage between the two has been halted by the cutting off of the Serb's penis by the Albanian relatives, but, in tragi-comic irony, we learn the bride-to-be is already pregnant. Despite immense difficulties for the film maker and for the couple, the film closes with the couple leaving Yugoslavia by train, "fed up" with the whole situation, and carrying the only print of the film of their troubled lives with them on request of the film maker. In the final sequence the couple toss the film out of the speeding train and in slow motion followed by a freeze frame we see the film unravel endlessly along the railroad track, discarded and abandoned.

Will this be the fate of post-Yugoslav cinema? Time will tell.

The immediate future has supported the bleak ending of this film, for Karanović's latest film, *Virgina*, is ironically about a Serbian girl brought up as a man in the Serbian section of Croatia at the turn of the century. This unusual drama was, furthermore, a Serbian-Croatian-French co production. Judged by many former Yugoslav film critics as one of the most important Yugoslav films ever made, the film has, as of this writing, been withheld from a general post-Yugoslav release not only because of the civil war, but also because of the in-fighting among the co- producers.[7]

Two final footnotes are worthy of attention, however. Lazar Stojanović, the only Yugoslav film maker to go to prison (three years) after the crackdown on the freedom of expression in the early 1970's, finally had his day of justice during 1991 when his long banned film, *Plastic Jesus* (1971), was finally released. This playfully irreverent experimental film which was made as a student thesis film under the influence of Stojanovic's teacher and mentor, Dušan Makavejev, played not only to praise in Yugoslavia, but also won the Critics' Prize at the 1991 Montreal World Film Festival and was screened widely around the USA and Europe. This self reflexive send up of Tito, the Nazis and all repression, emerges as a light at the end of a very dark tunnel for future young filmmakers in the various republics of

430   *Andrew Horton*

what was Yugoslavia who will, no doubt, find a way to create at last a new cinema with a name.

And in the midst of the current tragic war, Goran Markovic managed to complete a film with the provocative and evocative title of *Tito and Me* (1992). The film is both nostalgic and critical as an almost Italian neo-realistic tale of a young boy obsessed with Tito who wins a school essay contest for a "best essay on Tito" but who comes to see the hollowness of socialism and of the constructed Tito image. Such a work stands as a tribute to all post-Yugoslav filmmaking: despite war, hatreds, lack of money and materials, honest, moving, and artistically realized films may still be possible.[8]

Notes

1. Personal interview. Belgrade, June 1989.
2. Personal interview. Belgrade, February 1991.
3. Personal interview. Belgrade, June 1989.
4. Personal interview. Belgrade, February 1991.
5. The film was voted one of the top ten films of 1991 at the European Oscars ceremony during the Fall of 1991, with Marta Keler the young girl-boy receiving a "Felix" award. In 1992 it began to play the festival circuit including the San Francisco Film Festival and the Montreal Festival of World Cinema.
6. Personal interview. Belgrade, February 1991.
7. In *Virgina's* Belgrade release, it outsold *Terminator 2's* initial run.
8. For further discussions of this subject, see: Daniel J. Goulding (ed.), *Liberated Cinema: The Yugoslav Experience* (Bloomington: Indiana University Press, 1985); Daniel J. Goulding (ed.), *Post New Wave Cinema in the Soviet Union and Eastern Europe* (Bloomington: Indiana University Press, 1989); Andrew Horton, "Do You Remember Dolly Bell?" in *Magill's Survey of Cinema: Foreign Language Series* (Pasadena, Calif.: Salem Press, 1986), pp. 846–50; Andrew Horton, "Filmmaking in the Middle: From Belgrade to Beverely Hills," Graham Petrie & Ruth Dwyer (eds.), *Before The Wall Came Down: Soviet and East European Filmmakers Working in the West* (Lanham, Md: University Press of America, 1990); "'I'm A Yugoslav': National Images of Conflict on Film," in *Exquisite Corpse*, Vol. 34 (Winter 1992) pp. 27–28; Andrew Horton, "Oedipus Unresolved: Overt and Covert Narrative Discourse in Kusturica's *When Father Was Away On Business*," in *Cinema Journal*, Vol. 27, No. 4 (Summer 1988) pp. 64–81. Reprinted in Serbo-Croatian in *filmograf*, Vol. 14, No. 3 (Fall 1988) pp. 58–64; Andrew Horton, "The Whole Story: Yugoslavia's Multi-Faceted Cinema," in *World Cinema Since 1945* (New York: Ungar, 1986); Andrew Horton, "The Yugoslav Film Industry," in Tony Slide (ed.), *The International Film Industry: A Historical Dictionary* (Westport, Conn: Greenwood Press, 1988); and Arlene Pachasa, "Time For Kusturica," in *American Film* (March 1990) pp. 40–42.

18

The Catholic Church
in a Time of Crisis

Jure Kristo

Multiple are the "crises" to which the title of this chapter refers. It comprises economic hardships and shattering of identity and refers to the change of political system followed by a vicious war on the territory of former Yugoslavia, a war of aggression on Croatia and Bosnia-Herzegovina by Serbia and Montenegro using the Serb-dominated Yugoslav army and various irregular forces.

To a perceptive observer, the cracks in Yugoslavia were visible for some time, but they became life-threatening in the late eighties. The most vulnerable side of former Yugoslavia was the never resolved issue of equitable relations between its component nations. The official line that relations among the national groups were idyllic only succeeded in temporarily suppressing the feelings of frustration and anger.

What was the place of religion in the demise of Yugoslavia and in the Serbian aggression on Croatia? What was the role of the Catholic Church? I will take a closer look at this Church, which is the dominant religious denomination in Croatia and which has traditionally been a strong religious community in Bosnia-Herzegovina. My analysis will be focused on the political role of the Church, leaving its other aspects to mere cursory references. Moreover, I have assigned myself the modest task of following chronologically the activities of certain Church dignitaries who have had perceptible political impact. One has to bear in mind that ethnic Serbs in Croatia counted for less than 12 percent of the population (as of spring 1991), and most of them felt (and feel) at least a nominal attachment to the Serbian Orthodox Church. Ethnic Serbs in Bosnia-Herzegovina comprised over 30 percent of the total population. For this reason, the political role of the Catholic Church cannot be fully understood without at least an occasional reference to the Orthodox church.

432

Jure Kristo

At the outset, a frequently encountered assumption of Western journalists has to be dispelled: there is no religious war in former Yugoslavia. The war that is raging there is a clear-cut example of aggression intended to conquer a piece of real estate from a neighbor. But religious institutions have contributed a great deal to the creation of an atmosphere in which war became possible and in which its destructiveness was assured. Not surprisingly for a region where the identification of religion and national identity has been traditional, ethnic tensions have affected relations between religious groups.[1] Religions differ, however, as do their roles in society. (Serb) Orthodoxy has historically been mostly interested in promotion of the interests of the Serbian nation. (Croatian) Catholicism, even though opposed to equating faith and nationality, has regularly managed to be in the forefront of the defense of Croatian national interests. Muslims of Bosnia-Herzegovina have only recently even forged their national identity upon a religious basis. Hence, it was to be expected that contributions of these differing religious groups to the downfall of communism and the start of war would be different.

The End of the Communist Era

The Catholic Church under the communist regime in Yugoslavia went through various stages of coolness in its relationship to the state, but that relationship was invariably tense. Generally, the Church hierarchy was either persecuted or merely tolerated and the faithful were practically reduced to the status of second-class citizens.[2] It was not much different at the end of the 1980s, when communism began to crumble in Eastern Europe.

The first sign of trouble for Yugoslavia was material, as the country slid into deep economic crisis during the eighties. With the economic crisis, it became evident that this unhappy country knew but crises. This coincided with the departure of Josip Broz Tito, the President for life, but his departure was more an occasion for the appearance of weaknesses of the system which he had constructed than the cause of the crisis. The country had been passing, among others, through a trying spiritual crisis, a catharsis so powerful that it seriously threatened the society's very life. That crisis manifested itself in fanned Serbian nationalism and frustrated hegemony; its most visible manifestation was a vicious anti-Catholic and anti-Croat propaganda.[3] Although it is difficult to fathom the irrationality of this propaganda, its basic contours seem to be manifest: just as the communists had instinctively felt that the Catholic Church was an enemy which had to be defeated, so the Serb nationalists knew that the submission of Croats must go via the destruction of their Catholicism. The common thread

The Catholic Church in a Time of Crisis 433

of all of these literary products was the "misrepresentation of the past through various half-truths and mistaken interpretations of historical facts."[4] Its strategy was the portrayal of the Croatian people as Nazis, the implication of the Holy See in an alleged anti-Serb conspiracy,[5] and the accusation of Croats and the Catholic Church of allegedly endangering the Serb people in Croatia.[6] Many Serbian intellectuals became involved in this anti-Catholic propaganda, but the names of Vasilije Krestić, historian, Dobrica Ćosić, writer, and Amfilohije Radović, Orthodox bishop from Banat, stand out.[7]

The Catholic Church was aware both of the growing social crisis and of the tides of anti-Catholic propaganda. Its position was further complicated by the fact that it had to continue dealing with a hostile communist government. But by the end of the 1980s, the Croatian communists were experiencing a general malaise which lessened their traditional antagonism toward the Church. In fact, there was a favorable change in the communists' attitude toward religion, producing an atmosphere more tolerant of religious activities.[8] For example, for Christmas 1988, Zagreb TV for the first time ever extended good wishes to Catholic believers.[9] If one were to conclude that this move represented a genuine change of heart on the part of the Communist party toward believers (mostly Christians), it would be a wrong inference. The party apparatchiks even intensified their attacks on church buildings,[10] their interference with liturgical ceremonies,[11] etc. The party in Croatia persisted in judging the Church by traditional criteria: its stance toward "the fundamental values of the Socialist Federal Republic of Yugoslavia," i.e., "the brotherhood and unity and general stability of society."[12] Nonetheless, reality was forcing the Croatian communists to change certain of their attitudes.[13] They found themselves faced with Milošević's aggression (which was driven by a frenzied nationalism fueled and nurtured by the 1986 Memorandum of the Serbia Academy of Sciences).[14] And they were convinced that the unscrupulous anti-Catholic propaganda also represented an attempt to overthrow them. Thus, the more liberal wing of the party tried to avoid tensions between the government and the Catholic Church.

The Croatian communists could not, however, give the impression of siding with the Catholic Church. They resolved their dilemma by remaining ambivalent, and hence distributed the blame equally among the involved parties, in this case the Catholic and the Orthodox Churches.[15] This is clear from Celestin Sardelić's address at the meeting of Central Committee of the League of Communists of Croatia (CC LCC) of 22 May 1989. In the best communist tradition of inventing incomprehensible terms, Sardelic talked about the Catholic and Orthodox confessions exclusively as representatives of "clerico-nationalism," allowing no difference between the two sides in their defense of "national interests."[16] He was, of course, handi-

434   *Jure Kristo*

capped by the fact that the party allowed no consideration of any alternative political arrangements on the territory of Yugoslavia from those provided by the Yugoslav communists themselves.

More than equally distributing the blame, the Croatian communists made an ostensible effort to please the Serbian Orthodox church in Croatia. In the light of later developments, the consecration of the St. Dimitry's church in Dalj has a special symbolic value. The church renovation was financed by the Croatian government, and at ceremonies of consecration the old Orthodox patriarch, German, was present, which gave an added gravity to the occasion.[17] Only a few months later, after Serbia invaded Croatia, Serbs of this town massacred Croats, and the Serbian Orthodox Church not only did not condemn the slaughter, but one of its bishops saluted the forceful acquisition of Baranja by Serbia. No less symbolic was the renovation of a monastery near Knin. Unlike Catholic church buildings, the renovation of the monastery at Krk was financed by the Croatian government. The Croatian state even paved the 4.5 km. of the road to ease the access of Patriarch German when he came to mark the six hundredth anniversary of the battle of Kosovo. The celebration, held 8–9 August 1989 near Knin, was yet another occasion for local and visiting Serbs to celebrate Serbdom and to contest Croat sovereignty.[18] It was in Knin that Serbs began to erect road blocks and started an armed uprising with the help of the federal army.

Paradoxically, the Catholic Church had the easiest time in its relationship with the communist government since World War Two. The fact that Croatian communists were manifestly incapable of countering Serbian hegemonistic tendencies and anti-Croat propaganda made it much easier for the Church. The Church was faced, however, with new and more difficult challenges: on the one hand, it had to defend both itself and the Croatian people against inimical propaganda and, on the other hand—in the vacuum created by the indecision of the Croatian communists—it had to defend the nation's right to self-determination. In the turmoil of the end of 1980s, the Church plunged into both of these murky waters. Zagreb archbishop Franjo Cardinal Kuharić warned about the destructive behaviour of the Serbian leadership, which (in his words) seemed to be aimed at the abolition of the "natural and historical right" of Croats to sovereignty, and which directly threatened the coexistence of peoples in the Balkans. The Cardinal specifically cautioned about the destructive nature of anti-Catholic, anti-Croat, and anti-papal propaganda.[19]

Unlike his communist compatriots, the Cardinal was not timid about the defense of national sovereignty. The Catholic bishops were convinced that by defending Croatian sovereignty they were doing something good; national sovereignty belongs to the set of values the Church has always felt it has to defend. One such opportunity was the debate about the con-

The Catholic Church in a Time of Crisis   435

stitutional amendments concerning the name of the official language in the Socialist Republic of Croatia. Catholic priests, gathered at the Theological-Pastoral Week in Zagreb, backed the formulation found in the Constitution of 1974, where the official language was said to be the "Croatian literary language."[20] A similar statement was issued by the Catholic theological faculty in Zagreb,[21] followed by the statement of the Theological Society "Krščanska Sadašnjost" (Christian Present) in the same spirit.[22] The bone of contention was the adjective "Croatian" as the name of the language used in Croatia; ethnic Serbs of Croatia insisted that the official language should be called "Serbo-Croatian or Croato-Serbian." They were adamant about this, and their claims of national endangerment at this stage were based on the Croatian opposition to this constitutional amendment.[23]

The anniversary of the death of the late Alojzije Cardinal Stepinac, on 10 February, was traditionally a barometer for the status of the relationship between the Catholic Church and the regime. In his homily for the occasion in 1989, Cardinal Kuharić outlined what the church considered to be the good of a nation: "freedom to live and to develop its identity and its sovereignty in all areas of life: moral, spiritual, cultural, (and) material, finding its expression in statehood."[24] This is a clear language, leaving no doubt that the hierarchy of the Catholic Church looked with favor on the aspiration of Croatia's people to establish a sovereign state. Kuharić's position was soon bolstered by the collective body of Croatian Catholic bishops. From their meeting on 2–4 October 1989 in Djakovo, the prelates addressed to the faithful a letter in which they complained of an alleged "incessant strengthening of a program of *psychological terrorism* aimed particularly at the Croat people imposing upon it a collective guilt," which is creating in people a "feeling of anxiety."[25] The talk about "psychological terrorism" was strong language, but an idiom commensurate to the times and a realistic evaluation of the dangers threatening all Croatian people. By the same token, the Croatian Catholic bishops advocated not only a democratic transformation of Croatian society (free elections), but also a freedom of "association" as an expression of a 'culturally higher level of existence,' which particularly concerns the "building of coexistence in justice and mutual respect" with other nations.[26] This indicates that the Catholic bishops supported the idea promoted by Croatian and Slovenian politicians of a confederal structure for the Yugoslav state. This represented an example of "realpolitik" of Croatian Catholic bishops. The confederalization of Yugoslavia was at the time a high priority of Croatian politicans, to keep the constituent people relatively satisfied, help the Yugoslav quagmire be peacefully resolved, and eliminate the sources of future conflicts. As is known, the Serbian politicians, like Western power-wielders, not only rejected this idea outright, but undertook a military campaign to punish its advocates.

436   *Jure Kristo*

The Catholic Church in Croatia was, naturally, in tune with the Holy See in Rome. One of the concerns of the Church in modern times has been protection of human rights. Guided by this principle of defending human rights, the Catholic Church of Croatia not only countered the Serbs' anti-Catholic propaganda, but continued to protest the violations of human rights, particularly in the province of Kosovo. Moved by the strike of Kosovo's miners at the Trepča mine in 1989 and by oppression of the Albanian population by Serbs in this region, the Executive Board of the Bishops' Conference of Yugoslavia issued a statement on 27 February 1989 which called on all political factors not to favor any national interests at the expense of human life.[27] Cardinal Kuharić issued a personal statement in the same spirit, and the Slovenian regional bishops' conference sent a telegram of support to Skopje Auxiliary Bishop Nikola Prela.[28] The Bishops Conference of Yugoslavia again addressed the situation in Kosovo at its spring session (4–6 April 1989).[29] Its Justitia et Pax Commission discussed the human rights violations in Kosovo at its first meeting on 7 April 1989. The Commission expressed serious doubts that the emergency measures introduced in that province served to advance the protection of human rights; indeed, the Commission pointed out how those rights were even further curbed.[30] Cardinal Kuharić again issued a personal statement on 3 February 1990 asking for the respect of human rights in Kosovo.[31]

By comparison, the Serbian Orthodox Church disapproved of such apparently innocuous messages of humanitarian content. As a response to the actions of the Catholic hierarchy, the Theological Faculty of the Serbian Orthodox Church in Belgrade refused to send its delegation to the commemoration of the Faculty Day of the Catholic Theological Faculty in Ljubljana.[32] More than a mere pouting of a bruised body, this reaction of an important institution of the Serbian Orthodox Church represented the beginning of a retreat from its involvement in ecumenism. The evidence suggests that the Serbian Orthodox Church's ecumenical activity was motivated solely by the hope of political gains for the Serbian nation. This impression is confirmed by consulting earlier statements by Pribislav Simić, the Dean of the Theological Faculty in Belgrade. Commenting on the absence of its institution from the Ljubljana ecumenical encounter, he indicated that the interest of his institution in ecumenism ceases the moment that the partner in dialogue refuses to back Serbian policy in Kosovo. Simić emphasized, however, that the Serbian Orthodox Church supported the preservation of Yugoslavia. In the parlance of Serbian politics at the time, this was a variation on the theme that all Serbs must live in one state.[33]

The Catholic Church in a Time of Crisis　437

The Enticement of Democracy

The end of 1989 marks the beginning of a new epoch for the part of the world which outsiders somewhat condescendingly called "Eastern Europe," and whose peoples shared the experience of the domination of communist ideology and terror. By the end of that year, this ideology and the world it fashioned began to crumble.[34]

Even before the momentous collapse of communism, there was talk in Croatia and Slovenia about introducing a multiparty system and free elections. The religious communities, particularly the Catholic Church, actively participated in these discussions. There was also a general relaxation of the remaining communist regimes' policies toward religion. In Yugoslavia, this was evident in increasingly open discussions about making Christmas a national holiday.[35] The traditional New Year reception of religious representatives at the Croatian Parliament (Sabor) at the beginning of 1990 was very telling. It was particularly significant when compared with the previous such reception. Under the spell of the grandiose sudden changes in the European East, Andjelko Runjić, the president of the Sabor, sounded a conciliatory tone and wanted to be more than magnanimous to the religious communities, especially the Catholic Church.[36] Speaking in the name of the Catholic Church, Zagreb archbishop Cardinal Kuharić analyzed the "signs of the times," and offered his own views of political events in Croatia and Yugoslavia. Noting the consequential changes in Europe and saluting the more or less peaceful retreat of communist power from the world scene, the Cardinal underscored the importance of multiparty political systems as an essential pre-condition of democracy which was hesitatingly creeping into the territory of the Balkans. He advanced the principle that governs the Catholic Church in political matters which he had often invoked: "The Church is not a political party and does not intend to share power with any political party."[37] In order to dispel any doubts that the Church advocates a certain abstract democratism with no reference to concrete people, Kuharić underscored the national right "to a homeland, sovereignty and identity, which includes the right of cultural, economic, and security development."[38] The Cardinal spoke in moral terms and on the level of principle, but the political significance of his phrasing was not lost on his listeners.

Other church institutions were no less decisive in championing the advantages of democracy. The Catholic weekly *Glas koncila* frequently educated the readership how "democracy is the highest degree of the Gospel's application in social and state life."[39]

10 February 1990 marked the thirtieth anniversary of Cardinal Stepinac's death, and provided an excellent opportunity for submitting a balance sheet on the Church's relations to the state. *Glas koncila* made a

438   *Jure Kristo*

particular effort to show how Cardinal Stepinac had been unjustly persecuted by the communist state and sentenced to sixteen years of hard labor,
immediately commuted to internment. It published a translation of an
article from the Vatican daily *L'Osservatore Romano*, which had appeared
twenty years earlier and which had been the cause for the confiscation of
that issue. It also defied the ban on any mention of Stepinac and for the
first time in Yugoslavia published the statement Stepinac had made at his
trial. *Glas koncila* journalist Tomislav Vuković commented on the pastoral
letter of the Croatian bishops issued in September 1945, which the communists had used as a pretext for the persecution of the Church. Vuković
compared this statement of the Catholic bishops with a similar letter by
the Orthodox bishops which had never aroused communist ire.[40] Cardinal
Kuharić's homily, however, avoided mentioning any outstanding difficulties in the relationship of the Church with the communist government; the
Croatian communists were in such a state that they needed help, and the
Church showed itself to be more than willing to succor the communists.
The Croatian people, communists and non-communists alike, needed more
than anything a message of hope; consequently, the deceased archbishop,
Alojzije Stepinac, was portrayed as a man of hope.[41]

The Church found itself in a completely different situation at the beginning of 1990, which marked the commencement of pre-electoral party
activity. It should be noted that the hierarchy of the Church grew younger
by ordination of new bishops. At the end of 1989, Želimir Puljić was installed as bishop of Dubrovnik. At the beginning of 1990, Antun Tamarut
became the residential archbishop of Rijeka, following the resignation of
Josip Pavlišić. Also in 1990, Srećko Badurina, a younger scholarly man
from the Franciscan Third order, became the bishop of Šibenik.

It is apparent that the Church wholeheartedly espoused the prospect
of free elections in Croatia. The episcopal commission "Iustitia et Pax,"
presided by the Šibenik bishop Srećko Badurina, issued a statement about
free elections on 26 January 1990. Acknowledging that the recent formation of several political parties in Croatia represented a giant step toward
democracy, the statement reminded readers that this process must culminate in "free, direct, confidential, and valid elections." The statement
also underscored the need to secure equal financial means as well as access to public media for all political parties. Furthermore, it warned the
faithful that participation at free elections is their obligation.[42] The
Church's advocacy of free elections was a calculated move; it was certain
that the free expression of the people would mark the end of communism
in Croatia.

The new political life showed, however, the complexity of the Church
as an institution and the difficulties associated with applying clear principles in practice. Certain problems were specifically Croatian. On the one

The Catholic Church in a Time of Crisis

439

hand, Church guidelines forbid participation of the clergy in political party life. On the other hand, aware of the nonexistence of democratic institutions, the Church in Croatia wanted to be involved in the delicate process of initiating normal political life. True, Church legislation leaves it to the discretion of a local bishop to allow the participation of a cleric in politics,[43] but the church was also aware of the politicians' tendency to use the clergy for their own political purposes.

These became agonizing dilemmas with the emergence of multiparty political life in Croatia. At the founding convention of the Croatian Democratic Community 24–25 February 1990 in Zagreb, three Catholic priests were elected members of the party's governing body.[44] There were several other priests and one nun present at the convention, and it was public knowledge that the Croatian Democratic Community had many sympathizers among the Catholic clergy. One should keep in mind that Franjo Tudjman, the president of the Croatian Democratic Community, banking on his past as a partisan general, communist prisoner, and founder of the first anticommunist political party, and skillfully using good timing, began a national movement more than a classical political party, a movement which focused on a single goal: the establishment of full Croat sovereignty. This goal could be accomplished only through the defeat of communism. Such an aim was capable of mobilizing the public in Croatia, and people readily identified with the message of the Croatian Democratic Community. Beside ostentatious displays of the hitherto taboo Croatian flag and the denunciation of alleged "enemies of the people" by new arrivals from the Croatian diaspora, the novelty of this party convention was that its schedule included a daily mass at the Zagreb cathedral. The second day of the convention, Tudjman himself was present at the beginning of the mass. This was perhaps for him the beginning of still another personal transformation: from the partisan Bolshevik commissar to Croatian patriot searching for Christian roots.[45]

Politicians rarely hesitate to manipulate religion and the church for their political purposes. At least the Catholic weekly was aware of it; in an editorial entitled "The church does not allow itself to be manipulated," *Glas koncila* warned politicians who may have popular support that they cannot have unconditional and uncritical support.[46] The Church assumed this position of safe distance from the most popular new political party in Croatia, the Croatian Democratic Community. In addition to including a few priests in its executive board, the Croatian Democratic Community used Cardinal Kuharić's letter declining to attend the convention as an expression of the Cardinal's support for the party and its convention. The Catholic weekly *Glas koncila* had to deny such an interpretation of the Cardinal's action.[47] Kuharić himself explained that the presence of priests at the convention cannot be interpreted as the Church's support of the

440   *Jure Kristo*

party.[48] In any event, the Church leadership decided that no valid reasons existed for any political engagement on the part of the clergy.[49] The official church claimed that the continued involvement of two priests in politics was without deeper significance. Being a retired priest, the Sarajevo archbishop claimed that Anto Baković, a former priest of his diocese, could not be prevented from political involvement. Tomislav Duka took a leave of absence from his Franciscan order while holding a political appointment.

Other political groupings did not bypass religion in their programs and activities. The Croatian Social Liberal Alliance (CSLA) devoted a chapter in its program to religion. Reminding its readers of the injustices that religious groups, particularly Catholic Church, had suffered under communists, the Liberals promised their correction.[50] Not even the League of Communists of Croatia wanted to miss the opportunity to include religious people in their program. Of course, they needed either to justify or to criticize the practice of religious persecution under their direction. Certain Catholic circles, such as the Theological Society Christian Present, were still willing to give the communists a helping hand, at least by continuing to participate in discussions about religious freedoms under their sponsorship.[51] Communists even attempted to put the leftist priest Luka Vinčetić on their electoral list, which he declined.[52]

The official Church continued using its offices for shaping political environment. The Bishops' "Iustitia et Pax" Commission warned on 3 March 1990 of the "reappearance of fear-inducing methods" applied by communists. The Commission invited communists "to cease speaking in the name of people before their legitimacy is confirmed by free elections."[53] It also invited other parties to care more about "national reconciliation" than about narrow party interests and to avoid assuming the exclusive right to interpret recent Croat history.[54] Priests working with Croatian emigrants in Germany addressed a petition to the Croatian Sabor (on 8 March 1990) demanding permission for Croats working abroad to vote in impending elections.[55] The Croatian Catholic bishops had a letter read on 12 March 1990 in all churches concerning the approaching elections. The bishops advised the faithful to vote for "that program and those representatives who will most contribute to the good of the people and each individual."[56] The criterion for electing someone, according to the bishops, should be his or her prior accomplishments, and the criterion for choosing a program should be the likely veracity of the individual's promises. In any event, the Croatian electorate was fully cognizant of the communists' many broken promises and that in fact hurt the Communists' chances in the elections. It was, of course, also important whether a particular program allowed for the Church's freedom to operate in the area of its competency. Finally, the Church was aware that

The Catholic Church in a Time of Crisis 441

one of its important tasks was to dispel pervading fear in people if they opted for a party and before changes which a multiparty system would introduce.[57]

The Church also felt the need to educate people in democracy. In a pastoral letter addressed to all priests (dated 17 March 1990), Catholic bishops stated that the Church's presence in politics was the requirement of the Gospel. The priest is in a difficult position, having to help people discern which political program is the most promising and yet avoiding an endorsement of any particular political party. In any event, the faithful should be able to make their own political decisions regardless of options their priests might choose.

Given the above criteria, and provided that the faithful would listen to their bishops—which was not doubtful—it was already clear that the communist party still in power could not win free elections. Moreover, since the Croatian Democratic Community proposed a program which was the most directly opposed to that of communists, the outcome of the forthcoming elections in Croatia was already decided. The majority of the Catholic electorate had, indeed, opted for the Croatian Democratic Community, and against the coalition which ran on a platform suggesting less radical political changes.

Democracy and Its Opponents

The Catholic bishops promptly reacted to the results of the first democratic elections in Croatia in decades. From the spring session of their conference in April 1990, they urged the need "to accept with confidence and respect the expressed will of the citizens of Croatia." It was undoubtedly the communists and their sympathizers who needed this encouragement more than the faithful.[58]

Having free elections in Croatia behind them, the leadership of the Catholic Church transferred its attention to Bosnia-Herzegovina. Since the Bosnian situation was essentially different, the Church had to devise a separate strategy. It was readily apparent to anyone familiar with the Bosnian-Herzegovinan situation that only parties with clear national programs could succeed there. Moreover, ethnic affiliation there has long been closely associated with religious traditions. A considerable number of Yugoslavs, mostly offsprings of mixed marriages, were a lost group that had had the hardest time adjusting to the new political realities on the Balkans. One of the most challenging issues for political organization in Bosnia-Herzegovina was the fact that the constitution prohibited forming associations on the basis of religious and/or national partnership. Hence, the Catholic Church made efforts to strike that provision from the books.[59] At the same time,

442   Jure Kristo

the faithful were encouraged not to fear organizing themselves on a national and religious basis.[60]

The opening session of the new Sabor in Zagreb on 30 May 1990 represented also a reintroduction of the Catholic Church into its traditional place in the political life of the nation. Cardinal Kuharić presided over the mass in the cathedral. The mass was attended by the majority of parliamentarians, and other religious representatives arrived later (although the Serbian Orthodox clergy were conspicuously missing) for the first session of the Sabor.

The absence of Orthodox representatives from the opening session of the new Sabor was not accidental. Ethnic Serbs in Croatia, most of whom at least nominally belong to the Orthodox church, comprised a majority of the police and military and held a disproportionately large number of government posts, which also meant that most of them were members of the League of Communists. They, as well as their Church, felt that a communist electoral defeat would mean the disappearance of the privileges they had enjoyed. Moreover, the Croatian Democratic Community, headed by Tudjman, appeared particularly threatening, since its representatives did not hide the fact that they would curtail those privileges. Moreover, in order to secure the votes of the majority of Croats, Tudjman's party appealed to people's emotions; their promises ranged from the reintroduction of Croatian national symbols to the securing of Croatian sovereignty and self-determination. It was not too surprising that an ethnic Serb attempted to assassinate Tudjman during the electoral campaign.

There were also other ominous signs of tension between Croats and their ethnic Serb neighbors. The buses with Catholic pilgrims were occasionally pelted with stones and the travellers were maltreated.[61] The most painful incident was a seizure by the Orthodox Church of the Catholic church of Saint Savior in Cetina, near Sinj.[62] In March 1990, the Catholic weekly *Glas koncila* began a series of articles penned by Tomislav Vuković, which for the first time revealed, based on archival documents, the Serbian Orthodox Church's support of and collaboration with the Nazi regime in Belgrade during World War Two.[63] This was a Catholic response to the anti-Catholic and anti-Croatian propaganda of the Serbian Orthodox Church. Obviously, this did not lower the temperature in the already heated realm of Croat-Serb relations. The Catholic hierarchy and the press tried to warn against (Croatian) nationalism which would denigrate other nations and would raise the nation to the highest value.[64] But events were heading in a different direction. In any case, when Tudjman came out as a big winner, the Serbs and the Orthodox Church could not hide their disappointment.

In mid-August 1990, ethnic Serbs in Croatia erected the first barricades in the vicinity of Knin, Obrovac, Gračac, and Benkovac, and the Yugoslav People's Army obstructed the intervention of the Croatian police. This

The Catholic Church in a Time of Crisis

was the beginning of armed aggression against Croatia aimed at nullification of the results of free elections and the obliteration of Croatian sovereignty.[65] This was also the beginning of numerous massacres of Croatian victims and of the material devastation of sacral and cultural monuments.

The leadership of the Catholic Church was as baffled as the rest of the Croatian people. Their perplexity was increased by the fact that the Serbian Orthodox Church was an agent of instigation of this rebellion. In September 1990, the Serbian Orthodox Church in Croatia issued a statement which could only be interpreted as an escalation of hostility between ethnic Serbs in Croatia and the Croatian government; the Church effectively involved itself in the war against Croatia. From its meeting in Pakrac, the Orthodox bishops encouraged their faithful "to secure for themselves the right to life on their age-old hearths in Croatia by armed sentinels [and] barricades."[66] They justified the armed uprising of ethnic Serbs in Croatia as a response to "political-police pressure," which had allegedly manifested itself in "increasingly frequent, literally daily, cases of intimidation, threats, insults, job firings, demolition of houses and apartments, acts of arson, attacks and violence of every kind, and there were cases—in Dalmatia—of proven rapes and homicide."[67] The bishops did not provide any proofs; neither were the proofs provided after the Croatian government expressly asked for them. Apparently, no proofs existed. In a strongly intoned editorial, the Catholic weekly came short of calling the Orthodox bishops liars.[68] Indeed, with the exception of incidents which rarely had national connotations, the allegations of a systemic oppression of ethnic Serbs by the new Croat government were not based in reality. The only exception might have been the allegation of dismissals from jobs, but that almost exclusively concerned the police force, which had been disproportionately staffed by ethnic Serbs.

More than baffled, the Catholic Church representatives were as angry as the rest of the people. The official Church tended to support the president in his feisty rhetoric when actions were missing. But different accents were, nonetheless, noticeable. While Cardinal Kuharić expressed his hope for the preservation of peace and liberty of *all citizens of Croatia*,"[69] the Zadar bishop Marijan Oblak, the president of the Bishops' Conference Council for migrations, and Vladimir Stankovic, the coordinator of the pastoral work for the Croats in diaspora, expressly urged the president to prevent the creation of a Serbian autonomous province in Croatia, which would be tantamount to the negation of Croat sovereignty.[70]

The Challenges of Democracy

It was ever becoming clearer that the Catholic Church could not prevent the war against Croatia. Cardinal Kuharić delivered a homily in which he lamented the large number of war-related fatalities among both clergy

444   *Jure Kristo*

and laity. At the same time, he praised the police for their efforts to assure the security of Croatia's citizens and expressed concern that they too had had casualties in the war.[71] The Church also tried to prevent violent reactions of Croats against material goods of the Orthodox Church. Both the Catholic press and the highest body of the church deplored the lapidation of the Orthodox Church in Zagreb and interference with church services.[72] But these steps could not change much in the course of events; as is known, an all out war against Croatia would soon follow.

Surprisingly, in spite of the war, some democratic reforms were continuing. The Catholic Church was one of the most significant beneficiaries of these political changes. Soon after the new government assumed power, it offered to let the Church organize religious education in schools. Even though there was no unanimity among Catholics as to the wisdom of this move,[73] the hierarchy accepted the offer, and the first classes of religious education in primary and secondary schools were introduced by the start of the new school year 1990. In summer of 1990, the Faculty of Theology was again made part of Zagreb University. By the end of that year, hospitals, nursing homes, and homes for the elderly secured space for liturgical services. The most significant political event took place at the end of 1990: a new Constitution was promulgated in the Sabor. The Catholic weekly *Glas koncila* did not miss the opportunity to emphasize that its significance stemmed from the fact that it was not only the first non-communist constitution, but the first such document of Croatia as a sovereign state. Neither did the paper fail to endorse the new constitution, emphasizing its "secular" nature and its clear separation of the Church and the state. The paper's editorial lauded the document for its "humanness," its concern for the rights of all Croatian citizens.[74]

The political presence of the Catholic Church in the new democratic society of Croatia seems to follow the trodden path. It tries to stay away from party politics and direct political involvement in order to remain a powerful moral force.[75] The passage from a well structured and constrained atmosphere under communism to a looser democratic and pluralistic ambience of a young democracy has not unfolded without stress and problems. While the church has easier access to the public forum, it is at the same time being more readily challenged on several fronts. The issue of legalized abortion has already made waves. The Church has also been criticized for bolstering Croatian nationalism,[76] even though its manifestations are less marked. The communists have criticized the Church for being too visible in the media and for advancing the views of Catholic Croathood.[77]

Since June 1991, the foremost preoccupation of the Church, as of entire nation, is the Serbian war against Croatia and Bosnia-Herzegovina. And it is to the consequences of war that I return in concluding this chapter. Thou-

The Catholic Church in a Time of Crisis 445

sands of lost lives, more than 2.5 million refugees and homeless people, hundreds of destroyed national monuments, especially churches, mosques, museums, and libraries, substantial destruction of infrastructure, agriculture, and industry, and enormous losses of revenue—these are the sorry results of the aggression on Croatia and Bosnia-Herzegovina. The Church, as all Croatian people, is particularly frustrated because of the apparent inability or unwillingness of the Western democracies to stop the aggression, especially after they have recognized both Croatia and Bosnia-Herzegovina as independent states.

The most significant activity of the Catholic Church during this time has been distribution of food and other humanitarian aid. A few matters of potential political significance can, nonetheless, also be mentioned.

First, finding itself in an independent state, the Catholic Church has already begun thinking about its administrative structure in the Republic of Croatia. Unlike Slovenia and Bosnia-Herzegovina, Croatia was divided into three metropolises, and the Zagreb hierarchy wants now to see the Croatian Church organized around a single metropolis, which will undoubtedly be based in the state capital, Zagreb.[78] This will certainly imply a division of the Zagreb archdiocese, one of the largest in the world, into several dioceses. Only the war has prevented the bishops from moving more quickly with these administrative changes.

Second, the anniversary of Cardinal Stepinac's death in 1992, preceded by the recognition of Croatia by the European Community on 15 January, was the occasion for Cardinal Kuharić to note the Church's satisfaction that the Cardinal's figure ceases to be a political issue. His political "rehabilitation" was completed on 14 February 1992, when the Croatian Assembly (Sabor) passed a resolution declaring Stepinac's trial, together with other similar trials, to have been purely political and unjust.[79]

Third, in August 1992, Bishop Josip Bozanić from Krk, the head of the Council for Laity of the Croatian Bishops' Conference announced a conference to discuss the place of the laity in the Church. In addition to bad organization, other unexpected issues emerged when the conference was held in October. Although the meeting showed that there were many organizations of lay people among Catholics of Croatia, discussions and subsequent reactions demonstrated a deep dissatisfaction, even resentment, of some active lay Catholics with their treatment by the clergy.[80]

Fourth, while the country as a whole is preoccupied with securing its sovereignty over its entire territory (as defined by the republic borders of the SFRY), other issues press onto the agenda, such as the transition from the socialist to market economy, the return of Croatian refugees to their homesteads, the rebuilding of cities and villages, the rising crime rate. Thus, traditional Church and state issues are not the primary concerns of either partner. There are indications, however, that there is a great deal of good

446

Jure Kristo

will and mutual understanding on the part of the ruling Croatian Democratic Community and of the Catholic Church in Croatia—and this can only make for a Church-state relationship dramatically different from that of the communist era.[81]

Notes

1. Belgrade Catholic archbishop Franc Perko (a Slovene) warned how tensions in ethnic relations are causing "inter-confessional strains which prevent the development of ecumenical relations." See Franc Perko, "Suprotnosti našeg vremena," in *Blagovest* (Belgrade), Vol. 54 (December 1988).

2. See Jure Kristo, "Catholicism Among Croats and its Critique by Marxists," in Dennis J. Dunn (ed.), *Religion and Nationalism in Eastern Europe and Soviet Union* (Boulder, London: Lynne Rienner Publishers, 1987), pp. 77–95; Jure Kristo, "Relations Between the State and the Roman Catholic Church in Croatia, Yugoslavia in the 70's and 80's," in *Occasional Papers on Religion in Eastern Europe*, Vol. 2, No. 3 (June, 1982), pp. 22–33; and Sabrina P. Ramet, *Balkan Babel: Politics, Culture, and Religion in Yugoslavia* (Boulder, Colo.: Westview Press, 1992).

3. The indications of this systematic defamation of Croat Catholicism are numerous; they range from the Serbian Academy of Sciences and Arts analysis of causes and consequences of "Yugoslav crisis" known as Memorandum (1986) (see "Memorandum SANU," in *Naše Teme* (Zagreb), Vol. 33 (1989), No. 1–2, pp. 128–163) to numerous books and various media pieces. Mere titles of some of this production provide a gist of its intentions. A Belgrade publisher reprinted Viktor Novak, *Magnum crimen: Pola vijeka klerikalizma u Hrvatskoj* (Belgrade: Nova knjiga, 1986). An anti-Catholic pamphlet authored by a Croat, member of Free Masonry, which was originally issued as preparation for the trial of Zagreb archbishop Alojzije Stepinac in 1946 was also published. Dragoljub Živojinović and Dejan Lučić hurried with their "supplements for Magnum crimen" *Varvarstvo u ime Hristovo* [Barbarism in the Name of Christ] (Belgrade: Nova Knjiga, 1988). In 1987, Vladimir Dedijer published his book *Vatikan i Jasenovac* (Belgrade: Rad, 1987). The same year a Belgrade publisher issued the translation of a calumniatory booklet by Herve Lauriere, *Ubice u božje ime* [Murderers in God's Name] (Belgrade: Rad, 1988). Milan Bulajić, *Ustaški zločini genocida* [Genocidal crimes of the Ustashe] (Belgrade: Rad, 1988), and later in English. See Vladimir Dedijer, *The Yugoslav Auschwitz and the Vatican*, trans. into English from the German translation by Harvey L. Kendall (Buffalo, N.Y.: Prometheus Books, 1992). See also "Novi prilozi za istoriju bešćašća," interview of Luka Minčeta with Dragoljub Živojinović, "Novi prilozi za istoriju bescasca," in *NIN* (Belgrade), No. 1983, 1 January 1989, pp. 41–42.

4. Perko, "Suprotnosti" [note 1].

5. The Serb anti-Catholic propaganda was reaching the point of hysteria and paranoia. Belgrade newspapers seriously discussed how Josip Broz Tito paid the Vatican in gold to honor him with a feast (in the Catholic calendar, St. Joseph [Josip], the Worker on 1 May). (See P.Z., "Crkveni praznik koji zbunjuje čaršiju," in *TV Novosti* (Belgrade), 19 January 1990, p. 17.

The Catholic Church in a Time of Crisis   447

6. V. I. Mlivončić, "Crkve, cirilica, seobe," in *Slobodna Dalmacija* (Split), 7 January 1989, p. 6.

7. Amfilohije Radović said that the Croat people is "traumatized similar to a child that had a sadistic father." As reported by TV Zagreb, "TV dnevnik 3" (18 September 1989).

8. A significant contribution to this changed attitude toward religion not only in Yugoslavia but in "Eastern Europe" as a whole was made by the work of the reigning pope John Paul II. Not less important was the fact that the leadership of the Soviet Union was in the hands of Mikhail Gorbachev. A mutual encounter of these two men at the end of the eighties had a beneficial effect on the attitudes of communist regimes toward religion.

9. The well-wishing for Christmas 1988 was highly visible in the media; see *Aktualnosti Krščanske Sadašnjosti* (AKSA) No. 2/973 (13 January 1989), pp. 8a–9a.

10. For an attack on the church in Baška Voda near Makarska, see AKSA No. 3/974 (20 January 1989), p. 1.

11. See AKSA No. 1/972 (6 January 1989), p. 1 about the interference with the liturgy in Rab.

12. The Sabor's president, Andjelko Runjić, on the occasion of the New Year well-wishing ceremonies for the ecclesiastical representatives. Concerned for the "brotherhood and unity," he asked religious representatives about the status of ecumenism in this region. See AKSA No. 3/974 (20 January 1989), p. 3.

13. The communists even began to discuss the possibility of making Christmas a state holiday. Radio Zagreb, "Dnevnik" of 4 December reported about such a proposal by the Commission for religious questions. See AKSA No. 50/1021 (15 December 1989), p. 13.

14. See the chapter by Ivo Banac in this volume for details, and also the sources listed in note 3.

15. Luka Vinčetić, a Catholic priest of leftist leanings, felt obliged to react to such an equilibrated distribution of guilt: "I see a tremendous difference between, let us say, that everyday behavior of the Catholic Church in Croatia and elsewhere and the Serbian Orthodox church in Serbia and elsewhere"; see his letter "Stetna pacifikacija," in *Danas* (26 September 1989), p. 2.

16. See AKSA No. 21/992 (26 May 1989), pp. 4–5.

17. Zagreb Television, "TV dnevnik 2" (14 May 1989).

18. See Zagreb Television, "TV dnevnik 2" (25 June 1989); Marinko Čulić, "Kokarde opet sjaju," in *Danas* (18 July 1989), pp. 7–10.

19. The speech at the Sabor reception for religious representatives, as reported in AKSA No. 3/974 (20 January 1989), Prilog IV, pp. 1–5.

20. AKSA No. 5/976 (3 February 1989), p. 3.

21. AKSA No. 4/975 (27 January 1989), Prilog I.

22. *Ibid.*, Prilog II.

23. The Serb Orthodox clergy of the Dalmatian eparchy demanded the name "Serbo- Croatian or Croato-Serbian" as a sign that "the Serb people in Croatia are not discriminated against." See Meri Stajduhar, "Duhovi iz boce," in *Danas* (23 May 1989), pp. 35–37.

24. AKSA No. 7/978 (17 February 1989), Prilog I, p. 3.

25. See AKSA No. 40/1011 (6 June 1989), Prilog IV, pp. 9–11, my emphasis.

448   *Jure Kristo*

26. *Ibid.,* p. 11.

27. AKSA No. 9/980 (3 March 1989), p. 1. This declaration was signed by archbishops of Zagreb, Franjo Cardinal Kuharić, and Ljubljana, Alojzije Šuštar.

28. *Ibid.,* pp. 1–2.

29. AKSA No. 14/985 (7 April 1989), pp. 4–5; No. 15 (14 April 1989), p. 1.

30. AKSA No. 15/986 (14 April 1989), p. 3.

31. See AKSA No. 6/1029 (9 February 1990), p. 2.

32. Dragan Antić, "Iznevereni duh ekumenizma," in *Politika* (8 March 1989), p. 9.

33. Dragan Antić's interview with P. Simić in *Intervju* (Belgrade) (17 March 1989), p. 5.

34. It is probably too early to speculate about the most important contributors to the demise of communism, but it is not difficult to see that the leadership of the Catholic Church made a substantial contribution to that process. *Time* magazine implied that Pope John Paul II and former president of the USA, Ronald Reagan, had a kind of vow to work toward the goal of dismantling the world communism. See "The Holy Alliance," in *Time* (24 February 1992), pp. 12–19. There is no doubt that the pope in his formal appearances directly attacked communism, and in some of his apostolic letters equated naziism and communism as equally responsible agents for World War Two. See V. Inoslav Bešker, "Dvije iste dogme i bijeg od boga," in *Vjesnik* (Zagreb) (28 August 1989), p. 3.

35. Such discussions were conducted even in Bosnia-Herzegovina, traditionally more hesitant republic to initiate any changes whatsoever; see the letter of the Vrhbosna metropolitan to the Executive Committee of the Assembly of Bosnia and Hercegovina, AKSA No. 2/1025, Prilog II, pp. 12–13. In Serbia, Christmas was accorded generous publicity and celebrated there according to the Julian Calendar; see AKSA No. 2/1025 (12 January 1990), p. 6.

36. See "Čestitka predsjednika Sabora Andjelka Runjića," in AKSA No. 3/1026 (19 January 1990), Prilog II, pp. 13–14. It is also significant that the representatives of the Serbian Orthodox Church refused to attend this reception. Given the symbolic significance of this event, the Serbian Orthodox Church was in fact negating the Croat sovereignty. The reason for their absence was detectable from Runjić's congratulatory address: "the voices of darkness are coming from certain milieus, which would change borders, annul nations, regulate relations with other people according to their criteria, and provoke fratricide war." (*Ibid.,* p. 14).

37. "Čestitka kardinala Kuharića", AKSA No. 3/1026, 19 January 1990, pp. 14–16. The Zagreb archbishop often expressed similar views: the church "closes itself in no political party nor does it identify with it, but evaluates from a moral standpoint the values each party advocates." (Radovan Stipetić, "Božicni intervju s kardinalom Kuharićem," AKSA No. 52/1023, 29 December 1989, Prilog).

38. "Čestitka kardinala Kuharića" [note 37].

39. *Glas koncila* (13 May 1990), p. 2.

40. See *Glas koncila* (11 February 1990), p. 3.

41. "Govor kardinala Kuharića o kardinalu Stepincu," AKSA No. 7/1030 (16 February 1990), Prilog I, pp. 17–20.

42. "Izjava Komisije BKJ za pravdu i mir," AKSA No. 5/1028 (2 February 1990), p.1.

The Catholic Church in a Time of Crisis

43. Zakonik kanonskog prava, CIC, kan. 287, para. 2.

44. They are Anto Baković, retired priest of the Sarajevo archdiocese, Tomislav Duka, Franciscan friar, and Franjo Čuk, pastor of the Zagreb archdiocese.

45. In the interview for the organ of the Catholic youth magazine *Mi* (*Zbor. Prilog lista mladih "Mi"* Vol. II/1992, No. 1 (11), pp. 4–6), Tudjman talked about his Christian upbringing and about spiritual renewal on Christian foundations.

46. *Glas koncila* (4 March 1990), p. 2.

47. *Ibid*, p. 3.

48. This could not dissuade some of the reappearance of "political Catholicism"; See Ivica Mlivončić, "Politički katolicizam?," in *Slobodna Dalmacija* (Split) (27 February 1990), p. 6.

49. The Conclusion of the Executive board of the Episcopal Conference of Yugoslavia of 28 March 1990. See also "Predizborno pismo hrvatskih biskupa svećenicima," AKSA, No. 14/1037 (7 April 1990), Prilog I, pp. 14–15.

50. See "Religija integralni dio kultiviranog duhovnog života," AKSA, No. 9/1034 (16 March 1990), pp. 3–4.

51. The participant at the panel organized by the Zagreb City Committee of SKH "Religious rights and liberties" held 9 March 1990 was Josip Turčinović, the president of Catholic Theological Society Christian Present.

52. See *Glas koncila* (25 March 1990), p. 12.

53. "Izjava Komisije BKJ Iustitia et pax", AKSA, No. 10/1033 (9 March 1990), p. 1.

54. *Ibid*.

55. "Peticija Saboru za bira ko pravo hrvatskih iseljenika," AKSA, No. 11/1034, pp. (16 March 1990), p. 1.

56. "Predizborno pismo katoličkih biskupa Republike Hrvatske," AKSA, No. 12/1035 (23 March 1990), pp. 1–2.

57. *Ibid*.

58. "Priopćenje za tisak s proljetnog sabora BKJ u Zagrebu, 24–26 April 1990," in AKSA, No. 18/1041 (4 April 1990), pp. 1–2.

59. AKSA, No. 23/1046 (8 June 1990), Prilog II, p. 13; also AKSA, No. 26/1049 (29 June 1990), pp. 1–2.

60. AKSA, No. 26/1049 (29 June 1990), p. 1; also AKSA, No. 29/1052 (20 July 1990), Prilog I, p. 15.

61. See *Glas koncila* (24 June 1990), 2.

62. *Glas koncila* (3 June 1990), p. 5.

63. The first installment appeared on 18 March 1990.

64. See *Glas koncila* (1 April 1990), p. 5.

65. There were actually barricades erected at an earlier date in Eastern Slavonia, but they were not as massive, and thus less noticed.

66. The bishops still argued that they did not usurp the Croatian state, but only claimed their right to "national identity [and] spiritual and cultural autonomy."

67. "Saopštenje za javnost episkopa i svećenika Srpske Pravoslavne Crkve u Hrvatskoj," in AKSA, No. 38/1061 (21 September 1990), pp. 4–5.

68. *Glas koncila* (23 September 1990), p. 2.

450   *Jure Kristo*

69. AKSA, No. 34/1057 (24 August 1990), p. 1, my emphasis. This can be interpreted as cardinal's intentional attempt to strike a balance to president Tudjman's tendency to use the expression "Croatian people" when addressing the nation.

70. *Ibid.*

71. See *Glas koncila* (25 November 1990), p. 1, 8, about the murder of the Catholic priest Antun Grahovar in Sisak.

72. *Glas koncila* (4 November 1990), 2. The Catholic weekly openly wondered if the incident might have been the work of provocateurs.

73. *Glas koncila* (22 July 1990), p. 2; (30 September 1990), p. 2 and throughout.

74. See *Glas koncila* Editorial (30 December 1990), p. 2.

75. See the meeting of President Tudjman and Cardinal Kuharić in Jastrebarsko, *Glas koncila* (October 1990), p. 2.

76. See Luka Vinčetić, "Ljubav oltara i političara," in *Danas* (18 September 1990), p. 23.

77. Darko Plevnik, "Nacionalizacija Božića," in *Danas* (8 January 1991), p. 12.

78. See *Glas koncila* (5 January 1992), p. 2.

79. See *Ibid.* (23 February 1992), p. 1.

80. See *Ibid.* (25 October 1992), pp. 1, 2, 8–9; (15 November 1992), p. 2; and (8 November 1992), p. 6; Bono Zvonimir Šagi, "Laikat i svjetovna dimenzija Crkve," in *Kana* (Zagreb), Vol. 23 (september 1992), pp. 5–7; *MI* (Zagreb), Vol. 16 (1992), No. 10–11, p. 2; *Zbor. Prilog lista mladih MI* (Zagreb), Vol. 2 (1992), No. 7, p. 1.

81. See Jure Kristo, "Katoličko organiziranje i politika: Počeci Hrvatskoga katoličkog pokreta," in *Croatica Christiana Periodica* (Zagreb), Vol. 15, No. 28 (1991), pp. 86–104.

PART SIX

Conclusion

19

The Yugoslav Crisis and the West

Sabrina Petra Ramet

The interpretations presented in this book represent a diversity of assumptions and of opinion, and it would be illusory to leave the reader with the impression that these essays, taken collectively, lead to some identifiable and consistent conclusion. They do not. On the contrary, these chapters pull in different directions, and the presuppositions of any given author might be found to be incompatible with the presuppositions of others.

At the simplest level, Ivo Banac, Jasmina Kuzmanović, Jure Kristo, and I trace the conflict to the mobilization of anti-Croatian and anti-Muslim sentiment among the Serbs and to policy decisions taken by Serbian leaders—above all Slobodan Milošević, president of the Serbian Republic, and Radovan Karadžić, president of the Bosnian Serbs. Marko Milivojević, on the other hand, narrows the focus and declares baldly that "...the large Serbian minority population in Croatia...is at the root of this conflict," adding that by 1990, Milosević, for his part, "...hardly bothered to conceal his ambitions to reconstitute the Greater Serbia of December 1918." Kuzmanović adds a note of complexity (seconded by Rada Iveković and Dijana Plestina) in highlighting that the Croatian government of Franjo Tudjman has evolved in an authoritarian direction, embracing a variant of nationalism that is damaging to democracy, both in the short run and in the long run. Paul Shoup takes a minority view, however, urging that all sides shared culpability for the conflict (thus also blaming the ill-prepared Bosnian government of Alija Izetbegović). And Branko Pribičević, taking an implicitly systems theory approach, argues that the collapse of the Soviet bloc also contributed to the destabilization of Yugoslavia.

I propose to accomplish three rather diverse tasks in this chapter, and trust that the disadvantage associated with the lack of a single central argument will be outweighed by the advantages of these separate strands. First, I propose to review the principal controversies embedded in this book,

454   Sabrina Petra Ramet

highlighting issues related to the nature of the conflict, the turning points
in the descent to chaos, the question of culpability, the nature of the Western media, the legacy of the war, the meaning of nationalism, and the prospects for democracy. Second, I shall discuss the tortured American (and
Western) policy debate surrounding the Yugoslav war, and the sundry
misconceptions which have found favor. And third, I shall provide a brief
status report, updating the situation as of September 1993.

Diversity and Concord

The contributors' interpretations of the historical record show differences of emphasis. Rusinow, for example, characterizes the intercommu-
nal violence of World War Two as largely exceptional and suggests that
Serbs, Croats, Muslims, and others "lived in relative peace" in the same
towns and rural districts for many centuries. Shoup, on the other hand,
takes a more fatalistic reading, characterizing Bosnia as "a witch's brew of
ethnic Slav nationalities, who...could always be aroused...to communal violence and ethnic warfare." Shoup, thus, sees a fragility in which violence is
only to be expected — a sharp contrast to Rusinow's interpretation.

In spite of this and despite his further claim that resort to violence is a
"tradition" in the region, Shoup holds the West partly responsible for the
Bosnian war. Pribičević abjures this conclusion, highlighting, on the one
hand, the impetus to destabilization produced by the demise of the Soviet
bloc (as already noted) and, on the other hand, the responsibility of the
Yugoslav peoples themselves for the failure of their federation. In line with
this analysis, Pribičević underlines the deep reluctance of the Bush administration to recognize the breakaway republics or to become involved in
any way, and notes Bush's comment that he did not see what "objective"
would be served by using military force in the Balkans. Zachary Irwin
takes yet another approach, highlighting the diversity of opinions among
the West European states with regard to the war. None of the contributors
would be likely to quarrel with Irwin's documentation that the EC preferred to maintain a unified, federal Yugoslavia, rather than see the country break up. But once it was clear to all concerned that Yugoslavia had in
fact dissolved, was this because of the lack of a unified Western response
(as Irwin suggests), or because of Western bungling (as Shoup argues), or
because of diabolical Western scheming (the official Serbian policy line,
not articulated by any of the contributors per se), or was the solution of the
conflict simply beyond the capacity of outside powers? Shoup makes the
most categorical judgment here, holding that "*all* the actors in this tragedy,
including the international community, bear responsibility for the present
situation".

The Yugoslav Crisis and the West   455

What kind of war is it? Rusinow and Shoup characterize it as a war for land. Banac shows how the war has reflections in evolving intellectual debates. I have tried, in my chapter on the Serbian Church, to show that Church's contribution to stoking and encouraging war frenzy among the Serbs. Jure Kristo, for his part, dismisses the idea that this conflict should be considered a religious war in *any* sense, and emphasizes that the Catholic Church has not been implicated at all in the build-up to war.

The contributors to this volume, even while agreeing on the basic facts, take diverse views as to how the momentum toward war developed. Banac stresses the Serbian memorandum of 1986 as a key event, I highlight the importance of Milošević's takeover in late 1987, and Kristo prefers to emphasize the constitutional changes in Slovenia and Serbia in 1989, while Milivojević notes the dangers sown into the development of the JNA, by 1990, into "...little more than an instrument for the forcible advancement of Milošević's pan-Serbian ambitions." Rusinow, finally, underscores the importance of developments in 1990 and early 1991 in the gathering momentum for war. While all of these events were important, the difference of emphasis amounts to a difference in the assessment as to what was the decisive turning point (or perhaps, the most decisive turning point) in the spiral to war.

Interpretations of culpability also vary. Rusinow, for example, spreads the blame fairly widely, but traces the disintegration of Yugoslavia, all the same, to the alienation of Serbs from the Titoist solution, which, as he notes, they came to regard as an anti-Serbian "plot". Shoup, on the other hand, believes that "Serbia's role in precipitating the civil war is beyond dispute," and adds that "the attitude of Karadžić, supported by Milošević, was that of a reckless, violent man."

The media have inevitably become both actors in the war, and *ipso facto* the subject of scrutiny. The Western media in particular have made much, in the past, of their aspiration to something like "objective reporting". But some contributors score the media for shortcomings. Rusinow and Kristo, in particular, criticize the Western press — the former citing the media's circulation of misconstruals that the Serb-Croat dispute was of "ancient" vintage, and the latter criticizing the media's emphasis on religion as a supposedly causal element in the calculus of war. In the following section, by contrast, I intend to examine the role of the Western press in setting the tone for policy discussions. The American press, as I shall show, has published a wide diversity of views. And Kuzmanović, whose chapter is devoted to the media, denies the possibility of objective reporting altogether. She cites two reasons for this. First, whether the media are owned by profit-oriented corporations or by the government, their journalists are susceptible to pressure. Second, the journalists themselves cannot escape their own subjective value systems, prejudice, and at times, emotions.

456 *Sabrina Petra Ramet*

What will be the legacy of the war? Shoup, Kovač, and Adamovich offer optimistic prescriptions. Shoup focuses on structural-political schemes for creating autonomous zones and urges an international protectorate for Sarajevo as well as other regions of Bosnia-Herzegovina, suggesting in passing that democratization might still be a possibility in Bosnia. Kovač and Adamovich focus their sights on the benefits of economic cooperation. Kovač, in particular, urges that it makes economic sense for the Yugoslav successor states to agree to a customs union or some other form of economic integration, and notes that five of the six republics (not Slovenia) had tentatively agreed to this in November 1991, during deliberations at the EC-sponsored peace conference. Adamovich largely echoes Kovač's plea for cooperation, arguing for the possibility (in sequence) of a peace accord that will respect the basic interests of all sides and of an institutionalized framework for economic cooperation among the Yugoslav successor states.

A much more pessimistic note was struck by Slovenian economist Jože Mencinger in an address in Vienna in April 1993. Mencinger warned at that time that the combination of the breakup of the unified Yugoslav market and of the war itself had so thoroughly undermined the economic structure of the former Yugoslav republics that they now stood on the brink of economic disaster; in his view, cooperative plans among the six (five? four?) republics, even if feasible, would be too late to avert the disaster, which he believes will only be fully felt when the war is over. According to Mencinger's figures, industrial production in Slovenia in 1992 stood at only 70 percent of the 1989 figure, with corresponding figures of 55 percent in Serbia and 50 percent in Croatia. In terms of exports, the value of Slovenia's in 1992 stood at about the same level as in 1990, while in Croatia and Serbia there were declines of 25 and 50 percent respectively.[1] Likewise taking a pessimistic approach, I enumerated five consequences of the war, in my book, *Nationalism and Federalism in Yugoslavia*, among them warning that "...the war has sown much deeper hatred between Serbs and Croats than ever existed before...and that could last for generations...[And] as a result of the economic impact and the mobilization of ethnic loyalties, the war has seriously complicated the efforts by democratic forces in the republics to move toward stable pluralism."[2] Whether cooperation is possible among these republics at such point as the war may end is, given these considerations, open to question.

In this connection, Pribičević strikes a pessimistic chord, warning that not a single one of the problems that led to the disintegration of the country and the present interethnic war have been solved. On the contrary, the problems and conflicts are still escalating, assuming more dangerous forms and dimensions.

All of the contributors to this volume see danger sown into the very fabric of nationalism. Kristo, for example, writes of the nationalists' appeal

The Yugoslav Crisis and the West 457

to emotions, rather than reason, in the Croatian context, while Ivekovič and Plestina highlight the role played by nationalism in fueling intolerance and misogyny, and in undermining prospects for democracy. My own chapter on the Serbian Orthodox Church suggests that nationalism may become linked with specific alternative collective pathologies, facilitating the legitimation of violence, while Horton is perhaps the sharpest, among the contributors to this volume, in his condemnation of nationalism. Horton also provides an insight into the organic bond between machismo and national chauvinism in his account of Srdjan Karanovič's film, *A Film With No Name*. The film tells of the love between an Albanian woman and a Serbian man, and their marriage plans. The woman's relatives disapprove of the liaison and "solve" the problem by cutting off the Serbian man's penis, thus effectively scotching their marriage plans. Here, in graphic form, is the great fear of Serbian men, projected through an allegorical Freudian lens.

Rusinow, too, takes a critical view of nationalism and distributes the blame for the breakup of Yugoslavia among nationalist politicians in Serbia, Croatia, Slovenia, and Bosnia-Herzegovina. This leads him to nostalgic reminiscences about Tito's days. "Tito's strategy," he writes, "of containing divisive nationalisms through a combination of territorial-national autonomy and a balance of power and grievances among the contenders...may have provided a more viable solution to the national question than is generally recognized today." Shoup, on the other hand, views the process with a sharpened consternation, suggesting that "the future of...Europe is at stake," and warning that the conflict could spread and engulf the Balkans more generally.

Given the foregoing differences, the reader is entitled to ask what the contributors *do* agree on. In the first place, we would probably all agree that the relationship of nationalism to democracy is, at least in the Yugoslav context, deeply problematic at best. In fact, the prospects for democratization in the Yugoslav successor-states face at least six broad challenges. These are: nationalism (highlighted by Plestina), sexism (highlighted by Ivekovič), difficulties in freeing the media (highlighted by Kuzmanovič), economic deterioration (discussed, but not emphasized, by Adamovich), the absence of established institutions (highlighted by Plestina), and the war itself. In drawing together some of these threads, Plestina puts it best, writing, that the paradox of democratic transition"...is that the concentrated political effort needed to successfully restructure the economies of ex-communist countries, while avoiding social unrest, creates a need for power concentration which in turn undermines the democratic process, reproducing instead some form of authoritarian rule." And of course, where pluralist institutions are weak or not yet consolidated, right-oriented parties and other elite groups are more than ready to muscle their way in.

458   *Sabrina Petra Ramet*

The contributors to this book would further agree that the problems between Serbs and their neighbors (Croats and Muslims in particular) date back in time (Serbs generally trace the problems to 1941, Croats to 1918, and Muslims would likely trace the problems back to 1878, when Bosnia was annexed by Catholic Austria, and the Muslims lost their privileges). But we would insist all the same that there were no particular conflicts or tensions between Serbs and Croats prior to 1918 and thus that there was no direct line from the remote past to the disintegration of June 1991. On the contrary, we would agree, the decisions taken by various political figures in the course of the years 1986–91 pushed the country over the brink—to dissolution and conflict. *Which* political figures, you ask? But there we disagree. And I would venture that we might be able to agree that the parties to the conflict are unlikely to achieve peace without the helpful mediation of the international community. But what kind of mediation? with or without the use of force (and against whom?) and pushing toward what kind of peace? Here the differences among the contributors are in fact far greater than the book's framework (based on a topical division of labor) will reveal.

A Faraway Country Of Which...

Chamberlain earned eternal notoriety in 1938 for his decision to appease Hitler. In promoting his decision, Chamberlain called Czechoslovakia "a faraway country of which we know nothing." The same can be said of Yugoslavia, as seen through the American lens. Time and again, prior to 1991, newspaper articles and radio programs had to explain to the American public that Yugoslavia was situated in the Balkans, had a multi-ethnic makeup consisting of—and the groups were enumerated—and adhering, at one time, to a program of workers' self-management. If Americans had so little interest in Yugoslavia that these basics could not sink in, and required constant reiteration, it is no wonder that Americans at large have found the entire conflict perplexing if not inexplicable—although, thanks to the war, the public is now at least able to situate Yugoslavia in the Balkans.

Given this context, it is no wonder that the Yugoslav conflict has given rise to an unusual amount of sheer confusion not merely among ordinary citizens, but even among American politicians and writers (especially during the Bush presidency). Leslie Gelb, an editorial staff writer for the *New York Times,* for example, dismissed Slovenia's post-communist politicians, in a July 1991 op/ed piece, as "unknown quantities"—unknown *to him*— while describing the Croatian nation *as a whole* as "known more for its Nazis than for its democrats."[3] In a subsequent article, Gelb offered the advice that where non-recognition of Macedonia was concerned, "Greece has the

The Yugoslav Crisis and the West 459

answers to the Macedonian question."[4] Greece, of course, took the position that the region which had been called Macedonia for 3,500 years had no right to that name, because contemporary Greeks associate ancient Macedonia with the name of Alexander the Great, and choose to understand Alexander as a forerunner only of the modern Greek nation. In yet another editorial column, A. M. Rosenthal declared that there have only ever been Serbs and Croats in Bosnia: the so-called ethnic Muslims, he declared, were objectively either Serbs or Croats, regardless how they might view themselves![5]

Given this level of confusion, combined with absorption in the presidential race, it is not surprising that neither the American government nor the American public gave much thought to the Bosnian conflict during 1992. Interestingly enough, the West took the following steps with regard to the Yugoslav conflict. First, on the eve of the conflict, the commander-in-chief of NATO declared that Yugoslavia lay outside NATO's defense perimeter —signalling an intention to stay out of any eventual conflict. And at the same time, US Secretary of State James Baker visited Yugoslavia and announced, only a few days before Slovenia and Croatia seceded (according to a preannounced deadline known to Baker), that the US would, under no circumstances, recognize either breakaway republic. Second, Western Europe held up recognition of Slovenia and Croatia for six months (and the US held it up for 10 months), despite the Serb-Croat war and despite the fact, as Rusinow noted in his chapter, that Yugoslavia had in fact been dead for some time. Third, the West imposed economic sanctions and an arms embargo against all six Yugoslav successor republics, hurting only the more modestly armed Croatia and Bosnia, while actually helping Serbia and its allies, the heavily armed Serbian militias in Croatia and Bosnia, to maintain their advantage. Fourth, the West refused to accord diplomatic recognition to Macedonia, on the grounds that the Greeks objected to the country's name: the diplomatic embargo, reinforced by a tough Greek economic embargo against Macedonia, has sent the Macedonian economy into a free fall and has blown wind into the sails of home-grown nationalists. In fact, on 27 April 1993, the head of the CSCE's sanction-monitoring mission in Macedonia, Ambassador Norman Anderson, said that the economic repercussions of the dual embargoes could soon bring Macedonia's "economic survival" into question.[6] Fifth, the West not only refused to send arms to the besieged Croats and Bosnian Muslims, but actually took pains to block "illegal" arms shipments. In mid-1992, thus, German police rounded up persons who had been smuggling arms to Croatia while in early 1993, for example, Western naval forces intercepted a large shipment of weapons bound for the Bosnian government and confiscated them.[7] Even as late as March 1993, in the course of debates about the UN-imposed "no fly" zone over Bosnia, the Security Council decided

460   *Sabrina Petra Ramet*

to postpone authorization of NATO planes to shoot down military aircraft flying bombing raids (only Serbian aircraft were involved) out of deference to the embattled Russian President Boris Yeltsin.[8] And in fact, the first aircraft ever forced to land (by British forces) as a result of this "no fly" zone was a *Croatian* helicopter which was trying to bring weapons to local Croats.[9]

Given the consistency of these responses, it is no wonder that Croats, Bosnian Muslims, and Macedonians have been less than ecstatic about the West's role in the conflict. On the contrary, the Croatian government accused the West quite early in the conflict of pursuing an objectively pro-Serbian policy.[10] Bosnia's Muslims, who hooted at Cyrus Vance and UN Secretary-General Boutros Boutros-Ghali as "fascists" when they visited Sarajevo, likewise feel betrayed by the West. Most obviously, so too do the Macedonians. And the Serbs, for their part, thanks in part to the Serbian media's relentless propaganda barrage, portraying the West (and especially Germany, the US, and the Vatican) in the most hostile terms, view the West as engaged in the construction of a broad anti-Serbian conspiracy, inspired by the Catholic Church and spearheaded by Kohl's government —which Belgrade newspaper *Politika ekspres* has derided as "the Fourth Reich".[11]

What the West has wanted, above all, was not to get involved, not to have to think about the conflict seriously. London,[12] Paris,[13] and Washington[14] have all expressed deep reluctance to become militarily involved in the struggle, in any capacity. Some Western writers have promised that any effort to bring the Bosnian war to an end, even if limited to aerial strikes against Serbian forces, would necessarily involve Western or American troops in a Vietnam-type quagmire.[15] Dimitri K. Simes, usually known for his observations about Russia, highlighted the fact that there is no oil in Bosnia and warned that "a US-directed punishment of Serbia would be a blow to Russian democrats." In his view—in a nutshell—Russia is important, and Bosnia is not, genocide or no genocide.[16]

Yet another editorial writer—Fareed Zakaria, then a fellow at the Harvard University Olin Institute for Strategic Studies—claimed that casualties in the Yugoslav war were dwarfed by casualties in similar conflicts in Nigeria, Somalia, and Nagorno-Karabakh—a completely false claim, incidentally; rather the Yugoslav casualties dwarf any of the others—and accused all persons outraged at the Bosnian genocide of being motivated by *racism!* In Zakaria's words, "the great moral principle that the United States is being asked to fight for in the former Yugoslavia is not justice—but justice for Europeans alone. Orphans are killed by rival ethnic groups all over the world. *White* orphans are dying only in the Balkans."[17] For Zakaria, thus, standing by while, as he views them, "white orphans" are slaughtered and their "white mothers" raped, will strike a blow against racism!

The Yugoslav Crisis and the West

461

Perhaps the most resounding rejection of the argument for the use of force to end Serbian aggression came from General Colin L. Powell, then Chairman of the Joint Chiefs of Staff. "I do not know how limited bombing will stop the Serbs from doing what they are doing," he said.[18] These comments helped to reinforce a growing view in the US that nothing could be done to stop the Serbs, that any allied engagement including even massive aerial bombardment would have no effect on either the Serbs' resolve or their ability to wage aggressive war, and that the Croats and Muslims, by implication, were qualitatively inferior to the Serbs in combat ability. When one recalls how long the scantily armed Croatian defenders of Vukovar held off a literal Serbian juggernaut, one is disinclined to accept any such sweeping generalization.

From spring 1992 on, there was a growing tendency in the West, and most especially in the United States, to draw historical parallels. Bosnia was "another Vietnam", Western policy amounted to "another Munich", Vance was "another Chamberlain", Milošević was "another Hitler", Yugoslavia was "another Lebanon". I have discussed elsewhere the role played by these and other metaphors in Western policy responses to the Yugoslav conflict.[19] Rather than rehearse these again, I would prefer to note some points of comparison between the Spanish civil war of the late 1930s and the current conflict. The Spanish civil war, like the present conflict, involved considerable savagery and produced a high death toll, but neither threatened Western access to a major raw material (oil and chrome are probably the chief motivators) and neither seemed likely to ignite a more general war (or, if the present war should spread, it would be unlikely to spread beyond the Balkan peninsula and the countries of the Aegean basin). In both conflicts, the aggressor (Spanish fascists, Serbian militias) enjoyed significant military superiority from the very beginning, and continued to enjoy easier access to arms supplies (chiefly from Nazi Germany and fascist Italy in the case of the Spanish fascists, and from the Serbian Republic in the case of the Serbian militias, or, more remotely, from Russia and other states in the case of the Serbs generally). And in the Spanish civil war, the West responded by washing its hands and consigning the republic to oblivion. In the current war, the West has produced an enormous clatter and a great deal of self-righteous rhetoric and even some ominous-sounding threats, but ultimately, the behavior of the Western states in this crisis differs very little from its behavior in the Spanish war.

In both cases, the West responded with arms embargoes against the victims of aggression. In the case of Spain, not only did Britain lead the way in organizing an international arms embargo against all combatants (sanctimoniously holding to it even after it was public knowledge that Nazi Germany and fascist Italy were completely disregarding the embargo), but she would later compel France to cease all arms shipments to the Republic.

462

Sabrina Petra Ramet

Moreover, the US also responded by passing a Neutrality Act, which effectively imposed a US arms embargo on the Spanish Republic.[20] In the present conflict, British Foreign Secretary Douglas Hurd defended the arms embargo, at one point, by declaring that there were "enough arms" in former Yugoslavia already. The *Financial Times* of London had taken this same stance already in September 1991, in opposing the shipment of arms to Croatia. "If Croats cannot be defended by external force," the newspaper offered, "should they at least be allowed to acquire arms so that they can defend themselves? It is tempting to say yes. Yet there can be no guarantees that arms, once acquired, would be used responsibly or humanely in a region already bristling with them."[21] It is striking that the British, French, and Americans should have concurred twice in this century that the imposition of an arms embargo on the victim of aggression (in each case a legitimately elected government) was the appropriate response to regional conflict.

Alongside these repeated calls for isolationism, or, as one might put it, to "let Serbia be Serbia," there have also been calls for a stronger response. While advocates of isolationism fretted about the commitment of American and other Western ground troops, advocates of intervention largely focused on the uses of air power. In essence, the two sides have argued past each other.

It is striking how little was said about a Western military response as long as the conflict was confined to Serbs and Croats. The Americans and the French[22] fretted over Croatia's fascist past and pointed to human rights transgressions and abuses on the Croatian side as evidence that there was no "pure victim" in the Serb-Croat conflict. Serbia's expansion of the war into Bosnia changed all this. The virtually unarmed Bosnian Muslims, who lost 60 percent of their territory within a few weeks (amid widespread slaughter, now termed "ethnic cleansing") and another 30 percent of their land within the following months, could more easily be construed by the media as "pure victims" and it is at this point that Western voices started to be raised in favor of aerial strikes against appropriate Serbian targets.

In a dramatic move, George Kenney, the US State Department desk office for Yugoslavia, resigned his post in summer 1992 in protest over US inaction in the conflict. Kenney subsequently offered a plan (with Michael J. Dugan) outlining steps to entail "first, destroying Serbian forces in Bosnia and, second, using concentrated force against Serbia."[23]

Other voices seconded the idea, including former British Prime Minister Margaret Thatcher and former US Secretary of State George Schultz. In August 1992, Zbigniew Brzezinski and Alexander Haig gave separate interviews to CNN, and both called for aerial bombardment of Serbian artillery batteries and other military targets, with Haig adding that he felt that Belgrade should be bombed as well. I joined the chorus in August with an

The Yugoslav Crisis and the West   463

article for *Foreign Affairs*, in which I proposed, among other things, "...the imposition of an effective sea, land and air blockade, and the use of surgical air strikes to destroy Serbian hydroelectric plants, dams, bridges, army depots and arms factories in both Serbia and Bosnia (including an important factory in Serb-held Banja Luka), as well as certain farms operated by Serbian militias near the front."[24]

These calls went unheeded, however, for a number of reasons. First, the mediation efforts of Lord Owen and Cyrus Vance were still underway and many felt that any other recourse was, under the circumstances, at best premature. Second, there was a deep reluctance in London, Paris, and Washington DC to commit any of their own military resources, or even to become diplomatically any more involved than they already were via the mediation and peace conference. Third, where the US was concerned, the Bush administration had no intention of doing anything precipitous, until after the presidential elections were over, lest the incumbent's prospects be jeopardized. There were two further considerations that applied to the US case. The first of these was a widespread skepticism, extending into the ranks of the Departments of State and Defense, as to whether the US had any interests at all at stake in the conflict—whether economic or political or strategic—and an accompanying belief that the European powers should address the situation on their own. And second, in the morally jaded ambience of post-Watergate America, mainstream public opinion no longer believes that any conflicts can be in any sense black and white, and hence, many Americans assumed that if the Serbs were committing atrocities, the Croats and Muslims must be doing the same; and in any event, on *a priori* grounds, the several combatants should be treated as equally culpable and morally equivalent. As early as May 1992, after initial reports of Croatian-Muslim clashes, the *New York Times* felt constrained to publish a stiffly worded editorial entitled "Lean on Croatia, Too." Less than a month after the US' belated recognition of Croatia, the *Times* was recommending that "a threat to break relations and impose economic sanctions would give Croatia clear warning: Stop the fighting and renounce any territorial claims on Bosnia or, along with Serbia, face the consequences."[25] Later, in early 1993, a further string of reports about clashes between Croatian and Muslim forces[26] encouraged this moral relativism.

But then came confirmed reports of the systematic rape of (by EC estimates) some 20,000 Muslim women by Bosnian Serb forces[27] and of the continued operation of Serbian detention camps, in which Muslim and Croatian civilians have been held captive and tortured,[28] together with reports of "ethnic cleansing" mostly by Serbian forces and televised reports of relentless Serbian bombing of the Bosnian towns of Srebrenica, Goražde, and once-beautiful Sarajevo. In combination, these reports convinced many Americans that the Serbian and Bosnian Serb politicians and forces were

464   *Sabrina Petra Ramet*

behaving as international outlaws, and engendered renewed calls for action. George Schultz compared Serbian behavior in Bosnia with what the Nazis did at Auschwitz, while then-Secretary of State Lawrence Eagleburger declared that the world has "a moral and historical obligation not to stand back a second time in this century while a people faces obliteration."[29] Whether they realized it or not, the Serbs were increasingly being compared with the Nazis. In a lengthy editorial in August 1992, the *New York Times* drew the parallel:

> Serbian atrocities are one parallel with Nazi Germany. Another is Europe's peace at any price response. At Munich in 1938, Britain and France agreed to a "peace plan" that forced Czechoslovakia to surrender part of its territory, the Sudetenland, to Hitler. Today, the European Community wants Bosnia to agree to a "political solution" that would surrender part of its territory to Bosnian Serbs loyal to Mr. Milošević...Like their predecessors at Munich, Europe's negotiators proceed as if Serbia were negotiating in good faith, despite a string of broken promises and violated ceasefires.[30]

Five months later, as President Clinton took office, the *Times* again returned to the theme, writing: "That Serbian aggression in Bosnia defies the conscience of the international community cannot be in doubt. Not unless at the end of the twentieth century the world accepts mass murder, rape and terror directed against one ethnic group."[31]

For the American media, it was no longer possible, by early 1993, to express much concern about Croatian seizure of Bosnian territory, especially given that most of this occurred in southwest Herzegovina which has traditionally had a predominantly Croatian population, and the American public, broadly speaking, gradually came to view the Serbs as the villains in the Balkan drama. Inevitably, the Serbs cried out that American media coverage of the war was one-sided. For their part, the media professionals were by then convinced that this only reflected the fact that the war itself was "one-sided." After all, Belgrade was not under siege, and very few Serbian women had been raped. Nor have any battles taken place on the territory of FR Yugoslavia (Serbia and Montenegro).

A new obstacle to any serious discussion arose in early 1993, when the myth of the allegedly "ancient vintage" of the Serb-Croat quarrel was briefly revived. One was invited to imagine early neolithic cavemen in the region, already divided into Serbian and Croatian camps and squabbling over land. And if the quarrels were "ancient," it would follow that specific complaints and grievances are not really the source of difficulty at all, and further, that there was no point in anyone in the West losing any sleep over the conflict, let alone considering military options. This groundless misinterpretation of history—rebutted by Rusinow in chapter 1 in this volume—was repeated over and over again in the media, and even voiced by Clinton administra-

The Yugoslav Crisis and the West

465

tion spokespersons, who should have known better. It is no wonder that the myth of Yugoslavia's "ancient quarrels" crept into the public mind. Thus we find, for example, Judge Ellis Gregory Jr. of the St. Louis County Circuit Court in Clayton, Missouri, repeating this "popular wisdom". "True," he began, "there is terrible killing going on over there. But this is mostly a continuation of ethnic hatreds that have been boiling over for literally centuries..."[32] Or more precisely—one is tempted to add—since 1918.

Meanwhile, the Western powers continued to hope that the Vance-Owen plan (described briefly by Irwin in his chapter for this volume) could bring an end to the fighting. First, the government of Alija Izetbegović, and then the Bosnian Croats (led by Mate Boban) agreed to the plan. The Bosnian Serbs seemed, at one point in January 1993, to be about to endorse the plan too,[33] but gave it a preliminary rejection already in late March[34]

At the same time, American opinion-makers had to confront the paradox that the peace plan which they had promoted would require the deployment of some 65–75,000 "peacekeeping" troops, of which 25,000 would be American. Thus, in the supposed interest of avoiding the commitment of ground forces, the US was sponsoring a plan premised on those self-same ground troops. The *Christian Science Monitor* fretted that the Vance-Owen plan "may lack realism" and "*would* result in the quagmire [that] all want to avoid."[35]

The Bosnian Serbs' rejection of the Vance-Owen plan provoked a triad of responses in the West. First, it gave new force to the continuing debate about the arms embargo. Baroness Margaret Thatcher, the former British Prime Minister, and Reginald Bartholemew, the US envoy, both spoke in favor of lifting the embargo and arming the Muslims.[36] But officials from Britain, France, and Canada argued strenuously against any modification of the arms embargo.[37] British Prime Minister John Major, for example, told the House of Commons, "I share the view...expressed about the need to damp down and not increase the supply of arms [in the region]."[38]

Second, the UN Security Council approved a draconian expansion of the economic blockade against Serbia at its 18 April session. Thirteen members voted in favor of the resolution, with Russia and China abstaining.

And third, the option of air strikes against Serbian targets was now taken up by American officials seriously for the first time. Although the discussion of air strikes began earlier in the month, two developments on 22 April gave strong impetus to American hawks. First, at a dedication of the Holocaust Museum in Washington DC, attended by President Clinton, Nobel Prize winner Elie Wiesel delivered a speech in which he took time to denounce the "ethnic cleansing" in Bosnia, comparing it to the Nazi holocaust against the Jews. Turning to the president, Wiesel added, "Mr. President, this bloodshed must be stopped. It will not stop unless we stop it."[39]

466   *Sabrina Petra Ramet*

The second, rather unexpected, development on 22 April was the delivery of a letter to Secretary of State Warren Christopher, by the State Department's 12 top Balkan experts, calling Western diplomatic efforts a failure and recommending military action against Serbian forces. In a strongly worded passage, the experts wrote, "We are [so far] only attempting to end the genocide through political and economic pressures such as sanctions and intense diplomatic engagement. In effect, the result of this course has been Western capitulation to Serbian aggression."[40] About the same time, the American UN Ambassador, Madeleine Albright, wrote a memorandum to the White House, bearing the same message.[41]

But would air strikes against Serbian targets accomplish any useful purpose? Here opinions in the US and elsewhere in the West differed widely. Some worried that air strikes would not be perfectly surgical and expressed concern that innocent people might be hurt.[42] Others denied that they would either bring the Serbs to the negotiating table or end the fighting.[43] Still others argued that air strikes could effectively neutralize Bosnian Serb artillery positions and thus relieve the besieged Muslim towns.[44] And still others argued for a "full-scale military intervention" to involve both air strikes and ground troops.[45] Meanwhile, President Clinton told a press conference on 23 April, "There's never been a serious discussion in this country about the introduction of ground forces into an ongoing conflict there."[46]

There were also differing assessments about the likelihood of a Western military intervention. On 30 April, for example, the *Financial Times* reported comments by a senior NATO official to the effect that "the chances of decisive Western military intervention in Bosnia were fading."[47] Two days later, however, the *New York Times* reported that President Clinton an his advisers had "...decided in principle today to commit American airpower to help bring an end to the fighting in the Balkans," specifying air strikes against Serbian targets.[48]

But even as the White House gravitated toward a military option, the British conservative government fought down demands by the opposition Labour Party that air strikes be undertaken against Bosnian Serb positions. Foreign Secretary Douglas Hurd stressed his view that there was no such thing as a military solution to the conflict, while Conservative backbencher Sir Edward Heath (who served as Prime Minister from 1970 to 1974) demanded that the British government veto any move by Washington to obtain UN approval for the bombing of targets in Bosnia.[49] There was, in addition, strong opposition from British Defense Minister Malcolm Rifkind.[50] The French government gave in to American pressure about the same time and seemed to agree, albeit reluctantly, to support air strikes against Bosnian Serb positions and strategic targets.[51]

As these discussions continued, Serbian President Slobodan Milošević issued a strong endorsement of the Vance-Owen plan, and urged the Bosnian

The Yugoslav Crisis and the West 467

Serb "parliament" to approve it.[52] On 24 April, Karadžić rejected the Vance-Owen plan (for the third time), but when, in response to this, the West seemed to make some serious moves toward a military response, Karadžić suddenly changed his mind and hurried to Athens on 2 May, to sign the plan after all, noting only that the Bosnian Serb "parliament" would still need to endorse his concurrence. The Bosnian Serb parliament asked for negotiation about nine points in the plan, but US Secretary of State Warren Christopher argued, "I think it's another ploy to gain delay, and I for one will not be thrown off track."[53] Even Lord Owen, co-author of the Vance-Owen plan, declared (in early May), "It may be that military action now has to be contemplated as the only way of convincing these people that they cannot continue on their present course."[54] In these conditions, the Pentagon sent US Special Forces into Bosnia "to study potential targets for air attacks in preparation for military intervention there."[55] Meanwhile, US officials kept other options open, as NATO authorities simultaneously elaborated plans for the implementation of the Vance-Owen plan.

But by early May, the Western military threat was already rapidly evaporating, and on 6 May, the Bosnian Serb "parliament" rejected the plan. The rejection of the Vance-Owen plan by the Bosnian Serbs dramatically sharpened the crisis. But in an ostentatious display of defiance that, in typical Serbian fashion, rivetted on historical monuments of religious significance, the Bosnian Serbs chose this moment to dynamite two historic mosques in occupied Banja Luka: the ornately decorated Ferhad Pasha mosque built in 1583 and considered by many to have been one of the most beautiful pieces of architecture in the Balkans; and the Arnaudija mosque, built in 1587.[56] These mosques had survived the independence struggle of 1877–78, the Balkans wars of 1912–13, two world wars, and the Nazi occupation. Meanwhile, the Bosnian Serbs pressed forward with their siege of several Muslim-held towns, and began to close in on the Muslim enclave of Žepa.

Perhaps hoping to create the appearance, in Western eyes, of a rift between the Belgrade government and that of the Bosnian Serbs, Presidents Milošević of Serbia and Dobrica Ćosić of FR Yugoslavia criticized the Bosnian Serb rejection of the Vance-Owen plan, and in a statement released 6 May, declared that they would cut off all but humanitarian aid to their co-ethnics in Bosnia.[57] But the West remembered that these same figures had earlier indicated that the Republic of Serbia was not providing any military assistance to the Bosnian Serbs, that the Republic was not sending its aircraft to fly bombing raids against Muslim towns, and that Serbia was, in no sense, at war. Given the general Western conviction that these claims were not true, and the further record of broken promises and broken truces, there was a deep reluctance on the part of the West to take this statement at face value.

468   *Sabrina Petra Ramet*

By the end of the first week of May, contingency plans for strikes against Serbian targets were said to be "well advanced,"[58] and Clinton administration officials expressed optimism that the US and its European allies could soon agree on a common approach.

Avoiding a Reckoning

What the Clinton team had in mind was a two-part strategy involving allied air strikes against Serbian positions and lifting the ban on arms supplies to the Bosnian government. It was Secretary of State Warren Christopher's assignment to sell the US strategy to Britain and France: Germany had been calling for a military option for a long time and needed no convincing, and the Russians, it was thought (probably mistakenly), could be brought around, although Moscow was in fact emitting very mixed signals at this time. But Christopher returned from Europe empty-handed, with the British and French governments once again blocking any use of force against the Bosnian Serbs and insisting on the maintenance of the arms embargo against the Muslims.

The US government appreciated that it would be diplomatically costly (impossible, in some eyes) to press forward with a military option in the absence of a Western consensus. The Vance-Owen plan was quietly scuttled, and the EC instructed Lord Owen to return to the Balkans and negotiate an alternative settlement. Unable to act alone, the US backed away from the conflict. Secretary of State Christopher sounded the new note in American diplomacy, writing off the Bosnian conflict as "a humanitarian crisis a long way from home, in the middle of another continent."[59]

Torn between confusion and frustration, Secretary of State Christopher cast about for a scapegoat for the failure of Western diplomacy and, in an inexplicable *nonsequitur*, declared, in an interview published in *USA Today* on 17 June, that "the Germans bear a particular responsibility" for this failure, highlighting German pressure to recognize Slovenia and Croatia.[60] German Chancellor Kohl rejected this criticism as "unprincipled", while German Foreign Minister Klaus Kinkel reminded Christopher that the problem was Serbian aggression, not Western acceptance that the principle of national self-determination applied also to Slovenia and Croatia, as Christopher had charged.[61]

The US now tried to push a resolution to lift the arms embargo through the UN Security Council. To be adopted, the resolution needed eight votes in favor. But only six countries on the council voted for the resolution; the other nine countries, including Britain, France, and Russia, simply abstained, effectively killing the measure. The British delegate, David Hannay, in an inspired bit of diplomatic double-talk, gave classic expression to the

The Yugoslav Crisis and the West 469

British position: "The adoption of this resolution would [have left] the impression that the United Nations was abandoning Bosnia-Herzegovina and leaving its people to fight it out to the end."[62]

Western inaction encouraged the Serbian and Croatian sides to begin to look at each other as possible alliance partners against the Muslims. After all, from the Croatian point of view, if the West was not going to play a role in stopping Serbian expansionism, then why not take advantage of the situation to absorb Croatian-populated areas of Herzegovina long considered, by Croats, to be part of the Croatian homeland? Accordingly, by mid-June, the Serbian and Croatian governments were involved in intense negotiations to reach an agreement on the partition of Bosnia.[63] On 16 June, Milošević and Tudjman used the EC framework in Geneva to conduct bilateral talks at which they agreed on a plan for Bosnia, dividing it in three —with nominally a small mini-state left to the Muslims. Lord Owen, along with other Western leaders, advised the Muslims to sign whatever the Serbs and Croats offered, but Izetbegović initially refused.[64] Subsequently, on 19 June, Karadžić and Bosnian Croat leader Mate Boban met secretly in eastern Herzegovina; they were observed arriving and departing with maps in hand.[65] Against this, the EC, Lord Owen, and according to some reports, even the White House counseled Izetbegović to accept defeat and accept such terms as might be offered to him by the Serbs and Croats.[66]

Ultimately, the smaller West European states could be expected to follow the lead of NATO's "Big Four": the US, Britain, France, and Germany. But the US and Germany—by now both advocates of lifting the arms embargo against the besieged Muslims and of air strikes against Bosnian Serb militias—were unable to persuade Britain and France. Publicly, British Prime Minister John Major held fast to his maxim that there were enough weapons in the Balkans already; privately, he conceded to US President Bill Clinton that the real reason that he was insisting on the maintenance of the embargo and opposing air strikes against Bosnian Serbs was his fear that British public opinion would be unsympathetic to such moves.[67]

Meanwhile, Radovan Karadžić warned that if the Muslims would not participate in negotiations for the Serb-Croat partition plan, then Bosnia might end up divided entirely between Croatia and Serbia, with nothing left to the Muslims. As Serbian and Croatian bombardment of Muslim positions continued, with the Serbs closing in on Sarajevo, the Muslim side finally caved in, and on 30 July, agreed in principle to the Serb-Croat partition plan.[68]

By this point, Clinton had fully succeeded in putting together a consensus to prepare for air strikes against the Bosnian Serbs and on 11 August, the US announced that the ground controllers needed to coordinate air strikes were in place, completing necessary preparations.[69] But even now, NATO officials agreed that no bombing raids would take place with-

470   *Sabrina Petra Ramet*

out prior approval by UN Secretary-General Boutros Boutros-Ghali, Lt.-
Gen. Jean Cot of France (the commander of UN "peacekeeping" forces in
the Balkans), and all 16 NATO member-states.[70] Whether such a consensus
could in fact be obtained remained open to serious doubt, and such doubts
about the efficacy of the NATO threat were only reinforced by the Russian
Foreign Ministry's warning on 10 August against "uncontrolled actions"
in Bosnia and its restatement of Russia's support for "political instruments."[71] For that matter, less than a month later, French Foreign Minister
Alain Juppé and Russian Foreign Minister Andrej Kozyrev reiterated their
governments' continued opposition to any lifting of the arms embargo
against the Muslims.[72]

Bosnian Serb militias now began an elaborate test of wills with NATO,
repeatedly retreating and advancing on the hills overlooking Sarajevo.
NATO forces watched helplessly, as if transfixed. Meanwhile, the negotiations in Geneva continued, albeit with interruptions.

On 19 August, the three sides agreed that upon conclusion of a peace
settlement, Sarajevo would be placed under UN trusteeship for a period of
two years. The next day, Lord Owen and Vance's successor as UN mediator, Thorvald Stoltenberg, presented a new plan to the parties to the conflict. The Owen-Stoltenberg plan closely followed the lines set by the Serbs
and Croats, with some changes, largely at Croatia's expense. The plan
proposed to give the Serbs the lion's share—52 percent of the republic's
territory. The Muslims would receive 30 percent of the land, and the Croats
would receive the remaining 18 percent (mostly in the southwest).[73]
Izetbegović expressed horror at the mediator-backed plan, a plan he called
"worse than war."[74] Milošević, on the other hand, praised the new plan as
"an honorable compromise."[75] Meanwhile, Izetbegović, for his part, pointed
out that the Muslims had constituted almost 44 percent of the population
of pre-war Bosnia-Herzegovina, and accordingly, demanded 43 percent of
the territory for the Muslims. Karadžić dismissed this demand as "entirely unrealistic"; Karadžić and Boban offered the Muslims 28.7 percent of
Bosnian territory.

In spite of these disagreements and the complete lack of progress toward resolving them, the Western mediators once again expressed optimism that the warring sides were near agreement. But on 1 September, the
Muslims "unexpectedly" withdrew from the talks once again, when the
Serbs and Croats refused to cede them more land.[76] Later that month, the
Muslim-controlled Bihać enclave in the northwest, declared its autonomy
from the Sarajevo government, thus adding to the complications. Bihać
leader, Fikret Abdić, who first gained notoriety in summer 1987 as head of
the corrupt Agrokomerc Company in Bosnia, said in a statement on television that he wanted the Geneva talks to treat Bihać as a fourth player, and
to talk about a quadra-partite division of Bosnia.[77]

The Yugoslav Crisis and the West

471

Interestingly enough, in the course of negotiating strangely contorted land holdings linked by narrow "safe corridors", international mediators Vance, Owen, and Stoltenberg never asked themselves whether the formulas they were developing were conducive to stability. Many observers, including the present writer, viewed these schemes as impractical and hopeless—at best.

By late summer 1993, there were increasing numbers of voices in the West admitting that the West's policy in the Balkan war was nothing short of a fiasco. Even NATO General-Secretary Manfred Wörner publicly criticized the West's refusal to do something about the war. It was considered highly unusual for someone in his position to make such criticism publicly.[78]

Conclusion

Officials in the EC, in NATO, and in Moscow have, for months, been suggesting to the Croatian government that upon the conclusion of the war, it look to the Federal Republic of Yugoslavia (Serbia) as a partner for economic and political cooperation. Lord Owen even went so far as to suggest, in late April 1993, that the former Yugoslav republics should establish a "confederation". Given the firmness with which the Serbian Republic had resisted Slovenian-Croatian proposals for a confederal arrangement in 1990-91, and given the bitterness sown on all sides by the war, such a notion would seem to be utterly fanciful. At any rate, *Vjesnik* commentator Ivo Jakovljević took pains, in a May 1993 column, to dismiss such advice as unrealistic and unwanted. On the contrary, asserted Jakovljević, Croatia had no intention of resuming even economic, let alone political, cooperation with Serbia.[79] In the long run, of course, the Croats *might* decide to let by-gones be by-gones. But in the Balkans, whose peoples are famed for historical memories and grievances reaching back to 1389, it would be premature to bank on such a development before the war is even over.

I itemized the internal consequences of the Yugoslav war earlier in this chapter. I would like to close with a few remarks about the lessons and consequences of the West's failure to come to grips with the crisis. To begin with, it is striking that despite the warnings, over the course of years, by specialists, of the trouble brewing in Yugoslavia,[80] and despite an explicit warning by the CIA in 1990 that civil war in Yugoslavia was less than 18 months away, Western governments (except for the German government) were caught by surprise. In other words, the governments failed to absorb even the conclusions drawn by their own intelligence services, let alone by academic experts. If Western governments are serious about

472

Sabrina Petra Ramet

"learn[ing] the lessons of this saddening experience" in order to prevent the occurrence of "future Yugoslavias," as French Prime Minister Edouard Balladur put it in June 1993,[81] then the first step is to reorganize themselves so that they pay more attention to the advice of their experts. The resignation, between August 1992 and September 1993, of four of the US State Department's top experts on Yugoslavia, in protest over US inaction in the Bosnian crisis, is symptomatic and symbolic.[82]

Beyond that, the West's flaccid response to the Yugoslav war shows that, with the end of the Cold War, Western states are inclined to define "national interest" much more narrowly than heretofore, and hence, unable to see threats to the credibility of the Geneva Conventions[83] or the Helinski Accords,[84] even when they are flagrantly violated so close to their own borders. Or, one is forced to wonder, perhaps Britain, France, and the Netherlands—the leading opponents of either air strikes or arms supplies for the Muslims—have reached the conclusion that in the post-Cold War era, the Geneva Conventions and the Helsinki Accords are no longer necessary. And this, in turn, leads to the conclusion that regardless of the specificities of the eventual outcome of the war, the Yugoslav war is likely to cast a long shadow over European politics and European diplomacy for decades to come.

Notes

Portions of this chapter are drawn from my chapter, "The Yugoslav Crisis and the West: Avoiding 'Vietnam' and Blundering into 'Abyssinia'", in Takayuki Ito and Shinichiro Tabata (eds.), *Transformations in Eurasia and Emerging New World Order* (Sapporo: Slavic Research Center, Hokkaido University, 1994); also published in *East European Politics and Societies*, Vol. 8, No. 1 (Winter 1994).

1. *Neue Zürcher Zeitung* (22 April 1993), p. 15.
2. Sabrina Petra Ramet, *Nationalism and Federalism in Yugoslavia, 1962–1991*, 2nd ed. (Bloomington, Ind.: Indiana University Press, 1992), pp. 268–269.
3. *New York Times* (10 July 1991), p. A15.
4. *International Herald Tribune* (Paris ed.), 13/14 June 1992, p. 6.
5. *New York Times* (16 February 1993), p. A11.
6. Macedonian Information Liaison Service, MILS—NEWS, *Dnevni Vesti Angliski* (28 April 1993), p. 1.
7. *New York Times* (26 January 1993), p. A6.
8. *New York Times* (25 March 1993), p. A3.
9. *The Times* (London), 15 May 1993, p. 1.
10. *New York Times* (8 December 1991), p. 7.
11. See, for example, *Politika ekspres* (Belgrade), 2 August 1991, as summarized in Tanjug (2 August 1991), in FBIS, *Daily Report* (Eastern Europe), 5 August 1991, p. 53; and *Politika ekspres* (4 July 1991), quoted in Deutsche Presse Agentur (DPA), Hamburg, 4 July 1991, in FBIS, *Daily Report* (Eastern Europe), 8 July 1991, p. 59.

The Yugoslav Crisis and the West　　　　　　　　　　　　　　473

12. *Sunday Telegraph* (London), 3 January 1993, p. 1; and *Neue Zürcher Zeitung* (30 January 1993), p. 3.

13. *Financial Times* (11/12 July 1992), p. 3.

14. *Financial Times* (12 June 1992), p. 3; and *Wall Street Journal* (5 August 1992), p. A16.

15. See, for example, *New York Times* (15 January 1993), p. A17.

16. See Simes' editorial in *New York Times* (10 March 1993), p. A15.

17. *New York Times* (8 August 1992), p. 15.

18. Quoted in *New York Times* (28 September 1992), p. A6.

19. For elaboration, see Sabrina Petra Ramet, "The Yugoslav Crisis and the West: Avoiding 'Vietnam' and Blundering into 'Abyssinia'", in *East European Politics and Societies*, Vol. 8, No. 1 (Winter 1994).

20. Robert Dallek, *Franklin D. Roosevelt and American Foreign Policy, 1932–1945* (New York: Oxford University Press, 1979), pp. 135–137, 178–180.

21. *Financial Times* (18 September 1991), p. 14.

22. Re. the French on this point, see *Wall Street Journal* (1 July 1992), p. A6.

23. *New York Times* (29 November 1992), p. 11.

24. Sabrina Petra Ramet, "War in the Balkans", in *Foreign Affairs*, Vol. 71, No. 4 (Fall 1992), p. 97.

25. *New York Times* (13 May 1992), p. A14.

26. See, for example, *The Independent* (London), 16 January 1993, p. 8; and *Neue Zürcher Zeitung* (20 January 1993), p. 1.

27. *New York Times* (9 January 1993), P. 1.

28. *New York Times* (24 January 1993), p. 1.

29. Quoted in *New York Times* (18 December 1992), p. A23.

30. *New York Times* (4 August 1992), p. A12.

31. *New York Times* (22 January 1993), p. A15.

32. *New York Times* (2 May 1993), p. 18.

33. *New York Times* (21 January 1993), p. A3.

34. *Süddeutsche Zeitung* (Munich), 27/28 March 1993, p. 2, and 3/4 April 1993, p. 1.

35. *Christian Science Monitor* (12 February 1993), p. 20, emphasis in original. The troop figures come from *Süddeutsche Zeitung* (3/4 April 1993), p. 7.

36. Thatcher's comments are reported in *The Independent* (14 April 1993), p. 1. Bartholemew's comments are reported in *The Independent* (16 April 1993), p. 1.

37. *New York Times* (24 April 1993), p. 1. See also the comments by British Foreign Secretary Hurd, reported in *Financial Times* (30 April 1993), p. 9.

38. Quoted in *The Independent* (16 April 1993), p. 1.

39. Quoted in *New York Times* (23 April 1993), p. A14.

40. Quoted in *Ibid.*, p. A1.

41. *Neue Zürcher Zeitung* (25/26 April 1993), p. 2.

42. *New York Times* (29 April 1993), p. A18.

43. Misha Glenny, in an op/ed piece for the *New York Times* (29 April 1993), p. A19.

44. Gen. Merrill A. McPeak, Air Force Chief of Staff, as reported in *New York Times* (29 April 1993), p. A1.

474   *Sabrina Petra Ramet*

45. David Rieff, in an op/ed piece for the *New York Times* (29 April 1993), p. A19.

46. As reported in *New York Times* (24 April 1993), p. 5.

47. *Financial Times* (30 April 1993), p. 16.

48. *New York Times* (2 May 1993), p. 1.

49. *Financial Times* (30 April 1993), p. 9.

50. *Christian Science Monitor* (3 May 1993), p. 4.

51. *New York Times* (7 May 1993), p. A6.

52. *Financial Times* (30 April 1993), p. 2.

53. Quoted in *Seattle Times* (6 May 1993), p. A3.

54. Quoted in *Ibid*.

55. *Seattle Times* (4 May 1993), p. A1.

56. *New York Times* (8 May 1993), p. 1.

57. *New York Times* (7 May 1993), p. A1.

58. *Ibid*.

59. Quoted in *International Herald Tribune* (Tokyo ed.), 15 June 1993, p. 8.

60. *International Herald Tribune* (Tokyo ed.), 19/20 June 1993, p. 1; and *Le Monde* (Paris), 19 June 1993, p. 1.

61. *Vjesnik* (Zagreb), 19 June 1993, p. 1.

62. Quoted in *International Herald Tribune* (Tokyo ed.), 1 July 1993, p. 2.

63. *The Times* (19 June 1993), p. 10. See also *Vjesnik* (18 June 1993), p. 2.

64. *Le Monde* (18 June 1993), p. 1, and (19 June 1993), p. 1; and *International Herald Tribune* (Tokyo ed.), 10/11 July 1993, p. 2.

65. *Frankfurter Allgemeine* (22 June 1993), p. 2.

66. See, for example, the report in *International Herald Tribune* (Tokyo ed.), 22 July 1993, p. 1.

67. See the oblique reference in *The Times* (14 June 1993), p. 13.

68. Details of the plan in: *New York Times* (31 July 1993), p. 4.

69. *New York Times* (12 August 1993), p. A1. See also *Süddeutsche Zeitung* (10 August 1993), p. 1.

70. *New York Times* (12 August 1993), p. A11. See also *New York Times* (10 August 1993), p. A1.

71. *Süddeutsche Zeitung* (11 August 1993), p. 1.

72. *Süddeutsche Zeitung* (8 September 1993), p. 2.

73. *Danas* (Zagreb), New series, 24 August 1993, p. 33.

74. Quoted in *International Herald Tribune* (Tokyo ed.), 1 September 1993, p 4.

75. Quoted in *Süddeutsche Zeitung* (21/22 August 1993), p. 2.

76. Details in *New York Times* (2 September 1993), pp. A1, A8; and *Süddeutsche Zeitung* (2 September 1993), p. 1.

77. *Süddeutsche Zeitung* (11/12 September 1993), p. 9.

78. *Süddeutsche Zeitung* (11/12 September 1993), p. 1.

79. *Vjesnik* (4 May 1993), p. 13.

80. By this writer: "Yugoslavia and the Threat of Internal and External Discontents", in *Orbis*, Vol. 28, No. 1 (Spring 1984); "Yugoslavia's Troubled Times", in *Global Affairs*, Vol. 5, No. 1 (Winter 1990); "Serbia's Slobodan Milošević: A Profile", in *Orbis*, Vol. 35, No. 1 (Winter 1991); and "The Breakup of Yugoslavia", in *Global Affairs*, Vol. 6, No. 2 (Spring 1991).

The Yugoslav Crisis and the West

81. As quoted in *The Times* (21 June 1993), p. 9.

82. Re. the three resignations in 1993, see *Der Spiegel* (Hamburg), 16 August 1993, p. 108; and *Japan Times* (Tokyo), 25 August 1993, p. 5.

83. Adopted in 1949, the Geneva Conventions bound the signatories to observe certain standards in the wartime treatment of civilians and prisoners.

84. Adopted in 1975, the Helsinki Accords were signed by all European states, including Yugoslavia, and established the principle that European borders would not be changed by force.

About the Editors

Ljubiša S. Adamovich is a Professor of Economics and since 1972 Chair of the Department of International Economics, University of Belgrade. He received his BS from the University of Belgrade, MBA from Ohio University (Athens, Ohio), and his Ph.D. in Economics from the University of Belgrade in 1961. He is the author of several books, among them *International Economics Relations; International Trade Theory; Integration and Disintegration in the World Economy; The European Common Market and Yugoslavia;* and *Yugoslav-American Economic Relations Since World War II* (with J. Lampe and R. Prickett). Professor Adamovich has published many articles in professional journals in Yugoslavia and abroad (USA, Russia, Belgium, Italy, Greece, Japan, Mexico). He has lectured at some 40 leading universities in more than 20 countries and has participated in many international professional conferences. He is a member of the *Learned Society of Serbia, ASPEN Institute–Rome, Academy of Science and Arts of Montenegro,* and is listed in various publications, including *Who's Who in the World.* Currently he is Professor of Economics at the Florida State University (Tallahassee, Florida).

Sabrina Petra Ramet is Professor of International Studies, University of Washington. She recieved her AB in Philosophy from Stanford University in 1971, her MA in International Relations from the University of Arkansas in 1974, and her Ph.D. in Political Science from UCLA in 1981. She taught at the University of California at Santa Barbara from 1981 to 1983 and has taught at the University of Washington since then. She is the author of five books, including *Nationalism and Federalism in Yugoslavia, 1962–1991,* 2nd ed. and *Balkan Babel: Politics, Culture, and Religion in Yugoslavia* (Westview Press, 1992), and the editor of eight previous books. During the 1993–94 academic year she was a Foreign Visiting Fellow at the Slavic Research Center at Hokkaido University, Sapporo, Japan.

About the Contributors

Svetlana Adamović is an Assistant Professor of Economics, University of Belgrade, Yugoslavia. She received her BA in Economics from the University of Belgrade, her MS in Economics from Florida State University, and her Ph.D. in Economics from the University of Belgrade (1990). She was a Fulbright scholar at UCLA during the 1987–88 academic year. Dr. Adamović is the author of the book *High Technology and Structural Changes: Strategies of the USA, Japan and Western Europe* (1991) and has published articles in professional journals and presented papers at international conferences.

Milan Andrejevich was a research analyst and a Special Assistant to the Director of Radio Free Europe for Southeast European Affairs, Munich, Germany until the summer of 1994. He specializes in Yugoslav area affairs. He earned a BA in History with honors from Indiana University in 1975 and a MA in Modern European History from the University of Chicago in 1978. He has received two Fulbright-Hayes awards to Yugoslavia, in 1976–77 and 1983–84. He also taught at the University of Illinois at Chicago. He is currently working as International Affairs and Media Consultant in Washington, DC.

Ivo Banac is a Professor of History and Master of Pierson College at Yale University. He received his MA and Ph.D. in history from Stanford University in 1971 and 1975 respectively. He is the author of *The National Question in Yugoslavia: Origins, History, Politics* (Cornell University Press, 1984), which was awarded the Wayne S. Vucinich Prize of the American Association for the Advancement of Slavic Studies, and *With Stalin, Against Tito: Cominformist Splits in Yugoslav Communism* (Cornell University Press, 1988), which was awarded the Josip Juraj Strossmayer Award by the Zagreb Book Fair. He is the author of numerous collections including most recently *Dubrovački eseji* (Matica hrvatska, 1992) . He also edited five books and is a corresponding member of the Croatian Academy of Sciences and Arts and the editor of *East European Politics and Societies.*

Andrew Horton is a Professor of Film and Literature at Loyola University, New Orleans. He received his BA in English Literature from Hamilton College in 1966, his MA in English Literature from Colgate University in

480

About the Contributors

1969, and his Ph.D. in Comparative Literature and Cinema from the University of Illinois in 1973. He is the author of *The Films of George Roy Hill* (Columbia University Press, 1984), *Laughter with a Lash: Inside Soviet Film Satire* (Cambridge University Press, 1993), and *Writing the Character Centered Script* (University of California Press, 1993), and co-author (with Michael Brashinsky) of *Time Zero Hour: Glasnost and the Soviet Cinema in Transition (Princeton University Press, 1992)*. He is also editor of *Comedy/ cinema/theory* (University of California Press, 1991). He is also a professional screenwriter and has made three short video documentaries for TV channel 32 (WLAE) in New Orleans (1986–87)—two on neighborhoods and one on Yugoslav oyster fishermen.

Zachary T. Irwin is an Associate Professor of Political Science at the Pennsylvania State University, Erie, Pennsylvania. He received his BA in Political Science from Hamilton College in 1968, his MA in International Relations from the Johns Hopkins University in 1972, and his Ph.D. in Political Science from the Pennsylvania State University in 1978. He is the co-author of *Introduction to Political Science*, 2nd ed. (Prentice Hall, 1992). His articles have appeared in *East European Quarterly, Problems of Communism, Religion in Communist Dominated Areas*, and other journals. During 1993, he was a Research Fellow at the Woodrow Wilson Center for International Scholars, researching the foreign policies of the Yugoslav republics.

Rada Iveković is a free-lance writer and Indologist whose career has taken her from Zagreb to Paris. She earned master's degrees in Indian Studies and English Language and Literature at the University of Zagreb in 1969, and a Ph.D. in Buddhist Philosophy from the Delhi University, India, 1972. She also received her habilitation from the University of Paris in 1993. She is the author of *Rana budistička misao* (Masleša, 1977), *Druga Indija* (Školska knjiga, 1982), *Orients: Critique de la raison postmoderne* (Blandin, Paris 1992), *Jugoslawischer Salat* (Verlag Droschl, 1993). She has also co-authored *Briefe von Frauen über Krieg und Nationalismus* (Suhrkamp· Frankfurt: 1992) and has edited *Studie o ženi i ženski pokret* (Komunist, 1994), *Počeci indijske misli, 2nd ed.* (NOTLIT, 1991), and *La Croatie depuis l'effondrement de la Yougoslavie* (L'Harmattan: Paris 1994) . From 1988 to 1991 she was an Associate Professor at the University of Zagreb; since 1991 she has been teaching at the University of Paris.

Oskar Kovač is a Professor of Economics at the University of Belgrade and was Minister of the Federal Government of Yugoslavia, 1986–89, and Deputy Prime Minister in 1992. He obtained his MS and Ph.D. degrees in Economics from the University of Belgrade, spent one year of post-graduate studies at the London School of Economics, and a year of sabbatical at MIT,

About the Contributors 481

Massachusetts. He is the author of six books, including *Spoljno ekonomska ravnoteza i privredni rast: problemi i iskustva Jugoslavije* (Institut ekonomskih nauka, 1979), and co-author of several books, including *Stabilization and Development: Yugoslavia until 1985* (Jugoslovenski Pregled, 1982), *Privredni razvoj Jugoslavije do 2000, godine: makroekonomski model i projedcije* (Ekonomika, 1993), and *Effective Protection and Competitiveness of the Yugloslav Economy* (Institut economskih nauka, 1991).

Jure Kristo is Project Director of the Institute of Contemporary History, Zagreb, and chief editor of the journal, *Casopis za Suvremenu Povijest.* A native of Croatia, he received his BA and Masters of Theology from the College Dominican in Ottawa, Canada, in 1969 and 1970 respectively. He later earned an MA in Religious Studies in 1978 and a Ph.D. in the same field in 1979, both from the University of Notre Dame. He taught at St. Johns University in Collegeville, Minnesota, Aquinas College in Grand Rapids, Michigan, and Loyola University, Chicago between 1978 and 1990. He is the author of *Looking for God in Time and Memory: Psychology, Theology, and Spirituality in Augustine's "Confessions"* (University Press of America, 1991). His latest book, *Prešućena povijest. Katolička crkva u hrvatskoj politici 1848–1918* has been published by Hrvatska sveučilišna naklada of Zagreb.

Jasmina Kuzmanović is a staff writer for Associated Press in Zagreb. A native of Zagreb, she earned her BA in English Language and Literature and Comparative Literature at the University of Zagreb in 1984, and was employed, from 1985 to 1992, as staff writer for Zagreb Weekly news magazine, *Danas* (*Novi Danas*). In 1988 she won the Alfred Friendly Press Fellowship and spent six months in the United States, working for *The Nashville Tennessean* and *USA Today*. Since 1989, she has been a regular columnist for the cultural supplement, *Profil*, in the Split-based weekly newspaper, *Nedjeljna Dalmacija*, and in 1990, she became a correspondent for the US daily economic bulletin, *Eastern European Report*. In 1991 and 1992, she wrote as a war correspondent for *USA Today* and was chief stringer in Croatia for *Time* magazine. Since spring of 1992, she has been one of two section editors for Croatia on the staff of the Budapest-based periodical, *East European Reporter*.

Marko Milivojević is a free-lance writer and consultant on Yugoslav affairs. Since 1983, he has also been an associate editor and editorial board member of *The South Slav Journal*, published in London. In 1986, he became an Honorary Visiting Fellow in Yugoslav Studies at the Research Unit in Yugoslav Studies, University of Bradford. He recieved his BA from Manchester University, his MA from Warwick University, and his MBSc. From Manchester University. He is the author of four books, including *The*

482   *About the Contributors*

Debt Rescheduling Process (Frances Pinter, 1985), and is co-editor of *Yugoslavia in Transition: Choices and Constraints* (Berg. 1991) and other books.

Vukašin Pavlović is a Professor of Political Science at the University of Belgrade. He received his BA in Law from the University of Belgrade in 1966, his MA in Political Science from the University of Sarajevo in 1973, and his Ph.D. in Political Science from the University of Sarajevo in 1976. He is co-author (with James H. Seroka) of *The Trajedy of Yugoslavia: The Failure of Democratic Transformation* (M.E. Sharpe, 1992) and has been Fulbright scholar in the United States. He is currently Director of the Center for Socio-Economic Research and Documentation in Belgrade.

Dijana Pleština is an Associate Professor of Political Science at Wooster College, Ohio. She received her BA in French Literature from Carleton University, Ottawa, in 1970, and her MA in Comparative Literature, likewise from Carleton University, in 1973. She received her Ph.D. in Political Science from the University of California, Berkeley, in 1987. She is the author of *Regional Development in Communist Yugoslavia: Success, Failure, and Consequences* (Westview Press, 1992).

Branko Pribićević is a professor of Political Science at the University of Belgrade. He did his undergraduate work at the University of Warsaw and Zagreb in the field of Law, and earned his Ph.D. in Political Science at Oxford University in 1957. He is the author of *The Shop Stewards, Movement and Workers' Control, 1910–1922* (Oxford, 1959), *International Socialism* (Belgrade, 1982), *Socialism: Rise and Fall* (Belgrade, 1991), and other books. He was a Fulbright Scholar at the University of Oregon (Eugene) in 1984–85. He is one of the founders of the Faculty of Political Science at the University of Belgrade and the first head of its Department of International Studies.

Dennison Rusinow is a Research Professor and Adjunct Professor of History at the University of Pittsburgh. From 1963 to 1988 he was an Associate of the American Universities Field Staff, based in Belgrade, Zagreb, and after 1974 in Vienna. He received his BA from Duke University in 1952, and his MA (1959) D. Phil. (1963) from Oxford University. He is the author of *Italy's Austrian Heritage, 1919–1946* (Oxford University Press, Clarendon, 1969), *The Yugoslav Experiment 1948–1974* (University of California Press, 1977), and, *An Institutional Framework of a Federally Structured Cyprus* (American Universities Field Staff, 1978). He is also the editor of *Yugoslavia: A Fractured Federalism* (Wilson Center Press, 1988). He was a Rhodes Scholar at Oxford, and a Fellow of the Institute of Current World Affairs from 1959 to 1963.

About the Contributors

Paul Shoup is a Research Professor of Government and Foreign Affairs at the University of Virginia. He received his BA with honors in Political Science from Swarthmore in 1951 and earned his Ph.D. in Public Law and Government from Columbia University in 1969. He is the author of *Communism and the National Question in Yugoslavia* (Columbia University Press, 1968), compiler of *The East European and Soviet Data handbook: Political, Social, and Developmental Indicators, 1945–1975* (Columbia University Press and Hoover Institution Press, 1981), and editor of *Problems of Balkan Security: Southeastern Europe in the 1990s* (Wilson Center Press, 1990). His articles have appeared in *The American Political Science Review, Problems of Communism, Telos,* and other journals. He spent the 1992–93 academic year ad Radio Free Europe, Munich, researching the Yugoslav crisis, with support of a grant from the National Council for Soviet and East European Research.

About the Book

The fruit of a landmark international collaboration, this book focuses on the final years of socialist Yugoslavia and on the beginning of the country's breakup. With chapters devoted to each of erstwhile Yugoslavia's six republics, the book also offers a unique blend of thematic essays on political, cultural, economic, environmental, religious, and foreign policy issues. Bringing together renowned scholars from the United States, Great Britain, Serbia, and Croatia, the book shows how disintegrative tendencies penetrated and affected all spheres of life in Yugoslavia. The resultant war has, therefore, been fought not only on military and diplomatic fronts, but also at the level of economics, through literature and film, and in the spheres of religion and gender relations.

Index

Abbas, Mohammed, 370
Abdić, Fikret, 158, 470
Abortion, 201, 399, 400, 401, 404, 444
Adamovich, Ljubiša S., 456
Adriatic Sea, 305, 306, 312, 317, 321, 371
Adžić, Blagoje, 75, 76, 216, 377
Agh, Attila, 149
Albania, 22, 72, 73, 211, 216, 219, 224, 229,
    239, 336, 350–351, 352(table), 356, 357,
    358, 381
Albanian Democratic Alliance
    (Montenegro), 242
Albanians, 4, 57, 76. *See also under individual*
    provinces and republics
Albright, Madeleine, 466
Aleksandar (king of Yugoslavia), 16, 41, 52
Alliance of Reform Forces (B-H), 157, 158
Alliance of Reform Forces (Montenegro),
    242
Alpine-Adriatic Group, 352(table), 353, 363
Alps-Adriatic Work Community, 367
Amato, Guilano, 227
Anarchist parties, 398
Anderson, David, 18, 459
Andjelković, Zoran, 222
Andreotti, Guilio, 370
Antall, József, 363
Anti-fascist Council for the Liberation of
    Yugoslavia (AVNOJ), 107, 157, 165
Arabs, 103, 369, 383
Arkan. *See* Raznjatović, Željko
Arsenije III Carnojević (patriarch), 110
Assimilation, 44, 54
Association for a Yugoslav Democratic
    Initiative (AYDI) (Serbia), 396, 403
Association of Reformist Forces, 395
Austria, 78, 102, 110, 112, 155, 156, 189, 194,
    196, 197, 299(table), 335, 349, 352(table),
    353, 355(tables), 362, 363–364, 367, 376,
    383
Authoritarianism, 25, 149, 150, 453
Autocephalous Orthodox Church, 116

AVNOJ. *See* Anti-fascist Council for the
    Liberation of Yugoslavia
AYDI. *See* Association for a Yugoslav
    Democratic Initiative

Babić, Anto, 41
Babić, Goran, 47, 51–52
Babić, Milan, 131, 132, 173
Badinter Commission, 164, 165, 174–175
Badurina, Srečko (bishop), 438
Bajramović, Sejdo, 27
Baker, James, 30, 195, 459
Baković, Ante, 400, 440, 449(n44)
Balkan Foreign Minister Group, 352(table),
    356, 357
Balkan Pact (1954), 338
Balladur, Edouard, 472
Banac, Ivo, 119, 453, 455
Barrett, William, 103
Bartholemew, Reginald, 380, 465
Bavaria, 367
Bavčar, Igor, 204, 205
Bečković, Matija, 93
Belgrade (Serbia), 7, 59(n10), 111
    -Bar railway, 317
    demonstration (1991), 25
    economy, 271
    First Military District, 72, 75
    underground metro, 370
Benelux countries, 197, 352(table)
Berisha, Sali, 216, 381
B-H. *See* Bosnia-Herzegovina
Biber, Dušan, 57
Bihać (B-H), 157, 470
Bilirakis, Michael, 230
Bishops' "Iustitia et Pax" Commission
    (Croatia), 438, 440
Boban, Ljubo, 2, 57
Boban, Mate, 179, 469
Bogdanov, Vaso, 41
Boka Kotor Bay, 321, 322
Boras, Franjo, 158, 166
Borovo Selo (Slavonia), 29, 32

486 Index

Borstner, Ivan, 191
Bosanska Krajina (B-H), 165, 167, 172
Bosnia-Herzegovina (B-H), 15, 113, 454
  Arab soldiers in, 383
  armed civilians, 79, 117, 118
  capital. *See* Sarajevo
  Catholic Church, 431, 441
  censorship, 57
  censuses, 156, 181(n2)
  civil war, 155, 160, 170, 180–181, 408
  Communist Party, 57, 89
  and confederation, 26, 163–164, 166, 167, 168
  and Croatia, 4, 58, 135, 136–137, 155, 163, 179, 464
  Croats in, 21, 25, 69, 89, 136, 155, 156, 158, 163, 170, 172, 179, 469
  defense industries, 157
  and EC, 162, 163, 164, 165, 167–176
  economy, 8, 157, 295
  elections (1990), 24, 57, 157–158
  and environment, 301, 310
  film, 413, 420, 421, 423
  government, 7, 25, 69, 158–164, 453
  historians, 41
  and Homeric sites theory, 58
  independence (1992), 6, 160, 163, 164, 166, 168–169
  and Islam, 6–7, 21, 25, 172
  media, 84, 88–91
  mosques destroyed, 467
  Muslim nationalism, 102, 457
  Muslims, 25, 33, 34(n13), 44, 46, 69, 89, 136, 155, 156, 157, 163, 178, 180, 432, 463, 467, 469, 470, 472
  National Assembly, 158
  no-fly zone, 379, 459
  partitioned (1939), 157
  partition proposal, 164, 166, 173, 175–176, 178, 180, 469, 470
  political parties, 22, 24, 25, 69, 71, 73, 85, 88, 157, 160
  population, 156
  president, 69
  prime minister, 158
  refugees, 189, 200
  and Russia, 345
  and Serbia, 28, 85, 89, 90, 107, 116, 155, 157, 170, 179, 180, 181–182(n6)
  Serbian Autonomous Areas, 162, 183(n20)

  Serbian offensive against (1992), 136, 214, 379, 445, 464. *See also* Sarajevo, bombardment
  Serbs in, 5, 21, 25, 69, 73, 89, 117, 118, 155, 156, 158, 160, 161–162, 165, 166, 168, 169, 172, 179, 408, 431, 463, 467
  State Presidency, 24, 158
  Titoism, 157
  and UN, 379
  and U.S., 170, 173, 179, 186(n76), 343, 345, 472
  and YPA, 89, 245
  See also Serbia, expansionist war; *under* Montenegro; Slovenia
Boutros-Ghali, Boutros, 460, 470
Brzezinski, Zbigniew, 462
Bozanić, Josip (bishop), 445
Božić, Ivan, 45
Bozović, Radoman, 92, 224
Brena, Lepa, 417, 426–428
Brkic, Miljenko, 172
Brković, Jevrem, 238
Brownmiller, Susan, 408
Bucar, France, 191
Budiša, Dražen, 139
Bulatović, Momir, 29, 243–244, 246, 248, 249
Bulgaria, 206, 211, 213, 216, 219, 221, 225, 301, 308, 325, 350–351, 352(table), 356, 360–361, 362, 381, 398
Burzan, Danilo, 88
Bush, George, 342, 343, 345, 381, 454, 463

Canada, 102, 228, 465
Cantonization, 176, 177, 178, 181
Capital accumulation, 258–259
Carrington, Lord, 115, 167, 243, 244, 246, 377, 378
Catholic Church, 3, 40, 45, 110, 113–114, 402, 455
  clergy and politics, 439–440, 449(n44)
  and Communists, 432, 433, 437, 438, 440, 447(n13), 448(n34)
  and free elections, 438
  humanitarian aid, 445
  and human rights, 436
  and politics, 441, 442, 444, 446
  religious education, 444
  and Serbian Orthodox Church, 114–115, 118, 436, 442, 443
  and Yugoslav integration, 56, 57

Index

487

See also under Bosnia-Herzegovina;
   Croatia
Čavoški, Kosta, 49, 50
CDU. See Croatian Democratic Union
Cengić, Bato, 423, 424
Censorship, 44, 45, 57, 136, 144
Centralism, 2, 16, 42, 43, 45, 46, 131, 192, 273
Cerar, Miro, 201
CFC. See Chlorofluorocarbon
Chernobyl (Soviet Union) accident (1986),
   304
Chetniks, 2, 4, 41, 49, 50, 56, 60
Chlorofluorocarbon (CFC), 320, 322–323,
   328(n25)
Christopher, Warren, 347, 380, 466, 468
Church Slavonic (language), 110
Cirković, Šuna, 45, 51
Civil society, 126, 160, 310
Čkrebić, Dušan, 362
Clinton, Bill, 347, 464, 465, 466
Club of Rome, 325
CMEA. See Council for Mutual Economic
   Assistance
CNP. See Croatian National Party
COMECON. See Council for Mutual
   Economic Assistance
Comintern (Communist International), 54,
   62(n36), 107
Committee for Truth (Serbia), 94
Communism, 2, 3, 16, 22, 23–24, 49, 50, 56,
   126
   demise of, 129, 437
   Titoist, 24, 331–332
   See also Reform Communists; under
      Catholic Church
Community for Independent Former
   Yugoslav Republics proposal, 166
Conable, Barbara, 368
Confederation, 2, 21, 22, 23, 26, 31, 54, 55,
   166, 193, 194, 242, 382
Conference on Security and Cooperation in
   Europe (CSCE), 175, 227, 343, 344, 346,
   352(table), 364, 369, 375, 381, 459
Conservation, 326
Convertible currency, 256
Ćosić, Dobrica, 6, 433, 467
Cot, Jean, 470
Council for Mutual Economic Assistance
   (COMECON/CMEA), 286, 299(table),
   349, 351

Council for National Defense and
   Protection of the Constitutional Order
   (Croatia), 79
Council of Europe, 349, 352(table), 365, 376
CPP. See Croatian Peasant Party
CPR. See Croatian Party of Rights
CPY. See Yugoslavia, Communist Party of
Creation of Yugoslavia, The, 1790–1918
   (Ekmečić), 56
Crnćević, Brana, 93
Crnić, Zlatko, 137
Croatia, 40, 157, 221
   Agency for Reconstructuring and
      Development, 96
   arms imports, 78, 136
   borders, 97
   capital. See Zagreb
   Catholic Church, 57, 130, 431, 432, 433,
      434–436, 439–446
   censorship, 44, 57, 96
   civilian arms, 78, 117, 118
   Communist Party (LCC), 23, 44, 51, 52,
      57, 62(n36), 85, 125, 127, 128, 433–434
   Communist Party (LCC-PDC), 129
   confederation proposal, 22, 26, 54, 130,
      131, 159
   constitution (1990), 69, 124, 132, 133–135,
      138, 141, 147, 148, 404, 405, 444
   counties, 153(n40)
   defense minister, 67
   democracy, 123, 124–125, 126–127, 128,
      135, 137, 140, 143–144, 145, 149, 456
   and EC, 163, 164, 196, 215, 343, 376, 377,
      445
   elections (1990), 24, 57, 125, 127, 128–131
   elections (1992), 138–140
   elections (1993), 140
   electoral system, 137–138
   environmental issues, 305
   federal budget, 126
   federation proposal, 22
   feminist movement, 399, 407
   film, 52, 423
   foreign investment in, 354
   foreign relations, 366, 367, 383
   and FRY, 295, 471
   government, 71, 79, 115, 123, 124, 132–
      133, 135–138, 146–147, 152(n18), 453
   and Great Britain, 67, 462
   historians, 41, 43, 51

488   *Index*

independence (1991), 6, 30, 57, 123, 124, 133, 194, 377
industrial production, 8, 456
JNA attacks (1991), 123, 135, 136, 377
judiciary, 147–149, 150
leadership, 4, 19, 23, 127
majority rule, 128, 129, 138
media, 84–85, 88, 93, 94, 95–97, 98, 144, 146, 406
military, 79
military court, 147–148, 153(n45)
militia reserves, 67, 69
and Montenegro, 94, 243, 244–245
nationalism, 2, 6, 15, 19, 25, 44, 93, 103, 126, 129–130, 180, 444, 453, 457
-occupied Herzegovina, 4, 183(n20), 464, 469
opposition parties, 25
paramilitary special police, 29, 67, 78
Parliament (Sabor), 79, 123, 134–135, 137, 138–140, 141–144, 147, 437
political parties, 22, 25, 45, 67, 85, 93, 95, 124, 129, 139, 140, 150
president, 24, 67, 145–146, 147, 150, 376
privatization, 96, 97, 272
referendum (1991), 29–30, 133
refugees in, 135, 137
rural, 129
and Russia, 346–347, 380
and Serbia, 4, 22, 41, 43, 46–47, 52, 54, 55–56, 67, 68–69, 74, 92, 93, 94–95, 118–119, 127, 130, 171, 446, 455. *See also* Serbia, expansionist war
and Serbian Orthodox Church, 105, 114–115, 116, 118, 434, 442, 443, 448(n36)
Serbs in, 5, 6, 19, 21, 27, 28–29, 31–32, 33, 55, 61(n22), 68–69, 73, 93, 114, 117, 118, 131, 132–133, 136, 376, 431, 442
Serbs in Parliament, 141
and Slovenia, 30, 31, 79, 189, 190, 192, 196–197
sovereignty, 134, 382, 439
strategic location, 22
TDF, 71, 78, 79
and UN, 123, 137, 379, 460
unemployment, 8, 206
urban, 129, 140, 150
and U.S., 67, 343, 345, 459, 460, 462, 463
War of Croatian Secession (1991), 28, 29, 442–445

women, 396, 399, 400–402, 404, 405, 406, 407
and YPA, 67, 68, 71, 78, 95, 376, 442
See also Krajina; Slavonia; *under* Bosnia-Herzegovina
Croatian (language), 5, 89
Croatian Defense League, 176
Croatian Democratic Community, 89, 160, 164, 166–167, 439, 444, 446
Croatian Democratic Union (CDU), 67, 68, 71, 73, 79, 88, 93, 95, 96, 124, 126, 129, 131, 137, 138–140, 142–143, 146, 148, 157, 166, 172, 179
Croatian National Party (CNP), 153(n39)
Croatian Party of Rights (CPR), 139, 144
Croatian Peasant Party (CPP), 140, 153(n39)
Croatian Social Liberal Alliance (CSLA), 440
Croatian Social Liberal Party (CSLP), 139, 140
Croatian *Ustaše* (fascist), 2, 21, 28, 41, 56, 60(n13), 93, 114, 433
Croat Peasant Party (HSS), 41, 61(n22)
Croats, 26, 44, 112, 360, 456, 464–465
Catholic, 113–114, 431
population, 15
and Serb hegemony, 16, 28, 52, 458
and socialist symbols, 130, 131
Crvenkovski, Branko, 226
CSCE. *See* Conference on Security and Cooperation in Europe
CSLA. *See* Croatian Social Liberal Alliance
CSLP. *See* Croatian Social Liberal Party
Čubrilović, Vaso, 41
Čulinović, Ferdo, 41
Customs union, 293–294, 456
Cutilheiro, José, 167, 172
Cvetković, Dragiša, 41
Cviić, Christopher, 378
Cyprus, 361, 369
Cyrillic alphabet, 5
Czechoslovakia, 351, 352(table), 415. *See also* Czech Republic; Slovakia
Czech Republic, 196, 296

Dabčević-Kučar, Savka, 42–43, 44
Dalmatia (Croatia), 29, 68, 113
Damjanović, Pero, 41
Danube Commission, 352(table)
Danube River, 304, 305, 306, 307, 359
canal, 361, 367

Index

Deak, Ferenc, 428
Decentralism, 2, 17, 42, 43–44, 45, 283, 284, 332
DeConcini, Dennis, 229
Dedijer, Vladimir, 44–45, 46, 47, 48, 61–62(n34)
Degoricia, Slavko, 146
Delchev, Goce, 213
Delimustafić, Alija, 158
De Michelis, Gianni, 371
Democracy, 126, 360, 456, 457
  and anti-nationalist opposition, 396
  consensual, 127, 128
  majoritarian, 127–128, 129, 151(n13)
Democratic Coalition (Montenegro), 242, 248
Democratic Party (Slovenia), 193, 201, 202, 204, 205
Democratic Party of Serbs (Macedonia), 222
Democratic Party of Socialists (DPS) (Montenegro), 85, 87, 237, 242, 248
Democratic Union of Bulgarians, 222
Democratic Union of Magyars of Vojvodina (DUMV), 81(n25)
Demos. *See* Slovenia, Democratic Opposition of
Denationalization, 198, 260
Deus Pinheiro, Joao de, 225
Diaspora, 19, 21, 23
Distinctivists, 44, 45
Dizdarević, Raif, 361, 363, 365
Djordjević, Aleksandar, 427
Djordjević, Bora, 106
Djukanović, Milo, 88, 246, 247
Djukić, Djordje, 286
Djuranović, Veselin, 369
Djurdjev, Branislav, 41
Djuretić, Veselin, 56, 64(n71)
Djurić, Veljko, 114
Domestic resource costs (DRC), 300(table)
DPS. *See* Democratic Party of Socialists
Drašković, Vuk, 71, 72
Draženović, Ljerka, 94
DRC. *See* Domestic resource costs
Drina River, 314
Drnovšek, Janez, 200, 204, 205, 365
Dubrovnik (Croatia), 43, 61(n26), 113, 438
Dugan, Michael J., 462
Duka, Tomislav, 440, 449(n44)
DUMV. *See* Democratic Union of Magyars of Vojvodina

Duraković, Nijaz, 157
Durmitor National Park (Montenegro), 320, 321, 323, 324

Eagleburger, Lawrence, 176, 186(n72), 379, 464
EC. *See* European Community
ECU. *See* European Currency Unit
EEC. *See* European Economic Community
Effective rates of protection (ERP), 290–291, 292, 298(fig.), 300(table)
EFTA. *See* European Free Trade Association
Eisenhower, Dwight D., 338
Ekmečić, Milorad, 45, 46, 47, 56–57
Ellemann-Jensen, Uffe, 226
Elytis, Odysseus, 220
Energy, 315, 326, 346
Environmental issues, 301–311, 325–327. *See also under individual republics*
ERP. *See* Effective rates of protection
Ethnic cleansing, 118, 136, 177, 215, 379, 409, 463
Ethnic Forum (Belgrade), 177
Ethnic peace, 13–14, 155, 454
Ethnic politics, 2, 5, 7, 464–465
European Community (EC), 30, 179, 196, 277, 296, 346, 361, 373, 377, 380, 468. *See also under* Yugoslavia; *individual republics*
European Currency Unit (ECU), 373
European Economic Community (EEC), 286, 287, 293, 296, 299(table)
European Free Trade Association (EFTA), 197, 286, 287, 299(table), 349, 352(table), 354. *See also under* Yugoslavia
European Investment Bank, 373
European Monetary System, 294
European Parliament, 358, 378
Evren, Kenan, 75

Family planning, 319
Fascism, 2, 21, 28, 41, 49, 53, 98, 131, 132
FEC (Federal Executive Council). *See* Yugoslavia, government
Federal Defense Secretariat, 67, 74
Federal Environmental Division, 303, 305, 306
Federalism, 19, 42, 46, 47–48
Federal People's Army, 90

490   *Index*

Federal Presidency, 27–28, 29, 67, 68, 70, 72, 74, 158, 365
   and YPA, 75
Federal Prime Minster, 72
Federal Republic of Yugoslavia (FRY). *See* Serbia, and Montenegro as FRY
Federation, 17, 22, 26, 163, 177, 182–183(n16), 242, 246, 335
   asymmetric, 192, 214
Feminist movement, 396, 398, 399, 406, 407
Films, 52, 228, 413–417, 418–430, 457
   festival prizes, 413, 418, 419, 420, 429
Film With No Name, A (film), 416, 429, 457
France, 50, 102, 195, 196, 197, 218–219, 229, 299(table), 352(table), 355(tables), 367, 370, 378, 462, 465, 466, 468, 469, 472
FRY (Federal Republic of Yugoslavia). *See* Serbia, and Montenegro as FRY

Ganić, Ejup, 159
Gavrilo (Macedonian metropolitan), 113
Gavrilo (Serbian patriarch), 105
Gelb, Leslie, 458
Genocide, 14, 21, 28, 31, 32, 54, 55–56, 61(n22), 91, 460
German (Serbian patriarch), 104, 113, 114, 434
Germany, 195, 196, 197, 221, 229, 299(table), 352(table), 354, 355(tables), 371–372, 378, 417, 468, 469
Girenko, Yuri S., 196
Gligorijević, Branislav, 46
Gligorov, Kiro, 24, 26, 215, 216, 218, 220, 223, 225
Gočevski, Traian, 216
Godina, Carpo, 423, 424
Golding, Peter, 83–84
Gospić, Zoran, 420
Gotovac, Vlado, 43, 44
Grafenauer, Bogo, 41
Grdesić, Ivan, 140
Great Britain, 50, 67, 77, 102, 117, 195, 229, 299(table), 352(table), 355(table), 369–370, 378, 465, 466, 468, 469, 472
Greater Serbia, 26, 28, 29, 68, 69–70, 72, 73–74, 116, 157, 222, 455
   plan for B-H (RAM), 162, 176, 183(n18), 184(n28)
Great Serbian hegemony, 2, 40, 43, 46, 53

Greece, 8, 196, 219, 223, 224, 299(table), 335, 338, 356, 361, 367, 381, 415. *See also under* Macedonia
Greek Orthodox Church, 110
Green Party (Serbia), 403
Green Party (Slovenia), 191, 193, 201, 202, 205, 302
Grlić, Rajko, 413, 416, 418, 419
Grol, Milan, 51
Gross, Mirjana, 47
Grujić, Radoslav M., 112
Gypsies, 421–422

Haig, Alexander, 462
Hannay, David, 468–469
Hanrieder, Wolfram, 381–382
"Hatred as Pleasure" (Kernberg), 104, 109
Helsinki Watch, 92
Historians, 39, 41, 43, 45, 46, 49, 53, 57
Historiography
   congresses, 39, 51, 52
   ideology, 39–41, 43–46, 48, 51–52, 55–58
   institutional, 41–43
   revisionism, 48–49, 53
Hladnik, Bostjan, 415
Hodza, Mehmet, 357
Home Guards. *See* Territorial Defense Force
Horton, Andrew, 457
Howe, Gordon, 369
Hoxha, Enver, 358, 359
Hren, Marko, 191
Hribar, Spomenka, 199
HSS. *See* Croat Peasant Party
Human rights, 23, 30, 92, 148, 191, 196, 215, 353, 365, 373, 436
Hungarians. *See under* Vojvodina Province
Hungary, 78, 136, 189, 196, 206, 215, 296, 308, 349, 351, 361, 362–363, 383
Hurd, Douglas, 218, 462, 466

IBRD. *See* World Bank
ICFY. *See* International Conference on Former Yugoslavia
Ilinden uprising (1903), 213, 360
Illiescu, Ion, 360
Illyrianism, 15, 40
IMF. *See* International Monetary Fund
IMRO. *See* Internal Macedonian Revolutionary Organization
IMRO-DPMNU. *See* Internal Macedonian Revolutionary Organization–

Index

491

Democratic Party for Macedonian
National Unity
Inflation, 7, 8, 125, 126, 225, 226, 256, 269,
282
Internal Macedonian Revolutionary
Organization (IMRO/VMRO), 213,
222, 226, 383
Internal Macedonian Revolutionary
Organization–Democratic Party for
Macedonian National Unity (IMRO-
DPMNU), 69, 214, 221
International Conference on Former
Yugoslavia (ICFY) (1992), 178–179
International Monetary Fund (IMF), 197,
368, 369, 373, 374
International Women in Media Foundation
award, 91
Irdizović, Mirza, 420
Irenej (bishop), 112, 114
Irredentisms, 15, 20, 33, 211, 219, 358
Irwin, Zachary T., 454
Islam, 40. *See also* Muslims; *under* Bosnia-
Herzegovina
Islamic Declaration, The (Izetbegović), 172
Islamic fundamentalists, 5, 6, 24
Istria, 360
Italy, 102, 189, 195, 196, 197, 227, 299(table),
320, 335, 349, 353(table), 353,
355(tables), 366, 367, 369, 370–371
Iveković, Rada, 453, 457
Izetbegović, Alija, 7, 24, 26, 69, 89, 90, 158,
160, 161, 162, 164, 165, 169, 171, 172,
179, 469

Jakovljević, Ivo, 471
Janković, Dragoslav, 41, 51
Janša, Janez, 86, 191
Japan, 102, 229, 282, 368
Jaruzelski, Wojciech, 75
Jelinčič, Zmago, 205
Jergović, Miljenko, 89
Jevremović, Jela, 94
Jevrić, Nebojša, 94
Jevtić, Atanasije (bishop), 118
Jews, 109
JNA. *See* Yugoslav National Army
John/Jovan (Serbian patriarch), 105
Joint ventures, 354, 371
Jokanović, Vukašin, 222–223
Jović, Borislav, 27, 29, 67, 68, 71, 74, 366, 372,
377

Jovović, Ranko, 244

Kačin, Jelko, 86
Kádár, János, 362
Kadijević, Veljko, 67, 68, 70–71, 74, 75, 76,
162
Kálláy, Benjamin, 156
Karadjordjević monarchy, 40
Karadžić, Radovan, 89, 90, 160, 163, 165,
167, 168, 169, 171, 172, 179, 379, 380,
453, 467, 469
Karadžic, Vuk, 45
Karadžol, Boran, 354
Karanović, Srdjan, 416, 419, 429, 457
Kardelj, Edvard, 4, 54
Kasapović, Mirjana, 133, 144
Kaufman, Michael, 118
KDA. *See* Kosovo Democratic Alliance
Kecmanović, Nenad, 157, 158
Kenney, George, 462
Kenović, Ademir, 420, 424, 425
Kernberg, Otto, 104, 105, 108
Khrushchev, Nikita, 339, 340
Kilibarda, Nikoa, 244
Kinkel, Klaus, 468
Kljuić, Stjepan, 158, 160, 166
Kljusev, Nikola, 219, 224
Knezević, Gordana, 91
Knin region (Croatia), 28, 29, 68, 73, 135,
136, 434
Kocović, Bogoljub, 156
Kohl, Helmut, 371, 468
Kolar, Slavko, 47
Koljević, Nikola, 158, 166
Konade, Dragica, 86
Korošec, Antun, 17
Kosovo, Battle of (1389), 56, 57, 104, 105,
110, 113, 434
Kosovo Democratic Alliance (KDA), 73
Kosovo Province (Serbia), 19, 74, 370, 383
Albanians in, 2, 4, 19, 20, 35(n21), 44, 48,
72, 73, 91, 92, 106, 110, 111, 125, 135, 211,
357–358, 436
armed civilians, 79
autonomy abolished (1990), 72
censorship, 57
Communist Party, 57
and human rights, 23
and Macedonia, 211
media, 84, 92, 135
Montenegrins in, 20

492   *Index*

Muslims, 20
political party, 73
poverty, 20
problem, 19–20, 125
riots (1981), 2, 20, 48, 106, 111
and Serbia, 27, 28, 30, 32, 48, 69, 72–73, 75,
   91, 92, 106, 107, 125, 135, 215
Serbian name, 4
and Serbian Orthodox Church, 111
Serbs in, 20, 28, 54, 72, 106
striking miners, 374–375
YPA in, 72, 92
Kostić, Branko, 219, 245–246
Koštunica, Vojislav, 49, 50
Kotor (Montenegro), 238
Kotor, Bay of, 247, 321, 322
Kovać, Oskar, 7, 456
Kovačević, Živorad, 369
Kovačić, Zlatko, 286
Kozyrev, Andrei V., 346, 380
Krajgher, Sergej, 2
Krajina, Kninska, 162
Krajina (Serbian Croatia), 4, 8, 27, 28, 29, 32,
   123, 207, 376, 383
   as SARK, 69
Krajišnik, Momčilo, 158
Krčić, Shefket, 116
Krestić, Vasilije, 53, 55–56, 433
Kristo, Jure, 453, 455, 456
Krizan, Mojmir, 31
Krizman, Bogdan, 57
Krushevo Republic, 213
Kučan, Milan, 24, 30, 68, 190, 192, 205, 358
Kuharić, Franjo Cardinal (archbishop of
   Zagreb), 114, 118, 401–402, 404, 434,
   435, 436, 437, 439, 442, 443, 445
Kuljis, Denis, 96–97
Kulundžić, Zvonimir, 43, 47, 60(n13)
Kurspahić, Kemal, 91
Kustić, Živko, 114
Kusturica, Emir, 413, 414, 420–422, 425
Kusumagić, Ismet, 7
Kuzmanović, Jasmina, 453, 455

Language, 4–5, 14, 45
Latin alphabet, 5
Lavanić, Zlatko, 420
Lazar (tsar of Serbia), 104, 113
Lázár, György, 362
Lazić, Milorad, 114

LCC (League of Communists of Croatia).
   See Croatia, Communist Party
LCC-PDC (League of Communists of
   Croatia–Party of Democratic Changes).
   See Croatia, Communist Party (LCC-
   PDC)
LCM (League of Communists of
   Montenegro). *See* Montenegro,
   Communist Party
LC-MY. *See* League of Communists,
   Movement for Yugoslavia
LCY (League of Communists of
   Yugoslavia). *See* Yugoslavia,
   Communist Party
League of Communists, Movement for
   Yugoslavia (LC-MY), 71, 74
League of Communists of Yugoslavia
   (LCY). *See* Serbia, Communist Party;
   Yugoslavia, Communist Party
League of Reform Forces (LRF), 71
Liberal Democratic Party (Slovenia), 193,
   198, 200, 201, 202, 203, 204, 205
Liberalism, 49, 50
Liberal Party (Slovenia), 193, 201
Lijphart, Arendt, 127
Lim River, 323
Lithuania, 221
Livno Declaration (CDU), 166
Ljubljana (Slovenia), 4, 71, 190, 202
   archbishop, 200
   Liberation Square demonstration (1988),
   191
Lončar, Budimir, 349–350, 351–352, 353,
   356, 360, 365, 368, 376
Loza, Tihomir, 162
LRF. *See* League of Reform Forces
Lukanov, Andrey, 360
Lukijan (bishop), 118

MAAK. *See* Movement for all-Macedonian
   Action
Mačan, Trpimar, 44
McCloskey, Frank, 229
Macedonia, 4, 112, 164, 213, 219, 223, 458
   Albanians in, 87, 212, 213, 221, 226, 227,
   229
   armed civilians, 79
   Assembly, 215, 226
   and Bulgaria, 211, 213, 216, 221, 225, 229,
   360
   capital. *See* Skopje

Index

and confederation, 26, 214, 215
constitution, 214
constitution (1991), 215, 218, 222, 223
and Croatia, 221
and CSCE, 381
destabilization, 212, 229
diplomatic isolation of, 212, 221, 225, 229
and EC, 211–212, 215, 218–219, 220, 224, 225, 226, 228
economic embargo against, 212, 221, 225–226
economy, 8, 212, 225–226, 228–229
Egyptians in, 222
elections (1990), 24, 57
film, 228
foreign investment in, 265
and FRY, 295
government, 26, 69, 219, 226, 228, 229
and Greece, 211, 212, 218, 219–221, 226, 227–228, 229, 361, 381, 458–459
independence (1991), 6, 69, 214, 215–216
and JNA, 216, 217, 222
language, 213
majority rule, 128
media, 84, 86–87, 216, 228
Montenegrins in, 223, 224
multi-candidate elections, 214
Muslim refugees in, 383
name, 218, 219, 220, 226–227, 228, 229
nationalism, 102, 213, 226
non-party government of experts, 24
pluralism, 228
political parties, 22, 69, 73, 85, 87, 214, 228
president, 24, 215
and privatization, 214, 263–266
and Russia, 227
and Serbia, 52, 211, 212, 221–225
Serbs in, 212, 222, 223, 224
and Slovenia, 221
TDF, 216–217
Titoists, 213
and Turkey, 217, 221, 227
and Turks, 213
UN peacekeepers in, 227, 381
and U.S., 211, 218, 219, 224, 229–230
and YPA, 72
Macedonian Orthodox Church, 112–113, 223, 228
Macedonians, 44, 211, 219, 361
nationalism, 15, 21
Maček, Vladko, 41

McPherson, C. B., 126
Major, John, 465, 469
Makavejev, Dušan, 413, 415, 423, 429
Malile, Reis, 357
Mallikurtis, Stylianos, 224
Malta, 369
Mandić, Miroslav, 420
Manolić, Josip, 167
MAP. *See* Mediterranean Action Plan
Marinović, Mikan, 418
Marjanović, Jovan, 41
Market economy, 18, 260, 268, 274, 282
Marković, Ante, 23, 71, 72, 194, 242, 342, 349, 351, 359, 360, 363, 372
Marković, Goran, 416, 424, 426, 430
Marković, Mirjana, 74
Marković, Šima, 52, 54
Marotti, Miklos, 92
Marx, Karl, 308
Matić, Ivica, 424
Media
control of, 25, 83, 84, 88, 91, 93, 95, 96, 97
journalists killed, 94
liberal, 86
and objectivity, 83–84, 455
repression, 89, 92
war, 91–93
Western, 417, 455
See also Print media; Radio; Television; *under individual provinces and republics*
Mediterranean Action Plan (MAP), 369
Mediterranean nonaligned group, 367–368, 369
Mediterranean Sea, 306, 371
Memorandum. *See under* Serbian Academy of Sciences and Arts
Mencinger, Jože, 198, 456
Mercouri, Melina, 220
Mesić, Stipe, 29, 32, 136, 377
Mihailović, Draža, 41, 49
Mihić, Goran, 421
Mikasinović, Branko, 367
Milaš, Nikodim (bishop), 111
Milić, Goran, 85, 90
Milivojević, Marko, 453
Milošević, Slobodan, 5, 7, 19, 80(n9), 164, 192, 353
and collective state presidency, 27, 136
and Communist Party, 23, 53, 126, 192, 241
and dissidents, 53, 125

494 *Index*

and Europe, 367
and Greater Serbia, 28, 30, 68, 69, 73, 107, 125, 171, 433
and Greece, 219, 224, 225
leadership (1987), 3, 20–21, 25, 30, 56, 57, 91, 107, 455
and media, 91, 92, 136
opposition to, 74, 106
and Russia, 345–346
and SASA Memorandum, 55
and Serbian nationalism, 107–108, 131
and Serbian Orthodox Church, 111, 112, 113, 116, 117–118
and Serbian Party, 22, 32
as Serbian president (1989), 21, 67, 74, 211, 360
and SSP, 68, 71, 72
support for, 106
and UN, 162
and U.S., 186(n76), 379, 381, 466
wife, 74
and YPA, 71, 72, 73, 74
Misetić, Bosiljko, 148, 149
Mitrović, Andrej, 49–50, 51
Mitsotakis, Konstantinos, 196, 218, 219, 224, 226–227, 361
Mock, Alois, 363, 364
Močnik, Rastko, 199
Mojsov, Lazar, 353
Montenegrins, 20, 44, 115–116, 223, 357
in officer corps, 23, 240
Montenegro, 4, 20, 40, 94
agriculture, 316, 320
Albanians in, 238
armed civilians, 79
and B-H, 161
borders, 97
capital. *See* Titograd/Podgorica
clans, 237, 240
coastal area, 321
Communist Party (LCM), 69, 87, 237, 240–242
Constitution (1992), 248
Croats in, 135, 238
Development Fund, 262, 263
and EC, 242, 243, 246–247
as ecological state, 311, 312, 313–319
economy, 238, 242, 313–314, 318–319
elections (1990), 24, 87, 241, 242
elections (1992), 248–249

and environmental issues, 247, 301, 311–324
and federation, 242
foreign investment in, 262, 318
as FRY. *See* Serbia, and Montenegro, as FRY
government, 239
independence (1878), 238
industry, 247, 311, 317, 322, 382
media, 84, 87–88, 241, 243
multiparty elections, 239, 241, 314
Muslims, 238, 239, 249–250(n6)
National Assembly, 239, 242
nationalism, 102, 240
national parks, 313, 320
natural resources, 315–316
and OECD, 320
opposition parties, 241, 242, 248
and Orthodox Church, 116, 239
political parties, 85, 87, 237, 239, 242
population, 238, 314, 357
poverty, 238
president, 29
prime minister, 242
privatization, 242, 261–263
and Serbia, 6, 21, 27, 30, 32, 69–70, 107, 115–116, 125, 237, 239–240, 242–245, 248, 249
Serbs in, 238, 249–250(n6)
sovereignty, 243, 247, 248, 249
sustainable development, 318–320
tourism, 247, 316–317, 318, 320, 321–322
transportation, 247
and Turks, 238, 239, 240
Uprising (1989), 241
urban, 321
water supply, 322
and YPA, 72, 237, 240, 244, 245
See also under Croatia
Montreal Protocol (1987), 320, 322, 328(n25)
Morača, Pero, 41, 51
Morača River, 314
Morava River, 304
Moro, Aldo, 371
Movement for All-Macedonian Action (MAAK), 214, 361
Movement for Serbian Renewal (MSR), 71, 72, 74
MSR. *See* Movement for Serbian Renewal
Multiparty system, 51, 127, 130, 241, 437
elections, 22, 23, 24, 57, 127

Index

Muslim Bosnjak Organization, 163
Muslim Party for Democratic Action (B-H), 24, 25, 89
Muslim Party for Democratic Action (Montenegro), 242
Muslims, 5, 6–7, 15, 20, 21, 56, 73, 380, 458, 463. *See also under* Bosnia-Herzegovina

Nagy, Imre, 362
Nakayama, Taro, 368
Nasirević, Zoran, 428
National Bank of Yugoslavia (NDY), 76, 276, 285
National communities, 28, 40
National Democratic Party (Slovenia), 193, 201, 205
Nationalism, 1–2, 3, 8, 15, 19, 24, 43, 46, 54, 102, 211, 282, 285, 456–457
  and communism, 52
  and conservativism, 396
  and democracy, 129, 457
  and religion, 101, 105–106, 111, 112, 119
  traumatic, 105, 119
  typology, 101–105
  and women, 396
Nationalism and Federalism in Yugoslavia (Ramet), 456
National Liberal Party (Slovenia), 202
National Liberation Struggle (Tito), 14–15
NDY. *See* National Bank of Yugoslavia
NATO. *See* North Atlantic Treaty Organization
Netherlands, 195, 472
Nikezic, Marko, 46
Nikoliš, Gojko, 48
Nobilo, Mario, 166
Nominal rates of protection (NRP), 289–290, 291, 292, 298(fig.), 300(table)
Nonaligned Movement, 333, 341, 350, 351
North Atlantic Treaty Organization (NATO), 338, 350, 459, 460, 467, 469, 470, 471
Norway, 228, 229
NRP. *See* Nominal rates of protection
Nuclear power, 301, 304, 308, 370

Oblak, Marijan (bishop), 443
OECD. *See* Organization for Economic Cooperation and Development
Oil, 276, 310
Oluić, Željko, 149, 151(n8)

Oman, Ivan, 205
Opačić, Jovan, 131, 132
Organization for Economic Cooperation and Development (OECD), 286, 296, 299(table), 320, 349, 352(table), 355(tables), 365, 368
Orlandić, Marko, 360
Orthodox Church, 40, 110. *See also* Serbian Orthodox Church
Osterman, Anka, 204
Ostojić, Velibor, 88
OTEX (firm), 264–266
Ottoman rule. *See* Turks
Owen, David Lord, 179, 379, 380, 463, 467, 468, 469, 470, 471
Owen-Stoltenberg plan, 470

Pakrac (Croatia), 29, 74, 136
Pantić, Miroslav, 43
Pan-Yugoslav party, 23, 32
Papić, Krsto, 415
Paris Club, 368
Paroški, Milan, 222
Partisans (communist), 2, 18, 157, 336
Party for Equality (Montenegro), 242
Party of (Croatian State) Right, 45
Party of Democratic Action (B-H), 157, 158, 162, 164, 167, 176
Party of Democratic Change (B-H), 157
Party of Democratic Prosperity (PDP) (Macedonia), 73
Party of Democratic Renewal (PDR) (Slovenia), 192, 193, 202, 204, 205, 210
Party of Reform Forces, 23
Party of Yugoslavs in Macedonia, 223
Pašić, Nikola, 53
Paskalević, Goran, 424, 425, 426
Pavelić, Ante, 115
Pavić, Milorad, 109
Pavle (Orthodox patriarch), 115, 117, 118, 119
Pavlišić, Josip, 438
Pavlović, Živojin, 413, 415, 424, 428
Pavlowitch, Stevan, 14
PDA. *See* Slavic Muslim Party of Democratic Action
PDP. *See* Party of Democratic Prosperity
PDR. *See* Party of Democratic Renewal
Peasant Union (Slovenia), 191. *See also* Slovenia People's Party
Pekić, Borislav, 426

496   Index

Pelivan, Jure, 158
Pentagonale-Hexagonale, 352(table), 353,
    363, 367, 368
People's Democratic Party (Macedonia), 87
People's Party (Montenegro), 242, 244, 245
Perović, Latinka, 46
Pešić, Desanka, 52
Pesić, Slobodan, 416
Peterle, Lojze, 193, 195, 197, 199, 200, 203,
    376
Petković, Ranko, 350, 358
Petranović, Branko, 49, 51, 56
Petrović, Aleksandar, 413, 415, 421
Pirnat, Rajko, 193, 205
Plavšić, Biljana, 158
Plesković, Dušan, 198, 199
Pleština, Dijana, 453, 457
Pljevlja Valley, 323–324
Pluralism, 51, 128, 189, 310, 365, 366, 456,
    457
Poetry/poets, 43, 47, 93, 244
Poland, 75, 102, 196, 206, 296, 352(table)
Political culture, 151(n13), 310
"Policy of Environmental Protection and
    Promotion in Yugoslavia with
    Measures for Implementation, The"
    (1991), 305, 306, 319
Popov, Čedo, 51
Powell, Colin L., 461
Poznic, Andrej, 204
Prague Group (filmmakers), 415–416, 420
Prela, Nikola (bishop), 436
Press, freedom of the, 85, 86, 87, 95, 96
Pribičević, Branko, 453, 454, 456
Print media, 84–85, 86, 87, 93, 96, 97
Privatization, 96, 97, 189, 214, 253–257, 265,
    275–276, 278–279
    adjustment period, 261, 269, 272–274
    institutional ownership, 268–275
    opposition to, 268–275
    types, 254–255
    See also under individual republics
Pučnik, Jože, 70, 205
Puhovski, Žarko, 151(n8)
Puljić, Želimir (bishop), 438
Puttnam, 421

Quadrilateral Group, 352(table), 353

Račan, Ivica, 23, 127, 128
Radio, 84, 86, 87, 88, 91, 95, 203

Radović, Amfilohije (Orthodox bishop), 433
Radulović, Milutin, 88
Railroads, 317, 358, 373
RAM. See Greater Serbia, plan for B-H
Ramet, Sabrina Petra, 453, 455, 456, 462–463
Ranković, Aleksandar, 42
Rašković, Jovan, 131, 132, 133
Raznjatović, Željko (Arkan), 170, 186(n64)
Recycling, 304
Reform-Communists, 22–23, 24, 71, 139
Refugees, 8, 118, 135, 137, 189, 200, 207, 383
Regionalization, 176–177, 181
Religion. See Catholic Church; Islam;
    Serbian Orthodox Church; under
    Nationalism; Women; Yugoslavia
Remington, Robin Alison, 332
Ribnikar, Ivan, 199, 200
Rifkind, Malcolm, 446
Rigelnik, Hermann, 204
Rocard, Michel, 370
Rock'n'roll, 106, 420, 428
Roman, Petre, 359
Romania, 308, 352(table), 356, 357, 359–360,
    361, 367, 381
Rosenthal, A. M., 459
Rossanda, Rossana, 409
Runjić, Andjelko, 437
Rupel, Dimitrij, 193, 205, 366
Rus, Vojan, 51
Rusinow, Dennison, 454, 455, 457, 459
Russia (post-Communist), 196, 221, 227,
    343–344, 345, 346–347, 380, 460, 470

Sachs, Jeffrey, 198, 199
Saint Sava, 105, 111
Salinas Price, Roberto, 58
Samardžić, Nikola, 244
Samardžić, Radovan, 53
Sapundxija, Riza, 27
Sarajevo (B-H), 45, 91, 180
    bombardment, 90–91, 157, 169, 170, 215,
    463
    and UN, 470
Sarbanes, Paul, 230
Sardelić, Celestin, 433
SARK. See Serbian Autonomous Region of
    Krajina
SASA. See Serbian Academy of Sciences
    and Arts
Šaškar, Ines, 51
Sava River, 303, 304, 305, 310

Index

497

SDP. *See* Social Democratic Party (Croatia); Social Democratic Party of Slovenia

SDU. *See* Slovenian Democratic Union

Secession, 27, 28, 30, 33, 73, 180, 194

Šeks, Vladimir, 96, 137

Sekulovic, Aleksandar, 366

Self-determination, 2, 6, 19, 28, 129, 363, 375, 377

Self-management market socialism, 16–17, 18, 274, 275, 282, 284, 307, 333, 366

Selimoški, Jakub (Reis ul-ulema), 118

Serbia
Albanians in, 24, 30, 357, 358, 399
anti-communist party, 71
arms purchases, 117
army, 25, 27, 32, 57, 58, 76, 79, 136, 170, 172
Bulgarians in, 222
capital. *See* Belgrade
civilian arms, 3, 78, 106, 192
Communist Party, 20, 22, 42, 45–46, 49, 50, 52, 55, 63(n61)
and confederation, 22, 57, 196
constitution (1989), 22
constitution (1990), 69, 72, 194, 201
and EC, 377–378, 379
economy, 7, 136, 268, 269, 272, 456
elections (1990), 24, 57, 130
embargo against, 7, 8, 181, 327
and environment, 301, 306–307
expansionist war, 3, 4, 6, 7, 8, 68, 69, 85, 93, 94–95, 96, 97, 116–117, 124, 135, 136, 173, 175, 214–215, 376, 379, 408, 461, 462
and federalism, 48
Federal Presidency, 27–28, 29, 67
and federation, 22, 26
films, 414, 424
foreign investment in, 258, 271, 354
foreign relations, 357, 367, 383
government, 24, 25, 27, 266, 267
and Greece, 219–220, 223, 224
historians, 41, 49, 51, 52
language and alphabet, 4–5
majority rule, 128
media, 6, 72, 81(n24), 84, 85, 87, 89, 91–93, 95, 460
military industries, 78
and Montenegro as FRY (1992), 6, 7, 34(n7), 216, 248, 294, 295–296, 325, 327, 346, 347, 380, 464, 467, 471
Muslims, 73, 249–250(n6)
nationalism, 2, 3, 6, 7, 15, 16, 20, 21, 22, 25, 46, 55, 56, 57, 64(n71), 103, 106, 107–108, 115, 119, 180, 457
opposition parties, 25, 71
paramilitary militia, 72, 79
pluralism, 51
political parties, 53, 71, 85, 98, 269, 396, 398, 403
privatization, 257–261, 264, 266–268, 269, 270–274, 278
publishing, 51, 63(n61), 111–112
rural, 106
and Russia, 343–344, 345, 346–347
taxes (1990), 76, 270
TDF, 79
and Tito, 42, 46, 54
and Turks. *See* Kosovo, Battle of
and UN, 379, 383
unemployment, 7, 270
urban, 106
and U.S., 379, 380, 381, 383, 460, 462–464, 465, 466, 467–468, 469
and Western Europe, 50, 383, 460, 469–470
women, 396, 398, 399, 406
See also Chetniks; Greater Serbia; Great Serbia hegemony; Serbian Orthodox Church; *under individual provinces and republics*

Serbian Academy of Sciences and Arts (SASA), 20, 53, 55–56, 314
Memorandum (1986), 20–21, 53–55, 106, 125, 433, 446(n3)

Serbian Autonomous Areas, 69, 183(n20)

Serbian Autonomous Region of Krajina (SARK), 69, 73, 74, 78, 167, 173, 176, 244

Serbian Democratic Party, 51, 89, 131, 132, 152(n18), 157, 158, 159, 160, 162, 163, 164, 165, 166, 168, 173

Serbian Guard, 170

Serbianization, 16, 21, 34–35(n18)

Serbian National Bank, 374

Serbian National Guard, 176

Serbian Orthodox Church, 3, 113, 115, 223
and communism, 111, 434, 438
and Greater Serbia, 116, 117–118, 119, 436, 455
grecification, 110
and nationalism, 111, 112, 113, 114–115, 116, 432, 457
periodical, 106

and religious education in state schools, 112

and Tito, 104, 106, 107, 112, 115

and Turks, 105–106, 108, 109, 110

victim complex, 109, 110, 113–116, 117–119

and World War II, 104, 105, 108, 110, 112, 114, 115, 442

See also under Catholic Church; Milošević, Slobodan

Serbian Party, 22, 24, 32

Serbian Radical Party, 53, 98, 211

Serbian Republic of Bosnia and Herzegovina, 165, 168, 176

Serbian Socialist Alliance of Working People, 192

Serbian Socialist Party (SSP), 68, 71, 74

Serbo-Croatian (language), 4–5, 191, 435

Serbs, 6, 23, 44, 112, 223, 357, 360, 432, 453, 455, 456, 464–465

population, 5, 15

unified in a single state, 53, 55, 107–108, 131

See also under individual provinces and republics

Service sector, 271, 277, 283

Šešelj, Vojislav, 98, 211

Shoup, Paul, 6, 453, 454, 455, 456, 457

Shultz, George, 462, 464

Sidak, Jaroslav, 41

Sidran, Abdulah, 425

Sijan, Slobodan, 417, 424

Silajdžić, Haris, 158, 165

Simes, Dimitri K., 460

Šimić, Petar, 70, 72

Simić, Pribislav, 436

Skardar Lake, 247, 321

Skopje (Macedonia), 87

Škrabalo, Zdenko, 197

Slavic Muslim Party of Democratic Action (PDA) (B-H), 69, 71, 73

Slavonia (Croatian region), 28–29, 69, 107, 113, 114

Slovakia, 296

Slovenes, 15, 19, 26, 44, 112, 190

Slovenia, 15, 30, 156, 190, 229, 362, 363, 458

anti-communist coalition, 24, 192

arms imports, 78

Assembly, 68, 200, 202, 205

and B-H, 197

and Catholic Church, 57, 199, 200, 203

Communist Party, 189, 190, 191, 192

and confederation, 21, 22, 23, 26, 27, 54, 159, 192, 193

constitution (1989), 22

constitution (1990), 194, 201–202, 404–405

Croats in, 196

and democracy, 189, 191, 192, 201, 206–207

Democratic Opposition of Slovenia (DEMOS), 27, 31, 68, 71, 73, 79, 85, 126, 192–193, 199, 202, 366

and EC, 163, 164, 195, 196, 197, 206, 207, 215, 343

economy, 8, 126, 189, 191, 196, 197–198, 200, 202, 206, 207, 456

education, 203

elections (1990), 24, 27, 57, 136, 192

elections (1992), 205

environmental concerns, 302, 304, 310

and federation, 22

films, 423

foreign investment in, 354

foreign relations, 195–197, 221, 353, 366, 367, 369, 456

and FRY, 295

government, 27, 31, 70, 86, 202, 204–206

historians, 41

and IMF, 197

independence (1991), 6, 27, 30, 31, 57, 68, 180, 189, 194, 195, 375, 377

industrial production, 206, 207, 456

and JNA, 3, 125, 136, 195, 205, 214

media, 84, 85, 86, 94, 190, 191, 202, 203–204, 206

military, 79, 191, 194, 195

nationalism, 15, 21, 25, 102, 190–191, 206, 457

parliament, 193, 202, 399

police, 78, 79

political parties, 22, 24, 25, 191–193, 201, 205

population, 31, 189, 190

president, 24, 68, 192, 205

prime minister, 193, 200, 376

privatization, 189, 198–201, 207

refugees in, 189, 190, 200, 205, 207

sanctions against, 196–197

and Serbia, 46, 54, 61(n22), 93, 94, 192, 197, 377

sovereignty, 136, 192, 382

TDF, 71, 78, 79

Index

transport, 190
unemployment, 200, 206
and U.S., 195, 196, 343, 459
women, 396, 399, 403, 404, 405, 408
and YPA, 68, 70, 71, 86, 91, 94, 245
See also under Croatia
Slovenian Christian Democratic Party, 192,
199, 201, 202, 203, 204, 205–206, 405
Slovenian Christian Socialist Movement,
191
Slovenian Democratic Union (SDU), 191,
192, 193
Slovenian National Party (SNP), 205
Slovenian People's Party (SPP), 193, 201,
202, 204, 205
Smerdel, Branko, 128, 144, 151(n8)
SNP. See Slovenian National Party
Social capital, 259, 266
Social Democratic Alliance (Slovenia), 191
Social Democratic Party (Macedonia), 226
Social Democratic Party (SDP) (Croatia),
129, 139
Social Democratic Party (Serbia), 396, 403
Social Democratic Party of Slovenia (SDP),
192, 201, 202, 205
Social Democratic Union (Slovenia), 199
Socialism, 22, 24, 47, 49, 123, 193, 307–308,
310. See also Yugoslavia, Tito regime
Socialist Alliance (Croatia), 129
Socialist Party of Serbia, 24
Socialist Party of Slovenia, 193, 200, 201,
202, 204
Socialist Youth Organization of Slovenia,
190
Social product, 189, 212
Social property, 257–258, 263, 264, 268, 270,
271
Sokol, Smiljko, 128, 137, 151(n8)
South Adriatic Development plan, 320
South Slavs, 2, 13, 15, 19, 40, 55
Soviet Union, 49, 62(n36), 64(n71), 107, 196,
341–342, 350, 352(table), 424. See also
under Yugoslavia
Spaho, Mehmed, 157
Spain, 195, 352(table), 370
Speech, freedom of, 87, 89, 92, 96–97, 126
Špegelj, Martin, 67, 68, 74, 136
SPP. See Slovenian People's Party
SSP. See Serbian Socialist Party
Stalin, Joseph, 54, 123, 332, 335, 338
Stambolić, Ivan, 106

Stanisavljević, Djuro, 46
Stanković, Djordje Dj., 53
Stankovic, Vladimir, 443
Starčević, Ante, 45
Starčević, Ivan, 151(n8)
Stepinac, Alojzije Cardinal (Archbishop and
metropolitan), 48, 435, 437–438, 445
Stojadinović, Milan, 41
Stojanović, Lazar, 429
Stoltenberg, Thorvald, 470, 471
Štrugar, Vlado, 41
Sučeška, Avdo, 46
Sugar, Peter F., 110
Sulphur dioxide (SO_2), 304, 323
Šuštar, Alojzij (archbishop), 200
Šuvar, Stipe, 47, 51, 52
Sweden, 355(table)
Switzerland, 355(table), 367

Tadić, Jorjo, 41, 43
Tamarut, Antun (archbishop), 438
Tara River Canyon, 301, 314, 321, 323, 324
Tasić, David, 191
TDF. See Territorial Defense Force
Tedeschi, Emil, 96
Television, 25, 83, 84, 85, 86, 87, 88, 89, 90–
91, 92, 93, 95, 144, 146, 203–204, 413,
415, 417
Temperley, Harold W. V., 110
Territorial Defense Force (TDF), 71, 78, 79
Terrorism, 370
Terzić, Velimir, 42, 52
Thatcher, Margaret, 369, 462, 465
Theodore (bishop), 105
Tisa River, 305, 306
Tito (Josip Broz), 2, 5, 6, 27, 54, 61–62(n34),
334, 359, 362
biographer, 44, 48
and Serbian Orthodox Church, 104, 106,
117
and unified Yugoslavia, 40, 41, 42, 46,
107, 213
Titograd/Podgorica (Macedonia), 4, 248
Todorović, Louis, 417
Tomislav (king of Bosnia), 156
Tomislav (king of Croatia), 132
Tourism, 247, 276, 283. See also under
Yugoslavia; individual republics
Transportation, 190, 247, 317, 367
Trenevski, Martin, 87
Trianon, Treaty of (1920), 383

Tribalism, 310
Trieste, 371
Tripalo, Miko, 44
Tudjman, Franjo, 4, 24, 30, 31, 44, 67, 69, 71,
  79, 97, 131, 133, 139, 143–144, 145, 146,
  164, 166, 360, 366, 376, 439, 442
Turkey, 28, 75, 217, 221, 227, 338, 352(table),
  356, 361, 381
Turks, 105–106, 108, 109, 110, 156, 213, 238

Umek, Igor, 198
Unemployment, 8, 125, 126, 200, 206, 238,
  256, 313
UNESCO. *See* United Nations Educational,
  Scientific, and Cultural Organization
Unitarism, 42–43, 47, 57, 108, 131
United List (Slovenia), 205
United Nations, 123, 134, 137, 148, 179, 302,
  325, 358, 361, 459–460, 470
  pink protected zones, 123, 135
  embargo, 7, 8, 181, 217, 224, 344, 345, 378,
    380–381, 459, 465, 468–469, 470
  See also under individual republics
United Nations Educational, Scientific, and
  Cultural Organization (UNESCO), 314,
  323
United Opposition (Montenegro), 248
United States, 77, 117, 165, 167, 350, 460–461
  economic sanctions, 196, 380, 459
  films, 416, 417, 421
  press, 455, 464
  and Yugoslavia, trade, 286, 299(table)
  See also under Yugoslavia; *individual*
    republics
Universal suffrage, 145
Ustaše. *See* Croatian *Ustaše*
Uzelac, Alan, 148

Vance, Cyrus, 165–166, 175, 179, 379, 460,
  463, 471
Vance-Owen plan, 179, 347, 380, 465, 466–
  467, 468
Vance Plan, 166
Vasilije (bishop), 112, 118
Vatican, 40, 114, 438. *See also* Catholic
  Church
Videos, 413, 415, 416, 417–418
Vidović, Vjekoslav, 148–149, 154(n48)
Vinčetić, Luka, 440, 447(n15)
Vlahs, 28
Vllàsi, Azem, 365

VMRO. *See* Internal Macedonian
  Revolutionary Organization
Vojvodina Province (Serbia), 20, 27
  autonomy abolished (1990), 72, 363
  Hungarians in, 4, 44, 73, 81(n25), 92, 215,
    362
  media, 84, 92
  name, 110
  Ruthenians in, 92
  and Serbia, 27, 30, 54, 69, 72, 92, 107, 110,
    125, 215
  Slovaks in, 92
Vranitzky, Franz, 363, 368
Vrdoljak, Anton, 146, 423
Vučičević, Branko, 423
Vučinić, V., 417
Vukadinović, Radovan, 363
Vuković, Šćepan, 87
Vuković, Tomislav, 114, 438, 442
Vuković, Željko, 167

Waldheim, Kurt, 362
Warsaw Pact, 341, 350, 351
West European Union, 343
Wiesel, Elie, 465
Women, 106
  and the law, 398, 399, 403, 404, 405, 406–
    407
  pacifist movement, 407–408
  political participation, 395–399, 402–403,
    405
  and religion, 396, 397, 401–402
  right, 399–404, 405–406, 407, 410
  unemployment, 3, 399, 400
  violence against, 406, 408–409, 463
Wood, Andrew, 369
World Almanac, 228
World Bank (IBRD), 319, 322, 368
World Commission on the Environment
  and Development, 319
World War I (1914–1918), 40, 61(n22), 239,
  409
World War II (1939–1945), 13, 49, 64(n71),
  93, 104, 105, 112, 114, 157, 239, 362, 409,
  454, 461–462
Wörner, Manfred, 471

Yankelovich, Daniel, 103
Yeltsin, Boris, 346, 347, 460
YMO. *See* Yugoslav Muslim Organization
YPA. *See* Yugoslav People's Army

Index

Yugoslavia, 14, 26, 40, 44, 97, 123, 190, 281
  agriculture, 282
  army, 23, 41, 125. *See also* Yugoslav
    National Army; Yugoslav People's
    Army
  balance of payments, 283, 284, 285, 286
  and Balkan states relations, 356–364
  borders, 475(n84)
  bourgeoisie, 40, 41
  civil war, 2, 13, 15, 33(n3), 471
  and CMEA/COMECON, 353–354
  Communist Party (LCY), 17, 23–24, 39,
    42, 44, 46, 50, 70, 84, 339, 340, 360, 361,
    366, 372, 395
  Communist Party of (CPY), 40, 41, 44, 51
  constitution (1946), 240
  constitution (1974), 16, 18, 47, 54, 55, 303,
    308
  and CSCE, 352(table), 364, 369, 375
  currency (dinar), 284–285, 373
  defense expenditures, 76
  and democratic transformation, 309–311,
    327, 352
  and EC, 349, 352(table), 353, 354,
    355(tables), 365, 367, 368, 369, 371, 372–
    374, 375, 376, 382, 383, 454
  economy, 3, 16–17, 18, 125–126, 276–277,
    281–282, 285, 286–293
  and EFTA, 352(table), 354, 364, 365, 373
  environmental issues, 301, 302–311, 327
  Federal Republic of (FRY). *See* Serbia, and
    Montenegro as FRY
  film, 415–416, 426–428
  foreign investment in, 354, 364
  foreign relations, 349–354, 364–375, 382–
    383
  foreign trade, 283, 284–285, 286, 288(fig.),
    293, 297(figs.), 299(table), 353–354,
    355(tables), 372, 373
  GDP (gross domestic product), 277, 282
  geopolitical position, 332, 367
  GNP (gross national product), 277, 282,
    283(table), 285
  government (Federal Executive Council),
    23, 71, 374
  and IMF, 369, 373
  income, 276
  industries, 289–292, 300(table)
  lakes, 305, 306
  minorities, 5–6, 15
  monarchy (1918), 2, 14, 16, 40, 41, 465

  name, 4
  Nazi occupation (1941), 2, 14, 41, 52, 107
  and Nonaligned Movement, 333, 350,
    351, 366, 373, 382
  overseas workers, 283, 354, 355(table),
    363, 364, 371, 373
  population, 357
  poverty, 126
  protectionism, 289–292, 298(figs.),
    300(table)
  religions, 3, 4, 40, 43, 45
  research institutions, 305
  security, 350–351
  and Soviet Union, 62(n36), 107, 331–337,
    339–341, 350, 355(tables), 453
  split (1991), 6, 13, 14, 160–164, 341
  Tito regime (1945–1980), 2, 4, 6, 13, 14, 15,
    16, 19, 21, 40, 41–43, 44, 46, 106, 308–
    309, 331, 332–333, 335–340, 455
  tourism, 276, 355(table), 364, 371, 373
  and U.S., 333, 334, 336, 337–338, 340, 341,
    342–343, 344, 352(table), 354,
    355(tables), 358, 454, 458–460
  and Western Europe, 364–375. *See also*
    individual countries
  women, 3, 395
Yugoslav idea, 14–15, 16, 23, 39–40, 55
Yugoslav Muslim Organization (YMO), 157
Yugoslav National Army (JNA), 3, 114, 123,
  136, 407, 455. *See also under* Croatia;
  Slovenia
Yugoslav People's Army (YPA), 57, 58, 67–
  68, 71, 75, 76, 86, 89
  control, 70, 71, 76
  and Great Britain, 77
  Military Districts, 77
  officer corps, 70, 240
  in republics, 71, 74, 78
  and Serbia, 70, 72, 74, 75, 79
  Serbs in, 70, 79
  size, 77
  and U.S., 77
  weapons, 77–78
Yugoslavs, 156, 182(n7), 238

Zafronović, Lordan, 416, 424
Zagreb (Croatia), 7, 52, 118, 444, 445
  5th Military District, 67, 71, 76, 79
  Serbs in, 29
Zakaria, Fareed, 460
Zakelj, Viktor, 200

Zakošek, Nenad, 129, 130
Zavrl, Franci, 191
Žećević, Momčilo, 39–40, 46, 49, 50, 51
Zeta, 238, 316
  River, 248, 321
Zhelev, Zhelyu, 381

Zhivkov, Todor, 360
Zilnik, Želimir, 413
Zimmerman, Warren, 77, 175, 337
Zulfikarpašić, 163
Zwitter, Fran, 41